# JACK
# LONDON'S
# WOMEN

# JACK LONDON'S WOMEN

*Clarice Stasz*

University of Massachusetts Press

*Amherst*

LC 2001017156
ISBN 1-55849-301-8

Design by Mary Mendell
Set in Minion by Graphic Composition, Inc.
Printed and bound by Sheridan Books, Inc.

Library of Congress Cataloging-in-Publication Data
Stasz, Clarice.
     Jack London's women / Clarice Stasz.
        p. cm.
     Includes bibliographical references (p. ) and index.
     ISBN 1-55849-301-8 (cloth : alk. paper)
        1. London, Jack, 1876–1916—Relations with women. 2. Authors, American—20th
     century—Biography. 3. Women—United States—Biography. I. Title.

     PS3523.046 Z894 2001
     813'.52—dc21
     [B]
                                                                        2001017156

British Library Cataloguing in Publication data are available.

Some circumstantial evidence is very
strong—as when you find a trout
in milk.
HENRY DAVID THOREAU

Truth is rarely pure, and never simple.
OSCAR WILDE

# Contents

# *Preface*

My Introduction to Jack London was through his second wife, Charmian Kittredge. Raised in the mid-Atlantic states, I had never read any of London's works before moving to California in my late twenties. I ignored the Jack London State Historic Park perched on the eastern slopes of Sonoma Mountain, a mud volcano readily viewed from my backyard. Only a chance remark from a neighbor sent me up the winding road to the Beauty Ranch. "You must go there and look at the photographs of his wife. I know you will write a book about her."[1]

Entering the stone house Charmian had built for herself after Jack's death, I felt a resonance with the owner—that this was a home I would have built on that very spot. A large fireplace with conversation area dominated one end. In alcoves alongside were large leather banquettes that invited a long afternoon's recline with a book or a cozy tête-à-tête. Above one of the banquettes hung fencing rapiers and masks, as well as a reproduction of a classical Venus. Chairs and tables were in the plain Arts and Crafts style, of rich-grained, unelaborated wood. Drapes were fibrous tapa cloth printed with South Seas cultural motifs, the various shades of brown and beige adding to the sense of beauty existing in function rather than decoration.

Beyond sat a most inviting dining room, snug, with a wall of windows looking out onto a heavily wooded slope. The furniture here too was obviously custom-made, for its carvings borrowed symbols from the various South Seas artifacts scattered throughout the house. The walls were azure, and the white porcelain dining service in the cabinet was trimmed in a similar shade. The adjoining kitchen and butler's pantry repeated the sea green tones in tile, porcelain sink, and linoleum flooring.

Upstairs, Charmian's bedroom was so large as to dwarf the grand piano before the fireplace. The ceiling was coved and curve-beamed like a ship captain's cabin, and splashes of blue-green throughout further suggested the ocean. The closet revealed riding clothes, cloaks, and unique dresses, some beaded, some trimmed with lace, all bespeaking a daringly artful wearer. These gowns contrasted sharply with the many photographs of the owner in her typical attire of riding breeches and boots, or a loose muslin pants suit worn aboard a sailboat. A tiny galley kitchen, sufficient for preparing a simple meal, could be glimpsed beyond the dressing room.

The image that most entranced was a picture in a case along the stairwell landing. There a petite brunette stood sideways to the viewer, peering over her shoulder with a dazzling smile that exuded sheer joy in the scene surrounding her, that of a gathering of virtually naked Solomon Islanders. Perched on her hip was a tiny Colt pistol—an audacious reflection for me, recently enchanted by the nascent women's history movement. I would like to say that I also read the complexities of the signs—the sexuality, the white man's imperialism, the naive anthropology—but I did not. I was taken by this woman's obvious physical prowess, apparent in her well-toned arms and legs, and her adventuresome spirit.

My identification with Charmian appeared as counter-ego or Jungian shadow, a creature incorporating much I avoided or feared, through whom I might vicariously enjoy unaccustomed challenges and thrills. Within days I met Irving Shepard, then literary executor of the Jack London estate. Unclear to me until later was my propitious timing. Devoted to Charmian, Shepard had long wished that someone would honor her memory and contributions apart from her husband's. Another writer recently granted permission to write a biography had produced no results, so he welcomed my interest. During my first visit to the House of Happy Walls, as Charmian named her home, he took me around and explained little details of the design and how it so precisely reflected her values and personality.

At that time I also met the owners of a bookstore in Glen Ellen, Russ and Winnie Kingman, and purchased from them all of the books Charmian had written: *The Log of the Snark, Our Hawaii,* and the two-volume *Book of Jack London.* One copy even had her signature in a rounded backhand, along with photographs she had pasted on the end papers. When I spoke enthusiastically of my plans to write about Charmian, Russ belittled her with a tone implying naïveté on my part. Upon perusing existing biographies of Jack, I understood the reason for his low estimation.[2] Irving Stone, who had met Charmian, admired her physical courage yet portrayed her as both a clever shrew and a puerile annoyance. Richard O'Connor was less certain, sympathetic with Charmian for having to put up with an unfaithful, domineering man, yet also describing her as "subject to moods . . . sometimes sullen and demanding, sometimes openly possessive and jealous . . . largely self-centered." Forty years later, Kevin Starr wrote of her as affecting "a vaguely masculine outdoor atmosphere," becoming "petulant and demanding," and described by Jack as "our little child." Two biographers virtually ignored her role: Philip Foner and, more understandably, Jack's daughter Joan. The leading literary scholar Earle

Labor, as might be expected, did not much discuss Charmian, but acknowledged her favorably, as Jack did, as his "Mate-Woman."

It was Labor who warmly received my intentions and guided me through my first visit to the archives at the Huntington Library. That first brief glimpse into Charmian's diaries and letters convinced me that the biographers had been too quick to judge. (Only their notice of her vanity matched my evaluation.) The private Charmian revealed a woman consistently working, studying, and taking chances, even with her very life. That London loved and adored her, that the relationship persisted through tragedy and crises, was clear. Her notes also charted a deepening independence and sense of self throughout the marriage. In discussions with women colleagues at Sonoma State University, I found myself agreeing that she suffered the historical lot common to wives of famous men: shunted aside as of little consequence or condemned for being disruptive to the "great man's" creativity.

Charmian's writings also challenged me to shed an oversimplified perspective on gender relations prominent then which would have argued the opposite thesis: that the wife was equally responsible for the creative output and genius, an anonymous partner. A fascinating, complex woman such as herself must surely have been bound to an equally intriguing man. Jack London, it seemed, could not be the one-dimensional hard-drinking, womanizing, adventure-striving, suicidal personality depicted in works such as Irving Stone's *Sailor on Horseback,* and Richard O'Connor's *Jack London.* Andrew Sinclair's *Jack* avoids this caricature, yet also emphasizes the dark side of London's personality. The more I pored over Jack's works, especially his letters, and reflected on his nonliterary activities, such as his socialist propaganda and his ranch management, the less he fit the stereotype of the masculinist twentieth-century American novelist. There was much more substance to him than the self-destructive themes that overwhelmed even those narratives, notably by Stone and O'Connor, which incorporated praise as well. Consequently, what began as a biography of Charmian was transformed into the biography of a couple, *American Dreamers.* This was an examination of a marriage unusual for its day within the context of Bay Area artistic life, changing gender roles in the nation, and recently developed psychological concepts of interdependency. Although it incorporated a strong feminist framework, it eschewed simplistic explanations that cast the woman as victim.

That manuscript originally extended several chapters past Jack's death in 1916. When it became clear that publishers were not interested in Charmian's later life, I excised that material. Readers, though, did not agree with the editors, and kept asking when I was going to complete the story. I set the work aside while continuing to contribute to Jack London scholarship at conferences and in journals. It seemed prudent to pass beyond midlife myself before trying to appreciate fully the four decades of life Charmian experienced as a widow. The diaries of her later years were so imbued by her encounter with aging that I wanted to understand some of that experience myself before risking further estimation of her.

Twenty years after first encountering Charmian's home, I felt ready to return to the project, which I thought would be a simple matter of updating and expanding. Grace intervened, however, in the form of an angry caller who identified herself as Helen Abbott, daughter-in-law of the late Joan London, Jack's daughter. She charged me with having quoted from an unpublished manuscript of Joan's without permission. When she learned that the manuscript had been shown to me by Russ Kingman, she accepted my apologies. (Not until that moment had I recognized my error in forgetting to seek out the owner of the rights to Joan's unpublished material.)

Upon Ms. Abbott's invitation, I drove up into the gold country, portable copier in tow, and found placed at my disposal boxes of Joan's correspondence, manuscripts, photograph albums, and ephemera. Those contents demanded that I face up to another oversight on my part: that despite revising the commonplace view of Charmian, I had continued to propound one uncomplimentary to Jack's mother, Flora Wellman, his first wife, Bess Maddern, and his elder daughter, Joan. Furthermore, I realized that my understanding of Becky London, the younger daughter I had known casually during her final years, required revision. In writing about these figures I had unwittingly adopted the view of Charmian and Jack, and in the process had likely erred in some of my previous interpretation.

Within weeks, happenstance provided yet another revelation in the form of a manuscript copy of James Boylan's biography of Anna and William English Walling, later published as *Revolutionary Lives.*[3] Anna was the only person to co-author a book with London, *The Kempton-Wace Letters,* and in the process, though already married, he proposed to her. Because biographers have used only Jack's surviving correspondence, they have drawn one-sided conclusions. Apart from titillating arguments as to whether the two ever consummated the relationship, Anna is portrayed as alluring yet innocent, and possibly the victim of Jack's high-pressure courting. Boylan's work suggested a darker, more passionate figure, as desperate for Jack as he was for her. It also directed me to the Yale Library holdings, where Anna's correspondence and notes for manuscripts were accessible.

These discoveries required me to reread and reinterpret old notes in the file drawers. I also returned to library archives and double-checked my earlier summaries by retaking notes at the Huntington and other libraries, then compared them with ones made years earlier. To my relief, the notes displayed an agreeable consistency, but more important, in the process I picked up clues I had overlooked before.

Most necessary was a fresh outlook, a questioning of all I had previously assumed. Two conclusions became obvious. First was how much more problematic previous biographical scholarship had been than I had noticed. Even Russ Kingman, the most fact-driven of the biographers, ignored evidence that was inconsistent with his concept of London. That criticism included my own work, which depicted an overromanticized view of the couple, one they carefully constructed for posterity. Similarly, personal bias could lead investigators to accept one source and not another. For example, a common observation during scholarly discussions was the unreliability of Joseph Noel's memoir *Footloose in Arcadia*, because it was written after a falling-out with London. Now that I was more adept in historical methods, that conclusion seemed suspect. Checking Noel's memory against Charmian's diaries, I found correspondences that could not be ignored. While the tone of Noel's writing broadcast his animosity, the particulars of his accounts retained credibility.

Furthermore, my interpretation of London expanded, affording a better understanding of him as an icon of the Progressive Era, among the most famous men of his day, whose actions and writings reflected the pulse and contradictions of the culture. He was secondarily a representative of California to those outside the Golden State, a proselytizer for its Edenic promise. The more one examined the historical context, the more typical he seemed of others on the cusp of that era's change rather than an eccentric or a visionary. This applied in particular to the issue of masculinity, a prominent topic of controversy then. Most often he has been placed among the tough, brawny, and dominance-obsessed Bully Men of the day, the Teddy Roosevelt ilk, but I was aware of other elements of the discourse: a critique of such a view of manhood as destructive and an insistence that men change their ways.

Virtually everyone else in the recent boom of London scholarship being literary critics, my approach as a social historian was unique, and I hoped to correct assumptions concerning London's life and times. These scholars also were taking a revisionist approach to London as a writer, but none had access to the Joan London manuscripts, nor were they addressing much his relationships with the many females surrounding him. I was reminded of my biographies of the Vanderbilts and the Rockefellers, where the influence of the women disproved the myth of the masculine, self-made, solid American hero, a portrayal London carefully constructed to supplement his fame.[4]

Furthermore, I was the only London scholar living in California and immersed in the history of the state during his lifetime. Again, my research on the Vanderbilts and Rockefellers had also reinforced the significance of place in understanding a family culture. (No one can understand the Rockefellers without a study of the Burned-Over District of western New York or of the Western Reserve of Ohio.) The more one placed London and his relations within the national and local framework, the more clearly one could trace his curious complexity, and thus understand why he was very much a mirror reflecting to his readers their own questions, wishes, and confusions.

Social Darwinism, with its certainty that human types can be placed on a hierarchy of talent and skill, flourished during his lifetime, and racial matters would pervade much of his writing and thought. Through a brilliant stroke, fate delivered him two mothers, one white and one black, and, in a curious social anomaly, the latter of a higher class than the former. One stepsister became his devoted business manager, while the other fell into a life of dissolution and an early death. Before his first marriage he would love two women of very different backgrounds, one British-born, the other a Russian Jew. He may even have fallen in love with an African American woman. His two wives were exceedingly different in temperament, one linear and analytical, the other free-spirited and artistic. His two daughters inherited diametrically opposed halves of his makeup, with one becoming a self-sufficient, conventional business-woman who clung to a life of simple pleasures, while the other thrived on emotional drama and hell-raising in defiance of authority.

Since no one had made these women their focus, many commentators necessarily relied on commonly accepted sketches based on either London's own estimations or ready-made cultural constructions. The black mother devolves into the ever-devoted mammy, the real mother into a shrew; the British girlfriend is a fainting Victorian beauty, the Russian Jew a sultry intellectual. When planning this study, I was inclined to document page and verse of all the exaggerations and errors previously written about this amazing array of women. Eventually I understood that some of this deficient scholarship flowed from the lives of the women, especially the power London had by virtue of his gender to shape their identities well after his death and indeed their own.

By contrast, feminist historians directed me to reflect on the development and perpetuation of patriarchy. Key practices the awareness of which guides my analysis are *silencing,* the stilling or obliterating of women's voices; *self-naughting,* that is, following the precept to put others first and vanquish one's own needs; *suppressing sensuality,* which includes the stifling not only of sexuality and emotional intelligence but also of intuition; and *enclosing,* the actual and metaphorical walling in that excludes women from free movement in society. For each of the women here, London was a conduit for enforcing these precepts—or sometimes not, for he was not consistent. Indeed, what I found was that the choice whether to invoke patriarchal rules is itself a mechanism of control. Furthermore, the expression of that choice becomes a technique to divide and rule among women who might otherwise unite.

If feminist historians remind us that patriarchy is a dynamic system, they also challenge stereotypical reductions by revealing women's place as independent actors, not mere victims of a tyrannical social arrangement. As will be evident here, women internalize inferiority to varying degrees; hence their reaction to authority is differentially expressed. Some are complicit because they identify with the "rightness" of the arrangement. Some negotiate to achieve the best bargain from the inequality. Others find resources to confront or rebel against the patriarch. Less assertive ones implement techniques of passive aggression. All of these adaptations may be found among the women connected to Jack London.

Because this study covers three generations of women, the context in which they come of age is also significant. The first were migrants to California in the 1870s, who found new opportunities for self-assertion and participation in community life. The second generation, native raised, flaunted their physicality and education, and insisted on their right to speak out. The third generation reminds us how a context of increased women's rights and opportunities is not sufficient for all to enjoy the benefits.

To blend these profoundly private episodes in the lives of these women yet embed their stories within the context of their times requires a hybrid history. The narrative becomes the evidence and the argument. Begin with the mother line, the constructing of an identity and voice for two women. Position London as he was in life, part of a network in which his influence was greater than that of the women connected to him. Consider in turn how the women exerted a force on him and on one another. Examine how over time the connections strengthened, loosened, and in several cases were severed.

As a consequence, readers will find familiar themes in the story: of love unrequited, of promises broken, of children used as pawns by their divorced parents, of women becoming friends rather than jealous competitors, of marriage partners facing their fallibilities, of valiant souls puzzling through traumatic life transitions. History reminds us that life's daily challenges and promises vary little across time and culture; it is the resources and solutions available that particularize. To ignore the context of a life is to project one's own experiences, to self-satisfy and moralize, to apply a "presentist" bias. Too often this has been the case in biography, where the interpretive schemes devolve to the biographer's current-day value system, assisted by a smattering of psychological theory. The glare of the spotlight on the subject leaves the surrounding players and setting in shadow.

One consequence, as this book will demonstrate, is the creation and perpetuation of mythology built on specious reasoning. With regard to Jack London, the scholars' and biographers' ignoring, belittling, or misrepresenting the women in his life has had private as well as intellectual consequences. These are the parts of the project that have been most painful: reading documents that evince malice, deceit, and cruelty toward these women because of their affiliation with a famous man. Accordingly, given their particular relation with Jack, each woman was assigned a valence by him with regard to one another. Each was to absorb his view, and if she did not, to invoke a metaphor borrowed from his own intimate language, he would extinguish her star from his sight.

The danger in presenting London within this female constellation is that the very nature of patriarchal society casts him as dominant, of heavier gravity. While typing parts of the manuscript, my male assistant would whisper in exasperation, "What a bully!" Yes, he certainly was in particular circumstances, but often that bullying emerged from the frustration of trying to be a "good man" for his day, which he took to include financially supporting his first wife and daughters, his second wife and her eccentric aunt's household, his stepsister and her son, his nephew, his mother, a second nephew, and his surrogate mother. If patriarchs hold the power in theory, they must find the resources to fuel it in practice, and therein arises resentment. My hope is that, as in *American Dreamers*, London is revealed here not an outsized villain, hero, or tragic figure, but as a gifted man who, like any of us, made both wise and foolish choices.

In preparing this narrative, I avoided referring to *American Dreamers* so that I would be forced to begin afresh with my research materials. Some themes covered in depth there are not treated in detail here. These include exposition on Jack's and Charmian's youth, their separate development as writers, their South Seas adventure, and her role in his literary activities, both as a feminine persona in various stories and as a research assistant and editor. At the same time, I composed this book to be freestanding rather than a sequel, so that readers new to Jack London would find sufficient introductory material. Although I would change some conclusions of that earlier account today, I remain satisfied with the overall argument presented there, and am grateful to have the opportunity to expand my interpretations. After all, I have been enthralled by Jack London, for he loved strong-willed, questioning women.

CLARICE STASZ
*Petaluma, California*

# JACK
# LONDON'S
# WOMEN

# Mrs. Prentiss, Mrs. Chaney

THE STORY OF JACK LONDON's matrilineage begins at a most unexpected place, a slave cabin in Virginia. There, on an unknown day around 1832—the year is only a guess—a woman delivered a daughter later named Daphne Virginia by her owner in honor of her birthplace state. Her parents were sold off, and she would have no later recall of their presence.[1] Jennie, as she was known later in life, ended up in Tennessee, on a plantation in the Nashville area owned by John Parker. Her dire status was slightly softened by her assignment to the Big House, where she was to be servant and companion to the Parkers' youngest daughter, several years her senior.[2]

For many, plantation life conjures up scenes of Tara in *Gone With the Wind*. In one, a white woman in sumptuous, thickly petticoated dresses is waited on by a loving black mammy whose main joy in life is attending to her mistress. In another, the ladies of the house languish in the parlor and gossip. In a third, a house slave frets and cries childishly while the white woman belittles her fear. The surviving diaries, letters, and reminiscences of pre–Civil War southern women, however, sketch contrary scenes. Today we know that both white and black women were ensnared in the web of patriarchy that exploited slavery for private as well as economic purposes.[3]

The southern lady depicted at a ball with lavish hairdo and rich silk gown in reality spent most of her days at hard labor. She was up at five with her house slaves and worked beside them into the evening on an endless list of chores. She stood over heated pots making soap or rendering lard, slaughtered hogs, attended to the poultry, planted and weeded the kitchen garden, spun and wove fabric, sewed clothes for her family and slaves, dried fruits, salted meats, oversaw the kitchen, and handled numerous household maintenance chores. She nursed the sick, assisted in the education of her children, and directed the family's religious practices. In addition to the sheer physical labor, she was the major supervisor of Big House workers and was responsible for the living conditions of field slaves as well. She attended their births and deaths, settled disputes, distributed rations, and cajoled or beat her workers as was her wont.

As happens among the powerful, many resented the constant presence of slaves and their accompanying problems, which seemed to outweigh the value of their free labor. Some southern ladies did see their slaves as foolish, lazy, or childlike; some resented their husbands' use of slaves as concubines or prostitutes, with the ever-present reminder of mulatto children. Nonetheless, some felt a commonality that they were bound as tightly, though not as cruelly, by the rigidly patriarchal plantation system. Forced to ignore the sexual profligacy of the men, discouraged from seeking education and freedom of thought, more reflective plantation women displaced their hatred of slaves onto the institution itself. Thus they looked forward to its destruction, though they would confide such hopes only to their most trusted friends and private jottings.

Nor were the slave women in the Big House, those Jennie would have known as foster mothers and aunts, the big-hearted, good-humored mammies of the movies. They were often there instead of in the fields because they had special skills in cooking, needlework, or herbal medicine. Mulattos, too, were favored in an oblique acknowledgment of their blood relation to the plantation owners and white overseers. Typically, a caste system developed such that house slaves looked down on rather than sympathized with field slaves. Some, notably cooks, developed reputations as iron-fisted dictators over their domain, using their status to command and intimidate other slaves. Similarly, house workers applied their skills, talents, and intimate knowledge to resist and manipulate their owners to their advantage. Hardly obsequious servants, they would have been strong, self-confident models for a young motherless black girl such as Jennie.

Growing up in the Big House, Jennie was uniquely positioned. In the early years, as servant and companion to the Parker children, she learned reading and writing, as well as basic child care skills. By adolescence, she worked alongside Mrs. Parker and the house slaves to become an accomplished cook and seamstress. Less obvious was the ease with which she learned to move in the company of whites as well as blacks. She was thus among the few in bondage who became well equipped to succeed as a free woman in an integrated, urban society.

Furthermore, compared to the Deep South, upon which most historical research on slavery is based, in Tennessee laws and practices were less oppressive.[4] Slaves were chattel in civil law but persons by common law. Though civil law treated the slave as a property totally under the control of the owner, other laws allowed a slave some rights, such as to represent an owner in certain transactions. In practice, Tennessee slaves were often referred to as "hands" and less restricted from travel and education than slaves in the Deep South. Most slaveholders owned moderate-sized spreads, with fewer than ten workers in bondage, and kept their families intact. It was also more common for slaves to carry guns for hunting or to earn their own money. That Jennie's stories of slavery did not include accounts of cruelty suggests that the Parker plantation was run along such relatively humane lines.

Although her childhood was less degrading and laborious than that of a field slave, Jennie was nonetheless on permanent call to the child she served. By adolescence, she was assigned to accompany her mistress during domestic chores, which included "kitchen tricks" that would serve her well in later life. Perhaps as a result of Mrs. Parker's example, she acquired an aristocratic bearing and demeanor. Kept from the companionship of field hands, with their cultural practices closer to those of West Africa, she developed mannerisms more common to wealthy white southerners.

If Jennie's demeanor can be traced to her mistress, her life philosophy can be traced to older black women. Jennie would be a lifelong Christian, who saw "the Lord" as her constant friend and counsel. Jesus promised release, just as Moses had assured the freedom of the Israelites.[5] In slave society prayer meetings were practical occasions as well, providing the opportunity to plan and assist escapes, perhaps to find passage on the Underground Railroad and cross the "river Jordan," in this particular case the Ohio. Religion brought the slaves more than comfort and hope; it supported a sense of moral superiority based on criticism of their owners' un-Christian actions. This rock-hard foundation of belief suggests why Jennie not only refused to accept the mainstream view of Negro inferiority but also asserted the opposite, that the African race was superior to others.

What the hymns promising deliverance and freedom never mentioned were the particulars of what would transpire once the river Jordan was crossed or slavery ended. Certainly, at age eleven, Jennie could not imagine that about six hundred miles to the northwest in Massillon, Ohio, a white child was being born whose path would cross hers and bring a radical change into the life of each.

Flora Wellman was born on August 17, 1843, into a family whose ancestors could be traced back to the 1500s in England. Thomas Wellman as a young man was among the first generation of immigrants to New England. His offspring remained there for almost two centuries.[6] Then Joel Wellman, wife Betsy, and four children moved to Wayne County, part of the Western Reserve, the area of Ohio that was set aside as compensation to Connecticut citizens who had suffered severe losses from the British during the Revolution. Few took that offer, however, so Joel and Betsy Wellman were among those scattered stalwarts who created settlements in what was for them a cruel and threatening environment.

These daunting frontier conditions required self-reliance and courage to prosper. A family story survived, telling how Joel's young sons Hiram and Marshall embarked alone on a trip to Cleveland, which required a boat trip to a desolate island where another craft was scheduled to stop on the way to the port. It was late autumn, the last day the Cleveland boat was to run that year. When, for some reason, the boat failed to stop along its appointed route, the boys found themselves alone without food or shelter. Using rocks for tools, they constructed a raft out of driftwood and maneuvered themselves to the next town and to safety. Such behavior was a matter of course for frontier settlers, who either quickly adapted, died, or returned to the more protective environment of the East Coast. The same strong character would be passed on to Flora.

Those settlers who did stay and survive, and who foresaw the opportunities available, flourished. The Wellman men's foresight brought fortune. Flora's uncle Hiram owned a large warehouse on the Cuyahoga River, became a director of the Bank of Cleveland, and served as town marshal for eight years. Flora's father, Marshall, started out in Wooster as a cooper, a valued craft of the day, but foresaw more profits in canal building and became a successful contractor. Enjoying his newfound wealth, he settled his family in Massillon, the center of a rich wheat belt. There he and Hiram opened a mercantile warehouse on the new canal connecting the area to Cleveland and offered "cash for wheat." The brothers soon dominated the region and became the leading businessmen of Ohio's fastest-growing town on the inland waterways.

Marshall Wellman's wife, Eleanor Garrett Jones, presided over a staff of servants to care for a handsome seventeen-room house built of sun-dried, handmade yellow brick. From the street, a passerby looked through a filigree wrought iron fence to an imposing Federal facade bespeaking affluence. From farther down the street the great size of the house was more evident, for one could now see two extensions behind the main part of the building. Most likely one extension held the kitchen and functional rooms, including the nursery, and the other behind it, the servants' quarters. The main building, with its formal salons and ballroom, was the bailiwick of Walker, a black butler who wore a silk top hat as he went about his duties. Nearby, Flora's uncle Hiram built a similarly impressive mansion, a modified Greek Revival home with six tall columns supporting the entry portico.

Marshall and Eleanor Wellman loved children, as was evident in the double hand railing of their stairway, the lower one for small children to grasp easily when climbing up and down. Flora was the fifth child and the fourth daughter of a father who indulged her, particularly after Eleanor died when Flora was only four. His rapid remarriage to Julia Hurzthal, who bore four more children, left the girl spiteful that she was no longer the beloved baby of the family. Townsfolk came to consider her spoiled and willful. Neighbors spoke of watching her dash out in her nightgown to run several blocks to play at her cousins' house. When she was ten, she used a diamond ring to inscribe her name and the date on a stained glass window in her home. (The window, now in a museum, is all that remains of the mansion, so that desecration secured her memory in perpetuity.) Marshall and Julia Wellman nonetheless continued their unbridled pampering. They saw to it that Flora's clothes and toys came from New York so that she would always have the best and be at the height of fashion. Exempted from work of any kind, she acquired only one domestic skill, needlework, which she performed with unusual diligence and precision, though with little pleasure.

Liberal New England Protestantism, with its fostering of universal public education, temperance, women's rights, and abolitionism, dominated the Western Reserve. Massillon was a major stop on the Underground Railroad. Hiram Wellman's home was a well-known resting place for runaway slaves; later discovery of a storeroom under Marshall Wellman's driveway suggests the involvement of Flora's family as well in furnishing sanctuary. Despite her family's abolitionist activities, years later she deflected all of her granddaughters' inquiries concerning slavery. She was, however, always a strong supporter of women's suffrage. Accordingly, her family saw that she was given the best education, both home tutoring and private schools, along with piano and elocution lessons. She enjoyed being the center of attention, and developed a fondness for performing highly gesticulated dramatic presentations of poetry.

Less is known of Flora's religious education. New Englanders brought their piety with them to Ohio and quickly established Congregational, Baptist, and Methodist churches, which served as community centers as well as places of worship. Religious observances such as morning prayer, midweek church meetings, Sunday school, and Sabbath practices were believed to constitute the backbone of family unity. While the Wellman family likely belonged to a congregation, the extent of infusion of Christian practice and precepts into their daily life is unclear. Did they, like many families of the day, determinedly construct their lives around Scripture and prayer, or were they instead casual ritualists who joined in church activities for the sociability more than the spirituality? Whichever was the case, in later life Flora showed no concern for traditional religion or its trappings.

Flora's major adulthood belief system and practice was spiritualism. During her childhood, seances swelled in prominence, much as a result of the popularity of the three Ohio Fox sisters, whose fortune-telling and spirit sessions fed a press mania that brought them riches, medals, and public acclaim. Also active in Ohio were Victoria and Tennie Claflin, sisters whose mother was addicted to evangelical prayer meetings, speaking in tongues, and mesmerism. Her daughters aped the Foxes and would become even more famous as adults, even gaining the confidence of Commodore Vanderbilt. Just when Flora determined that she also had "the gift" of foresight and communicating with the dead is unclear, but it is likely that the Fox and Claflin girls played a part in awakening her to the possibility.

Flora's first twelve years were blessed by a loving family and many material comforts, yet they could not protect her from the childhood diseases that struck often without warning, incurring disability if not death. In 1855 Flora was felled by typhoid fever so severe that her growth stopped at four and a half feet, her hair fell out, and her eyesight failed. A wig and thick glasses gave her an owlish appearance. No doubt fancy silks, pearls, and furbelows compensated for some of the humiliation. Still, to understand Flora Wellman is to imagine her daily struggles to be recognized and respected in defiance of her childlike stature. She could, for example, stand among a group of peers, conversation passing back and forth above her, feeling ignored while the others simply did not see her below their line of sight. Her struggle for notice would take many forms later on.

Of other serious disruptions in Flora's life one can only conjecture. Her father lost much of his fortune in the financial panic of 1858. The sudden end to the fountain of luxury may have strained relationships within the family. In 1860 she left home and moved in with a married sister, Mary Everhard. Although she told one granddaughter that she fled because of an argument with her stepmother, local history hints at an affair with a married man. Despite her tiny stature, she had the buxom torso and tiny hands and feet treasured at the time. Was she complicit in an affair, or a victim of sexual assault? In later years she refused to talk at all about this episode—further evidence that the cause was either very embarrassing or very traumatic.

After some time Flora returned to Massillon to nurse another sick sister; yet she was never fully reconciled with her family, and expected to leave when her service was no longer needed. Meanwhile, many townsmen were taking off to support the Union cause, thus lessening the opportunities for a woman of her age to court and marry. Flora bided her time waiting for the war to end by joining in Sanitary Commission activities such as making bandages out of old linens and sheets. The family ballroom's chandeliers still blazed some evenings, lighting farewell dances as prospective soldiers took their departure. One of those departing was her father, who would be captured and spend time in a Confederate prison before returning home.

For thirty-year-old Jennie Prentiss the war brought tribulation before vindication. Following the Union victories at Forts Henry and Donelson in February 1862 and the capture of over fourteen thousand prisoners, the Confederate Army withdrew from central Tennessee, leaving Nashville vulnerable. Sweeping through that part of the state, Union troops under General Don Carlos Buell rampaged and burned a swath through an area including the Parker spread. What transpired was so horrific that Jennie would say only that two survivors remained: her mistress and herself. With no money or food, and only the clothes on their backs, they headed out of the war zone toward St. Louis, where Mrs. Parker had relatives.

Jennie grubbed for food, fruits, vegetables, and roots found along the way, and begged from strangers to keep her and her mistress alive. In later years she spun frightening stories of the journey, of hiding in woods to escape soldiers, of people weeping by the roadside, of the smell of burned houses, barns, and slave quarters, of rotting bodies. She was so close to starvation that she would often awake at night startled from a dream in which she was just about to bite into a sweet potato dripping with butter.

Once in St. Louis, Jennie was left on her own, for Mrs. Parker's people would not take her in. Consequently, she hired herself out as a domestic worker, a job for which she was well prepared.

At war's end, Jennie returned to Nashville, where she found work as live-in housekeeper for Ruth and Alonzo Prentiss. The Prentisses were originally from Putnam County in northwestern Ohio.[7] There he had run a successful carpentry business, while Ruth took care of their three children. When war struck, Alonzo signed up for three years' duty with the Forty-ninth Ohio, and served as a first lieutenant. The first regiment to enter Kentucky, the Forty-ninth was received by Union supporters in Louisville with fanfare and hurrahs. From there, they started the march southward, battling the Confederates at Stones River. When the unit was sent on, however, Alonzo was dispatched to Nashville, where on February 15, 1862, he was subject to a Board of Examiners hearing. The honorable discharge of a healthy, uninjured man could arise only from unusual circumstances. Apparently someone had revealed that Alonzo's mother, though apparently Caucasian, was in fact a mulatto.[8] Consequently, despite his very pale complexion, Alonzo was legally a Negro, which made his enlistment fraudulent, and his presence in the all-white fighting force illegal. Black regiments did not yet exist, so a transfer to one was not an option. In light of his good service record to that date, however, the board allowed him to resign with a full honorable discharge on March 10.

It was then that Ruth brought the children to Nashville, where the couple decided to stay while Alonzo resumed his carpentry—a skill much needed in a war-stricken community. By the time Jennie came into their household, the marriage was in collapse. After the war ended in 1865, Ruth took the children in July, moved back to Ohio, and sought an annulment. (She must have kept in contact with her former husband, however, because thirty years later he was aware of his daughter's married name.) Alonzo then courted Jennie, whom he married in March 1867. Their first child, William, was born late that year.

Although Alonzo was legally black, his pigmentation allowed him to pass as white, which meant that the couple appeared to be practicing the dreaded crime of miscegenation. Jennie was not just of African descent; she had an ebony complexion and deep-set dark eyes that strongly contrasted with her husband's coloring. Somehow the couple became acquainted with the wealthy mulatto abolitionist John G. Jones, who helped them, along with others, move to Chicago. There Jennie was active in the Berean Baptist Church and gave birth to a daughter, Priscilla Anne, in 1873. This was also the year of a major national financial collapse, which may have motivated the Prentisses to head west to San Francisco, a boomtown that would provide much work for Alonzo. They settled in a four-room redwood frame house at 17 Priest Street, just south of Market, with its bustle of shoppers, parades, torchlight marches, and spectacle. Having been settled by a motley array of people from various cultures, classes, and races, this was a city more tolerant of couples such as the Prentisses, perhaps more so than anywhere else in the nation.

Flora reached her thirties unmarried. Sometime in the early 1870s, following several years of wandering, she arrived out west as well, in the frontier town of Seattle, where she boarded at the home of Mayor Henry Yesler. Living with the Yeslers placed her at an advantage to meet many residents and visitors. One evening in their parlor she was introduced to William H. Chaney, a stocky, powerful-looking man with a leonine head and strong, unconventional opinions expressed in a forceful tone of voice.[9] His sense of humor and genial laugh countered the darker side of his nature, which by his own admission could be uncompromising and vengeful.[10]

Chaney was twenty-two years older than Flora, having been born in a log cabin near Chesterville, Maine, on January 13, 1821. His New England ancestors were independent yeoman, farming families who for generations had eschewed the more cosmopolitan seaboard towns. Chaney's father owned 1,500 acres, and as the only son Chaney stood to inherit this property holding. His good prospects ended at age nine, when his father died in an accident, and his mother was left with no one to run the farm. In a short time the family's fortunes faltered, and young Chaney, like his sisters, was bound out, essentially sold as labor to another farmer. Defiant of his virtual enslavement, and more an intellectual than a laborer, he was traded among seven farmers before he reached the age of sixteen, when he escaped for work at sea. There followed a stint on a fishing schooner for two years, then nine months in the navy, which he deserted, a brief fling at piracy on the Gulf Coast, clerking at a store, reading law, editing newspapers, writing novels and poems (long since lost), making stump speeches, preaching sermons, and generally wandering about.

Chaney seemed incapable of holding onto a thought or an acquaintance for long. While attracted to an idea, he was principled and resolute, but a new slogan could pull him off to a new short-term fidelity. He was in turn a Congregationalist, a Methodist, and a Baptist. His political affiliation switched from the abolitionist Whigs to the prejudice-based Know-Nothings. His wives, who by his own count eventually added up to six, did not last long either. Yet despite his mercurial ways, he was constant to his humanitarian ideals and devoted to the improvement of mankind.

Chaney's first wife died tragically right after their marriage in 1851. He was married again by year's end to a well-to-do woman, but that marriage broke up after six years. In 1857, two wives behind him, he landed penniless in Boston. Nothing is known of the next nine years, until 1866 or so, when in New York City he befriended and moved in with Luke Broughton, an immigrant British doctor who had quit medicine to popularize astrology. Broughton had already been chased out of Philadelphia on a charge of fortune-telling for distributing his *Monthly Planet Reader and Astrological Journal* at four cents a copy. New York appeared more hospitable, and Chaney proved the disciple Broughton needed, one vigorous at oratory, charismatic in crowds, and persuasive in writing. The acolyte had been bitter over his difficult life until he discovered astrology, which read in his natal chart the likelihood of persistent poverty. That knowledge freed rather than frustrated Chaney, for he realized that simply by chance of a favorable birth, modest intellects could make a fortune; thus his own lack of financial success was no reflection on his character. Indeed, he would remain contentedly in poverty the rest of his life, committing every spare coin to the promulgation of the celestial doctrine.

Astrology, Chaney asserted, was "the most precious science ever made known to man." It could hasten the development of humankind by bringing about sturdier and more intelligent children, whose education could be more precisely directed by planetary guidelines. Knowing a child's horoscope, one could train him or her "to dwarf the evil propensities and develop all that is good."[11] Implicit in Chaney's system was the notion of eugenics, the doctrine that the human race could be improved by identifying and applying scientific laws. Underlying this impulse was a belief in the superiority of Anglo-Saxon culture and blood, which implied a repugnance for immigrants from "lesser" cultures, notably those subscribing to the Roman Catholic Church. His was a theory of racialism, that is, one of prejudicial beliefs without implying harmful actions toward those who were deemed inferior. Herbert Spencer's best-sellers would reinforced and spread such racialist ideas across the country and would much influence Chaney's only offspring.

Eventually even New York City decided that Broughton's popularity was too threatening to the Boss Tweed machine which protected the Irish. Consequently, the astrologers found themselves unpopular with a vociferous segment of the citizenry that decried them as "anti-Papal," a valid charge in light of Chaney's claim that the Bible was the creation of medieval monks. Broughton's landlord rid himself of his disreputable tenants by leasing the floor above to a crew of Fenians who spent day and night drilling and singing on behalf of a free Ireland. When Chaney complained to authorities about the Fenians' rowdyism, they jailed him instead.

During his many months languishing at the Ludlow Street prison, Chaney converted a female inmate to astrology but resisted marriage to her because "Venus [was] in evil aspect with Jupiter." Nevertheless, she eventually became his third wife, though she should have listened to his warnings. Not soon afterward, Chaney learned of the interest western miners and homesteaders had in visits from peripatetic phrenologists and spiritualists. Feeling called to "serve as the angel of astrology on the Pacific Coast,"[12] he left his wife, who did not want to accompany him, and headed to the infant settlement of Portland, where he established a lively practice. Since his freethinking included support of women's rights, he befriended the most influential suffragist in the Northwest, Abigail Duniway. She may have introduced him to the Yeslers, who were also supportive of feminist causes.

During his wanderings, Chaney lectured, trained students, and prepared an updated and corrected ephemeris, the reference essential to calculating accurate natal charts. He also drew the rancor of traditionalists when he modified Broughton's doctrines, which followed the English astrologers' deterministic assertion that heavenly alignments determined human actions. In a very American reinterpretation, Chaney held that the configurations merely indicated the characteristics of the client, who had the free will to apply the information wisely or not. His lectures and writings often attacked the British through use of witty arguments. In one lengthy example he asked why Queen Victoria's son, the Prince of Wales, was depraved and unsuitable despite his mother's laudable character. Poking fun at the British love of the ancients in their horoscope interpretations, he noted how "modern authors make a mistake in citing Claudius Ptolemy, who lived in Egypt and flourished nearly two thousand years ago, as authority to show what business or occupation Young America is likely to choose."[13]

Chaney achieved his goals, for he was very much responsible for bringing respectability to astrology, both by spreading its doctrine throughout the nation and by producing guidebooks instructing readers how to cast charts on their own. From the viewpoint of serious astrologers today, Chaney is a major figure who shifted the practice from quackery to a more rigorous method.

Exactly when Flora Wellman and William Chaney became lovers is unclear because our only source is his autobiography, with its vague and sometimes inaccurate chronology. Whatever the precise timing, Chaney claimed he lived in Oregon for several years, then in October 1873 moved to San Francisco. While there, he says, his third wife wrote from New York that she was divorcing him, "but if I ever married again she would have me imprisoned. This aroused my ire and on June 11th, 1874—three weeks later—I took another wife." They settled at 314 Bush Street, and later moved to 122 First Avenue. "We lived together till June 3rd, 1875—then separated."[14]

This wife would have been Flora Wellman. Since most San Francisco civil records were destroyed by the great fire of 1906, no document of proof exists. The question whether the union was legal or not is complicated by the fact that the partners were key members of a countercultural group that was, according to its publication *Common Sense: A Journal of Live Ideas,* "pro labor, pro-Negro, pro-Grange," for free love and freethinking, and against religious revivalism based on emotionality. "The emancipation of labor from the chains of capital" was another common theme. It was, for its day, radical both politically and socially, though not unusual for the Bay Area, where extremists of every sort found a hospitable crowd and tolerant coverage by the press.

Although some members invoked Victoria Woodhull's principles of free love, it is not clear that they were sexually promiscuous with one another. "Free love" for Woodhull meant rather monogamy without state sanction. Apart from vague anecdotes that Flora was "loose" during this time, nothing substantial suggests that these friends traded sexual partners or treated sex lightly. For example, one participant recalled of Flora's sexual conduct during this time that "she never meant to be immoral; she was merely unstable," and Chaney himself later claimed that Flora was also seeing another man, Lee Smith.[15]

Chaney did, however, legalize several of his other marriages, and Flora is mentioned throughout *Common Sense* as "Mrs. Chaney." One advertisement identifies her as "Flora Wellman Chaney, Teacher of Elocution and Instrumental Music," at 409 Stevenson Street. She is also listed that way as editorial assistant to the publisher Amanda Slocum.

Chaney advertised himself as an astrologer and lecturer, and attracted notoriety for his spirited defense against those detractors who debunked his beliefs as phony fortune-telling.[16] One of his more infamous talks concerned his claim that the Bible was hokum, and that Christ had no more reality than Santa Claus. Another speech answered in the negative the question "Does Christianity Promote the Highest Civilization?" In line with his previous Know-Nothingism, he had special venom for "Romanism," a derogatory term for Catholicism. During the winter he took these and other lectures, including several in favor of prison reform, on tour to inland California communities.

One of Chaney's arguments was that women had advanced little under Christianity. This feminist concern was evident in the group's practices, for when Amanda Slocum took over the Woman's Publishing Company, a printing firm, she hired only women and paid them wages equivalent to men's. Slocum's firm specialized in pamphlets and books emphasizing equal pay for equal work.

Although Chaney was the major intellectual of the group, by May 1875 the editors of *Common Sense* had decided that his astrology was more a hindrance than a help to their larger cause. In response, Chaney attempted to form a rival society called the Philomatheans, while *Common Sense,* short on funds, soon ceased publication. Chaney proposed that his new group be "a fraternity, etc. for mutual improvement, so that their children may prove superior to themselves and thus continue to improve the race until in a few generations vice and crime will almost disappear."[17] Unfortunately for Flora, he did not apply this axiom to his own life. When she became pregnant, Chaney, it was alleged, told her to get an abortion.

What transpired led to lurid headlines and a provocative melodramatic story in the *San Francisco Chronicle* of June 4, 1875:

A DISCARDED WIFE

WHY MRS. CHANEY TWICE

ATTEMPTED SUICIDE

The account described Flora as the victim of a cruel charlatan, a man who had taken all the money she'd earned and then told her to "destroy her unborn babe." As if that were not devilish enough, he then sold the household furnishings and deserted her. Distraught by the abandonment, she took laudanum, and when that failed to work, shot herself with a tiny pistol aimed at her forehead. The ball glanced off, producing only a flesh wound. The Slocums rushed in, prevented any further suicide attempts, then delivered her to a Dr. Ruttley's rest home. Questioning how Flora could be attracted to a man known for his "harsh words and unkind treatment," the reporter concluded that she had been struck by "a mania like . . . that which drew Desdemona toward the sooty Moor."

If the *Chronicle* mocked Chaney's "hybrid doctrines" and his blasphemy, it allowed that astrology was "highly valuable," the only problem being that there were too many practitioners in the city to provide any one of them a good living! Though his failing as a provider was judged deplorable, Chaney's major sin was held to be his abusing Flora's goodwill and affection. That said, the story became a moral to warn women against men of weak character.

Further circulating this story was Abigail Duniway, who upon hearing of Flora's plight began a public campaign against "this uncouth yet erudite Ishmaelite."[18] Chaney looked to astrology to find reason for Duniway's newfound hostility toward him. He determined that she had Scorpio rising and Mercury on the ascendant, and for years afterward he would use her case in his lectures as the example of a troublesome disposition caused by the stars.

Despite the public outrage reported in the newspapers, Chaney remained in San Francisco, moving into his business office on Bush Street. His coolness toward Flora was perhaps best explained later by a woman who was likely his granddaughter, who spent years ferreting out his full story. Given the cruel circumstances of his childhood, she ventured, he simply had no ability to relate to children. They existed for him only in the abstract, as members of the species to be molded for the betterment of the race.

The facts of Flora and William Chaney's relationship are more complicated than the tabloid news stories described. Key documents are missing, the memories of participants sparse and contradictory.

In his astrological primer Chaney often referred to his own chart and history, and discussed his amatory life explicitly so that readers could learn from his experience. There were to be two more women after Flora. All his wives, he regretted, "were simply unfortunate in having their paths intersect with mine, and they should be pitied instead of blamed." His acquaintance with marriage suggested that it was an institution made not in heaven "but in that other place." He never blamed his wives, explaining that it was "a coward and sneak who will try to injure the woman who has borne his name, no matter if she has been in the wrong, for it is ten to one that he is equally so." Rather, he attributed his habitual marital difficulties to his combative disposition. "You may as well try to turn Niagara upstream," a friend had commented of him, and he confessed it was true.[19]

The *Common Sense* devotees rejected the need for social sanctioning of a relationship, and believed that living together without benefit of clergy was more advanced than having a legal contract. So perhaps Chaney's assertion of marriage to Flora referred instead to a common-law union. Indeed, over twenty years later Flora would swear that she had never been married prior to meeting John London.[20] Yet her statement was for purposes of getting access to a pension, and her supporting witness was an out-of-state sister who would not necessarily have known the facts of Flora's status regarding Chaney. In fact, her next marriage certificate would list her as "Flora Chaney"—though she could have been using that name to retain a semblance of legitimacy for herself and her son. Given all these complexities, whether the couple legally wed or not remains problematic and is unlikely to be resolved.

Further perplexing the issue is Chaney's own later denial of paternity. He claimed to have been "impotent," which could be taken to mean "sterile," for despite his many sexual dalliances, he fathered no other known children. Years later Chaney offered his own version of the story, namely, that Flora had been nagging him to let her have a child by "a good, nice man" yet remain his wife with the child bearing his name. He rejected the idea. A month later she told him she was pregnant, but he thought it was a ruse. After they fought all night long, he said she could never be wife to him again. He had been thinking of leaving her well before this, but because of her temper, not her loose morals. Nevertheless, Chaney added, other than gossip he had no direct evidence of indiscretion on Flora's part. Their relationship had simply turned so sour that at one point he had thought of killing both her and himself. Unfortunately, Chaney's version is so contaminated by self-defense, and was offered so long afterward, that its credibility is difficult to determine.[21]

Flora's voice concerning this period, her memories and her rejoinder to Chaney, is silent. She hid the truth so well from her only child that he would not learn of Chaney's putative paternity until adulthood. Her granddaughter Becky believed that Flora loved Chaney to the end in spite of his cruelty. What supports Flora's naming Chaney as the father of her son are, first, the indisputable fact of their cohabiting during the time of his conception, and second, the absence of any suggestion on the part of her associates that another man could have been responsible. Finally, except in cases of extreme promiscuity, it is rare for a woman not to know the father of her child.

Nevertheless, unless DNA evidence is introduced, whether or not William Chaney was the biological father of Jack London cannot be decided. Putting aside the sensational news articles, which haunted Chaney for years, and the paucity of other evidence, a cautious investigator can conclude only that Flora Wellman Chaney had an anonymous conception. Chaney would, however, be considered by her son and his children as their ancestor. For that reason, whether valid or not, he must be included in the full story and treated as such.

Deserted, bereft, confused, Flora found solace in the Slocum household. There, while the child grew within, she recovered sufficiently to earn her keep by giving music lessons and sewing custom-made clothes. Her favorite sister, Mary Everhard, shipped out a full baby layette, and the Common Sense group gathered round to support her emotionally.

Flora receded into anonymity until a public notice, a birth announcement, appeared in the *San Francisco Bulletin*. "In this city, January 12 [1876], wife of W. H. Chaney, a son." Chaney remained in the city yet never acknowledged the baby as his own. Later that year he moved to Oregon, where he would take his fifth wife, as well as continue his battle with Abigail Duniway, whom he would successfully sue for maligning his reputation.

Flora's delivery had been difficult and prolonged, and she was unable to produce much milk. Her doctor attributed her poor lactation to mental fatigue, and recommended a long rest for her emotional as well as physical restoration. He advised that she send the baby to live with a wet nurse, a woman whose own recent child had been stillborn. That woman was Jennie Prentiss, and the baby delivered to her breast would forever proudly call himself her "white pickaninny."[22]

# 2

## *Johnny, Jack*

JENNIE PRENTISS'S MEETING with Johnny Chaney seemed fated. On January 12, 1976, she had delivered a stillborn daughter, yet in her grief agreed to nurse and care for Flora's newborn. Consequently, the boy lived at the Prentiss home, where he became a substitute sibling to Will and Priscilla Anne for the child who had died. When as the result of an illness his dark hair fell out, it grew back so light that Jennie called him her "Cotton Ball." The former slave now had a white child of her own to nurture.

Her attachment quickly deepened. As an old woman she recounted with outrage the time when Alonzo invited a couple over on the mistaken assumption that the baby was available for adoption. The visiting woman "went near crazy-like over my Cotton Ball . . . and he was scared and began to yell—and he *could* yell." After the couple left, she gave Alonzo a tongue-lashing for inviting them in. With regard to the "teenty, helpless angel," she knew "no difference between that baby an' my own Will, I was set on him. It most killed me when I had to wean him, and his folks took him with them out yonder to Bernal Heights."[1]

Flora did not visit her son often. To Jennie she seemed hard driven, set on getting ahead by teaching piano and sewing custom clothing every moment of the day. Tired and fiercely angry toward Chaney, yet mourning his absence, she had little emotional currency left to spend on her son. Nor were the traditional motherly behaviors—cooing, cuddling, playing, praising—congenial to her character. Yet one could not help admiring this tiny woman with her outsized energy and determination to prevail despite the unfavorable times.

The year 1876 was notable for making one of several sudden and deep collapses in the mercurial Gilded Age economy. Fortunately for the Prentisses, it less affected carpenters, who were needed to turn out San Francisco's Gothic, Queen Anne, Italianate, and Stick Style homes, with their distinctive ornamental trim. These expensive houses featured elaborate interior paneling and molding, built-in cabinetry, window seats, and gleaming parquet floors. More common were the workers' homes, put up quickly and cheaply for the wave of new immigrants. While the depression, which tossed thirty thousand men out of work, brought private crises to many San Franciscans, Alonzo was not among them. Joining the unemployed, however, was a friend by the name of John London, who would be introduced to Flora by the Prentisses.

Forty-seven-year-old John London was relatively new to starvation poverty. His early years on a farm in Clearfield County, Pennsylvania, had been uneventful, his early adulthood spent as boss of a railroad section gang.[2] After marriage to Anna Jane Cavett, he farmed in Wisconsin, Illinois, and Missouri. In November 1864 he enrolled in the 126th Illinois Volunteers in time for the Battle at Duvall's Bluff in Arkansas, but, following repeated bouts of pneumonia, measles, and infections that left his lungs permanently damaged, was discharged.[3] He then took his family to Iowa, where he supervised construction of a bridge across the Cedar River. Seeking more independence, he and Anna Jane played gypsy for two years, living out of a prairie schooner before finally resettling to homestead on a section of land outside Moscow, Iowa. There John learned the language of the neighboring Pawnees, hunted for meat, tilled the soil for food, and was kept busy with the dawn-to-dusk chores that filled the frontiersman's life. Though his was a back-wrenching lifestyle, the opportunities to test himself may have fulfilled him as he gained skill to survive in that harsh environment.

Less sturdy, Anna Jane eventually succumbed to the burdens of frontier life. Over a twenty-year period she gave birth eleven times, and thus was always either pregnant or nursing. Weakened by consumption, she died on December 19, 1873. Without a wife to watch his two small daughters and son still at home, John was forced to give up his land and set out for the West. Eleven days after arriving in California in 1874, his son, Charles, died. Soon after he left his daughters, Eliza, eight, and Ida, five, at an orphanage in Butte County, while he moved on to San Francisco to work.

By now wartime injuries had severely restricted London's stamina, placing him at a distinct disadvantage in a city where most unskilled jobs required ten or twelve hours a day, six days a week. Indeed, upon noticing his labored breathing, Jennie Prentiss guessed correctly that, like her daughter Priscilla, he too was suffering from consumption.[4] Having lived all his life in small towns or farming areas where familiarity bred trust, John London was also unaccustomed to the chicanery of commercial city life and was easy prey for deceivers. It was a poignant letdown for a man so well equipped to survive the dangerous, unpredictable plains that he was thought to be of little value in the safe, orderly city. Eventually, he became a canvasser for a local emporium, hiking the steep hills into the various ethnic neighborhoods. These experiences nourished a storytelling inclination that made him welcome company at the end of the day.

Out of place, kindhearted, and sympathetic to the underdog, John London found Flora's vulnerability attractive. After her unhappy experience with Chaney's bluster and inconsistency, Flora correctly saw in John London fifteen years her senior, a man ready to take on responsibility without rancor. They discovered a shared willingness to take risks, an interest in gambling and games, and a fascination with spiritualism. The courtship could not have been a long one, for they were married on September 7, 1876, before Justice of the Peace James C. Pennie in San Francisco.

The reality of their commitment set in quickly. On February 19, 1877, John brought Eliza and Ida home from the orphanage. He had not told his daughters much about their stepmother, and they naturally had idealized her appearance. Since Flora had given up wearing wigs, she looked even more odd and stern. The girls' disappointment must have shown in their response to her. Neither was ever to warm up to their stepmother, nor she to them. John would also soon discover that Flora had a temper and a domineering manner; she learned in turn that his physical condition could not match his drive for success.

Despite these surprises, the couple proved highly compatible. Of even temperament, he humored her, appreciated her energetic spirit, and deferred to her strong dominant streak. He was the only person who could elicit a softness from her, and she became increasingly protective as his chronic illness progressed. No stories survive of this curious couple disputing or growing alienated from each other—quite the contrary. If anything, as will be seen, they were too oriented toward each other to attend to their children's pressing needs. Particularly uniting them was an optimism, unvanquished by past experiences, that tempted them with the typically American promise of wealth to those who work hard and diligently.

The extent of the daily challenges facing this newly blended family is reflected in their moving six times around the city over three years. Part of this peripatetic restlessness reflected Flora's conviction that a better place was always to be had, perhaps down the street or over the next hill. Even their rare "good" houses, which she could describe in detail to grandchildren years later, did not hold her interest for long. Meanwhile, John took whatever odd jobs he could, including that of door-to-door salesman for the Victor Sewing Machine company, while Flora continued her efforts to raise money.

Exactly when baby Johnny joined the London household is unclear. He may have lived with the Prentisses as late as the age of two, for at the time weaning was postponed until much later than today. Furthermore, Jennie's emotional bond to the child was strong, and she would not let him go easily. After he departed, she determined to maintain contact with him and his family.

Near-tragedy in 1879 compelled the Londons to move across the Bay. Three-year-old Johnny and nine-year-old Eliza fell victim to diphtheria epidemic. The children were so near death, and the family so poor, that Flora explored the possibility of burying both in the same coffin. When the children recovered, John London joined in a partnership to open a produce store at the corner of Seventh and Campbell streets in Oakland, and moved the family to a truck farm near the eastern shore of San Francisco Bay. Oakland was thought to be a much healthier environment, and thus attracted growing families to fill its rapidly developing streets. When within a year the store failed, the Londons moved to a twenty-acre farm in Alameda, a seven-mile-long island nestled along the estuary west of Oakland. In 1880 the census taker noted the presence of a Chinese cook living in the household, so it would appear that the family had rebounded from their losses.

Significantly, at about the same time Alonzo and Jennie Prentiss moved to Alameda and lived within easy distance. Escape to a more accepting community and promise of more economic opportunity may have been their motive, for the East Bay was especially congenial to blacks.

Unlike African Americans in other states, after the Civil War, California blacks had an ironic advantage as a minority thanks to the presence of the Chinese, who outnumbered them ten to one. Consequently, various efforts to ensure blacks their rights, though up against strong opposition in the state legislature and city councils, resulted in significant successes for an era when segregation was becoming institutionalized throughout the country. In contrast to the scapegoated Chinese, blacks could point to their being "native Americans," Christians, and loyal to the country. Despite the racial prejudice that held blacks to be less intelligent and capable than whites, their counterargument facilitated the passing of laws to desegregate public schools and public conveyances.

Within California, the East Bay provided special opportunities. With the completion of the transcontinental railroad, which terminated in West Oakland, black porters and railroad workers settled nearby. The steadiness of the jobs and good pay enabled these workers' families to buy homes and enjoy a middle-class lifestyle. They built the Shiloh African Methodist Episcopal Church at Seventh and Market streets in Oakland, which would serve as an important community center for political organizing, conferences, clubs, socials, and educational activities. By founding institutions parallel to those of whites, they created a cosmopolitan, nature-loving, open-minded community. They considered themselves full citizens of the Athens of the West, as Oakland proclaimed itself, and took pride in that status.[5]

A countrified extension of Oakland, Alameda offered children broad sweeps of fields, woods, marshland, and waterfront for play. Single-family homes were larger than those in San Francisco and had bigger yards for gardens, poultry, and even some livestock. This smaller community included over a hundred black families, who were not segregated in one section. Town fathers bragged about Alameda's being crime free, its jail usually empty save for the weekend drunk or troublesome vagrant. Alamedans pronounced themselves hardworking, good-natured, and kindhearted, in other words, better than their cosmopolitan neighbors in Frisco. The town boasted a factory that made the thickest rope in the nation, a brick works, the Clark Pottery and Tile Works, a brewery, and several dairies. Most important for Alonzo Prentiss, it was attracting affluent families who wanted large, well-built Victorian homes. The Prentisses' own house, a modest two-story Gothic dwelling, was comfortable and well kept.[6]

Johnny often visited the Prentiss household, where Jennie was always ready with fresh pastries and hugs. "Will and Annie were like cousins," he recalled years later, and he was for some time ignorant of the meaning of their different skin color. He recalled how, when during a tomato fight he bashed Will's nose, he cried out in the derogatory language of the day, "Oh, gee! Willy! I've made your nose as flat as a nigger's."[7] In the fictionalized versions of his life story provided to book publicists and reporters, however, these "cousins" do not exist. Nonetheless, throughout his childhood he played with the Prentiss children, even long after understanding the repugnance toward their race felt by his white companions. To do so, of course, he had to hide his time spent with the former from the latter, to dissemble and deceive. In the process, he perhaps grew intrigued by the dramatic elements of having a "secret life," for variations on this theme would reappear in other guises throughout his life and his fiction.[8]

Daily existence was clearly harder for the Londons than the Prentisses. The Londons were typical of working-class families of the time in adopting a cooperative model. When family expenses exceeded the wages of the male head of the household, wives and children used whatever talent or means available to bring in extra money. Accordingly, major decisions on relocation, work, and education required members to subordinate their personal desires to family needs.

Such deferral of dreams was not always accepted easily, and all three London children were unhappy with their lot. Perhaps because their father was more easygoing, they made Flora the object of their complaints, the reputed cause of their various sorrows. It is not that she beat Eliza, Ida, and Johnny, or in other ways directly abused them. Nor could their strong feelings be attributed solely to her being more of a disciplinarian than John. Rather, one suspects they had absorbed her constant longings for more comfort, her account of fate as heaping undeserved abuse on her, a victimized view of life that was countered by a restless search for relief. In an era when mothers were held up as virtually angelic beings, serene ladies whose attention was devoted solely to their brood, any woman whose circumstances prevented that lifestyle was vulnerable to censure.[9] Flora displayed her caring indirectly, and probably believed she was doing a good job as a mother by adding to the family's income. After all, her own parents had always shown their love by giving her things, and she was literally wearing her fingers raw to provide for her family.

Children's narcissism prevents perception of their parents' limitations, and in some cases never wanes to be replaced by a more compassionate stance. Whatever the realities, each child had particular grievances. Being the eldest, Eliza bore most responsibilities. (As an adult she would say the happiest time of her childhood was in the orphan asylum.) With Ida, she handled domestic as well as field work, while their little stepbrother had easier chores and more leisure to daydream and read. Having been wrenched from the stable Prentiss household and thrust into a vagabond one, the finely tuned Johnny was, however, the most insecure. Among his earliest memories were sense images of sounds and sights that aroused dark and lonely feelings. In one he was left alone in a dusty room, boxes filled with items for the next move, frightened by the sound of the woman next door beating a rug.[10] As with so many artists, this extreme alertness to the physical environment would serve him well in his craft, though at great cost to his emotional stability.

If the relationship of mother and son was little marked by warmth, it was nonetheless strong. It was Flora who taught him to read by age four, and he always respected her for introducing him to books. She also gave him and her stepdaughters piano lessons. As he grew older, Johnny complained about some of her demands—what child does not?—yet acknowledged that she was the only one always to have utter faith in him, to nurture his latest youthful dream. Consequently, he never fully severed his filial feelings or the precept that a good son cares for his mother when she is in need.

He bonded well with his stepfather, and together they used teasing to demonstrate their alliance against Flora. One evening Frank Atherton, a friend of Johnny's, came to dinner—thick steaks served on a table covered with newspapers for easy cleaning. John and his son pretended that the food came from charitable neighbors and commented on the odd tablecloth. Flora, taking the bait, showed Frank the linens in the closet and refuted their claims of poverty. Finally she realized that they were "full of the old nick" and joined in the laughter.[11]

Until adulthood, Johnny assumed that the kindly man who had taken him out on the bay and entertained him in the evenings with long, colorful stories was his "Papa." Though never adopted, he thought his legal name was John London, Jr. He had accepted Eliza and Ida as his natural sisters and would refer to them as such throughout his life. Nor was Johnny the only one affected by the suppression of his origins. Eliza denied that she was other than his natural sister and maintained that her father was Johnny's father. One day she went into Flora's trunk, removed all the letters and other evidence of Chaney's presence in her stepmother's life, and burned them. She had, after all, been absent through the pregnancy, delivery, and marriage, and this may have been what she was told. She coddled, praised, and spoiled Johnny so that he felt ever grateful for her many kindnesses. This exceptionally close sibling bond, however, excluded Ida, who grew increasingly alienated from the family.

After two years' residence in Alameda, the Prentisses moved to Oakland, to a section close by the estuary that was becoming more concentrated in its black population. Although some were squatters or lived on houseboats, most lived in relative comfort. Son Willy apprenticed in the carpentry trade under his father, while the ailing Priscilla Anne continued her schooling. With both children growing up, Jennie had more time to devote to her church and African American community organizations.

For both the Prentiss and London families, daily household tasks were unceasing and fell upon the female members. Although canned goods and some domestic appliances were now available, they were not often affordable to families such as theirs. This meant that food was prepared from scratch, some of it homegrown, then harvested and preserved, mostly through the long, hot process of canning. Poultry kept in the yard provided eggs; unproductive hens faced the axe. Clothes were mostly homemade, not store-bought. For such families, the Sears catalogue was just a "wish book" (and a source of outhouse paper). Carpets had to be beaten by hand, laundry sudsed in tubs, the water heated on the stove, and coal stoked in the oven. These chores were more laborious for tiny Flora than sturdier Jennie. It is not surprising that by her forties, Flora was afflicted by the onset of joint disorders and skeletal collapse.

At the Prentiss home Johnny found a family less plagued by financial worries, and more united by the parents' well-defined and expressed Christian values. Whereas Flora was unconventional in her spiritual beliefs, Jennie was a faithful member of her church and was devoted to reading the Bible. Whereas John could not seem to hold to a job, Alonzo was steadily employed. Whereas the Londons were always grasping for a perch they could not seize for long, the Prentiss family had found its niche in the middle class.

Johnny's opportunity to escape to the Prentiss home ended in 1883 when his family moved to a ranch near Moss Beach on the San Mateo coast south of San Francisco. After some small success, by 1885 they had profited enough to buy a larger spread in a more favorable growing area, the warm Livermore Valley, over the range to the east of Oakland. Wisps of the children's memories hint at

the parents' leaving the youngsters alone for days at a time, of unruly houseguests, of both parents drinking, of earnings spent on Chinese lotteries and fly-
by-night schemes. Nevertheless, the Londons did well enough to expand their
holdings to over one hundred acres in Livermore, where they raised olives,
grapes, and fruit and were able to afford hired hands. How much of the parental
neglect is true, how much apocryphal, is unclear.

As the parents labored and schemed toward a better life, and with Jennie
Prentiss far away, Johnny came to view Eliza as his surrogate mother. There are
no large events, no significant episodes he would recall later in honoring her
devotion. But her place in his heart, in his indebtedness, was set enduringly. It
was thus a terrible loss for him when widower and sea captain James Shepard
approached Flora with the possibility of boarding his dependent children on
the farm. She explained that she did not have room for three more youngsters.
During his visit, however, he took note of sixteen-year-old Eliza. He courted her
for several months and then proposed. She accepted despite his being more
than twice her age, for his position promised a better standard of living and escape from the chaotic London household. Shepard bought her a home near the
Prentisses in Oakland, where she took happily to raising her stepchildren.

Though too young to marry, Ida threatened to run away rather than have to
absorb all of Eliza's chores. Eventually she did so, marrying and bearing a son,
John Miller. She would not follow her older sister's happy model, however, for
her husband would later desert her, and she her own son.

Johnny's response to the family's unsettled life was to bury himself in books,
such as Washington Irving's *Alhambra*, which set in his mind a dream of a magnificent home on a hill. Another favorite was one of Paul duChaillu's *African
Explorations,* which inspired the boy to add travel to exotic lands to his list of
longings. Most influential was Ouida's *Signa*, whose portrayal of a musician
suggested the appeal of a life in pursuit of beauty. (Pages containing the tragic
ending of suicide were fortunately missing from his copy.) Johnny's displeasure
with farm chores arose not out of laziness so much as aesthetic repugnance, and
he came to hate the countryside and farming until later in life.

Although the Livermore farm had thrived enough for John London to add
acreage, one addition, that of poultry, doomed the entire enterprise when an
epidemic killed all the chickens. Salvaging what they could following foreclo-
sure, John and Flora moved back to Oakland in 1886, to a home in the working-
class area known then as Brooklyn. Eliza and the Prentisses lived nearby. Still
leaning toward feminist and social causes, Flora proposed building a house
large enough to take in female boarders from the nearby California Cotton
Mills so that the women workers would have decent housing. The concern
proved so successful that John constructed a second house on an adjoining lot.

Unfortunately, given the erratic national economy, hard times soon returned. John London applied for a Civil War pension, claiming war-related disability, but was denied owing to lack of any evidence in his files to corroborate his lung injuries. By 1887, for unknown reasons the boardinghouse scheme collapsed. Between 1886 and 1891 the London family moved ten times around the Brooklyn and West Oakland neighborhoods. As their fortunes waxed and waned, home could be a neat bungalow with large yard and picket fence, or an unadorned cottage of a single room's width crowded between other tiny domiciles. In 1888 the Civil War Pension Office reevaluated John's appeal and awarded him four dollars a month.

West Oakland was a neighborhood remarkable for its diversity. Whereas many other cities in the nation had segregated racial and ethnic enclaves, this area included the skilled and unskilled, educated and uneducated, English and non–English speaking. Portuguese, Germans, Irish, Asians, and blacks lived alongside one another. Some class distinctions were evident in the location and appearance of houses. Working-class cottages were small, plain, fenced, inward-looking, and closer to the rail lines; middle-class homes addressed the street more openly, with large, unfenced lawns showing off their distinctive Norfolk pines and palms.[12]

Unlike in the Massillon Flora had known, the better homes were not limited to white occupants. The broad range of employment related to the railroad, the waterfront, and companion industries meant that successful immigrants and African Americans could afford well-appointed domiciles. (One of the most sumptuous houses in the neighborhood was that of Captain William Shorey, a black whaling captain.) Having grown up pampered by black servants in an abolitionist family, and having befriended Jenny Prentiss, Flora found the presence of African Americans less objectionable than that of Italians, Irish, and Chinese.

Another person in Johnny's life who may have had nativist leanings was Eliza. First, her father, with whom she identified, made much of his long heritage and his family's place in the nation's birth. Second, as a result of watching her father's decline from his Civil War injuries, Eliza became active in the Woman's Relief Corps, an auxiliary of the Grand Army of the Republic. During the 1890s the WRC pioneered the observance of Memorial Day; campaigned to fly the American flag over every school, urged the daily pledge of allegiance in classrooms, and erected memorial halls and monuments throughout the land. The WRC also provided more traditional women new opportunities in political life to march in parades, write and distribute flyers, meet with city officials, speak from podiums, and gain a strong voice in major public discourse. Although being white was not an official requirement for membership, in practice the organization condoned segregation and would increasingly identify patriotism and Americanism with Protestant Christianity—the whiteness of the early Anglo-Saxon settlers.[13]

If resettlement in Oakland brought little stability to the London household, Johnny now had Jennie and Eliza nearby. The unanswerable question is what values he took away from each, along with those of his parents. While one can only conjecture, it is clear that he had three very different older female role models, and their sometimes conflicting manners and preferences must account for some of the strong contradictions and equivocations in his later life.

Jack London's later autobiographical notes always emphasized "hunger" and "loneliness."[14] When as an adult he often recounted his starving childhood, both Flora and Eliza disputed his claim. There was always plenty of vegetables, they countered, in itself unusual fare for a working-class family. When meat was not available, chicken was. The much poorer Frank Atherton warmly recalled dinners at the Londons', where Flora served thick pan-fried steaks, mounds of potatoes, and bread with butter. Thus, despite repeated setbacks, the family was never dirt poor, not like the "shanty Irish" in the city or the "wops" in San Mateo, whom Flora despised in the derogatory terms of the day. As economic historians have discovered, families such as the Londons—those with a piano, vegetables, and linens—were among the better-off members of the laboring class.[15] Still, foolish spending, encouraged by his parents' indefatigable optimism, introduced anxiety into daily life, and Johnny's constant worry was that rather than their realizing sudden riches, all could disappear. There would never be enough in his life as a consequence.

At least in Oakland a ten-year-old boy could earn some money of his own. Here once again Flora exerted her sway. When Johnny developed nervous tics, she suggested that a job after school would help calm him down. As was common then, he turned most of his earnings over to his parents. He took odd jobs throughout his grammar school years, from yard work to setting pins at a bowling alley and delivering newspapers at three dollars a month. He spent his small sums on boyish pursuits of the day, such as collecting trading cards from cigarette packages (the images depicted prizefighters, actors, racehorses, national flags, and colorful birds). Though as an adult he would claim to have been overburdened as a youth, in fact he discovered that work brought satisfactions well beyond the income. Work introduced order and structure, which Johnny preferred over confusion and surprises.

Despite the continual disruption of moving, Johnny found several other sources of stability in his life. One was the Cole School, where his talent for writing first appeared. There, during singing classes, his tin ear proved so disruptive that he was excused by the principal to work alone writing essays instead. One of these compositions described the cruel labor conditions in the quarries of Rutland, Vermont, an early indication of his interest in this subject. It also suggests his awareness of the raging labor warfare during his formative years, which included the Haymarket riot, railroad worker strikes, and the rallying of the Knights of Labor for an eight-hour workday.

Cole's principal, J. P. Garlick, recalled Flora as "a remarkable woman" who had "a wonderful command of language," a "bright, cheerful philosophy of life," and "best of all, knew the nature of her boy thoroughly." She frequently came to school to check on Johnny's progress. One day she noted that her son was unhappy with school but he would not tell her the reason. She intuited that his teacher had "not the mother love," an impression Garlick himself had formed, and as a result counseled the employee. "Mrs. London's wonderful tact and friendliness was shown by the change in that teacher," he remarked. He found the Londons "poor but respectable and cultured people," not of the slums. Although he had little contact with John London, he concluded that the boy "got his talent" from Flora, and that John was "a poor provider."[16] Frank Atherton agreed. His many mentions of Flora in his memoir of his childhood days with Jack depict an affectionate woman, worried about her son yet kindly despite his rebellious ways.

Also significant for this introverted child was the discovery of the Oakland Library, located on Fourteenth Street next to City Hall. There another woman, librarian Ina Coolbrith, noticed the reticent youngster, who asked permission to read any book that caught his fancy. Then in her early forties, Coolbrith was a noted, widely published poet. She was one of what was called the Golden Gate Trinity, the others being writers Bret Harte and Charles Warren Stoddard. She had befriended Mark Twain before he returned east after working on the *Overland Monthly,* as well as the eccentric poet Joaquin Miller. All these men eventually found broader fame when they left California for the East or Europe, but Coolbrith felt obligated to support her mother, an orphaned niece and nephew, and Calle Shasta, the half-Indian daughter Miller left on her doorstep one day.

When Johnny met Coolbrith, she still retained her often remarked beauty— her pure olive skin, bouncing dark curls, and large dark eyes. Like most others, he would not know of her tragic private life, her past marriage to an abusive husband and the death of an infant. Later, other prominent Oaklanders, including Isadora Duncan and Gertrude Stein, would similarly credit her guidance in their development. Not only did Coolbrith lead Johnny to classic literature, but also she was a forceful, intelligent woman with a caring bent. Years later he thanked her for being "a goddess" to him. There he was, "raw from the ranch," and yet she praised the ten-year-old for checking out a book about Pizarro in Peru.[17] That encouragement reinforced his addiction to reading, and he set himself a goal he usually surpassed of two books a week.

Johnny's love for books became an obsession. He read during lunchtime, during school recess, and every evening. When on a trolley car with Frank Atheron, he would pull out his book and ignore his companion until reaching his stop. He pressured Frank to read more, and proudly showed off his well-worn copy of Shakespeare and other books given him by his parents. When Frank's reaction to the wealth of the Oakland Library was to wonder at the impossibility of exhausting its supply, Johnny answered that just "because a person can never learn everything to be learned, it's no reason he should be a moron all his life."[18] Thus Frank was not surprised that when an explosion in a gunpowder factory forced the evacuation of their school, Johnny rushed to save the books.

Johnny also introduced Frank to theater and opera—then much more affordable and popular among the working class than today. Flora's influence shows here too, for she, unlike John, had a rich artistic education which she would pass on to her son. Johnny and Frank would clamber to the heights of the top balcony and swoon over a particularly melodic line. As a result of this exposure to culture, Frank took up the violin and later became a music teacher. Though lacking in musical talent, Johnny remained an avid fan who would enjoy drama and opera all his life.

His favorite form of aggression was verbal—teasing and embarrassing his victims. His bookishness tempted school bullies, who would taunt him for his intellectuality. Also, after his stepfather became a special officer on the waterfront, members of the local "Fish Gang" tormented the boy in retaliation for his father's role in making arrests. While not one to start fights, Johnny was a fearless and adept boxer, whose barrel-chested torso supplied a power his slender limbs belied. Not surprisingly, it was news of barehanded boxing events, not the national sport of baseball, that most interested him, though he would outgrow his own fisticuffs.

During his free time Johnny also wandered the estuary waterfront or rowed out in a small rented boat with his stepfather to fish for rock cod. When he was twelve the family could finally afford its own fourteen-foot decked-over centerboard skiff, on which he'd sail out into San Francisco Bay. He was most at peace on the water, and would escape to boats all his life. While sailing to Goat Island, John would tell his stepson stories of being a Civil War scout and spy, of hunting buffalo. Often Johnny would bring along his dog Shep, one of several the boy cared for during his childhood.

The estuary and marshes were favorite hunting and fishing sites for Frank and Johnny, who made pellets out of scrap lead and shot them at ducks with slingshots of their own design. Believing that the Chinese were too stupid to tell mud hens from ducks, they dreamed of getting rich from selling the easily cap-

tured coot. The scheme of course proved to be a fiasco. Another time they decided to go after mountain lions in the Piedmont Hills, again in the mistaken
belief that the Chinese would buy them for ceremonial purposes. Experiences
of selling junk to ragmen and buying a defective pistol from a pawnshop owner
reinforced their stereotypical beliefs that "dirty old Jews" were out to cheat
them. In regard to these prejudices, they were growing up like most Californians of their day, for even newspaper comics emphasized humor based on ethnic caricature.

The waterfront was also the location of clip joints and saloons, which did not
exclude children. John London took the boys to bars such as Heinhold's Last Saloon, where they ate free lunches and drank soda water while he downed his
whiskeys. Following their first visit, Jack explained to Frank that though his father had "quite a number of saloon bills" in the neighborhood, he only got
"jingly," never fully drunk.[19] Trips from the Livermore farm to Oakland meant
stops at roadhouses for whiskey, but since sipping beer by mistake at age five,
he wanted nothing to do with alcohol. Frank observed how in the evenings John
London would unfurl marvelously graphic accounts of hairbreadth escapes in
battles with Indians, stories that flowed more readily as the whiskey glasses
added up.

Despite his hyperbolic memoirs, Johnny London was very much a typical
boy of his time and place. One exception, however, was omitted from accounts
of his "blighted" youth. He continued to visit the Prentiss family, and made
friends within Oakland's African American community. When Johnny went
swimming in the estuary or pirating coal with a gang of boys, these other boys
were just as likely to be Ed and Joe Dewson or Charles and William Disard as
his white pals. These youths' mothers were Jennie's best friends, as well as members of the A.M.E. Church. Johnny even attended church with Jennie's family at
times, and was thought by some members, given Alonzo's light coloration, to
be her natural child.[20]

The few printed witnesses to Jennie's voice appear in the memoirs of white
women—Jack London's second wife and his daughters—whose perceptions of
African Americans were similarly molded by the racialist attitudes of the day.
To their ears she speaks in dialect; in their memories her actions are those of the
mammy, always loving, noble, sacrificing for her white children. So written, she
can be consigned to the footnotes of history, if mentioned at all. After all, she
was merely doing her job. This has been the standard treatment of Jennie in
biographies: a few brief references to her nurturing Jack London. Perhaps
her presence, and that of the Oakland African American community overall,
planted the seeds of doubt about human difference that appear in his later writings, his weighing and questioning the inevitable and superior consequences of
white domination. Though within a few years he would harden his beliefs into

an Anglo-Saxon chauvinism and uphold the superiority of his corner of the white race, he also expressed doubts over such beliefs throughout his life.

When Johnny graduated from eighth grade in 1889, he changed his name to Jack. His education was considered complete for the occupations available to him. (Fewer than 4 percent of children then graduated from high school, and scarcely half of adolescent boys attended school at all.) His stepsister Ida, for example, worked in a laundry after her graduation. Yet instead of striking out immediately for a full-time job in a factory or as a laborer, he spent the summer in Auburn, where the Atherton family had moved. When that idyllic vacation with his friend ended, the fourteen-year-old signed on at Hicamott's Cannery, to stand alongside adult men and children as young as seven stuffing pickles into jars throughout twelve-hour days. The pay, ten cents an hour, went mostly to his family, for his ailing stepfather was earning very little as a night watchman.

Similar to some boys today, Jack soon saw a more lucrative alternative with the Oakland gangs, pirates who raided the oyster beds in the bay. Some years earlier the widely despised Southern Pacific Railroad had usurped government lands and leased the beds back to select oyster growers, thus establishing a monopoly that kept prices inflated. Consequently, both the public and the police looked the other way while adolescents took their skiffs out to harvest the oysters and then sold the stolen goods at lower prices than those in the stores. Thus this form of delinquency was also his first politically revolutionary act.

Needing a boat, but lacking enough money, Jack turned to Jennie Prentiss for the funds to buy a sloop, the *Razzle Dazzle*. Her willingness to give him the $300, many months' income for a workingman's family, has often been portrayed unquestioningly, as though it were natural for his "mammy" to treat her foster son so lavishly. A more tragic motive may have spurred her generosity. In 1890 her only son, William, died suddenly at age twenty. Jack's dependence thus enabled Jennie to transfer her bereaved maternal feelings to the white boy she had long treated as kin.

Jack moved to his sloop and lived there most of the time, spending his leisure in contradictory pursuits. On the one hand, he drank and raised havoc with fellow pirates. In bars he also eavesdropped on the tales of sailors and other adventurers, while observing the male-defining rituals. Also frequenting the waterfront, though missing from his later accounts, were artists—writers, painters, musicians—who found the neighborhood picturesque as well as inexpensive. These bohemian types sometimes lived in shacks they built from scraps and recycled goods, and thus suggested a different lifestyle from Flora's bourgeois aspirations. On the other hand, he would sneak off to the Oakland library, bring back a stack of books, and hide in his bunk reading and eating candy.

Always an extremist, never one to do things halfway or unhesitatingly, Jack made a complete turnabout. Realizing that his next stop could be San Quentin if he continued his unfettered ways, he joined the Fish Patrol in Benicia, which enforced the law on San Francisco Bay. In practice, patrols focused their enforcement on Chinese shrimp fishermen using illegal nets, and these encounters further reinforced the young man's anti-Asian sentiments.

By 1892 Jack was living in Oakland again, drifting around the waterfront, returning home, rarely, for a hot meal or shower. He became a bar loafer, and likely engaged with other young men in illegal means of obtaining the price of another evening's round of beer or whiskey. Although he drank heavily, he did not enjoy the consequences, and was perceptive enough to recognize that he would end up like other dissolute men were he to continue this way.[21] Consequently, at seventeen he signed up as an able-bodied seaman with the sealing vessel *Sophia Sutherland*. The ship left in January 1893 for seven months' hunting in the Pacific waters along the northern coast of Japan, an experience that confirmed his love of the sea, if not the sailor's life. He would return with little money, however, because in ports such as Yokohama, he would visit bars and brothels. He had, however, been highly attuned to life aboard the ship, and would later cull these memories for financial profit well beyond his imagining at this point.

As adolescents often are, Jack was rather oblivious to the lives of others. Jenny and Alonzo Prentiss had suffered yet another tragic loss in 1891 when their only surviving child, Priscilla Anne, died at age eighteen. Alonzo was too old now to do construction work. Meanwhile, John London's health was so poor that he and Flora moved into a tiny cottage built of materials salvaged from dismantled buildings. Both families were now living primarily on army pensions, which fortunately had increased. In 1890 the Dependent Pension Act provided relief to honorably discharged soldiers who suffered any disability, no matter how it had occurred, and regardless of their financial status. Eliza's husband, the Oakland liaison for invalided Civil War veterans, filed the papers for John London, now in his sixties and disabled with pulmonary disease; his allotment doubled to eight dollars a month. Alonzo's files included an affidavit from a leading Oakland jurist, Judge Jacob Samuels, who testified to Prentiss's "moral hability."

The money could not have come at a better time. In 1890 the concentration of wealth in the nation had resulted in 1 percent of the people possessing more capital than the remaining 99 percent together. The federal government initiated annual unemployment counts that year, and announced that the rate was relatively low, only 4 percent. What this statistic failed to convey were the terrible working conditions—the lack of regulations guaranteeing safe conditions at work, the long hours, the child labor, the stagnation of wages. In 1892, when sixteen-year-old Jack London was carousing on the waterfront, labor unrest and police violence burst out around the country. In the bloody Homestead strike at the Carnegie steel mills, ten workers were killed and many wounded by Pinkerton detectives hired by management. In 1893, while Jack was at sea, financial panic hit after securities suddenly dropped on the New York Stock Exchange, and the value of the U.S. silver dollar fell precipitously several weeks later. By the time Jack walked off the gangplank in August 1893, unemployment had tripled to 12 percent. In just a few months, dozens of banks had failed, thousands of small businesses collapsed, workmen been forced out of work, and families cut adrift. Unemployment would rise to 18 percent over the next year.

Given this inhospitable climate, Jack returned not to his old buddies on the waterfront but to his parents in their ramshackle home. His earnings from the sea did not last long, He soon found a job in a jute mill, where he stood by rows of rotating bobbins, moving from one bobbin to another to attach the cord and begin another spool. The workday ran from 6:50 A.M. to 5:50 P.M. with a half-hour lunch break, over a six-day week. The spinning room was noisy from all the tightly aligned machinery, and filled with the lung-clogging debris of the jute fibers. The close juxtaposition of the revolving machines with moving belts all around led to accidents, the loss of fingers and even arms. Pay for a white male was typical of factory work, about a dollar a day, with fines averaging a quarter for each work rule violation. Overall, jute mills were cited by the California Department of Labor Statistics for their use of child labor, unsafe conditions, and insensitive management.[22] Leaving that job, Jack found another equally bad, shoveling coal twelve to fourteen hours a shift for the Oakland steam railway.

Very possibly Jack London would have drifted along as a working-class laborer, a dependable, industrious wage earner, had it not been for his mother's vision and drive. One day she read that the *San Francisco Call* was running an essay contest, with a prize of twenty-five dollars, more than half her son's monthly earnings. Worn out in the evenings from his factory work, he resisted her insistence that he write up some of his experiences on the sealing ship for the competition. Finally, perhaps to quiet her, over two nights' time he composed "Typhoon off the Coast of Japan," a compelling, realistic portrayal of nature's fury. The essay won first prize, ahead of contributions from Stanford and Berkeley students.

Any further publishing was in the distant future, however, because Jack had discovered women. With his friend Louis Shattuck, a blacksmith's apprentice (a sorry craft to choose the year the first automobile rolled off the line), he attended public dances and picnics and hung around ice cream parlors. He later told of meeting his first love at a Salvation Army meeting: "He has called her Haydee, and never divulged her true name. She was somehow different from the other good little girls he flirted with. . . . [H]er brown sweet eyes and tip-tilted nose, her pretty brown hair and petulant rosy mouth, were the loveliest he had ever seen."[23] But Haydee was not his only early love interest. There was another one he left out of his reminiscences: Lucy Cauldwell.

Lucy's grandfather, Isaac Cohen, had left his Jewish family back east to marry a young black woman, Lucy Craddock, and then changed his name to Cauld-well. They arrived in California in 1855 and eventually settled in Oakland. Their children married within the local black community. These children of light complexion (Cauldwells, Disards, Dewsons) formed a tight group with the similarly light-skinned Prentiss offspring, and thus came to know Jack well. Lucy's cousin Jane Disard Wright recalled, "We thought of him as one of us." Sometime in the 1890s he "was often seen with one of our group, a beautiful girl [Lucy]. . . . They were so close and such a beautiful couple together that some of us believed there would be a marriage."[24] Exactly how long the relationship lasted, or why it ended is unknown. Jane Wright implied that the breakup was a result of Lucy's taking up with Edwin Dewson, whom she later wed.

It is questionable whether any of the black women Jack knew in Oakland would have considered marrying him, for they were of better social standing. The London family's status was well known, and provided only a partial excuse for Jack's often unkempt appearance among a group for whom neatness was a major virtue. A surviving photograph of Lucy from this time reveals a well-dressed young woman with a large, elaborate hat and leather gloves, perhaps a church outfit. Being among the more affluent members of the community, she was raised to take on leadership roles in charity activities and present herself as respectably middle class. Although the Cauldwell cousins may have found Jack's energy and cleverness appealing, he was not really one of them—not when it came to marriage.

During this time it would have been difficult for Jack to commit to any woman, because his primary concern was money. By 1894 the national unemployment figures listed one of five workers, with no relief available apart from charity. Coal miners' strikes led to more violence and deaths. Wheat prices fell to half their usual rate, ruining grain farmers. Gold reserves in the federal treasury shrank. More bank failures, factory closings, and railroad bankruptcies followed. While some of the aggrieved rallied behind the campaign for Free Silver, others took up the banner of Jacob Coxey, who called for unemployed workers to gather at Massillon, Ohio, for a march on Washington, where he hoped the demonstration would convince Congress to pass public works bills. In the West, Charles Kelly organized an "Industrial Army" to ride the rails cross-country and eventually meet up with Coxey's group. Not much for politics, eighteen-year-old Jack signed on for the adventure, though he would return with a strong social conscience.

Eliza provided ten dollars to start him off, and Flora promised to send more money ahead. Arriving too late to depart with Kelly's group, Jack accompanied a gaggle of tramps familiar with riding the rails and quickly took to the thrill and danger. Once he caught up with the marchers, he joined a group of noisy scalawags who caused so many problems for Kelly that in Missouri they were ordered to leave the group.

During his absence, Flora sent a loving letter that drifted around midwestern post offices until it caught up with him. One of the few surviving statements in her own hand, the document poignantly expresses feelings she seldom stated directly: "When we did not get a letter for three weeks I worried so that I could neither eat nor sleep, but Papa would always say 'never mind Jack, he knows how to take care of himself, and he will make his mark yet.' . . . Be careful of fever and ague that is the bane of the East. Keep your liver and kidneys all right and you need not fear it. . . . Now my dear son take good care of yourself and remember our thoughts and best wishes for your success, happiness and safe return are always with you. With lots of love, Papa, Mama, and Sister."[25]

Having learned that other letters and money awaited him in Chicago, Jack visited his aunt Mary Everhard and her husband, Ernest. They were taken with the youth's love of reading, and were impressed that he was keeping a journal of the trip. Along with a daily account of his activities, he scribbled down snatches of conversation, jokes, copies of poems, riddles, and an ongoing glossary of tramp vernacular, all of which he would use in later writings, notably *The Road*.

From Chicago, Jack wandered to Washington, D.C., and up through the major northeastern cities. Attending the public speaking forums on street corners and in parks, he listened to the speakers, some unemployed workers, some professors, harangue on the evils of class conflict. They gave a name to their perspective, socialism, and thereby a model to help explain the young man's own troubled work history. Whenever an orator mentioned a particular book or writer, Jack would stop off at the local library and look it up. His exposure to leading social theorists and historians led him to conclude that education was the key to advancement in life.

A more traumatic insight struck as the result of his thirty-day stay in New York's Erie Penitentiary on the charge of vagrancy in Buffalo. Scant justice took place in the courtroom, where he was summarily sent off to jail without a chance for defense. Sadism marked both the official practices at the prison and the interactions among the inmates. A handsome young man, he was a potential victim for sexual assault; he later held homosexuality to be repugnant. These encounters ingrained in him a contempt for the justice system and a lifelong sympathy for the plight of prisoners, whose brutality to one another was encouraged by the authorities. He returned home with a fervor for underdogs of all kinds.

Back in Oakland, Jack found that his stepfather's health had improved enough for him hold a regular job. Consequently, the family had moved to a charming bungalow ornamented with unique architectural details, including a keyhole entry to the porch. When Jack spoke of his desire to return to school—first high school, then the university—his parents were quick to support him. Flora furnished her son's room comfortably to serve double duty as a den. She arranged a spacious daybed, for he liked to read and take notes while reclining. Eliza advanced him money to buy a worktable, reading lamp, and bookcases. His obsession with order required that his bowl of fruit, cigarettes, and matches be placed just so, and he would rail at his mother whenever in cleaning she moved objects slightly awry. This fastidiousness, the need for order around him, perhaps provided an important visual grounding for his quick, wandering mind.

Many mornings Jack would cycle over to Eliza's house for breakfast before heading on to Oakland High. One day she chastised him for chewing tobacco, whereupon he showed her his mouth, riddled with cavities. She offered to pay for the dentistry provided he quit chewing; he accepted the money, though not her lectures about the importance of brushing his teeth. When a bicycle accident resulted in the loss of his front teeth, she paid for the upper plate. Eliza was the one person capable of giving back to Jack more than he gave out, and he avoided yelling at her as he did at his mother.

Seeing that Jack was always looking for ways to make money, whether mowing lawns or beating carpets, Eliza used her influence to get him a position as janitor at the high school. This was not easy, given his quickly established reputation as "Boy Socialist of Oakland." This title was the result of his meeting the reference librarian Frederick Bamford, who, though small and frail, brought to mind the street corner philosophers Jack had admired during his tramping back east. Bamford introduced the youth to Oakland's socialists, and he readily propelled himself into the center of their activities, drawing headlines in the process.

At that time socialists typically fell into two separate groups within a community. The European immigrants, often Jewish, read Hegel, Marx, Engels, and others in the original German, classic texts that had yet to be translated into English. Their firsthand acquaintance with anarchism in Europe convinced them of the necessity for revolutionary action. The American-born socialists relied on others' interpretations of the original works, often finding the jargon opaque and the European historical examples hard to appreciate. Consequently, they leaned toward utopian discussions of the class struggle and new models for society, rather than urging violent change. They particularly emphasized the sharing of goods and services and other cooperative ventures. It is this latter group that dominated the Oakland branch of the Socialist Labor Party. Among the works on its reading list during the 1890s were Edward Bellamy's *Looking Backward,* Oscar Wilde's *The Soul of Man under Socialism,* Lawrence Gronlund's *Cooperative Commonwealth,* and Max Nordau's *Horace Greeley and Other Pioneers of American Socialism.* Bamford introduced Jack to these works and to members of the party.

Two younger members became longtime friends: Herman "Jim" Whitaker and Frank Strawn-Hamilton, who had developed a technique for attracting crowds to the city hall steps, where they sought to make converts. Pretending to start an argument, they would shout and gesticulate so violently that people gathered in anticipation of a fistfight, then remained to listen to the propaganda.

Although Jack accepted the party dictum that cooperation was the key to human survival, he was more attracted than his comrades to revolution as a means to utopia. Never one to be a purist, whatever the system, he adopted ideas higgledy-piggledy from various authors without regard to internal logic. This was apparent in his own missionary work on the Oakland city hall steps. An article in the *San Francisco Chronicle* of February 16, 1896, noted that he defined socialism as an "all-embracing term—communists, nationalists, collectionists, idealists, utopians, altrurians [followers of Bellamy], are all socialists, but it cannot be said that socialism is any of these—it is all." Similarly, he shocked many of his younger classmates at the high school with his provocative talk of toppling the social order, that is, their own fathers' businesses.[26]

There is no evidence that Jack's parents found his increasingly extreme political leanings unusual or lamentable. This was after all a decade of popular ferment against authority, from the Free Silver farmers to the striking miners and the suffrage-seeking women. Bellamy's book, which praised government ownership of the means of production, with the citizenry reaping its rewards and cooperative organizations easing life for all, was a best-seller. The general public did not use the label "socialist" pejoratively as it would years later, but rather saved condemnation for those it called "anarchists," a euphemism for Jewish socialists. The Socialist Party retained respectability in part because its platforms featured popular reform goals, such as the municipal ownership of utilities, safe working conditions, and public health initiatives. These ideas would appeal to working-class people like John and Flora London, who knew firsthand the consequences of unbridled monopoly capitalism. Those members of the middle class frustrated by the failure of government to meet social needs were more likely to think of themselves as Progressives, who seemed too conservative to the Londons' impatient son.

In reflecting on Jack London's youth, what one perhaps finds more significant than social class was its rootless quality. His parents had been part of the footloose generation that wandered westward during the nineteenth century. The boy might hear stories of Massillon or western Pennsylvania, but he had no direct acquaintance with either, nor with the relatives left behind in those places. His family's constant moving about increased his sense of the world's impermanence. No wonder he found books, a permanent record of communication from another human being, a source of solace. Yet even these lodestars could not fix his own restiveness, his search for identity and acceptance.

His curiosity and impulsiveness left him a perpetual novice, whether twisting jute in a factory, heaving sails on a sealer, or hopping onto moving railway cars. He seemed to understand that these were just stops on a longer journey, that none was his soul's nest, none worth understanding beyond a basic familiarity. For when it was time to take root, to persist and hold fast despite constant rejection, he would do so, and prove the many doubters wrong. Still, most observers shook their heads over this mercurial young man and presumed, wrongly, that he was rejecting opportunities out of rebellion or shiftlessness.

Fortunately his path crossed those of a few cosmopolitan adults who caught glimpses of the young man's talents. With his shabby dress, unkempt wavy hair, large blue-gray eyes, and utter sincerity, they must have felt an irresistible urge to take him aside and counsel him. They recognized his unusual polymath curiosity, his willingness to challenge authority, and his determination to achieve on his own terms. He had a natural gift for logical argumentation, and an economy of language that enhanced his rhetoric. He was also headstrong and too ready to grab onto ideas without careful scrutiny, but most youths are.

His socialism, curiously, would not show him a connection between his family's history and the context of his life. He came away from factory labor with a determination to escape his class, and to fight against injustices perpetrated on the powerless. Yet he seems never to have thought of his parents within that frame. Perhaps only an exceptional child could reflect so. In time he became philosophically committed to cooperation and unity in social life, yet fully absorbed the stubborn individualism of the West. These two impulses fought within him to the end, usually without self-awareness. In practice, the individualist creed prevailed.

In moving about so frequently, he experienced isolation, whether from lack of playmates or from too brief a stay in a neighborhood to develop them. He complained throughout adulthood of that handicap, yet it also nurtured in him a comfort in being alone with words, a chance to adventure vicariously and dream even larger than his parents. That loneliness also left in him an enormous ache for attention, acceptance, and acclaim. He was determined to prove to his parents, particularly his mother, that he deserved such things. The irony is that his long reach was largely her doing, inculcated by her fierce unexpressed love. Solitude also twisted around those feelings of hunger and insecurity a vine of enormous self-confidence, which could appear to be bravado or braggadocio. He was certain of greatness, and would not be surprised when it came—only that it took so long.

# 3

# *Those California Women*

WHILE JACK LONDON was flirting with ideas of social reform and revolution on behalf of workers, he discovered a parallel world, that of the cosmopolitan middle class. Within its comfortably decorated parlors and dining rooms he would meet two women who would further shape his self-development. The first embodied traditional feminine values formed during the early 1800s, which emphasized purity, domesticity, and piety, though not as strictly as during the highly corseted Gilded Age. The other was what would be known as the New Woman, a forerunner of the Roaring Twenties' free-spirited flapper, more forthright in her independent beliefs and actions, her commitment to women's education, rights, and suffrage. Given the nature of California, both models of womanhood, conventional and rebellious, were less conformist than their eastern counterparts.

Perched on the Pacific rim, California clearly deserved the reputation of an elusive Eden. Its mild climate and abundant natural resources nurtured the relatively peaceful coexistence of indigenous groups so small and differentiated that, hundreds of years ago, over sixty distinct languages and hundreds of local dialects were spoken. Their practice of sustainable agriculture, hunting, fishing, and gathering little changed the landscape and its bounty. More interested in exploiting the land, Spaniards, and later Mexicans, introduced herds of cattle and crops that thrived in the sweeping valleys they irrigated.

The 1846 Bear Flag revolt picked this "ripe pear," as it was called, for the United States. The 1849 Gold Rush introduced a bourgeois segment, made up of migrants from all over the nation, black and white, as well as Asians and Europeans. Within a few brief years these immigrants introduced the elements of a long-settled society. They adapted their varied cultural experience to revolutionize local agriculture, both the methods used and the crops grown. Significantly, production farming rather than small homesteads would prevail. They also recreated their original hometowns and cities, built schools and churches, encouraged a distinctive art and literature, constructed water systems, crisscrossed the state with railroads, and devised a vibrant political system.

Despite the national unifying forces of the telegraph and the railroad, Californians were in their own and others' minds distinct from the rest of the nation, even their sister western states. The discovery of gold had stirred a deep symbolic longing for new opportunities and the end of privation. One suspects this uniqueness would not have been projected upon, say, the less geographically grand Arkansas, had the luminous veins been discovered undulating through its hills. Though the rush was brief, enough new arrivals thrived that the state's image as the land of promise remained.

Among those tempted by this opportunity to start over and prosper, as we have seen, were Jennie Prentiss and Flora Wellman. They belonged to the generation of community builders, the dreamers, however ultimately disenchanted, who were willing to test their optimism. In a twist on the usual American plot, circumstances more favored Jennie, the African American woman, than Flora. Their trajectories crossed, the former slave rising to own her own home, the spoiled rich girl descending to rent modest cottages without indoor plumbing. Joined by happenstance, they shared the role expected of new California women: to establish order in a society dominated by the presence of so many men.[1]

The first generation of pioneering Californian women, those arriving in the 1850s and 1860s, found themselves a tiny minority in rough-and-tumble male settlements, cities as well as mining camps, where rule by brawn and fist prevailed. Those who had not come as prostitutes, con artists, or petty crooks found their lives restricted by men's narrow views of respectability. Married women had the protection of their husbands to attest to their decency, but even they had to watch their behavior on the streets. Single women sought protection in boardinghouses and hotels where public rooms provided a tacit chaperonage.

Like westering women in other states, most set out to recreate the social order and culture of their previous communities. They used what influence they had to quell disorder, to foster well-run civic institutions, to build churches and schools, and to encourage the arts. Key organizations such as the Women's Christian Temperance Union furnished resources and guidance, as well as opportunities to develop skills in administering good works or lobbying politicians.

These women corseted themselves, literally and figuratively. Even in tiny crossroads settlements there evolved "society," that segment run by women determined to vanquish for good any remnants of Indian, Spanish, or male adventurer ways of life. By the 1870s, when the proportion of "respectable" women entering the state increased to 30 percent, the foundation for a femininity based on Christian piety and propriety was firm. Ladies enjoyed their pedestals, their lives above the fray. (Thus Flora earned sympathy as a moral woman abused by a nefarious man.) "Decent" women coddled their children, ruled their husbands with a velvet glove, spurned any thought of employment, and spent their excess energy on public benevolence. Self-supporting or working-class women found that their domestic skills brought a good price, and were less pressed than in the past into prostitution for income.

Despite the surge of moral Victorianism, California women behaved in some ways that would surprise their East Coast cousins. For one, they were less committed to their marriage vows. California led the nation in divorce, and as a result, more of its women found themselves on their own, especially since child support was neither guaranteed nor often generous. Add to this group the numbers of adventuresome single women who determined to make it on their own as their Gold Rush brothers had, and a counter-current to the "lady" role becomes evident. As a consequence of this trend, some of the key players in California agriculture were middle-class women. For example, Sarah Money developed the first commercial orange nursery in the San Bernardino Valley. In San Francisco, an ex-slave, Mary Ellen Pleasant, became a major holder of real estate and a key political power broker. Some married women, such as *Common Sense* editor Amanda Slocum, owned women-only businesses. Though exceptional, these women were well known, and they were less disparaged than their counterparts elsewhere in the nation.

More common were the otherwise conventional women who took avidly to wilderness pursuits. By 1878 a half dozen women had scaled Half Dome in Yosemite, and Anna Mills that year conquered 14,494-foot Mount Whitney. Accordingly, California women adopted unorthodox clothing, such as bloomers. "We girls wear boys' clothes [when camping]," remarked a young Gertrude Atherton to Ambrose Bierce. "We wear short trousers, long loose legins, and a tunic to our knees."[2] One such young woman, Charmian Kittredge, designed a split skirt similar to culottes for riding astride rather than sidesaddle, itself an audacious act. Although many communities had laws forbidding women to dress in men's clothing, some did so to pass as men and work in male occupations. In these ways they anticipated the New Woman—the self-assertive, athletic, comfortably clothed model of the early 1900s.

California women also fought for their rights earlier and with more success than their eastern counterparts. In 1874 San Francisco women teachers lobbied successfully for a state law guaranteeing equal pay with male teachers. In 1867 women gained the legal right to practice medicine, and in 1878, following a difficult fight, to practice law. Also in contrast to their eastern sisters, in their political and volunteer efforts they emphasized social reform rather than moral reform. Thus, the California WCTU worked more for the vote (which women received in 1911) than against saloons.

Overall, the typical California woman of the late nineteenth century was bound by and followed tradition, yet she was also aware of restrictions on her civil and economic rights and did not think it unladylike to seek redress. Although most women drew the line at wearing pants or mountain climbing alone in the Sierras, enough of them took exception to tradition to define a model of respectable rebellion for younger women. The middle-class California woman might dress in silken flounces and invite a man to tea, but she would speak her mind, and on the weekend join heartily in a strenuous hike through the golden hillsides.

By age nineteen, when he entered high school, Jack London had few serious flirtations behind him. His experiences in the virtually all-male worlds of oyster piracy, Fish Patrol, urban gang, saloon, sealing ship, rail riding, and the penitentiary had left him ill prepared for genteel rituals of meeting and courting young women. His initial sexual experiences would have been those of the Oakland tough: brief encounters with poor girls. He may have had his first experiences with prostitutes in Japan, and certainly witnessed, if not participated in, homosexual activity on shipboard and in prison. His proud survival of potentially life-threatening experiences in the world of men had nevertheless left him gauche and loutish in the female world of parlor and church hall.

While attending high school, Jack disguised his feelings of inferiority and shyness by flaunting his difference from his classmates and condemning their sedate, ordered lives. He did not bathe often, nor did he care about his clothing. Add to this his argumentative manner and talk of revolution. In class he would act bored and uninvolved. Few working-class youths attended high school, and his classmates kept their distance from this curious, shabby older student who swept the floors and washed the windows when the schoolday was over. They would have been astonished had they known of the proper families that welcomed him in their homes in the evenings. These families had recognized the latent talents of the shy, surly youth and were determined to guide him in achieving his goals.

The better known of these middle-class invitations arose from Jack's visits to the Oakland Library, where he came to know a slightly built, bespectacled young man of serious countenance. Fred Jacobs had been working in the library since grammar school and was attending night school toward earning enough credits to enter the university. Fred was scientifically inclined and little interested in socialism. Nonetheless, he found much in common with Jack, who was so well read of his own volition. Fred taught Jack photography, a craft that would assist him in later years, and more important, introduced him to his friends. One of these was Ted Applegarth, whose formal manner and British accent gave away his origins. If Ted was offended by Jack's vulgar talk and rough style, he did not show it.

One evening while out walking, Jack came across Ted and a companion, a tall, slender black-haired woman with large, expressive hazel eyes. She was introduced as Elizabeth Maddern, though she preferred to be called Bess. During their conversation, she asked if he were the same John London who had won the newspaper writing contest with a story about a typhoon, a question certain to flatter. The pair were on their way to a Salvation Army meeting and invited Jack to join them. When he said that he had been to enough of those of late, Bess suggested a concert at the First Congregational Church, and he assented. Afterward, she asked Jack to walk her home and enjoy some dessert, but he excused himself, more out of awkwardness than lack of interest.

Bess was attending night school in hopes of entering the University of California in the fall of 1896. Such plans defied the wishes of her parents, who like most of their generation saw little purpose in women being well educated. After she completed grammar school, despite her objections, they sent her to business school to learn bookkeeping, a profession just opening up to women. Upon completing the course, she refused to seek an office job but instead became a self-employed tutor. As word spread of her patient, thorough instruction in English and mathematics, she acquired a steady clientele. Since teaching was an acceptable feminine occupation, her parents, who otherwise were very loving toward their daughter, did not impede this enterprise.

Bess's effectiveness as a teacher was due in part to her eloquent expression and warm, mobile features. She had inherited a family talent for drama, for her aunt was the famous actress Minnie Maddern Fiske, who had brought a realistic style of acting to American theater, and a cousin, Merle, would also enjoy success on the stage. But Bess's parents soon quashed her childhood dream of performing behind the footlights as unsuitable for a lady. Less apparent to observers was the fact that Bess's forthright behavior was a mask for frequent doubts. More traditional than she appeared at first, she was self-effacing and would avoid any conflict, whatever the cost to herself. Thus when Jack London first met Bess, he deduced wrongly that she was self-assured, an impression that strengthened as he learned of her enthusiasm for athletic activities. An avid hiker and amateur naturalist, while cycling around Oakland she drew taunts from strangers for wearing bloomers instead of a skirt. Her unconventional dress, however, was more for practicality than rebellion.

One of Bess's good friends was Ted Applegarth's older sister Mabel, whose curly blond hair, clear blue eyes, and delicate hands presented a vision of feminine beauty. Mabel's mother was a stalwart British countrywoman, full of vigor, game to sport with her adult children, and solidly in control of any situation. She was untiring on long bicycle trips and undeterred by woodland bugs or stinging nettles. Perhaps because her daughter was consumptive, she raised her to play the parlor-bound lady par excellence. Whenever Jack visited, he found

Mabel languishing on the sofa, quick to quote snatches of memorized poetry in her precise diction. When feeling strong, she played capably at the piano. Her innocence, inexperience, and frailty, her very dissimilarity to other women he knew, soon stole the young socialist's heart.

Their relationship brought to mind that of Elizabeth Barrett and Robert Browning, among Jack's favorite poets. He imagined saving Mabel in the same way, freeing her from her afflictions to enjoy life fully. There was on her part some maternal, protective response. Not only was she several years older, but also she was obviously better educated in topics that mattered to him, particularly grammar and literature. Calmly she corrected his diction, coached him in his use of the proper fork, and expanded his appreciation for opera. The attraction was heightened all the more by the rules of courtship, which fostered long hours of companionship, but always under the guidance of a family chaperone. This was a new ritual for Jack, who was used to taking out working-class women without supervision. The memory of sitting on a trolley holding their coarse, callused hands lost all charm compared to the touch of Mabel's soft fingers brushing his as she turned the pages in a book of poetry they were reading aloud to each other. The isolation brought on by infirmity kept Mabel innocent about love and sexuality. Although Jack was in no way the ideal mate for her class, his breadth of experience in a rougher world aroused her passion. She would reach over and stroke his bare neck, a daring and improper gesture. Despite herself she reciprocated his love.

The contrast between the genteel Mabel and Jack's waterfront bluntness spurred him to try to fit into her world. Despite his ideological inclination to defend the working class, Jack London readily followed the siren call of bourgeois comforts. He quit going to saloons and no longer drank, learned to play chess from Ted, took ballroom dancing lessons from Bess and Mabel, and attended the French Club, a literary salon run by Mrs. Applegarth. On weekends and many weeknights he accompanied the Madderns or the Applegarths on picnics, hikes, and bicycle trips through the East Bay hills. During the summer of 1895, he camped with the Applegarths and their friends in Yosemite Valley while Mabel convalesced from a serious illness. (One imagines Flora much approving these connections with upstanding, financially successful families.)

That fall Jack returned to Oakland High, where he continued to write stories for the school magazine, the *Aegis*. But as he joined in more socialist activities, he spent less time at the Applegarths'. Years later he would memorialize his infatuation with Mabel in his novel *Martin Eden,* where she appears as Ruth Morse, tracing to it his eventual disenchantment with all she represented: convention, parlor morality, superficiality. She had been necessary for his creation of a self-presentation that would serve him well in polite society, for he need no longer sweat over how to place his napkin or use a finger bowl. If he appreciated that his unrestrained sailor's manners had been leashed somewhat, he nevertheless resisted thoughts of taking a regular job, however clean the office or well paid the work. He would not be "sensible" or "reasonable" in the ways expected of middle-class men. He argued with Mabel over a life devoted to earning money when what mattered above all, he asserted, was love. Martin Eden conformed to the fictional Morse family style much more than Jack London did to that of the Applegarths.

Jack's appeal to these families was likely based on those characteristics mentioned throughout his life by those who encountered him. He was "boyish" in the most positive sense of the word. He had verve, a sense of wonder, and an enthusiasm to learn all he could about the world. Other terms that often appear in acquaintances' accounts include sweetness, gentleness, and generosity. His physique matched his personality. He was slightly below average in height for the day, about five foot seven, with tousled light brown hair and well-formed lips quick to shape an engaging smile. Most often remarked on were his eyes, "blue blazing" or "cheerful gray." Though he was broad chested, he did not give an impression of brawn; he little resembled those "great blond beasts," the male heroes splashed across popular magazine illustrations and stories. His physical presence thus softened the effect of his direct, candid, sometimes provocative conversation.

During this time Bess Maddern accepted Fred Jacob's proposal. Fred had decided to attend the University Academy, a "cramming school," to prepare for the university entrance exams. Once again Eliza provided tuition so Jack could attend as well, though he did not stay long. Because of his extensive reading, he was optimistic about passing the upcoming tests in literature, philosophy, economics, and sociology. Fred helped him with physics and chemistry, and Bess tutored him in English grammar and algebra. As a result of that preparation, in August 1896 Jack passed his entrance exams and was accepted as a special student in the class of "Naughty Naughts," 1900.

The University of California had originated in Oakland in 1868, and in 1873 moved to an isolated rural hillside in Berkeley. Unlike most eastern colleges, it opened its programs to women on equal terms in all respects to men. By 1896, given the new boom in the economy, the school was suddenly overrun with students and ill prepared to handle the overflow. Some classes met in tents, and the budget was too strained to light the library at night. There were too few instructors, and they were overworked with the large classes. Having idealized the college experience, Jack was quickly disillusioned and became a desultory student. He took three English courses without earning a grade, and two European history classes, achieving a B and an A. Neither Bess (who did not enroll, as she had hoped) nor Mabel could interest him in any activities beyond standing on the sidelines at several college dances. Though political topics abounded in the student newspapers and informal debates, he did not participate. Instead, Jack spent his free hours with socialists and wrote letters to the editors of local papers concerning political issues.

Jack withdrew from the university in February 1897 and immediately challenged authority through a nonviolent protest. Two years earlier Oakland had passed an ordinance, inconsistently administered, that forbade public speaking on the street without the written permission of the mayor. In February, Jack took to his soapbox and was promptly arrested. When the case was tried two weeks later, the jury acquitted him of the charge. In March he ran unsuccessfully for the Board of Education on the Socialist Labor ticket, garnering 552 votes.

That spring he also began writing in earnest, primarily poems, jokes, and brief stories he hoped to sell to help support his family, since John London was earning little as a door-to-door salesman for a portrait company. Eliza's stepson Herbert Shepard helped him get a job in the laundry at Belmont Academy, which strengthened his determination to avoid a life of hard labor. Thoroughly steeped in socialist rhetoric, he revolted against what he perceived to be the overprivileged instructors by starching their wives' underwear.

Since his leaving grammar school, Jack's relationship with his mother had been one of convenience. When home, he expected and received from her nourishing meals, clean laundry, and other domestic chores. He had been away for months at a time, to return for a period of recuperation, as it were, from the waterfront or the sea or tramping. Flora was ever ready to help her only child, no matter how wildly or inconsiderately he had behaved. In May 1897, however, her place in his heart grew slighter.

That month one of John London's daughters revealed to Jack the truth of his birth, that he was a bastard born of an irresponsible father. Stunned by this news, he confronted Flora, who verified it and named Chaney as his father. By now Chaney was married to his sixth wife, Daisy, and living in Chicago. As a result of pouring all his meager income into his astrological annuals, *Chaney's Primer of Astrology,* he was impoverished. Nonetheless, he remained well known and respected among his peers.

Jack wrote using the Applegarths' as his return address to prevent Flora from seeing the correspondence. Chaney replied that he had lived with though never married Flora, and that he was impotent "due to hardship, privation and too much brain work."[3] During that time, he added, gossips had told him of Flora's involvement with Lee Smith, a lodger in their house, and with a married stockbroker named McKinney, who later affirmed this relationship. Either of these might be Jack's father, he suggested, although he had to admit that he'd never believed Flora guilty of loose morals. Despite these detailed if confusing accounts, Jack believed that Chaney was his father, and the denial of paternity brought added humiliation. Chaney's response, heartless to Jack, has some justification. A man of seventy-six would hardly welcome a reminder of an episode that had so publicly besmirched his reputation. Nor could he afford to help Jack financially, if he thought that the real reason for the contact.

Most biographers argue that Jack became alienated from his mother at this time, though that does not fit all the facts. His concern for her material welfare is evident, for he could have left her to bum around or live with friends, but he did not. More significant are his inscriptions to her in his books several years later. In 1901 he wrote in a copy of *The God of His Fathers,* "To my Mother— Who has travailed sore with me in the making of men and women to breathe and move and do things in the printed pages of a book." And two years later, in *The Call of the Wild,* he noted, "You have always loved your son, and things with us always will be well. Your loving son, Jack London."[4]

Easily distracted, Jack readily gave up on further pressing Chaney, for he had been bitten by the new epidemic, "Klondicitis." The fever struck the Bay Area on July 14, 1897, when the *Excelsior* arrived in San Francisco to disembark one very grubby man loaded down with a thirty-pound pack of gold dust. Within hours policemen, clerks, and trolley men quit their jobs, doctors and lawyers shut their offices, and preachers left their congregations to stampede the steamship ticket offices and outdoor goods emporiums. Jack's friends were dismayed that he would want to raise a grubstake and join the mass of ill-prepared men heading north on the steamships to Skagway, the starting point for the trek inland toward Dawson. Mrs. Applegarth and Mabel beseeched him to reconsider. Flora was noncommittal. Then Eliza's husband decided that he would join Jack and staked them both to supplies by mortgaging his home. On July 25 they were among the first rushers boarding the *Umatilla* for Port Townsend, then transferred to the *City of Topeka,* which set them on the docks of Juneau on August 2. There followed a hundred miles of paddling canoes through glaciated valleys that, he wrote Mabel, reminded him of Yosemite. Upon reaching Dyea, Shepard admitted that he was too out of shape for the long trek ahead and returned home.

Jack was among the one in five men who actually completed the inland trip, though not among the one in seven who found any gold at all, let alone broke even. The Yukon would further test him and refine his materialist bent. Though familiar with harsh environments, whether factory, ship, rail riding, or prison, he was awed by the unforgiving Arctic wilderness, where ignorance or neglect of a simple law of the trail, such as keeping one's feet dry, brought speedy death. Ultimately Nature ruled, and she was no gentle goddess strewing flowers in sunshine and sending rainbows after showers. Survival required cooperation, a theme that would resonate throughout most of his writings and reinforce his socialistic leanings.

To get inland, Jack faced the tortures of the Chilkoot Pass, under pouring rain joining in lockstep the men who paid the toll to cart a small portion of their nearly two tons of goods up the 1,500 "Golden Stairs," only to slide down and start up again with the next load. Then followed almost six weeks of canoeing and portaging his outfit to arrive at Dawson on October 18, just in time to set up camp and spend the winter holed up in a cabin with newfound friends. Gold was a paltry reward in light of these achievements. He proved himself a good comrade, helped others in distress, and won over his companions with his sweet smile, spirited conversation, and generosity. When the weather was good, he went to town to observe the various local characters—the prostitutes, the natives, the prospectors, the women on the trail, the business proprietors—and filed their stories in his memory. During the darkest part of winter he read from the books he had brought along—Milton, Darwin, Spencer—and eagerly lent them in exchange for others, such as Shakespeare. Much like the forty-niners, these adventurers were a literate lot.

In October 1897, Flora wrote her son the sad news that John London had succumbed to his lung disease, but he did not receive her letter until the thaw the following spring. Upon his return in July 1898, empty-handed and weakened by scurvy (the result of a diet of beans, bacon, and bread), he found her in yet another house, this one on East Sixteenth Street. Worse, he discovered her caring very affectionately for a little four-year-old boy, his stepsister Ida's son, Johnny Miller, a relationship he resented. (Ida's husband had deserted her soon after the child was born.) Jack, now twenty-two, was tired and bitter.

The mood of the country in 1898 had turned around, partly as the nation rallied toward the approaching war with Spain. Feeding the nation's optimism were advances in technology that eased everyday life. More families could afford purchases from the Sears catalogue, which burst with consumer goods that promised a better future, from organs to electronic energy belts, washing machines to opera gloves. Neighborhoods were being electrified, the outhouses torn down as sewage lines snaked through the blocks. Electric trolleys eliminated the smell and refuse of horse-drawn carriages. Average housewives found canned goods and ready-made clothes finally affordable. An industrial production boom was under way as well, with factories expanding to feed the new markets overseas and revive the one at home.

Yet economic growth had not trickled down to the workers in the form of better conditions or a significant share of the profits. The labor movement was fragmented, with the only strong survivor being the crafts union, the American

Federation of Labor, whose policies were protectionist on behalf of white native-born men. Thus, had he wanted to go into a skilled trade, Jack London would have found himself advantaged by virtue of his gender and ancestry. Given his education, he was even better situated for one of the many emerging white-collar occupations. At the urging of Eliza, who personally knew the value of a government job, he applied to take the civil service exam to become a postal carrier. Expecting that such a steady, respectable position would lead to marriage, Mabel Applegarth also pressured him.

While waiting for the test results, Jack began writing, creating about a story a week beginning in September 1898. The first few are not familiar titles to London aficionados: "From Dawson to the Sea," "The Devil's Dice Box," "The Test," and a poem, "The Clondyker's Dream." What is extraordinary is how quickly he then produced some of his masterworks. In October he composed "The White Silence"; in November "To the Man on the Trail." He also wrote ghost stories, children's stories, and mood pieces, sending them out to all the major magazines, including *Black Cat, St. Nicholas, Youth's Companion, Munsey's, Cosmopolitan, Lippincott's, Godey's,* and *Overland Monthly,* as well as newspapers in New York and San Francisco. It was an audacious act by a poor man forced to hock his bike to buy postage stamps. When a story came back, as it did inevitably, he repackaged it and sent it to another editor.[5]

During this lonely apprenticeship, London followed a mechanical or factory-based system of labor. He set himself a quota of a thousand words a day; one day's shortfall was added to the next; one day's surplus was not. He worked for speed rather than quality, eliminating extensive revision beyond perfunctory editing for spelling and punctuation. (His friends warned him to attend more to editing, but he discounted their criticism.) He festooned his room with strings and clips so he could hang notes and lists of vocabulary words for easy reference. He set up an accounting procedure for each manuscript so he could calculate its cost based on the expense of postage until the time of acceptance. He stratified his market so that a work went first to the top tier, not going to less prestigious or poorer-paying ones until later in the distribution process. (Once he became successful, he mocked how quick publishers were to accept his previously rejected, mediocre work.)

This obsessive, efficiency-based approach to writing reflected his philosophy. He was working not out of the need for artistic or creative expression but simply for the money. By setting a daily quota, he avoided having to labor long hours. This is clear from the tremendous amount of reading he achieved. He immersed himself in popular magazines to understand what would sell, and marked up arcane monographs in biology, economics, philosophy, and sociology. His reading was always more skewed to nonfiction—to ideas or scientific reports—than to literature. He followed this model throughout the rest of his life, with the result that he generally wrote only three to four hours a day. In this sense he was a very humane employer who never demanded overtime from his worker!

Jack's letters to others during this winter were understandably full of self-pity and egocentricity. Part of his melancholy was likely physical, the consequence of his stressful year in Alaska. Also, he felt very isolated because the Applegarths had moved to Palo Alto, forty miles away by bike and ferry. Nonetheless, he showed little empathy for others and had limited capacity to put his life in perspective. When news came of his friend Fred Jacob's death from fever in Manila, he wrote Ted Applegarth not a elegiac remembrance but: "So be it. He has solved the mystery [of death] quicker than the rest of us."[6] To Mabel Applegarth he provided a whining summary of his life of suffering through various jobs only to have to give all his money to his parents. He had worked "thirty-six straight hours, at a machine, and I was only a child." He "could have killed himself" the night his mother showed up asking for five dollars. As for his father, "How often as I swept the rooms at High School, has my father come to me at work and got a half dollar, a dollar, or two dollars? . . . The imps of hell would have wept had they been with me."[7] This is an odd reshaping of reality from a youth who, apart from several brief episodes, always did whatever he wanted, whether his family approved or not.

Here were the echoes of Flora's voice, her resentment at the injustices that life had dealt her, yet, while complaining, not giving up either, nor seeking self-destructive escape. For all his self-centeredness, he accepted adulthood's precepts. He claimed to hate "DUTY" but never shirked it. He did not escape to the waterfront again or drown himself in cheap whiskey at Heinhold's saloon. For who was his model, if not Flora? Who was bringing in what meager income there was during this period to put food on the table and even, as on the day he wrote his pathetic letter to Mabel, feed his friend Frank Atherton as well? He gave no acknowledgment of Flora's efforts, of her sitting by the keyboard with a piano student or kneading bread to sell on the street.

It was also Flora alone who stood behind his dream of becoming a writer. While Ted, Mabel, and even Eliza urged him to take on a secure, decent-paying job, she encouraged his dreams. On January 7, 1899, when the postmaster announced that Jack had scored well on the civil service test and an opening was likely within a few months, everyone but Flora found this news a cause for celebration. A job opened in April, which he refused. By then he had had two Yukon stories published in the *Overland Monthly*, "To the Man on the Trail" and "The White Silence." Although several dozen other works continued to circulate among the publishers without success, by September he had earned enough to put thirty dollars down on a new bicycle. The months of dealing with the pawnbroker (described to friends as "my Hebrew uncle") and budgeting pennies for stamps was over. By the conclusion of 1899, he would have published twenty-four stories, articles, poems, and jokes, a remarkable success for a novice.

At the same time his relationship with Mabel Applegarth waned. In a display of dominance, he often criticized her writing. When she neglected to send him a birthday card, he sulked that only Eliza had sent him birthday wishes. Gradually he rationalized that Mabel's eloquently stated opinions were formulae, pat conclusions shaped by style, not deep reflection. He continued to visit the Applegarths, and even spent the 1899 Christmas holidays with them, but the romance was over. He wrote to his closest correspondent, the journalist Cloudesley Johns, of how people could not resist him, but complained that he was always getting caught up in his friends' lives. He invited friends such as the impoverished Frank Strawn-Hamilton to stay, then wrote that they irritated him. Despite his complaints, his self-confidence was growing, his depression lifting.

One of the editors of *Overland Monthly,* Netta Wiley Eames, contributed as well to Jack's growing self-esteem. She was a handsome woman in her fifties whose short-cropped, curly hair signified that she was not as conventional as her dress implied. It was likely she who cooled Jack's wrath the day he appeared at the *Overland*'s office to demand the long-delayed payment for his stories. He readily warmed to this hardworking, capable woman of independent mind.

During a visit to her home, he met another New Woman type, her niece Charmian Kittredge, petite yet voluptuous, with golden brown wavy hair and a ready, welcoming smile. Charmian wrote a flattering profile of Jack for the *Overland Monthly,* albeit with Netta listed as author, as well as a laudatory review of his first book for that journal.[8] Little did he guess the role these two women would play in his life.

Netta had been born in the Wisconsin woods to Yankee parents who taught their children so well that by age twelve they were writing stories in French and German. Her sister Daisy's stories and poetry idealized romance to such an extent that her view of reality was veiled by these fictions. Some of these pieces were published in prominent women's magazines such as *Godey's Ladies Book.* Following the end of the Civil War, the Wileys set out west in a wagon train. Daisy kept a diary of that journey, recording with her steel-nib pen the wonders of the changing landscape and contrasting scenes of inviting Indian villages with scenes of Indian carnage against earlier trains passing along the route.[9] The family settled in Salt Lake City, where Netta, Daisy, and sister Tissie established the first non-Mormon school. By the end of a year, though, they realized that they were not welcome and set out again, this time to southern California.

Daisy remained behind to marry a cavalry captain, Willard ("Kitt") Kittredge, a lifelong bachelor more than twice her age. He failed to meet her heroic standards, and her writings turned to more tragic themes, particularly after Daisy fell in love with a Colonel Johns. Eventually the Kittredges moved to California.·

In 1871 in Wilmington, California, Daisy gave birth to her only child, Clara Charmian, who inherited her mother's curly hair and heart-shaped face. Following the child's birth, Daisy was too depressed to care for her, and handed the infant over to Tissie and Netta at the Wiley homestead. After Daisy recovered, Kitt moved them to Petaluma, a busy port town north of San Francisco. There he ran the premier hotel. Daisy felt proud to be among the leading families. Then, when Charmian was three, a stable fire spread to the hotel and burned it down, a catastrophe that drove Daisy to total nervous collapse. Returning south to live with her Wiley relatives, Daisy never recovered, and took to a source of relief common to women of her day—laudanum and opiate drugs. Netta, recently married, took the toddler into her home. When Daisy died in 1876, the clannish Wileys wrenched Charmian from Kitt's custody and sent her north to Oakland, where Netta and husband Roscoe Eames had just moved.

Netta had no children of her own and was not maternally inclined.[10] On the one hand, she taught Charmian at home and inculcated her with her beliefs, which incorporated vegetarianism, socialism, and Woodhullian free love feminism. On the other, Netta constantly reminded the child of her indebtedness to her aunt which she must repay as an adult. Toward that end she had the girl learn Roscoe Eames's shorthand method to equip her with skills to support herself. Her method of child rearing was one of belittlement and criticism; even when Charmian was an old lady, her aunt would still refer to her as "Childie."[11] As a consequence of this upbringing, Charmian felt bound to her aunt, appreciative for being raised to be independent, yet also resentful that she was always viewed as flawed.

Besides mastering shorthand, Charmian also became a speedy, accurate typist, able to produce over a hundred words a minute. Those clerical skills gained her a position with Susan Mills, president of the school she and her husband had founded. In exchange, Charmian was able to attend Mills Seminary for two years of college-level education, focusing on courses in the humanities and arts. Very few women even completed high school then, and one with college experience was considered peculiar. For the course Charmian took, the entrance requirements included knowledge of the major Latin works and their commentaries, French or German, and mathematics, and the ability to write a simple essay according to the rules of grammar and rhetoric.

After two years Charmian left Mills, having found dormitory life and campus regulations too stifling. To support herself she became the only female office worker for shipping firms across the bay in San Francisco. She rented two rooms in her aunt's house on Parker Street in Berkeley, hired a Swedish woman to do her cleaning and laundry, and bought a horse she rode in the hills on weekends. Pedestrians hooted "Brazen hussy!" at her for refusing the sidesaddle and riding without a chaperone.[12] Her love of horses and riding led to an engagement to a man named John McNab, who won her over with a gift of horse and saddle. Eventually she realized it was the horse and not the man that had won her heart, and left him heartbroken when she returned the ring.

Given that Charmian was almost six years older than Jack, and was now involved with a man called Will Minstrel, no romantic or erotic sparks passed between them. After editorial consultations with Netta on Parker Street, however, he would often visit Charmian, who was an avid reader of modern literature and was quick to offer thoughtful commentary. She was also a virtuoso pianist, frequently invited to perform at local concerts, admired for her skill as an accompanist and her sweet singing voice. Having been one of Flora's notably unsuccessful piano students, Jack admired her expressive playing and enjoyed singing along with her. To Cloudesley Johns he commended her as "a charming girl who writes book reviews, and who possesses a pretty little library wherein I have found all the late books which the public libraries are afraid to circulate."[13]

It would be several more years before this aunt and niece played more than a peripheral role in his life, though this is not to discount their influence from the start. They set in his mind the image of another type of woman, one different from Mabel, one who managed to pass in conventional middle-class society while defying some of its cherished standards. Such women worked, had affairs, and in other ways, as with Charmian's spunky athleticism, challenged the limits of women's role. Though in the minority, they were quintessential California women, exhibiting behaviors on the cusp between tradition and modernity.

The *Overland Monthly* exposure thrust Jack into the spotlight as much more than a local soapbox orator railing against government corruption and for a society based on cooperation. There soon followed a contract with Houghton Mifflin for a collection of his stories, *The Son of the Wolf*. Announcing this boon, the *Oakland Tribune* featured a photograph of him in one of his bicycling knickers suits, and applauded the success of a man "equipped with only a high school education" who was "supporting not only himself but his mother and nephew from the sale of his literary wages."[14] *The Son of the Wolf* would be one of Houghton Mifflin's top five sellers in 1900, selling over seven thousand copies. A trade magazine referred to "Jack London, the young westerner who is making a reputation so rapidly as to be the envy of many and the marvel of all."[15] One major essay at year's end predicted that Jack would be recognized as a writer "as forceful as Kipling and discerning as Lafcadio Hearn," the latter a popular author and translator of fantastic tales.[16]

Among these acclamations was a thoughtful essay by George Hamlin Fitch, literary critic for the *San Francisco Chronicle*, who viewed London within an emerging trend, a new literature inspired by the unique landscape and history of California. Observing that Californians were cosmopolitan and literate, "people who read with more care and thought than those in New York and London," he predicted that "all [the ingredients] are here to reproduce the Hellenic masterpieces." Singling out London, Fitch declared that he would rather "have written 'The White Silence' than anything that has appeared in fiction in the past ten years." He was concerned, however, that with regard to California writers, "the timid Eastern publisher cannot see the virtues of a book that is off the beaten track."[17] London's writing, in particular, with its brutal realism and exposure of the savage side of human nature, would in fact disgust those accustomed to afternoon tea literature and the violet prose of Victorian romances.

If Fitch was correct that New Yorkers cast California writers into the pot of "regional literature," he need not have worried about London. Carefully rewriting his life story for journalists, Jack presented himself as the son of a scout, soldier, trapper, and frontiersman, in other words, John London. There was implied a literary reference here to a figure revered even by the urbanites, that of James Fenimore Cooper's Leatherstocking. This ideal frontiersman was a romantic reminder of what civilization threatened to destroy: virtues of fearlessness, fidelity, prudence, self-reliance, and ethical action. But London updated this model by emphasizing the characteristic of race. Urban reviewers could identify with London's brutal Northland tales because they provided exemplars of Anglo-Saxon masculine dominance. As one noted of the collection, "Nothing . . . proves that a man is a man more conclusively than his ability to stand the North."[18] As others noted more explicitly, the "Wolf" was the white man, and pride of race was the major motif. Tellingly, around this time London took up the wolf as a totemic symbol for himself, and would be called Wolf by his male friends.

Though repugnant to twenty-first century readers, London's Anglo-Saxonism compensated for his political radicalism. He proved as conservative as the easterners in proselytizing scientific racism, a belief that an individual's moral, intellectual, and social development could be determined by his or her physiognomy, such as jaw structure or skull size. Basing their arguments in the pseudosciences of craniometry and phrenology, its advocates published compelling evidence, however flawed in retrospect, that racial differences were set in biology. Such studies identified "racial weakness" among Catholic and Jewish immigrant groups as well, indeed, among any of non–northern European stock.

Even more influential in Jack's thinking was Herbert Spencer, who added to Darwin's theory of evolution the notion of "survival of the fittest," the inevitability of the persistence and dominance of the more "civilized" human races. Spencerian morality posited that it was more ethical for the development of the human race to neglect the disadvantaged than to ameliorate their conditions, which would only perpetuate their weak genetic stock. (One sees in Spencer as well the roots of William Chaney's interest in astrology as the basis for proper breeding and child rearing.) London did not favor such benign neglect, but offered instead the promise of improvement found in socialism.

Socialism now seems a curious companion to these elitist and racialist beliefs. But most American socialists held that capitalism was a stage of evolution, with socialism being the final stage.[19] They preferred Spencer's gradualism to Marx's revolutionary anger, for it suggested that workers could not achieve justice on their own, but needed the assistance of enlightened intellectuals. In this curious way they accepted that workers were inferior, best suited to play a subordinate role in society, yet deserved some improvement in their lives. In one of his many assertions of these views to Cloudesley Johns, Jack explained: "You mistake. I do not believe in the universal brotherhood of man. . . . I believe my race is the salt of the earth. I am a scientific socialist, not a utopian, an economic man as opposed to an imaginative man."[20]

Though Jack would be a lifelong socialist, he was always more propagandist than activist. Throughout his dozens of letters to friends at this time, one searches vainly for commentary on national or international issues. One would never infer the range of major events: President McKinley's decision to "civilize" the Philippines by force, the responding anti-imperialist outcry, John Hay's trade doctrine (later known as the Open Door), the unabated rise in the number of lynchings, congressional passage of the gold standard, the Hague peace conference, the presidential campaign of 1900. He had no aspirations to be a leader, but lent his writing and oratorical experience to the cause. However fervent the prose, for much of his life he seems to have been, if anything, apolitical, indifferent to actual policy and events. It was as if the excitement of socialism lay in the ideas, not the reality. Events could stir his passion to speak out against oppression of Russian peasants, but he was not drawn to the barricades. This distancing of himself from direct activism would leave him vulnerable to criticism from his socialist comrades, particularly in later life.

London's interests went well beyond the "science" of racial differences or socialism. His letters to friends in the late 1890s abound with enthusiasm and opinions about the arts and literature as well. Here one is reminded how unusual he was in terms of his self-education, how he was much more than a narrow ideologue. For example, in early 1899 alone his letters referred to the works of the British literary critic Frederic Harrison, the philosopher Spinoza, the

Russian novelist Ivan Turgenev, the British writer Richard Le Gallienne, the French traveler Paul Bourget, the poet Charles Edwin Markham, and the historical writings of Theodore Roosevelt. He observed how Robert Louis Stevenson, unlike Rudyard Kipling, never wrote a bad line because he had the income to support his craft, while Kipling had to do journalistic hack work. (London would put himself unapologetically in Kipling's camp.) He often quoted poetry, from John Keats to Helen Hunt Jackson, recommended recently published short stories, and reviewed plays he had seen.

An example of his appetite is evident in his reading pile of April 30, 1899, which included Arthur Saint-Armand's *Revolution of 1848,* William T. Brewster's *Studies in Structure and Style,* David Starr Jordan's *Footnotes to Evolution,* John Williams Tyrrell's *Across the Sub-Arctics of Canada,* and Eugene von Bawerk's *Capital and Interest.* With such a collection, to be consumed within a few days, it is understandable why he would have left Berkeley. In 1899 he was certainly reading more serious literature, science, philosophy, and history than a student would have covered in four years of classes. It is little wonder that he was welcome in parlors and meeting rooms where lively intellectual discourse was valued.

# 4

# "*Gitana Strunsky*"

LATE IN 1899, the Socialist Labor Party held a commemoration of the Paris Commune of 1871 at the Turk Street Temple in San Francisco. There in the dusty gaslit hall, decorated with pictures of Marx, Engels, Ferdinand Lassalle, and other revolutionaries, British-born Austin Lewis's eloquent re-creation of the conflict at the barricades left a young woman in attendance convinced that "the People would rise. . . . We were builders of the future." She joined enthusiastically at the conclusion in singing the "Marseillaise" and the "Internationale." Her name was Anna Strunsky, and her life would be marked from this day forward by her being introduced to "a Comrade who has been speaking in the streets in Oakland."[1]

When Jack shook her hand and looked her in the eye, Anna felt "as if I were meeting in their youth, Lassalle, Marx, or Byron, so instantly did I feel I was in the presence of a historical character." Her idealization of him, "the Platonic ideal of man, the body of the athlete and the mind of the thinker," would stay with her lifelong. Jack remarked how good it was that people like Austin Lewis, the "best and finest had crossed the barriers of class to side with the people." They did not talk long, however, because he had to catch the last ferry to Oakland.

Like other men in their circle, Jack was struck by Anna's vivacious, radiant manner. She was more handsome than beautiful. Her dark, heavy-lidded eyes took hold of the observer while she spoke effusively and passionately about injustice and revolutionary philosophy. Though unconventional in her assertiveness and participation in politics, she was very conventional with regard to a woman's personal relationship to a man. Consequently, she could mislead men by being open and forthright in her behavior, yet she was clearly not a New Woman where sex was concerned. She seemed vaguely aware of her temptress qualities, and enjoyed the attention, but was in her sexual mores quite Victorian. As one of Jack's friends later observed, "It would have to be marriage" with Anna, because "what a hell of a fuss these little intellectuals make about their virginity."[2]

Several days after their introduction, Jack wrote Anna a remarkably candid and daring letter in which he summed her up as "a woman to whom is given to feel the deeps and the heights of emotion in an extraordinary degree; who can grasp the intensity of transcendental feeling, the dramatic force of situation, as few women, or men either, can."[3] To let her know he was similarly well read, he mentioned Robert Browning, to whom she had referred during their meeting. Her reply included an invitation to the family home the following Saturday evening, which he accepted. "Take me this way," he cautioned, "a stray guest, a bird of passage, splashing with salt-rimed wings through a brief moment of your life."[4] Little did she realize how accurately that metaphor predicted their future relationship.

Jack could not have known from their brief encounter that Anna had spent her childhood until age nine in a Russian village of hovels.[5] She had been born on March 21, 1877, in Babinots, deep within the czar's pale of Jewish settlement. Her father, Elias Strunsky, was a well-read businessman who often traveled away from home. Inspired by a Russian translation of Alexis de Tocqueville's *Democracy in America*, he decided to emigrate. His pregnant wife and six children packed what little could be taken, their treasured featherbeds and cooking implements, and made their way to Germany then through Liverpool to New York City. There, on the Lower East Side, Anna's older brothers helped support the family by sewing shirts, and in the process became acquainted with socialism. After two years the family moved uptown to Thirty-ninth Street, where Elias started a wholesale grocery business.

Anna's mother (also named Anna) put great emphasis on education, and insisted that her children go to college. Max completed his medical education at Bellevue Hospital and set up his practice in their home. Anna earned notice in the *New York Herald* as the brightest student at Public School 49, her teachers praising her fluency in languages and her writing. Younger sister Rose, who would be her lifelong confidante, was similarly accomplished. The children's achievements were enhanced by the salon atmosphere at home. Elias Strunsky's evening ritual was to share wine and food with friends while they expressed and disputed a wide range of ideas. These "formative forces," Anna recalled, included "budding genius, refugees; revolutionists; broken lives and strong lives, all made welcome, all met with reverence and with warmth."[6]

Advised for health reasons to leave New York, in 1893 Elias moved the family to San Francisco. Though the timing, in the midst of depression, could not have been worse, the new Strunsky enterprise was wholesaling liquor, a commodity little affected by economic downturns. Consequently, Elias was able to buy a large house at 901 Golden Gate Avenue. Unlike in other parts of the country, Jews in California faced little prejudice. Because they had joined in the Gold Rush and experienced the same hardships and successes as the other settlers, their acceptance paralleled that of other ethnic whites in the Bay Area. From among them came leaders in the economic and cultural foundations of San Francisco and Oakland. Consequently, the Jews here felt less need to turn inward, and mixed more socially with those of other religions.

At the Strunsky home the soirees continued, attracting Jews and non-Jews alike. A prominent segment consisted of émigrés of socialist bent. Many were followers of Daniel de Leon, who preached suppression of immediate pleasure for the sake of political work. Despite her father's protests, around age sixteen Anna joined the Socialist Labor Party, and a few years later sister Rose followed.

In 1896 Anna graduated from Lowell High School and enrolled at the recently founded Stanford University, listing her proposed career as writer and lecturer. Her professors included such eminences as the psychologist William James and the sociologist E. A. Ross. James was so impressed by her essay comparing the conversion to humanism to his own theory of religious conversion that he asked her to prepare a lengthier version for his forthcoming book. She also formed a lifelong friendship with her literature professor, Melville Best Anderson. Her favorite teacher, however, on whom she developed a crush, was the historian Mary Sheldon Barnes, whose unexpected death in 1898 left Anna bereft for months afterward.

Despite these exceptional intellectual opportunities, Anna did not fulfill her professors' expectations. Any woman attending Stanford would have felt somewhat second class. Though Stanford had a relatively high proportion of women for that day, over one fourth, male students were its priority. Add to this Anna's Jewish heritage, which placed her very low on the scale of aptitude in the minds of the university's social Darwinist instructors, including Ross and the school president, David Starr Jordan.

In December 1898 the university suspended Anna. Her grades were part of the problem, for she apparently had suffered some kind of collapse that resulted in her passing only one course that semester, with three ambiguous "conditional" grades and three "deferred." Two causes seem likely for her academic failure. One could be grief over the loss of her "friend, sweetheart, lover" Professor Barnes.[7] The other was that she was committed less to school than to socialism. She was secretary of the party's Central Committee during her entire tenure at Stanford, worked on special projects, and traveled about the Bay Area giving speeches. So fervent and frequent were her talks that the local press dubbed her the "Girl Socialist of San Francisco." Thus it is curious that her path did not earlier cross that of Boy Socialist Jack London.

Their first evening together the couple sat by the fire at her home, where, she later recalled, the flickering light "flowed on him. I had never before seen a face at once so strong and so sensitive."[8] Anna admired Jack's wavy hair, his arresting large blue eyes with their unusually long lashes. His several missing teeth did not disfigure his smile, but in her mind only added to the boyish charm of his appearance.

Jack suggested they start a Karl Marx club, to meet at Anna's house regularly and read the original sources. She sensed his fervor for the abolition of class differences, the identification and destruction of "the enemy" that fostered divisiveness and grew fat off the spoils of inequality, though she was less certain of his backing women's equality. Later in the evening he picked up a copy of Rudyard Kipling's *Seven Seas* and read aloud the "Song of the English." (As part of his self-directed development as a writer, Jack had copied out pages of Kipling as a way of absorbing the master's style into his own.) She agreed with him that despite Kipling's imperial cry, he deserved praise for being "the first who sang of the soldier and the sailor in their own language."[9] They viewed the writer as having democratized literature by bringing beauty and significance to the voice of the commonplace, and compared him to Dante, who wrote in vernacular Latin. They next read Swinburne together. When Jack left, Anna stood by the window to watch him move quickly down the street in his rolling sailor's gait.

Reading aloud became the focus for many of their encounters: Wordsworth's sonnets, "Tintern Abbey," and "The Excursion," along with Browning's "My Last Duchess," "Saul," "Caliban," and "The Ring and the Book." As he would repeatedly with friends over the years, Jack returned for inspiration often to these poets, along with the novelists Thomas Hardy and Joseph Conrad. He wrote to Anna of staying up all night reading and crying over *Jude the Obscure,* and of identifying with Maksim Gorky's "Twenty-Six of Us and One Other" when it appeared in translation.

The companionship expanded into a more public realm. Jack, one of the organizers of American Friends of Russian Freedom, was elected president while Anna was voted secretary. Whenever the Strunsky family went to a play, he asked that they obtain a ticket for him to join their party. Consequently, Jack and Anna spent many evenings in theaters watching Shakespeare and Ibsen, Pinero and Barrie. They often went to the home of aesthetics professor Melbourne Green, where they participated in the reading of pre-Elizabethan plays. Their fellow actors included the humorist Gelett Burgess, socialist Jane Roulston, poet James F. Morton, Jr., and Marks Green, the physician wife of the host—once more a gathering of stimulating, original thinkers.

In between visits, Jack's letters teased and tempted. (Hers to him do not survive.) When she admonished him for including as characters in a story several haggling Jews, he discounted her criticism by noting that they were based on real people he knew well. (He was no doubt thinking of his childhood encounters with ragmen and pawnbrokers.) When she realized that she would never complete her degree at Stanford, where she was now an unmatriculated student, he wrote sympathetically, reminding her that "one's works are not measured by a college career and record but by a whole life."[10] By January 21, 1900, he could address her "Dear Miss Strunsky:—O Pshaw! Dear Anna. . . ."

He sent her books and flowers. They hiked the hills together during the day and joined the partying bohemians at Coppa's restaurant in San Francisco in the evening, where she was admired for her uniquely sorrowful voice. In February he offered to be her literary mentor, to "stand over you with a whip of scorpions and drive you to your daily toil."[11] He shared his writing drafts as well, and sought her commentary. But Anna was more captivated by Jack's charisma and political fervor than his literary aspirations, and this preference would be part of her undoing.

On February 20, Jack mentioned that he would be attending a funeral, that of Fred Jacobs, whose body was finally being returned from Manila. This news would have consequences beyond Anna's imagining, for it seemed clear that he was courting her. Several weeks later, he met her after a class at Berkeley, where she was hoping to complete her degree. There they conversed outside North Hall, his bicycle leaning against the wall. They were discussing Kant's Categorical Imperative when she sensed an atmosphere of crisis overwhelm them. He passed his hand through her hair; she blushed, and her hand shook in his. Terrified that he would think her bold or demanding if she responded in kind to his gesture, she stared into the distance and tossed off an irrelevancy about hoping to travel to Russia. Her upbringing held her back, when she in fact longed to embrace him and accept a proposal of marriage. It was a moment she would still remember in detail in very old age, down to the light breeze on her face and the color of the geraniums on the wall.

Instead, a few days later she received a brief, impersonal letter. Jack had proposed to Bess Maddern. They would be married right away, on April 7, at her parents' home. The impulse had come to him as she helped move him into a two-story house on Fifteenth Street in Oakland. "It was rather sudden. . . . For a thousand reasons I feel myself justified in making this marriage," he wrote to his editor at the *Overland Monthly*, Netta Eames (and thus to Charmian Kittredge). "Sunday evening I opened transactions for a wife; by Monday evening had the affair well under way." The reasons he gave were consistent with masculine ideals of the day: he would be "a cleaner, wholesomer man because of a restraint being laid upon me in place of being free to drift wheresoever I listed."[12] Anyway, it was a practical issue. The household (including Flora and Johnny Miller) would have to be supported whether he had a wife or not, so why not have one?

Anna was stunned. She had not known that when Fred Jacobs left for war,

Jack had agreed to take over Bess's protection. During the past frustrating year, Bess had shared Flora's optimism, expressing certainty that Jack's chosen path of a writing career was the right choice, that he would not fail. Her constant loyalty and support, combined with her undemanding temperament, made her the kind of companion his other friends could not be. More athletic than Anna, Bess joined Jack for long cycling outings, handball games, and even wrestling matches. As Jack once recounted to Clousdesley Johns of that period, "Last night, threatening rain, we wandered off into the hills, cooked our dinner (broiled steak, baked sweet potatoes, coffee, etc., crab, French bread, and a patty of dairy butter), and were a couple of gypsies. Tomorrow we may jump on our wheels and ride off forty or fifty miles. And yesterday we may have taken in the opera and dined fashionably."[13] Bess also shared his pleasure in photography and working in the darkroom. When Jack proposed, he reflected, "We [have] had so much fun together."[14] That argument easily won Bess over then and through difficult years ahead.

Both acknowledged publicly that they were not marrying out of love, but from friendship and the belief that they would produce sturdy children. Neither was a sentimentalist, yet they were confident that their mutual affection would grow over time. The wedding was a simple Saturday morning service officiated by Bess's minister. Afterward they mounted their bicycles and took off for a tour of the northern part of the state, Bess in a fashionable dark skirt, white shirtwaist, and beribboned porkpie straw hat. Despite some initial sexual difficulties, by the end of the month, Bess was pregnant. Jack was now earning over a hundred dollars a month as a writer, well beyond the average laborer's wages. All boded well, until they settled down to keep house.

Flora viewed Bess as an interloper in her home, and her temper flared. Having been Jack's primary material and spiritual support throughout his difficult year of apprenticeship, she now found herself shunted aside. For one who loved taking center stage, it was an affront to watch another woman be granted the role of Jack's official hostess. When reporters came to call now it would be Bess, not Jack's mother, whom they would naturally want to interview.

Having worked since leaving school, Bess had few domestic skills and little understanding of how to meet the needs of two adults and a small boy used to living together. Yet she was determined to run the household as well as handle Jack's typing, editing, and clerical chores. An obvious solution would have been to ask Flora, who understood the preferences and peculiarities of the household members, to cover the domestic duties. Instead, Bess bowed to years of her mother's teaching and felt impelled to handle everything, in the process making everyone unhappy. Since Jack groused at his mother for setting an ashtray a few inches from its appointed spot, one can imagine that he would not have spared Bess. Adding to her confusion, she was in the early stages of pregnancy, and so her newlywed days were hardly idyllic. One night Flora slipped into a trance at the dinner table and Bess splashed a glass of water on her in frustration.

Eventually Jack arranged a costly truce between the women, though it added significantly to his monthly bills, by resettling Flora and Johnny in a cottage a block away. The plan worked. Flora became a frequent and welcome visitor, who taught a more willing Bess how to cook Jack's favorite pan-fried steak. Whenever company came over, Flora sat quietly in a corner, since Jack had made it clear that she was never, ever to entertain with one of her elocutionary performances. As a consequence, Flora and Bess discovered, if not fondness, at least a compatibility in their mutual reserve, their difficulty in expressing affection directly or responding to a heated remark in kind. Although Jack did not consciously note this similarity, it would prove a special disadvantage to Bess when further trouble arose.

The trouble came soon and in unexpected ways. "All is not contractual in the contract," wrote Émile Durkheim, the nineteenth-century sociologist, whom Jack likely read. By that aphorism Durkheim was reminding us that no statement of terms is ever inclusive, that any contract has implicit elements which may be interpreted differently by the contractees. When Jack and Bess agreed to have a scientific marriage, he emphasized the first word, she the second. Yes, let us marry out of friendship to raise healthy children for the sake of the race, she agreed, yet let us also be married in conventional ways. Yes, let us marry because it is appropriate from the viewpoint of nature, he thought, but I can go on and live my life as before, free to do as I wish. He felt obligated to be the wage earner and seed provider, but little more, while she expected his full companionship and thought he should give family an equal place in his life with his writing.

"For a thousand reasons I think myself justified in making this marriage. It will not, however, interfere much with my old life or my life as I had planned it for the future," he wrote to Anna Strunsky on his wedding eve.[15] While Bess managed the house and prepared his manuscripts, Jack went out for exercise with his friends: bicycling, boxing, fencing, swimming, and tossing Indian clubs. He had become enamored of the physical culture fad inspired by such bodybuilding celebrities as Benarr McFadden, and, like many of that ilk, posed for portraits in briefs to show off his body. Bess's advancing pregnancy also explains why he would hike and bike without her.

There was also the Ruskin Club, the Political Equality Club (a women's suffrage organization), the American Friends for Russian Freedom, and Socialist Party meetings in the evenings. Just three weeks into the marriage he lectured on "The Question of the Maximum" in San Jose, and soon afterward on

"War" to the Ebell Club. These appearances increased in frequency during 1900. Men dominated the podiums, with Jack the most frequent speaker. Anna gained in prominence for her radiant delivery. On rare occasions she was allowed to orate, while Bess's role, when she attended, was that of official hostess.

In June, Jack signed a contract with McClure, Phillips to write his first novel, *A Daughter of the Snows*. Set in the Yukon, the story tells of Frona Welse, a Stanford graduate and physical Valkyrie, who upsets her wealthy father's Yukon community with her forthright conversation and brazen befriending of the town prostitute. Jack told Anna that she was the model for Frona, and the signs are evident in the character's passion, her nonconformity, and her support of women's rights. Her very speech mimics Anna's florid use of language and introduces ideas from writers they read together in the Strunsky parlor, such as Browning and Ibsen. Yet Frona is interested in Anglo-Saxon advance, not socialism, and her physicality recalls the California woman, not the urban Jewish intellectual. In transforming Anna into the daughter of a splendid monopolist of Welsh stock, Jack erased the essence of Anna's identity, her culture, and her political commitments. She never acknowledged this profound distortion, however, and what it ultimately meant for Jack's understanding of her, which was always as a "Russian Jewess."

It is not that Jack viewed Jews as particularly inferior stock. The well-informed Jewish socialists he read or knew disproved that image. Still, his racialism left him uncertain where to place them within his human cosmology. Though inclined to stereotype, he did not sanction anti-Semitic acts. (Certainly he would have spoken out against the Holocaust, had he lived.) He seemed unclear about the historical role of Jews in capitalism. Were they essential yet defamed moneylenders in collusion with capitalists, or victims of them, an unfairly marginalized class? With regard to Anna, he admired the cosmopolitan and intellectual qualities of her "race," yet emphasized her "proud breast," her "black eyes," her "Assyrian profile," that is, her exotic sensuality. Hence, transforming her into Anglo-Saxon Frona was a way of expressing control over that threatening sexual appeal.

In addition to *Daughter of the Snows*, Jack expanded his Frisco Kid stories by twenty thousand words to produce a full-length juvenile book, *The Cruise of the Dazzler*. The Frisco Kid adventures were based on his oyster pirate days. Assuming that his readers would be middle-class boys, London developed the character of Joe, a wealthy young man fed up with school and rules who escapes to the waterfront to join the Kid. By the conclusion he has a clearer view of the world and humanity, and has come to appreciate his father's authority. He has become a boy headed for the clean, wholesome life London believed marriage had brought himself.

However much Jack insisted that he would be happy under the restraints of wedlock, his less conscious longings found ready expression. After the honeymoon, he sent Anna a letter as if there had been no change in their relationship, and inquired what evening he could come by and visit her. While sitting before the fire at the Strunsky parlor, he explained how he had worked out a new, modern form of marriage, in which "one married for qualities. He would found his marriage on that friendship in which love resolves itself." Psychologically astute, Anna quickly perceived a defense mechanism at work. "It was as if he had been saying he could be happy without happiness."[16] He continued to write her, to treat her as his literary protégée.

It was the Socialist Party that served as the catalyst for reviving his suppressed passion for Anna. She was present at the many party meetings and was invited to the Wednesday night socials Jack and Bess hosted for their friends. On May 2, Anna must have welled up to read, "How enthusiastic your letters always make me feel. Makes it seem as though some new energy had been projected into the world and that I cannot fail gathering part of it to myself."[17] By the end of July she could not help but read commitment between the lines. "Comrades!" he wrote her. "And surely it seems so. For all the petty surface turmoil which marked our coming to know each other, really, deep down, there was no confusion at all. . . . The ship, new-launched, rushes to the sea; the sliding-ways rebel in weakling creaks and groans; but sea and ship hear them not; so with us when we rushed into each other's lives—we, the real we, were undisturbed."[18]

Anna accepted Jack's more frequent invitations to his home. When he went sailing with Bess, she sometimes accompanied them. On one of these trips he argued with Anna about eugenics and the importance of making sure one was not in love with one's mate. As she later recalled: "Jack proposed that we write a book together on eugenics and romantic love. The moon rose, paled, and faded from the sky. Then the night came awake and our sails filled. Before we landed we had our plot, a novel in letter form in which Jack was to be an American, an economist, Herbert Wace, and I an Englishman, a poet, Dane Kempton, who stood in relation to him of father to son."[19] They would collaborate by sending actual letters to each other, Jack representing his scientific model, Anna the romantic. All this passed in the presence of Bess, who must have wondered at his proposition and believed that Anna would be attacking the very basis of her marriage. Fortunately for her, the plan did not require the co-authors to meet together to accomplish their goal—or so she thought.

In what would become *The Kempton-Wace Letters,* Jack argued an updated version of the Madonna/Whore dichotomy. Man should marry not the object of his lust, who was essential to his creative inspiration, but the Mother Woman, "made preeminently to know the lip clasp of a child."[20] This may have been the source of a clash between him and Anna, for, in her words, "a chill crept over their exchanges."[21] He finally healed the breach on December 26 by writing about their "white beautiful friendship," how the world could not conceive of such ties between a man and a woman.

Jack was not far off the mark, for the leisure rituals of the day emphasized all-male gatherings, whether in clubs, lodges, saloons, wilderness trips, or sports. A respectable woman would not consort even in an innocent way with a married man, yet that is what Anna chose to do. Societal disapproval served the purpose not just of condemning sexual impropriety but of protecting what was seen as threatened masculinity. This was a period of tumultuous debate around gender roles. Men had become so removed from the home since the Civil War that now preachers, journalists, and women in general were demanding that they return to their domestic responsibilities and become companions to their wives, not just breadwinners. With the advent of the New Woman, the independent, educated woman reviving the suffrage cause, men drew in their ranks even tighter to defend against perceived threats to manliness, which by definition required even more participation in male-only activities.

Thus, when Jack went off in the evenings and left Bess alone, he was not behaving in a manner that women of her class would have found in itself unusual. This is not to imply, though, that she tolerated all these absences any more than other wives would. Men's going to saloons and brothels had political consequence as well, for the major supporter of anti-suffrage activity was the liquor industry. Less often stated out loud, yet implied in the writings of temperance advocates, was the real threat to women of contracting venereal disease from their errant spouses. Furthermore, Bess had violated their agreement and fallen in love with her husband. He might have encouraged that impulse, as spouses behaving deceptively are apt to do, for she believed that his oft-demonstrated affection implied loyalty.

Despite his patronizing view of women and his predilection for nights out with his buddies, Jack eventually came to be firmly in favor of the vote for women. It was probably socialists such as Anna, Jane Roulston, and even Bess who enlightened him here, for in the late 1890s he had confirmed anti-suffrage beliefs. "Moral and formal logic" argue for woman's suffrage, he admitted, but "higher logic says she shall not . . . because she is woman," and women by nature were deferential to men.[22] By 1901, however, his attendance at the Political Equality League meetings signified a clear shift in his position, although he was never to speak out loudly on suffrage as he would regarding workers' rights and municipal ownership of utilities.

Complicating Jack's ambiguous, sometimes contradictory opinions regarding the female sex was his avid support of talented, intelligent women. This encouragement is perhaps one reason why Anna could not stay angry at Jack for long. Thus she accepted his peace offering to resolve their latest disagreement and appeared at his twenty-fifth birthday party on January 12, 1901. Confiding his hope that his first child would be a boy, he specified that it must be "no whining puny breed. It must be great and strong. Or—the penalty must be paid. By it, by me; one or the other. So be."[23] This strange prenatal dare was not a flight of literary bombast. He meant it, and would live by it. After all, what would it say of his own blood and talents were his children merely average? On January 15 the child was born, a nine-and-a-half-pound daughter—"a damned healthy youngster," Jack wrote Cloudesley Johns. He and Bess had achieved their purpose, a sturdy Anglo-Saxon child.

Except it did not quite happen as he described.[24] When Bess's labor began on January 14, she lay down in their double bed with its ornate headboard to deliver. As her labor became protracted into the early morning, Jack grew so hysterical that neither the doctor nor Melissa Maddern, Bess's mother, could calm him. Desperate, the doctor pulled out the forceps, yet even then the delivery was difficult. The baby emerged with her head misshapen, her temple dented, and one ear torn, and seemed lifeless. While Melissa Maddern tried various means to stimulate the baby to breathe, Jack cried out, "Let it die! Let it die!" Despite immersion in hot and cold baths, drops of brandy on her tongue, and Melissa's mouth-to-mouth resuscitation, the child remained lifeless. Discouraged, Melissa put the baby over her shoulder one last time, and suddenly a tiny wail came out. The child arrived not on her father's birthday, as he had hoped, but on that of the grandmother who saved her.

While Bess recuperated, she meditated on possible names, for tellingly only one had been selected ahead of time: Jack. She observed her husband's wariness around the baby, his referring to "it," not "she," his disinclination to touch or pick her up. After several days she recalled a note Jack had made on a scratch pad: "Heroines—favorite names, Eve and Joan." Bess was undecided which to choose until Jack appeared in her room to ask if he could get her anything. "Yes, will you bring Joan to me?" He lit up in delight and exclaimed what a perfect choice the name was, then picked the baby up for the first time. Significantly, Bess also acquired a nickname from her husband then, "Mommy Girl," and she reciprocated by calling him "Daddy Boy."

His hesitation should not be interpreted as displeasure or unhappiness with either Joan herself or her gender. Just twelve hours after the baby was born he took a portrait of her and bought a photo album he titled "Joan—Her Book." Throughout her first two years he took, developed, and printed photographs, pasted them in the album, and added whimsical comments in an archaic voice:

> Joan meditateth on the Mystery of Things, Vieweth life Pessimistically, And striveth hard to be Reconciled—all at Three Weeks Old. . . .
>
> At Six Months Joan sitteth on the Beach at Sunny Cove and looketh Sphinx-like. . . .

At Nine Months she Biketh [perched in the front basket] with the Pater, who is the Pater no longer, but Daddy. Behold Joan's House in the Distance. . . .

And at Twelve Months, which is her Second Birthday, she holdeth her First Birthday Party. . . .

Nineteen Months—While Daddy is away, Joan trieth to break the Commandments, her Neck, and the Mater's Heart [by clambering over a fence].

The album reveals the early life of a well-fed, much-loved child. Usually uncomfortable in front of a camera, Bess smiles proudly. Jack's wonder over his daughter, whether pulling a splinter out of her finger or holding her up to show off her clothes, is undeniable.

The year 1901 would prove to be a time of fulfillment for the young couple in other matters as well. In just the first three months Jack earned $1,100, enough to support his and Flora's households in comfort. His stories appeared in such nationally prominent magazines as *McClure's*, *Cosmopolitan*, and *Youth's Companion*. His writing continued apace, not only short stories but also the Yukon novel, the collaboration with Anna, and essays for socialist journals (for which he received no payment). Then in July, newspaper editor William Randolph Hearst took note of this local writer and gave him an assignment to cover a Schutzenfest, or shooting match. Out of this minor event Jack produced ten stories for the *San Francisco Examiner* and earned the respect of the powerful publisher. (He made fun of himself for making money off "the Yellow [journalism]" and complained about its cutting into his other work, yet certainly he knew the value of having Hearst in his corner.) In November, Hearst assigned Jack to cover the Ruhlin-Jeffries boxing match, an event he portrayed with such color and insight that it led to other assignments over the years and established London as among the most gifted reporters in that branch of sports journalism.

Sympathetic with the additional demands Joan brought into Bess's life, Jack hired a nursemaid as well as a cleaning woman. Now aware that Jack was spending ahead of his income, Bess sought tutorial students to help pay the daily bills. She did so with pleasure that she was assisting his career, and in expectation of future comforts his eventual success would bring. Bess similarly enjoyed entertaining and preparing the large buffets for their Wednesday evening parties, where guests found her friendly and a welcome contributor to the high level of intellectual banter.

Though Jack was willing to play the capitalist's game to make money from his writing, he continued his political activities. As the Social Democratic Party's nominee for mayor of Oakland, he stumped to explain why voters should support a third party and reject the major ones. For all their talk of municipal welfare and ownership, neither the Republicans nor Democrats would act, he argued, because both were ultimately at the beck and call of the economically powerful. Thus, any workingman who voted a standard party ticket was throwing his vote away. (Jack garnered 245 votes in the election.) He continued to deliver lectures throughout the Bay Area—"Competitive Waste" and "The Restaurant Worker's Strike"—which had been organized by his friend Frank Strawn-Hamilton. By the end of 1901, he was writing less from his Yukon experiences and had turned almost entirely to social issues, particularly as informed by his tramping and prison encounters.

This had been among the best years of Bess's life, and Jack's as well, and its final months were particularly gratifying. There had been a brief disruption in March when their Oakland home flooded and they had to moved into La Capriciossa, a fey Moorish structure designed and lived in by sculptor Felix Peano and his family. Though picturesque on the outside, the house with its dark, tiny rooms cramped family life. Relief came in June, when the Londons went to Forestville, a summer resort town on the Russian River, to enjoy the easy tent-cabin life at Camp Reverie. Bess thrived in the outdoors, particularly enjoying being near water, and Joan proved an easygoing infant in this new setting.

Located in a grove of redwoods along the Russian River, Camp Reverie was an extension of the Chautauqua movement, with its emphasis on education-based leisure. Jack was one of the lecturers, invited to speak on political issues. During their stay, he and Bess acted in the camp play, "Manitoba Jim's Revenge," with the cast of characters reading "Irresistable Villain—Jack, Son of London" and "Deserted, but admiring wife—Queenie London." Adding to what would prove to have been ironic casting in retrospect was the presence of the "Mediator—Gitana [Gypsy] Strunsky."

Following the summer idyll, the couple searched for another home. They chose a large, elegant house on Bayo Vista, which as the name implies was in the foothills above Oakland, and the newest fashionable neighborhood. Bess always recalled this place affectionately, later repeating to her daughters during difficult times, "Perhaps it would have been better if we had stayed there and not moved to Piedmont at all."[25] She had a large garden to draw her outdoors, and space for the houseguests who always seemed to be pressing upon their hospitality. Yet only four months after settling in, Bess learned from Jack that she should pack up again.

Along with his growing fame, Jack attracted a new set of friends. Chief among these was George Sterling. Seven years older than Jack, Sterling was a fascinating mix of prankster and propriety. This slight, medium-height man with the prominent beakish nose had been born to an affluent family on Long Island. Serious about the possibility of entering the priesthood, he performed brilliantly at Carroll College in Maryland, where he received a rigorous classical education combined with theological courses. One of his mentors recognized that George's real calling was literature, for he had a lyrical, sensual inclination better suiting him to the lay life. Consequently, George joined his family, who had moved to Oakland, and became private secretary to his uncle George Havens, a prominent East Bay real estate mogul.

Exploring the Bay Area literary scene, he succumbed to the influence of Ambrose Bierce, the domineering, misanthropic cynic whose approval or censure was the final word in one's local reputation. Fully absorbing Bierce's pessimism, George announced himself a reincarnation of the romantic Lord Byron, his new philosophy "sine qua non to discard morals" that he "might bathe in moral slime."[26] Nonetheless, all who knew him remarked on his exemplary character, his kindness, loyalty, and generosity to friends. He took his poetry seriously and labored for Havens for seventeen years without stint while leading a bohemian life away from the office. His wife, Carrie, pushed him to be a successful businessman, while his companions pulled him toward a more carefree life dedicated to art. The struggle would ultimately resolve in tragedy.

Jack had little in common with George, in terms of either life experience or philosophy, yet the two felt a sympathetic understanding that overcame such differences. In time they would become like brothers, "Wolf" confiding in "Greek" (so dubbed for his profile), and assisting each other through very ticklish situations. In addition to meeting at restaurants, parties, and other events, they sometimes caroused in San Francisco's Barbary Coast, where Chinese prostitutes were kept in cages and clubs spiked the drinks so employees could roll victims for money. George kept a hideaway apartment on the Montgomery Block, or Monkey Block, where many historic figures going back to the young Mark Twain had resided. In the late hours both men smoked hashish together, though who introduced whom is unclear. Their favorite drug was alcohol, with George the more susceptible to its allure.

In March 1902, on George's recommendation Jack moved his family to a sprawling, multilevel redwood shingled house nearby on Blair Avenue high in the Piedmont hills. A large vine-covered veranda created an outdoor living room overlooking the spread of Oakland, marshy Lake Merritt, the Golden Gate with tall-masted ships moving in and out, the Farallon Islands far out in the Pacific, and, to the north, the undulating prominence of Mount Tamalpais. Five acres of orchards, fields, eucalyptus groves, pine trees, and gardens sprawled around the house on the slopes of the hill. The property included a large barn, chicken coops, a pigeon loft, separate laundry and creamery buildings, and even a steep-roofed cottage for Flora and Johnny Miller. Because this was country, abutting cattle ranges run by cowboys, the rent was only thirty-five dollars a month. Though a stunning spread and capacious house, it was also isolated, making Bess's trips to the grocer or the doctor with baby Joan a long one.

There is a rare mention of Bess in one of Jack's stories from this time, "The Golden Poppy." The story begins with the two enjoying the resplendent sweep of orange and yellow plants carpeting the fields alongside their new home. "We shall have great joy," predicts Bess, who agrees that all the "No Trespassing" signs posted by the previous owner must come down. But, like "flood-beset rats," the city folk invade the field to pick poppies, or worse, pull them up by their roots. Jack and Bess reach for ever more desperate measures to stop the desecration, but without success. One sentence foreshadows the irony concerning race that would build in his fiction over the years: "We are a race of land-robbers and sea-robbers, we Anglo-Saxons, and small wonder, when we suckle at the breasts of a breed of women such as maraud my poppy field." This charming story, full of self-mockery, also hints at London's rediscovery of the countryside, a place to live in "fresher and more vigorous ways."[27] By the time this story appeared in print, he and Bess were no longer living together.

Now the Wednesday gatherings expanded from a half dozen or so guests to several times that many. Having grown up in a large, gregarious extended family, Bess found these crowds a familiar, comforting way to spend free time. Inviting one guest, she advised, "We just wear all the old duds we can find, so just come over and have a jolly good time."[28] Entertainment was homegrown: quoits, boxing, fencing, musicales, reading aloud, flying kites, even ducking for apples and other children's sports. One youngster admired Jack's fascination with blowing bubbles and his search for ever more interesting bubble pipes. In accord with the absorption of physical culture into the New Woman role, both fencing and boxing matches were coed and served as highly competitive simulations of the larger battle between the sexes.

Prominent at the Wednesday gatherings now were the brilliant Partington siblings, who included drama critic Blanche, noted portraitist Richard, and opera singer Phyllis (stage name, Frances Peralta). Other artistic types joined in, such as lawyer-turned-writer Jimmy Hopper and journalist Joseph Noel. Living not far from Jack and George in Piedmont was Jim Whitaker, who, despite years of poverty and struggle to support seven children, finally broke through as an income-earning writer in 1901. Jack had encouraged Whitaker and helped the family financially through hard times when he could hardly support himself. As a way of acknowledging all who had helped him over the years, Jim invited other impoverished artists to pitch tents on his property rent free. Carlt Bierce lacked his brother Ambrose's misanthropy, and with wife Laura formed another popular pair.

Perhaps the most eccentric companion was Mexican-born Xavier ("Marty") Martinez, recently returned from six years of art study in Paris. His corduroy coat, baggy pants, black velvet beret, flowing red tie, and large mustache made him the most colorful figure of the group. Marty's vivid appearance and brilliantly colored paintings marked him as the most visible representative of bohemianism to the more staid Bay Area denizens. Martinez also kept rooms in a high-ceilinged, many-windowed building on the Monkey Block, and would soon take over a sprawling bungalow very close to those of London and Whitaker in the Piedmont hills.

Some evenings the Crowd, as it came to be known, joined with San Francisco writers and artists at their unofficial clubhouse, Coppa's restaurant, noted for its black cat logo. Its genial Turinese proprietor and chef, Giuseppe Coppa, generously served mountains of spaghetti and full glasses of red wine on credit, often free, to those lacking the price. He also welcomed the growing array of sketches, mural paintings, and poems they left behind on the walls. Devoted to her new daughter, Bess was unlikely to have joined her husband at these raucous dinners. Nevertheless, despite some of the temptations entering Jack's life, the marriage remained companionable.

Being of an older generation, Netta Eames came less often to these gatherings of the Crowd, and her niece Charmian Kittredge not at all. Charmian had broken off her engagement with Will Minstrel to take up with Harry Dugan, whom Netta disliked. Fed up with her aunt's constant intrusion into her private affairs, Charmian went to live with paternal relatives in Maine, and also took the grand tour of Europe then requisite among the well read. Though no longer an editor, Netta remained an influence on Jack, who adopted a filial stance toward her. Slowly she was superseding the place of Eliza, Flora, and Jennie as a maternal figure.

Neither was Eliza attracted to the overheated play of the Wednesday set. When with age her husband became irascible and difficult, she devoted herself to her civic causes. She was more likely to see Jack when he found a few minutes to stop by her house and visit. Nor did Flora seem to have gone to these socials, for she does not appear in the various remembrances of those who attended.

Another who appeared infrequently at the Londons' gatherings in Piedmont or at Coppa's was Anna Strunsky. In 1901 she descended into what appears to have been clinical depression. Her notebook entries shifted to the themes of death, loss, futile effort, and the relentless passing of time. One set of sketches was for a never-written collection of stories called "Studies in Suicide." She also worked on plans for a novel that was to introduce in chapter 1 "John Torrance at 12. Fury then gentleness. Oakland—selling papers. Incident of the candy."[29]

It was clearly a story of childhood poverty based on Jack's life as she understood it, for it included his acceptance into a "Group of noble Dames"—the Applegarths, no doubt.

Jack's encouragement of Anna's literary bent continued, for it had been his vision of her as a great writer that had started her off on this career. Yet his blessing, as it were, turned into a curse. Anna would spend her life starting writing projects but rarely seeing them through. Despite urging from William James, she did not expand her essay on political conversion for his book. The reasons are unclear. It was not that she lacked talent, for even Jack admitted that her portions of *Kempton-Wace* were superior to his. Nor did she lack for role models, support, or inspiration. Her family both encouraged her intellectually and provided the material support to allow her freedom to write. Did she sabotage herself with thoughts of inadequacy? Was she lax in self-discipline? Or was it, as one friend reflected, her very personality that interfered, that allowed her to gain attention and rewards without having to produce a work or an act of substance? Perhaps it was simply that her bouts of despair and melancholy depleted the energy required to carry a project to its completion in a timely manner.

Jack was cognizant of her "soul sickness," though not of his role in aggravating it. For with the appearance of Joan, and Jack's obvious joy in fatherhood, Anna realized that she must once and for all repress her longing for more from him than approval of her literary style. Accepting her love as unrequited, she flirted with another member of their socialist group, Cameron King, who proposed to her in the winter of 1901. Anna then forwarded her suitor's letter to Jack, explaining that she had spurned the offer yet felt guilty about doing so. Jack's lengthy, thoughtful response assured her that she had injured King less by refusing him than by accepting what would have been an unhappy commitment. He cited examples to prove that Anna was superior to King, whose affection he discounted as "puppy love." "Your growth has been greater than his," he wrote. "You dare not, cannot, do else than remain the star."[30]

Jack's reference to "the star" would reappear as part of his courtship language with at least two other women in his life. The reference is to his and Anna's favorite poet, Robert Browning. "My Star," in which the beloved is conceived as a celestial object, concludes, "Mine has opened its soul to me; therefore I love it."[31] Thus Jack and Anna were writing in coded messages, though whether they did so consciously that December of 1901 is unknown. She should not marry another, he implied, for she was his star, and he confessed that his year had been "tumultuous and bankrupt," an odd comment from someone who was telling others that he was a successful, happily married man.

In 1902 Anna moved north across the Golden Gate to San Rafael, intending to write her novel and complete her sections of *Kempton-Wace*. When Jack attempted to see her, she rebuffed him or refused invitations to his gatherings. On

March 22 he tried to tempt her with news of another guest, Charmian Kittredge, "charmingly different from the average kind." Charmian had recently returned from her long absence and now lived in Berkeley at the home of her uncle Harley Wiley. Having healed her breach with Netta, she too began to appear at the Londons' parties and went sailing with the couple on the bay. Charmian was considering the proposal of a man she had met back east. As Joseph Noel observed, she cut quite an alluring figure in fencing gear, but so did other young women hoping to catch Jack's eye. While he romped and flirted with such women, his mind was on Anna. Flora also befriended Anna, addressing her as "my dear daughter," and welcomed her to stay the night whenever she wished.[32] Was she aware of the growing infatuation between the collaborators, or simply hoping to curry Jack's favor by being gracious to his friend? In any event, she would soon show support for the romance that developed between the two.

In May, Anna agreed to stay at Jack's home while they worked together on the final editing of their book. Here is where two surviving accounts of what transpired diverge. According to Anna, Bess was cordial at first, then seemed to adopt a cooler though not unkind attitude. Feeling uncomfortable, Anna decided to leave and was surprised when Bess as well as Jack objected. When she did depart, Bess's farewell was affectionate. According to Bess, however, Anna and Jack would arise at 4:30 in the morning, work in his study until breakfast, then wander off for the rest of the day. One day she discovered Anna sitting in Jack's lap and realized that more than a literary collaboration was under way.

Bess's version agrees with Anna's on one point: that after the visit Jack asked Anna to marry him. "When he spoke and urged her to accept his love," Anna recalled, describing the scene in the third person, "there was a tumult of joy in her heart and she promised to marry him." After discussing the matter with her mother, who urged her to imagine the consequences of the scandal and its effect on their relationship, Anna reconsidered. Several weeks later, Anna retracted her acceptance of his proposal. "I was afraid to take my happiness at the expense of his wife and baby," she later explained, yet she could not blunt her longing for him.[33]

What she did not know then was that Bess was expecting again, in October. Somehow Jack had left that complication out of his proposal. Undaunted, he responded to Anna's rejection with increased ardor. His June 10 letter read in its entirety: "I shall be over Friday afternoon. I am doing 2000 words a day now, & every day, and my head is in such a whirl I can hardly think. But I am sick with love for you and need of you."[34] Anna affirmed that she still loved him, but was cautious, and arranged that their meetings were chaperoned.

During this time Bess found a sympathetic new shoulder among the Crowd: Charmian Kittredge. Jack's friends had never fully accepted Charmian into their inner circle because she was not willing to submit to her secondary role as a woman. Within the Crowd, women could be only wives or whores, and Charmian failed to fit either slot. She was an odd mix of propriety and sensuality, of independence and cozening up to men. Being in the midst of a complicated romance herself, she and Bess were drawn closer because of their similar difficulties.

Anna and Jack's romance was interrupted when, in July, he accepted an assignment to interview officials in South Africa regarding the Boer War. This opportunity was also a useful excuse to escape Bess and her recriminations. Upon reaching New York City, however, he learned that the project had collapsed, and arranged instead a project on the London slums, to be called *The People of the Abyss*. With so much publicity surrounding the coronation of Edward VII, he saw an opportunity to challenge the fantasy of a prosperous England well run by the benevolent, paternalistic aristocracy.

Neither wife nor collaborator had seen Jack off at the train station when he departed Oakland. He wrote Anna brief notes from New York and London, and worried increasingly that she was not writing back. On August 25 he received two letters, one chatty, the other, written on a later day, a tempest. She now rejected his stories about the failure of his marriage, for she had learned of Bess's pregnancy. The source was likely Flora Wellman, who had written Anna and asked her not to visit for the time being. Bess, Flora said, had proved "a heavy cross to carry" and "made my heart bleed" through her "cruel misrepresentations" and "constant effort to turn my son against me." But because Bess was pregnant again, Flora did not want "to cause her a single heartache." Thus she pleaded with Anna, "Let us both do right that good may come of it."[35]

Characteristically, Jack ignored his duplicity. "You are one of the cruelest women I have ever known," he chastised Anna. "Also, you have 'pitied' me and my children. . . . I would rather be called a liar, even by you, than to have you pity Joan. Do with me what you will, but leave Joan's soul alone."[36] He soon apologized for the harshness of his response, explaining that he was very blue and tired when he wrote it. "When I get warm I make a mess of it. . . . Yours was the last clean, pure warming light I shall ever receive I imagine."[37] It was three weeks before he received her next letter, a casual one filled with news. They stumbled back into a friendship. He commiserated that she had received two rejections of their *Kempton-Wace* project, and urged her to "plug right in" and keep writing. Holding himself up as a model, he proudly noted that he had completed the 63,000 words of *The People of the Abyss* by the end of September.

Looking back on this episode years later, Anna reflected of herself, "She would of course realize her cruelty later and be overwhelmed with remorse. She would never again write anything to anybody in criticism."[38] She decided to accept an offer from Gaylord Wilshire to work in New York City at his socialist magazine, *Wilshire's Monthly*. Elsie Whitaker and her father, Jim, were among those who saw Anna off at the station. Elsie was fascinated by Anna's dress, of a "soft smoke-colored material with a red ornament at her neck and a red belt buckle." When she came to know Anna better, she realized the dress was connected to the romance with Jack, for Anna said, "It's the only dress I have ever loved and have never forgotten."[39]

# 5

# Damned Hard on the Woman

IN OCTOBER 1902 BESS WAS due to deliver, yet Jack did not return home from England. Instead, he went off on a rapid tour of Europe, taking photographs that are remarkable for evoking emptiness and isolation. The streets are vacant, as though he went out haunting at daybreak.[1] Consequently, he was absent when Bess bore a second daughter, her namesake Bess, who would come to be known as Baby B, and eventually Becky. At some point in her life Becky would learn that her father had stayed away when she was born, that her arrival was not good enough reason for him to return to his family. Worse, one day in anger Bess would blame this younger daughter for causing the marital difficulties. Had Becky not been conceived, she implied, she would still be married to Jack.[2] These cruelties, however, were still in the future.

Upon returning to the States, Jack spent several days handling business matters in New York. It was only on the westward train, where he opened mail held for him in New York, that he learned Anna was heading east, and they had missed each other by a day or two. He wrote her a lighthearted note about the missed opportunity, and on November 9, 1902, sent George Brett, their Macmillan editor, a letter of introduction to his collaborator on *Kempton-Wace*. "I am sure you will find her charming. She is a young Russian-Jewess, brilliant, a college-woman, etc." He assured Anna she could do the final editing, though in fact over the next few months he revised all the work, and left it to her to accept or reject each change he had made in her portion of the manuscript. He was scrupulous, though, about her receiving her own contract with Macmillan, one equal to his. He also deferred to Anna's idea for a prologue, which Brett eventually cut from the final version.

Jack walked through the door of his home a vanquished man. He was deeply in debt, for despite earning a comfortable income, he continued to live on credit, namely, his publishers' advances. Despite a habit of keeping account books of his expenses, he omitted the key information—the flow of income. He could never refuse his impulsive desires, whether to feed dozens of friends, buy a sloop, or give money to needy suppliants.

With Anna gone from the scene, Bess was ready to accept her errant husband back. She may have realized that the romance had never been consummated, and was ready to avert her eyes from signs of his carnal encounters in the city. And as he pointed out, they were both still young, only twenty-six, and there would be more opportunities to have a son. Never unmindful of the burdens Bess bore, he brought Jennie Prentiss into the household to help care for the girls. (Alonzo was very feeble now—he would die a few months later—and the opportunity to care for her beloved foster son's children was most welcome.)

Bess quickly extended the understanding and support Jack had come to expect from women as a result of the combined coddling of Flora, Eliza, Jennie, and Netta. Until the final upswelling of his infatuation for Anna, he had been a good companion. He secluded himself with his family, assured Bess that the next child would be a boy, but that he loved Baby B just as she was. He spoke of buying a boat and taking them all around the world, and told Jennie she would be included too. To Cloudesley Johns he wrote in a self-congratulatory mood: "By the way, I think your long-deferred congratulations on my marriage are about due. So fire away. Or, come and take a look at us, and at the kids, and then congratulate."[3] Inscribing *The Children of the Frost* to Bess, he noted: "'The first book of mine, all for your own,' you said. But what matters it? Am I not all your own, your Daddy-Boy?'" So he would always be to Bess, and could win any demand by sweetly calling her "Mother-Girl."

That winter his letters to Anna grew prickly. Though only twenty-six, he wrote with haughty self-pity: "I am fifty years old to-day. The mystery of man & woman is behind me. I am deep in the mystery of father & daughter. You do not understand this. You are about seventeen to-day. And between seventeen and twenty-seven you will linger until you die." This taunt was another of his remarks that would seem so powerful as to turn into an incantation—and not only for Anna. Observe that he referred only to *a* daughter, and otherwise in the letter spoke of "Joan—great, wonderful, glorious Joan."[4] Becky, the child responsible in a sense for the loss of Anna, would never be described in such fulsome ways by her father.

Part of Jack's bad mood was the result of a box of books falling and striking him "in a vital place," with the result that he was laid up for several weeks. While recuperating he formulated what would become the plot of *The Sea-Wolf*. As he explained to George Brett on January 20, 1903, the story "shall have adventure, storm, struggle, tragedy and love. . . . My idea is to take a cultured, refined, super-civilized man and woman . . . and throw them into a primitive sea-environment where all is stress & struggle and life expresses itself, simply, in terms of food and shelter; and make this man and woman come out of it with flying colors."[5] *Kempton-Wace* was not even in print, yet he was already composing a story in which he argued the opposite philosophy: that love mattered.

Anna's brother Hyman and his wife, Mary, visited Jack's sickbed, evidence that he was still part of the extended Strunsky family. For his twenty-seventh birthday Anna sent a volume of W. E. Henley's poems that she had received previously from their mutual friend Jane Roulston. She inscribed warmly how much she loved the book and "the woman who gave it to me," that it helped her recall "yet other times when others who were close read [it] with me."[6] But Jack grew angry and attacked her for including two slips of paper inserted on pages that contained passages he interpreted as commenting on their breakup. No such meaning had been intended by these accidental placements, and he was quick to apologize, particularly upon learning that Mary Strunsky had suddenly died. The apology was backhanded, though, for he mocked Anna as "one who will always titillate with desire . . . who is content to pursue without attaining," and "a child as saliently as you are a woman."[7]

Anna finally just refused to explain herself anymore. Even before her sister-in-law's death she had once again jotted suicide themes in her notebook, and in January she was struck with a flu so severe that she was bedridden until March. She contacted Jack then only because the proofs were due at Macmillan; he responded briefly and to the point about editorial matters.

That winter Jack most likely learned of his putative father's death, though he left no hint of it. On January 12, 1903, the *San Francisco Call* featured on its front page an article headlined "Horoscope Forecasts His Death." The forecaster was William Chaney, who, though in vigorous health, had the previous Thanksgiving Day predicted his demise before witnesses and prearranged his funeral. He was buried in Elmwood Cemetery in Chicago. Despite a howling blizzard, a dozen men and women, some in the purple robes and regalia of the Masonic order, carried out his plans.

To the end Chaney had continued his efforts on behalf of astrology. In 1900 the editor of *The Adept* described a visit by Chaney "in his 80th year and as active as a man of 30. . . . [W]hile not lecturing or teaching he enjoyed working 18 hours a day," a schedule he maintained through a lifetime habit of brief rests. Chaney was still deriding religion, particularly Christianity, with gleeful sarcasm, and drawing critics to rejoin with tart venom. In "The Origin and Evolution of Religion," he argued that worship originated in fear and ignorance. "Many need a religion, even a devil and hell to make them behave themselves." A fellow adept who practiced "Bible Astrology" accused Chaney of "drinking something besides Chicago lake water," and listed his many faults, including "wives by the octave."[8] Thus to the end Chaney fought his intellectual wars and, though impoverished, did not die lonely or unappreciated.

By spring of 1903, the Piedmont bungalow was a joyful, friend-filled place, though the guests now included hangers-on and sycophants whom Bess did not always like. Toddler Joan had a proclivity to wander off and worry her parents, who rushed over the acreage searching for her. When Charmian Kittredge visited, Joan would grab her hand and pull her to the piano to play. Joan heard such stories later from her parents and Jennie. What she remembered most about this time, however, was the sensuality of the landscape, the changing colors of the flowers, the scent of eucalyptus and herbs, the feel of the afternoon breeze rolling up the slopes.

Interestingly, it was during this period of reconciliation that Jack wrote his masterpiece, *The Call of the Wild*. If in *Kempton-Wace* he voted for eugenics and scientific mating, in *Call* he gave himself over to the immaterial phenomenon of love, for it is Buck's love for John Thornton that is central to the dog's individualization. Through this mythopoeic novella, Jack renounced his earlier beliefs, and would seem to have been ready for a deep union with his wife. Unfortunately, given her upbringing and personality, Bess was incapable of titillating Jack with a thousand desires, as Anna had done. In this regard, he still retained his *Kempton-Wace Letters* characterization of women: Bess was "the Mother Woman, the last and highest and holiest in the hierarchy of life." He respected and honored her, while she longed for romance and fidelity.

With Anna, the model for the "wanton. . . . Mate Woman," gone, the situation was ripe for another to take her place. Hints of what was to come appeared that spring in a *Sunset* article, "Jack London Afloat," written by Charmian Kittredge. There she described his postponement of a South Seas adventure in favor of local sailing. To that end he had just purchased the *Spray*, a thirty-foot sloop, which he had equipped with all his writing paraphernalia and comfortable living quarters. "Mrs. London expects to accompany her husband a goodly portion" of the time, along with both daughters, the article reported. Yet Charmian's conclusion was more prescient, that "lusty yachtsmen skimming familiar waters of San Francisco bay" should be alert to sounds "as Jack London sails his boat and weaves romance."[9] The romance would not be fictional.

Bess watched other women flirt with her husband, yet he did not lead her to suspect he was going to stray again. For one thing, there were his future plans for the family. For another, his days were consumed with juggling the writing, editing, and marketing of various books and essays. Living on credit had started him on a race toward an ever-receding financial goal. In letters to his editors he begged for advances or larger payments, giving melodramatic accounts of his situation. Writing to publisher Frank Putnam, for example, he wove a story of how his trip to England had been financed by a $300 loan from Flora. "Now my mother who came from the East when she was a child, who is old & has never been back to the old home & the old places & faces wants to go back once before she dies," taking her grandson with her.[10] (Flora never took such a trip.) Two weeks later, on March 26, he recorded receipt of $925 from five different sources, yet was so desperate for money that he sold Macmillan all book rights to *The Call of the Wild* for $2,000, which meant that he would never make another penny from its phenomenal success.[11] He never regretted that decision, because the success of the book guaranteed him prominence in the literary constellation.

In late May, Bess, the girls, and Jennie packed for a trip to Glen Ellen in Sonoma County north of San Francisco Bay. Netta Eames had bought a place there named Wake Robin Lodge, whose expansive grounds included tent cabins for family vacations. Similar to Camp Reverie, Wake Robin would offer lectures as well as family entertainment. Californians were so enamored of fresh air for their health that the homes built during this time often included porches off the bedrooms for sleeping outdoors. Camping out was thought to extend the health benefits, as well as encourage "the simple life," a key principle of the Arts and Crafts movement in vogue among artists and professionals in the Bay Area.

Jack stayed behind—to complete some work, Bess believed, though he was actually intending to "find any woman I could get ahold of" from among a dozen eligibles.[12] As Jack's friend Joseph Noel had observed that spring, Jack was once again "tugging at the leash of matrimony." During nights out with the men, Jack often criticized Bess as "devoted to purity," code words for her fear that he was consorting with prostitutes and might bring home venereal disease. During one party, Noel followed Jack to look in on an ailing Becky. The sight of Bess sitting by the child's crib, staring into space, left Noel with a sense of "tragedy stark, impalpable, hovering over that household. All the decencies that one may possess were ranged with Bessie."[13]

In mid-June, Jack visited the Sterlings in Oakland. A carriage accident injured his leg, forcing him to cancel his meeting with an (unidentified) woman. Upon hearing that he was returning to Wake Robin to recuperate, Bess called Charmian Kittredge and asked her to buy some goods for Jack to bring up with him. When Charmian arrived at the Piedmont bungalow, she helped Frank Atherton pack Jack's trunks. Watching her, Jack thought, "Here was my chance," that she was among the women who would "suit me in an illicit way." Consequently, he kept her on the porch for about half an hour while they "talked philosophically," and he "was busy telling [her] some of the things in her that I didn't like." When Charmian rose to leave, Jack kissed her.

Charmian received a note asking her to meet Jack at George's the next weekend, unaware that he was also planning to take a sailing trip with another woman. Bess caught Jack with a telegram from his paramour, and the ensuing argument only hardened his determination to stray. Bess's discovery of his philandering pricked his masculine pride; he would be tamed, but only on his own terms.

Charmian later destroyed her diary for this year, so one can only surmise her feelings, let alone validate Jack's version of the meeting.[14] Since 1900 she had watched a disheveled, self-conscious young man turn into a polished, confident adult. Meanwhile, she had been involved with a string of successful, even prominent men, though the relationships never felt right to her. She preferred vegetarianism, tended toward socialism in principle if not active practice, and did not condemn sex outside of marriage. Fiercely self-disciplined, she kept up a regimen of music lessons, exercise, and a program of reading classic literature, philosophy, and modern psychology, all the while supporting herself when it was considered déclassé for a woman of her middle-class status to do so.

Despite her eccentricities, she was popular in the Berkeley social scene, which centered on families of professionals and university professors. Others could not help applying the pun in her name, as Jack had with Anna, that Charmian was charming, a well-informed, sprightly conversationalist who made everyone feel at ease. Her brilliant smile, sparkling hazel eyes, and wavy brown hair with golden glints made up for a lack of traditional beauty. Admittedly vain, she affected striking, feminine clothes, whether seductive kimonos, the current rage, or suits exquisitely tailored to her hourglass figure. Though even in old age she would stir male observers' lust, she did not alienate other women at the dances and musicales she attended. Essentially an introvert, happiest when solitary, she was gifted at putting others at ease and making them feel admired.

Blessed with exceptional coordination and natural athleticism, she perceived life most fully through her body, whether diving from thirty-foot platforms at public pools or making love. She also experienced "beatitudes," her terms for fugue states in which she found herself living in past times and cultures. More imaginative and intuitive than rational, she ached over the opportunities in life denied her as a woman. She did not play coy with lovers.

Complex, dramatic, multitalented, she clearly wanted a man of good income, yet ultimately found the life professionals offered less appealing than her independence. The shenanigans of the Crowd were thus a welcome escape. Carrie Sterling, however, was instrumental in determining which other women on the scene were acceptable, which not. Suffering from an unfaithful husband, Carrie battled the sybaritic elements in the Crowd, and correctly saw Miss Kittredge as untrustworthy.

So imagine Charmian, thirty-two years of age, never married, just finished with a long-term relationship, and receiving seductive signs of interest from a similarly vibrant, highly sensitive man who was earning enough to support several households well. At least he would be more fun, and certainly more fascinating, than her businessmen lovers. At most, well, what possibilities in the great unlikelihood he would leave his wife and marry her! What was amazing was how quickly he determined to do just that.

It was the sex that turned his head, but that was not all. Within days of their meeting at the Piedmont bungalow they were in rapture under the trees at Wake Robin. Trained in the art of love by her aunt Netta, experienced with other men, Charmian offered herself to Jack "with no shock, no fear, no surprise, nothing but good nature and sweet frankness." That lack of coyness, that directness undid him, leaving him "vanquished before the battle." He understood her as one who was "game," who took chances in life regardless of the painful consequences. "You are more kin to me than any woman I have ever known," he wrote, and Charmian delighted him when she repeated those words aloud. He felt "for the first time loved," and one suspects the same was true for her, the orphan in thrall to a demanding, difficult aunt, the young woman unable to settle for less than what her grand imagination promised.[15]

Among the extraordinary letters he wrote over the next few weeks, one best captured his insight into his needs and desires, and his recognition of the same in Charmian. Whatever womanly love might be, he longed for something that "made those woman-loves wan things and pale," a dream of "the great Man-Comrade." What he had been seeking, he realized, was not possible: a male companion who offered delicacy and tenderness as well as bravery and "the glow of adventure, unafraid of the harshness of life and its evils."[16] It was the narcissist's dream, of course, of a lover just like himself, yet it was also audacious in light of the gender strictures of the day. Although George Sterling came closest to fulfilling this dream, he ultimately held back part of himself from Jack and frustrated him in doing so. The women in Jack's life were even more constrained, so the thought of finding such a comrade among the female sex seemed a sheer impossibility. Then Charmian appeared, and it was her good fortune that she well matched his projections.

Still, his mind was not so settled as his ardor proclaimed. He invited Cloudesley Johns to Wake Robin to stay at least a month. The cheerful presence of Joan and Becky so tugged at Jack's heart that he led Bess into conversations about their moving to southern California, away from the Crowd. Consequently, she was utterly unprepared one evening when he told her that he was leaving her, without saying why. Deserted at the tent, she had to deal alone with breaking camp, caring for her daughters, and finding a new place to live, for apparently she was not even to stay at the beloved Piedmont bungalow.

Returning to Oakland, Jack cleared out his belongings and, with Frank Atherton's family, rented 1216 Telegraph Avenue, which would be his pied-à-terre until the end of his life. Jack offered his friend free rent in exchange for meals and caretaking. Nearby he found a house for Flora and her grandson Johnny Miller. In early August he wrote Cloudesley Johns, "Whatever I have done I have done with the sanction of my conscience, that I have performed what I consider the very highest of right acts." He admitted only to having been "a hypocrite grinning on a grid," for while a man might marry philosophically, "it's damned hard on the woman."[17] In the end, though, once Jack London made up his mind, he was close to intransigent. If visits to Bess and his children stirred his natural compassion for those in need, he refused to allow such feelings to challenge the moral certainty of his decision.

In *The Kempton-Wace Letters,* Jack argued that irrationalities are born in extreme passion. Now, swept up by his thoughts of Charmian Kittredge, he gave in fully to frenzied excitement. Typical of amorous letters, Jack pronounced their love unique, among the "rare loves, such as the Browning love, once in a generation of folks." A trivial reminder would send either into reveries of longing for the absent one. The moments of separation were "all dead and utter loss."[18] Each grew impatient over tiny delays. (Mail then arrived twice a day, and for a letter not to receive a response by afternoon post was upsetting!) They wallowed in their mutual delight, oblivious to events and people around them. It is a familiar story in human experience, and among irrationalities often a splendid one.

This was unfortunately also an adulterous affair, which meant that it welcomed mendacity as part of its fuel. This plot, too, is a familiar one. It begins with lies to spouse or friends, then invites confidants to join in the deception. The duplicity is rationalized as necessary in service of the great love, and thus adds to the titillation. Little attention is paid a conscience that would normally ensure more scrupulous behavior. The lies become easier, to the point where the lovers may even lie to each other. Such deceit would play a large role now in Jack and Charmian's lives and the lives of those around them.

Bess was bereft and confused. *The Kempton-Wace Letters* had been published. Could it be that Anna's departure had not ended the flirtation? Here the lovers encouraged Bess's mistaken assumption. To further mislead her, Charmian visited often to offer sympathy, and even talked Bess into moving to Berkeley, where she stayed for a month. After these visits, Charmian reported back to Jack. "B. has apologized five times, over the telephone, for . . . talking about you as she did. . . . She says I am the 'nearest and dearest' friend, and so forth, and you can imagine how it makes me feel. But it is all a part of the big tragedy of living, and I begin to think I have fair histrionic abilities. But it isn't funny."[19]

For the next year Bess and the girls moved from one Oakland flat to another. The Madderns gathered round in support, Melissa spending long hours with grandchildren Joan and Becky, while urging Bess not to give up hope. Her siblings came by to offer support, yet she remained in shock and grief, while hiding her feelings from her daughters. Jennie Prentiss was a daily member of the household as well, and now widowed, moved to a bedroom in Flora's cottage.

Two-year-old Joan was vaguely aware of the confusion, the sudden changes in her life, the whisperings of her mother with others, the sudden packings and unpackings as they moved from Grandmother Maddern's home to a flat, and soon after to another. Both she and Becky were often sick; Joan was prone to respiratory infections throughout her childhood. One illness almost changed Jack's mind, but even bedridden daughters could not weaken his newfound passion.

Not all of the girls' memories of this period were unhappy ones. Grandmother Maddern passed a lasting legacy to Joan by teaching her how to shell lima beans, not just to get the chore over with, but to do so with reverence. "Under her spell, I saw the limas as ovals of pale jade, heard the music they made as they fell rhythmically into the colander, which had magically become a burnished silver bowl, and watched the swift, precise movements of her hands and fingers weave the patterns of a dance. With the skill and art of an alchemist, she was transmuting a humble domestic task into the color and shape, the sound and motion, of beauty." Joan would fully absorb Melissa Maddern's philosophy and see that "beauty was everywhere," even in the act of cleaning windows or darning a sock. As a consequence, she would take lifelong pleasure in the domestic arts.[20]

Joan's first acquaintance with racial prejudice occurred about this time. She made friends with a much older African American girl, Annie, who taught her how to play jacks and read books aloud to her. One day some boys walking by Annie's porch stopped and mocked Joan for "always want[ing] to play with that nigger," taunting her that a "dirty old black woman" was in her house. Joan shouted back, "She's not black," and ran inside to get Jennie and bring her out as proof. But when she reached the hallway and faced Jennie, she realized the boys were right, and burst into tears. Jennie calmed her down, told her to ignore the boys' taunts, and gave her two cookies. Bravely Joan went out, crossed the street, and handed Annie a cookie in clear defiance of the boys' intimidation. Sometime later Joan asked Jennie why her father used the term "mammy." When she heard the explanation, she asked if white women were also called by that title. Told it applied only to black women, Joan decided to drop the usage and called her "Aunt Jennie" from that day on. Thus was born her lifelong commitment to racial equality.[21]

Gifted with a natural curiosity and high intelligence, Joan had more resources to adapt to the chaos than her younger sister. Becky was sweet-tempered and seldom querulous, but oddly mute at a time when she should have been joyfully pointing at objects and struggling to form the syllables that identified them. Only Joan could read the grunts and gestures of Becky's private language. Bess used every technique she could to encourage her younger daughter to speak, but she refused to do so. Becky also showed scant recognition of Jack as her father, as though in those early years she was cognizant of how insignificant she was in his life. The contrasting temperaments of the two girls would cast the more phlegmatic Becky in her parents' eyes as always somehow lesser than Joan, whatever the measure.

It must not have helped Bess to see Jack's star shoot suddenly higher with the serialization of *The Call of the Wild* in the *Saturday Evening Post*. Dozens of critics agreed that the "gripping" and "enthralling" book was "a piece of lasting literature," a work of "force and individuality," an "epic" from "one of the most original and impressive authors this country has known."[22] Of special delight for him must have been the *San Francisco Chronicle* caption beneath his photograph: "His books are strong meat for the anemic generation that worships at the shrine of Henry James." Bess had contributed much to the conditions that led to Jack's fame, and now she was denied any of the rewards.

His success was most welcome, given the feeble reception to *The Kempton-Wace Letters*. Upon that book's publication in May, Gaylord Wilshire had honored Anna in a lecture at Astor House, and invited various eminences from the New York literary world. The *New York Times* found it "the old sex problem again" in a story lacking "human personality or appeal." There were kinder reviews, but they lacked enthusiasm. The work was "sane, clean and stimulating," its debate unusual and profitable." The book sold poorly, despite Macmillan's investing over $2,000 in publicity. Nonetheless, George Brett sent Anna $500, a sum equal to Jack's advance.

Hard at work on a novel tentatively named *Windlestraws,* Anna wrote Brett of her plan to travel to Europe and meet major revolutionary figures, in the expectation that she could incorporate the material "into a book which will be the Uncle Tom's Cabin for the capitalist regime."[23] Brett encouraged her, for he had been successful in marketing writers with leftist views, and was convinced, based on her *Kempton-Wace* writing, that she could produce an appealing result.

Accompanying Anna were friends Gelett Burgess and his sister Ellie. The humorist teased the ship's captain by sending him amorous verses in Anna's name. This lighthearted ruse, along with the shipboard balls and concerts, lifted Anna's spirits. As the trio progressed from London to Paris to Florence, however, Anna grew more somber. Gazing out the window of the train rolling through Italy, she mused, "Truth and love and death—I am finding them all. The Trinity surrounds me."[24] Understandably, the most lasting memory would be not of her visit with the revolutionary Kropotkin, but of walking through Père Lachaise cemetery in Paris. There, at the tombs of the tragic lovers Héloïse and Pierre Abélard, she imagined a shrouded figure placing flowers on the grave. This scene would inspire later efforts at a novel.

More entries about death followed; for example, she imagined herself underground with relatives who had preceded her. Returning to San Francisco after an absence of almost a year, she visited Mary Strunsky's grave and imagined how easy it would be to join her in death. Even the local press's warm welcome of the return of "The Divine Anna" did not brighten her spirits; if anything, it added to her self-imposed burdens. The novel she was writing for Macmillan gave her an escape into work, yet high expectations undermined her confidence. She feared she might not prove to be the woman Jack believed her to be.

Fellow socialist Cameron King had sent Anna clippings concerning Jack's separation from Bess, so she arrived in Europe well informed of that fact. Since it had occurred so soon after publication of *The Kempton-Wace Letters,* upon learning the identities of the anonymous authors, reporters conjectured, as Bess did, that Anna was the cause of the breakup. Anna wrote to tell Jack how sorry she was for his unhappiness, that she knew he was a dreamer who only meant to do good, never to hurt anyone. In her idealization of her greatest love, Anna never considered his record of duplicity, that he might already have another lover. If he'd lied to his wife in order to see her, would he not also lie for other purposes? He would, and assured Charmian that Anna had taken the news "in a sisterly fashion," proof that she would not cause any trouble for them and, by implication, could be counted on to take the fall for them.

That autumn Charmian moved to Wake Robin Lodge to disguise further any hint that she might be the real mistress, though Jack visited often in secret, having rented a cottage on the property from Netta. He completed *The Sea-Wolf,* often writing outdoors on a redwood stump, and passed his hand-scrawled pages on to Charmian for typing. She received frequent letters from Jack affirming the inevitability of their mating and his constant longing for her presence, which brought him "a restfulness born of perfect intimacy & sureness." His hunger for her, significantly, was "greater than any hunger for food I have ever felt." They talked of living in Japan, and he even researched Kobe, which he discovered had "enough white people" and a snowless climate.[25] Though this plan was not carried out, it was an indication of their shared interest both in escape and in travel to exotic lands. In early October he and Cloudesley Johns took off on Jack's sloop *Spray* for two months of wandering around the Sacramento Delta, while Charmian spent her days on long hikes and piano practice.

Anna meanwhile withdrew into herself so much that she even avoided her socialist friends. Scraps of notes for *Windlestraws* hint at her continued obsession with Jack. The book would be a way "to reach the man," to reveal her wish to give him "every heart-beat of my youth, every ray of my smile, all the dew of my tears. . . . Why does he fear my free gifts."[26] To her family and corespondents, however, she gave no hint of her longing and regrets.

On December 2, 1903, Anna wrote to a friend, Dr. Katherine (Katia)

Maryson, that she was going to visit with Jack and Cloudesley, yet mysteriously provided no account of the meeting, if one occurred. Evidence of a reunion is clearer for January 1904, when Anna began to negotiate with the *San Francisco Bulletin* to be named a war correspondent so she could travel with Jack, recently hired by Hearst's *Examiner* to cover the Russo-Japanese War. His contract for stories and photographs promised close to $1,000 a week plus all expenses. George Brett was in town, and unsuccessfully tried to dissuade Anna from the dangerous plan, urging her to stay behind and complete *Windlestraws*. All she could think of, though, was sailing off on the *Siberia* on January 7 with Jack.

Anna's plans understandably further inflamed rumors that she was planning to recapture the writer's heart—which, given her private writings, may indeed have been her unconscious goal. Her hopes were dashed, she explained to Katia, when she asked for "a ridiculously enormous salary" in light of Jack's contract. The truth may have been otherwise, that this was a ruse the *Bulletin* used to put Anna off. Jack's passion for Charmian had erased any memories of his previous lust for Anna, and it would have been in character for him to pull strings to keep her off the ship.

With Jack now gone for an unknown period of time, Anna escaped to a hideaway in the Santa Cruz Mountains, away from the support of her family, in order to complete her novel. She accomplished little apart from patches of scenes and episodes. In April she returned home for Passover and the comfort of family and friends. *Windlestraws* remained uncompleted. As for Jack in Korea, she wrote, "Sometime in life I will find him again and him me, sometime when we are both old, in the barren years when there will be nothing to gain! How shamed we will be before each other at our shameful renunciation! Will we stop and make apologies?"[27] In old age she would regret that even this dark prediction would not come true.

Before embarking on the *Siberia*, Jack directed George Brett to send his Macmillan advances monthly in two checks: $127.50 to Bess and $22.50 to Charmian. It was a risky plan in light of the mystery that surrounded his separation, but he had sent other letters to Brett which identified Charmian, along with George Sterling, as editors of *The Sea-Wolf*. Consequently, were these payments ever to become public, they would be presented as Charmian's wages for typing and copyediting. This would have been true, for Jack did not want her labor to be a gift. Yet the payments were not commensurate with what she would have earned in less entangled circumstances.

Not that Charmian felt cheated; she delighted in being the "typewriter woman" he required. While often self-absorbed, Charmian was not conceited; nor did she overestimate her talents and abilities. Essentially artistic and intuitive, she recognized that she lacked "a certain something," a creative spark. She could sketch graceful images, though not invent original designs; she could accurately play the technically exacting Chopin Études, but she missed the expressiveness. She was thoughtful about what she read, yet was disinclined to compose essays to formalize her ideas. Nevertheless, she was a crackerjack typist and stenographer, an accomplished horsewoman, and an entertaining conversationalist, so why not enjoy using these skills?

In time, Charmian conceived a philosophy whereby her life was her art, and her mission was to set an example for others to absorb life fully and express themselves fearlessly. Only a few can be artistic geniuses, she would say, but anyone can be a genius at living artistically. As a result of her conscious plan for living, Charmian seldom compared herself to others or expressed envy. Furthermore, she protected a very private core while portraying to the world a smiling, supportive, if self-dramatizing demeanor. Appearing rather superficial to some, and utterly enchanting to others, she gave extreme and contradictory impressions, though overall the favorable ones dominated.

Now she had the most favorable opinion of a man who was unafraid of her complexity, who welcomed the fact that, unlike Anna, she was "game," whatever the consequences of their affair. It can only have helped that in the few months since their first rapture, *The Call of the Wild* became a best-seller, and *The People of the Abyss* was receiving praise for its harrowing, poetic descent into the London slums. If Jack's new success increased his allure, it was an added benefit, however, not the sole draw. Ultimately, these were two unusual people convinced that they were meant for each other, and, in the final reckoning, they appear to have been correct.

With Jack away, Charmian followed through on a jointly agreed plan: she would stay with a friend, Lynette McMurry, in Newton, Iowa, until just before Jack's return, which was expected to take a year. Lynette was the daughter of the widower Edward Payne, Netta Eames's lover, and she had lived in Netta's household during her adolescence. While in Iowa, Charmian spent pleasant days practicing piano, sewing, playing whist, and writing long letters to friends. She heard often from Jack, and was frustrated that so few of her letters reached him in Japan and Korea.

To facilitate the correspondence, Jack had arranged for it to go by way of the newspaper office, where a friendly editor was to take care of forwarding their letters. His first letter confessed how observing her, "all abandon, there on the stringer-piece of the pier kissing your love to me," had left him convinced that he should see "until I die a picture of a woman's gray form" there.[28] On April 4, 1904, Jack learned why he had not heard much from Charmian: through a mix-up, her unsigned letters to him had been forwarded to Bess. And because Jack had never confided about his affair to his stepsister Eliza, she reinforced Bess's suspicion that the anonymous writer was Anna. (In fact, Eliza had returned from seeing off the *Siberia* to tell Bess that Anna had been on the wharf.)

Jack apologized to Charmian for not informing Eliza of their relationship. He would ask her to urge Bess to apply for a divorce on the basis of desertion. Certain that logic would sway the different Eliza, he laid out his argument as systematically as an Oxford debater. To wit, he loved another woman and wanted to marry her. Were Bess to refuse a divorce, "how can she tell Joan someday that her father is living in shame with another woman because she [Bess] will not let him marry that woman?" Joan would then, he hypothesized, ask why her mother was making him live in shame, hence forcing his daughter to live in shame. If Bess applied for divorce on his terms, he would pay all expenses, pledging that the girls would never want "so long as I live, and if I die there are the insurance and my copyrights." Bess knew of the will he had made just before taking off. It had put her and the children first. To prove his good intentions, he enclosed a power of attorney for a maximum of $500 for Eliza to use toward covering the legal fees.[29]

He did not stop with Eliza, however, for he copied his letter to her in the text of a similar request to Will Maddern, Bess's brother, and his wife, Corinne. Urging them to speak to Bess on his behalf, he added, "I am honest myself in the matter, acting to the dictates of what I consider highest right conduct." Furthermore, he asked Will to cooperate by not telling Bess or Eliza of this letter.[30]

Will responded with a sharply worded attack on Jack's character. A year previously he had watched Jack's "inexcusable conduct [develop] into concrete intention and show us the real man to be dealt with." Will had urged Bess then not to accept any further reconciliation from "the aggressor in this injury." He chastised Jack: "I will not discuss your unmanly and cowardly effort to include her as an instrument in the making or unmaking of a mistress for you." While respecting Jack's individualism, Will reminded him that respect "is conditioned by the rights of others." As for Jack's repeated statements of intent to support Bess and the girls, well, Will feared that the courts could not enforce just allotments "where there is no conscience to act upon."[31] His fear proved prescient.

Will's voice was that of middle-class standards, yet his was a chorus of one, for Jack was fully encircled by collaborators. Among these was Netta Eames, who from the start of the affair had provided her home in Glen Ellen for trysts, in return for which Jack now called her "Mother Mine." Frank and Maggie Atherton knew about the affair because they lived with Jack, and now, so did Eliza. (Interestingly, the members of the Crowd were less favorable toward divorce; the men among them might stray, but they wanted constant wives of good repute.)

Neither the wail of the popular press against divorce nor any religious doctrines gave Jack pause. The most important voice, Charmian's, agreed with him that individuals should determine their own happiness and defy convention if necessary. Each was unapologetic about their right, indeed their duty, to do as they wished, without regard for Bess, the children, or Mrs. Grundy. They were not thoughtless; quite the opposite. Their beliefs shaped an ethic at odds with that of the average American, but it was an ethic nonetheless. They were being supremely rational, but omitted from the equation consideration for those affected by their behavior. What counted most, Jack asserted, was his happiness, to which Will Maddern responded: What of Bess and the children? Do they not have the same right?

Having directed his volleys homeward, Jack turned to his frustrations with the Japanese army, which was so restrictive of his movements that he had even been arrested at one point for defying their orders to stay out of Korea. Perhaps because his experience in Japan and Korea had much less influence on his writings than his Yukon, sealing, and tramping experiences, it has been largely ignored by biographers and critics. On reflection, though, that half year's isolation spent on journalism rather than fiction had long-term significance for his final maturation.

Despite his cleverness, daring, and determination during this assignment, Jack London felt himself a failure. He worried that he was not earning Hearst's money. He was dissatisfied at having to compose stories peripheral to the real one, the battlefront, and in the process grew hostile toward the Japanese. By the end of his trip, his Californian prejudice toward the Chinese had generalized to the threat of "the Yellow Peril." He foresaw the eventual dominance of China and Japan as capable of eliminating Western colonial control in the Pacific. At his most apocalyptic, he imagined a war in 1976 in which the rest of the world would eliminate the Chinese behemoth through bacteriological warfare.

Paradoxically, while his racialism toward Asians hardened, his admiration for Asian culture increased. Specifically, during the boring days away from the front he observed local agricultural practices and concluded that the Japanese and Koreans were much more capable farmers than Americans. Their two thousand years of cultivating the land under often harsh conditions had resulted in soil conservation through erosion prevention (such as terracing of hillsides) and replenishment (through use of manure), as well as carefully planned irrigation practices. In contrast, he believed that American farmers were wasteful of soil and water, and neglected ways of reusing materials to their benefit. Just as Jack London had left the Yukon with a store of experiences to nourish his fictional imagination, he would leave Asia with a challenging vision for American agriculture.

This pilgrimage had profound consequences for others in his life after he returned. His missing Becky's transition from infancy to toddlerhood further diminished her presence for him. His separation from Bess had solidified his disparaging beliefs about her, and reinforced his view of himself as the victim of a woman preoccupied with "purity." His separation from Charmian, by contrast, prevented any reality from dashing his idealization of her, and she had no need to worry about other women taking her place.

A seemingly trivial skill acquired during the trip bonded him even closer to Charmian. To get around, he had had to ride horses, an anachronism for a city boy used to bicycles, ferries, and trolleys. Knowing how accomplished a rider Charmian was, he wrote her often of his favorite horse, Belle, and his overcoming the hardship of saddle sores. "I'm riding all kinds of Chinese ponies, with all kinds of saddles, in all kinds of places . . . and live to tell the tale." He promised they would "have glorious rides together."[32] Having now experienced firsthand the equestrian challenge, he had found new grounds for admiring her, as well as a genuine love for horses.

In addition, he brought back Manyoungi, his cook and valet, who dressed like an English butler in his black jacket, stiff collar, tie, and shirt studs. In effect, Jack entered Japan a middle-class American and returned an aristocrat, who found shaving himself too menial an act, one to be performed by an inferior. To be fair, that is how others often interpreted his hovering male companion, whereas Jack saw his manservant as a sensible and practical means of saving his own energy to spend on grander matters. He never understood why his socialist friends criticized him so for keeping a personal servant.

A very different man embarked on the *Siberia* for the return home in late June 1904. Although he had cause for self-satisfaction, he was ruled by "disgust," part of which had a physical basis. Accidents had aggravated previous injuries to his legs and feet, tiny for a man his height and girth, and restricted his mobility.

While he was still on shipboard, Bess had him served notice. She had gone to court on June 28 and had a lien placed against all his earnings and possessions. Her charge was cruelty, as well as Jack's infecting her with gonorrhea and consorting with Anna Strunsky. By filing before the year was up, Bess foreclosed the possibility of suing on grounds of desertion, as Jack would have preferred. As he later explained to Charmian, Bess's motive was "to have [the] Court give her a whack at all I possess in division of community property."[33] Despite her launching a divorce suit, he knew that Bess was not really committed to a permanent break. But if standing up to Jack was only a ploy to get him to return, it had the opposite effect. From this point, Jack cast Bess as a viper, a harridan out to get his money, a formidable adversary to be stopped by any means whenever she blocked his interests.

For Bess, though, the situation was much more complicated. Jack had made an agreement that she had fulfilled; he was the one who broke it. A key provision was her mothering his Anglo-Saxon children, and her children remained foremost in her mind. She also understood that despite his impulses and philandering, Jack had a deep-felt need for security and domestic life. He had shown it from the first in their marriage, through his voiced admiration for her creating a congenial place to live, and his exuberant fathering of Joan. She was willing to take him back. She foresaw that he might well return to her and the girls. Her real anger was toward Anna, whom she named as corespondent in her suit, thus providing the newspapers with a field day when Jack arrived home at the end of June.

It had been arranged that George Sterling would cable Charmian of Jack's impending return so she could meet him at the dock. When Bess took the offensive, however, Netta told Charmian to remain in Iowa to avoid being entangled in the scandal. Throughout the month of July, caught between the opposing pressures of aunt and lover, she deferred to the former. This decision put her in a position of having to ask forgiveness, something Jack was not quick to grant anyone.

Though Charmian saved her reputation, Anna did not. The newspapers promulgated gossip that was especially cruel to a woman who had never known the ultimate intimacy with the man she had regretfully spurned. The story the press built on was true: Jack had asked Anna to marry him, and told Bess so; Anna had wanted to join him on the *Siberia*. What the reports embellished, however, was her Jewishness, invoking the stereotype of an exotic bohemian, by implication a loose woman. Never fond of Bess, Anna responded loyally on behalf of Jack. To reporters she averred that he was "blindly in love with his wife," that the stories of Bess finding the couple making love were "silly." She even lied, insisting that she had seen Jack in person only "three or four times" since 1901. In a thoughtless snipe, Anna added that Bess was "very well-educated . . . but is bound by rigid conventions," thus unable to appreciate the demands of his literary work and the "hero worship" he received from "a lot of silly girls."[34] She confided to friends the belief that Bess was using her as a pawn, hoping to make divorce impossible by blackmailing Jack to prevent injury to Anna's reputation.

Thus Anna behaved as Jack expected, while he did nothing to quell the weeks of rumor and innuendo against his onetime collaborator. Cameron King, still in love with Anna, told her that Jack had another woman and was planning to remarry. When Anna asked for an explanation, Jack was disingenuous. Such information was "news to me," he assured her, something Cameron had "imagined." All the gossip would soon die away, he promised. The closest he came to an apology was, "I wander through my life delivering hurts to all that know me."[35] Hence Anna remained ignorant of Charmian's role in the matter.

Throughout July, Jack negotiated to be divorced on the less sensational grounds of desertion. The final agreement seemed reasonable at the time, yet left significant loopholes that each participant would later rue. He bought a lot at 519 Thirty-first Street in Oakland, and ordered the speedy construction of a bungalow for Bess and the girls. He would provide a maintenance allowance of $75 a month (down from his previous $127.25), which was to increase as needed. She would have care and control of the children, granting him the right to visit at "reasonable and proper times as may be agreed upon between the parties." Community property would be severed, with Bess giving up all rights to his royalties, past and future. Finally, Jack would continue to maintain certain life insurance policies with the girls as beneficiaries.

By today's standards, it was a shoddy contract with too many indeterminables. Divorce law was in its infancy, however, so the settlement should not be judged by current practice. California had one of the most liberal statutes at the time regarding ease of divorce. Unlike states to the east, the California Progressives who had shaped the laws believed it was wrong to coerce couples to stay together. With regard to alimony or child support, the courts had had as yet few opportunities to apply Progressive policies, and the majority of California women received little. Even when wives were the complainants and there were children to support, the amounts were typically under fifty dollars a month. From this perspective, Jack's financial arrangement of paying for a home plus maintenance was a generous one that assured Bess and the girls a comfortable if not affluent lifestyle. That custody reside with the wife and visitation be open-ended was common, for it reinforced the notion that woman's proper role was domestic and maternal. (This was a recent shift in American law, for previously men had been granted custody in recognition of their role as patriarchs.)

Yet why would Bess abrogate any interest in Jack's royalties for works completed during the marriage, as would be her due under laws of community property? One possibility is that she exchanged those rights for a dependable monthly income, which would have been sensible, given Jack's record of poor financial management. Also, it would have been unwieldy to monitor these royalties, commingled as they would be with others from Macmillan and various magazines. Furthermore, Jack's will likely included his daughters as beneficiaries of any royalties that survived his death. Although his early 1904 will is not available, the one he wrote in July 1905 indicates his state of mind. Essentially his property was to be divided four ways, among Charmian, Flora, Joan, and Becky. Charmian and Flora were to enjoy only the interest, not the principal. Ultimately, everything would "in the end pass undiminished" to Joan and Becky, upon Charmian's remarriage or death and Flora's death.[36] So at the time of the agreement, Bess had no reason to suspect that Jack would ever skimp or neglect their daughters. Her trust proved misplaced.

On July 17, 1904, Charmian received a cable from Jack advising her that it was safe to return. He enclosed the fare for the train. Still she did not leave until July

27, arriving in Oakland on August 1. Her diary entry for that day was "! ! ! ! ! ! ! !" Following several days' blissful reunion in Glen Ellen, Jack returned to the East Bay. So far as Charmian was concerned, nothing had changed between them during his long absence. But Jack may have been having second thoughts. Whether out of anger over Charmian's delayed return or the sudden encounter with the real rather than the idealized woman, he was soon flirting with another member of the Crowd, the beautiful Blanche Partington. Or perhaps he was using Blanche, who had long been infatuated with him, as a ruse to draw attention away from his true love. The evidence suggests both motives were at work.

Jack's letters to Blanche resemble those to his previous lovers in several respects. He compliments her newspaper writing and encourages her to tackle plays. He offers what seem to be previously secret self-revelations and references to his failings ("I know my own weakness too well under the splendid farce that conceals it").[37] He admires her frankness. Yet the tone is more playful and sexually teasing than in letters sent to Anna or Charmian.

Meanwhile, Charmian was in Glen Ellen typing *The Sea-Wolf* and *The Game*, a boxing novel. She read the same authors Jack was reading, including George Bernard Shaw and Friedrich Nietzsche. She found no hint of trouble in his brief visits, except that they were less frequent than she had hoped. Sometimes she would go to Oakland to stay with the Sterlings, who knew about Jack's affair with Blanche but said nothing to Charmian. (Carrie had been along on the yachting trips Jack took with Blanche, and knew of their frequent dates at plays and parties. Carrie in fact schemed to get Jack to leave Charmian.) In the midst of the affair, Jack wrote Charmian that he thought they were in a "trying stage" because the "ardor & heat & ecstasy" of their affair had been tempered, while at the same time they were "denied the growing comradeship which should be ours right now."[38]

Meanwhile Anna continued to pine over the loss of Jack. She escaped with her mother to a health spa at Agua Caliente, a spring not far from Glen Ellen. From there she wrote her friend Katia of Jack's divorce, how happy she was that he had obtained his freedom, for he "has suffered bitterly." As for herself, "I have the Semitic temperament that gives up over readily. . . . I must be fought for gallantly to be won and I think Jack would rather wait than fight."[39] One wonders how she felt when Eliza sent belated thanks for the "noble manner in which you stood your trial," which had resulted in the admiration of both Jack's friends and the world at large.[40] Cameron King continued to woo her, but could not compete with his idealized rival.

For Bess and the girls, Jack's lodging with his mother three blocks away meant frequent visits. Bess even agreed to allow Manyoungi to live in an attic room. Joan quickly grew fond of the kindly valet, who played with the girls, and taught them acrobatics. On days when Jack did not appear, she would probe him for information about her father's activities. When Jack came for dinner one evening, she was puzzled that he would not allow Manyoungi to join the family for dinner, and it was some years before she understood how the racism toward African Americans applied to Asians as well.

Jack's appearances, often in the afternoon, thrilled his daughters, who would run to him wildly for the opening ritual, a rambunctious tussle that set them shrieking and laughing. The free-for-all had strict rules: no kicking, biting, scratching, or hair-pulling, and most important, no crying. From the start Jack instilled in both girls total intolerance of cowardice or fear. They rose to the challenge, and as adults recalled with pride that he had molded them to be dauntless. This hurly-burly was treasured, too, because it was their only physical contact with him, their only chance to smell a hint of Bull Durham tobacco or shaving lotion, fragrances that marked him and no one else as "Daddy." According to Joan, "he did not bathe us, or carry us off to bed, or spank us when we were naughty or touch us in any of the dozens of ways common to young fathers. He might have read to us or told us stories . . . taken us for walks, but he did not."[41] She wrote this later in life, at a time when a more active model of fathering was prevalent in the culture, so whether Jack was unusual in his distant relationship with the girls is uncertain. Mothers were supposed to bathe children, read aloud to them, and take them on walks, all of which Bess did. Yet even if Joan was applying excessively high standards in retrospect, the emotional consequences of Jack's desertion were intense. Just as he had seldom known real hunger yet recalled hunger as the essence of his childhood, so Joan would always recall paternal deficiency, his absence at the core of her being.

Bess agreed with Jack regarding physical toughness and courage. In crises she responded coolly and without concern for herself, as when a vicious fight occurred between a strange dog and the two that Jack kept in the backyard of the house on Thirty-first Street. Joan never forgot how her mother grabbed a clothesline pole and tightrope-walked on a high fence stringer to beat the aggressive mutt away. Whenever the girls were frightened by a bogey, real or imagined, Bess knew how to calm them and erase the fear. Her even disposition, her steadiness and cool temper, her calm provision of an orderly life created needed psychological ballast. What rankled Jack in a wife soothed the daughters.

During this time the rancor between Jack and Bess lessened. Joan would lie in bed some evenings and listen in on her parents' conversations. Sometimes they sat by the fire, Jack reading aloud to Bess. Other times Joan heard laughter from both. This congeniality confused Joan, who was not told about the divorce decree, and was perplexed that her father lived three blocks away with his mother, yet behaved as in the past whenever he came by. These friendly exchanges also confounded Bess, who, like Anna, was unable to sever her emotional dependency. She continued to believe that he might return to her before the divorce was final. She did not realize that his amicability was premised on the finality of the break, that it was only because they were no longer intimate that he could once again enjoy Bess's company. She read much more into his kindness than he intended.

At least for cheery, towheaded, two-year-old Becky, Jack's return from Korea marked the end of her silence. Joan recalled how, during one of his first visits, he approached Becky in her crib, and she exclaimed "My Daddy!" These were purportedly Becky's first words, and others spilled out easily from that point on. She too would be captivated by his allure, and despite his clear preference for Joan, would become a lifelong defender of his character.

By November 1904, Jack's flirtation with Blanche Partington was over. Though the reason is unknown, it is likely that her attitudes clashed too much with his. Several years later Blanche would become a fanatical practitioner of Christian Science and upset him with her firm opinions. She would never marry.

The granting of the interlocutory decree allowed Jack to reflect again on his relationship with Charmian. She began to appear more frequently in the East Bay, joining Jack and the Crowd at restaurants. By the end of the year, several times she had written in her diary of "lovely understanding time" with her "Mate."

# 6

## Deceivers and Deceived

EARLY 1905 FOUND ANNA STRUNSKY secluded once again in a cabin on Kings Mountain west of the Stanford campus. Having given up on *Windlestraws,* she embarked on her socialist story. The inspiration came from her visit to Paris's famous Père Lachaise cemetery; hence the title, *Violette of Père Lachaise.* As in the previous year's seclusion, she did not accomplish much writing; nonetheless, this retreat set the stage for a life-changing epiphany.

Late in January on a very stormy day Anna set off on a hike and lost her bearings. Exhausted at one point, she even lay down in a road to recover her strength. When darkness approached, she grew fearful of scurrying animals and the haunting appearance of the skeletal trees. Having successfully made her way back to her cabin, she arose the next day to repeat the adventure, hiking five miles to Woodside, then wandering fourteen miles back after losing the road during a downpour. On returning, she reflected on her experience and transformed it into an elegy on Jack's love, "The Road." Here she likened the terrifying images from her mountain hikes to the struggle to find her lost love. The road ended at "the trysting place," but he was not there. "I turned my face and took the bitter length again / And groped my way, forgotten by my love."[1]

Three days later history delivered the news that would change her life and clear her mind of Jack for almost a decade. On January 25, 1905, Cameron King wrote her of the revolution in Russia, and inspired her with the notion that they could die together for the cause in St. Petersburg. "Bloody Sunday" completed Anna's epitaph for her love for Jack. The next day she took off exuberantly through the woods, unafraid of getting lost, purposely experimenting with her route, and thinking of Russia and its possibilities.

Returning home, Anna devoted herself to the newly formed Friends of Russian Freedom. Although Jack was on the executive committee of that group, along with Cameron King, George Sterling, and Austin Lewis, his services seem to have been limited to lending his now impressive name to its publications. Among Anna's first endeavors was a fundraising brochure calling for "sympathy and help" for the victims of Bloody Sunday and the subsequent exile of protesters to Siberia. One of its New York City recipients was a tall, slender, elegant man with deep-set eyes, William English Walling.[2]

Born into a prominent, wealthy Indiana family, English—as he preferred to be called—had graduated from the University of Chicago, then a hotbed of liberal Protestantism with inclinations toward socialism. Disgruntled by his subsequent experiences at Harvard Law School, he returned to Chicago to study sociology and economics under Albion Small and Thorstein Veblen. He even moved into a tenement near Hull House and tried to live on the wages of a typical workingman. Receiving over $10,000 a year from a trust fund, he left school to commit himself and his wealth to social policy. English had crossed paths with Anna briefly when she was working for *Wilshire's Magazine* in New York, and he recalled meeting her at a socialist gathering during a trip to San Francisco in 1904. After a picnic on Mare Island, the two had become so engrossed in talking late into the evening at the railroad station that twenty-four trains passed before they relented and got on board for their separate returns.

English dashed off a note praising Anna's brochure as "the best yet" and inviting her to meet other women socialists living on the East Side were she to return to New York. In August he sent a postcard from Geneva, letting her know that he and a friend, Arthur Bullard, had set up a revolutionary news bureau there.[3] Meanwhile, Anna found much to do in the Bay Area to further the cause, and became the most prominent speaker on Russian events. She was praised for her animation and intensity, her fluency and flow of beautiful English, and her ability to inspire her audience about subjects in which they were not vitally interested.

Anna's younger sister Rose was having an exciting year as well. Now attending Stanford, she was in the midst of a passionate relationship with the flamboyant ladykiller Xavier Martinez. To remedy scoliosis, Rose had spent five years on the couch in her bedroom rather than attending school and leading a normal adolescent life. Although she thought it wrong to marry one's first amour, Martinez forced her to reconsider.

English Walling's correspondence with Anna brought a drastic and unexpected change in Rose's life. Anna was determined to go to Europe and work for his news bureau in Geneva, but her parents adamantly refused, and relented only on condition that Rose chaperone. Rose was upset at first about having to leave both college and Martinez, but suddenly changed her mind and joined in Anna's enthusiasm for the overseas adventure. Anna must have been very relieved the day she received her sister's letter of consent, which concluded, "What a wonderful glorious life God is giving me! He is opening the gates of Paradise with full swing."[4]

Jack was also thinking of Russia. His latest manuscript for Macmillan was a collection of essays, many based on his socialist speeches, for a volume to be titled

*The War of the Classes.* Brett welcomed such additions to his list, for he had positioned the company as the major publisher of socialist writings for a broad audience. He searched for ideologues like Jack who could present their arguments without the arcane theoretical terminology of the European immigrant socialists. Jack's essays were hardly ideologically pure, and drew criticism from some in the movement, but others appreciated that his concise, driving argumentation spoke to a less intellectual readership. They were willing to forgo issues of correctness to keep his powerful voice on their behalf. Book reviewers agreed, and praised London's essays in terms such as "genuine," "virile," and "combative." The Socialist Party had quadrupled the number of presidential votes for Eugene Debs in 1904 over 1900, and members were optimistic that its rise to major party status was close at hand. Jack's forceful propaganda appeared to the party members a boon toward that end.

Several days before Bloody Sunday, Charmian watched Jack mount the podium at the University of California in Berkeley to deliver his most popular and incendiary speech, one he would give repeatedly over the next year. "Revolution" was his most vitriolic attack on the capitalist system. In recent months he had grown disheartened by fellow socialists' shift toward reform rather than radical change, and by their adopting rules and procedures similar to those governing more staid institutions. The Berkeley crowd had expected a talk on literature, but instead were greeted with the information that he now addressed letters "Dear Comrade" and signed them "Yours for the Revolution." He accused the students of being "asleep in the face of the awful facts of poverty I have given you, asleep in the greatest Revolution that has come to the world. Oh, it is sad! Not long ago revolutions began, grew, broke out in Oxford. Today Russian universities seethe with revolution. I say to you, then: in full glory of life, here's a cause that appeals to all the romance in you. Awake! Awake to its call!" After recounting the strength of the movement overseas, he turned to the case of the United States, where now "10,000,000 people [in poverty] are perishing, are dying, body and soul, slowly, because they have not enough to eat." He then cited specific cases of sweatshop garment workers, of child labor in southern textile mills. How could so efficient and inventive a society allow men, women, and children to live and die like beasts, he asked? "The capitalist class, blind and greedy, grasping madly has made . . . a management prodigiously wasteful." Since the working class outnumbered the capitalists, through its revolt it would succeed and repair the ills of society.[5]

If Jack's speech signified his break from moderate colleagues, notably the Christian socialists, his decision was not idiosyncratic. The year 1905 marked a split in the movement nationwide, with one faction pressing to build a vote-getting machine to legitimize the party, through alignment with Samuel Gompers and the American Federation of Labor, an exclusionary crafts union. Jack threw his support to the more militant who urged organizing the mass of workers, the unskilled ignored by the Gompers faction. The most radical of this element were the Wobblies, or International Workers of the World. They raised a magnificent propaganda machine of posters, songs, and orators to battle their bête noire, the capitalists. London regarded the Wobblies as a welcome addition to the cause, although he never joined them in going so far as to recommend sabotage. Their influence on him would grow, however, for theirs was the first notable outcry against such potential corruptions to the Socialist Party as its growing preoccupation with parliamentary procedures and organizational structure. Jack agreed, yet failed to reflect fully on the contradictory implications of a mass movement based on anarchism.

The Berkeley event was personally significant for Charmian, for it marked her first appearance with Jack in public. As she sat in the front row, her twinkling admiration struck perceptive observers as more than a love for politics. That week she accompanied him to various events: Carrie Sterling's birthday party, swimming at the Piedmont Baths, the theater, and a restaurant lunch with Eliza. This sudden visibility may have been intended to suggest that they had just begun dating, so that the eventual marriage would look less precipitate. Bess would learn of these appearances, and realize that she had a serious rival who threatened her hoped-for reconciliation with Jack. Worse, she soon discerned that Charmian's friendship for her following the separation had been feigned.

Jack gave many socialist speeches over the next few months, and ran once more for mayor of Oakland, this time garnering almost a thousand votes. Yet he was deeply depressed. Later he referred to this time as the "Long Sickness," and modeled the tragic trajectory of the semi-autobiographical *Martin Eden* on this experience. Martin pulls himself up from the dregs of society to become a famous and well-paid author only to discover life's illusions vanishing to the point of absurdity. Neither the work, the fame, the money, nor the women matter. Turning inward in this existential crisis, he commits suicide. When others criticized his ending his hero's life so damnably, London replied that Martin lacked what he had: the "PEOPLE" and the love of a woman, meaning Charmian.

Charmian was cognizant that he was not the "old Jack," and that she must adjust her own needs to his. Early that February she became quite ill, quit her job, and moved to Glen Ellen permanently. In her absence, Jack's melancholy darkened, and when he came to visit her in early March, Charmian granted him his freedom from any prior commitments to her. This offer so amazed him that, as they rode together through mountain canyons toward the train in Napa, he experienced an epiphany. Grateful for Charmian's caring and selflessness, he reaffirmed his pledge to marry her. Soon afterward, she learned that Jack's distress was more than existential angst: he had been suffering bowel discomfort for some time and, based on his usual self-diagnosis after searching the medical texts, was convinced he had cancer. Returning to Oakland, he consulted a doctor, learned that he had a case of raging hemorrhoids, and underwent successful surgery.

❧

While recuperating at his mother's home, Jack begged Bess to bring the girls by for a visit. They had never been to 1216 Telegraph Avenue before and never would again. Upon their arrival, Flora and Manyoungi pulled Bess into the parlor and an argument ensued. Dressed in their best outfits and full of anticipation, the girls grew upset to hear their mother say she would not let them visit their father after all. Eventually Bess gave in, but only on condition that she stay down in the parlor while the other adults escorted the girls upstairs. When they entered, the room was dark, lit by a single rosy-shaded bedside lamp. Joan noticed someone sitting in a dark corner, quietly watching. When their father failed to introduce the stranger, Joan became curious. Afterward she asked her mother, who said it was just an old friend of their father's. It was twenty years before Joan would meet Charmian again.

While Charmian nursed Jack, he decided to prove his commitment to her by moving permanently to Glen Ellen. He told Macmillan to increase Bess's monthly allowance to $100, as though that could compensate for his absence. Old enough to understand that a distance of seventy miles was well beyond her reach, Joan mourned that she could no longer sleep secure knowing that her father was only three blocks away. When she asked her mother whether she would ever go to see him, Bess responded, "I don't know," then added harshly, "Probably not!"

Their deceit had caught up with the lovers, and would ultimately infect the innocent. Bess was intransigent, insisting that her daughters be barred from seeing Charmian, who never afterward gave the slightest hint of understanding her role in this tragic decision. One might scan hundreds of pages of her diaries and letters and never guess that Jack was a father. Of course, it was that utter devotion to him alone that so appealed to Jack. The move to Glen Ellen reinforced his growing alienation from his daughters. Seventy miles was not that long a journey by train and ferry; yet more often than not, his trips to San Francisco and the East Bay did not include a trip to Thirty-first Street.

Jack's isolation extended beyond his immediate family, for he also saw less of his friends from the Ruskin Club, the political groups, and the Crowd. He wrote George a wistful letter regretting that there had always been some incompatibility between them, that in effect his hope that George would be his great comrade had been dashed. He was nevertheless proud to be sinking an anchor, and reinforced his decision by writing a kind of sequel to *The Call of the Wild* called

*White Fang* to depict the "call of the tame." Disgruntled with people, even socialists, Jack London was embarked on a new adventure: the stewardship of the land.

With other nativist Americans of the day, he revived the Jeffersonian vision of agrarian freedom and purity. The city was to them a fetid, frightening, corrupt place, overrun with filthy, defective immigrants of inferior stock. Some fled to suburbs, while Jack, like others affluent enough to purchase large tracts of land, chose a regression to yeoman farming. It was a notion particularly encouraged among boys in the late 1800s: the importance of physical labor, exposure to the outdoors, not overloading oneself with "brain fag." If the city was a den of iniquity, then time spent away would inculcate decent morals. In 1905 this dream of a new landed Eden was just a will-o'-the-wisp to Jack, but it would grow to embody the central mission of his life.

Within weeks of moving to Glen Ellen, Jack purchased the Hill Ranch, 128 acres on the lower slopes of Sonoma Mountain. Close to a century later this landscape retains its haunting appeal, stimulating atavistic memories. Blood red and wine red trunks of manzanita and madrone twist and curl alongside the pathways; towering fir and redwood enclose dark sanctuaries; bay laurel releases its mildly exotic scent; wispy pale green Spanish moss drapes to make ghostly statuary of majestic live oak, tanbark oak, black oak, and white oak. Deep canyons cut through the slopes, carved by water rushing and tumbling down from above during the rainy season, riffling and whispering the rest of the year. It was a landscape to attract poets, and would seduce Jack and Charmian with its atmosphere of wonder.

This first parcel of what would expand to become the Beauty Ranch cost $7,000, with the accouterments of horses, cows, turkeys, wagons, plows, harrows, and such for an additional $600, all of which he paid for in cash. The money was part of a $10,000 advance from George Brett, although it is not clear why Jack needed to borrow so much, for partial records show that he earned at least $14,800 during 1905. Of this, Bess received $1,800, yet he was quick to complain to Cloudesley Johns of being "flatbroke" because of her latest request. It seems she had asked him to pay for a horse, surrey, and backyard stall, for she wanted ready transport to take the girls not only around Oakland but also up in the hills away from the noise and distractions.[6]

Despite his grumbles, Jack met Bess's request, and she bought an apparently well-tamed nag of indefinite age. Throughout the summer she took the girls, often accompanied by Flora and Jennie, up winding dirt roads through fields full of cows, past hedgerows of roses and hollyhocks. Along the way she taught the girls botany, showed them how to identify edible plants, and named the birds flying overhead. They absorbed Flora's and Jennie's stories of their youth, the contrast of the candlelight of crystal chandeliers lighting balls in Massillon against the rampaging Union soldiers at the Parker Plantation. For Joan in particular, these jaunts encouraged her delight in nature. Even at the end of her life she could easily evoke the "silver rippling grass . . . the sweetbriar whose delicate leaves were fragrant as spice, minty yerba buena, gold-back ferns, and the small, dark-red wild strawberries that tasted so much better than the domesticated kind."[7] Had he known what pleasures the horse would bring, Jack might have been less mean-spirited.

Blaming Bess for his problems became part of a general pattern of reinterpreting events to deny his responsibility. That May, for example, Charmian learned how the Crowd had conspired against her by fostering Jack's affair with Blanche Partington. The story, filtered through Jack, left her "sad to find dear friends (?) treachrously small."[8] Charmian interpreted the episode as if the Crowd bore full responsibility, and excused Jack of any complicity, at least on a conscious level. Blanche and Carrie, however, had not finished with their machinations. During that summer each wrote Jack to accuse Charmian of breaking up his marriage and of bad-mouthing the Crowd. Jack felt relieved of culpability, and he responded by rewriting events to release Charmian as well from their blame. The Crowd's problem, he countered, was that they believed the word of "one of the most colossal and shameless liars I have ever known," Bess, whom he claimed was responsible for spreading stories. Look at how she had dragged Anna Strunsky through the mud. Was it any wonder he would shield Charmian? That was why he'd counseled Charmian to remain friendly with the "eagle-eyed, jealous" Bess during the separation. As he piled up these justifications, Jack convinced himself, if not Blanche and Carrie, that he and Charmian were the victims of Bess, pure and simple. "I don't consider it a crime for any woman to attempt to cut out a man from under the guns of another woman."[9]

If friend and biographer Joseph Noel is correct, the real threat Bess posed to Jack was not that she was talking about Anna or Charmian, but that she was telling others of his illegitimacy: "As a matter of fact the separation originated in Jack's setting his face against [Bess's] mean gossip against his mother and his birth."[10] This was a direct challenge to stories he was telling reporters about his bloodline. In a day when eugenics had reached its pinnacle, he was always careful to describe himself as having been born of "perfectly strong and vigorous" stock—that of the Pennsylvania Londons—to emerge "the king bean" in the pod. Both his parental lines were prerevolutionary, he asserted, and he referred to his family as having been "the only American" one among the Irish and Italians in his neighborhood.[11] For Bess to reveal that John London was not Jack's father was also to expose Eliza as other than his blood kin.

At the time of Bess's first accusations of infidelity, Flora had criticized her daughter-in-law to reporters, asserting that Jack had been "loving, generous, and affectionate to a fault," that Bess made too much of the "silly girls who wrote letters" to him.[12] With Charmian's irresistible pull now obvious, she re-aligned with Bess. It was most likely around this time that Jack's estrangement from Flora occurred. Thus, when she took up baking and selling her bread again, he complained that the public would think he was not supporting her well enough. Even Jennie fell out of favor for backing Bess and the girls. While Jack remained throughout life a most generous man, quick to help strangers and friends alike, he turned his back on his mother and foster mother, and saw only to their most basic needs from this point on.

Through an Orwellian twist of language, Jack had solved the paradox of his infidelity and his break with Bess and his daughters. Despite her history of love affairs and sexual liberality, Charmian was "pure" and made him feel "clean," while Bess, who had been faithful to him and tolerant of his casual sexual pec-cadilloes, was more "devoted to purity" than to himself. Charmian had col-luded in his deceptions, yet it was Bess he called a "shameless liar."[13] He applied similar illogic to Flora and Jennie. Though both had been instrumental in his development and eventual success, he rewrote his past as conceived in and of himself. The anonymous conception was transformed into an immaculate con-ception, one achieved without the participation of women at birth or during infancy.

It all made sense from his viewpoint. He was the noted writer, the prominent socialist. It was he who collected the hundred-dollar checks, not any of the women. He worked diligently seven days a week, sick or well, in order to pro-vide for three households and seven people, not to mention the frequent gifts to friends such as Netta or the Atherton family. He was full of the blessing and curse of patriarchy: gifted with fame and riches, but burdened by what seemed to him hangers-on, people who were not carrying their share—except for Charmian. It seemed to him an uneven exchange, and resentment was natural. But it was uneven only if one accepts society's devaluation of the others' work, only if one measures effort by income. He was doing more for his family than most men in his circumstance, but he criticized his dependents, not the neglect of other men, or the society that structured gender relationships in so skewed a manner. Patriarchy invokes the same psychological twists as slavery, with the patriarch, like the plantation mistress, coming to hate the responsibilities con-nected with the benefits of power. Displacement of grievances upon the less powerful is a convenient and common response.

Though recipient of Jack's unremitting praise, beatified as it was, Charmian had difficult expectations to meet. One was the problem of living up to the "Man Comrade" vision. Lurking in the background was the need to provide an heir eventually, even a spare. For Charmian, now thirty-four, this was not a certain feat. Furthermore, having to maintain Jack's ideal image of her could be exhausting. This situation forced her to negotiate a way to preserve her long-maintained independence without threatening the relationship. Several factors assisted here. One was that since she could not become pregnant until after the wedding (though birth control was illegal, it was available to those in the know), unlike Bess, she had a period of adjustment free from maternity. Also, she was more unconventional than Bess, not at all domestic (apart from sewing), and more experienced in clerical skills. With regard to sex, work, and play, she and Jack were "Mates."

Nonetheless, Charmian faced situations where she had to bend to Jack's will when she would have preferred to do otherwise. She was more self-disciplined when it came to health; she maintained a vegetarian diet, got plenty of daily exercise, and avoided tobacco and alcohol. Their differences here would be the crux of most of their arguments, and to strengthen her cause she would raise women's trusty swords: manipulation, cunning, and bargaining. In other matters she simply complied. He determined where they would go, what they would do. He controlled the finances. (She never signed a check or knew about their accounts.) His opinions became hers. She controlled any hint of furious emotion, since Jack could not stand "hysteria." It reminded him of his mother, he said.

It would be wrong, however, to conclude that Charmian was bullied or oppressed. That patriarchy granted Jack the ultimate power implies neither that he enforced it nor that any of her "submissive" behaviors were unwilling. Society provides a model; exact conformity is problematic. Charmian very consciously deferred, was for the most part satisfied with her choices, and would have objected had anyone tried to fit later notions of victimization to her situation. Jack's desires were primary in the relationship because they brought such obvious benefits. Incorporating him into her life meant that her needs would be fulfilled in a way that would have been impossible with almost any other man. She did not have to domesticate herself, for Jack provided servants. Better, she found a partner to meet her own dreams of adventure. Who wouldn't compromise? she might challenge.

Though clearly in charge, Jack acceded to Charmian's preferred way of life, a life out of the city. He adopted her relatives as his own, such that one or another was often staying at the ranch. When she complained that his reading at night aggravated her chronic insomnia, he agreed to separate bedrooms. As payment for her clerical work, he gave her his handwritten manuscripts, aware that they would be of value one day. He was inordinately proud of her, fascinated by her very different way of approaching life, her ease with living in the moment.

The daily schedule they developed that summer of 1905 became a well-known ritual to servants and guests. Jack retreated each morning to work on his stories, while Charmian typed his manuscripts and correspondence. Sometimes she played piano to provide background for his work. They preferred sex during the day—her diaries documenting frequent "lollies"—perhaps because their sleeping habits were so different. Lunchtime often included guests. Afterward they would ride their horses or romp with campers and locals at the town swimming hole. Jack taught children to swim, and played a game with them involving the retrieval of objects dropped to the bottom of the creek. He taught others, women as well as men, to box. After dinner, recreation was more sedate: sing-alongs, reading aloud, word games. Once in their separate bedrooms, Jack would read until well after midnight, writing notes in the margins and on odd slips of paper, while Charmian also read to tempt the often elusive sleep. This daily routine would last throughout their marriage, wherever they were or whatever their state of health. (When given a single room while traveling, one or the other would sleep in the bathtub.)

They made a habit of reading the same books, and that summer one book that fell into their hands was Joshua Slocum's *Voyage of the Liberated,* in which he recounted how, following the wreck of his boat, he set sail with his wife and children from South America in a canoe. This led them to read Slocum's *Sailing Alone around the World* and *Voyage of the Spray.* These accounts of the lone sailor's circumnavigation evoked a "thrilling pulse" in Jack to build a boat and repeat the voyage in perhaps five years. Charmian avidly assented, arguing that they should not wait but take off sooner, postponing building a new house on the ranch to build the boat instead. She was "game," the quality Jack admired above all others. Wherever his compass pointed, she would gladly accompany him.

Notably ignored during this discussion were Joan and Becky. Until recently men had long followed occupations separating them from family, whether taking to the sea, prospecting for minerals, adventuring in the fur trade, or fighting frontier wars against the Indians. Factory and later office work tied men to the clock and their hometowns, but at some cost to their sense of masculinity, so they turned to sports, scouting, and lodge memberships for all-male camaraderie.[14] For a majority of men, the camaraderie included alcohol; hence the alliance of the women's suffrage movement with prohibition. Though a social radical, London was reactionary with regard to masculinity. He longed for the bully life of physical adventure proselytized by Theodore Roosevelt. It was a style available to ever fewer men, generally those either willing to lead the life of the homeless tramp or wealthy enough to take off on long hunting trips.

In response to the separation of men from the household, and the injurious effects of drinking on family life, reformers, ministers, and experts in giving advice were preaching that men could become more active in the home without challenging their brawny masculinity. Proponents of this new model argued that men should do more than just provide material support. Rather, they should take time to mold and guide their children's achievement, provide discipline (thought not physical punishment), and make more of an effort to express warmth and kindness at home.[15] The very magazines London studied and wrote for espoused these ideas, so he could not have been ignorant of them. He, however, followed a more Victorian model, judging himself as a father primarily by his financial contributions. When Bess challenged him to be more of a participant in the girls' upbringing, suggesting that he sacrifice some of his own happiness for their sake, she was expressing the latest Progressive ideals of family life.

Jack's eschewing the domesticated model of manhood can be seen in how readily he forgot his daughters following the breakup. As a result, his intermittent interventions seemed to Bess and the girls nothing more than thoughtless interference. A typical example concerns his behavior upon learning about a problem with the horse he had bought them. Abruptly one rainy day, with the girls in the saddle, the animal broke loose from Bess's control and thundered wildly toward home, leaving the girls thrilled by the bouncing and sliding of the leather seat. Afterward Bess learned that the horse was a young one that had been mistreated, although it regained its spirit under her care. Having handled the runaway capably, Bess proudly recounted the story to Jack, who then insisted that she send the ornery beast to the ranch. He promised a replacement, but never followed through. Jack's neglect may have been unintentional, but it was not forgotten. Her dependency on his goodwill prevented Bess from making any direct expression of disappointment, but her grievances mounted.

As the date for finalizing the divorce approached, Charmian did not see the wedding as any more than a legal requirement. As far as she was concerned, she and Jack became man and wife early in their relationship. Consequently, the couple agreed to take advantage of a special tour and fit their nuptials and honeymoon into their work schedule.

The opportunity arose on September 12, 1905, when a group gathered in New York City to form the Intercollegiate Socialist Society. Although he was not present, Jack was elected president, perhaps on the urging of Upton Sinclair, who admired the writer, and who would do the actual organizational work as vice president. Other organizers included lawyer Clarence Darrow, journalist Lincoln Steffens, economist Thorstein Veblen, economist Charlotte Perkins Gilman, and poet Edwin Markham. They were, in other words, the liberal intellectual elite, and their honoring London indicates the degree of his achievement despite his unconventional education.

To further the organization's cause, Jack signed with the Lyceum Bureau to arrange speaking engagements for him throughout the country beginning in late October. The timing could not have been better, because he and Charmian had already decided to marry out of state and honeymoon back east. He departed alone, to lecture at the University of Kansas, while Charmian went by train to stay with Lynette McMurry in Iowa. Jack stopped there briefly, then continued on as far east as New Jersey and from there to upstate New York, then down through Pennsylvania and Ohio. On November 17 Jack received word that his divorce was final. Charmian met him in Chicago, where they were married on the nineteenth at ten in the evening at the home of a justice of the peace. The next day they boarded a train to Wisconsin, where Jack gave two lectures.

The public view of divorce and remarriage was soon evident in the sensationalized response. Several sponsoring groups canceled Jack's appearances in protest of his immorality. Preachers damned the couple from the pulpit. Newspapers described Charmian in the most unseemly terms, including one that declared children ran from her in fright.

The tour paused in Iowa, but by early December the couple were traveling around New England. In Maine they visited various relatives of Charmian's father. Later that month Charmian beamed at the standing-room crowds in Boston and at Harvard University, where labor leader Mother Jones came to the podium to plant a kiss of benediction on Jack's cheek. Blood red posters announcing his "Revolution" speech inflamed his notoriety among the conventional. On December 27 the couple (accompanied by the ever-present Manyoungi) boarded a United Fruit Company cargo ship, the *Admiral Farragut*, for a honeymoon in Jamaica and Cuba. Throughout this busy public journey Charmian proved adept at public relations. In contrast to Bess, she welcomed the spotlight and knew exactly how to phrase an answer to Jack's best advantage. She unstintingly accompanied him to the Chicago stockyards, and later to observe dissections at a medical school. She complained about the "capitalist press" and its refusal to criticize libraries that were removing his books. Although Jack was ill several times during these frantic months, Charmian proved to be of strong constitution, and a good nurse.

In later commemoration of his love, Jack created in his novels female heroines who incorporated many of Charmian's qualities: physically brave and intellectually strong, sexual and sensuous. Incidents and people in their fictional lives were taken directly from Charmian's experiences. Her courageous side became Avis Everhard in *The Iron Heel,* her secretarial world in *Burning Daylight,* and her eroticism in *The Little Lady of the Big House.* One of the last stories London ever wrote, "The Kanaka Surf," was conceived in admiration of Charmian's spunk and athleticism. Yet despite this constant homage, over the years Charmian felt impelled to record in her diary verbal expressions of love he had made to her, as if she were never completely certain of his love. More likely, she never felt fully deserving of his love.

Given his remarriage, on December 4, 1905, Jack composed a new will and later added several codicils.[16] The stipulations emphasized that everything ultimately was to go to his daughters. He added instructions that Jennie Prentiss be supported "whenever she expresses a willingness to enter [an] Old Ladies Home." Eliza's growing prominence in his life was evident in his leaving her $1,000. As in his July 1905 will, Charmian was to receive the horses and various personal belongings, but Bess was to receive his sets of Robert Louis Stevenson, James Barrie, and Rudyard Kipling. Both women, as well as Flora, could continue to use the houses he had provided for each, which ultimately would revert to Joan and Becky. If Bess remarried, she could rent the house from her daughters; if Charmian remarried, however, she lost all use of the ranch. There were also special life insurance policies, and all the women were to share in his royalties according to a formula he set down. The implied intent was to balance the bequests to Charmian and Bess respectively, and to see to the maintenance of Flora and Jennie, with a clear priority given to the daughters. "Each of the legatees is to receive enough to keep her from going hungry; if any are to go hungry, it shall be the three adult legatees." His "primary consideration" was Joan and Becky; the executors were to understand the latitude he was providing them. "By education I mean equipment in life[;] . . . should Joan or [Becky], desiring to study music or art or anything else, here or abroad, ask for the necessary money," the executors must provide it. Later that day Jack added a codicil stating as a "note of explanation" that Charmian had "of her own initiative and volition" added a codicil to her own will bequeathing to "Joan and Bess [Becky], all property willed to me by my husband."

On December 6 Jack added "my beloved sister, Eliza Shepard" as an executor, the others being James G. Read (a longtime friend) and George Sterling. Another codicil allowed that should the daughters predecease Charmian, she would become the beneficiary, with the proviso that she "see that my sister, Eliza Shepard, is always adequately provided for." This requirement hints at changes in Eliza's marriage, which was deteriorating partly as a result of her husband's drinking. With her stepchildren grown, and one child of her own, Irving, now seven, she was preparing to become self-supporting. Though her formal education had been cut short by her youthful marriage, Eliza had gleaned a rich harvest of business and legal skills from her government job as well as her work in community organizations. Her patient manner served her well in setting goals, negotiating deals, and executing plans. Jack's filial love for Eliza, whom he always referred to as his natural sister, was increased by her feelings for Charmian. The two women were quite different in temperament and personality, yet perhaps it was that very dissimilarity that nurtured their friendship, which would grow into deep affection.

Upon returning from the honeymoon, Jack resumed his round of socialist speeches, while editing the story collections that would become *Moon Face* and *Love of Life*. Perhaps most significant for Charmian was the short story "Planchette," which incorporated elements of their fateful ride through the Napa mountainside when Jack reversed his course, realizing the depth of his need for her.

Around this time he bought a house at 490 Twenty-seventh Street in Oakland for Flora and Jennie. This two-story structure in a solid middle-class neighborhood was richly decorated with Greek Revival columns and pilasters, a large bay window by the dining room, and that key sign of status, a palm tree in the front yard. He and Charmian reserved two rooms upstairs as a pied-à-terre for their frequent overnight visits, which did not include much interaction with Flora, for it is clear that Charmian had absorbed Jack's view of his mother as troublesome. Jennie was still helping Bess with the girls, and worked in the African American community as a midwife. Flora thrived in her new, larger home, and became more gregarious, attracting younger friends who appreciated her unusual personality and sparkling conversation.

Another new large expense would be the *Snark*, the boat in which they planned to circumnavigate the globe. Jack provided the design, a radical departure from most yachts of the day. He chose a high-bowed ketch, forty-five feet on the waterline, equipped with a seventy-seven horsepower motor.[17] The Beauty Ranch had hay fields to tend and farmhands to pay. Their decision to press ahead with their nautical adventure, regardless of bank statement, increased the financial pressure on Jack, and by implication on Charmian, to churn out more magazine serializations and full-length books. Neither seemed to consider postponing a new, great, and costly scheme.

With her new cause and a new suitor to please her, Anna felt no resentment toward Charmian. Nor did she hold the couple responsible for the scandal implicating her in the divorce. Characteristically, just before the marriage Anna sent Charmian a bouquet of lilies of the valley, accompanied by a letter in which she remarked, "I find you and wrap you in love. Then I kiss you full on the lips, and say farewell." She was writing on a night spent sleeping under the stars with her sister Rose. "That is my honeymoon, Charmian, but the Milky Way is wide enough for you and Jack too."[18]

Now her life seemed to have a purpose. Anna spent much of the fall of 1905 lecturing, this time for a fee, to raise funds for the trip to Geneva. "My work will consist of writing mostly, and I am happy to be of any service to the cause to which I have devoted my life," she told a reporter, who described her a "fearless socialist."[19] On November 23, when several dozen members of the Ruskin Club met to pay tribute to her, she delivered an impassioned address concerning the Russian cause. The next evening, members of the Crowd met at the Strunsky home for a more intimate gathering. George Sterling read a poem he had composed for her, while Xavier Martinez hung around his beloved Rose, perhaps hoping she would decide not to leave.

On November 28 the sisters left for New York. Anna's suitor Cameron King and another socialist friend saw the sisters off and got drunk afterward, drinking curses to Walling. Martinez wrote, but did not send, a letter urging Rose not to go on to Russia, for he would not meet her there for fear of getting his head blown off on the barricades. He wanted her to understand that for him, art came before politics. As it happened, he showed the letter around to enough people that Rose eventually heard of its contents, and her feelings for him cooled. Martinez obviously knew what most members of the sisters' family did not: that they intended to go all the way to St. Petersburg and join William English Walling. Anna anticipated that their father and brothers would never allow them to travel beyond Geneva, which is why she gave misleading stories to the press. Their mother, however, did everything possible to help her daughters prepare, and by indirection suggested that she knew the truth about their plans.

Anna was also misleading Cameron King, whom she asked to remain behind to study French and German in preparation for his own trip to Geneva.[20] When Elias Strunsky withheld proof of his daughters' naturalization, King used his legal connections to get the travel papers they required. Unaware of Anna's true destination, King in one of his letters described the plot of a story running through his mind, concerning a young man turned socialist giving thanks to the woman he loved. Despite his revealing and ardent letters, upon reaching Europe, Anna no longer responded.

In March 1906 Cameron learned the truth. Anna had gone directly to St. Petersburg, where within a few weeks she had become engaged to English. From the beginning, she and Rose had been caught up in Walling's energy and commitment. When he learned that Anna had no more ties to Jack London, he proposed to her in the presence of her sister. Anna was speechless, but gathered her wits sufficiently to say that she felt as he did. As Rose observed, the couple were so affectionate in public that others had assumed Anna was already English's mistress. On January 19, 1906, Anna wrote to her parents of meeting a man who loved her "tenderly as mother," and who had opened her mind to new vistas. In her private jottings she noted that at last she was free from her worst fear, that of being alone.

Distraught over Anna's deception and the silence of those who could have alerted him, Cameron King sent her a cruel telegram, then followed it with a repentant apology. In remarks that were generous yet thoughtful, he trusted that her love for Walling was genuine, that she had not confused her feelings for him with the romance of the struggle they shared. King also feared that English's parents would disapprove because she was Jewish. In fact, upon later meeting Anna, the Wallings welcomed her; any subsequent in-law difficulties would arise from the extremely close ties between English and his mother. It was Anna's parents who were upset that she had chosen to marry a non-Jew in a civil ceremony.

Cameron's letter may have provoked Anna to reconsider her precipitate decision to marry, for she replied warily of fearing "vitally to displease [English] in the end." Cameron found her comment puzzling, since it hinted at an incompatibility much deeper than the usual daily conflicts couples face. He mocked that she had become "submissive enough in love to honor and *obey*." Quoting Browning, he wrote, "I will speak thy speech love / Think thy thought."[21] Under the circumstances, he advised her to marry quickly. She did, becoming English's wife on June 28, 1906, with only her sister Rose to represent friends and family. Karl Marx's grandson Jean Longuet was their other witness. In keeping with her political convictions, Anna refused to change her last name or to wear a wedding ring.

To friends and family the couple wrote of their marriage as a partnership committed to "the work," as they referred generically to socialism. For several months Anna rejected English's overtures to consummate the marriage. Before the wedding, the idealism that brought the two together also prevented their exploring everyday matters that would affect the relationship. Anna soon discovered that English, used to being coddled, was not inclined to treat her with the equality their socialism commanded. He in turn learned of her frequent descent into dark, uncommunicative states during which she would write angry or suicidal thoughts in her diary. In response, he shut himself in his den to write and excluded her from the collaboration she expected. There would be episodes of kindness and warmth that eventually resulted in physical intimacy, but the dominant motif was one of mutual isolation.

At the time of the wedding it had been nine months since Anna received a letter from Jack London; she would not get any congratulations from him, nor hear from him for some years. She thought she had put his influence behind her. English was similar to Jack in being a man of high energy, determination, intelligence, and charisma. And, as with those who knew Jack, friends would always forgive his less endearing qualities. Having spent the past few years among some of the key women leaders of Progressive causes, English was comfortable in the company of well-educated women committed to action. In Anna he had found a partner as single-minded as himself concerning the plight of oppressed

Russians, and one who embodied an unself-conscious feminine sensuality. As he explained to his parents, she had a nature larger than his own, totally lacking in his "faults of disposition—temper, coldness, hardness."[22] He also was a man who liked being in charge, supremely confident in his opinions and abilities.

Cameron King had been prescient in his reading of the relationship. Whereas Anna wrote of equality in their relationship, of their collaborating in the cause and their plans to write a book together, English's letters home hinted at her lack of organization and weak domestic skills. Anna complained to Rose that English did not trust her to buy the simplest things. He clearly saw himself as responsible for educating and directing her. "Of course she is a Jewess," he told his parents, "but I hope to improve that—at least in private life."[23] In describing him as her "supreme comrade," Anna aptly yet subconsciously acknowledged through that oxymoron the inconsistency of her position.

This is not to imply that English was cold or insensitive so much as analytical and methodical, inclined to discount intuition and sensation. He adored Anna's ability to create warmth wherever she went, to provide a soothing, nurturing setting. He admired her purity of values, her rejection of luxury, her courage to live a life out of the ordinary on behalf of others. Still, though he knew his own faults well, he was more inclined to bend others to him than change himself. Unfortunately, Anna was willing to bow to his wishes, yet could not acknowledge that the resulting submersion of her needs was also a fault that would make compatibility very difficult. Charmian, by contrast, was much better at getting Jack to think that he was in charge while taking insistent stands against him when it mattered most to her.

For now, however, the potential disagreements between the Wallings were barely noticeable. Caught up in the turmoil of opposition to the czarist regime, the couple saw themselves as fortunate to be participating in history, to defer their private pleasures for the opportunity to risk their own lives in the midst of current events. Approaching Petersburg, she sat in the train, "drunk with the [Russian] language, with the winter landscape."[24] Having heard Russian émigrés' stories of torture and rape during her 1903 visit to Europe, Anna knew what potential dangers lay ahead. A week after their arrival, they saw an officer murder a student who refused to sing in honor of the czar. Very quickly they connected with the anti-regime underground, which helped hide those who were being sought by authorities, arranged for false papers, and assisted flights to freedom through Finland. During their two years in Russia, Anna, English, and Rose defied the authorities by traveling to troubled areas so they could report to the world at large the truth about the autocratic regime. This was particularly dangerous at times for the Strunsky sisters, Russian-born Jews, such as when they entered towns wracked by pogroms and had to deal with unpredictable military men. Despite the challenges, they were certain they had arrived in time to witness the success of the Revolution, the overthrow of the czar and his oppressive feudal regime in favor of socialism.

Life in the Bay Area that summer of 1906 was fraught with turmoil of a different kind. At dawn on April 18 the earth shook violently throughout the area, awakening people, tossing many out of bed, dropping mirrors and bureaus on others. Startled awake in Glen Ellen, Charmian and Jack quickly dressed, mounted their horses, and rode to the top of Sonoma Mountain, from which point they could see fire and smoke rising from Santa Rosa to the north and San Francisco to the south. Not ones to miss a major news story, they took off for the city. Before leaving, Jack called Bess to make sure everyone was all right. She assured him that apart from some fallen chimney bricks and a toppled walnut bedstead, she and the girls had suffered no harm.

It had nevertheless been a more frightening experience for Oakland residents than for those in Glen Ellen. During the quake Bess had crawled into bed with the girls to explain what was going on. She calmed them despite horrid screams from the East Bay Sanitarium, a four-story building on the nearby corner that had collapsed into rubble on top of its patients. She described what to do when quakes hit, how to avoid harm caused by fear and foolishness. Soon the house was filled with relatives and friends: Flora, Jennie, various Maddisons, and "Uncle Charlie" Milner, who was in the early stages of courting Bess.

Charmian and Jack rode a train to Sausalito, and then ferried into the ravaged city, where they wandered for two days with little rest, photographing the damage and speaking with the victims. They went to the apartment of an aunt of Charmian's who was out of town so Charmian could retrieve photographs of herself with her long-deceased father. They passed by a store owned by her former love Herbert Dugan, Charmian "burying hatchets" about him in her mind, aware now that his business would likely go up in flames. They napped on a doorstep, and were later invited in by the owner, who gave them cake and pie. In perhaps the most poignant encounter, Charmian sat at the piano of a home and played on it for the last time for its owner before they all fled the approaching flames.

At the Strunsky home in San Francisco, all of Anna's belongings, including her draft of *Windlestraws,* were destroyed. The Londons' own loss consisted of damage to a barn under construction. More significant was the impact the quake would have on the construction of the *Snark.* Now both supplies and workers would be scarce, and the cost would be well beyond Jack's initial calculations, by some accounts over $20,000 at a time when the average family survived on $500 a year.

In frustration Jack left the supervision of the boat building to Netta's husband, Roscoe Eames, who was to be their navigator, and returned to the ranch, where he embarked on one of his most productive periods of writing. He completed *Before Adam,* a science fantasy of pre-human society; *The Iron Heel,* his dystopian critique of capitalism; and *The Road,* an account of his tramping days most notable for its section on the Erie Penitentiary. Interspersed with these was a variety of short stories and essays.

Among the most personal essays was "My Castle in Spain," later renamed "The House Beautiful" when it was included in *Revolution and Other Essays.* Without any direct reference to the term, London cast his vote with the Arts and Crafts aesthetic currently thriving in parts of California. This tradition, born in England under John Ruskin and William Morris, had transplanted readily to America, which had a long tradition of countercultures espousing the simple life. Simplicity implied ease, efficiency, lack of waste, conscious beauty, and honesty. Earlier, similar expressions had occurred among Puritans, Quakers, Transcendentalists, Shakers, and Mennonites, as well as in domestic advice books of the nineteenth century. The Progressives added another reason for the simple life: escape from the false and corrupt values of urban capitalism.

Two California centers for the movement were the East Bay and the Pasadena Arroyo, both with lively artist populations. While growing up in the East Bay, London was surrounded by the more ornate Victorian style wherever he went. Charmian, by contrast, became exposed to Arts and Crafts precepts through Edward Payne, who had been a founder of the short-lived utopian community of Altruria in Santa Rosa. Wake Robin Lodge exemplified the aesthetic. Throughout her life Charmian would be content with functional furnishings, plain meals, and minimal fuss. She doubtless influenced Jack's coming around to the belief that "I worship utility and believe that utility and beauty should be one." To him, the house at 490 Twenty-seventh Street was a monument to all that was wasteful and false in society, for its Greek Revival pillars had "no use, no work to perform," hence "lied and cheated," as did residents of such buildings "in their business lives."[25]

Though explicitly committed to the simple life, Charmian and Jack were not dogmatists. Charmian's dress, which drew criticism from some as ostentatious, also fit this aesthetic. She viewed her clothes as works of art, and often they were. Throughout her travels she acquired unusual fabrics and trim to bring back for self-decoration, and became an avid collector of opals for custom-crafted jewelry. For a time she was influenced by the Orientalist rage, whose kimono-influenced style combined comfort and beauty. For special uses she designed practical garments, such as split skirts for cross-saddle riding, and set about making several sets of muslin pants outfits for the *Snark* trip.

Less able to curb his impulses, Jack deviated more from the simple life. Indeed, he would invoke his philosophy of simplicity, then incur debt to achieve his aims. If the utilitarian is beautiful, then cost is insignificant in satisfying one's aims. Simple did not necessarily mean inexpensive, particularly for the Arts and Crafts movement, with its emphasis on exquisite craftsmanship and the best materials.

Members of the Crowd had also flirted with Arts and Crafts ideas, but it was not until Jack moved to Glen Ellen in the summer of 1905 that they acted more seriously on these principles. That summer, following Jack's example, George Sterling decided that he would escape to the country too, but in another direction—southwest to the tiny community of Carmel on the coast. As George explained to his mentor Ambrose Bierce, he was going to wrest a living from the soil and hole up with "just one girl," Carrie, who was no doubt relieved by this aspect of his plan. If Jack could hear the call of the tame, so could George. The two men's intimacy in part involved this press toward a purer life. Over subsequent years they would report in their letters how many weeks or months had passed since they had imbibed alcohol. With their respective moves to the country, both implicitly denounced their earlier jaunts into the dens of the Barbary Coast.

With the help of friends, George began building a simple redwood house with huge chalk rock fireplace on a plot about a thousand feet above the old Carmel mission and a half mile from the ocean. It would be the next summer before the house and surrounding three-acre garden, complete with vegetables, Belgian hares, hens, bees, and squabs, was fully inhabited. "I'm not worrying much as to my ability to keep alive in Carmel," George reported. "Again let me say that Carrie and I love the simple life—the simpler the better."[26] There were quail and deer in the pine forests to hunt, wild berries to pick, salmon and perch to hook. Most of all there were abalone for feasts with friends, who one afternoon had little trouble filling almost fifty sacks with the delicacies.

Visitors to Carmel were numerous, particularly such old Crowd members as Carlt and Laura Bierce, and Dick Partington with sisters Blanche and Gertrude. The noted photographer Arnold Genthe constructed an enormous house nearby, supported by four redwood trunks with bark left on. Mary Hunter Austin, well known for her paean to the desert, *The Land of Little Rain*, arrived alone after a broken marriage and stayed. George's closest friend in Carmel was the athlete and journalist Jimmy Hopper, who rented a cottage in the dunes at only six dollars a month for his growing family. The colony had its playful, eccentric moments, but for the most part it consisted of a set of hardworking friends committed to the plain life and to art. Jack would honor these friends fictionally in *The Valley of the Moon* in an episode in which his main characters encounter a similar colony in Carmel.

In November 1906, Charmian and Jack arrived on the scene. The Londons spent one day with the Crowd in the Sterlings' thirty-by-eighteen-foot living room indulging in what George called "book indigestion." The next day included a carriage ride over the Seventeen Mile Drive to a party, the third a coastal jaunt and abalone feast. The partying was an exception, for despite their reputation the Carmel artists spent most of their daylight hours in solitary chambers plying their craft.

Mary Austin was surprised to find Jack "sagging a little with the surfeit of success," turning down a hike, no longer the well-muscled, fit young man known for his boxing, fencing, and sailing. She listened to him discuss the creative endeavor, including his belief that artists required an occasional love affair. Her sprightly rejoinder was, "I never needed a love affair to release the subconscious in me." (The conversation may have been a typical ploy of Jack's, to take a position sure to inflame his listeners just for the fun of provoking lively dialogue.) At this and other meetings Mary observed that "women flung themselves at Jack, lay in wait for him," and he was aware of his attraction. He explained to her that women preferred to marry up, and would take "the tenth share in a man of distinction to the whole of an average man."[27] Charmian knew of these beliefs, and made certain that she claimed much more than a tithe portion of her husband. Whereas those women flinging themselves at Jack had sent Bess into despair, Charmian let potential interlopers understand that they could not defeat her. As Jack's assistant, she had reason to go with him everywhere and drop reminders about all the work to be done. Thus it is not surprising that the couple left Carmel after only three days. They never considered living there.

Though rooming just a few blocks from the girls, Jack did not visit often that winter. It is unclear whether he was even aware of the care Bess was taking regarding their education. Long fascinated by the writings of Maria Montessori, Bess decided that Joan was old enough for her to apply the Italian pedagogue's methods. Thus at age five the girl surprised her father with her ability to read aloud, and soon was pleased that she could master Kipling's *Jungle Book*. Becky was even more a natural reader, able to discern words by age three. Writing was a struggle for Joan, but she stubbornly practiced "the ugly markings that horrified and enraged me." Joan's second letter to her father, written on October 13, 1906, hinted at what would become a complex correspondence, sometimes distressing to both. "Why did you not write me a letter?" she rebuked. Although her mother had offered an excuse for his laxity, forthright Joan would not let him off. The note contains another line that would be repeated over the years, with variations: "Bess [Becky] and I send you a big kiss and hug." Conscientious in her role as elder sister, Joan served as Becky's representative to their father over the years. Even after Becky was old enough to write on her own, she did not often do so. Consequently, she remained much more of a stranger to her father.

Christmas of 1906 was the first Joan would remember, and among the happiest in her life. Jennie and Bess had teased the girls with stories of a wonderful holiday secret. In the afternoon Jack arrived with large boxes which, when unwrapped, revealed yet another box, like a set of Russian dolls. The final boxes held the same present for each: a muff and tippet of gray and white squirrel. Even better from their perspective, Jack did not look at his watch and rush off, as he usually did, but stayed until they were ready for bed.

For the most part, though, their father's visits were unpredictable, and when he did come by, he seemed unable to relax. Joan concluded that he was bored, as she was at times with him. Sometimes she would listen as her mother disagreed with Jack, often about his planned voyage, one theme being that he was letting the *Snark*'s contractors take advantage of him. Bess also pointed out that Roscoe Eames was a poor choice of navigator, since he had only bay sailing experience. She turned out to be correct on both counts, but Jack discounted her observations. He blamed the earthquake for his financial overruns, and assured her that Roscoe would be a fine crew member. He also seemed obsessed with fear that strangers would break into the bungalow and rob Bess and the girls while he was gone.

Although Jack earned over $3,000 just in the month of January 1907, he borrowed $5,000 against Flora's house to pay more *Snark* bills, for they could not sail until they owned it free and clear. Charmian was also unhappy because he was drinking more heavily than usual. Furthermore, Blanche Partington was in the picture again, so much so that Charmian composed a long letter to Blanche explaining what she and Jack meant to each other.[28] Blanche appeared at Glen Ellen soon afterward and upset Jack with her sharp comments, but after several days she and Charmian had "a great talk" and cleared everything up. Charmian admitted that she was a jealous person, and she knew that no woman who had loved Jack had ever gotten over it. Their reconciliation became the basis for a lifelong friendship.

With the *Snark* construction encountering one delay after another, the Londons went to Carmel again in late February 1907 for a second reunion with the Crowd. Upon their return, Jack learned that Joan was very sick and went to sit by her bedside. But he was soon off again with Charmian to Los Angeles and Las Vegas. These and other intermittent trips meant that he could not see the girls as much as they wished. "How long it was before I was able to admit and understand my childish resentment that I occupied so small and casual a place in Daddy's life," Joan reflected in old age.[29] Being so young, Becky would have little memory of this period to develop such thoughts.

By mid-April it was clear that the voyage could finally be under way. They planned to be away for seven years. Jack appeared in a gay mood to bid farewell to the girls, then grew saddened when he realized that Joan would be thirteen and Becky eleven by the time he returned. He promised to send them curios, letters, and dolls. When it was time to leave, he returned to his obsession that strangers would attack. He gave Bess a package that contained, to her horror, a revolver. As soon as Jack departed, Bess asked Charlie Milner to come over. While waiting for him, she tossed everything in the linen closet onto the floor. She had Charlie shove the package far to the back of the top shelf, then locked the door and informed the girls that she would hide the key in a secret place. She would protect them from harm without Jack's gun.

In the days that followed, Joan concluded that her father had simply abandoned her, that he was off seeing strange new places with which she must compete for his attention. During a bout with pneumonia, she determined to campaign vigorously for his attention and would do so with the only resource available, her pencil. But Joan's letters would take a long time to reach him, and the girls soon found another man to take their father's place.

# 7

# Like Children at a Circus Parade

BY 1907, THOUGH THE *SNARK* was not yet finished, Jack decided it was seaworthy enough to commence the voyage. He planned an ambitious itinerary. Hawaii was the first port of call, to be followed by a wandering journey through the South Seas, down to New Zealand, over to Australia, then through the Philippines and West Indies to Japan. After travel in Korea, China, and India, the *Snark* would sail through the Suez Canal to meander the Mediterranean. (Africa seems not even to have been considered.) There would follow explorations of countries along the Black and Baltic Seas, and trips up various rivers, including the Danube, Seine, and Thames. He wanted to spend at least one winter in port at St. Petersburg. The journey would end with an Atlantic crossing to New York no less than seven years later.

At a time when luxury steamships were now available for travel to Asia and Europe, journalists mocked the plans. Forecasting a dire end, they overlooked how experienced Jack and Charmian were in handling small sailing boats. Furthermore, they much underestimated how game both were to face the challenge of unpredictable events. They might consider it a great romance, as Charmian called the voyage, but they were much better prepared and less idealistic than the Wallings on their equally courageous political venture.

On April 22, 1907, friends crowded aboard the deck of the *Snark*, and well-wishers lined the dock to celebrate. This was to be their last meeting for seven years, the intended length of the trip. Unexpressed were thoughts that this could well be a final encounter with the Londons, for the trip was believed by many to be folly. Perhaps more open with their worries were Bess, Flora, and Jennie, none of whom attended the farewell party. They tried hard to distract Joan and Becky, who had not seen their father in three weeks, from the news accounts of the event.

In the many photographs taken of the occasion, Charmian beams with delight and enthusiasm. The only woman aboard, she would prove to be the most capable of the crew. Although she had only bay sailing experience, she readily handled her assignments at the wheel or on deck, and displayed sturdy sea legs and stomach. Her good humor and capability would earn all the crew's admiration. Bert Stolz, a Stanford engineering student who was to handle the engines, later revealed that his theoretical knowledge did not guarantee practical acumen. Since Manyoungi believed the venture to be suicidal, he had quit Jack's employ, to be replaced by Tochigi (later known as Paul Murasaki), a willing worker yet prone to seasickness. Martin Johnson, a young man from Kansas selected from many applicants around the country to handle the galley, would be the only member of the original crew to complete the entire journey with the couple. Unfamiliar with the sea, and not much of a cook, he nevertheless had the same thirst for adventure as his employers and was agreeable to doing whatever was asked.

Three weeks out, navigator Roscoe Eames proved Bess correct in her predictions of incompetence. He revealed that he was operating on a then faddish theory that the *Snark* was sailing on the inside of the earth's crust (curiously, in 1900 William Chaney had accepted a $100,000 challenge, never acknowledged, to disprove this odd cosmographic theory). Worse, he was just tossing out numbers to fool the others into thinking that he knew what he was doing. To save their lives, Jack and Martin taught themselves navigation. Spending much of the day laboring over charts and books, they assigned the wheel to Charmian, who found herself even dreaming of steering compasses.

Charmian dubbed the boat the "Inconcievable and Monstrous" for its numerous problems in construction that resulted in key parts breaking, the plumbing to fail, and much of the food to be spoiled by leaks. One day she punned on the final blow: "My great earthen bean-pot, my noble bean-pot . . . has gone to pot!"[1] It was not so funny in fact. Nonetheless, when the wind was good, the *Snark* ran like a racehorse, which encouraged the Londons' optimism that with repairs she would prove well fit for the task ahead. Charmian kept a detailed diary, steering with her feet in pleasant trade winds so she could keep up her notes. "Oh, the big sapphire hills of water, transparent and sun-shot, are topped with dazzling white that blows from crest to crest in the compelling wind." Over such waves the *Snark* slid easily "without jerks or bumps."[2]

When not on nautical duty, both Jack and Charmian continued their schedule as though on land. The *Snark*'s construction had ballooned from an estimate of $7,000 to almost $25,000, and improvements on the Glen Ellen ranch continued apace throughout the journey. (Jack had appointed Netta Eames as his business agent and property overseer, a decision he would later rue.) These expenses, not to mention the ongoing costs of the journey, had forced London to mortgage his mother's home and press George Brett again for advances on his Macmillan books. During the crossing to Hawaii, Jack wrote the majority of the Yukon stories that would make up *Lost Face,* along with more than half of the futurist tales to appear in *When God Laughs.*[3] Charmian typed the pages of manuscript scrawls, the letters he dictated, and her diary, as well as read background material to aid Jack with the magazine articles he had contracted to write as a way of paying for the voyage.

Their favorite recreation was highly competitive games of cribbage, for which Charmian kept detailed records, with the scores serving a basis for daily teasing. It was during such a game on May 17, 1907, that they spied land, a faint sighting of the volcano Haleakala. Three days later the *Snark* drifted past Diamond Head into Honolulu harbor, to the surprise of reporters who had already announced their demise.

Meanwhile, during these first six weeks Bess had prevented her daughters from becoming anxious about their father's fate. Looking back years later trying to understand this time, Joan reflected, "Too long denied by her [Bess's] passive acceptance of Daddy's wishes and desires, her inner need for direction and purpose was at last asserting itself."[4] On the wall by her vanity mirror, Bess pinned a copy of Henley's *Invictus:*

> Out of the night that covers me,
> Black as the pit from pole to pole,
> I thank whatever gods there be
> For my unconquerable soul!

Bess took a small legacy out of her savings and began to spend recklessly. "We'll go to someplace in the country where the sunshine will make you little girls well and strong, and where there will be no telephones or newspapers," she announced.[5]

With Jack gone, she was free of his beguilement, his control of her through his coy affection. She took the girls wandering around the Bay Area, spending a few weeks in the Santa Cruz Mountains, then to Carmel to stay with the Hoppers, up to Camp Meeker along the Russian River, and down to a farm in Marin County. The girls loved these and later travels, which Bess documented extensively with her camera. Her attention to their appearance is evident in their well-tailored homemade dresses and decorative hats, and their affection for one another is clear in the candid shots. Usually uncomfortable as the subject of a photograph, Bess smiles warmly in one picture as she rests languorously by a wooded stream.

Accompanying the girls was Glen, a puppy born of Brown Wolf, their father's favorite dog. While building sand castles on the Carmel beach one day, the girls were greeted by George Sterling, who told them that Glen had wolf blood in his veins. George's romantic evocation of the contrast between civilized dogs and primitive beasts fascinated the girls, although they could not see much evidence of wolf heritage in benign Glen.

Their father's letters being brief and infrequent, Joan and Becky had little to hold onto as memories of him. Being outdoors so often provided much exercise and improved their health. Bess continued to teach them wherever they went, turning hikes into field trips and any incident into an opportunity for a moral. But what most deflected any sadness over their absent father was Charles Milner. He too could have been the reason for the new happiness in Bess's face.

Milner had known Bess for many years, and was now courting her in earnest. He was a slender, handsome man with dark brown hair and mustache; his manner was patient, kind, and open. Never married, he held a well-paying job with the railroads, and would take Bess and her daughters to the best restaurants, where they ate foods with foreign names and used finger bowls. An accomplished French horn player, he introduced the girls to the delights of classical music and escorted them to matinee concerts. He amazed them with his hammered metal decorative pieces: bowls, vases, candlestick holders, and trays. His agile hands seemed able to repair anything. He was, in other words, very different from Jack London, and easily won the hearts of all three residents of the Thirty-first Street bungalow.

Jack and Charmian were oblivious to these changes occurring in the Oakland household. Once in Hawaii, they settled in for a long stay while work on the *Snark* was completed, repairs were made, and a new crew was hired. Their temporary home was a three-room canvas-sided cottage at the Seaside Hotel on Waikiki Beach. They were swamped with invitations from different segments of the Hawaiian elite, including military officers, plantation owners, ranchers, and businessmen—those most responsible for the recent overthrow of the Hawaiian monarchy —as well as members of the deposed ruling family. Jack gave his "Revolution" speech to comrades and capitalists alike, while Charmian announced that were she to be a martyr to anything, it would be socialism.

They most preferred visits to ranches, where they could enjoy the isolation and hospitality of a family, as well as daily horseback riding. Their favorite was Haleakala Ranch, managed by Louis von Tempsky. His teenage daughter Armine, a budding writer, was surprised to find Jack a "breezy, boyish-looking man with . . . a mop of rather untidy hair. Intelligence, vigor, and a gusto for life emanated from him." For ten days she joined the couple on horseback. Jack rode "like a sailor," while Charmian was "such a finished performer that I lent her Bedouin, who had never carried another woman on his back." Jack read one of Armine's manuscripts and dubbed it "tripe," but added that she had "a streak of fire" that promised success once she understood that writing was the hardest work in the world.[6]

The Londons' social schedule belies the amount of work they were accomplishing. Despite fancy dress balls, surfing, horseback riding, plantation visits, socialist lectures, and a stay at the Molokai leper colony, both continued writing. Jack completed several short stories, embarked on the novels *Martin Eden* and *Adventure,* and submitted magazine essays that would eventually be collected and published as *The Cruise of the Snark.* The original purpose of Charmian's diary was to have copies to send round-robin to friends and family. Once he read her first entries, however, Jack concluded that she had the makings of her own book and encouraged her to compose with that goal in mind. She did not always take his criticism well, and sometimes found him a tough taskmaster. Mostly, though, she took pride in his confidence that she could be an accomplished author. During the 1890s she had published several articles as well as photographs of Yosemite, and had become an experienced editor, but she had never taken her potential writing talent seriously.

Charmian's eventual published version of this part of the trip, *Our Hawaii,* conveyed its adventurous and romantic side. They were among the first whites to try surfing, which was done then on heavy twelve-foot boards, and they became enamored of the sport. She recorded poignant incidents of their stay with the lepers, such as the sight of a young girl playing the piano with stubby remnants of fingers. (Jack's essays on Molokai, which would appear soon after in *Women's Home Companion,* upset the Hawaiian elite for their frankness, yet went far toward demythologizing the disease among the mainland public.) Though Charmian viewed the Japanese farm laborers in stereotypical terms— as happy-go-lucky primitives—she admired the Polynesians for their beauty and their imaginative culture. Despite her prejudices, she recognized the feudal nature of the society, and realized that the pleasures she shared with the elite class were bought with the backbreaking labor of the field-workers.

Her private diary, kept faithfully and often cryptically in tiny day books, charted the emotional weather of her relationship with Jack. On the trip over to Hawaii, Jack was frustrated by his promise to set sail without cigarettes or alcohol. Once ashore, he returned to chain smoking, despite getting sick from the nicotine, and demanded that Netta rush him five hundred boxes of Imperiales, his favorite brand. With so many social activities involving cocktails, his intake of liquor increased. By July 31 Charmian was completely disheartened: "Mate criticizes diary; misunderstanding my attitude, and I shed many tears. My eternal loneliness. I mold myself in-so-far as I can to him; but I cannot stand irritability—nor will I mold myself so far. . . . And the cursed smoke!" On September 16 he went out alone to go drinking, then returned home to guests at dinner, where he spilled coffee all over himself and went to bed without saying good-bye to anyone. In early October he got into a fight at a bar.

Quick to take the blame, Charmian concluded that Jack resented her for revealing some things about him to others. For one who was so careful to create a public myth, even to some extent with the Crowd, such revelations were a major breach of trust. For example, he was angry that she had mentioned his smoking in her letters. (When, after his death, she published *Our Hawaii,* she noted in the preface that she had reinserted material about Jack that he had taken out because she believed that the public had the right to know all the details.) She also attributed much of his irritability to outside causes: the terrible disappointment when a work was rejected, as happened with a proposed serialization of *The Iron Heel;* the frustration over the continued breakdowns and problems on the *Snark* and the unexpected cost of the repairs.

For the most part this emotional storminess was occasional, while the shared daily rituals ensured long stretches of calm. Regardless of these flare-ups, they were committed to their mutual work; they shared similar leisure interests; they read the same books and listened to the Victrola together; they played furiously competitive games of cards; they kept up their honeymoon frequency of lovemaking. Public and private diaries each slant the story; together they remind us of the complexity of intimate relationships, and thus warn us not to depict them simplistically.

On October 7 the five-month Hawaiian idyll ended and the *Snark* set sail by an uncharted route to the Marquesas. Two weeks out Jack learned from the *South Sea Directory* that, on account of adverse wind and sea currents, their route was an "impossible traverse." However frightening, squalls were less troublesome than the doldrums, where the lack of wind frustrated the crew over the lack of progress, and the increasing tropical heat irritated them. To allay the boredom, Jack read aloud from Herman Melville and Joseph Conrad, Robert Louis Stevenson and Rudyard Kipling, Sappho and Robert Browning. Lacking a piano, Charmian entertained with songs accompanied by ukulele.

Charmian's letters to friends emphasized the natural wonders that diverted her mind, however briefly, from cockroach-ridden beds and weevil-infested food. She played up the fun of observing the dolphins and flying fish that accompanied them for days at a time, the thrill of capturing shark, albacore, and sea turtles. A crack shot, she practiced on the sea birds gliding by. "We are all like children at a circus parade," she exulted, and found contentment dangling her legs over the edge of the bow. She also limned word paintings of the seascape: "The world was a wound blue ball swathed in clouds like a jewel in white floss, covered by a blue bowl . . . and through the silent picture our white-speck boat moved upon her quest for palm and coral and mountain-isle and pearls and strange simple peoples."[7]

Fortunately, given the demands of this leg of the trip, the new crew functioned better than the first. (Eames and Stolz had been fired in Hawaii, and Tochigi quit.) Tsunekicci Wada ably devised tasty dishes from the various sea creatures pulled up on the lines or off the harpoons. The only survivor of the first leg, Martin Johnson, shifted his role to that of an able-bodied seaman. A Dutch sailor, Herrmann Visser, was well experienced and professional in attitude. Only one crew member became troublesome: J. Langbourne Warren, an ex-convict whose bad temper matched his nautical skills.

The most valued addition was Yoshimatsu Nakata, Jack's new valet, who became so attached to the couple that they became virtually inseparable for the next eight years. Charmian found him physically odd, a "brown cherub" whose black glossy hair resembled a "roughly used shoebrush," and who seemed to have "more teeth than the rest of us."[8] Despite her anti-Japanese prejudices, she soon singled him out for more praise than any other crew member. "His frank expectance of kindness, as expressed in his winning bearing, bring him goodwill all round. The captain has to hide his face repeatedly, for the sake of dignity and discipline, at some evidence of frisky humour on the part of the little brown mannikin with the homely face that his smile made beautiful."[9] Nakata and Charmian shared a zest for adventure and a pride in work, no matter the task nor one's state of mind. In her he seemed to recognize that what seemed like sacrifice to others was willing service in exchange for the exceptional life she shared with Jack London.

As on the first leg, the *Snark* did not always cooperate. The water supply leaked once more, leaving everyone unable to wash. Eventually rations became so meager that the possibility of dying from dehydration loomed grimly. The flying jib took off in a squall, and the oak beams ordered from New England were apparently somewhere else because the ones on the *Snark* were discovered to be pine. After what seemed endless hot, thirsty weeks, rains came, along with the flying fish foretelling landfall.

Approaching the South Sea islands, Charmian wondered what devastation might have resulted from the colonizing of Typee, sixty years having passed since Melville's storied evocation. On December 7 they set anchor in Taiohae Bay, where the port of Nuka Hiva welcomed guests to the Marquesas. Once again their appearance was unexpected, for newspapers had been conjecturing "Jack London and Wife Lost at Sea?" and "Old Sailors Talk of Treachery of Pacific."

In Nuka Hiva the Londons would find French bread at a bakery and a dry goods store that provided Mother Hubbard dresses to hide the women's bodies. The natives' chronic coughing was a sign of the local tuberculosis epidemic. Most Marquesans displayed other evidence of encounters with traders and intruders from Europe, who had left behind blue or green eyes, blond or straight hair. This was a far cry from the days of Melville's description of these people as the most beautiful in the South Seas.

Nonetheless, over subsequent days the adventurers were rewarded by opportunities to participate in native feasts and rituals, and to sleep in a cottage once lived in by Robert Louis Stevenson. Typee, being less contaminated by European culture, albeit ravaged by tuberculosis, was a source for carved king posts and tapa cloths, calabashes and anklets of human hair. Charmian kept meticulous notes on the weather, the customs, and the many artifacts, until she felt more like an archaeologist than a tourist. These details would provide a vivid journey for the vicarious traveler of many decades later.

Despite collecting letters from home during port stops, the Londons received no information on the fate of Anna Strunsky, who continued to live in St. Petersburg with English and her sister Rose. The trio's expectation that Bloody Sunday would lead to the czar's abdication or overthrow had proved false. Nonetheless, all three Americans remained optimistic that change would soon occur. Anna sketched an article on what was transpiring, "Russia Today," while English composed a book, to be published in 1908 as *Russia's Message.* Anna documented the denial of civil rights under the czarist autocracy, the stifling of political criticism, the jailing and exiling of protesters, and the economic exploitation of peasants. High on her list, too, was the spreading of religious intolerance, by which she meant the treatment of the Jews, who were denied education, entry into professions, and most property rights, were restricted in movement and place of residence, and were victims of state-provoked violence. She hoped that the United States would provide assistance just as the French had done during the American Revolution. English's book was to be the first of twelve he would complete and publish over the next twenty years. Anna's article would be one of many she would work at yet never see in print. The self-inhibiting patterns exhibited with her aborted novel *Windlestraws* would mark all her attempts as a writer. Blessed with frequent inspiration, she was nevertheless weak on execution.

It was not all Anna's fault, though, that she would not achieve her goal. English was judgmental, arrogant, and condescending toward her as both a writer and an intellectual. He was that way with almost everyone he encountered, and it was only because of his excess of other qualities, such as his energy, commitment, and devotion to a cause, that associates tolerated him. He seemed oblivious to the effects of his abusive commentary on others, and doubtless believed that he was merely offering logical counterarguments or supportive suggestions. But the tone of his critiques could be brutal, and they were not reserved for private encounters. Anna's melancholy left her vulnerable to his dinner table affronts, and she was temperamentally incapable of either standing up to him or turning a deaf ear.

Given this marital dynamic, it is not surprising that Anna would pull Rose closer, that her most intimate relationship throughout her life would be with her younger sister. In turn, Rose was to enjoy the advantages of being related to English, such as the opportunity to participate in this momentous episode in

Russian history, as well as at times partake in the comforts of his wealth, though without bearing the costs Anna paid.

Once Anna realized that her husband was not like Jack, that is, frankly encouraging of a woman's interests and talents, she swallowed her pride and concluded that other things were more important than fulfilling her own destiny. For one, with peasants, protesters, and professors being rounded up and tortured, she could not feel sorry for herself. She also understood that English's ill temper was in part the result of frustration over his helplessness in the presence of so many who were suffering. He had a martyr's passion, single-minded and ready to sacrifice anyone, even those he dearly loved, for the sake of a larger cause. Furthermore, she believed that his talents should go first to the cause, and it was her position to serve the cause by seeing to his needs.

Anna and Rose became even more fearless in gathering information and providing intelligence to activist groups. Pogroms executed by the Cossack "Black Hundreds" increased, and random violence spread as a result of the deliberate dissemination of fictions such as of Jews sacrificing Christian children during their worship services. When Odessa became the center of anti-Semitic fervor, then Anna made certain that she went there to see for herself. When friends asked them to hide a comrade who had escaped a Riga prison, Rose nursed the man's broken ribs and saber wounds, and Anna took him in a sleigh to a Finnish railroad station, lying to authorities that he was her husband. Anna's notes reveal her special admiration for the Russian women, who "stood shoulder to shoulder with the men, marched to Siberia and mounted the scaffold." A particular heroine was poet Vera Zusalich, who inspired listeners "in the glow of her beauty, somewhat dulled after several years of suffering, personifying the glory and greatness of the Movement."[10]

Although Anna met the now sainted Leo Tolstoy, giving him a copy of *The Kempton-Wace Letters,* still on the shelves of the Yasnaya Polyana museum, she thought his theories naive. Rather than attacking class inequities, he provided his peasants with education, medical aid, and good food. She preferred Maksim Gorky, who, unlike Tolstoy, did not try to merge himself with the people, but wrote of the people's struggle. Gorky introduced the Wallings to other Russian artists, and they in turn arranged for him a literary tour of the States. Anna was moved to note how "vanity and career are completely worthless and naive attributes . . . to the Russian [writers]," who merged themselves with the Revolution.

On October 21, 1907, while the *Snark* crew was reveling over the sight of a coppery moon in a purple sky, the Strunsky-Walling trio was placed under arrest. They had been dining at the Hotel de France with four members of the Finnish Progressive Party, who had also been taken in by the police. Their rooms and baggage were searched, many of their books confiscated, and much of their documentary material carted away. English was accused of financially supporting the revolutionists and was sent to prison. Rose, considered the most important captive, was locked up in a new jail, built recently for use by the government's secret police. Anna was sent to the Women's Prison.

Their incarceration could not have been a complete surprise, for the secret police had been trailing them since their arrival. English had just returned to Russia after spending several months in Germany and France, where he had attended conferences of various socialist organizations. His reappearance, and the potential consequences of any new information and plans he might have brought, perhaps provoked the police action. But it could also be that Rose, so involved with the Finnish revolutionaries, was seen as the real threat.

Being Russian-born Jews, the two sisters must have had particularly frightening moments, for they could not be certain that the government would honor their American citizenship. American papers broadcast the arrests— "Arrest of Wallings Forces U.S. Protest to the Czar"—and Secretary of State Elihu Root cabled the American embassy in Moscow to get the three out. Within two days, all three were released from prison and sent packing out of the country. There would be no martyrdom on the barricades after all.

Oblivious to the trials of the Wallings, on December 27 the Londons sailed into the harbor at Papeete in Tahiti. There an enormous pile of mail awaited, much of which outlined a financial morass that would require Jack's direct intervention to untangle. Without Jack's approval, Netta Eames had canceled several bank accounts on which he had continued to write checks, spent thousands of dollars on unauthorized renovations to her home, doubled her salary, and made a mess of several writing contracts. She had even allowed a bank manager who had read a false report about the *Snark* being lost at sea to foreclose on Flora's house. The only welcome enclosures were the newly published copies of *Love of Life* and *The Road*. Netta would later blame Eliza Shepard for some of her bad decisions, an accusation that suggested her determination to keep her supremacy over Eliza in Jack's eyes.

Thus, on January 13, 1908, Jack and Charmian interrupted their journey and set sail for San Francisco on the *Mariposa*. The Crowd met them at the dock, celebrated with them at dinner, and then joined them at the Orpheum Theater for a show. Most of the couple's time during their ten days in the Bay Area was passed with friends, Charmian's relatives, and Eliza. One afternoon they visited Mabel Applegarth, now an invalid with an advanced case of tuberculosis.

Jack visited the girls only once, and even then in a perfunctory manner. One night Joan felt her mother nuzzle her awake. She opened her eyes to see her father. Hugging him brought back the long-suppressed feeling of loss, and she quickly spilled out stories of recent happenings until she became breathless. He apologized for not sending the dolls he had promised, and slipped a gold coin under her pillow. Thoughtlessly, he did not even awaken Becky. Although Joan waited expectantly for his return that week, she did not hear from him until a phone call the evening before he sailed.

During that brief visit Joan unwittingly planted the seed for a vine of cruel emotions that would entangle most of the extended London clan. During her tale-telling she had mentioned the fun they'd been having with "Uncle Charlie." In previous letters Joan had described how he had built them a coaster that both she and Becky enjoyed riding, in another how he was teaching her to swim. London had reason to be jealous, for as Joan later recalled, Charles Milner was "for a brief time, more of a father to us than Daddy would ever be."[11] Indeed, Milner represented the new Progressive ideals of fatherhood, taking an active interest in the children's activities and development. Joan looked forward to his becoming a stepfather. He would never replace her daddy, she believed, but his was a presence she treasured.

What she did not learn until years later was that Jack had come upon Bess and Milner in the parlor that night, and a furious argument ensued over ownership of the Thirty-first Street bungalow. Until then, Bess had not realized that the divorce agreement granted her use of but not title to the house. She wanted to secure the place so the girls would not have to move if she remarried. As a result of the argument, Jack signed an agreement with Bess and Milner that upon their marriage, they could buy the house for $4,500. For Joan to refer innocently to "Uncle Charlie" right after that dispute thus aggravated an already heated situation.

London's subsequent actions are so obsessively focused on money as to suggest reasons beyond finances for the almost paranoid vindictiveness that followed. He was feeling financial strain at the time, but he was also increasingly ill throughout this period. Upon returning to Tahiti, Jack wrote to Eliza and asked her to consult his lawyer with regard to his divorce settlement. Would Bess be able to sue for her insurance policies and have the other two policies revert to the daughters? Would his entire divorce agreement be declared null and void, meaning that Bess and the children "could participate in all my estate at time of my death, and in royalties, past, present, and future, on all my writings?"[12] He also wrote Bess and Charlie from the *Snark* that, were they to sell the Thirty-first Street house, he was to get the profits. In other words, Bess would buy not the house but only a life interest in it.

In a rare act of self-assertion, Bess challenged these new demands.[13] The arithmetic made no sense. If she and Charlie married, Jack would receive $4,500 in cash, which he could invest, while the couple planned to put $2,000 into improvements in the building, making their outlay $6,500: "In other words you want the profit on $11,000 for the use of $4500. What do you think of that?" Furthermore, she reminded him, "When I marry your little girls will have their share of Charlie's estate just the same as they have of yours. Do be just Jack."

Next Bess criticized his decision to change his life insurance policies. At the time of the breakup, he had six life insurance policies, four naming Bess and two the girls as beneficiaries. He was considering changing the policies to benefit Charmian instead of Bess. During the January visit he had challenged her to consult a lawyer concerning his plan; she now responded that her lawyer had advised her against it. "Jack, I signed away my rights to your community property with the understanding I was to have the insurance instead." Reminding him that she had "worked hand in hand with him from the beginning," she asserted that she had the right to more than just the "little furniture" she had received at the divorce. Bess made a counteroffer, whereby she would give him $1,000 cash additional for a life interest in the house outright and give up all claims to $4,000 in life insurance. This letter did not reach him for six months, until the fall of 1908. By that point, the couple had decided to build their own home, but the matter was not over so far as Jack was concerned.

When Jack read Bess's much-delayed letter, he responded with a counteroffer of his own.[14] He was not out to take advantage of the couple; he wished only that the contract for their purchase of the house should grant him a right to buy the place for $4,500, and he would also pay for any improvements they made. He was not trying to make a profit from them, he argued. Rather, he was making the couple a gift, the use of the house for twenty years. If they wanted a house that was an investment, they should "go out in the market and buy one on more favorable terms."

The tone of this lengthy letter was vitriolic. Jack attacked Bess for assuming that she could remain a beneficiary of his insurance despite her forthcoming marriage, thus sidestepping the fact that this was among her few rights under the divorce settlement. He harangued her and Milner for being "out to drag money out of me" and "rob" him, to "mulct me of several thousand dollars for use of yourself and your second husband." Referring to the divorce complaint, he accused her of "damnable lies" that blackened not only him but also the children. In case his repetitious fury did not make its point, he countered that he would "fight, fight, fight until there is not a penny left for anybody to get."

In concluding his diatribe, Jack advised that owing to the *Snark* expenses, he was cutting his monthly contribution back to sixty-five dollars a month (which he soon learned he could not do legally). True to his word, he instructed Netta Eames to change his insurance policies so that all those naming Bess as beneficiary would now substitute his daughters, while all those naming his daughters would now substitute Charmian and Eliza. He had all his property homesteaded in Charmian's name "so that it is untouchable" to Bess. Should Bess show signs of a fight, Netta was to sell his mother's home and "work out a scheme where the money is untouchable," even place it in a foreign bank if necessary.[15]

The next day Jack sent Becky a letter in which he enclosed "two ear-rings which the savages here [in the Solomon Islands] wear." He remarked that he was writing a novel (*Adventure*) in which he had named the lead character Joan, and that in the future he would name a girl in a book after her (though he never did so).[16] This letter was typically brief, lacking in any account of his adventures, and, in Joan's words, "failing utterly to bridge the space and time that lengthened steadily between us."[17] Other notes offered repeated excuses for not yet having sent them the promised dolls.

On February 24, 1909, Jack wrote his sister Eliza that he had not heard anything from Bess or his daughters since sending the "hot letter," and added that he intended to "make things warm for [Bess]" when he returned home.[18] These threats were made despite the fact that he'd received no evidence that Bess was going to press her case. In fact, by then she and her daughters were focused on the future. Joan continued to write her father sporadically and dutifully, and was not surprised later to discover that he never kept those letters from her.[19]

Bess and Milner were not formally engaged until April 22, 1909, a year after their disagreeable encounter with Jack. "I wish to cremate memory of Jack London and have a home with children . . . my highest resources," she added to her public announcement.[20] Eventually they decided to build their own home rather than stay on Thirty-first Street. After dinner every evening the family would gather around the table and discuss the plans Milner was designing. Almost every Sunday they would walk to the lot on Jean Street, overlooking small farms and a creek running through what was then called Pleasant Valley (now bustling Grand Avenue). He would pace off the plot and point out to the girls the location of the French doors leading to the back garden, their bedroom, study, and bath suite. The girls, and no doubt their mother, looked forward to the day when they would move into this marvelous, sunny home, never suspecting that their father would interfere.

One cannot help but wonder that this situation might not have spun out of control had the various actors been in proximity. When Bess's assertive letter caught up with Jack, it was already moot, but he had no way of knowing that. And it could not have fallen into his hands at a worse point in the journey. London's short stories inspired by his South Seas sojourn follow the arc of Joseph Conrad's "Heart of Darkness." One of Jack's favorite tales, it concerns the white man's horror at entering the territory of seemingly savage people. Jack and Charmian encountered a similarly heightened sense of threat and terror as they traveled westward from the melting pot culture of the Marquesans through

Tahiti and Samoa to the islands of the Melanesians, where colonialism had imposed slavery rather than neat imitations of European village life.

The couple's scientific readings naturally colored their observations. They had absorbed Ernest Haeckel's racial hierarchy, which categorized humans by skin color and hair texture. To Haeckel the lowest sub-races were woolly or fleecy-haired; Charmian's diary entries noted that the Fijians were "frizzle-headed man-eaters." Invoking the parlance of the day, the Londons remarked on the naked "niggers," the "grinning, apelike creatures" who pierced their ears with clam-shells, keys, even doorknobs. They would espouse these views in their separate books on the journey, like the French filmmakers they encountered who were composing a documentary on what seemed to them fearsome, beastly peoples.

These derogatory beliefs, however, did not deter the couple from spending several days visiting Melanesian villages, where they were entertained by dancers, joined fish dynamiting expeditions, and traded for artifacts. Charmian and Nakata needed several days to clean and pack beautifully wrought pearl shell fishhooks, carved boxes of wood and bamboo, woven basket bags, turtle shell nose rings, finely etched clamshell armlets, and other curios bartered for tobacco and beads. Jack was taken to a men's house; he teased Charmian for being a "taboo Mary," forbidden to enter. Their hosts boasted in pidgin English of the men they had killed, but all denied ever having eaten human flesh. Charmian's account blended disparaging descriptions of this people's appearance with admiration for their art. What seemed the ultimate proof of their inferiority was not their odd decor nor even their history of aggression but their physical dirtiness. She washed her hands after returning from a visit with a chief, not because he was a murderer, but because his hands were so filthy. And as with all the cultures she documented, she gave an unusually sympathetic account of women's lives under the rule of patriarchy.

Still, ideology confronted just enough reality to seem fully valid. When Jack wrote Sterling that the Solomon Islanders were "about the rawest edge of the world. Headhunting, cannibalism, and murder are rampant," he was exaggerating though not fully inventing.[21] Tribal culture incorporated revenge murders, and it was natural that these people, hunted down for copra plantation enslavement, would use their weapons and wiles against their white oppressors as they did against their island enemies. One day the Londons took a ride on a slave-catching vessel and were ambushed by islanders. (They refused to use their guns when serious violence seemed imminent, but resorted to stratagems to end the onslaught.) Several Westerners the Londons stayed with were later murdered—one beheaded—by indigenous people. Jack would incorporate Haeckel's theory into Adventure, much of which is constructed around their stay at Penduffryn Plantation on Guadalcanal. In that novel Hawaiian-born Joan Lackland, sympathetic to native peoples because of her experience with

Polynesians, is shipwrecked on a copra plantation in the Solomons and gradually comes to accept the harsh racialist views of the owner.

As in Hawaii, the Londons enjoyed the company of the islands' elite, this time plantation managers living in heavily armed stockades. At Penduffryn Plantation there were lazy days of partying, including a costume party, and a several-day binge on hashish. Such cavorting seemed necessary to offset the ever-present fear of attack from the plantation workers.

Equally threatening in this part of the Pacific was disease. Since leaving Samoa, the crew had been beleaguered by multiple ailments, including malarial fever, yaws (an ulcerous skin condition), and "scratch scratch," another nasty skin disorder. They took quinine tablets and doctored their skin with peroxide and corrosive sublimate. Martin Johnson may have acquired a venereal disease on an island where, Charmian noted, he also likely left behind a future offspring. A crew member picked up in Samoa almost succumbed to the often fatal black-water fever. Nakata suffered terribly from hemorrhoids, as did Jack, whose gums also became inflamed and infected. Most troublesome were Jack's hands, which swelled so badly that he could not hold a pen, while the skin peeled continually, and the nails on his fingers and toes grew exceedingly thick, probably from a fungus. Being the hardiest of the bunch, Charmian overworked herself, seldom slept, and developed neurasthenia. In time no one could manage much more than the minimal tasks necessary for survival. ("Jack is sleeping with one eye half open, and I wish he would either close it or wake up, he looks so ghastly.")[22]

The trip would have to end, though it would be several months before that conclusion was accepted. Leaving the *Snark* behind in Guadalcanal for repairs, Charmian, Jack, Martin, and Nakata took a steamer to Sydney, where they expected that expert medical care would return all to full enough health to return to the *Snark* and continue the circumnavigation. But "how blindly we plan," wrote Charmian. "How little we thought, that starry, musky night under the Southern Cross . . . that this would be the last time we should ever descend her teak gangway ladder."[23]

On November 14, 1908, they reached Sydney and immediately underwent medical treatment. Jack's bowel problems were diagnosed as fistulas which would need to be removed; his skin condition was diagnosed as psoriasis. The problem with his hands and nails remained puzzling. Charmian's intermittent malarial fevers, nervous anxieties, and heart palpitations continued to distract her, but she stayed with Jack and slept in the other bed in his hospital room throughout his recovery from surgery. In December he told her of his decision to end the adventure; he needed to return to his native climate. A year later he would come across Charles Woodruff's book *The Effects of Tropical Light on White Man*, which argued that racial types were adaptations to particular environments; hence the white man could not thrive in the tropics, whereas darker-skinned peoples did. That pseudoscientific text reassured him that his physical reactions had been predictable.

Adversity seldom defeated Charmian or Jack, whose insistence on returning to a normal life protracted rather than hastened their recuperation. They went out to plays and restaurants. Jack tried to write as often as possible and took on assignments for Australian newspapers. The most notable of his journalistic work was his coverage of the Burns-Johnson fight, which Charmian attended in drag because women were not allowed at boxing matches. Indeed, throughout their stay she drew attention for her outspoken refusal to submit to Australia's strong gender discrimination. Continuing to suffer from fever and pain, they went to a resort in Tasmania for a month, yet seldom rested.

Jack's unabated anger toward Bess revealed itself in a new will composed in Tasmania on February 6. He appointed George Sterling, Eliza Shepard, and a lawyer as executors, with the specification that they were to consult Charmian on any matters concerning his books and translations. Bess was to have the use of the Thirty-first Street home, but maintain it herself. The girls were to be supported from the insurance funds according to a detailed schedule whereby they would get twenty dollars a month at age fourteen and up to a maximum of fifty dollars at age twenty. In his most serious attack on Bess, Charmian was to "personally house and manage" the girls. She was also to inherit all property, which was to go to Joan and Becky at her death. If she remarried, the girls were to receive only his "peculiarly personal" belongings, such as photographs and his manuscripts. As in his earlier wills, he provided for support of Flora, Jennie, and Eliza, who was to be business agent and manager of the estate.

Charmian could have no better proof of his devotion, though what she valued most were his inscriptions to her in presentation copies of his books. Inside the copy of *The Road*, he wrote:

> Whose efficient hands I love—the hands that have worked for me long hours and many, swiftly and deftly, and beautifully in the making of music; the hands that have steered the Snark through wild passages and rough seas, that do not tremble on a trigger, that are sure and strong on the reins of a thoroughbred or of an untamed Marquesan stallion; the hands that are sweet with love as they pass through my hair, firm with comradeship as they grip mine, and that soothe as only they of all hands in the world can soothe.

Despite all Bess Maddern's good qualities—her honesty, intelligence, steadfastness, devotion to her daughters—she could never have garnered such moving ardor from Jack. And now, with his latest will assigning care of his daughters to Charmian, he was even denying her the one role he had always honored, that of Mother-Girl.

It was April 8 before Jack and Charmian felt well enough to board the *Tymeric* for the journey home. Before departing, Jack advanced Martin Johnson money to carry out his own plans to continue around the world. Martin was now inspired by having met the filmmakers on Penduffryn to make a career combining his skills in photography with adventure.. He also resolved to find a wife like Charmian: brave and enterprising yet cheerful and feminine. When Nakata expressed his desire to stay on with the Londons, Jack obtained the papers from the Japanese consul in Sydney to help the young man enter the United States.

The *Tymeric* was a coal freighter, not a passenger liner, so the Londons and Nakata officially signed on as crew. It was six weeks, mid-June, before the ship reached Guayaquil in Ecuador. From there they took what is still the most dangerous train trip in the world and found it deserving of that reputation, what with avalanches crashing down across the tracks and news of train wrecks ahead. Following three weeks in Quito, they slowly wended their way northward through Central America. Jack wrote Joan that he would be home soon, news that surprised her because she had been marking off the days until 1914 for his return. It was July 21, 1909, before the Londons stepped down from a train into the Oakland terminal. In typical fashion they went not home to rest but out to dinner with Eliza, to the Idora amusement park with nephew Johnny Miller, and then to the Orpheum Theater. The next day Jack arranged to meet his daughters and take them to luncheon with the Sterlings.

According to Joan, the reunion was somewhat strained. George was familiar to the girls, but Carrie had disappeared from their lives at the time of their parents' separation. Jack seemed uncertain what to say to his daughters, now eight and six. George and Jack kept ordering rounds of martinis and lemonade for the girls, who were intimidated by the accumulation of full glasses before them. (Becky later denied that their father ever drank in their presence.) At the end of the afternoon Jack realized that the girls had not had much fun listening to him banter with the Sterlings, so he made it up to them by taking them to the city the next day. It was a day Joan never forgot, and was never to recur. Jack gave his undivided attention to his daughters, asked them about their interests, and took them on a shopping spree that included engraved coin purses from a jeweler and strands of colorful ribbons. Becky loved to see how her father was greeted on the street, how friendly he was to all, and generous with his tipping. Their daddy was back, and all was forgiven.

Upon returning, the Londons caught up with news of Anna and English. For Anna, the arrest in 1907 had been a heady conclusion to her stay in Russia. She left full of hope, for she was six months pregnant, and expected to complete a book on her Russian experiences in time for the birth of the baby. The couple moved to a fashionable residential hotel in Paris, where English insisted on the best physicians and most luxurious comforts for Anna. On February 8, 1908, Anna gave birth in her hotel bedroom to a daughter, Rosalind. Five days later English found their perfect child blue and cold on Anna's breast. Afterward, she blamed the nurse for the infant's illness and for failing to call the doctor. Over the years, stories of the nurse's culpability grew more sensational—that she poisoned the child, for example. What really occurred, and whether anyone was to blame, is unclear, for English had passed those days alone in the den writing, while Anna was too exhausted to know much about the baby's care.

Characteristically, Anna's grief was so dramatically expressed as to worry family and friends about her stability. They counseled her to put it all in perspective. Her mother, after all, had lost four children. Anna rebuffed their attempts and turned to her in-laws, whose sympathetic correspondence reinforced her sense of victimization. In thanks, she decided to adopt their name, and now called herself Anna Walling.

In Paris, both socialism and art drew her back into society. There were meetings with Russian exiles, café evenings with endless conversation about politics and gossip, and visits to studios of artists such as Picasso, guided by her friends Gertrude and Leo Stein. That summer, on the return trip to America, English took her on a tour of the British Isles. There she conceived a philosophy of their relationship. They would be lovers, yet not husband and wife, best friends, yet enjoy their partially separate ways. She would have his children, do her work, see her own friends, and travel, knowing that he would be alongside "as far as he loves me . . . as far as his life permits."[24]

Soon after they settled in New York, a frightful episode occurred in Springfield, Illinois, that would change the direction of Anna and English Walling's lives. While preparing for the centennial of the birth of that city's most famous son, Abraham Lincoln, on August 15, 1908, a violent and bloody race riot exploded in response to the sensational news of a rape. Frustrated when the alleged perpetrator was swept off to another jail for his protection, a mob burned black-owned businesses, beat up blacks, set fire to their residential area, attacked those who tried to flee, and ultimately turned on the police as well. Bullets were fired on all three sides—rioting whites, blacks, and police—resulting in the death of four white spectators. Rioters then shot, hanged, and mutilated an elderly black barber, and cut the throat of an eighty-four-year-old black cobbler. Not even battalions of state militia could quell the violence, although their presence enabled many members of the black community to escape to safety.

Among those who reported on the outbreak was English, who rushed to the city with Anna as soon as they heard the news. Having witnessed Cossack raids in Russia, they were outraged that similar behavior was occurring in their own country. Both composed articles about the event, but characteristically it was English who finished his and got it in print. His powerful report in the *Independent*, a journal popular with social activists, presciently observed that the event was part of a coming "race war." Noting that the black population was too small to be a threat to white supremacy, he blamed the Springfield press for inflaming public opinion. Most egregious for him were the news articles hinting that in the South, people knew how to respond to such a crime, that is, through lynching. Equally shocking to him was that white residents remained defiant and unashamed of the national notoriety. Even after the rape victim recanted and admitted that a white man had been the assailant, they continued to deny their responsibility. They refused to let blacks return to their jobs, and storekeepers would not allow them to make purchases. Walling deplored the standard northern reaction, that mitigating circumstances had resulted in the murders. "Who realizes the seriousness of the situation? What large and powerful body of citizens is ready to come to [the blacks'] aid?"[25]

Although there had been some rallying around racial issues in recent years, thanks to such spokespeople as Ida B. Wells, Booker T. Washington, and W. E. B. DuBois, few listened. Just as Jack London had been convinced of black inferiority, so too were most whites. The Supreme Court had sanctioned segregation; social scientists had "proved" racial inferiority; professors taught racialism at the leading universities; politicians continued to devise restrictive laws. Even most blacks supported the gradualist ideas of Booker T. Washington, based on the premise that they must prove themselves, mainly in the workplace, before they could expect their rights. Thus when English Walling called for new action, he was defying deeply held beliefs, analogous to Einstein's announcing that time was relative.

All the more amazing was that English had, up to the time of the riots, been a rockbound racialist. His maternal ancestors had been Kentucky slave owners. In college he was insulted when he had to share a table one day with a black person, and his letters invoked the typical derogatory terms and stereotypes. Anna's thoughts on race were notable for their absence: she was oblivious to racial issues in the United States. It was her own ethnicity that was most on her mind. But having observed the terrors in Russia, the murders, exiles to Siberia, imprisonments, and executions, both feared that a similar fate could await blacks in the United States. They suddenly saw the world as more complicated, with societal problems based on more than just class inequities.

Soon after the publication of English's article, a white socialist social worker, Mary Ovington, sought him out. She had been studying the conditions of blacks in New York City for over four years, and, being descended from abolitionists, was a fervent supporter of civil rights. As she recalled of Walling, "Here was a white man who called upon both races, in the spirit of the abolitionist to come forward and right the nation's wrongs."[26] She met the couple after a lecture English gave comparing Russia and America, and suggested that the three of them work together on an idea he had conceived, that of a national biracial organization to right the wrongs of racial injustice.

During a meeting, the threesome decided to draw up a strong statement, to be published on Lincoln's birthday, calling for a conference on racial issues. Already well connected among activists in New York, they were able to draw in well-known white educators, publicists, social workers, churchmen, and writers to sign "The Call." Oswald Garrison Villard, grandson of abolitionist William Lloyd Garrison, wrote the statement, which reiterated the wrongs Lincoln would find were he to appear again. The white press mostly ignored the proposal, but word of mouth spread through the activist communities of both races. In particular, those blacks who were unhappy with the more conciliatory Booker T. Washington's dominance of racial policy were quick to participate. Over subsequent months the gatherings at the Walling apartment grew so large that they had to find a new meeting place. The organization would come to be known as the National Association for the Advancement of Colored People.

Though over the next few years Anna would join English at conferences and make her own speeches on behalf of black rights, she did so despite further private sorrow. Several days before "The Call" was published, and on the first anniversary of Rosalind's death, she miscarried at three and a half months. Eventually she put partial blame on her own brother Max, who had prescribed a medication for nausea just before the miscarriage. But her immediate response was that she was ill fated, and that she could not survive the horror of the loss. Just as she had accepted Walling as her surname after the death of Rosalind, this time she decided to wear a wedding ring, engraved "English—June 28, 1906." Now strangers would no longer misunderstand their relationship.

Perhaps she saw the ring a talisman, a necessary sacrifice to the gods of conventionality for a child. She would be pregnant again within several months, delivering daughter Rosamund in January 1910. Three other healthy children would follow. Each pregnancy, though, was marked by uneasiness over the outcome, and each newborn baby was hovered over for weeks until its vitality convinced her of its survival. Socialism and civil rights, those great callings, still mattered, but could not help but seem paltry at times in comparison to the possibility of a new, unique offspring of her and her beloved's mating.

# 8

# Mother-Girl, Mother-Not

"WILL WE EVER BE ALONE? Where is the quiet of the country? And our old long days on horseback in the hills?"[1] Their return to Wake Robin and Glen Ellen in July 1909, Charmian discovered, brought little solitude. Guests arrived and, for her, outstayed their welcome. Cloudesley Johns brought his wife for a month, and when they finally left, Charmian commented in her diary that they had "grown fat" on her hospitality. George Sterling showed up drunk one day, made a scene over a woman, and was ordered by Jack to leave. Another evening at dinner a woman, likely Blanche Partington, angered Jack so much during a conversation that he threw beer in her face. Such prickly responses were unusual for the couple, evidence that they were still suffering nervous exhaustion from their various tropical ailments and grief over their aborted trip.

While Jack was off at the Bohemian Club Hi-Jinks, the annual camp and "fol-de-rol" in the redwoods near the Russian River, Charmian had a few days of quiet. August and September are the hottest months in the Valley of the Moon, a time of high fire danger because most years no rain has fallen for three or four months. "I've had a funny feeling of fire and catastrophe for some time now," she admitted in early August.[2] Her apprehension proved correct when a fire was set accidentally on the ranch by two teenage boys who had been using the swimming pool below the dam Jack had built on Graham Creek. Although several ranch workers came upon the fire soon after it started, some acreage burned. Thanks to an eyewitness account, Charmian located the youths and calmly explained that they had to be more careful. The boys were very repentant.

Though she handled this crisis with equanimity, within a month Charmian feared that her mind was going. Friends suggested that she find some quiet retreat to calm her shattered nerves. Consequently, in October, when Jack went off on a long sailing trip with the Crowd, Charmian went to Burke's Sanitarium, a nearby rest spa. She dreamt of Jack leaving her—understandably, given what had transpired on his last cruise with his friends—and of fires and earthquakes. Jack wrote loving notes, and praised her bravery through her depression, her willingness to face her demons and take the cure. While away, he bought her a

.22 caliber Winchester automatic rifle and five hundred rounds of ammunition, and reminded her that Eliza welcomed any call for assistance.

After a month's absence, Jack returned and crawled into bed beside Charmian to confess that he had not been well either. They read aloud H. G. Wells's *Ann Veronica*, a novel that had led many in England to ostracize the author for challenging Victorian norms of sexuality. The heroine of the novel defies her father, flees from home to attend a scientific school, where she falls in love with a teacher whose marriage is failing. Though demanding to be free, she settles for a conventional marriage. The attraction of the book for the couple is apparent; Jack commented that it seemed to portray their own relationship, their worship of each other. This reaffirmation may have influenced their decision to leave Wake Robin and move onto the ranch property as soon as possible.

Charmian was now suffering indigestion and bloating, with her periods arriving every two weeks. She wondered if her liver was the cause. On December 29 she realized that, at age thirty-eight, she was pregnant. "Mate's proud as a peacock and I'm pretty interested and happy myself," she wrote in relief.[3] They decided on the names Mate for a boy, Joy (the meaning of the Greek "Charmian") for a girl. Jack was composing the final scenes of *Burning Daylight,* whose main character, Dede Mason, incorporates Charmian's personal history and character. As was his habit, he wove into the plot this latest incident from his life, the expectation of a child.

In February 1910 the couple went to Carmel, by now a most self-conscious artists' colony owing to the arrival of new blood from outside the Bay Area. One newcomer was fellow socialist Upton Sinclair. He arrived with a pack of followers, most of whom had belonged to his short-lived experimental community in New Jersey, Helicon Hall. The Crowd ridiculed Sinclair as a zealot for all his causes, whether for Kellogg's vegetarian diets, enemas, opposition to smoking, or, worst of all, teetotalism. (Years later Sinclair would pay them back in kind by denouncing members of the Crowd for having sacrificed their talents to the goddess of drink.)

Accompanying Sinclair were the socialists Mary and Gaylord Wilshire. Despite his politics, Wilshire specialized in real estate deals, some of them shady. A major boulevard in Los Angeles would be named in his honor. London and others in the Crowd, along with Sinclair, were soon among Wilshire's victims, for who better to exploit than fellow socialists hoping to make a killing in capitalism? Charmian and Mary, however, found the pursuit of money and fame less interesting than the pursuit of women's friendship.

One of Sinclair's young acolytes made a better impression. Carrie described the recent Yale graduate to Blanche Partington as "homely as Broadway in Oakland. He's tall, red-headed, has a bad complexion and bulbous nose, but is lively company and bright."[4] The young man, Sinclair Lewis, known then as "Hal," shared a cabin with William Rose Benét, who would also one day achieve literary fame. In 1910, however, they were living impoverished in the midst of more established artists, in expectation that some of the success would rub off. Benét was busy writing poems, but Lewis, profligate in spinning plots, had yet to acquire the self-discipline to fill them out in the day-to-day slog of writing a novel.

When the Londons arrived, they were accompanied by two Japanese servants and Ernst Untermann, a socialist painter who had recently translated Marx's *Das Kapital* into English for an American public. Mary Austin had moved to Europe, where she was cutting a swath through English society while, she thought wrongly, dying of breast cancer. Consequently, she left no reminiscences from this period. Hal Lewis took Austin's place, hanging around Jack, seeking to learn how he could become like his ideal, a self-made, well-off artist, adventurer, and successful writer. He was surprised that, after hours of writing, Jack preferred to play bridge, that he had "become a country gent," interested in pig breeding and polite literary conversations. The high point for Lewis was when Jack read aloud from *The Wings of the Dove,* "James's sliding, slithering, glittering verbiage," eventually to slam the book down and wail, "Do any of you know what all this junk is about?" London then gave a spontaneous lecture on the clash in American culture "between Main Street and Beacon Street," a rift that remains today.[5]

Aware of Lewis's impecunious state, Jack offered to buy some of his plots at five dollars per story line. Lewis agreed, and Jack wrote a check for seventy dollars. When Jack shared one of the stories with Charmian afterward, she commented that it was "*awful, astounding*—worse ever."[6] London used ideas from only three of the fourteen plots, though he continued to correspond with the young man afterward and bought other unused ideas. His motive was, according to Mary Austin, who had earlier seen Jack buy plots from other writers, "chiefly a generous camouflage for help that could not be asked . . . otherwise."[7]

Following one raucous dinner with the Crowd, Charmian grew deadly tired of everyone getting drunk. George had discovered a new French liqueur, Amer Picon, and devised a lethal punch which he poured liberally at meals. Jack's alcohol consumption always surged in George's company, where Charmian could not exert her restraining influence. Jack grew testy one day and exclaimed that he wished she wouldn't make him love her in public, a charge that puzzled her. There may have been some basis to his complaint, for she sometimes left observers with the impression that she was forcing the image of a great romance. Whenever Jack became upset with Charmian, he usually followed up with a present as an apology, in this case the Steinway baby grand piano she had always desired.

The pregnancy was not an easy one, leaving Charmian to feel more harassed than blessed by the growing addition to the family. When she felt particularly ill, Carrie Sterling gave her rubdowns. (The years' separation had resolved any remaining ill feelings between Carrie and Charmian.) Carrie was eating humble pie, for George had fallen in love with another woman, which was much harder for her to bear than his usual brief sexual flings. In April, Charmian welcomed visits from both Carrie and Blanche to the ranch, for the three found they had a common bond the men in the Crowd could not disrupt. Now they were all less willing to play supporting cast, and had outgrown their youthful cattiness toward one another.

Another woman Charmian enjoyed was Emma Goldman, who arrived on April 30 with her lover Ben Reitman. She found Emma "not remarkable intellectually, but . . . a good, clean, wholesome, loveable woman—though many may not guess it."[8] As a token of friendship, she gave her guest a fine lace hanky. Emma found Charmian witty, very intelligent, and spirited, sewing "on the outfit for the baby while we argued, joked and drank into the wee hours of the morning."[9] Jack was his usual boisterous self, quick to prick the ideological balloons of his anarchist guests and play practical jokes on them. Goldman admired Jack's "humanity, his understanding of and his feeling with the complexities of the human heart." He argued without rancor, and his warmth belied his oft-stated mechanistic philosophy. Later she wrote to Reitman, "I think, if you loved me as Jack loves [Charmian], I too might yearn [for] a child."[10]

In May 1910 the Londons celebrated the addition of seven hundred acres to their ranch, which provided frontage on three creeks, thick timberland, and fields that swept a swath up the eastern slope of Sonoma Mountain. The property was the Kohler and Frohling Ranch, once a winery, now neglected and soil-depleted. This purchase, which cost $26,000, not including the livestock and equipment, brought their total holdings to almost a thousand acres. Appropriately, London's latest novel captured the arc of their life to this point.

In *Burning Daylight*, the eponymous hero, a hard-living, money-grubbing capitalist, unsuccessfully courts stenographer Dede Mason, who is unimpressed by his wealth and achievements. He would be "money's man," not her man, were they to marry, she rebukes him. One day he is struck by an epiphany when he rides to the top of Sonoma Mountain, where he realizes that the bounties of its wild, varied landscape satisfy more than the thrill and challenge of the corrupt yet rewarding business world. Though his transformation is not immediate, he eventually submits to the rural life and wins the hand of his reluctant lover. So complete is his conversion that upon discovering a vein of gold on his newly purchased mountain farm, he covers it up and tells no one about it.

This tale fit well with the Country Life movement of the day, with its revival of the yeoman myth, which can be traced as far back as Hesiod and Virgil through its most important American proponent, Thomas Jefferson. The sentimental side of the movement proclaimed farmers to be the best in society—intelligent, energetic, law-abiding. Concerned over the exodus of farmers to the city, proponents of the movement extolled the health and moral benefits of rural life. Some reformers, including Jack London, added social Darwinism to the equation by suggesting that Anglo-Saxons should retake the countryside as a way to preserve American native stock and, by implication, move away from the new immigrants, viewed as the source of urban decay.

This idealized, nostalgic view permeates *Burning Daylight* and a later novel, *The Valley of the Moon*. But Jack was just as committed to another, somewhat contradictory branch of the movement, one emphasizing the application of scientific knowledge and expertise to make farms more efficient and productive. For many reasons American agriculture was in a bad way, but with the closing of the frontier, a farmer could not simply leave his burned-out soil and move westward to fresh acreage. Characteristic of the Progressive Era, this impulse emphasized the improvement of rural areas by educating farmers and increasing their skills so that they would be more productive and competitive with foreign producers. Thus, proponents urged, farmers should listen to soil conservationists, entomologists, botanists, chemists, and stock-breeding specialists. By improving farming, the exodus from the countryside could be halted, and at the same time the Anglo-Saxon stock be attracted back to its roots.

London's correspondence emphasized this scientific rationale for his decisions. He would rebuild the soil through composting and manure spreading. He befriended Luther Burbank, who lived in nearby Santa Rosa, and took his advice on planting. The horticulturist found him "a big healthy boy with a taste for serious things, but never cynical, never bitter, always good-humored and humorous . . . with fingers and heart equally sensitive when he was in my gardens."[11] Jack regularly consulted with scientists at the nearest land-grant agriculture school, the University of California at Davis, as well as read and heavily marked up their numerous research bulletins. Partly as a result of their reports, he was in the midst of planting tens of thousands of gum eucalyptus, a rapidly growing Australian species thought to have numerous construction and industrial uses.[12] He genuinely believed in the benefits to the spirit of country life, but took just as avidly to the business of ranching, and would come to enjoy that part of his daily life much more than the writing. Members of the Crowd and their socialist cronies for the most part never understood this shift in his passions, and found it dreadfully hard, he acknowledged, to appreciate his curious delight in shire horses and hay crops, in pigs and Burbank's spineless cactus.

🍃

Unlike Burning Daylight and Dede Mason, the Londons had not settled for the simple life of fourteen acres and some chickens and managing the chores themselves. Instead, they bought into a grand dream of a showplace spread, one that was to prove costly to acquire and costly to support. Jack had supplanted his fervor for improving the lot of workers with a zeal for revolutionizing agriculture, and in time he would integrate his socialism into his farming administration. But for now he needed to slave at his desk, and turn out admittedly hack work if necessary, to pay for the land, the trees, the seeds, the livestock, the machinery, and the farmhands.

"Mother Mine," as Jack called Netta Eames, continued to complicate their lives, both in her role as business manager and as a relative. She would use their money for her own purposes, and issue confusing notes on who owed whom what. She hired a cook for herself, made changes to Wake Robin, and paid for them through Jack's accounts. She urged Jack to move Flora to a "cheap house" to save money, and neglected to follow through on some of his instructions. She took money out of Charmian's real estate earnings to pay a debt owed to Jack "because she, dear child, remembers that I gave her my last three-hundred dollars once to buy her a piano and typewriter."[13] She threw fearsome fits anytime the couple failed to meet her demands.

Netta's intimate life was just as chaotic. Her lover Edward Payne lived with her and Roscoe Eames, who was seeing other women. This curious ménage broke up in January 1910. Netta and Roscoe finally divorced, and he was remarried the next day to Elide Penazzi, a much younger woman. He moved into another cottage owned by Jack, and expected the Londons' continued financial support. Though fed up with Netta's ongoing furies, Jack and Charmian decided to pay for her November 1910 wedding to Payne, but after that they would revoke her authority as business agent and decrease their support. This break would not end Netta's demands, however.

More annoying to Jack, because the behavior was public, were Flora's attempts to make money. Like Bess, she sought ways to augment the basic income Jack provided. He had chastised her in the past for hawking small goods at a booth in downtown Oakland, and now complained because she had bought a new stove for her breadmaking. Although her behavior humiliated him, he did not take the obvious step of simply increasing her monthly stipend. If Flora had hoped to embarrass him into such a move, she failed. Charmian agreed with him that his financial problems were the fault of ungrateful women, that he was doing more than his duty to them.

Flora's endeavors were part of a larger pattern of self-confidence that set in while Jack was off on the *Snark*. Her granddaughter Joan observed that, with the famous son gone, the mother could once again feel free to talk to journalists. Several of them became part of a group of regular visitors who enjoyed Flora's company, her thoughtful, unconventional opinions, and her dramatic personality. Until physical ailments brought frailty, she created a satisfying independence. She and Jennie each had their own friends and interests, but shared a common cause through devotion to Bess and the girls. One wonders about the conversations that must have passed between these two women of such different backgrounds, whose meeting through childbirth on January 12, 1876, melded their lives together in so astonishing a way.

With the expansion of the ranch demanding so much of Jack's earnings, he sought sources of income beyond his usual stories for magazines and books for Macmillan. He spent much of early 1910 composing a play, *Theft*, which made the rounds of New York dramatic agencies without success. In his compulsion to earn money from any source, Jack agreed to cover a major boxing match, the Jeffries-Johnson bout in Reno, scheduled for the time of Charmian's delivery in June. She supported his plan, even though it meant that he would have to be away for almost two weeks to cover the preliminaries as well as the fight.

All her life Charmian had preferred alternative treatments to medicine. She relied on healthy habits to prevent illness, and rest cures when sick. (Her resistance to medical doctors was not unusual; it was only during the Progressive Era that physicians were able to establish the beginnings of their monopoly over health education and care.) Much against her instincts, Charmian succumbed to pressures from various women to have her child delivered in Fabiola, an Oakland hospital, by a physician rather than at home by a midwife.

At noon on Sunday, June 19, 1910, just before Jack was to leave for Reno, Charmian bore a healthy, full-term girl whom they named Joy. The delivery was very difficult, perhaps a breech or transverse presentation. Charmian caught only a glimpse of her daughter's head and heard her cry before she was taken to the nursery. Jack was beside her through the "terrible hours," and gleefully reported to Eliza his delight at having a child "just like Mate's and mine. Anglo-Saxon through and through!"[14] That she was not a boy no longer mattered. More of concern was Charmian's health, for the placenta did not deliver and she went into shock. Doctors warned Jack that she might not survive. And to add to the horror of what should be celebration, the doctors told him that Joy's back had been broken during the delivery and she too was dying.

When Charmian recovered from surgery, she found Jack and Eliza poised on either side of her bed to tell her that her "perfect child" was "gone in the twilight of the morning." Characteristically, Charmian "did not make it harder for [Jack] than I could help" and advised him to leave for Reno to cover the fight. She recuperated alone, on a ward of "ten mothers with nine babies."[15]

Heartbroken over the loss of the child and still unsure of Charmian's survival, Jack went to a bar, got into a fight with the Irish saloonkeeper, and ended up in jail overnight. This besmirching of his reputation would be aggravated when Jack wrote letters to the press spewing vitriol upon the "sheeny" judge, who, he discovered, was the bar's owner. Even though the judge had dismissed the charges of assault against both men, Jack was aggrieved and played on then-common anti-Semitic stereotypes. Yet his coverage of the famous match between James Jeffries, the Great White Hope, and the black boxer James Johnson was more equivocal. London had previously seen Johnson defeat the giant Tommy Burns in Australia and respected his skill. He referred to Johnson as a "care-free boy" and Jeffries as "a thinker," but did not predict certain victory for the white man. When, to the consternation of most Americans, Johnson won, London praised him for the deftness and agility that had led to the victory. And ever the radical, to those voices decrying the brutality of boxing, he asked why they ignored the brutality of factory owners, munitions manufacturers, and producers of adulterated food.

When Jack returned from Reno in July, he spent his afternoons at Charmian's bedside in the hospital, where she would remain until the twenty-second. She spent her days listening to other babies' cries and, perhaps to force her grief, insisted on holding others' infants. After her release, she recuperated at a friend's home for several weeks. There she checked the galleys of *Burning Daylight*, corrected the proofs, and kept to herself how she really felt—as if the bottom had fallen out of everything. When she was finally able to go riding, Jack took her out and proudly showed off the new bridle trail he had had constructed during her absence.

The girls' dream house on Jean Street with their own suite of rooms and Charlie Milner as a stepfather was not to be. A month after returning from the voyage of the *Snark*, Jack found Milner at the dinner table with Bess and the girls, a scene that may have revived his animosity toward the upcoming marriage. When in the Bay Area he more often included a stop at Thirty-first Street, and in the winter spent Christmas Eve, Christmas Day, and the day after with his daughters, the only holiday season he spent with them. He sent brief notes on postcards and made prearranged phone calls. If he had little time, he would settle down to play jackstraws or work puzzles with the girls; on longer visits he would take them to a matinee at the theater or to a vaudeville show, to be followed by a stop at Lenhardt's ice cream parlor in Oakland, where black-clad waitresses with frilly white aprons and caps delivered luscious macaroons and ladyfingers along with the ice cream delights. Movies were still a novelty, and less interesting to the girls than the stage, with the singing of larger-than-life Sophie Tucker, a clown act, jugglers, tap dancers, and smart-mouthed comics.

Two days before the birth of Joy, Jack took the girls on their favorite outing, to Idora Park, an amusement center that included a theater, skating rink, Crazy House, boat ride, roller-coaster, Ferris wheel, shooting galleries, cages of monkeys and bears, and even a large baseball park with bleachers. When the girls proved terrified during their first ride on the roller-coaster, Jack bought what seemed a yard of tickets and took them on again and again to prove the ride was safe. From that day they liked the "scenic railway," as it was called, the best of all. The overriding lesson he pressed during his visits was that they not be afraid and never cry. Both daughters grew up proud that he had instilled in them this self-confidence and bravery.

Becky particularly remembered his emphasis on writing and language, his insistence that words were a powerful force in society.[16] He taught them to treasure books as physical objects, never to dog-ear them but to find something thin, like a matchstick, to mark one's place. He encouraged their love of fairy tales, which he said were good for children, then shifted them to classical mythology when they outgrew them. He extolled his work habits, the importance of completing tasks early in the day and not putting them off until later, of being well organized and keeping a schedule. Thus, although he was still a rather detached father, he managed nonetheless to instill values and practices that served his daughters well.

On June 25, 1910, significant in its proximity to Joy's death, Bess spoke to an *Oakland Tribune* reporter for over an hour, "dramatically and forcefully" asserting that "the man has not been born yet that she would wed." Jack, she averred, was devoted to the girls and deserved all the credit he earned. She claimed to be the model for Ruth Morse in *Martin Eden,* "a woman who can love [implying Jack London], and loving cannot forget." In fact, she had already told Jack that she had broken off the engagement with Milner, who would remain a friend, during a visit in January of that year.

In later years, when Joan asked her mother about this decision, Bess could not explain why she would cancel what promised to be a fully satisfying marriage, offering the presence of a kindly stepfather. Joan suspected that her mother was too fearful of Jack's temper, that standing up for herself by letter had been rare enough. Bess would occasionally say, "I wonder what made him call me 'Mother Girl' at the beginning of such a letter [the one attacking her house purchase request]?" She seemed genuinely puzzled that he never called her by that affectionate term again. Joan intuited that her father's manipulation during that time had been meant "to keep the special bond between them intact, to change nothing, to [have Bess] remain his mother-girl."[17] Despite all that had transpired, Bess still loved Jack. She would brook no injury to him, and displaced her hostility upon Charmian. Joan observed that for the rest of his life Jack expressed the same hatred toward Milner that her mother did toward "the Beauty," as she referred to Charmian.

Nineteen ten had been a notable year for the girls in other respects. Bess had allowed them to leave their tiny private school and transfer to the Grant School, the same one their father had attended. They also began dancing lessons, and Joan took up piano. In addition to lending the girls her copies of their father's juvenile literature, Bess introduced them to the works of Charles Dickens, Robert Louis Stevenson, and William Thackeray, though warned them against Honoré de Balzac (whom Joan would sneak off to read at age twelve). Jack also sent them subscriptions to *Youth's Companion* and *St. Nicholas Magazine,* as well as surprise boxes of books from time to time. Both girls would become avid readers, with Becky especially attracted to fiction.

Although the girls were happy to have their father around again, they had been aware from whisperings and head-shakings among their mother, grandmother, and Jennie that a "deepening shadow" lurked in their life. "Not until the danger had passed . . . did we know what they, as well as Daddy, had kept from us. This knowledge was so incredible, so bitter," wrote Joan. Jack had never told his daughters of Charmian's pregnancy, even when he visited them just before the delivery, and had ordered the others to keep silent as well. That the women kept his secret hints at how powerful his hold remained. Once Joan learned of the baby, and that it had died, she felt a nine-year-old's secret gratitude that she would have no other competitor for her father's love. In a short time, however, she would realize that Joy London "was inextricably woven thereafter into the cruel pattern from which we could not escape."[18]

The "cruel pattern" began with a well-meaning impulse. While recuperating in the hospital, Charmian noted in her diary that her mind was "full of Joan and Bess [Becky] and the possibilities."[19] She discussed with Jack the idea of moving Bess and the girls to the ranch, where he could have more contact with them. Perhaps Charmian's obstetrical complications and her age had forced them to consider that there might be no more Anglo-Saxon offspring. And given their commitment to the spiritual and physical superiority of country life, the couple could only imagine the offer as one Bess must accept.

Around this time Jack went out riding with a godchild, Adela Rogers, the eleven-year-old daughter of a local friend. When he mentioned his idea, Adela questioned whether Charmian would like it. As he explained that his current wife and his ex-wife needn't see each other, she thought that he didn't understand how women behaved. What about Joan, she asked. She wasn't very communicative with him, he responded, adding angrily, "I'm her father." To which

Adela retorted that *being* a father was different from *behaving* like one. "If my father had gone off and *left* me—when a person has showed they can live without you for years and go all over the world, it isn't so easy to believe all of a sudden they can't live without you any more." Jack snapped back that it was presumptuous for a child to judge a father. Adela countered that Joan's defense of her mother was only appropriate, that he was oblivious to the effects of his behavior on a little girl. At the end of the ride, when Jack cruelly announced that he no longer wanted to be Adela's godfather, she realized that instead of listening to her child's wisdom, he had treated her as he would have Joan.[20]

Of course Adela was right: Bess would not move, for it would mean subjecting her girls and herself to the presence of Charmian. It may have been this refusal that led Jack to another period of heavy drinking. During a show at the Orpheum Theater, a comedy sketch involving a maternity ward caused him to break down. He was more irritable than usual with Charmian, loving one minute, turning against her the next.

During one of his visits, Joan apparently became nervous while playing the piano. Afterward, Jack informed Bess that he would no longer pay for piano lessons since they were too much of a strain on the girl. Bess rejoined that Joan simply got frustrated when she made a mistake. The fact was that Joan enjoyed the lessons, and music soothed her nervous inclinations. Please talk to the music teacher, Bess begged, before denying Joan. "I have never let anything stand in either of the children's way that was in my power to do for them," Bess reminded him in a letter. Changing the topic, she thanked Jack for rail passes he had provided for taking the girls to Los Angeles over Christmas, but explained that Becky's chronic throat problems had "used up all vacation money and more besides."[21]

Several days later Joan wrote her father a cheerful letter, making no reference to her piano studies. Rather she discussed dancing class, Becky's health, and manual training at school, where she had made a fish line winder. What may have impelled this note, though, was a new responsibility laid upon the child, for she was now to notify Jack about various expenses, including dancing lessons, school transit fare, and school supplies, and send receipts for reimbursement. What at first provided a convenient reason to communicate regularly with her father would turn into a cause for conflict, for Jack would question any change in normal expenses.

In December, Bess finally did take the girls on a quick trip to Los Angeles, their first. Joan wrote her father of bumping her head so violently in the train's upper berth that she saw stars, an experience she hoped he would never have. They returned two days before Christmas, their excitement heightened by the streets and stores blazing with holiday lights, the sound of bells, and the throngs of shoppers. They decorated the tree on Christmas Eve, while Jennie prepared the turkey dinner for the next day. Charlie Milner called to say he'd learned that the famous coloratura Luisa Tetrazzini was making a special appearance that evening in San Francisco and asked Bess and the girls to join him. The girls begged to go, and Bess almost capitulated, until she realized that Jack might show up that evening. They stayed home, but he never appeared; only his surrogate, a box of rosy South Seas coral jewelry, arrived instead. Though he did not come on Christmas Day either, Joan wrote a long thank you letter, being certain to describe every other gift she received, including the "safety pin holder from Mr. Milner." If she were disappointed by her father's absence on the holiday, she did not imply it, and closed sending "lots of love."[22]

Over the holidays Jack's mood improved, and he was repentant with Charmian for his recent impatience. The newest medical literature made them hopeful once more of having another child, and they spent hours discussing the house they were having built on a ridge from which they could look out over the valley. They were living in an old wooden farm cottage, a warren of dark, narrow rooms, with the dining room and kitchen in an old stone winery building nearby. Guests, farmworkers, and their families stayed in an enormous remodeled winery building that provided living space above the farm equipment storage stalls. The Londons were ready for a place of their own, where they could have more privacy and convenience. As architect for their new house they had chosen Albert Farr, who designed a massive, rugged lodge, to be called Wolf House, built of volcanic rock and stones taken from the ranch, as well as redwoods from its woodlands. Although there were no rooms designated for children, Farr included a "guest suite" of three rooms with a sleeping porch, clearly meant for Becky and Joan, if not Jack and Charmian's own offspring. Planning their new home could not distract either Jack or Charmian fully from the blow of losing Joy. Into her seventies Charmian continued to record Joy's birthday and wistful what-if musings.

That spring Charmian scribbled a note: Jack had gotten drunk, "but it's Prohibition Ticket for me!"[23] (She was clearly anticipating the franchise later that year allowing California women the vote.) Jack would transform this episode into the first chapter of *John Barleycorn*, his brilliant, semiautobiographical exploration of alcohol abuse. Part of the reason for his distress was the usual burden of having taken on too many financial commitments. The new house would cost tens of thousands of dollars. But in a familiar pattern, Jack displaced worries about his overburdened budget onto his first family.

The situation boiled over in early 1911, when Bess asked that Jack raise her monthly allowance to $100. Even with her own income from tutoring, she owed $70 to Becky's doctor and another $12 to the dentist. Jack had apparently complained about Joan's frequent dental visits, for Bess went into detail concerning Joan's "soft teeth." She explained that the girls' growing older meant higher costs for clothes and school supplies. On a hundred a month, Bess could pay for their dance lessons instead of constantly requesting reimbursement.[24]

Jack responded spitefully. Admitting that he was too busy during Bay Area trips to "do anything more than take a passing look at [Joan and Becky]," he demanded that she allow the girls to visit him on the ranch. Her attitude was resulting in "a process of alienation from my children, a process that leads to lack of interest in my children." He refused to sacrifice his fatherly interest to her "narrow prejudice" and "sexual shortcoming." He reminded her that their marriage agreement was never based on love, so she could not fault him for finding someone else, someone who earned half of every dollar to pay for each "piece of bread, butter or chunk of meat you put in your mouth." Charmian had no wish to alienate the girls from Bess, he added, and he was not "so stupid, so vilely rotten" that he would warp his girls' minds were they to visit. Several times he attacked the Madderns in general as a small-minded brood.[25]

Jack and Bess had created a dynamic that would become a familiar one decades later when divorce was more common. What loving father would not want his daughters to visit him in his own home? What caring mother would not want a comfortable level of support? The divorce agreement gave neither much room for legal maneuvering. Consequently, Bess fully controlled visitation rights, while Jack was not bound to a specific level of financial support. Neither would concede nor compromise, and in the process they harmed the children they were fighting to protect.

Several weeks later, during one of Jack's visits with the girls, an accident occurred that left unpleasant memories. Joan was sick on the couch with a bad cold, and in her drowsiness she overheard her parents arguing, something they had never done in her presence before. Becky kept interrupting to ask her father to romp with her. As Joan recalled, in his frustration Jack threatened that if Becky didn't leave him alone, he would put her through the window. When she persisted, he picked her up and swung her around, and her legs went crashing through the front window. Joan was shocked that he would punish Becky when she had not done anything wrong, and worse, he did not say he was sorry.[26]

Becky's account was that during the romp, Bess chided Jack for playing so rough. He replied, "Baby B trusts me," and said to his daughter, "If I ask you to put your hands in mine and I would swing you through the window here, you'd do it and trust me, wouldn't you?" Becky said yes, and put her hands in his. As he swung her near the window, her foot hit the glass. She was not hurt, and he responded admiringly, "You know you can always trust your daddy." It was, Becky recalled, a "tempest in a tea cup."[27]

Whether accident or not, the consequences were not minor. Almost a month later Joan wrote her father that Becky was limited to arm exercises in gym class because "her leg is worse than you thought. An abscess formed on it and it is not well yet."[28] At home, the incident was allegedly forgotten and never spoken of afterward, for Bess assured the girls that he had not meant to hurt them. And from that point on, he was always gentle with them, although the romping they adored ended for good.

Though Becky always defended her father afterward, Joan was traumatized. As proof of the incident's seriousness, she pointed to her sister's permanent scars, "even if recognition of their existence is steadfastly refused by those who bear them [Becky]." Neither Joan nor her mother could discern the meaning of Jack's curious inscription in a copy of *When God Laughs* sent to Bess several days later: "God often laughs—especially at windows." Was he being flippant or remorseful? Becky's response reflected how well she had learned not to be a crybaby. Similarly, in a letter to Jack enclosing the glazier's bill, Joan bragged that she had pricked her finger at school and made it bleed. Was this not proof that she—like Becky, is the implication—was also "a tiger"?[29]

From that point on, Joan was more cautious around her father, more careful in the opinions she expressed, and at the same time more ready to "question his wisdom and even doubt his kindness."[30] Her letters that year were brief and contained two kinds of information: reminders about bills for dancing lessons and news of various achievements. (She wrote the best essay in class; Becky danced a fine sailors' hornpipe.) Joan was wary, yet she longed to return to the earlier days of the relationship and contrived ways to earn her father's praise.

Charmian recorded nothing in her diary of this episode, and may never have known of it. Rather, she glowed at Jack's showering her with gifts. When some of the Crowd arrived for a long visit, she was happy to note in her diary that George was "on the water wagon." A long cruise alone on their sloop *Roamer*, with the ubiquitous Nakata, had countered the strains of too much company. Construction had started on the new house, further balm for their grief.

Misfortune provided an exceptional new assistant for Jack. Her marriage having failed, Eliza had accepted his invitation to move to Glen Ellen and work as both ranch supervisor and overseer of the Wolf House project for fifty dollars a month in addition to room and board. She brought her eleven-year-old son Irving, who would become as committed to Jack's Beauty Ranch concept as his mother. Astute and efficient, Eliza was the perfect choice to translate Jack's unending ideas into practice, while at the same time she provided Charmian with much-valued female companionship. One of her first accomplishments had been to purchase an island of acreage in the middle of the ranch containing various buildings that once had belonged to the old Kohler and Frohling Winery.

This ten-acre plot included the cottage in which Charmian and Jack were living until Wolf House was completed.

On May 24, 1911, Charmian noted matter-of-factly that Jack had written a new will. Still resentful of Bess's refusal to allow the girls to visit the ranch, Jack drastically cut his first family's legacy. To Bess he granted only five dollars, while his daughters were to receive only twenty-five dollars monthly support each until reaching twenty-one or marrying. Anything else would have to come from the bequest of Charmian, who was to inherit his entire estate. Unlike his earlier wills, this one did not require that all property and literary rights eventually pass into the hands of his daughters. After accusing Bess of alienating his children from him, he had acted accordingly. Had he felt any ambivalence concerning the reordering of Charmian and his daughters in his priorities, they were now removed. His first family, however, had no knowledge of this decision.

Jack wanted to make a trip up the California coast through southern Oregon and back down the California valleys to collect research for his proposed novel *The Valley of the Moon*. On June 2 the four-horse trip up the coast began. The route took them winding through wilderness spotted with logging camps, north to Bandon, Oregon, inland to the Willamette Valley, southward over the Cascades and through the northern Sacramento Valley, then back home. Most of the journey was idyllic, with stops at tiny inns and hotels, daily fishing for the evening meals prepared by Nakata, and spontaneous receptions for the celebrities. When convenient, Jack attended socialist meetings and gave several anticapitalist speeches.

Within days of their departure, Joan was felled by diphtheria and put in quarantine for two weeks. A bad reaction to the antitoxin left her paralyzed for several days. Apparently she did not realize that her father had already left on his trip, because in a letter she mildly rebuked him for not being in touch with her, and as if to show that it did not matter, went into a lengthy description of the attention she was getting from friends and medical staff. When the letter finally reached him, Jack immediately had Eliza send skates to the girls, as they had requested. Although in the past he might have interrupted his journey to visit Joan's bedside, this time he did not. Upon his return, he found her haggard and bone thin from the ordeal.

After the three months of travel were over, Charmian experienced false symptoms of pregnancy and learned that she needed some further minor surgery if she hoped for another child. During a long visit at this time George Sterling became particularly troublesome as a result of his drinking. That meant that Jack was drinking too, so Charmian made an offer: limit himself to three drinks a day and she would have the surgery and stop using birth control. He agreed, and she followed through accordingly. Circumstances would soon prove his promise a weak one.

Despite their private troubles, 1911 was a highly productive year for Jack. He was writing short stories at a steady clip, and continued to do so during his travels. Charmian had a tiny Remington typewriter that went everywhere with them, and she assisted as well by jotting descriptions and impressions he would incorporate into his writings. Jack's income continued to increase. He told a friend that he had sold twelve stories to the *Saturday Evening Post* at $750 each, and delivered nine to *Cosmopolitan* at the same price. In fact, he sold many stories for as much as $900. He earned much from the republication of several stories in England, and royalties continued to pour in from his books. A conservative estimate of his income for the year is $32,000 for a writing week of thirty hours, in contrast to the $1,300 earned annually by skilled workers employed for a fifty-five-hour week. He was among the highest-paid writers in the country, and if not in the class of the Rockefellers or Vanderbilts, he clearly deserved the description "rich."

Nonetheless, he constantly complained that he was in debt, and warned Bess that he was earning less than in the past owing to his "socialism, my going out of vogue, and my natural and inevitable deterioration as a writer."[31] Including the extra payments for dance lessons, bus fares, and such, Jack contributed a little more than $1,000 to his first family that year, in addition to providing housing. He sent less than that to Flora and Jennie, while also providing a home. His dependents lived comfortably, though without many extras. Jack spent more on eucalyptus trees during 1911 than on his Oakland kith and kin.

As the intermediary, Joan became the focus of his ill temper. He examined bills microscopically and was often late in paying. "What has happened to you?" she wrote him. "You said that you would be down in about two weeks. Daddy, did you overlook those bills that I sent you for the gym?"[32] He stopped paying for Joan's music lessons that fall. When she provided a list of possible presents for Becky's birthday, she added a nervous postscript assuring her father that her sister did not want everything on the list, just one item. Jack's alienation was further evident in his ignoring their pleas that he take them to Idora Park before it closed for the winter. Two weeks later he appeared and took them to San Francisco, then did not see them again until Christmas Eve.

Despite his coolness, Joan once again sought to revive her father's interest in her life. She described her efforts at writing, the contests she'd entered in *Woman's Companion* and *St. Nicholas,* and her Sunday school writing competition. She set up a sewing table in the attic to use as a desk where she wrote her stories, and found a chest where she kept her "manuscripts, as I call them." She sent him copies of her stories for his comments, requesting that he be hard on her in response. But in particular, "however busy you are, never forget Bess [Becky] and I," she reminded him on February 10, 1912.

His daughters would not be much on Jack's mind during the first half of 1912. In early January he and Charmian arrived in New York City, where he had various business and legal issues to settle. Learning from Sinclair Lewis that his royalty rates were lower than those of other authors such as Edith Wharton, Rudyard Kipling, and Theodore Roosevelt, Jack asked George Brett for an increase. When Brett refused, Jack explored a move to Houghton Mifflin or Doubleday, neither of which came to fruition. He did sign to do four books for Century, a contract he would later regret, and which sent him penitently back to Macmillan.

Jack was also involved in an investment concerning the Millergraph, a new printing process, though he would eventually be squeezed out of the deal. One of his colleagues in the negotiations was an old friend from the Bay Area, Joseph Noel. In a memoir written much later, Noel described Jack's behavior during those weeks in New York as debauchery. While overly dramatic and reductionist, Noel's account matches Charmian's diary entries on enough details to support his conclusion in part. These two months would be the nadir of her marriage for Charmian. As Noel perceptively recalled, "With Jack's wife it was the problem of an incorrigible husband toward whom she felt all the responsibility of a mother toward a wayward son."[33] He found her much changed from the days of the Wednesday fencing matches—her pallor gray, her voice tired, her smile withered.

The couple stayed at the Morningside Park apartment of F. G. Hancock, better known as "The Blasphemer" to his friends. Many nights Jack went carousing with Noel and Hancock and others he met through their introduction. There was a visit to the composer Victor Herbert at his studio, dinner with the painter John Butler Yeats, and numerous outings with Michael Monahan, editor of the literary magazine *Papyrus*. One evening of pub hopping took Jack to "the Flatiron Building, rendezvous of the town's male harlots . . . with little dabs of rouge on their cheeks and mascara on their eyelashes."[34] Despite their admiration for the works of Baudelaire and Oscar Wilde, Jack and Monahan agreed in their view of homosexuality as a perversion, a sign of inward decay. There were frequent trips to burlesque theaters and serious plays, sometimes with Charmian accompanying, others not.

Soon after arriving, in New York, Jack met journalist Sophie Irene Loeb of the *Evening World*. Thirty-five and divorced, Loeb had much in common with Anna Strunsky, being another vivacious Jewish brunette with a strong commitment to social causes, in this case child health, school lunches, and economic assistance to single parents. During an interview with Loeb, Jack criticized New York as "wild maelstrom," a place where impressions mattered more than making good. Its women, he added, were too possessive, driving their husbands to unhappy labor in order to afford material comforts. He also decried city women's dislike of their own sex.[35] Charmian met Sophie one evening, but more often Jack saw her in the company of his male companions. Sophie is less likely to have stirred Charmian's jealousy and fear of Jack's philandering than the anonymous young women he was meeting at the clubs and theaters.

Jack drank heavily, with the result that he swung sharply between thoughtlessness toward his wife and tenderness, as if to apologize for his loutish behavior. The observation in Charmian's diary "Jack goes out on a mystery bent" leads to "Mate the lover, but I am so hurt, I can't rise."[36] Then he would buy her fox furs, or spend an entire day in bed with her, only to disappear the next evening without explanation. Part of the reason for his behavior may have been frustration over his unsuccessful attempts to find a new publisher and settle the business deals he had planned. Charmian similarly went to extremes. One day she would sit alone in the apartment in self-pity, and another she would take off to visit Emma Goldman, Mary Austin, or Arnold Genthe, all of whom were now residing in New York, or engage in other pleasant pursuits.

While it is true that both were emotionally distraught and unpredictable, it would be unfair to characterize this period purely—as some suggest—as bad times brought on by booze. Interspersed between moments of high drama were intermissions usually involving socialists and activists. One evening Jack spoke at a dinner attended by the most radical feminists of the time, including Alva Vanderbilt Belmont (who urged women to "take to rifles" if necessary to get the vote), Inez Mulholland (who would die of exhaustion during a suffrage lecture tour), and Charlotte Perkins Gilman (whose books included the female utopia *Herland*). They visited the Rand School of Science, a leading center for socialist thought. They met with Alexander Berkman, who asked Jack to write an introduction for his forthcoming book, *Prison Memoirs of an Anarchist*. Jack enjoyed his whiskey while Big Bill Haywood of the Wobblies recounted his various bouts with the law, and his acquittal of conspiracy to murder the governor of Idaho. Both men agreed that Samuel Gompers was leading the American Federation of Labor down a reactionary path, that the workers needed to wake up and throw him aside. Though Jack was no longer an active socialist, his commitment to the working class and the defeat of capitalist oligarchy remained strong.

The couple went to visit Anna and English Walling, who now lived in a country estate in Cedarhurst, Long Island. Anna, who had recently given birth to a new Anna, her second and namesake daughter, wrote Jack to say that she thought it "a beautiful omen that you were about to appear again in the life of the old [Anna]. This is a wonderful year that brings me my daughter and my friend again." As for English, he was "most usually where I am—I say in foolish and boastful woman-pride."[37]

Jack admired English's approach to socialism, his accusing socialist conservatives of undermining the party to reshape it to a reform platform. Although he was correct in his charges, they would result eventually in the expulsion of the radicals from the organization. Jack was similarly disenchanted with changes in the party, which he adroitly interpreted as suffering from its own success. In recent years socialists had been elected to local and state offices, and those in power had become more interested in preserving the organization and its hierarchy than in achieving its revolutionary ends.

That English shared these feelings was evident in Anna's later letters to Jack. After English became a member of the editorial board of *The Masses*, a new magazine appealing to "both Socialist and non-Socialist with entertainment, education, and the livelier kinds of propaganda," Anna wrote with enthusiasm about the venture.[38] Underwritten by wealthy rebels such as Mabel Dodge and Alva Vanderbilt Belmont, in its brief life *The Masses* attempted to cross politics with culture. If Jack could not serve as a contributing editor, Anna hoped "with all my heart" that he at least would send a statement of support.[39] He declined to contribute or play an active role, perhaps wisely, because he did not fit in with the cantankerous Greenwich Village bohemians who ran that publication.

The two wives would form a lasting relationship. What could have been a clumsy reunion for Anna was otherwise. "[Jack] came and it was as if he had never been away," she noted. "He is very happy in his marriage, but they had the sorrow of losing their baby." Charmian recorded, "Splendid talk with Anna in which she tells me several things."[40] Their each having lost an infant daughter led to easy intimacy between the two women, though that was not the only basis for their empathy. (Perhaps seeing Anna's tiny daughter stirred Charmian to note that Joy would be one and a half years old.) In a thank you note, Charmian remarked that she couldn't shake the vision of "Anna's happy home with its beauty, and its love, and its patience and sweetness." Women were superior to men for being able to rise above bodily torture, a more intimate awareness of birth and death than a man could know. Yet she was quick to compliment Anna's "big, big husband" and say how much Jack admired him as well.[41] Charmian's reference to "patience" suggests that she saw Walling's darker side. In fact, Jack suspected the couple were not compatible and expected that Anna would one day leave Walling.

It is unclear whether Anna shared with Charmian the story of her recent humiliation attached to a scandal involving English. Before their marriage he had been involved in Paris with Anna Berthe Grunspan, leading her to believe they would marry. In 1909 she sued him for $100,000 for breach of promise. The case, which dragged on for two years, was the kind of story yellow journalists liked to splash on the front page. Anna, refusing to stay away, attended the trial, often laughing during the reading of Grunspan's letters. She even petitioned the judge to let her be a witness when Walling's lawyer refused to place her on the stand. Her testimony, combined with weaknesses in Grunspan's case, led to a vindication for English. The notoriety, however, caused him to lose esteem within the NAACP, and his formal role in that organization was much weakened.

Meeting Charmian, observing how much of a partner she was in Jack's life, Anna fell into a deeper depression. "I think I love English more romantically than even that first spring in Moscow," she wrote her sister. "But I want time, I want space, to live a passionate, personal life and my whole personality is submerged, hangs on a thread."[42] However much joy she found in motherhood, it seemed also to leave her powerless because, having lost the first so tragically, she understandably hated to leave her babies. Anna shared English's commitment to civil rights and socialism, yet rarely joined him at meetings and conventions. Worse, he was writing—his second book was about to appear—while her novel languished, and her study of the 1908 race riots would never see print.

Anna was successful in publishing several articles in 1911, though the stimulus came from others, not from English. Her siblings Rose and Hyman had embarked on freelance writing careers, and their letters encouraged Anna to try her hand more seriously. As in the past, tragic events provided the topics. One was the murder of their good friend David Graham Phillips, whom Anna eulogized in the *New York Call* and the *Saturday Evening Post.* Her treatment by the press during the Grunspan trial led to an acceptance by *Collier's.* She was less successful placing a piece about the Triangle Shirtwaist Company fire, where 140 seamstresses burned or fell to their deaths. After rejections by major magazines, the *National Post* so severely edited the work that she considered it "completely ruined."[43]

This period of productivity did not last. Doubtless one reason was her experiencing two more pregnancies in quick succession. Yet she had domestic help, and it was common for Progressive women of means to leave their children in order to attend reform functions. She preferred the dream of what might be, and the bittersweet sense of loss, to the challenge of testing herself. Perhaps more significant, she was unwilling to stand up to English, who, unlike Jack, did not want to share his fame. Unlike Charmian, Anna would never find herself featured in women's magazines as a personality in her own right. English hectored Anna to write, yet also badgered her about her household responsibilities, which he held up as primary. (He often portrayed himself to his parents as having to make domestic decisions that should have been hers.) English would not invite Anna to collaborate with him, as Jack did when he asked Charmian to do research or write up experiences to incorporate into his fiction.

Though Anna complained about the restrictions of motherhood, she never conveyed that frustration to her children. While English's public career expanded, Anna increasingly found delight and fulfillment in her children. She would add two more to her brood: Georgia in October 1913 and William Hayden in 1916. By the time of her son's birth, Anna and English would be on the verge of a seemingly irresolvable disagreement in political philosophy. But at the time of Jack and Charmian's visit, she was still hopeful that her marriage would in time match her high expectations. Reality had not corrupted her romantic view of life.

# 9

## Bitter Harvests

BY THE END OF FEBRUARY 1912, Charmian was at the breaking point over the "filthy unhappiness" of New York. She had expected to be out of the city much earlier, but the shipping company with which they had booked passage home, via Cape Horn, balked for weeks at having a woman aboard, until she convinced them of her seaworthiness. (Presumably the captain's wife, who normally joined him on voyages, did not count as a female.) And Jack did not want to wait the time out in Baltimore, where the ship was when he had so much business and entertainment in Manhattan.

When the good news of their departure finally arrived, Charmian and Nakata packed seventeen boxes of clothes, books, and other paraphernalia for their trip around the Horn on the *Dirigo*, a tall ship embarking on its last trip, since engines had now supplanted wind for energy, and in any event the Panama Canal would open in two years. Following a short stay in Philadelphia, the couple and their valet arrived in Baltimore. They went immediately to the Customs Office to complete the necessary paperwork, then signed on board, with Jack designated as third mate, Charmian as stewardess, and Nakata as assistant steward.

The influence of "filthy New York" left a nasty reminder their first morning in Baltimore, when Jack went out alone and returned with his head shaved clean. Charmian broke down in tears and refused to speak to him, but at the end of the day he brought her a terrier puppy she named Possum. Appeased, she gave Jack a stocking cap to cover his bald pate and agreed to accompany him to a ceremony at the Edgar Allen Poe monument, where photographers centered them in their shots of the gathering. With Charmian wrapped in fox furs, arms thrust into a large fox muff, and Jack in well-cut overcoat and felt hat, the couple fit right in with the prominent, affluent crowd. One would never suspect that they were about to isolate themselves for six months on a spartan, potentially dangerous cruise.

Charmian kept two diaries during the voyage, her private jottings in her tiny diary, and an extended, typed version to be edited later for an intended book publication that never occurred. The latter document included details that aid in deciphering the more abridged musings of her tiny handwritten daybook.[1]

The *Dirigo* was the first of the Sewall Company's noted steel-hulled ships, three thousand tons and powered by the sails of its four square-rigged masts. The journey carrying coal around Cape Horn to Seattle would cover 18,000 miles without landfall, encountering much variation in weather. There was blissful travel over mildly rolling indigo waves; boring, debilitating periods of torpid tropical heat and humidity; bone-shaking, nerve-shattering hours of fighting snowy squalls. The three hardy guest crew members, little frightened by the uncertainties ahead, were pleased to be assigned separate narrow cabins adjoining the officers' mess and captain's quarters.

Charmian's journals reveal the extent of her shattered self-regard until she was sure Jack had returned fully committed to her: "He doesn't realize how worn out I am. I actually believe he has forgotten that past two months, or that he never realized what they were meaning to me. He called me Kid-Woman [to-day] and it almost hurt."[2] She was preoccupied with designing and embroidering "fripperies"—lacy underwear and caps—and repeated to herself how much Jack enjoyed dainty, feminine clothing. She transcribed his spontaneous proclamations of love, as though to assure herself by making a permanent record she could look back on. Determined to regain the full energy she had missed in the two years since the loss of Joy, she daily climbed the ropes to the tops of the masts and hiked several miles on deck.

Though the initial weeks were marked by minor ailments that preoccupied each, including Charmian's horrendous attack of bedbug bites, by April they had fallen into a familiar pattern. In the mornings Jack worked on *The Valley of the Moon* while Charmian typed his previous day's writings and wrote up descriptions for him to use in the novel: segments about the four-horse trip, descriptions of the Carmel landscape, and accounts of various events from her own life, such as learning about sex from her aunt Netta (transformed by Jack into the bewitching Mercedes). She also typed poetry written by her late mother, Dayelle Wiley, which Jack would weave into the novel. "Many a novelist depends upon his mate for woman's viewpoint on his characters," she commented.[3]

Work was the couple's main refuge. Sick in both body and soul from his bingeing in New York, Jack promised Charmian that he would prove he was not an alcoholic by drinking nothing stronger than tea or coffee while aboard. He also discussed with her his plans for *John Barleycorn*, a semiautobiographical tract based on his misadventures with drink. "[Jack] is all for youth being deprived of the chance to learn a taste for alcohol, to make the world a fitter place for YOUTH."[4] With temperance came an improvement in his health and his mood, which in turn lessened Charmian's long-standing insecurity and nervous condition.

They spent long hours reading aloud from an impressive variety of works, including James Barrie's "Peter and Wendy," Friedrich Nietszche's *Ecce Homo*, three volumes of Robert Louis Stevenson letters, several books by Anatole France, Max Nordau's *Interpretation of History*, Robert Browning's poems, Walter Weyl's *New Democracy*, Theodore Dreiser's *Sister Carrie*, Ouida's *Signa*, and the now forgotten Ellis Butler's *Kilo*, which left both with sides aching from laughter. Their other recreation was usually competitive, either games of double solitaire and cribbage, the results carefully recorded, with bragging rights often going to Charmian, or boxing bouts, watched admiringly by the crew. "And we never make an ending of Making Love," she noted in mid-May.

In late May, Charmian admitted that neither had recovered yet from Joy's death; she still waited patiently for "the day when I should feel satisfied in my state that would tempt me to undertake another child." Though feeling "tremulous" over the possibility of facing motherhood again, she thought the half-moon hanging above portended good news. Yet she waited a week before revealing to Jack her decision that they should create "a child of love, deliberately, in loving intent, to replace the little lost girl that never had a chance against an ignorant and unsure doctor." His immediate delight was echoed "as if in jubilation" by fine winds and an "amazing sunset that took the whole sky, painting the vast dome with living turquoise and greens and blues; the clouds overhead reflecting a horizon that was a long burning city." The next day he exclaimed, while discussing a nursery for Wolf House, that he didn't care whether it was a boy or a girl, just that it be "YOUR baby, OUR baby, that's all that matters."[5]

By late June, with the knowledge that Seattle was just a few weeks away, Charmian spent many hours writing letters by hand to drop in the mail as soon as they reached shore. Her longest and warmest was to Anna. "You are a gracious, generous creature. I love you to death." She confessed her desire for a child, though did not mention her growing belief that she was already pregnant. She urged Anna to read more of Jack's books, and to comment honestly to Charmian what she thought of them, and not feel compelled only to praise. With the journey's end in sight, she added, Jack "dreams, nearly every night, that we're on the ranch again. How he worships that country! It's all wrapped up in him." In a rare comment about Bess and the girls, Charmian praised Joan's "fine spirit & loyalty concerning her mother," though wondered how the girl would develop, given her "sensitive & knowing heart & mind." She was certain Joan "would suffer" as a result of the situation with her parents. As for Becky, "The other one is different—rather a puzzle to Jack."[6]

The final weeks at sea were particularly busy for Charmian. Quite unexpectedly she developed the idea for a short story, "The Wheel," which went through several rewrites under Jack's encouragement and editorial advice. She was surprised by this sudden burst of creative expression. She had often been frustrated that her fertile imagination was not accompanied by the skill to transform fantastic ideas into substance, whether a story, poem, or drawing. This effort so increased her daily chores that she brought Nakata into the typing pool, so that he could work on both Jack's manuscripts and hers while she attended to composition and editing.

Nakata had been with them seven years now. Charmian hoped he would marry and bring a wife along to add to his service. During the voyage she reflected that he was "inexpressibly precious to us both. We have, we Three, been through hell and high water together."[7] She thought of all the times he had nursed them through illnesses, and they in turn had once saved his life from food poisoning. The patronizing tinge to such comments, which run throughout her diaries over the years of Nakata's employ, cannot disguise the sincere warmth Charmian felt for this man. There was also an erotic undertone in her record of his giving her neck massages when neuralgia struck, his careful washing of her handmade blouses and underwear, his hours carving intricate hairpins and combs out of turtleshell, his brushing her waist-length hair. He seems to have read her moods and needs perceptively, and one wonders about the feelings likely to swell, given such close and constant proximity.

Ironically, because of the principles of scientific racism, this handsome bachelor was allowed intimacies unimaginable to a white man of similar age and attractiveness. That Nakata accepted his station as Oriental servant is evident in the fact that it took him seven years to "talk back" to his employers, an outburst so shocking to the couple that they excused his insolence, blaming it on the nerves all were suffering late in the cruise. Apart from this one incident, there are no signs of his ever crossing the master-servant line. From the couple's viewpoint, he existed only to serve. Even helping him to find a wife was meant to ensure that he would continue in their employ.

The final weeks on board, the deteriorating health of Omar Chapman, the ship's captain, called Charmian to further duties. He was growing pale and weak, and suffered such severe gastrointestinal problems that Charmian correctly diagnosed stomach cancer. When he finally became bedridden, she spent hours by his side, providing reassurance through her very presence and attending to what nursing tasks she was able to perform. In secret she worried that he might die before reaching shore. As it happened, he hung on, only to be taken directly to the hospital, where he died before his wife could arrive for a final farewell.

Though the trip ended under the shadow of tragedy, Charmian and Jack were full of hope. She was in fact pregnant; he had "proved" he was not alcoholic. One novel was completed and another book was under way. They were returning to their ranch, readying for harvest, both literally and metaphorically.

George Sterling and Charmian's favorite cousin, Beth Wiley, met the couple when they disembarked in Oakland on August 2, 1912. Jack went right off to see his daughters. Since he had been at sea for so long, he had received only three letters from Joan. During his absence, Becky had suffered a serious case of the mumps, and Bess had been sick much of that spring, perhaps from ovarian cysts, since she mentioned to Jack the loss of her second ovary.

The girls were active at Trinity Episcopal Church, where Joan also participated in a sewing circle and competed in Sunday school essay contests. Both girls took dance and music lessons as well. Having prominent actors in their maternal family line fed the girls' fascination with the stage, and thoughts of a career there. Minnie Maddern Fiske always came by whenever she was performing in San Francisco, and encouraged the girls' curiosity about the performing life. It was likely after one of Fiske's appearances in *Becky Sharpe* that young Bess changed her name to Becky. With lives so full of activities and friends, and so many relatives nearby, the girls had less time to miss their father, but his return rekindled their need for his attention.

Joan was ready to put in place a grand design to win him back. It had started with two letters scheduled to reach him upon his arrival in Seattle. In them she played up her interest in writing, and included a story for his comment, "Discontented Teddy," which concerns a dog who lives on a ranch with a woman named Elizabeth and her two daughters.[8] As in Joan's real backyard, chickens and other fowl roam about, including Mr. Cock, a haughty rooster whose pride at talking to the sun makes Teddy angry. Furious, too, that his mother rations his breakfast, he escapes to the wood, which in daytime enchants with its orioles and squirrels. Night is frightening, however, and Teddy returns home, never wanting any more than his allotment of breakfast and no longer teasing Mr. Cock. Joan would not be like Buck, called to stay in the wild, she seemed to say. This tension between rebellion and domesticity would mark her entire life, though her solution was to weave both together, much to the puzzlement of her politically activist friends.

At their reunion Joan may have shown her father the den she had created in the attic, with her sewing table used also as a writing desk, and a little Korean chest he had given her to hold her "manuscripts." Perhaps she and Becky also showed off their latest recreation, roller-skating. Though the initial visit lasted but a few hours, the girls were once again swept up by their father's magnetic pull.

Once home, Jack and Charmian faced months of unanswered correspondence, demands from friends anxious to see them again, and the lack of a cook. When Jack decided to go to the Bohemian Grove Hi-Jinks before settling down to work, Charmian returned to their Oakland flat. She was helping Nakata with his arrangements for a wife, which fell through when they learned that the candidate had an eye disease and would not be allowed to enter the country. Four days after seeing her doctor about her pregnancy, Charmian began bleeding, and Jennie nursed her through three days of labor that eventuated in the miscarriage of a son. Off sailing with the Sterlings after the Hi-Jinks, Jack sent Eliza to Oakland to comfort Charmian. During his three-week absence Charmian repeatedly noted her dismay over Jack's silence. But, dreaming "every night I am in Mate's arms," she was quick to forgive him when he appeared with a team of horses to drive her home.[9]

Among the many guests on the ranch that fall were Martin Johnson and his new wife. Following the collapse of the Snark cruise, Martin had set out to become "as big a man in my way as Jack London is in his" through a career as a travel lecturer.[10] Without informing the couple, to whom he owed $478.63, he and a pharmacist partner transformed an Independence, Kansas, drug store into the Snark Theater, the first of several in a chain. This was in violation of an agreement all the crew members had signed which stipulated that they could not make commercial use of their experiences without first clearing their writings through Jack. When the Londons eventually learned of Martin's chicanery, they excused it as the thoughtlessness of a young man. Martin had been the stalwart of the crew, and his assertion that his lectures would bring publicity to the Londons' own forthcoming books on the Snark appealed to their self-interests.

Despite its location in rural Kansas, Martin's theater attracted large crowds to his talks illustrated by his hand-colored lantern slides created from his several dozen black and white photographs. To fill out the time, Martin showed nickelodeon movies and vaudeville acts. One performer was a sixteen-year-old soprano, Osa Leighty, with whom Martin eloped within weeks after meeting her. The reason for Martin's attraction to Osa, besides her beauty and sweet disposition, was her resemblance to Charmian. She was spirited, game, and ready to join and assist her husband, whatever his endeavor. Even better, from Martin's view, were Osa's more traditional ideas about a woman's role, for she did not aspire to equality in her relationship with him, as Charmian attempted to achieve, however unsuccessfully, with Jack.

By 1912 the Johnsons were part of the acclaimed Orpheum Circuit, and with appearances scheduled in San Francisco, Osa would finally meet the woman held up to her for two years as a model that would be hard to beat. ("It's too bad she hasn't got a sister," Osa reputedly snapped at Martin one day.) Feeling as if she were under glass during the visit to Glen Ellen, Osa remained miserable throughout their stay on the ranch. She was unaware until the good-byes how much she had enchanted the couple, who assured her of their delight in Martin's choice of a mate.

A year later the Londons were less delighted with Martin, to whom they had given their own *Snark* photographs, including, as he requested, "the album of Samoan girls (nude studies)," along with various native artifacts, when he billed his act "Jack London's Adventures in the South Sea Islands." Worse, in 1913 he presented them with his book, *Through the South Seas with Jack London,* which they found amazing for its "criminal innacuracy."[11] Meanwhile, Osa's life on tour, for she no longer appeared on stage, became one of sitting alone in hotel rooms while Martin garnered the glory he sought, the farm boy's dream of fame fulfilled.

By September 1912 the ranch resembled a not particularly exclusive resort, where hobo socialists sat down to dinner beside sugar mogul Adolph Spreckels, and on the other side actor John D. Barrymore. Across the table might be the fledgling journalist Allan Dunn, or the Australian concert pianist Laurie Smith. Since the loss of a second child, Jack seemed even more hyperactive, engaged with plans for the ranch, business ventures, and his new book on alcoholism. Thus Charmian found herself drawn to her handsome younger guests. Smith arrived on September 27, "full of enthusiasm over the lovely moonlight ride up [Sonoma Mountain]." Being a "splendid rider" as well as a musician, Smith spent much of his time with Charmian. They played piano and sang together. Dunn arrived soon after and stayed intermittently that winter. In the late afternoons Jack would join his guests, and dominate the scene by reading aloud literature of interest, such as Conrad's "Youth" or Shaw's "Getting Married."[12]

On October 2, after she had sung to Laurie's accompaniment, Jack gave Charmian his newest book of short stories, *Smoke Bellew.* Within he inscribed, "I am still filled with the joy of your voice that was mine last night when you sang. Sometimes, more than any clearly wrought concept of you, there are fibre-sounds in your throat that tell me all the loveableness of you, and that I love as madly as I have always loved all the rest of you." This unexpected gift made her "move all day in a dream." She would soon awake to face inconceivable reality.

Health problems broke the round of entertaining. Jack's few remaining teeth were rotting and lose. Since he needed several days of dental work in Oakland, Charmian went to Merritt Hospital for further gynecological repairs. Jack held her hand while she went under the anesthesia, and visited her over the several weeks she spent in the hospital recuperating. While there she wrote poet Benjamin de Casseres, who had been one of Jack's companions during their last

New York visit. That time, she said, "seems a faraway, self centered nightmare," but everything was now "normal and healthy." Jack was busy writing "his alcoholic memoirs"—*John Barleycorn*—and "doing great things on the ranch." Addressing de Casseres's struggles as a young writer, Charmian acknowledged the special treatment she had received as "Mrs. Jack London." De Casseres had sold for $25 a story she thought a treasure, while ironically, her first story, "a padding out a theme . . . a slight incident," sold twice, to the *Monthly Magazine Section* in the States and the *Yachting Monthly* in England, earning her $155. "I'm not likely to lose my head over my phenomenal success (!)—especially as I am aware of the conjuring name I bear."[13] She did not want him to read her story, and refused to tell him its title, "The Wheel." Her evaluation of the piece was not mere modesty. Though competently crafted, it was little more than a wisp of a humorous incident at sea.

Jack's hospital visits to Charmian were followed by visits to Joan, who had been stricken with typhoid, a common killer. Just days before he had taken the girls to their favorite place, Idora Park. Now she lay semiconscious in an "icy nightmare" that would last for weeks. Upon stirring to brief awareness, she often found her father anxious-eyed by her side.

Possibly this experience, with its potential for the loss of another child, chastened London, for he began to pay more attention to his daughters. Bess convinced Jack that her home was in an unhealthy neighborhood, damp and contaminated by the nearby hospital, so he agreed to build them a new one. The three-story brown shingle on a promontory overlooking the entire Bay Area was virtually around the corner from the old Piedmont bungalow. He paid the girls allowances of two dollars a month, a good sum for that day, although they still had to send him receipts for expenses such as trolley fare to school or dancing lessons.

Jack was also building a brown-shingled bungalow for Eliza and twelve-year-old Irving on a ridge near the old cottage where he and Charmian now lived. Consequently, including Wolf House, he was paying for three construction projects that winter, and more than ever was pressed to find the money to keep up with the contractors' bills. But he could hardly stint his stepsister, who proved a loyal support no matter the trouble, and a shrewd, efficient administrator of the ranch and its workers as well. She had come to love the land and made many friends in Glen Ellen. Given her organizational acumen, she had also risen to become regional department secretary of the Woman's Relief Corps, a paid position that oversaw the business records of the almost six thousand members.

Eliza's patriotism actually complimented Jack's socialism. His complaint had always been with the political economy of capitalism, the inequities and abuses, not with representative democracy. His program of socialism never included overthrow of the American government and replacement by a dictatorship of the proletariat. He had run for office and supported the Socialist Party's conventional participation in politics, to win its case at the ballot box. His stepsister's efforts on behalf of loyalty to country appealed to his own confidence in the superiority of his homeland. Nonetheless, there was a subversive element to Eliza's choice of vocation. She was not an avid socialist, and by working for the WRC she could distinguish herself from her sometimes notorious stepbrother.

By moving to the ranch, Eliza deepened her friendship with Charmian, who, she could now see, was a woman of more substance than her public display of frills and light conversation suggested. If the less playful Eliza at times found Charmian's behavior frivolous or juvenile, her irritation was short-lived. Both women overcame their temperamental incompatibilities toward the service of their common purpose, Jack. As a result, they came to call each other "Sis."

Events that winter of 1912–13 formed the scaffolding for Jack's most curious and erotic novel, *The Little Lady of the Big House*. The story line involves a plot device he had used previously, that of a triad consisting of two men competing for one woman's love. It was the theme of his first novel, *The Daughter of the Snows,* and recurred throughout his stories and other novels up to his latest, *Adventure*. What makes *Little Lady* unique is its frank borrowing from his life with Charmian, and his candid admission of error. He uses himself as the model for rancher Dick Forrest, the antihero whose preoccupation with business and masculine pursuits leads to the suicide of his long-suffering and devoted wife. Before taking her life, Paula Forrest is tempted by the allure of a young house guest, Evan Graham, an athletic adventurer who enjoys Paula's dramatic style and superb physicality.

London would invest this story with great intensity, and in the process break from his earlier style. His main characters are no longer rooted in the nineteenth century—frontier adventurers or nostalgic escapees from the city—but are frankly modern types. Dick is the scientific, managerial rancher, who spends his days plotting and planning, studying research reports, tracing the bloodlines of his prize-winning stock. Paula is the unapologetic, New Woman, immodest about her many talents and conscious of her sexual needs. London dissects their relationship like a pathologist, with sharper diction and more clipped syntax than in his earlier writings. Perhaps it was the starkness of the realism, the radical disrobing of masculine values, that accounted for the critical rejection of the novel in its day and its exclusion from much literary scholarship in later decades.

If it is psychologically valid as a mirror of events during that winter, it nevertheless distorts the particulars, for obvious reasons. London set the story in the Central Valley, not Sonoma County, and made his lead character the heir of a great silver fortune rather than a self-made man. It is thus not autobiography, nor would London have wanted to hurt his rival, Laurie Smith, whom he held dear. Furthermore, Smith was not the only guest who touched Charmian's lonely heart, for Allan Dunn's more direct flirtations tempted her too.

With the loss of a second child, very likely the last chance for a child by Charmian, Jack shunned grief. Instead, he directed near-maniacal energy toward his Grand Scheme, that of creating a model ranch. As Eliza later recalled, his ambition "was to develop a model farm; one of the best all-round ranches in the state, combining a stock ranch, fruit, grain, vegetables, vineyard, and the like . . . [H]is enthusiasm was unquenchable."[14] With the final addition to the property, four hundred more acres in January 1913, he owned a swath clear up Sonoma Mountain from the town of Glen Ellen to the northern summit.

His agricultural project began with the construction of barns and stables for livestock and equipment. Hay was his first crop. In 1911 he followed the advice of both federal agricultural bulletins and the agronomists at University of California at Davis by starting a eucalyptus plantation. Eucalyptus, the Australian gum tree, was seen as a way to replace forests denuded by California's rapid growth in the late nineteenth century. Unfortunately, the experts proved to be wrong, because they failed to distinguish sufficiently among varieties of the tree. Jack, however, would glean no indication of error from the agricultural bulletins he marked up. This fast-growing, easy maintenance crop seemed to London and many other land-rich Californians a wise investment. He hired "floating workers," usually Italian immigrants accustomed to the work involved, to build his stone farm buildings and plant over 65,000 of the trees.

Once Eliza became his permanent superintendent, Jack turned to livestock raising, of which he was quite ignorant, though he was passionate about farm animals, felt a joy in their presence, and took a deep satisfaction in the challenge of a scientifically based endeavor. "Seven snow white pigs, not as long as this sheet of paper!" he wrote a convalescing Charmian in November 1912. In the postscript he mentioned several horses, including a new mare, "a bute."[15] Always believing that what was beautiful was also functional, he preferred the massive shire, a sturdy and powerful working horse.

Jack's first adviser in the care of farm animals was his former brother-in-law Ernest Matthews, whom he had hired to handle chores for Bess. Despite Mathews's marital relation to the Maddern family, Jack admired the man as someone he would "trust with anything & everything I had."[16] He appreciated Matthews's work ethic and hoped to help him break away from his regular occupation, a coffee sales route in the East Bay. Jack authorized Matthews to buy the working horses for the ranch, and asked his advice on a variety of matters from the use of chain harness to the identification of spavin.

Being new to serious farming, Jack was not hampered by long-standing ideas in animal husbandry currently under challenge, such as pure breeding, instead basing his management on the application of genetics and hybridization. Possibly the work of his friend Luther Burbank, the great plant hybridizer, influenced him here, providing visible proof, albeit in plums and cactus, of what the new stock breeding pamphlets argued. When it came to starting his own line of shires, he went to the best of breed from the 1912 state fair, a 2,300-pound British stallion named Neudad Hillside. He paid $2,500 for the horse, and $750 for another shire in foal. These joined the twenty draft horses he already had at work pulling lumber wagons, plows, and other farm implements. Then he turned to cattle and pigs, purchasing Jerseys, Shorthorns, Berkshires, and Cochin Chinas, and eventually angora goats. Charmian was equally involved in the husbandry, and Jack appreciated her eye for good conformation when it came to buying new stock and choosing which animals to breed.

As though this activity were not enough, Jack mapped out drainage, developed a gravity-fed irrigation system drawing from the mountain creeks into a small lake high above the pastureland, plotted and scheduled grain plantings, and kept a close eye on the workers, while Eliza took his directions and executed the particulars. All this was in addition to his daily writing and hawking of his stories. He boasted of keeping "a half dozen persons working overtime handling the work I map out and turn over to them. If I live to be five hundred years I should never be able to do the work I have already mapped out 100 novels and possibly 500 short stories."[17]

This determination to exert his will powerfully on the land, to prove his superiority through dominance of the earth and its creatures, was the essence of the fictional Dick Forrest as well. When Paula interrupts Forrest at work, he keeps his finger on the page he has been reading and glances at the clock. And, like Jack at this point in his life, Forrest has failed to sire children, while his beef cattle proliferate in the pasture. Meanwhile, a frustrated Paula displays her physical appeal and hunger by diving astride her mighty stallion into the pond and emerging as though naked in her water-soaked flesh-colored bathing suit. That vision brilliantly captured Charmian's mood and appearance that fall and winter of 1912.

When Jack hired his sister Ida's estranged husband, Jack Byrne, to take over some of Charmian's secretarial duties, she felt pushed aside (Ida was mortally ill and would die the next year. Byrne brought along their daughter, Charmian Eliza, better known as Tommy, who would be raised by Eliza and remained with her even after her father later remarried.) Thus, in late February 1913 she decided to "raise the spectre of adultery" and call Jack's bluff regarding monogamy, a state he was known to mock during conversations with guests as being unnecessary for those of the "higher classes."[18] Among these couples, he averred, divorce should follow when one of a pair has fallen in love with someone else. He had even confessed to Charmian at least one overnight fling. Some discovery, perhaps finding Allan Dunn and Charmian together at five in the morning watching a sunrise, forced a showdown. "Feel very much of a battle ground. But what men," Charmian confessed. "I can't help pouting out my chest. But I am heartbroken over Mate Man's suffering. Just the same—he has learned about women from me."[19] He once again became the avid lover, even taking Charmian on the living room floor.

Despite this passionate reconciliation, Jack failed to absorb Charmian's message. He did not slow down his ranch plans; he carried on a protracted contractual conflict with Century publishers; he pursued various business deals, none of which would result in a profit; he fought over dramatic rights to several of his works. Then offers from film producers in Los Angeles added a new source of distraction. He continued to use the Dictaphone and, over Charmian's objections, invited many friends to stay. One of the guests was again Allan Dunn, whose return was marked by "great days—full of beauty and interest and situation. Blue-eyed men."[20]

On May 3, 1913, Charmian recorded in her diary, "Eliza's husband shoots up the ranch." Though long estranged, James Shepard had come to visit, probably to see his son Irving. Meanwhile, Eliza had invited Charmian, Jack, and Jack Byrne to dinner. For some reason Shepard did not want Byrne present and ordered Eliza not to let him in the house. She refused, and when all three arrived to dine that evening, Shepard pulled a revolver and threatened to shoot his wife. Fortunately the gun went off without injuring anyone. The men wrestled Shepard to the ground, and Jack threw him off the ranch. The next day Shepard had the sheriff arrest Jack and Byrne for assault, though they were not jailed. A week later the case was thrown out of court. Although Shepard tried to reconcile with Eliza after that, she rejected all his overtures. In 1915 he would sue her for divorce, which was granted on grounds of desertion.

A month later a different sensational story would be splashed across the local papers. Allen Dunn had been arrested for stealing jewels from a noted society hostess and attempting to pawn them under the name of Elbert Hubbard, the noted essayist and craftsman. Also found in his possession were several pairs of Jack London's pajamas, a rather interesting theft in light of his flirtation with Charmian. A year would pass before he apologized to the Londons for his foolishness. He had been naive in failing to realize how much time would pass between the acceptance of a magazine article and the final payment, he explained, and hence had overreacted to his temporary financial straits. "Some of the playboy has been buried," he assured them, and thanked them for continuing to say kind things about him to others despite his churlishness.[21]

The first serious query from the movie industry came from Sidney Ayres, a handsome actor with the Balboa Amusement Company, one of seventy-three film companies now active in the Los Angeles area. In February, Jack assigned movie rights to his novels to Ayres, and in late April the Londons sailed south on the steamer *Lark* to discuss a possible contract. Charmian would once again be partner in the many negotiations that followed. She was excited by the prospect of a large income to pay for their expanding ranch dream and Wolf House, and was caught up in the glamour of the entertainment business.

Their agreement stipulated that Ayres was to produce four films by July 1, one of which must be ready for exhibition by mid-August. Though the time frame seems ludicrous by present standards, it was typical then, at a time when the public's voracious demand for one- and two-reel films had producers grinding them out. Like the eucalyptus investment, the movies seemed an easy path to sure profits. The monopolistic Edison Company had recently lost a patent suit against independent producer William Fox, which meant that independents like Balboa believed they could now compete against the giant. Whereas the short-reel scenario writers earned $50 to $500 for a script, novelist Roy Mc-Cardell received $30,000 from American Film for a single story. Jack was aware that the stakes favored established writers. Among them was Rex Beach, whose career Jack followed closely, to the point of saving clippings concerning Beach's film successes in his scrapbook. Thus the timing seemed perfect for both Balboa and London to profit from a new epoch in moviemaking, now that audiences sat not in tents for a few minutes, but in comfortable and commodious theaters and watched lengthy plots unfold. Americans had even proved willing to pay the astronomical admission of one dollar to sit through nine reels of the Italian extravaganza *Quo Vadis*.

The couple was ripe for exploitation. Ayres's plan was to become a director, and he hoped to use his rights to London's works to gain that position at Balboa. Yet his letters to Jack suggest little understanding of the production process, and he disparaged Balboa's owner, H. M. Horkheimer. Untroubled by these signs, London approved production of *The Sea-Wolf*, but objected to filming *John Barleycorn* until its book sales had peaked and its stage version had finished its run. Disagreement and mistrust between Horkheimer and Ayres built, however, and London was not always a reliable correspondent. By June he was losing confidence in the likelihood that quality work would result from his partnership, particularly after hearing that the first effort, *A Piece of Steak*, revealed Ayres's clumsy directorial skills.

When Horkheimer asked for an extension of the contract beyond July 1, Jack invited him to the ranch for face-to-face discussion. Before the meeting could get under way, Jack was felled by appendicitis and rushed to Oakland for emergency surgery. Even this mishap fed the ongoing national news commentary which often treated London's latest activity humorously. The *New York Herald* suggested that losing his appendix would have no effect on Jack's "overwhelming impudence," while the *Boston Transcript* joked that his next novel would be "a romance with an appendix for a hero." Charmian glued these news clippings into his oversized scrapbooks along with the recent favorable film reviews of *The Valley of the Moon* and *John Barleycorn*. Comfortable manipulating the press to his advantage, Jack did the same with editors, and now movie producers. (Charmian enjoyed watching his scheme unfold.) What Ayres and Horkheimer did not know was that a competitor, another member of their company, had been working behind the scenes. Sent by Balboa to find a boat in San Francisco on which to film *The Sea-Wolf*, Hobart Bosworth contacted Jack and persuaded him to reassign the movie rights to a company he was forming.

Bosworth had several advantages in Jack's eyes over the Balboa partners. He had grown up in Ohio, home state of the Wellmans, gone to sea, became a landscape painter, then a successful stage actor. By the time he met Jack, he had acted in over a hundred films, written almost as many, and directed over eighty. Backing Bosworth was Frank Garbutt, an astute Los Angeles capitalist made wealthy by real estate and oil dealings. Charmian was taken by the charm and experience of these two men, but also significant was their Anglo-Saxon heritage. (In her diary and later accounts, Charmian included a reference to "the wily but ingratiating Hebrew, Mr. 'Porchclimber.'") On July 26 Jack signed his movie rights over to Bosworth in exchange for half the profits. He was led to believe that this would bring in ten to fifty thousand dollars per picture.

Even before gaining the contract, Bosworth had worked subversively within Balboa to persuade its actors and technicians to join him. He even proposed to destroy the original negatives of *A Piece of Steak*, though this did not happen. Balboa now had two other movies ready to distribute: *To Kill a Man* and *The Sea-Wolf*. Bosworth had his own ideas for the latter story, and set about immediately to film his own version. One of his clever marketing ploys was to use footage of Jack on the ranch as an introduction to each movie, in effect an imprimatur. On August 14 Bosworth arrived to shoot these scenes, then invited the Londons to watch the filming in Sausalito harbor. They left confident in their new director, and celebrated by going to the movies that evening with

Blanche Partington. The capital they needed to support their grand scheme, their ranch experiment, now seemed secure.

The year 1913 was also marked by a revived intimacy between Jack and his daughters, particularly Joan. On February 22 Bess had apparently allowed them to visit the ranch. Charmian made a catty entry in her diary concerning the "awful surrey" and the terrible horses who could hardly make it up the hill, as though owning such inferior stock were Bess's fault, not Jack's. But she also described the lovely way the girls decorated the cottage with almond blossoms.

Curiously, in later reminiscences neither daughter ever mentioned this visit, their only one to the ranch during their father's lifetime. It is unclear whether Bess accompanied them, or whether Charmian was around during their stay. Yet it made an obvious impression on Joan, who began writing her father letters filled with stories of the garden and livestock at their own home. In one letter she expressed delight in news of his new goats and colts, and described the chicks hatched in their backyard.[22] She hoped he would approve the expenditure of nine or ten dollars for a chicken yard at their new house so their chickens would not be endangered by running loose. In another she exulted over the blooms on their apple, pear, quince, and cherry trees. Though the tone hints at seeking her father's approval, Joan's affection for gardening and animals was genuine.

Now twelve, Joan remained protective of her little sister. "My heart has been in my mouth for these last two days," she reported when delivering news of Becky's sudden collapse with what appeared to be scarlet fever. Sent to a neighbor's house, Joan expressed her great loneliness over separation from her sister, and her fears on waking up in a strange room. What calmed her were the sights and smells of the wisteria, lilac, and cherry blossoms outside the window, and "the whole world seemed to breathe of Spring joy and hopefulness."[23]

Joan displayed further identification with her father through her political interests. She recounted hearing a speech against the Alien Laws aimed at restricting Japanese immigration, and was reminded of her father's similar objections. She wrote of hearing an address against women's suffrage and of joining the audience to ridicule the speaker. Sometimes she tweaked her father humorously to make a point and express anger in an oblique way. In requesting three dollars so she and Bess could see a play based on one of their favorite series, the Oz books, she explained, "Mother's purse isn't ready to move. Purses are very stubborn sometimes. Does yours ever act that way?"[24] Another time she wondered if he fed his publishers' rejection letters to his goats.

As Joan's letters grew more revealing and self-confident, she included more requests for extra money for herself, her sister, and her mother, such as $4.50 to attend *Peter Pan,* starring Maud Adams, $1.65 for a month's dancing school lessons, and several dollars for concrete benches. These were often paid. But when she asked for $9 for the move to the new house and $21 for cleaning and laying carpet, she used an argument that infuriated her father. She was making the request, she said, without her mother's knowledge. The money was needed because the doctor's bills for the girls' illnesses that spring had exhausted Bess's funds, along with her own health. "Mother has borne everything on her shoulders the past twelve years and now I am trying to help her. I am trying to drive away those nasty wrinkles in her face." She begged for his understanding. "I wouldn't go to you if I could help it but you are my own Daddy so I'm sure you won't mind." She must have known otherwise, though, because she concluded, "Now don't forget don't scold mother but me."[25]

Jack sent the check, accompanied by words honed to a sharp edge. Self-pityingly he noted that Joan had failed to see all the wrinkles and tiredness in his own face, and that it was wrong of her to draw conclusions about him and her mother. "Don't you realize how you & I are practically strangers?" he asked, adding that she probably knew her uncles better than she knew him. He might be her daddy, who paid many bills, but they were at best "speaking acquaintances." He protested the tone of her request, which implied that he became angry when asked for money—an ironic protest in light of the anger clearly running through his letter. He closed with a cool remark that he anticipated acknowledgment of his *Peter Pan* money and allowance.[26]

Joan immediately apologized and thanked her father for his recent checks. She added that her mother was dumbfounded to receive the money for the move, and had explained to her daughters that her pained appearance had been the result of physical discomfort, not anything their father had done. On the day of the move in late May, Joan thanked him for their "magnificent" new home. Then she added, "Mother wants me to tell you that I became a woman yesterday. She says that you will understand. Lots of love from your Big Girl."[27] Jack's response was his shortest ever, yet rich in feeling. "Dearest Joan: Hurrah for the moving! And bless you for the other news you told me. All Love, Daddy."[28]

Joan once again loosened her caution and sought counsel on a key decision. What courses to take in high school? she asked. English, French, algebra, and history was his response, and a year of science later on—all courses leading to entry into the University of California. Now more aware of Joan's intense energy and nervous temperament, he added, perhaps as a warning to himself as well, "By all means don't over work."[29] Joan's excitement over her approaching grammar school graduation stirred her hopes that he would appear. Having written the class history and prophecy, which she would read at the ceremony, she reminded him, "Your big girl shall only graduate from Grammar School *once*."[30] In another letter she told him that the principal, Mr. Dunbar, also wished Jack would attend and say a few words to the students.

When Jack did not appear, Joan wrote a nineteen-page description of the event that well evokes the period just before the loss of America's innocence in the First World War. The girls wore dresses they had made themselves, with colorful ribbons to adorn their long hair. The event began with various musical numbers, including a song by the school janitor, who then led the audience in "The Trail of the Lonesome Pine." At this the audience "broke down utterly" over the love the students showed the janitor. As Joan received her diploma, she also was handed a bouquet of American Beauty roses, a gift from her drama teacher. Joan did not read the prophecy after all, but let her best friend, who had helped on it, have the honor. At a celebration dinner party hosted by a friend, Joan declined to join in the "ragging," not caring for that kind of dancing. In a more pointed description of her various gifts, for her father had sent none, she singled out the one from her mother, who had had a raw pearl Jack had sent from Samoa set into a ring. What a pleasure it would be, Joan cajoled him, to receive from him a silver watch, for she had so often heard of her mother's delight in receiving such a gift at her grammar school graduation.[31]

Why Jack missed his daughter's graduation is unclear. Had he been ill, Joan would likely have expressed her concern, as she had in the past. Nothing in Charmian's diaries hints at anything to prevent his attending. Rather, Charmian's notes focus on ranch operations and ongoing negotiations with the film industry. Joan's long letter suggests that she had discovered a subtle new way of expressing her displeasure with him, for there is not a hint of pique.

In July, when Joan heard of her father's emergency appendectomy, she immediately sent a cheery note and asked when she and Becky could visit him in the hospital. She added a long account of a hike she, Becky, and her mother had taken; scanning the distance, they'd noticed a red spot on Mount Tamalpais, which grew into a major fire down its slopes. In August she complained about the unusual heat, 110 degrees in the shade. These accounts are echoed in Charmian's summertime diaries as well, their concern was understandable, for the greatest natural threat in Northern California is not earthquake but fire.

During that unusually hot August the workmen had only finish work left to complete Wolf House, mostly sanding and oiling the extensive woodwork used throughout. The interior was not ornate as in the mansions going up elsewhere in the Bay Area, but was in the austere Arts and Crafts style. It was the culmination of Jack's vision of the "House Beautiful," built almost entirely of materials available on the ranch, and equipped with the latest domestic technology to reduce the labor of maintenance. The walls were of black and reddish-brown rocks thrown up in the era when the mountain had been a mud volcano; its great beams were of redwood with the bark left on for a rustic appearance. Huge untrimmed tree trunk columns supported the front portico. Cement walls and partitions, such as around the manuscript vault in the basement, and a water tower were details meant to help fireproof the structure. Because the house was U-shaped—surrounding a deep pond for stocking fish—and composed of such massive materials, it appeared larger from the outside than the interior proved to be.

The design carefully delineated the main functions of the house: work and play. The basement and first floor incorporated the servant quarters and work-rooms, a dining room, guest rooms, a two-story-high living room with music alcove, a library, and a stag party room for less formal activities. The second story was the private area, containing Jack's workroom, two unspecified "extra rooms"—one perhaps for a nursery—and Charmian's apartment, which included a large bath, dressing room, and sleeping deck. Above her room was a sleeping tower and private bath for Jack.

Charmian and Nakata used all their rare free moments to pack and prepare for the move in late August. The furnishings from their cottage would well suit their new home. Unornamented furniture of Hawaiian koa commissioned from sculptor Finn Frolich, along with decorative objects from the South Seas and hangings of hand-dyed tapa cloth, complimented the natural materials of the building. Charmian's dried flower displays and animal skins used as throws or rugs added to the aesthetic of natural simplicity. Their bedrooms would have functional iron bedsteads with modest side tables to hold their nighttime reading materials.

Embedded in the Arts and Crafts ideal was the ethic of combining beauty with function, which included labor-saving layouts and equipment. Having found physical labor so repellent, Jack always sought means to reduce the workload of his ranchhands and house servants. (His design for a circular piggery was meant to facilitate efficient feeding of the animals and cleaning of the pens.) Accordingly, Wolf House was designed with six stairwells to save time in changing levels, and had such up-to-date equipment as a central vacuuming system.

Charmian and Jack rode on horseback daily to the site to marvel at their latest dream made reality. On August 20, several days before they were to move in, she noted that she was again hoping to become pregnant, that there were "all sorts of reasons for the nursery." They were as usual spending more money than was coming in, but Charmian had no reason to fear now, given the movie deal, Jack's ongoing lucrative contract with *Cosmopolitan* magazine, and the imminent move to their rock-solid dream home.

"At midnight Eliza comes to tell us of fire," reads her diary for August 22. "And our Wolf House is destroyed. Mate and I are cheerful enough until we get back, at about 5 am. Mate breaks down completely."

# 10

## A Ruined Colt

FOLLOWING THE DESTRUCTION of Wolf House, Jack's despair was so extreme it tainted his relationships, especially with Joan. Receiving no word of sympathy from his elder daughter, he accused her of ingratitude. "Am I dirt under your feet? Am I beneath your contempt in every way save as a meal ticket?"[1] Forgive me, she replied. Though Joan had not heard of the fire right away, she admitted that the excitement of starting high school and her period had her "head swimming," and she'd been unable to calm down and write. "You are the goal which I sometimes hope to reach. The goal which is attained only after years of hard work like you have done." She begged him to understand she could not come to Glen Ellen so long as that meant seeing people other than him, that is, Charmian. She closed, "Your sorrowful & repentant Joan."[2]

Her father's response likely crossed her next letter, twelve pages about her high school experiences, for his tone remained angry. He refused to understand why she would not come to the ranch, and urged her to be more explicit. "Don't be afraid of being harsh. Don't be afraid of being true."[3] Joan's next, newsy note enclosed the first poem she had attempted. Chastened, he called it "dandy, splendid," and expressed the wish that he had the opportunity to teach her rhythm and form. In a loving postscript he added, "I used to write for the *Aegis* [Oakland High's literary journal] long ago. I dreamed a daughter would write for it."[4]

Clearly aware by now of Joan's talent and drive, Jack more than ever wanted to have her visit him on the ranch, where he could show her a very different world and teach her his views on life. Joan again pleaded for his patience; her feelings, however much he failed to understand, were *her* feelings. Perhaps it would be best, she suggested, that he stop making these demands and wait until she was older.[5] Yet several days later, during a visit to Oakland, he again urged her to tell "the truth," that is, to be frank regarding Charmian's role. Joan recounted how Bess had hidden the fact of the divorce from the girls and had led them to believe that their father had gone on a long journey. Eventually they learned that another woman had intruded in their mother's place, and suffered embarrassment at school when classmates taunted them for being children of divorce. "Bess [Becky] and I feel that we have one of the best Mothers in the whole wide world," she emphasized.[6]

When Joan refused to back down from her position, he warned, "The less I see of you and Bess [Becky], the less I would be bound to be interested in you." What Jack did not consider was his own complicity, how he had remained incommunicado during extensive travels, and how his treatment of Bess had forced his daughters to defend her. Instead he accused Joan of adopting her mother's "sex jealousy," and thus becoming a "little person." He knew Nakata, who had shared danger and near-death, comfort and laughter with him over seven years, "ten thousand times better." Continuing to discount her earlier statements, he charged her with being the silent one on the matter.[7]

This would have been a difficult letter for an adult to receive, let alone a twelve-year-old girl. It further documents his sheer lack of understanding of youth, its sensitivities and its needs. His other correspondence during this time is similarly direct and tough, but it was written to lawyers or businesspeople accustomed to blunt talk. Despite his newest threat, Joan reiterated her loyalty to her mother. What is better in the world than a "good mother," she asked. She begged him to stop forcing her to write "these awful letters."[8] To this Jack responded that he would send no extra Christmas money, which in the past the girls had used to buy presents for others, nor would he send tickets for them to see the play *Little Women*.

Having so little direct knowledge of Jack's daily life, neither Bess nor her daughters could appreciate how complex it had become, particularly now, with his involvement in movies. This endeavor, which was to provide the capital for the ranch, was proving more troublesome than its meager profits justified. During this time, too, his physical ailments increased, including the first signs of the kidney disease that would take his life. (Various hypotheses have been offered for his decline, including an undiagnosed tropical infection, lupus, or overuse of Salvarsan, an arsenic compound used to treat syphilis.)[9]

Nor did his family know that he suspected arson in the loss of Wolf House, as Charmian revealed to Anna in her account of the aftermath, referring to the "wanton destruction of so much beauty" and "the indisputable fact that it was set afire by some enemy." The Londons would never know that their suspicions were baseless, that the fire had resulted from spontaneous combustion of oily woodworking rags.[10] Consequently they could not help but consider "a thousand easy conjectures." Understandably, Charmian was feeling "a sharp keenness with reference to Jack" about "the precariousness of life." Fear of his death shadowed her days, not because she was a coward, but because it seemed "as if I were responsible for his existence and that we must preserve ourselves against all common fates that overtake other mortals! Laughable, perhaps, but deadly serious."[11] Her instincts were not unfounded.

Jack increased his work to avoid brooding over the loss. He completed *The Mutiny of the Elsinore* a week later, "making the ending where I [Charmian] suggested."[12] When not writing, he poured his efforts into the ranch. He kept his workmen busy realizing his program of self-sufficiency. They built silos with rock from his own land, which was towed to the crushing area by his livestock. Only the cement was brought to the site from outside. Other workers made ten-inch drain tiles for the alfalfa field, and designed a dam farther up the mountain to store 7 million gallons of water for both irrigation and fire protection. When the local blacksmith went out of business, Jack bought the entire shop and moved it up to the ranch, much to the consternation of his Glen Ellen neighbors who needed its services. Demonstrating that he could restore the worn-out soil, he terraced the hillsides extensively to prevent the topsoil from eroding in the rainy seasons to the creek far below. Borrowing from the Chinese experience of farming "forty acres without fertilizing," he rotated crops with plantings of green manure. A roofed enclosure collected manure from the animals, which, after fermenting, was spread on the fields in a liquid form delivered through a piping system. He revitalized a dozen acres of old French prune trees, and tore up the old winery vines to plant barley. Even visiting acquaintances joined in the ranch activities, such as filling a new silo with his and his neighbors' corn.

While Jack appeared cheerful to others, Charmian knew his secret anguish, his chest pains and nervous symptoms. One day he admitted to her that he had not passed the physical examination for a new life insurance policy. She suggested his cardiac problems could be due to excess smoking, but he argued the contrary and refused to give up his cigarettes. Worry over her husband's failing physical state further exacerbated Charmian's own heart palpitations and nightmares.

In late September a new threat appeared in the form of a lawsuit. Earlier that month Hobart Bosworth and Jack had sued H. M. Horkheimer to prevent him from distributing the films he had made, since their version of *The Sea-Wolf* was now ready for distribution. The financially strapped Horkheimer countersued, claiming that London did not hold the copyright for film versions of his works. Jack warned Charmian that they could lose everything if the case went to trial. If so, he assured her, they would buy a boat large enough to carry her grand piano, and leave the country forever.

London's position was uncertain legally.[13] Copyright law did not yet explicitly cover film, and an expert had convinced a judge that London's magazine se-rializations in effect made his work public property. In ensuing months Jack prompted the Authors' League of America to join in his complaint against Horkheimer, and tried to get publishers such as Macmillan involved as well. As usual, Jack cast himself as the total innocent, when of course he had been deceptive and duplicitous toward Horkheimer during their partnership. Nonetheless, his efforts on behalf of the larger copyright issue evince a sincere concern for authors' rights. Unfortunately, neither the Authors' League nor the publishers were willing to join his battle.

Meanwhile that fall the Horkheimer/Balboa Company versions of London's stories were siphoning potential income from the new Bosworth productions. With his investment clearly threatened, Frank Garbutt urged Jack to spread the word among exhibitors that only Bosworth's versions were authentic. In time, Garbutt intervened between the hotheads on both sides of the controversy to achieve a compromise. Thus, by the time the suit reached federal court in early 1914, Garbutt had persuaded Jack to pay Horkheimer $10,000 and allow con-tinued marketing of the Balboa films, though under new titles. Each side agreed to pay its own attorney's fees.

Even then the Bosworth venture proved of little value. His five productions failed to include any stars, and audience reactions were not favorable to Jack's tragic endings. Ultimately, the Londons' income from these films would amount to $9,300, far less than the profit originally projected from a single film. The time spent on resolving all the movie issues in 1914 meant, too, that other income sources could not be pursued.

Wolf House had been insured for much less than its value, yet bills remained to be paid, along with mortgages on homes for his extended family. Unsuccess-ful so far in garnering income from his movies, stage productions, or business ventures, Jack was vulnerable to promises of quick returns. One day he told Charmian that he planned to gamble by investing in fifty shares of a Mexican land stock; he lost several thousand dollars in the deal. Willing to take money from any source, he signed on as a celebrity endorser for products. A full-page *Cosmopolitan* ad for Royal Tailors in New York depicted London "before" in the baggy work clothes of an able-bodied seaman, and "after" in a trim suit unlike the loose tailoring he favored. Crafty in public relations, Jack understood the concept of "hype" long before it entered general consciousness.

In January 1914 Jack faced yet another serious challenge concerning copy-rights. Years before he had granted his friend Joseph Noel dramatic rights to *The Sea-Wolf*. Now living in New York, Noel had tried unsuccessfully to get his script produced. Then, having run into financial difficulties, Noel had bor-rowed money against any future receipts on the play. The agent holding those rights now went to court to claim that they included movie rights. He demanded $40,000 in compensation. Jack would have to go to New York to work out his legal problems.

Perhaps to further protect the ranch from losses as a result of this lawsuit, before leaving Jack transferred all title to livestock, farm equipment, and $450 to Eliza "for services rendered."[14] Charmian's name was now on the deeds to the ranch properties. Without informing Bess, Jack also transferred the deeds to her old house in Oakland to Charmian and the new 606 Scenic Avenue house to Eliza. These transfers marked the increasing role Eliza played on the financial side of Jack's affairs, where, unlike Charmian, she would have some decision-making power over property in her name.

Unable to afford train fare for his wife, Jack went east alone. Charmian was so strapped for funds that she had to borrow $150 from the visiting Osa and Martin Johnson to meet some of her household expenses. She not only repaid that debt quickly, but also took over the bills for an emergency operation Osa needed. While Jack was away, he sent telegrams advising her of the troubled progress of the negotiations. "Outlook dark" and "Situation ticklish" left her anxious until the final message almost five weeks later announced his success in talking the agent down to accept about $4,000.

Also worrying Charmian was knowing that "no one ever saw Jack London Himself in New York. Out of the very bliss of existence, as say on the yacht, or on the Ranch, he would plunge into an existence full of actions almost negating his other personality."[15] This trip was no exception. Before Jack's departure, as in other winters they sailed the *Roamer* for many weeks on the Sacramento Delta waterways, during which they worked, fished, and read aloud to each other. There his boyish side prevailed through such gleeful games as bets with their servants Nakata and Sanna over their respective fishing catches. New York brought out the darker side of his personality, the one drawn by the allure of devil-may-care entertainment.

On the train out, Jack composed one of his most ardent letters in years to "My Woman." He regretted having to do his thousand words a day and the effect it had on him, and thus on her. She was his "*dearest* possession . . . count[s] for everything. All the space of words occupied by all my books would not furnish the details of the account that makes you so count with me."[16] Perhaps this explains why she was not worried when Flora received a curious telegram and showed it to Charmian. "London is spending all his time with a woman who lives in the Van Cortland [sic] Hotel on Forty-ninth Street." It was signed "Amy." Yes, he admitted, he had been at the Van Courtlandt "with Tammany men, prize-fighters, street walkers, managers of theatres . . . also leading ladies, kept women, etc. etc. etc. More room for Scandal I guess." Despite encountering such women, he assured Charmian, he kept the vision of her "sweet, beautiful body, of the spirit that informs it to such quick eagerness." She was a thoroughbred mare, and he had never been "infatuated by cows."[17]

Exactly what transpired on another night in New York is unclear. Jack went with male friends to a nightclub in Harlem and invited several women performers to join them afterward for dinner downtown. At around one in the morning a limousine struck their cab. The occupants, though cut and bruised, refused hospitalization. Newspapers printed a story that omitted their identity. Perhaps there was a payoff to a reporter, or the editors were unwilling to expose prominent white men in the company of black women. Even yellow journalism had its limits regarding sensationalism. The following day Jack composed for Charmian a dramatic account of the episode: broken glass in his mouth, suffocating at the bottom of the pile of bodies. He left out key information, however, such as what happened afterward and just what he was doing with a group of black burlesque performers in the first place.

The frankness and free expression of these two long letters is disarming. To conclude that Jack was dissimulating requires an enormous level of cynicism. That he had not always been sexually faithful to Charmian was, by her own acknowledgment, true. But his straying had been a transient expression of lust, of a kind familiar to Charmian from her own single years of sexual freedom. What haunted her during his unruly periods was not the physical release he sought with other women but the possibility that he might fall in love. "Adultery" to both Jack and Charmian meant psychological and spiritual intimacy, not sexual intercourse. What these two letters from New York reflect is a new maturity following that most terrible year, when Charmian brought Jack up short with threats of her own infidelity, and their intimacy deepened through consolation over shared losses.

Charmian's correspondence with Anna during this time also hints at her confidence in Jack's devotion. Congratulating Anna on the birth of Georgia in the fall of 1913, Charmian wrote of her fear for Jack's life, "because any accident that would break up the combination that is ours, seems so utterly disastrous."[18] Anna, four-year-old Rosamund, and baby Georgia came in from Cedarhurst to visit Jack in New York. One day she, Rose, and Jane Roulston (model for the heroine of *The Iron Heel*) met Jack at the Hotel Astor for lunch. Afterward she let Charmian know how movingly Jack had spoken of his belief in love—in other words, he had capitulated to the romantic stance he had rejected in *The Kempton-Wace Letters*. That he would speak this way in New York reassured Charmian that "he has found out some things that I did not believe he would ever quite sense." Anna's message was proof that he "had not lost his real self" in that city of temptation.[19]

To English, Anna reiterated Jack's insistence that "nothing in the world matters but love." He was no longer interested in her career because he feared it "would interfere with my love for you and the babies." She acknowledged that Jack had "large and obvious" faults, but his outlook on life remained admirable, "his nature generous and practical."[20] Her remark led to a rebuke. "When you are working you are not loving(!)" English's response was candid. He recognized that Anna could not bear to part company with Jack, that her tendency was to see him always as youthful and energetic. He believed that she was swayed too much by Jack's personality, but he was in fact "constantly on a false road" and "so often wastes himself."[21]

Jack sealed his devotion to Charmian in a letter to Joan sent on February 24, 1914. He opened by complaining, probably with little hyperbole, that he had only $3.46 in his checking account after sending her a check for fifty cents. He admonished her for charging schoolbooks to his account at an Oakland bookstore without his permission. Then he introduced the real purpose of the letter by stating that he had always found that by being frank and true, "no thing is difficult to say." What he did not consider was the effect of his candor on his thirteen-year-old daughter, who would spend most of her life trying to understand the "relentless, calculating cruelty with which he wrote to me."[22]

Jack admitted that all his life he had had a pattern of developing disgust toward things in which he'd lost interest, and explained his feelings in terms of animal training. When a colt shows bad traits like kicking or balking, one tries patiently to train away the undesirable traits; when the colt persists, "I say Let the colt go. Kill it, sell it, give it away." He had warned Joan's mother that he would develop a similar loss of interest in the girls if she kept them from him. In his mind, Joan was "a ruined colt," the result of her mother's being a poor trainer and "born stupid." Consequently, although he would continue provide "food in your stomach, a roof that does not leak, warm blankets, and clothing to cover you," he was no longer interested in her or Becky. He would pay for them to go to the University of California, provided it was not "merely in recognition of the bourgeois valuation placed upon the University pigskin." He was even withdrawing his opposition to Joan's interest in a career on the stage. In return, he wanted no news of her "markings in High School, and no longer send me your compositions." Were he dying, he would not want her at his bedside. He signed the letter "Jack London."

For once his conditioning the girls not to cry failed Joan. When she received the letter, she could not control the tears, and simply denied his rejection. Two weeks later he advised her to send all schoolbook accounts to Eliza for reimbursement from then on. He also recommended that she file her letters to read when she was older. "Me of course you will be unable ever to understand, because you have never had an opportunity to be with me. The same will be true of yourself. When you are a woman you and I will talk different languages."[23]

Stubborn as her father, Joan responded with a single sentence: "I received the check for the car fare and allowance safely and I thank you very much."[24] She was determined to stay in his life, however much he defamed her mother and extolled Charmian. Joan continued to send brief notes to him, though more often to Eliza Shepard. Joan's requests typically began, "Mother asked me . . ." or "Mother wanted me to tell you. . . ." Eliza closely surveyed the accounts, and asked for explanations of discrepancies in small expenses, for example, questioning the number of schooldays in computing trolley fares for school. Over two years would pass before father and daughters came face to face.

Although the "ruined colt" metaphor was addressed to Joan, it had obvious implications for Becky as well. Jack's thoughts of his younger daughter, if measured by his infrequent mentions of her to others, were almost nonexistent. About the closest Becky came to expressing her own feelings is a passing comment that her father was in some ways ruthless, and "disappointed in anybody who didn't live up to what he thought they were capable of doing."[25] The reasons for her silence can be found as much in Becky's temperament as in her father's attitude.

Becky was now eleven and old enough to have established her own correspondence with her father, yet she had not done so. In contrast to her handsome, dark-complected older sister, she was blossoming into a classic beauty with fair skin, curly blond hair, and a winsome smile. Where Joan was quick, curious, intense, even overly dramatic, Becky was pleasant, even-tempered, lighthearted, and admittedly lazy. Though bright, she did not exhibit interest in ideas or theories, and preferred novels to the historical and political tomes her sister enjoyed. Well behaved and compliant, she disguised any feelings of anger or resentment where another child might lash out more directly. No doubt she thought that being the "good girl" would earn her favor with her father, but it only made her seem dull compared to Joan.

Resentment developed at some point, for in later life she recalled having been as a child under the control of her mother and sister in collusion against her. She saw herself as unfavored, though little hard evidence supports this perception, at least in material terms. She received the same treats as Joan: the same outings with their father, the same beautiful dresses and coats hand-tailored by their mother, the same presents from their father, the same trips with their mother. Joan's letters display only affection and protectiveness toward her sister. Nonetheless, it makes sense that Becky would resent her sister's special relationship with their father. Viewing Joan as the elder sister with commensurate responsibilities, Jack sent few notes to Becky alone. Yet by making Joan the intermediary, he made her the unfortunate messenger of his rejections, such as the news that he had denied some request or other.

There is some truth in Becky's perception that Bess felt closer to Joan, who as the elder daughter would naturally have understood more. Furthermore, Joan not only resembled her mother physically but also shared her more intellectual interests. And Joan was such an achiever, whether practicing piano, competing in essay contests, or raising chicks, that her accomplishments consistently outshone Becky's. Becky shared her mother's conventionality, yet that very steadiness was not likely to draw attention or special praise. In adopting her mother's avoidance of conflict, Becky also conveyed a misleading congeniality that would prevent others from recognizing her anger and frustration. There is also a familiar dynamic here of the younger sibling struggling to be seen in the older one's shadow.

True to her temperament, in later years Becky never referred to the troubling aspects of the girls' relationship with their father. Consequently, we know nothing about her reaction to Jack's mean-sprited letters to Joan. She certainly knew, however. Bess shared information frankly with the girls, though her pattern was to delay until she felt they were old enough to understand. Thus it was in the midst of this conflict that she sat the girls down one evening to explain the truth about Jack's paternity. Much later in life Joan reflected that "nothing in his own childhood had prepared Daddy to understand the plight of a sad, confused little girl."[26]

Now Jack's letters to Joan meant that Becky was denied communication with her father, and she placed the blame for that on her sister and mother. She came to see her father as so marvelous a personality that her mother, fearing the girls would like him better, had deprived them of contact with him. "So I never learned to ride a horse," she remarked at eighty-six, still resentful over the loss.[27] This interpretation, while partially valid, avoided what at some level she must have known, that in her father's eyes she was less important than Joan. After all, he had not even bothered to appear at her birth.

A breach was developing between the two girls, who as children had been such close and warm companions. When Joan told their father that "Becky and I" retained an allegiance to their mother, she was really speaking only for herself. What, one wonders, would have happened had Becky asserted herself differently to her father at that point?

Jack's financial difficulties worsened. His note on Wolf House required payments of $1,000 a month. The ranch payroll and regular expenses averaged another $2,000. In March 1914 he received over $8,000 from various publishers, but this income was only enough to stave off bankruptcy. Then, when he asked for an extension on his state taxes, he was refused.

Worse, the expected profits from the Bosworth films were not materializing. Despite the popularity of the Italian *Quo Vadis,* distributors resisted showing full-length feature films. In defiance of the lawsuit settlement, Balboa was still advertising *Hell Ship* as a Jack London movie. And although *John Barleycorn* was endorsed by ministers and social workers for its warnings against drink, film censors in major cities demanded cuts to remove what they considered to be salacious content. Garbutt was losing his own considerable investment in the endeavor, and could not convince Jack that he was not hiding the profits.

In his scramble to find new sources of funds, Jack signed up to sponsor, though not directly invest in, the Jack London Grape Juice Company. The tie-in was with his increasingly public stance in favor of prohibition and national women's suffrage. "London Will Fight Booze by Making Grape Juice" blared the headlines. The spirits and beer industries were the major underwriters of the effort to prevent women from getting the vote, understandably fearful that they would support a prohibition amendment. Jack had the sense this time to see to it that he had no liability, and thus was not held responsible for debts when the company failed in 1916.

All was not bleak in the spring of 1914. *Collier's Weekly* had arranged for Jack to go to Japan to write a series of articles on agricultural conditions there—although, as he explained to a friend, the book would really be about conditions in the United States. This was characteristic of his work, to embed a more serious motif within a superficial story or account, even if, to his dismay, only a few ever glimpsed the serious point. Charmian and Nakata would go along as well, and were busy preparing for the journey. Given a new national crisis, however, *Collier's* withdrew its offer and requested that Jack instead go to Mexico, where several American sailors had been arrested by the government of Victoriano Huerta in early April.

In support of the constitutionalist opposition to Huerta, President Wilson had ordered warships to Vera Cruz, where a battle for the Customs House ensued. On April 25 Jack left Galveston on a transport ship to Vera Cruz, while Charmian and Nakata boarded a fruit boat to meet him there. But by the time they arrived, Huerta had apologized and the war was over. Consequently, instead of writing war correspondence, Jack was pressed to find human interest stories.

In Vera Cruz the markets, balls, and bullfights continued in spite of the influx of refugees and injured men and the news of continued revolutionary skirmishes. Jack joined several expeditions to retrieve refugees from behind the lines, as well as a sortie to find a hidden machine gun. Meanwhile, with other American wives, Charmian explored tourist haunts such as cathedrals and shops, and temporarily sated her vanity with purchases of lace, jewels, and custom-made dresses. She was also the only American woman allowed to visit a hospital ship, where she observed an amputation, and she spent long days observing a court in session, all to provide detailed notes for Jack's articles. At times she accompanied him into the countryside with the anti-Huerta forces.

Once more Jack's weak constitution brought a precipitate end to an adventure that Charmian wished to continue. Struck down by dysentery, Jack responded poorly to the "dope," and found only brief comfort in the three daily enemas she administered. When pleurisy struck as well, she insisted they return to Galveston so he could get hospital treatment. Describing his almost fatal attack to a friend, she added, "It's just such huskies as Jack who get the sickest—especially when they're very finely strung and sensitive."[28]

At least *Collier's* did not balk at paying him $1,100 a week plus expenses for his articles. What surprised many old associates was the position he took. Three years earlier Jack had published a letter in support of those rising up against the dictatorship of General Porfirio Díaz, announcing, "We socialists, anarchists, hobos, chicken thieves, outlaws, and undesirable citizens of the United States are with you heart and soul."[29] A few months earlier he had questioned the use of war as a means of resolving international problems, yet his *Collier's* essays championed American intervention, which he believed would be best for the average Mexican citizen in the long run. This view naturally incensed the socialist press, which saw him now as a Yankee imperialist, a dupe of the oil interests.

Once again London presented a contradictory view of himself to the world. What could account for the change? Some friends, such as Emma Goldman, believed that wealth had caused him to lose contact with the people, yet this is not true. London continued to support prisoners' rights, to help the downtrodden who sent him begging letters, and to offer room and jobs on his ranch for the hard-up. Rather, what seems more likely is that he was swayed by his companions in Mexico, mostly American military officers. Jack had shown a similar blindness concerning Hawaii, where he and Charmian socialized with the military and capitalist elite, and adopted the imperialist stance of Anglo-Saxon superiority toward the Polynesians and Japanese. Jack was extolling a popular Progressive Era belief that America's technology and organizational brilliance gave it a moral duty to assist the "less civilized" nations. Charmian reinforced these racist convictions and was pleased when various military personnel later confided their approval of Jack's position regarding Mexico.

That Jack had been very ill is evident in the frequency with which he referred to his "rotten bacillary dysentery" to correspondents. To one he affirmed his agreement with Ernst Haeckl's scientific positivism: "I believe that when I am dead . . . I am just as much obliterated as the last mosquito you or I smashed."[30] That death was on his mind is further evident in a codicil he added to his will at the start of the Mexican trip. (One oddity is its being datelined "Glen Ellen," when the couple had left two days earlier for Galveston.)[31] The addition was a technical one, dropping George Sterling as executor.

Life had turned sour in recent years for Sterling. Even Jack had come to recognize that he was not going to be the great poet once prophesied. His mentor Ambrose Bierce was similarly disenchanted and simply cut off contact. For years Carrie had responded to her husband's adulterous flings and drinking by moving out, only to return and reconcile. In November 1913 a scandal concerning George and an adolescent girl was the final blow. Carrie filed for divorce, leaving George bereft. He fled to his childhood environs of Long Island.

Jack and Charmian still intended a long visit to Japan, but world events intervened. With the outbreak of what would become known as World War I on July 28, 1914, he hoped for the possibility of a war correspondent assignment in Europe. Also, he was finding a new burst of creativity, which culminated in two novels. *The Star Rover* follows the projection of a prison inmate undergoing "the jacket," a form of torture used in San Quentin. He finds himself transported to other times and places, becoming a dashing late Renaissance French count, a boy in a wagon train attacked by Mormons in the Mountain Meadow Massacre, a Roman legionnaire at the time of Christ's crucifixion, and a nineteenth-century sailor cast away on a desert island, among others. Through this entertaining series of tales he hoped to remind readers of numerous forms of tyranny, in particular the abuse of convicts, but most came away believing he was a spiritualist. The other was *The Little Lady of the Big House,* his dissection of masculinity under rationalized capitalism, a book few would read.

Whether it was his unexpected confrontation with death or his revived financial and emotional health, following the trip to Mexico, Jack responded warmly to a letter from Joan. She knew he did not want to hear how she was doing, she wrote, but she just had to tell him she had been elected president of the literary club at school. Congratulating her, he sent an extra ten dollars for her and Becky to use during their vacation at the beach. "Sorry I cannot see you: Sorry so much good country up here going to waste in which I could see you."[32] A tentative reunion by post occurred, as Joan sent cheerful accounts of her and Becky's latest accomplishments, yet she was always careful to thank him repeatedly for any allowance or reimbursement, and was sure to send meticulous accounts to back her requests for such expenses as trolley fare.

In high school Joan excelled in extracurricular activities. In addition to earning high grades, she held offices in the dramatic society, the French Club, and a humanitarian service group, and was an editor for the *Aegis*. Inspired by the actors in the Maddern family, she performed in half a dozen plays, including *Coriolanus* and *The Admirable Crichton* by Sir James Barrie. She also performed at church, such as in a play produced to raise money for the Belgian Relief Fund.

Academics at first challenged her, perhaps because she entered high school early, at the age of twelve. Soon she was able to boast to her father that she had pulled up her grades quickly in the first two quarters of her freshman year, even in the "nightmare" course of geometry. As for French, she could understand the language without mentally translating into English. A teacher had even asked her to serve as her secretary: "And Daddy, she chose me because my English work was so good. I'm so proud."[33]

Jack applauded her many accomplishments but could not help referring to his own experience at Oakland High. Walk around the building and note all the windows, he wrote, and remember that he had to wash them all, inside and out, during his tenure there, as well as sweep every room "from garret to basement." It was a good reminder to a daughter who knew little of working-class life. In a rare expression of affection, he concluded the letter with a lyrical refrain:

> I now want to sing you a song:
> You are my daughter
> You do not know, yet, what that means
> Have you no intellectual stir, no mental prod, no heart throb
> Impelling you to get acquainted with your dad:
> Oh, my dear, I am very old, and very wise, and I can set you four square
>     to this four-square world.
> I have nothing to offer you in the way of dollars and what dollars can buy.
> I have everything to offer you and show you in the way of the spirit and
>     what the spirit never buys, but commands.[34]

Joan included *Aegis* clippings in her letters to demonstrate her writing skill. One story survives with many editorial marks on the published copy in her handwriting, evidence of her self-criticism and attention to language. "The Horrors of the Unknown" is clearly derivative of her father's work, and hints at the difficulties she would have in her later effort to establish a career as a writer. The plot concerns a seaman whose boat lands in the fog late at night, not at San Francisco but at Richmond. As he wanders the unfamiliar dark streets searching for a hotel, he realizes that he is being followed by "chinamen." One confronts him, a very old man, "withered with sharp, beady eyes and cruel mouth partially covered by a long, drooping mustache." His "long, yellow finger nails" grasp a roll of paper and tear it up. The protagonist then, like the drowning Martin Eden, loses consciousness, his dying awareness being that the "chinaman got me." Feeling something dreadfully cold on his back, he awakens from his apparent nightmare "to find my dog pressing his cold nose into the small of my back."[35]

The story is a typical adolescent's surprise ending in an attempt to appear clever. Even aside from the anti-Chinese sentiment, which would only be seen as appropriate among nativist whites, the story fails to achieve the suspense it attempts. Key elements, such as the contents of the roll of paper, remain unexplained. The sentences are well crafted grammatically, but there is no indication that the writer has creative promise. She is ardent and serious, yet lacks "the certain something" Charmian also missed in her own art. Whereas Charmian acknowledged her creative deficiencies, however, Joan confused craftsmanship with artistry and would struggle many years before she accepted that her forte was nonfiction.

During this period both Charmian and Anna were busy completing their own books. Charmian reworked her round-robin letters from the Pacific crossing to shape *The Log of the Snark,* while Anna returned to *Père Lachaise.* Writing was much more difficult for Anna, surrounded by small children. So little gets finished, she told Jack, because "it is the blessed babies who do all engulf me and take all my time and strength and give me only happiness in return."[36] Her pregnancies and deliveries were always difficult. Although after the birth of Georgia she wrote him that she would have no more children, that she was fortunate to be alive at all, William followed in 1916.

The Wallings moved from Cedarhurst to a similarly large home in Greenwich, Connecticut, in 1914. Most of the time Anna was housebound, while English was frequently absent to attend conferences or to visit for weeks at a time with his mother in Florida. When home, he sequestered himself to write, between 1912 and 1916 completing six volumes on various socialist issues. Though aligned with more radical socialists, he was also a devotee of Samuel Gompers of the AFL. Anna would proudly send the Londons notices of English's latest publication or endeavor, and fostered the impression that her marriage was a blessing. In fact, English was not as available emotionally as Anna needed, nor was he very supportive of her desire to participate in socialist enterprises. Though a member of local branches of the Equal Suffrage League and pacifist organizations, she seldom visited New York City, with its lively community of Greenwich Village socialists and its headquarters for various groups and publications such as *The Masses.*

By late 1914 Charmian noticed in herself a curious self-acceptance, an ability to be more comfortable both in her marriage and among others. Her diary makes less mention of Jack's claims of love, and more often records descriptions of pleasant activities they enjoyed together. When she had yet another miscarriage, she was philosophical about the loss. She remained troubled over Jack's declining health, which now included rashes on his face described as "razor burns," episodes of "rheumatism," and hints of gout, all symptoms of kidney dysfunction. She seldom mentioned his drinking, for in fact he had cut back considerably in favor of juice or water.

When guests crowded the ranch, Charmian no longer complained about their presence, but noted her delight at visits from Carrie Sterling and their "ragging together" to songs from the Victrola. Although it is London on whom posterity placed the label of womanizer, it was George Sterling who much more deserved the title. Many friends would recall his gallivanting, among them the poet Robinson Jeffers, who noted that George would take up with "the most unattractive, most sexless females imaginable" because they loved poetry.[37] It was also George who was much more beholden to "the Noseless One," the taunting pessimist of Jack's drinking days evoked in *John Barleycorn*. Following Carrie's final departure, he lost all will to reform his drinking habits. Once again Charmian found herself befriended by a woman who had previously defamed her now that Carrie sought her out as a confidante.

Between weeks of hosting on the ranch and brief trips to the city, Jack and Charmian hid away on the *Roamer*. With *Little Lady* completed, he started *Jerry of the Islands*, another story about dogs, and its sequel, *Michael, Brother of Jerry*. Each was intended to heighten public awareness of the mistreatment of animals, and would in fact result in the spontaneous development of Jack London Clubs devoted to animal welfare. Charmian's love of animals inspired Jack to take up this new cause, and she assisted him by doing background research. She also helped him compose a play that would become *The Acorn Planter*, while Jack offered corrections on her writing as she always had with his.

Unable to get a journalistic assignment in Europe, Jack agreed to cover President Wilson's battleship trip through the Panama Canal to attend the 1915 Panama Pacific Exposition in San Francisco. Since Charmian was not permitted aboard the naval vessel, she arranged a short trip to Hawaii to visit her favorite cousin, Beth Wiley, who was wintering there. Given the developing horrors of the war overseas, which most had expected to be over quickly, Wilson canceled the tour at the last minute. Consequently, on February 24 Jack joined Charmian and Nakata aboard the *Matsonia* for a three-week vacation that extended to seven months.

Soon after their arrival in Hawaii, Nakata met a cousin who lived in the islands, became engaged to her, and announced that he was leaving the Londons' employ to study dentistry.[38] In spite of that disappointment, the couple retraced the steps of their 1907 trip, including visits to friends' ranches and the much-changed leper colony at Molokai. The moderate tropical climate improved Jack's health considerably. When not traveling, he spent the mornings at their cottage dressed in a kimono and working on the draft of *Jerry of the Islands*. Charmian, asserting her independence, would take off alone for several days to visit one friend or another. Sometimes Jack left to play poker, and she did not mind his going off without her.

One of their new Japanese servants was now typing Jack's manuscript since Charmian was preoccupied with the galleys of *The Log of the Snark*. She embarked on a second volume, which would build on her 1907 diary to discuss changes in the island observed during their current visit. *Our Hawaii* would document her new awareness of the rot underlying paradise. Though she associated with the wealthy, cultured elite, and like them expected to be attended by several house servants, Charmian acknowledged that their wealth was based on a feudal labor system of "coolies and peasants" who possessed no vote. She questioned the claims of the high-ranking military that the island would remain under American administration, and predicted that one day a Hawaiian-born Japanese would rule as governor. With regard to tourism, she deplored the changes brought by the influx of short-term visitors, whose numbers were resulting in new hotels, unattractive commercialization, and a faster pace of life.

Jack shared these ideas, and was intrigued by the Pan-Pacific Union, an organization started by their old friend Alexander Hume Ford for the purpose of developing mutual interests among the Pacific nations. London was impressed by the racial mixing on Hawaii, which he found a verification of animal and plant husbandry practices that emphasized hybridizing. The pure Polynesian might be quickly vanishing, he acknowledged, yet the quality of those produced by mixed racial unions was clearly superior, if one looked at the case of Hawaii. Again, he may have been influenced by Luther Burbank, who had argued that the plant breeder "finds among descendants [of cross-breeding] a plant which is likely to be stronger and better than any ancestor. . . . [A]nd so we may hope for a far stronger and better race if right principles are followed."[39] Thus, when a congressmen arrived on a junket in May 1915, Jack used this opportunity to express his growing dismay over the behavior of the Germans and his hope for world peace. During one speech he presented Hawaii as a model for the rest of the world: "When every race realizes that all men have the same ultimate goal, they will come to know each other and cease fighting."[40]

It may have been during their separate activities that Jack became acquainted with an American family within the network of Queen Liliuokalani. The timing is unclear—whether it occurred this time or on a subsequent visit to the islands is unknown—but photographs corroborate what scholars have discounted to date. Namely, after Jack's death, George Sterling gossiped that his late friend had fallen in love with a woman in Hawaii and was torn between his love for her and Charmian. Evidence exists in photographs passed down to the woman's granddaughter showing Jack and the woman in a pose reinforcing family history that he had been the woman's "beau."[41] Such a circumstance might explain Jack's decision to remain in Hawaii months longer than they had originally planned. They even considered buying a house there.

Whether Charmian knew of this relationship is unclear. She did not know that Eliza had earlier collaborated with Jack on his dalliances. For example, in 1910, when they embarked on the four-horse trip, Jack advised his stepsister, "There's a girl writes me from Los Angeles, strange handwriting and blue envelope. Please forward her letters unopened."[42] He had deceived Bess through similar arrangements, and may have continued the practice after his marriage to Charmian. The absence of almost all such incriminating letters is understandable, for it was Charmian who chose what would remain for posterity. Thus, if any survived Jack's death, she had the opportunity to destroy them.

Charmian did observe that Jack was unusually tense and argumentative during this trip, not only with her but with others as well. This irritability could have been a consequence of his uremia. Or it could have been evidence of the difficulty of leading a double life.

# 11

# *Your Silence Is Now Golden*

In late July 1915, upon returning from Hawaii the Londons invited many friends to meals or longer visits on the ranch. The longest-staying guest was the sculptor Finn Froelich, who built furniture as well as shaped busts of Jack and Charmian. One of his more fanciful creations was an evocation of the Little Lady of the Big House, a woman in a form-fitting suit riding a massive stallion that appears to be diving into a pool. George Sterling arrived periodically, bringing a woman named Stella. For the most part the guests were relatives of Charmian's: cousin Beth Wiley and her parents, Aunt Netta and husband Edward Payne, or nearby neighbors. Celebrities, artists, and socialists were less frequent visitors than in the past.

In October, the scenarist Charles Goddard came to work with Jack on the book version of a script titled *Hearts of Three*. Goddard, who had originated the *Perils of Pauline* series, had a plot idea involving gold adventures in Central America. Mistaken identity, false murder accusations, and a cast of evil Mayans beset the main characters, two men and a woman. Even Jack acknowledged that the book was a joke—a rollicking, high-spirited adventure story. Indeed, ridiculous as the story sounds today, with its Valley of Lost Souls and flooding Cave of Chia, it foreshadows popular cartoonish adventure films such as *Raiders of the Lost Ark*. Jack was paid $25,000 to write a serial version for the Hearst newspapers, income that allowed him to pay off mortgages and gain relief from so many overdue bills.

That fall Eliza faced a difficult time in the Santa Rosa divorce court, where she was being sued by James Shepard for divorce on grounds of immorality and cruelty. Countersuing on grounds of cruelty, she must have felt touched when London testified on his stepsister's behalf. He commended her generosity when he was growing up, which had left him grateful to be able to help her out financially in recent years. At one point Shepard became so disruptive that the judge threw him out of the courtroom. In the end, the judge granted the divorce to James, not Eliza, on grounds of desertion, yet he concluded that all the property was hers, that no community property existed to be distributed.

On Thanksgiving Day 1915 Jack and Charmian dined with Harry and Bess

Houdini following a performance in Oakland by the magician. The four posed for a studio shot in which Bess stares out blankly, Charmian looks up adoringly at Jack, whose smiling gaze reciprocates Houdini's. In her diary at the end of the evening Charmian gushed: "Charming Houdini. I shall never forget him."[1] What she did not note was that Jack had also attended a matinee performance of Houdini's earlier that day, in the company of Becky, who had asked her father to join her. This was perhaps the only outing the two ever had alone together. Joan had been the intermediary, buying the tickets and leaving one at Flora's home so Jack could pick it up on his way to the dentist, where he spent over four hours before heading to the theater.

Becky's request and Jack's capitulation were further evidence of renewed interest in his daughters. No longer a young man, his dreams dashed, his health troublesome, his hope for a child with Charmian recognized as futile, Jack did not become, as has often been portrayed, a bitter, pessimistic man. Rather, all the signs suggests that he had become more philosophical about life, less harried by disappointments and threats from others, more open to the deceptively simple, rich pleasures of mundane life. Without apologizing directly, he demonstrated his remorse to Joan, and by implication Becky, through a series of heartfelt letters of advice. Some of the old patterns remained: the wrangling over meager sums of money, the failure to appear at the girls' various dance or drama performances. Missives often began with reminders of how busy he was, his hundreds of correspondents. Yet these naggings and oversights recede in light of his obvious desire to provide the attention and guidance he had long neglected.

Becky was now a freshman, a "scrub," at Oakland High, a year ahead of her age group. Joan's letters included proud commentary about her little sister. For example, in relating how both had saved money for some favorite things, Joan noted that Becky was much the more economical of the two, able to save fifteen dollars in one year whereas it had taken Joan three years to save five. She persuaded her father to increase Becky's allowance now that she was in high school, but was unable to convince him to let Becky have her own charge account at the school supplies store. Of course, Joan also used the letters as an opportunity to demonstrate her own achievements, which included a major role in a drama club play, winning two dollars in a newspaper essay contest, her fluency in speaking and understanding French, and her many invitations to play the piano at gatherings.

Jack's advice was wide ranging, from suggestions on ways to make her swimming stroke more efficient to directions on the kind of postage to use on packages. On August 25, 1915, he reminded Joan that he disapproved of her interest in a dramatic career, and added that she should not go into teaching either, for "that way lies hell." Others have suggested that he gave this advice as criticism of Bess, but he may more simply have been warning Joan away from a profession that paid women significantly less than men while holding them to onerous regulations concerning their private life. Also, Jack's own view of teachers was generally uncomplimentary; he had considered his Berkeley professors "boneheads" for their narrow-mindedness. For him, life was the teacher, and the best instructors were those one encountered along the way, whether a kindly librarian or a fellow worker in a jute mill.

He also responded to signs that Joan was on the cusp of adulthood. She increasingly asserted her contrary opinions and seemed less the small girl showing off to win attention. When he berated her twice for using the ungrammatical "Bess and I," she countered that it was vacation time, a period when she and Becky "were murdering the King's English uproariously." Furthermore, even her English teacher allowed that there were times to permit exceptions to the rule. Jack replied that he was pleased she was not being swayed by the "dry, old professors" who refused to accept English as a living language. He acknowledged that while the subjunctive mood was passing from everyday usage, her slip-up regarding "Bess and I" remained a grammatical error not to be excused. He then added that, owing to a miscalculation in a discussion of money he owed them, he was making up the amount twice because "whenever your Daddy finds he is mistaken he doubles up in order to make even."[2]

When Joan let him know that the unexpected money had gone toward French-heeled slippers, Jack was inspired to write about femininity and bodily pride. "No matter how wonderful are the thoughts that burn in your brain, always, physically, and in dress, make yourself a delight to all eyes that behold you."[3] He held up as bad examples his philosopher friends who did not bathe or change their socks. He was, in other words, recommending a bourgeois model of womanhood.

Joan felt enough trust to confess to having a boyfriend, Edmund de Freitas, a senior, and editor of the *Aegis*. She even included a picture of "Brownie," as he was known for his "big brown eyes and brown hair." Jack agreed that he was fine looking, but reminded her that they were both still young. He hoped "some day, some time, [to] get together so that I may be able to give you advice about the world of men."[4]

Perhaps to stand out from her older sister, Becky wrote to request a renewal of *St. Nicholas Magazine,* and asked permission to have all her well-worn copies bound. She described how she had played with soap bubbles before the fire, and signed her letter "Your little, Baby Bee."[5] Yet she was now thirteen, studying algebra and French, not the child one might conclude from both the content and the simple language. Becky had good reasons not to rush into maturity, among which was the awesome model of her very accomplished and popular older sister. She would form her identity as the opposite of Joan's rather than try to emulate her. As she recalled in old age, "I was never jealous of Joan. I never wished to be like her in any way—physically, mentally or emotionally."[6] Also, since Joan had been given all the responsibilities, Becky found she could protract her childhood to extract further benefits from that status.

At least part of Jack's advice would have especially affected Becky. She loved dressing up in costumes, and must have known that his warning not to pursue a career in drama applied to her as well.

Despite the growing affection between Jack and his daughters, for the third year in a row they would not see him at Christmas. He had explained, "I shall be forever unable to see you and Becky at your Piedmont home. As you know, the ranch is always open to you."[7] As further sign of his softening, both rancor toward Bess and coercive demands had vanished from his correspondence. On December 16 he and Charmian left for Hawaii. The tropics were once again calling him away from his Beauty Ranch dream.

From Charmian's diary of this visit to Hawaii, one would conclude that the couple were merely social butterflies, flitting to this dinner, that luncheon, treating and being treated by the cream of Hawaiian society. They went to concerts and Charlie Chaplin movies, savored Geraldine Farrar in *Carmen*, and relished auto tours in a friend's Pierce Arrow. There were bridge parties, men-only poker games, rooftop dances, teas, and midnight swims. Their dining table, accommodating twelve, was full so often that Charmian kept seating diagrams and menus to manage the complicated protocol. On May 17, 1916, Charmian noted, "Love fest—Mate and me. Most wonderful of love days with Mate."

Life should have been easy in the bungalow on Kalia Road in Waikiki, where they were waited on by four servants and a chauffeur. But scattered among the diary pages are hints of the harsher reality of their lives. Charmian suffered repeated unidentified illness, in one case impelling her to go away for a rest cure. Jack was sick many mornings, unable to eat, listless. Sometimes he vomited. During the long dinner parties he'd push his food around his plate to disguise the fact that he was not eating, and when caught, proclaimed that the talk interested him more than the meal. The same Jack who a year earlier had dragged Charmian out to the deepest surf now made excuses not to join her in swimming, instead urging her to enjoy her mornings without him.

Consequently, Charmian was not aware of the seriousness of his condition until he passed a kidney stone. During his consultation afterward, the doctor warned her that Jack must change his high-protein diet, thus give up his beloved oysters, raw tuna, and scarcely cooked duck. Indeed, that information was not even noted in her diary. Following that episode Jack enjoyed six weeks of heartiness, which, though temporary, misled her again. Only in retrospect did she realize that his "insatiable ego" had given up, that for unfathomable reasons he had deliberately chosen to ignore all the doctors' advice of recent years.

Whether one can deduce that he was suicidal is debatable. Irritability and depression are common psychological effects of uremia, which induces biochemical changes that influence emotions, over and above the sheer discomfort of bloating. This is evident in his nasty letters to onetime friend Spiro Orfans, whom he belittled in unprecedented tones. Jack's pain was so debilitating that the doctor provided him with morphine for self-injection as needed, which he did out of Charmian's view.

If a suicidal current swelled at times, prominent too were the opposing tides of his valiant attempt to defeat "the Noseless One," the demon of his drinking days. He was restless with plans. He wrote Joan that he had decided to live in Hawaii, that he looked forward to her visiting him there. He spoke with Charmian of buying a three-masted schooner and taking off for another around-the-world voyage. They discussed a trip to New York in the fall, to Japan the following spring. He kept pace with his plans for the Beauty Ranch, which increasingly took on the outlines of a utopian community of happy, productive workers. In conversations he seemed obsessed with the war in Europe, and spoke out against America's self-protective "Safety First" policy, which seemed an abomination in light of the atrocities being committed by the Germans in Belgium.

War was their main topic of discussion. Once the writer of inspiring antiwar passages, Jack had determined that Germany was "a paranoiac," deluded by thoughts of persecution and fed by religious mania. Although the war was not good for individuals, it would be so for humanity in that it was serving "a pentecostal cleansing of the spirit of man." America had to align with the Allies, for the very foundation of civilization was at risk. As for the isolationist presidential candidates Woodrow Wilson and Charles Hughes, he believed that there "was nothing to hope from either of them, except that they will brilliantly guide the United States down her fat, helpless, lonely, unhonorable, profit-seeking way to the shambles to which her shameless unpreparedness is leading her." He supported Theodore Roosevelt, for exalting "honor and manhood" over the "peace-lovingness of the worshipers of fat."[8] His provocative and inflammatory rhetoric suggests his now uncontrollable irritability.

In a widely publicized and denounced move, Jack resigned from the Socialist Party on March 7, 1916. He was frustrated by its "lack of fire and fight," and believed that the selfishness of individualism prevented the collective action requisite for the revolution. He remained a socialist, but no longer aligned with the formal body. Taunting his plans, his desperate struggle for control over his failing life force, was a specter recurring in his dreams, a figure who descended a cascade of stairs toward Jack, its very presence questioning his self-mastery.

Jack's reading during this period centered on Wilhelm Fliess, Sigmund Freud, and especially Carl Jung. Jack read Jung's recently translated *Psychology of the Unconscious,* heavily marking the volume, which consisted of essays on personal transformation and symbols of the libido. There he found a system of meaning to battle the frightening dream figure, and suddenly shifted from his hack writing to more serious literature. The result would be among his most moving and provocative short stories. Returning to the inspired state he had once enjoyed while writing his Yukon tales, he quickly dashed off "The Red One," a haunting story of a man's journey into primordial darkness which concludes with a sphinx-like puzzle. Charmian later reflected that her "sick and dying" husband had revealed more of himself through that story than he would consciously admit in the scientist purged of his excessive irrationality to be redeemed by seeming savages. "The Water Baby" is even more haunting for its repeated use of the number signifying London's age, forty, in a plot concerning death and resurrection. Other stories, such as "The Bones of Kahekili" and "On the Makaloa Mat," invoked Jungian ideas through images from Hawaiian mythology and history.

Just as the hero of "The Red One" descends through a terrifying landscape to achieve spiritual knowledge, so did Jack delve into his own and Charmian's psyches in a form of amateur psychoanalysis. Obsessed with the challenge of Jungian interpretation, he kept Charmian listening for hours to his self-analysis, and demanded similar self-evaluation from her. Sometimes his goading left her resentful. As the demands he made on himself further strained his health, Charmian came to recognize the extent to which she had deferred to him, and some of her usual nervous discomforts waned. Her signs of independence— for example, her determination to devote more time to her manuscript on Hawaii—naturally surprised and perturbed him. She was in effect preparing herself for widowhood.

In correspondence, Charmian made no mention of Jack's deterioration. Letters to Anna, her most intimate woman correspondent, speak of lighter matters. Hearing of the acceptance of Anna's novel for publication, she congratulated her. "It is just sweetly wonderful that you and I, Anna and Charmian, so bound by dear ties, should each have a book published in the same year."[9] There would be different consequences for each.

Charmian's growing self-confidence must have been encouraged by the extensive, universally positive response to *The Log of the Snark,* published by Macmillan in the States and Mills and Boon in England. The book provided a daily journal of incidents and events that occurred from soon after the departure from Oakland to the final day in the Solomon Islands, when they left for

Australia, still believing that they would continue the journey once Jack recuperated from his various ailments. Three large sections of the journal were omitted. The five months in Hawaii were excised, to be used in a separate volume. A section concerning Penduffryn Plantation that included accounts of the masquerade hashish party and another on their half year in Australia and Tasmania were also omitted.[10]

Charmian's topic—travel to exotic places—was enjoying a heyday, and her choice of the Pacific was additionally pertinent in light of American imperialist activities there. Her style engages from the first paragraph, with her description of dangling her feet over the edge of the lifeboat and the first attacks of seasickness upon the crew. Aware that her readers are likely landlubbers, she explains any unfamiliar nautical terms—guny, heave to, jib—as well as the cultural practices of the various islands. Amusing anecdotes, including those that make fun of Jack and herself, relieve the celebrity focus. Interspersed are accounts of the genuinely life-threatening events to which the crew responded with pluck. Although *The Log* is also a "subjective biography," its intense naturalism reveals a narrator much more immersed in the real sensate world than Anna's romantic *Père Lachaise.*

Like much effective travel literature, *The Log* is accurate about what it portrays while omitting material that is too personal, tedious, or possibly uncomplimentary to the writer. That Jack concentrated hours daily on his prodigious output while Charmian grew weary of typing all his writing and hers is hardly mentioned. Unhappiness with certain crew members, documented in letters, is little evident. The encounters with various indigenous cultures reflect a mix of imperialist condescension and genuine curiosity. Always drawn to the women's lives, Charmian comments astutely on gender roles, and gently mocks taboo systems that serve to reinforce male superiority. In several encounters with native women, her descriptions border on the homoerotic. With such rich and complex material, the book retains its appeal today.

Although Jack's presence in the account ensured that prominent reviewers would address the book, they declared Charmian to be deserving of praise in her own right. She had "the rare gift of giving close attention to detail without at the same time spoiling general effects." She wrote "charmingly and full of color," and "with humor and clever anecdote enlivening each page." She was a "gifted woman" who told the story with "vivacity" in a "crisp and sparkling" style. Her "jaunty and merry mood" made "light of danger and hardship, and few books of travel or adventure are better worth rendering."[11] The strong sales led to additional printings, and George Brett pressed her to complete the volume on Hawaii as soon as possible.

Anna's novel, *Violette of Père Lachaise,* was published by a minor firm, Frederick A. Strokes, after being rejected by Macmillan in 1911. What impelled Anna in early 1915 to complete a manuscript begun in 1905 was the war. As in previous winters, English's long absence to visit his parents in Florida left her buoyant and energetic. In a world devastated by death and destruction, she thought it important to complete her story of individuals who remain strong despite all the odds against them. She doubted that the book would be widely read but needed to unburden herself of it.

The story concerns an orphaned girl raised by her poor grandfather in a cottage next to the famous Père Lanchaise Cemetery in Paris. Perhaps influenced by writers such as Henry James, Anna adopted a psychological approach to embody her "conception of the modern philosophy of love and revolution, idealism and democracy" through her lead character. Direct quotes from her 1903 diary can be found, with their emphasis on themes of death, grief, sentimentalized love, and passion for revolution. The writing is repetitive, flowery, and overwrought. The key characters are so without flaw that they are uninteresting, and striking for their lack of corporeality.

The writer Gervaise, who guides Violette's philosophy, is presented in the novel as "perfect in his idealism, freed of superstition," with the face "of one marked with wisdom and love," in other words, similar to Jack London as Anna perceived him. When he first meets her, she is chanting, "Tell me, shining star, do you see me, dear, do you know me?" Gervaise's wife is dead, killed in a demonstration against hunger. He eventually leaves Violette not for another woman but for the cause. Violette conveys her love through the language of enclosure, of being swallowed up. She wants his full love, yet knows it would change Gervaise, distract him from his larger purpose. So defining the situation, with or without Gervaise she sacrifices herself, either to him or to the cause. The real-life relationship brought to mind by this dynamic is that of Anna and English.

Violette repeatedly wanders about the cemetery, and is drawn particularly to the tombs of the actress Rachel and the tragic lovers Héloïse and Abélard. Her behavior abounds with projection. Despite his political and literary commitments, the much-older Gervaise repeatedly visits Violette because she is "the fountainhead of [his] inspiration" and he basks "in the effulgence of her mind." Since she is his muse, when he leaves he also loses his art and sacrifices himself for the revolutionary cause. The plot represents the theme of Western romantic love at its most archetypal: love unfulfilled.

In contrast to Charmian, who filled large scrapbook pages with reviews from all over the country, Anna had few clippings. The *Conservator* remarked that the novel expressed "a passive acceptance and a passive resentment in an active world."[12] The *North American Review* compared Anna to novelist Walter Pater, popular for his use of "insubstantial narrative . . . personal in its interest, but tenuous in that it subordinates detail to subjective truth." It praised her nonetheless for depicting "an inner life wholly natural and lovely both in its joy and distress," with delicacy and sincerity.[13] Overall, reviewers favored this "subjective biography" for its belief that commitment to love, revolution, idealism, and democracy gave worth to a life destined ultimately for annihilation.

World War I profoundly affected both Anna and English in ways that increased their incompatibility, though one would not know it from a book English edited in 1915, *Socialists and the War*. This volume was a scrupulously balanced presentation of the views of various socialist parties and leaders in Europe, Russia, and the United States regarding participation in the war. This objectivity and evenhandedness in his formal writing contrasted with his character in person. One would not guess from his editorial remarks in this volume that he was aligning himself with the pro-war faction, and would eventually so disagree with the Socialist Party's neutral stance that he tried to start an alternative, the Socialist Democratic League. English saw the war mobilization as an eventual boon to collectivism among capitalist governments, hence a step toward democratic socialism. That he favored American participation is evident in a letter Emma Goldman wrote Anna in June 1915 stating that she hoped English was not as "rabid" regarding the war now, for she found it inexplicable that revolutionists could be so blind as to support those they had been fighting.[14]

Anna took her husband's side meekly at first, and despite her involvement in the Woman's Peace Party, even wrote a letter to the *New York Times* parroting his views.[15] Eventually she switched to align with the other American socialists. Despite his scholarly writing, English could be uncivil to any who disagreed with him, and damned his former colleagues in letters to editors. In contributing to the hysterical patriotism that swelled once the United States joined the Allies, English redefined his reputation. He was, comrades decided, a shallow socialist, when in fact he had come to his position based on a particular view of socialist theory. Two years later Emma Goldman decried men like him, the "reddest of the reds," for becoming "lackeys of Wall Street and Washington."[16]

Friends observed that Anna grew more intense and serious at this time. They thought her fidelity to both English and socialism overblown and lachrymose. Although she was more sincere and constant in her political beliefs than English, she was ineffectual as a national activist, partly because he made her so. He had successfully chipped away at what little self-esteem she had remaining, even to the point of accusing her of being a bad mother. Guests noted his cruel belittling of her, yet realized that she was unwilling to admit his frailties and stand up to him. (One of her letters recounts that he threw a box at her, injuring her bare foot while she was breast-feeding their son. Her brother and nanny afterward both advised her that she would suffer less if she stopped showing English so much love.)[17] Her failure to be recognized as a writer only sealed her husband's condemnation.

Despite English's subversion, Anna carved out a small arena for self-expression through public speaking, usually when he was away on long trips. She spoke to Jewish groups concerning the pogroms in Russia, to women members of the Wobblies, to a gathering arranged by Jane Addams on pacifism, and to a birth control meeting at Carnegie Hall. The last was an invitation from Emma Goldman, who admitted it was ironic that Anna supported the movement yet was herself so frequently pregnant.

Following the birth of her son William Hayden in 1916, she signed on with the William B. Eakens lecture bureau, which specialized in left-leaning orators. Among Anna's topics advertised one year were "The Coming Woman," "Socialism—A Way of Life," and specialized talks on Walt Whitman, William Morris, Victor Hugo, Leo Tolstoy, and Peter Kropotkin. (English was also on the bureau roster, speaking on more theoretical issues in socialism, as well as on philosophers such as Emerson and Nietzsche.) That these talks were important to her can be seen in the difficulties she endured to make them; for example, one presentation in Michigan took three days by train to get there and back for just a few hours with her host group.

During the spring of 1916, Joan received the warmest communications yet from her father. Jack challenged her to read his books and give him a frank evaluation. He asked her to learn the songs "Sing Me to Sleep" and "The Perfect Day" so he could hear her play them when he returned to California. He offered to take her boyfriend Edmund de Freitas surfing during his expected visit to the islands that summer. Most touchingly, he expressed anticipation of introducing her one day to his friends in Hawaii.

Gifts flowed as well. He authorized Eliza to send the girls fox wraps, belated Christmas presents, as well as theater tickets and money for new shoes and vacations—all without his ritual rant about the expense. Charmian bought silks, crepes, and a Philippine fabric made of pineapple, which Jack sent in a large package for the girls to use for dresses, along with Japanese scarves and mandarin-style summer coats. When Joan requested money for sweaters and pins for herself and Becky, he asked Eliza to send the check.

Joan read *Adventure*, whose lead character was named in her honor, though modeled after Armine von Tempski, daughter of Hawaiian friends, who would one day become a writer herself. He was pleased that a reading club Joan belonged to had selected Herbert Spencer's *First Principles,* and offered to speak about the philosopher at their meeting in September, though this never happened.

Upon his return home in early August, the girls joined their father at a play, *The Great Divide,* the story of a ruffian civilized by the wife forced upon him.

Almost eight months had passed since he had seen them, during which time Becky had matured physically. Although she was almost thirteen, he seemed surprised by her having grown up. In a letter addressed to both girls afterward he noted, "Dear Becky, keep it up and you will skin Joan out in spite of the fact that she was born into the world before you."[18] His younger daughter was to remember this day with her father more than any other.

Having gained confidence through her many successes in high school, Joan now exhibited the forthright, feisty side of her personality that would serve her well in later years as a political activist, though it would prove to be a detriment in her private life. She asked for a new piano, but when Eliza offered her Steck, Joan demurred, explaining that it would not match the Mission golden oak in the family living room. She wanted a grand piano one day (like Charmian's?), and would save for years if necessary to have one. Joan's defiance may have been in response to the requirement that she go to the ranch and look the piano over, which she perhaps saw as a ploy to force her to defy her mother. Having become the check writer and go-between on money matters with Joan, Eliza could not help but draw the conclusion that Jack's elder daughter saw her father as little more than a source of material benefits. It was a false conclusion, but one structured by the relationship Jack had imposed on both.

Joan was humiliated by having to account for every item to the penny, and believed that it would be easier for all if the monthly allowances were changed. She had also become even more concerned with safeguarding her mother now that she was mature enough to appreciate all Bess had sacrificed. Adolescence incurred increased expenses for both girls, and war inflation had reduced the value of Jack's monthly support. What had served as a comfortable income in 1905 would not go far in 1916. Furthermore, doctor bills accumulated as a result of repeated attacks of pneumonia afflicting Joan and chronic glandular and throat problems besetting Becky. Following an operation that spring, Bess exhibited symptoms of heart disease. Joan was understandably worried about the health of her mother, who had been ordered by her doctor to stop tutoring.

With these points in mind, at lunch with Jack and Becky in early September, without informing her mother, Joan presented the case for doubling the monthly $75 allotment. She handed her father a detailed account of the family expenses, which were approaching $1,700 a year. There followed on his part "accusations, upbraidings, erection of straw dummies that were instantly demolished, self-justification that sank finally into self-pity."[19] Joan responded in the most reprehensible way possible for him, by crying. Before departing, he agreed to look at the figures, gave the girls perfunctory kisses, and left to meet Charmian. Joan's impulse was to run up and hug him as he walked away, until he turned and looked back, unsmiling. It was the last the girls would ever see of their father.

Soon afterward Joan attached a detailed account of family expenses to a chatty letter that bowed and scraped accordingly for bringing up the request, then described her excitement over being a senior and proposed Dramatic Club events. Although Jack balked at the girls' excessive purchase of erasers and their beginning the school term with eleven pencils, he did agree to send each $37.50 a month on top of the $75 to their mother. Bess, however, was to sign papers relinquishing the endowment of two life insurance policies worth a thousand dollars. In response, Bess acknowledged that Jack had paid extra bills over the years, but noted that she too had covered many expenses, such as the trip to southern California so Joan's lung condition could improve in that milder climate. She reminded him that the insurance policies were part of the community property assigned at the divorce, in exchange for which she had forsaken any claims on income from his writings.

Jack pounded back with his usual list of seemingly rational arguments that in the process ignored Bess's valid points. Recalling a mean-spirited refrain from earlier years, he taunted her regarding Charles Milner—how she'd let the girls call him "uncle," how she'd joined with Milner in a "shake-down." Furthermore, he noted, because two years earlier she had dared to accuse him of "women" when the girls were outside the door listening, he was sending them a copy of this letter rejecting her claims. Since she had considered them "ripe enough to listen to such talk" then, surely she thought them ripe enough now to read his letter. At the top of the page he wrote, it "is due to you two girls, as well as due to me, that you read the contents thereof."[20]

What Bess could not know was the state of Jack's failing health. Upon returning from Hawaii, Eliza was shocked by his appearance and remarked to Charmian that the real Jack no longer existed. During September he spent two long periods in bed as a result of his uremia. The first attack caused such swelling that he could hardly walk and had to leave the State Fair early. His letters that month and through October mentioned that he expected to go to New York on business "in a few days," though his departure was continually postponed. His anger toward even those dearest to him increased. He was upset that Charmian had decided to stay home and work on her book rather than join him in New York. She forced herself to sit through his unprovoked attacks, accusations, and rants until he simply wore himself out. One such rant at George Sterling left his best friend bitter in return. He even had a fierce argument with Eliza over livestock practices.

His irascibility was aggravated by a court case involving neighbors and Charmian's aunt Netta regarding water rights. They objected that a dam he had constructed for irrigation and swimming cut the flow, and hence interfered with their rights to the use of Graham Creek. It was particularly galling to have Netta participate as a plaintiff after all he had done for her and her husbands. In an eerie mirroring of his failing health, his favorite shire horse, Neudad Hillside, died suddenly in late October. That loss sent him into such despair that he cried all day, and dropped his work on *Cherry*, a new novel, to sketch a book in honor of the horse.

Though dark moods prevailed, episodes of youthful exuberance recurred for brief periods. He proposed new writing ventures, including an autobiography in serial form that would emphasize his experiences as a writer, and an article on man-eating sharks. He pursued, unsuccessfully, the project of getting *Hearts of Three* adapted for film. He more often requested that Charmian play music, especially, in line with his recent fascination with race consciousness, folk songs and Negro spirituals. He and Charmian discussed their proposed trip to Japan, a chance once more to flee the pressures of California.

In anticipation of the New York trip, Jack corresponded with Sophie Loeb, the *World* reporter he had met there in 1914. She inquired whether he was interested in covering the World Series for her paper, though her final sentences hinted at more than a professional relationship. "I saw a star last night—a new star—like no other yet discovered. I will give you three guesses as to what I have named it. As ever, Star."[21] Once again that celestial image, that reference to the Browning poem Jack used in his romantic relationships, reappears. This is hardly a sentiment to be expected of a woman noted for her single-minded writing and lobbying on behalf of social welfare. Divorced, independent, highly accomplished in her career, Loeb had all the qualities that appealed to London more than sheer physical attractiveness. And, too, she was that exotic, forbidden creature, a Jewish woman. Whether any intimacy had occurred or whether there was a flirtation in progress is unclear, but certainly something more than a shared interest in journalism passed between them.

By early November, Jack was suffering dysentery and edema. He was listless; his skin shone a pearly gray. Some days sheer willpower filled him with manic energy, as when he testified on the water trial in Santa Rosa. On the stand for two days, he gave long, fluent statements concerning his agricultural philosophy. When challenged that he was a novice gentleman farmer, he reminded the court that he had lived on farms until age ten, that for years he had studied agronomy, soil science, and livestock breeding and consulted with leading scientists. When challenged that the character Billy in *The Valley of the Moon* states that "the ginks and boobs of Glen Ellen" would be dependent on him for water, Jack retorted that Billy was a fictional character selected to perform the functions necessary to tell the story. (The judge forbade further use of London's fiction as evidence.) His animated, jovial manner distracted observers from perceiving how ill he was, that he was again suffering from the passing of a kidney stone. When he arrived home after testifying, he had Charmian inject him with morphine.

Charmian's awareness of the gravity of his condition emerged when a small act on his part took on a new significance. He inscribed in a book to her cousin Beth: "When you were here, the world was here, and the world was very much and too much with me. Darn the Wheel of the world! Why must it continually turn over? Where is the reverse gear?" When two film cameramen came to the ranch, and he posed animatedly while showing off his farm implements, horses, and baby pigs, Charmian nevertheless glimpsed something in Jack's face that struck her with fear. By November 19, their wedding anniversary, she had secluded herself in her room in a state of nervous collapse.

The next day Jack tried unsuccessfully to cajole Charmian into joining him on a ride up the mountain to look at another piece of land he hoped to add to the ranch. He returned excited over the quality of its soil. He hoped that he could sell a planned autobiographical work in New York to pay for the project. The day after that he slept, except for a discussion with Eliza on his plans for a general store, school, and post office on the property. He wanted the ranch "self-sustaining for every soul upon it."[22] Eliza confided in Charmian her concern that Jack was overworking his brain with his manic plans. That night Charmian calmed him down when he pointed to the piles of reading stacked by his bed. These included a hog catalogue, an economic study of tractors in the Corn Belt, the *Psychoanalytic Review,* and a catalogue of magic tricks, along with books on Hawaii, psychology, Henry VIII, and, in his hands, *Around Cape Horn, Maine to California in 1852.*

Upset by his almost delirious behavior, Charmian went for a walk under the stars and returned, much relieved, for find him asleep, the book on his chest. The next morning Eliza and house servant Sekine awoke Charmian to say that Jack was unconscious. She found him lying sidewise, doubled over in agony, in her mind "plain symptoms of [food] poisoning."[23] The telephone did not work, so Jack Byrne rode the eight miles into Sonoma to collect two local physicians, as well as call the family's San Francisco doctors. In the meantime, the women forced coffee into Jack in an attempt to wake him. Despite their efforts and eventually, those of four doctors, he died in the evening without gaining consciousness, other than the wisp of a smile toward the end.

Charmian dressed the body in a gray suit similar to the one she had first seen him in, while Sekine placed in his hand a note he had written: "Your Speech was silver, your Silence is now golden." Friends and farmhands gathered for a last look at the body, which seemed oddly small to the new widow. The next day ranch workers took the casket down to the railroad station, carrying it as if it were "a fragile flower," wrote a local reporter, and townspeople gathered in tears to watch Jack depart for his last trip to the East Bay. Charmian had decided that the funeral should be held there for the sake of Bess and the daughters, while she stayed behind on the ranch.

The girls first learned of Jack's collapse from the newspapers. They were on their way to a movie with friends and their mother when they noticed a headline, "Jack London Very Ill," above a quarter-column article. Returning home, they discussed calling, wondering whether they should disturb him. A few hours later Eliza phoned to say he had died.

Bess took the girls to meet the train. Their one consolation was his last letter, dated November 21, an invitation for lunch and sailing before he departed for New York. The cortege drove to an Oakland crematory, where Edward Payne gave a brief nondenominational address, and George Sterling followed with a poem written for the occasion. "I refused to believe it for years," recalled Becky. "I didn't, wouldn't, couldn't look at his coffin."[24]

On November 26 George arrived at the ranch bringing the urn, which Charmian and Eliza wreathed with ferns and yellow primroses from the cottage garden and withered leis from Hawaii. They placed it on a high carriage seat and walked behind over a mile down the steep slope through a forested part of the ranch to a knoll covered with white oaks, manzanita, and madrone to a spot that Jack had mentioned once, beside the graves of two children of the pioneer Greenlaw family. No word was said as the oldest ranch hand set down the urn and cemented it in place. Then other workmen rolled an enormous red lava block over the spot. Writing for the papers, George Sterling remarked that during the interment "all nature seemed at hush, as if in realization of the great power that had turned from life to have endless peace on her bosom." He read a poem he had written for the occasion, which praised the "Unfearing heart, whose patience was so long! / Unresting mind so hungry for the truth!" Sterling also predicted that the "United States have yet to learn from his greatness," as was already occurring in France, Sweden, Germany, and Russia, though George himself would be responsible for promoting stories about his great friend that ultimately undermined London's reputation at home.[25]

London's mother, Flora Wellman, as a young woman. Unfortunately, no satisfactory photographs of his African American foster mother, Virginia Prentiss, exist. Courtesy of Helen Abbott.

Anna Strunsky's vibrancy is evident in this portrait from the 1890s. Bancroft Library.

Bess Maddern, London's first wife, around the time she met him. Courtesy of Helen Abbott.

Ninetta Wiley Eames Payne, the *Overland Monthly* editor whom he called his "Mother Mine." Courtesy of Milo Shepard.

Charmian Kittredge in the 1890s was a secretary, writer, and photographer.
Courtesy of Milo Shepard.

Jack's personality included a generous, sensitive side often overlooked by biographers. Courtesy of Milo Shepard.

Joan, Becky, and Bess, ca. 1905, after the divorce. Courtesy of Milo Shepard.

Jack had a much stronger affinity for Joan than for her sister.
Courtesy of Milo Shepard.
Joan, Bess's fiancé, Charles Milner, and Becky on an outing.
Courtesy of Helen Abbott.

Jack during a visit to Joan when she was recuperating from
typhoid fever. Courtesy of Helen Abbott.

Seeing off the *Snark*, 1907. Carrie Sterling at far left, Charmian, James Hopper,
George Sterling (with his hand on Hopper), and Jack. Courtesy of Milo Shepard.

Charmian, Colt pistol on her hip, at a native market in the
Solomon Islands, 1909. Whereas modern viewers might respond
to the imperialist elements of this image, London's readers
objected rather that it was too erotic. Courtesy of Milo Shepard.

Charmian and Australian pianist Laurie Smith, partial model for the
other man in *The Little Lady of the Big House*. Courtesy of Milo Shepard.

Yoshimatsu Nakata, ever-present companion to Jack and Charmian, 1908–15. Courtesy of Milo Shepard.

Jack just days before his death, showing off a piglet, 1916. Courtesy of Milo Shepard.

Charmian and Jack several days before his death in 1916. Courtesy of Milo Shepard.

With noted actors in the maternal Maddern line, Joan and Becky both aspired to the stage. Seen here in costume for *Maid of the Argonne*, 1918. Courtesy of Helen Abbott.

Teenage Joan and Charles Miller, whom she would marry thirty years later. Courtesy of Helen Abbott.

Becky Fleming, children Jean and Guy, and nephew Bart Abbott, ca. 1930. Courtesy of Helen Abbott.

Charmian in her sleeping porch at the ranch cottage. Courtesy of Milo Shepard.

Jack's stepsister and ranch manager, Eliza Shepard, who avoided cameras, at the pig palace. Courtesy of Milo Shepard.

Charmian London, at back left in fur coat, and Anna Strunsky in white turban at front right, for launching of SS *Jack London* in 1943. Courtesy of Helen Abbott.

Charles Malamuth, Joan's second husband and noted Russian scholar. Courtesy of Helen Abbott.

Joan and E. E. Cummings in Moscow, 1930. Courtesy of Helen Abbott.

Bart and Joan with Clark Gable on the set of *The Call of the Wild*, 1934. Courtesy of Helen Abbott.

Barney Mayes, Joan's third husband, on left, and "Little Wop,"
as he was affectionately called,
their protector against Harry
Bridges's hit men. Courtesy of
Helen Abbott.

Percy Fleming, Becky, Charles
Miller, and Joan, ca. 1949.
Courtesy of Helen Abbott.

# 12

*Widows*

CHARMIAN REFLECTED HOW STRANGE it was for widowhood to seem so natural, as if she had known all along that she would soon be in that state. There followed the inevitable days of regrets: how sad that she and Jack would never again sail the seas together in small boats, how frustrating it was to follow the war news without Jack to help inform her. "I wander through the upstairs rooms, where Mate and I lived and loved after our return from the Snark voyage; where I carried my-our baby, and where I wept with the loss afterward. Truly I live without fear; for the worst has happened. . . . Well, I still have Eliza, and she is Jack's and my true sister."[1] Through Eliza she found an answer to the repeated question, "Why do anything?" The answer was found for them both in carrying out Jack's ranch dream and marketing his writings.

Most immediately complicating these new plans, though, was the settlement of the estate. Within days of the funeral, she sent Eliza as her emissary to Bess and the girls to communicate her concern that Jack's daughters come out well in the proceedings. Eliza advised Bess to take out guardianship papers to protect herself from the ambiguity in the will that intimated Charmian should have actual physical custody of the girls. She reported back that Bess had no hard feelings toward Charmian, who in turn hoped that all the legalities would be resolved quickly because money was so short.

To Jack's executors, Eliza and Charmian's uncle Willard Growall, however, Charmian confessed her mistrust of Bess, who she believed was ready prey for some avaricious lawyer. One of her first questions was whether the contract Jack had drawn up with Bess was legal. Growall assured her that it was not, because it had not yet been signed by both parties when Jack died. Nonetheless, to outsiders Charmian conveyed a staunchly supportive attitude. When news of Jack's insulting bequest to Bess of five dollars hit the headlines, Charmian wrote several friends to say how unfair that publicity was to Bess. She confided in Frederick Bamford that she could readily prove to the world why Jack had treated Bess so rudely, but she would not do anything of the kind unless dragged into an "unfair fight."[2]

Exactly what Bess's feelings were is unknown, for apart from court documents and news articles, nothing in her hand exists. Nor did she ever share the particulars of the negotiations with her daughters, even after they were older. One can only surmise what it was like for her to deal with her daughters' and her own grief, and Jack's betrayal in his failure to provide for the girls as promised at their last meeting. She soon discovered that he had also changed the beneficiaries on three insurance policies, dropping Joan and Becky and naming his executors in their place. Although the estate would eventually transfer that money to Bess and the girls, it would be a protracted process. At least she had no fears of Charmian's insisting that the girls move to the ranch.

The timing of Jack's death was particularly inauspicious. He was in one of his "bust" periods financially, $18,000 in debt. He had been counting on movie deals, business propositions, and books in progress to cover these expenses, which is why he had been about to head to New York. The nation was shifting toward a wartime economy, with its consequent shortages and inflation. In the publishing industry, the price of paper and other costs swelled, causing restrictions in the number of books produced. Drawn into a flurry of patriotic activity, from bandage-wrapping brigades to victory gardens, the populace also had less leisure for reading.

To Charmian's dismay, the negotiations over Jack's intellectual property rights were out of her control and under that of the executors.[3] In practice, this meant primarily her uncle, Willard Growall, who had hired the leading San Francisco firm of Metson, Drew, and Mackenzie. (Being owner of a prestigious tailoring and shirtmaking firm, Growall was well connected to the city's business elite.) Charmian was eager to see some of Jack's earlier works reprinted, for she knew it was important to keep him in the public eye. Growall balked when the publishers, citing wartime inflation, offered a lower royalty rate than usual. On this and other contract matters, Charmian found her wishes being discounted, though she voiced strong objections.

She also discovered that she could not use the estate toward maintenance of Jack's other major legacy, the ranch. Her commitment is evident in how quickly Charmian sought to publicize Jack's agrarian philosophy. Soon after his death she wrote a letter to a group of his friends who were planning a memorial service for him, encouraging them to include in their discussions "the tremendous importance to him of his great agricultural dream and the working out of this dream here and on the side of Sonoma Mountain." Pointing out how his socialism had been reborn in his uncompleted plans to create on the ranch a schoolhouse, post office, and other services for workers, she worried that these dreams were now being ignored. "Is everybody going to lie down and mawk about this and that and the other, and let the living reality of his biggest, warmest work lapse on the hillsides? I am begging you now, with all my heart, not to let the world (and your words carry far) forget that he laid his hand upon the hills of California with the biggest writing of all his writing and imagination and wisdom. . . . Don't seal your lips on this aspect of Jack London, which is so vital an aspect of him, living or dead." She hoped that the information would draw from others support for a "fitting memorial," such as a school of agriculture at the ranch.[4]

The recipients thought Charmian daft. City men such as George Sterling, intellectual men such as Upton Sinclair, could not appreciate her plea. They treated her like a sentimental widow for claiming that she knew more about Jack's values than they did. Patiently she responded. To Sinclair she wrote that Jack's interest in agriculture was hardly the "last minute one" he claimed it to be. As for his accusing her of trying to get others to contribute to the support of her property, she replied that she had inherited Jack's patriarchal responsibilities for four households and other unattached individuals. To Frederick Bamford she offered assurances that she was neither as tired nor as ill as he had sensed. "As Jack turned from the world of men and women more and more, to me, it was because I understood him—his heart and intentions." Her request, she insisted, was "worth thinking over."[5] Only Bamford remained loyal to Charmian; Jack's other male friends must have taken her letters as proof of their belief that she was lacking in perception. After all, to them it was Jack's writing and politics that were worth preserving, not his manure pits.

Like many others, these men were possibly misled by the sight of the ranch property and recent news reports into assuming that Jack had left Charmian a rich widow. Most of the assets—land, farm implements, intellectual property—had little liquidity. Her diary now records a new topic in scattered notes of sales and purchases: a Jersey bull sold for $1,500, a cow bought for $2,000, a horse sold for $600. (She and Eliza would prove themselves at the next State Fair, where they garnered a First in Show for their bull Roselawn Choice and top awards for other cattle.) The receipt of over $9,000 in insurance money could not keep the ranch solvent.

Up at dawn, Eliza spent her days hiking up and down the acreage, as well as monitoring market prices for the crops, purchasing machinery, overseeing the hands, and attending to myriad business papers. She tired out a reporter one day with her determination to show off the ranch. She "showed all the supple and exhilarating signs of outdoor life" and was an "enthusiastic and persistent walker," he wrote. When the reporter suggested that they walk downhill instead of up, Eliza replied with a twinkle in her eye, "You're a tenderfoot." The tour included the terraced farmland, storehouse, blacksmith shop, dairy, and "specklessly clean slaughter house." She explained Jack's plans to develop a model farm, which she hoped to fulfill as her spiritual inheritance from him.[6]

As is evident from the prices cited in Charmian's diary, stock raising required considerable capital, as did the other ranch activities. Expecting that the estate could help out, in January Charmian wrote Growall that she had her heart set on two shorthorn heifers and requested $1,500 for that purchase. He replied that she had inherited the ranch and everything on it, and was therefore responsible on her own for its maintenance and management. Although her lawyers did save on tax bills by treating the ranch as her residence rather than as Jack's business, Charmian soon realized that the $1,500 a month support awarded by the court could hardly begin to meet the ranch needs, let alone her responsibilities to Bess, the girls, Jennie and Flora, along with Netta and Edward Payne. (In fact, it would be months before Eliza would receive her own one-time $1,000 bequest.) Selling the ranch was out of the question. Rather than be overwhelmed or discouraged, Charmian saw this situation as an opportunity. She re-mortgaged her rental properties in Berkeley, and when not answering each one of the hundreds of condolence messages, devoted herself to completing *Our Hawaii*.

Charmian was determined that Jack's first family be treated right, but she overlooked how prone lawyers are to dispute and thus to protracted proceedings. During the two years of negotiations over the will, all monies from Jack's previously published work went into the estate to be held in trust. In June 19717 it appeared that a settlement had been reached. The *San Francisco Chronicle* printed a front-page story, "Widow Willingly Makes Liberal Concession to Former Wife and Children," reporting that the negotiations were being carried out "in a friendly spirit." Charmian explained to a reporter that the will had been written five years earlier "while Jack was in a passion of anger that soon passed off. . . . I feel certain that if he knew the old will existed and felt his end was so near, he would have provided more generously for his children in a new will." Showing all the signs of being planted by Charmian or her attorneys, the account was incorrect. Bess had expected Jack to increase her support payments. But he had not, and as Growall advised in a July 7 letter to Charmian, his failure to do so wasn't "helping our side. . . . [S]he should have been paid off the additional money." He noted that Bess had been cooperative about the delay in the insurance payments, and it put their side in the wrong to hold up her increase.

If Growall thought that Bess's Oakland lawyers, Chapman and Trefethen, would be easy opponents for the estate, he was wrong. Bess pressed a suit against the estate for $10,000—the amount of the canceled life insurance policies. When Charmian complained in January 1918 about the delays in settling, Growall blamed the situation on both Bess and uncontrollable technicalities. Among the delaying tactics was the estate attorney's request that Eliza desist from sending any support money to Bess until the settlement was completed. This was hardly a strategy to ensure a quick resolution.

Two months passed with no progress. In order to pay off Bess's claim,

Charmian was advised by Growall to arrange for extended payments. She did not agree. "I have myself been looking over the documents, letters, etc., and it seems to me it's worse than before, instead of simpler. I'm getting disgusted, and have just about made up my mind to let the suit stand—to pay the $10,000 and be free of the whole thing. I'm utterly disgusted with the shilly-shallying of lawyers."[7]

In March, Eliza wrote a traveling Charmian that Bess now wanted the estate to continue to support her after the girls reached maturity. By now what would become the final agreement was almost in place. As Growall explained to Eliza, "The 'will' is to be ignored and any bequest or payment to the girls mentioned therein to be void. . . . They get no security from anything except from royalties."[8]

By April 1918 Charmian was so frustrated by Growall and the various lawyers' decisions that she insisted an agreement take place directly between her and Bess, with no intervening agents. She wrote Eliza, "I have shown, in every possible way, *and at my own sacrifice,* my intention toward Jack London's children, as well as his divorced wife." She wanted Eliza to show Growall and all the attorneys her letter, stating her determination to carry out "*the intent of Jack's will,*" that is, her willingness to extend herself beyond what he had specified.[9]

With regard to real estate, Charmian also compensated for Jack's stinginess. First there was the problem of his having transferred the property at 606 Scenic Avenue into Eliza's name, which meant that it was no longer included in the estate. Eliza signed over the property to Charmian so that it could be given to Bess. At the time he wrote the will, the Scenic home had not yet been built; thus he had specified that Bess should have occupancy of 519 Thirty-first Street, but be responsible for all taxes and repairs. Were she to marry, she must leave. (That he mentioned only the Thirty-first Street house in the will would later set Jack's daughters wondering why he had not added a codicil at least regarding 606 Scenic.) Charmian deeded both that property and the 606 Scenic house to the daughters, with mortgages paid off.

The most important issue concerned royalties. According to California law, the girls were entitled to half the royalties on all of Jack London's copyrights, because all his writings had been completed while they were minors. Somehow this division had been avoided. Once Jack died, the royalties went into the estate and could not be used by Charmian. Determined to pay off all claims, she arranged an agreement in which Macmillan would advance her a lump sum of $20,500 in exchange for her waiving her rights to royalties from Jack's work for a six-year period. Given that Macmillan was Jack's primary publisher, she was losing her one dependable source of income. Nonetheless, she went against her advisers' recommendation and used half the money to pay off Bess. According to Joan's friend Robin Lampson, who was close to the scene, Bess was too bitter to institute a claim ensuring that her daughters would always receive half of the royalties.[10] It is unclear from the correspondence, which has gaps, whether either side was even considering enforcing this aspect of the law. It may also be that Bess's attorneys saw the estate as too encumbered to make further claims. In October 1918, Eliza confessed to Growall that she feared foreclosure on the Hill Ranch, but he was able to renew the mortgage for $10,000.[11] Even with clever accounting, however, back income taxes had accumulated to over $7,000.

In December 1918 the girls signed the final document, allowing them $75 a month each for support, which money was to come from royalties only, plus the deeds to both houses and $10,000 as recompense for the expected insurance money. Bess received $350 previously owed for repairs on the Scenic Avenue property. With the insurance money and rental income from Thirty-first Street, the arrangement must have looked generous at first to Bess and her daughters. But with both girls in college, an inflationary economy, and recurrent illness that interrupted Bess's tutoring work, most of the money went to pay bills, and the rest likely was invested for future income. And after Becky came of age, there would be no money at all. By that point the daughters, exposed to the numerous newspaper accounts regarding Jack London books and movie projects, would wonder why their mother had not demanded much more.

Despite the coarse thread of the estate negotiations running through Charmian's life for many months, she was at base contented, wondering at one point if Jack that last night had perceived that she would live out her life more or less happily. How, she mused, would he have responded to "his Kid-Woman writing a book, unaided, and no servant in the house. When I finished typing what seemed a fairly good piece of writing I stood up happily and said, aloud, 'Good Girl, Charmian!' and then cried suddenly, thinking of my darling and how pleased he would be."[12] On her few allotted days away from her desk she would visit Blanche Partington, her Wiley cousins, her uncle Willard and aunt Emma Growell, or attend art exhibits, ballets, plays, and operas in San Francisco.

Charmian was still being featured in magazine and newspaper articles about women, and would cooperate with any journalist as a way of keeping Jack's work in the spotlight. Eleanor Gates, a popular speaker of the time, created a talk on "Four Superwomen" who she felt served as inspirations to other women. These were Ann Blount, who explored Arab lands; Sarah Bernhardt, the magnificent actress; Ruth Law, an aviator; and Charmian. Gates argued that these were among the best examples of women who refused to be restrained. With her usual self-mockery, Charmian penned alongside one copy of this speech, "Ha, ha. Now aren't you [Jack] proud of me?"[13]

Only a few of Jack's old friends retained ties with her. Socialists Mary and

Gaylord Wilshire visited, fresh from a stay with Carl Jung, and Charmian prodded them for all they could tell her about psychoanalysis. Finn Froelich arrived to create more sculpture and furniture. Carrie Sterling and Blanche Partington also to provided comfort and assistance. George Sterling developed a duplicitous relationship, engaging her directly while mocking her to others.

Eliza's son Irving was now a strapping young man, out of high school and eager to contribute to the ranch. Having lived part of his youth in the presence of Jack London, he was set on assisting his mother and beloved aunt in their determination to preserve the land for agriculture. Modernism and the city held no appeal to him, for understandable reasons. Glen Ellen retained its idyllic nineteenth-century qualities, with its unpaved roads, creeks for swimming, horses for transportation, the First Congregational Church with its Mayflower Hall for social events. Whether ranchers, quarry workers, or railroad men, residents lived close to the land and shared in seasonal rural activities and celebrations. Given the local culture of respect, people were free to hunt, fish, and ride horses throughout the mountains, crossing property boundaries without fear of angering the owner. There might be nine bars, but saloons were the men's clubs, and with the approach of Prohibition, residents were well equipped to make their own wine and spirits. Thanks to its being off any main highway, Glen Ellen retained this neighborly isolation until after World War II.

Jack's death incurred more than financial loss for his first family and the psychological wounding of his daughters. His first family was often ignored now altogether. When the May 1917 *Overland Monthly* was devoted completely as a memorial edition to Jack, no one approached Bess or the girls for reflection, nor were their photographs included. The sole reference to them was in an interview with Charmian, who remarked that her plans included "assisting as best she can the education of her two step-daughters."[14]

Charmian and Joan haltingly began to build an epistolary relationship, much of which centered on gifts from Charmian and requests from Joan for favors for herself and Becky. During 1917 Charmian voluntarily sent several of Jack's books, offered the girls a puppy from the ranch, paid for Joan's high school graduation dress, arranged for theater tickets, gave them rings custom made by a local jeweler, and money beyond the usual support payments. She agreed to the daughters' request for other copies of their fathers' books, one of his old valises, a miniature she particularly treasured, and fabric to make into dresses. Each package usually included a brief piece of personal news to soften the mercenary theme. The only hint of discomfort would arise when neither Joan nor Becky acknowledged receipt of a gift. Nevertheless, Charmian continued to offer presents and accepted their excuses of "I thought I had . . ."

Expressions of a growing trust, however tentative, are evident. One of Charmian's first acts was to sort through Jack's letters to find those Joan and Becky had written and return them. She described the ranch and her hopes that they would enjoy it one day. When an unfavorable article appeared about Jack, Joan wrote Charmian how furious she was that people would say "unkind, absolutely unjust and untrue things about Daddy," who was such "a big man." She and Becky thanked her "for defending his memory so beautifully."[15]

Given the delays in the settlement, and so many past-due bills for Bess to pay, the girls had to piece together the funds to go to the University of California at Berkeley. Joan entered in the fall of 1917, and took on whatever work she could—coaching, serving as a French governess for two little girls, mending handmade lingerie for a wealthy woman—to pay for books and expenses. Nowhere in Joan's mass of lifetime papers is there any suggestion that she felt she deserved to be supported through college. She knew that her father had worked his way through high school and one semester of college, that her mother had intended to do so, and that Charmian had supported herself at Mills. Paying one's way was a sign of maturity, and Joan enjoyed working because of the independence it brought. Besides, she would recall, "We had always had a very small income from my father and were used to it. And we were young!"[16]

By the time Joan entered college, her dream of a stage career was over. When she was growing up, others would ask whether she wanted to be a writer like her father, and she thought, "Never!" Raised to be self-supporting, she rejected secretarial work or teaching as a career, and settled on social work. Eventually she decided to major in English, although her favorite courses were in history, and her sophisticated application of historical analysis remained evident throughout her life's writings. Her academic work was, as in the past, of highest quality, and would earn her a Phi Beta Kappa key.

There was one way in which her relationship to her father would be kept in the public eye—through the local tabloid press, with its emphasis on judging moral character. In "London Bridge," an unpublished reflection written in her twenties, Joan noted that being Jack's daughter had brought some advantages, such as access to the best seats at the theater or opening a charge account. But it had also brought ostracism from those who disapproved of what he had represented, and the inheritance of the notoriety attached to his name. "London Kin Balks at Middies," read one disapproving headline when she voted in favor of evening gowns for her high school graduation. Another more approvingly announced, "London Kin Registers at University." The stories ignored Joan's own views and instead presented her as a reflection of her father, whether for good or ill. What also rankled her was how the press ignored her mother's role in raising her to do well. "Is it the popular idea, I wonder, that writers produce their own offspring unaided, or that they marry morons?"[17]

Somehow Becky would not fall into this web. Perhaps it was her less assertive ways, her less frequent participation in activities that came under public scrutiny. She was mentioned in several local articles featuring her and Joan in dramatic productions, such as *The Three Fates,* a university pageant staged to raise funds for disabled war heroes. Photographs contrast the two strikingly, for the dramatic face of dark-complexioned Joan, with deep-set eyes, heavy brows, and full lips overwhelmed Becky's more conventional blonde prettiness. In one major patriotic parade, Becky had the starring role; photographs show her dressed as Columbia alone on the float.

Both young women easily attracted men's attention, though once again Joan would reign. Robin Lampson met her in 1916 when he attended for the first time Ina Coolbrith's monthly poetry group. As he recalled, "The remarkable thing that day is that I saw Ina Coolbrith at all" because Joan was "something more marvelous" even than the esteemed seventy-five-year-old California poet laureate holding forth in her lace mantilla.[18] Although Joan had a male escort, Lampson sought her address and permission to write her. He soon discovered that she had a rich singing voice, accompanied herself well at the piano, and was a wonderful conversationalist, vivacious and witty. Though he would never capture Joan's heart, their friendship would last almost sixty years.

A more serious suitor was Charles Miller, the strikingly handsome son of German immigrants, a young man of such splendid athleticism and physique that sculptors used him as their model of classical male form for public artworks. (His form graces the friezes on the Oakland Civic Auditorium.) Charles fell madly in love with Joan and expected to marry her when she finished college. But when the United States joined forces with the Allies, he went off to fight, his absence leaving a large vacuum for other young men to fill in her life.

However successful Joan was in attracting suitors, she made school her first priority, for she had formulated a firm philosophy of woman's independence. She enjoyed the flirtations, and expected to marry, but on her terms, which meant establishing a career so that she need never fear being dependent as her mother had been.

While Joan accumulated A's and academic honors, Becky, who also went on to Berkeley, mainly gathered suitors. Continuing to define herself as "not Joan," she was less driven to achieve at school, where she majored in anthropology and literature. Priding herself on having her father's sense of humor (something Joan was not known for), she was more frankly out for fun.[19] Since Berkeley's mascot was a bear, she tied a large teddy bear her father had given her to the front of a car on the way to football games, and carried it with her into the stands. Her joviality and optimism, combined with her gracious, well-bred manner, allowed her to draw suitors who found Joan's forthrightness unwomanly. Becky filled her photo album with portraits of young men, some in uniform—Carlton Kendall, Walter Plunkett, Kenneth Flad, Harold Wurts, Stanley Truman—several signed "with love."[20]

Joan later called this the happiest period of her mother's life. Now in her forties, Bess was more matronly, her hair turning gray. Despite all that had happened in recent years, she appears relaxed and contented in photographs taken on various excursions and vacations with her daughters. Determined to improve her knowledge of mathematics, she hired a private coach from the university to help her study geometry, algebra, trigonometry, and calculus in more depth. This training enabled her to widen her tutoring clientele to include college students. (In defending her against the Crowd's claims that Bess was not very interesting, Joan would respond that "it was the best they could do in an attempt to comprehend a person whose talents lay far from their own.")[21]

Though no suitors appeared at the door for her, Bess took delight in the simple pleasures of family and travel. Her girls had matured into lovely, accomplished young women in whom she could take pride. Her mother, Melissa, remained healthy and fit enough to take long trips with the girls during school breaks. Becky's album was filled with evidence of these enjoyable excursions, including numerous trips to favorite California spots such as Carmel, Yosemite, and the Russian River, and more extended ones east to Washington, D.C., to visit Maddern relatives in New Jersey, to New York, and many points in between. One cannot help but wonder if Jack's death brought a greater release for Bess than she had at first anticipated. There would be no more conflicts, no more competition with "the Beauty." True, there was no more Jack; but did she at some point appreciate the freedom resulting from the breaking of that earthly bond? The photographs answer a resounding "Yes!"

At least one person other than Charmian benefited from the will: Jennie Prentiss. In fact, during the negotiations with Bess's lawyer, Charmian at one point offered to waive her own support and work for a living, but she refused to sign a contract that did not include the care of Flora and Jennie.[22]

Jennie had remained vigorous into her early eighties, still attending as a midwife in the black community and contributing her services to the Federated Negro Woman's Club of Oakland and to her church. In 1917, when she was no longer able to keep house for herself and Flora, she requested that the estate provide her expenses to live in a rest home. Charmian quickly agreed, and Jennie moved to a place in Beulah Heights operated by a former sea captain, William T. Shorey. That move did not prove satisfactory, for she refused to conform to his many regulations. Through friendship with the publisher of the *Oakland Sunshine,* John H. Wilds, she found a room back in her old West Oakland neighborhood in the home of Mariah Bridges, until a fire caused by a coal stove brought an end to the arrangement. Although the house was not destroyed, the near-tragedy unsettled both women, particularly Jennie, who began to act confused and cross, much unlike her usual self. Friends found her another room, but in time her neighbors realized that Jennie could not live on her own, that her senility was too far advanced. She had outlived her husband, her children, her beloved "Cotton Ball," and most of her friends. Consequently, Jennie accepted commitment to Napa State Hospital, where Bess and the girls visited her periodically. She approved this arrangement because she was aware of her mental lapses, and during periods of lucidity would discuss her situation dispassionately. Bess and her daughters were among the few visitors she had. When less immersed in reality, she spoke as though her long-deceased family and her foster son were still alive.

Jennie died aged ninety-one on November 27, 1922. Charmian signed for the release of her remains, which were taken to a West Oakland funeral home. Among those who paid their respects were sister club and church members, along with Eliza, Bess, Joan, and Becky. (Charmian never attended funerals.) She was then buried next to Alonzo and her children in Mountain View Cemetery.

Though supported by the provisions of the will, Flora's final years were lonely, particularly after Jennie left. Her grandson, Johnny Miller, enlisted in the army and moved out. Flora lacked the community support that saw Jennie through her deterioration. Apart from Bess and her daughters, she had little companionship.

Flora's behavior did not so much change with age as become more hardened. By the time the girls were old enough to know her well, she was in her seventies. Joan remembered her as solitary, self-contained, undemonstrative, and seemingly incapable of smiling. But Johnny Miller recalled Flora as always warm and generous. (Johnny had also received letters from Jack, who falsely accused him of not working to help support Flora and Jennie.) Indeed, Miller was the one family member who never had an unkind word for his foster mother.

By her mid-seventies Flora was too crippled from arthritis to use her hands on needlework or at the piano, and her eyesight was so worsened as to limit her reading. After a short stay in the hospital in late 1921, she died on January 4, 1922. A local obituary focused on the "many tributes" Jack had paid "during his literary career to his mother and his sister Mrs. Eliza Shepard" for their encouragement before he became famous. Nothing else was said of her life apart from her son. Eliza, Bess, and the girls paid their respects at the sparsely attended service. But they felt less saddened by the loss than by what had become of a life once so promising and full of spirit. In passing the news to Anna, Charmian recalled that Jack had never loved his mother, and that she herself had "underplayed [Flora's] strangeness in writing about Jack's childhood."[23] Charmian's view of Flora, so colored by Jack, would be the one handed down to posterity. So many misunderstood this woman, so radical for her day, so passed over in the circumstances of history and the fame of her son.

A stranger appeared at Charmian's home during the summer of 1917, Rose Wilder Lane, a struggling writer and journalist. The daughter of *Little House* author Laura Ingalls Wilder, Rose told Charmian of the tragedy in her young life: two small children dead and a divorce. Now a *San Francisco Call* news reporter, she hoped that *Sunset* magazine's assignment for an essay on Jack would provide the spur her career needed. Charmian found her young and interesting, and with a good understanding of Jack, so she extended her full support. Several weeks later Rose wrote to explain that *Sunset* actually wanted a full-length serialized biography. She apologized for having appeared under false pretenses, but she could not afford to turn down the offer. Although Charmian was planning to write her own biography of Jack, being sympathetic with Rose's personal situation and admiring her obvious intelligence, she agreed.

The first installment in October 1917 appeared under sensationalized advertising, and its content consisted of sordid episodes from Jack's youth. Eliza was particularly furious about the discussion of Jack's dubious paternity and insinuations that his father was a drunkard. Charmian complimented Rose on her "charming fiction."[24] Rose responded that she was only trying to show truthfully the obstacles her hero had had to overcome in his struggle for success, and that in fact the information had come from Bess and Flora. The letter played on Charmian's sympathies: how difficult it was to write on top of holding a full-time job now that the man she had hoped to marry had gone off to Canada to join the air force.[25]

At her request, Charmian received proofs of the next installment from *Sunset* editor Charles Fields. When she marked the numerous errors and threatened to sue, he responded untruthfully that Lane had been forced to use other informants because Charmian had been uncooperative. As for the advertisements, yes, they were in regrettable taste, but could anyone prove they were lies? Certainly not everything in the story was true, he admitted, but Jack's devoted public were eager for anything, and were not very particular whether it was fiction or fact. He cynically proffered every apology, assuring her that no harm was intended toward the family, and he hoped that some remedy other than a court case could be found.[26] The wrangling continued on both sides until Fields agreed to publish Eliza's objections in one issue. But when the women received the galleys of that statement, they found that Fields had appended an editorial note discrediting Eliza. When they again threatened a lawsuit, Fields deleted the note, assuring Charmian that this only proved his good intentions toward the women.[27] Yet just a few days later a gossip column in a Bay Area paper tattled about the brouhaha, adding that *Sunset* had sent galleys to the women only as a ruse and had no intention of using their corrections. This is indeed what happened. Charmian labored over the worksheets and returned them by the next mail, only to be informed that pages were already in press by the time her corrections arrived.

During this contretemps Charmian reached a clearer understanding about how Jack's life should be handled. "The 'right to discuss' a famous man is a far cry from the right to misrepresent him. Rose Lane is a brilliant woman, but what woman or man, however brilliant, can be worked to death with journalistic work, and simultaneously write a biography of a great man inside of a few weeks?" she asked Fields.[28] She challenged him, as she was to challenge many in the future, to prove that certain of Jack's writings, such as *Martin Eden* or *John Barleycorn*, were completely autobiographical. From this point on she developed a new role, that of Jack's defender, a part she played till her dying days. As in this case, it often proved a losing battle, because writers and publishers were often more determined to tell a good story than a reliable one.

Many months later Rose Lane asked Charmian for permission to publish her serial in book form, and dangled the plum of a share in royalties as an incentive. Charmian not only refused but also threatened a lawsuit. In subsequent letters each woman softened her language, though not her position. Charmian finally thought the matter ended. Being no fool, Lane made sure to get full benefit of her labor. In 1925 it appeared as the novel *He Was a Man*. Despite the pseudonyms, most reviewers and readers took it to be a valid biography of Jack.

This bitter episode colored all of Charmian's future dealings with would-be biographers. Thus she warned one hopeful, "I have had a world of trouble and distress through unauthorized persons trying to write biographies of my husband, endless trouble that has taken us into courts. And I have edited the darnedest rot, written about my husband that you can imagine. So lady, lady, you go ahead with your German Prison and other stuff, and keep off Jack London. I'm tellin' you, as Jack used to say."[29]

More than the steady influx of bills stirred Charmian to write as a way of increasing her income. She had published nonfiction articles and book reviews for western magazines before meeting Jack, and refined her craft under his tutelage. Soon after Jack's death she resumed their familiar work pattern of writing all morning, and rapidly completed the manuscript of *Our Hawaii*. In December 1917 she read the published version while riding a train cross-country to New York, where she thought it best to negotiate contracts in person for her future work and Jack's unpublished writings. Her critical eye roamed unhappily over "repetitions and overuses of words that escaped me. Some silly typo-graphical errors. It's a good-*looking* book in the main."[30]

Personal reasons impelled her east as well. Since Jack's death she had ex-changed frequent and lively letters with the poet John Myers O'Hara, and clearly the exchange had grown flirtatious. "This slightly erotic experience at 3,000 miles distance is actually sapping me a bit. But it's terribly interesting. I guess I'll live through it," she noted in her diary.[31]

O'Hara was a dapper bachelor, a Chicago lawyer who became a Wall Street broker. His real love was language; he knew over twenty languages and dialects, and applied that erudition in his poetry. Jack had introduced *The Call of the Wild* with one of O'Hara's quatrains, and the couple had especially enjoyed reading aloud his translations from Sappho.[32] An avid bibliophile, O'Hara had included Jack's works among his private collection from their first appearance. His favorite poetic form was the sonnet; his best-known book was titled *Pagan Sonnets*, which gives a good clue to his style—gushingly romantic with re-pressed eroticism.

Though Charmian destroyed his letters, some of his later book inscriptions and poetic inserts, written long after the flirtation was over, hint at why she de-cided he might be "dippy." In one he penned, "Roses of Persephone! Roses she strews on the tombs of singers of the past. Immortal flowers! Kin of amaranth and asphodel! Roses of the days and joys that shall never return! Come back, as ghosts, in memory, with the pallor of long ago. Unseal your cassolets of dream! Waft your undying perfume to my heart!" He sent finely lettered copies of his and others' poems to her. One, decorated with cutouts of sprightly nudes, in-cluded this verse: "Where are you now, / O Dyad of my dreams, / My dancing girl? . . . There is no wine / of sateless lips, voluptuously sweet, / No passionate hearts to meet, / No ecstasy of night."[33]

Unlike in her previous visits, when she had to deal with Jack's carousing and mysterious disappearances, New York now shone with possibilities. Charmian attended over thirty plays, recording brief reviews in her diary, and visited many old friends. Both Merle Maddern and Hobart Bosworth were starring in dramatic productions; Martin and Osa Johnson had an apartment where she stayed part of the time; Arnold Genthe often accompanied her to cultural events. Mary Austin, now immersed in war support work and women's causes, introduced her to the refuge of the National Arts Club overlooking Gramercy Park. After one of several visits with Sophie Irene Loeb, she wrote cryptically in her diary that their conversation "stirred me to the deep. A sense of tremendous discrepancies in the past."[34]

With Anna very ill from her eighth pregnancy, one that would end in mis-carriage, Charmian frequently went to Greenwich to sit with her and reminisce. Anna shared her indignation over the inaccuracy and hyperbole of Rose Wilder

Lane's articles, and was so upset that she had lent Rose her letters from Jack that she now wanted to burn them. Charmian in turn admired Anna's own memoir which she had published in *The Masses*, portraying Jack as a romantic revolutionary, an unusual blend of boyishness, assertive manhood, and poetic sensitivity. This was Anna's daring affront to socialists who had condemned him during his final years, as well as a quiet statement of independence from English, who had broken from *The Masses'* editorial collective.

Business matters were settled quickly and satisfactorily. George Brett urged Charmian to attempt a "big book" about Jack, words he would one day rue. *Metropolitan* editor Carl Hovey and his wife, Sonia Levien, who would later gain fame as a screenwriter, corralled Charmian in their apartment for days, prodding her on the organization and style of the book. "They don't let up on me a minute about what they want me to do, and they're getting me interested—which is a good thing. I'm apt to get scared of myself and fall into a sort of apathy."[35] When two magazines began bidding against each other for serial rights, she knew at last money would be coming in, which she assured Eliza would be used for the ranch. Further hope, she wrote, was offered by Hobart Bosworth's discussion of movie prospects that might add to their coffers.

What Charmian did not convey to Eliza were the events that consumed most of her daily diary entries, her complex contredanse with male admirers. Soon after arriving in New York, Charmian met O'Hara for dinner, but the meeting had the opposite effect on each. Her fantasies of any intimacy vanished, while his soared. Conveniently for her, he became very ill soon afterward, and he was also preoccupied with a move to a new apartment. She had more than enough company, and certainly did not regret his absence.

On January 17, 1918, the man Charmian had said she would "never forget," Harry Houdini, sent tickets to his next Hippodrome performance, and an invitation to call on him in his dressing room afterward.[36] To her surprise, he approached her warmly and charmingly, paying her the considerable compliment of saying that she looked like a young girl. Later he called her hotel to leave the mysterious message that "a letter within a letter" would soon reach her room. He must have used some unperfected trick, for the note never arrived, and Charmian neither heard from nor saw him for several days. In the meantime, O'Hara, now recuperated, again became "chummy" with her. Houdini's note finally arrived, and she accepted an invitation to dine with him and his wife, Bess.

Understandably, Charmian was startled the following morning to receive an amorous telephone call from the illusionist. "HH's declaration over phone rather shakes me up." So began a chain of visits, usually in the afternoon or late at night, but frequent and obviously for more than purposes of polite conversation. Charmian sent a brief note to O'Hara suggesting that they call off their involvement for the present. Clearly she preferred her Magic Man, as she re-ferred to him in her diary, to O'Hara the Pagan Poet.

Or did she? For O'Hara and Houdini were not the only romantic suitors in her life. Taking advantage of Houdini's many hours at performances, she filled some of the time with Cloudesley Johns, now living in the East. These meetings also included more than friendly banter, although eventually guilt over the adultery forced Charmian to douse his passion.

Houdini pressed on with the wild declarations of the day that seem so ridic-ulous to modern ears: "Now I know how kings have given kingdoms for a woman. You are gorgeous—you are wonderful. I love you." Or "You don't seem human to me—I wonder if you have to eat."[37] The highest praise came the day that greatest of all mama's boys said that, yes, he would even tell his mother about his new love. His intensity soon overwhelmed Charmian, provoking in-somnia and dreams of the world engulfed in catastrophe. One evening she went out, knowing that he was to be at a benefit and could not see her. When she re-turned late that night, the news that he had come by only worried her further. She chose to flee.

By late March, both Houdini and O'Hara were filling her ears with pleas of love over the phone when she refused to see either of them, while she allowed Cloudesley Johns, more reconciled to her sexual rejection, to escort her about. To free herself from her zealous admirers, she went to Maine to visit her father's family. Upon her return, she refused to see Houdini, who left sorrowful mes-sages begging to see her once more. She would not. She left in April, gratefully enjoying the solitude of the train to work on the biography of her late husband. Love affairs added surprise and drama to life, but they were not to take prece-dence over her work.

# 13

## Every Woman Should Fight to Accomplish Her End

ONCE HOME FROM NEW YORK, Charmian ignored the persistent letters of affection from her suitors to focus on writing and ranching. She remained insecure about the former. The latest royalty check from her British publishers included only a few dollars in payment for her *Snark* log, which had been split into three volumes, one sensationally retitled *A Woman among the Headhunters*. That year the *London Pictorial* solicited from her an article, "British Women in Wartime," but no further offers followed, and she was unable to reprint the article in an American source. The reviews for *Our Hawaii* were mixed, and correctly compared the work unfavorably to her *Log of the Snark*. In Hawaii itself, however, the book was well received, one reviewer calling it "the best book since Mrs. [Mary Bird] Bishop's [*Six Months in the Sandwich Islands*]. As Boswell proved to be much cleverer than Johnson, so has Mrs. London beaten her brilliant mate."[1] The book would not bring in the royalties she had hoped for, but she was pleased that the Hawaiians appreciated her presentation of their society.

Despite the weak outlook for financial gain, Charmian had no choice but to move forward with the biography of Jack. For one thing, the episode with Rose Wilder Lane had taught her the importance of placing her version of Jack's life in the public eye before others exploited his memory. Furthermore, given crop failures as a result of weather and the expenses of developing the livestock herds, she had no other income source.

Within a month of returning home to Glen Ellen, she completed three chapters of the biography. Netta, Edward, and Eliza all praised her initial efforts, and promised full cooperation. Cloudesley Johns lent his extensive correspondence with Jack, which proved most important for understanding his attitudes during the early years of struggle and failure as a writer. Though supportive of the project, Anna refused to lend Charmian her letters, but eventually they too arrived in the mail. Anna later apologized, explaining that family illnesses and other problems had aggravated the great psychological resistance to opening the long-sealed box. "You never had a friend more hungry-hearted for your living presence," Anna added.[2]

By late 1918 Charmian and Eliza had cleared the remaining debts from the estate. Admitting that current circumstances prevented the ranch from becoming profitable purely as an agricultural concern, they were nonetheless determined to preserve the property in a manner honoring Jack's intentions. Given the instabilities in the economy and the costs of settling the estate, they hoped optioning Jack's stories for movies would help. Once again the chaotic nature of the film industry would result in a frustrating cycle of raised hopes dashed, only to be lifted once more.

The full account of Charmian and Eliza's dealings in the film industry is extremely complex, and has been scrupulously laid out in a monograph by the film scholar Tony Williams. As he demonstrates, despite their considerable acumen and caution, the women were swept up, as so many were then, by currents beyond their control. A combination of incompetent producers, ruthless film executives, changing public tastes, and problematic adaptations of Jack's stories undercut almost all the hoped-for income. Thus, while contracts, legal correspondence, and news stories regarding these years imply that Charmian and Eliza were getting very rich, the facts were otherwise.

In 1917 Spencer Valentine of the New York Picture Corporation wired Charmian requesting motion picture rights to Jack's short stories. Although nothing came to fruition there, he explored other possibilities as well. These included Charmian's writing screenplays for William S. Hart, having her own books made into films by Paramount-Artcraft, and directing her own stories if they did not sell outright. He even suggested marketing his own stories under Charmian's name, an idea she rejected. Although he was unsuccessful in these efforts, Valentine became an advise to Charmian and Eliza for over three decades and helped them market stories in response to changing public interests.

By contrast, the conflict between Hobart Bosworth and movie producer Frank Garbutt only complicated matters. In late 1917 Bosworth created a stage presentation of *The Sea-Wolf* in which he used some footage from his 1913 film production. When his tour of the material brought much applause around the country, Garbutt rereleased the earlier movie, and also initiated discussions with Charmian about a new version starring William S. Hart. Determined to be the only Wolf Larsen extant, Bosworth warned against that scheme and urged the women not to sign. Garbutt reminded them that he still owned the movie rights, and pressured them into a less remunerative contract for any subsequent screen adaptations. In 1918 Hart starred in a movie titled *Shark Monroe,* advertised as "the Sea Wolf of the Pacific," the first of a series of movies based on Jack London stories without any legal right. Although Bosworth believed that he had exclusive use of the Wolf Larsen role, it was Noah Beery who would star in the next film production, a 1920 version. Even Garbutt admitted that it was shoddy works, a loss for all involved.

Bosworth frustrated Charmian in other ways. First, although he was supposed to pay her $100 a week during the production of his play, he fell into arrears and complained that such royalties were excessive in light of the costs. Second, in his determination to play Wolf Larsen on the screen, he proposed a sequel to *The Sea-Wolf—Buck McAlister,* to be a collaboration between himself and Charmian. She agreed, so long as Jack's name be mentioned nowhere in publicity and that she be recognized as "Charmian London," not "Mrs. Jack London." The eventual product, released in 1921 as *Brute Master,* was publicized contrary to her wishes, and worse, infringed on the rights of Charles Shurtleff, who had by then signed a long-term contract for movie rights to Jack's stories. This breach of agreement, Charmian angrily protested, "imperils my living, Hobart, my very bread and butter."[3]

Shurtleff benefited by appearing in early 1919 at a point when Eliza and Charmian were clarifying the estate's movie rights with various individuals. After discontinuing the 1913 contract with Frank Garbutt, Charmian spent a week in San Francisco with her lawyers before approving an agreement whereby Shurtleff would pay $10,000 every three months over a three-year period for rights to make films "of the highest quality of artistic production and that every care shall be taken that said productions shall reflect credit on the work of the said Jack London."[4] Were Shurtleff to default, he could exhibit only those works for which he had paid. There was a potential to make $120,000, but as in the past, the women would see very little.

Within two months Charmian was questioning the wisdom of the decision to form the Jack London Film Corporation with a man clearly devoted to London's stories but unprepared for the complex task of moviemaking. His accounts of the first productions under way, *The Star Rover* and *The Mutiny of the Elsinore,* were not encouraging: costs exceeded budget, and a director had to be fired. His May payment did not appear until late September, by which time Charmian had given him an extension on his August installment. By the end of 1919 Shurtleff had moved his company to Hollywood, yet wrote that production problems remained, as well as difficulties with his British backers, and *The Star Rover,* he advised, needed much reshooting.

Over the next two years a pattern emerged of payments delayed or missed altogether and films of mediocre quality. Charmian's diary expressed financial worries, the Macmillan advance had covered only about half her debts. Furthermore, in anticipation of Shurtleff's success she had made some plans and purchases that now she could not pay for. "No good news from Shurtleff" was the refrain. "I am broke but hoping for the best" was another. Just as frustrating was reading the screenplay of *Burning Daylight* and discovering that it omitted any horseback scenes, which were essential to the novel's message. *The Star Rover* degenerated into a shabby crime melodrama that included only two of the prisoner's incarnations and omitted the key chapter of Christ's crucifixion. The film version of *The Little Lady of the Big House* concluded with Paula not committing suicide but embracing her husband. Overall, the productions were so shoddy that Charmian and Eliza disliked having to view them.

Anna also apparently received overture regarding a film of *The Kempton-Wace Letters*. When Charmian refused permission to release her half of the rights, Anna wrote of her distress: "It might have meant for me what Jack has enjoyed in life but never I—fame and success." Nevertheless, she assured Charmian that as a socialist she could not allow business to lay its "unctuous and clasping hands upon our friendship." Anna was true to her word, and increased the terms of affection she used in her letters to Charmian, such as "dearest," "beloved," and "sweetheart." It was such a relief, Anna said, to know there could never be any misunderstandings between them since they were unafraid to speak out simply and clearly to each other.[5]

Charmian's romantic intrigues continued. One day the mail brought a letter to "little woman removed" from Cloudesley, to "my darling nymph" from O'Hara, and the greeting "How I miss you—the magic of memory" from the incomparable Magic Man. At that time, too, she learned that the man she had loved most before meeting Jack, Herbert Dugan, had divorced. Others escorts appeared, mostly San Francisco men associated with the arts or the military. By early 1919, Charmian's frequent visits to the city resembled her New York trip, with the company of numerous men in one day at dinners, dances, symphonies, plays, and operas. She seemed little drawn to any of them. One even moved to a cottage on the ranch to do small chores on the property, but Charmian's involvement with him seems to have been ambivalent, for many days passed without her seeing him. As it was, he departed after several months, most likely because of his excessive drinking.

However many other men sought Charmian's attention, it was Jack who dominated her thoughts. One evening she reread *The Little Lady of the Big House* from beginning to end in one sitting, and wept because it was the most profound fictional statement of their love. She worked lovingly to prepare two volumes of Jack's short stories. Editing *On the Makaloa Mat* for posthumous publication, she noted, "So much of it is mine—paragraph after paragraph," a tantalizing suggestion that she was more of a co-author of those works written during the months of Jack's decline.[6] She finished preparing "The Red One" for *Cosmopolitan*.

One August day brought startling though not fully surprising news: Carrie Sterling had committed suicide by taking poison. Since divorcing George she had worked at small jobs, such as assisting at a library, but gradually lost interest in life. She went about her death methodically, first by writing farewell notes to her best friends, then walking to the Chinese pagoda on her sister's estate, playing a favorite melody on the record player, swallowing cyanide drops, and lying down to wait for sleep. Blanche Partington urged Charmian to write a memorial article, but she refused, explaining simply, "What is there to say?" Carrie's death would add fuel to the myth that the Crowd had all made a pact to die by suicide.

❧

For more than two years Charmian had fretted over the ranch, Jack's literary reputation, the financial obligations to several households, and the emotional needs of others. At times she labored so prodigiously on the biography that she would collapse sobbing over her typewriter, exhausted by both the physical tedium and the emotional dredging. She told Anna that she was working harder than during her married life, and was in need of a change.

As a reward, she wanted to build herself a new house. Charmian found her little cottage to be "damp and grave-like," filled with ghosts. Pack rats rustled about, stealing little objects, hiding them in corners or nooks, scampering through the house at night and awakening her. The roof leaked, and in foggy weather the house stayed much too damp for Charmian's attacks of neuralgia. Eliza was hesitant about investing in a house at this time, but, sympathetic with Charmian's need to have a safe home, a home of her own, free from the past, soon relented. Charmian in turn bought Wake Robin, the house where she and Jack had first resided, and gave it to Eliza as an Easter present. They anticipated that the Shurtleff movie deal would underwrite construction of Charmian's new house, a decision they rued.

While the exterior was going up, Charmian expressed to Anna its meaning to her beyond comfort. For one thing, it was constructed of a mossy gray stone with steel window frames so that it would "never burn." For another it would be "my house, Anna, not Jack's nor another's—my own expression of myself and the life I seem led to live. It's quite wonderful, this new self of mine—sometimes I think Jack would have liked this new, real Me—tho' she's perhaps less clinging!"[7]

Indeed, the house would be a unique expression of Charmian's personality. Apart from its rough stone construction, it little resembled Wolf House despite being designed by the same architect, Albert Farr. It was a two-story house, rectangular, with a large porte cochere at the entrance. One entered a first-floor living room of grand scale, approximately twenty by thirty feet. To the right were a den and doors leading to the dining area, kitchen, and stairwell; to the left a large fireplace, its hearth sunk several feet below floor level, providing a cozy pit where one could sit on pillows to talk or read by firelight. Two ten-foot-windowed alcoves on facing walls were fitted with large upholstered platforms for seating or even sleep. Large tapa cloth curtains could be drawn across these banquettes for privacy. Behind the fireplace wall was a small guest apartment with two bedrooms and a separate bath. Upstairs one passed another set of guest bedrooms and bath, then entered Charmian's large bedroom, covering much of the upper floor, with its stone fireplace decorated with small naked infants, and the ceiling curved and beamed like the interior of the captain's cabin of a sailing vessel. This room was flanked by a sumptuous dressing room and closets, her private bath, and a kitchenette, plus a secret spiral stairway connecting to the den below. Thus the house was planned to retain a curiously satisfying mixture of expansive, free spaces with enclosed, intimate, private areas. Many years would pass, however, before it was completed, because money problems would constantly interfere.

In a further sign of a new self-confidence, Charmian finally stood up to her lifelong nemesis, Aunt Netta, who had revived the water rights dispute. Once the estate was settled, Charmian explained, she had no money and was having a difficult enough time meeting her own responsibilities, let alone increasing support for her aunt. Netta remained so insistent and obstinate that Charmian finally "turned down the page," as she had seen Jack do with his daughters, and decided to have no further communication with her.

Regarding Eliza, she felt complete trust now. As she reflected privately, "I think Eliza did not like me—for many years; I think she has outgrown the dislike. I do not know whether she really loves me or not. She is very good to me, and very useful, and heaven knows she gets very little out of it for herself. I am quite sure she would like to retire out of my affairs, and get some rest herself."[8] Eliza showed her caring indirectly by sewing dresses for Charmian or remaking old clothes when money was tight, and perhaps most tenderly, by massaging her neck and head with oils. Further drawing Charmian into Eliza's affection was her fondness for Irving, now married to a local woman, Mildred Ranker. Irving exhibited the same strong, upright character as his mother and shared with Charmian, whom he adored, a passion for the land and the livestock.

For two years Charmian had urged Joan and Becky to visit the ranch. "It is so great an achievement of your father's that it will be a pity if you do not see what he did here," she wrote Joan. Nothing would please her and Eliza more, although they understood it would be up to their mother's approval. In April 1919 Joan wrote that she and Becky were going to be staying with some friends in Glen Ellen and asked if they could stop on the ranch to be directed to their father's grave by Eliza. Charmian urged them to think about spending more time to look over their father's workroom, "sad pleasure though it be," and all their father's things. If they could not see their way to meeting her, she added, she would understand, and hoped they would change their mind one day.[9] Joan's reply, that they appreciated Charmian's extension of hospitality but would only see Eliza, was worded with sensitivity and wisdom unusual for an eighteen-year-old.

On May 3 the young women arrived with their mother and friends, and after viewing Jack's grave found a place on the hillside to enjoy a picnic lunch. While out riding with a male companion, Charmian came across a ranch hand who mentioned a gathering of strangers who, when he came in sight, suddenly jumped up and turned their backs to him. Charmian surmised that it was the daughters, whom she did not want to embarrass by accidentally coming upon them. Thus, when she later saw them through some trees nearby, she changed her course to pass to the left of them. At that point, as she described it to Anna, "on my own land, mind—they all three jumped off the ground where they were picnicking and turned their back in a row!"[10] She thought this not only rude but also ironic in that the week before the girls had written for extra money and furs, and gotten them.

From the daughters' perspective, it was Charmian and her companion who had snubbed them, for she seemed to rear her horse on purpose and take off in a cloud of dust. Stunned by her apparent rudeness, they had jumped up in embarrassment at being treated so unkindly. For Charmian, turning their backs was the unforgivable rudeness. To that point she had believed Jack wrong to have given them up "in the end, as hopeless." She felt like a fool for having attempted to befriend them, and concluded that they had expressed interest in her solely for mercenary purposes. Although she wrote a long letter to Joan decrying their behavior as "inexcusable, prideless, and very short-sighted," she never sent it.[11]

In retrospect, a terrible misunderstanding seems to have occurred. Neither intended to insult the other. Rather, out of a scrupulous desire to avoid an awkward situation, each behaved in a way that could be misread. Silence followed from each side. It would be some years before, as Joan had once expressed to Charmian, both would "just try and understand the other."[12]

During 1919, behind the record of pleasant diversions enjoyed with friends and lovers, or just on her own, lurked signs of deeper disturbance. Charmian's dreams were splashed with visions of lost purses, missing addresses, and catastrophic accidents. Aging preoccupied her, leading her to record those incidents when people took her to be younger than forty-eight. She shuddered at having to buy a corset for the first time in her life. Constant exposure to sun, and the structural effects of gravity, sculpted her face into wrinkles and hollows. Given her vanity and physicality, she would see aging as an opponent to be vanquished as long as possible by any means.

Charmian's anxiety was shared by many, for the great flu pandemic was causing fear and changes in daily life. Becky's high school closed down for so long that it was unclear whether the seniors would have enough course work to graduate. At the Wallings', the children and English were all infected. Fewer visitors arrived at the ranch, and those living there went out less often. Fortunately, none of Charmian's close friends or relatives succumbed to the disease that was randomly taking entire families in other settings.

As Charmian approached the completion of her voluminous manuscript on Jack's life, persistent nightmares jolted her out of bed to compose in the middle of the night. Even George Sterling, as well as other, more loyal friends, encouraged her to ease back, fearful she would suffer a nervous collapse. If, as others reported to her, George despised Charmian, she had no hint from his treatment of her. Understanding perhaps more than anyone else George's complex personality and the demons that made him so self-destructive, she preferred to return his behind-the-back slander with kindness. Thus she asked him to complete Jack's mystery novel *The Assassination Bureau,* paying him seventy-five dollars a month, until he decided that he could not do the work justice. During this period Charmian often went to Oakland for day-long editorial sessions on the biography, and appreciated his counsel and full support.

Perhaps through others' instigation, in late November 1919 Charmian boarded a ship to winter in Hawaii, her first time there alone. The three New York admirers cabled love messages across the ocean, as usual, to no avail. Prone to dizzy spells and periods of weeping, she accepted all of the many social invitations in order to escape her fears. Nonetheless, the anxieties surfaced in her daily jottings, suggesting that leisure brought not rest but the full expression of grief suppressed by hectic activity. One house she had loved so much now seemed "full of age and wretchedness." Looking in the mirror one day, she decided that she "might as well leave off the war paint." While she appreciated the quiet retreats of old friends, it was not the same Hawaii. They were visibly older, a reminder of her youth now over. Many of these same friends had spurred the islands toward what were for her unattractive goals ("Commercialize! Modernize!"). Yet these very changes helped her to reflect, "No ghosts. I am laying them fast." No ghosts, few bittersweet reminders of earlier visits. As the year ended, she thought back to the men who had pursued her, to the many new acquaintances she was meeting. Approaching the new year, she turned toward the future, bolstered by the many rainbows that arched over the mountains of Maui in those final days of 1919.

If Charmian awoke cheerful on New Year's Day 1920, it may also have been because she had danced every dance save one the night before at the von Tempski ranch. Through much of her stay she had worked helpfully with Louis's daughter Armine, now a young woman with literary aspirations. Like many good editors, Charmian could improve others' work, though not her own. Soon referring to Armine as her protégée Charmian used her literary connections to assist the younger woman in what was to become a satisfying, modestly successful career. (In later years, when marriage brought Armine to California, she eventually filled the space in Charmian's heart that Joy would have filled had she lived to adulthood.)

One of the many books Charmian read in that tropic land was Frederick O'Brien's *White Shadows in the South Seas,* a best-seller about the author's adventures among those few tribal groups that avoided colonial intrusion. This popularized amateur anthropology rode on the interest spread by Martin and Osa Johnson's wildly successful 1918 film, *Among the Cannibal Isles of the South Pacific.* Still binding his reputation to Jack's, Martin used as the opening scene for that movie a hand-cranked shot he had taken of Charmian waving from the dock. Charmian was obviously moved by the film, and wrote a heartfelt letter of praise for the "sheer perfection" of the work and the "splendid photography."[13] Her response to O'Brien's book was similarly appreciative. Upon returning home in March 1920, Charmian looked up the author and sent him a brief letter of admiration.

Refreshed by the Hawaiian trip, her usual high energy returned, she now anticipated work with pleasure. John Hervey, editor of a horse magazine published in Chicago, joined Sterling in correcting her drafts of the biography, yet both combined could not keep up with her frenzied production. Despite her disappointment that construction of her new house was being delayed by lack of funds, she was much more contented than before her Hawaiian retreat. She reflected on the small delights of home, the tinkling of Korean bells, the sound of the fountain, the scent of the lilacs. That romantic eye would soon have someone to fix upon, for Frederick O'Brien was coming to the Bay Area.

In May the South Seas writer wrote to say that he kept a little blue house in Sausalito, across the bay from San Francisco, and would be spending some time there to work on a sequel to *White Shadows.* In turn, Charmian invited him and his wife—if he had one—to visit her on the ranch. O'Brien did have a wife, though he seldom saw her.

Charmian knew from photographs how handsome O'Brien was, but she found his complex personality and rich experiences the real appeal. In a recent sketch for *Bookman,* he had described himself as "a Marylander, first a sailor and then a law student at a university; laborer, tramp, reporter, war correspondent, newspaper editor and publisher in the United States, Hawaii, and the Philippines, correspondent and traveler in Asia, Africa, and Europe, gardener and keeper of chickens, goldfish, and goats, beachcomber in the South Seas, political writer, publicity utility expert, acting state food administrator of California, and one of Herbert Hoover's assistants in Washington; and always a lover

of sunsets on far shores, of books, of men and women and animals, of speculation on life and morals, customs and reactions, and of a merry song and a brave
deed, and also of being alone."[14] He further elaborated his proverbial good nature and laissez-faire attitude toward life; he never learned from experience,
and he wasted precious days and months in dreaming and in planning futures
for himself that would never come to pass. It is doubtful that Charmian had
read this self-description, but his brief, interesting letters to her conveyed many
of these characteristics.

O'Brien was small in build, trim-figured, and silver-maned, with "a profile
that any sculptor would be happy to perpetuate on a medallion." His smile and
ready wit attracted many women, and he cut a figure among the New York writing crowd as "the Lothario of middle age." He put "Pelleas in a back seat," made
"Shelley seem even a cruder boy than he was," and convinced others that
"Dante was an amateur when it came to women."[15] His wife, of French birth,
lived in Hawaii, childless. Her Continental upbringing had prepared her for an
arrangement whereby O'Brien had his freedom and she had his name for respectability. Very little can be learned about O'Brien otherwise; he refused to
list his birth date for his *Who's Who* entry and joked about being mysterious
and self-inventing. Although Charmian never noted the similarity, O'Brien's
charisma, wanderlust, and self-creation were also touchstones of Jack London's
temperament.

The name of at least one of his possible amours was also familiar to
Charmian. O'Brien had written *White Shadows* many years before its publication, keeping it in a closet despite the frequent urgings from his longtime publishing friend Morgan Shuster. He claimed to have left it casually with the Century Company, Shuster's firm, in 1919. In fact, O'Brien's submission could not
have been so casual, for he had sought the assistance of another writer to help
him prepare the final draft. And life always permitting plot twists not acceptable as "realistic" in fiction, it happens that the woman who had helped him was
Rose Wilder Lane. It is difficult to believe that two such personalities as Lane
and O'Brien would have worked together without some deeper involvement.
Charmian and O'Brien, or "David," as she usually referred to him, did not
know of their common previous acquaintance with Rose Lane, and would not
know for many months.

O'Brien similarly grew fascinated by this creature who displayed the same
sense of drama and self- fictionalization that he enjoyed. At first, after he arrived in Sausalito in May, the two did not meet but wrote letters and spoke often on the telephone. Finally, in June he sent Charmian a "frank letter" inviting
her to visit him the next day. He was all that she expected and more. "Something
new has come into my life. I know that someday we are going to be on a
schooner together," she reflected.[16] He returned with her to the ranch for sev-

eral days while she went about as though in a mist, showing him the many remnants of her life with Jack, her almost completed book manuscript, her horses and her piano. When he left, he gave her a copy of *White Shadows* inscribed, "As the odor of the tiare Tahiti are you to me."[17] She could not work for several days, but dawdled about, guilt poking at her. Charmian was in love.

One night she dreamed that her house was on fire, causing her to rush in to save the books Jack had given her. Later that month she was awakened by the fire gong. A tar pot at her new house site had caught fire, which spread to nearby lumber. Though little damage occurred, the reminder of the Wolf House fire left her unusually nervous. O'Brien came to her rescue, arriving for a long stay to read over her manuscript, give his corrections and approval, and watch her pack it off to Macmillan—enough material to fill two large volumes. That labor completed, Charmian devoted August to assisting "David" with his current project, a play script. Thus she did for O'Brien what she had done so many years for Jack: typed and edited manuscripts. Both being intensely private persons, O'Brien returned to his home for periods of solitude. Even on the ranch they slipped comfortably into days of working apart, then coming together for brief moments of relaxation and meals.

One day in mid-August, O'Brien called to tell her that he planned to depart for Tahiti two days later. When Charmian had first met him, he had mentioned his intention to visit the South Seas again, but once the affair was under way, he no longer discussed the plan. The precipitous announcement stunned her. When she met him at the docks, he shook her hand, said "Au revoir," and walked up the gangplank without once looking back. Accompanying her was Mary Clare O'Brien, his sister, who invited Charmian home, where, as women are wont to do, she offered comforting thoughts and repeated messages of affection men may not always express directly.

To ease the hurt, Charmian remained in the city and went dancing that night at the Palace Hotel. In subsequent days she thought of O'Brien often, but except for troubling dreams, his memory did not disrupt her other activities. Over two weeks passed before she received word from him, a wire stating his intention to return in mid-October. Exhausted by all that had transpired, Charmian left the final section of her book, a comprehensive bibliography of Jack's writings, to a woman named Beatrice Barrangon to finish. Barrangon's compendium was neither complete nor accurate, and though Charmian corrected many of the errors, she was too distracted to catch all of them. Scholars inevitably fault her *Book of Jack London* for these errors and omissions.

Much more distressing than O'Brien's desertion were repeated nightmares of losing her purse that coincided with the deterioration of the Shurtleff movie deal. Literary grave robbers overseas were in full force, pirating and reprinting Jack's works with abandon. In France, unauthorized translations of the most inept and irresponsible sort were rolling off the presses. One "translator" there went so far as to take one of Jack's essays, retitle it as a preface to one of Jack's novels, and sign his own name to the stolen introduction. With much vigilance Charmian was able to control the American rights, but she could not stop the theft of his serials by Canadian magazines.

Individual frauds of other sorts continued throughout these years. In 1918 Charmian learned from the photographer Annie Brigman, who had taken the marvelous portraits of Jack and Charmian in their oilskin slickers on the *Snark,* that a friend of theirs, George Wharton James, had "borrowed" plates of her photographs of Jack, made up prints, and was peddling them in New York City. Charmian intervened on Annie's behalf, warning James to stop or else she would expose him. Among other shams, she discovered through a tiny news item that the Oklahoma Historical Society had purchased a collection of supposed artifacts of the *Snark* voyage from a man who had never known them, let alone been on the trip.

Then George Brett at Macmillan wisely informed her that her biography was too long, and cited the wartime paper shortages as a reason to cut it. This explanation did not ring true, for her English publisher, Charles Boon, had just advised her it was so absorbing that he would put the book into press in its entirety immediately. Even George Sterling had praised the book, especially the ending, with its "powerful and effective close to a most absorbing Fall."[18] By the end of 1920, Charmian had decided to bypass Macmillan and offered the book to Century, which serialized a portion in its namesake magazine, and promised to advertise it as its "big feature" in 1922. A tidy advance in December nevertheless only temporarily caught up with ranch bills.

When O'Brien returned in mid-October as promised, they had a joyful though ultimately frustrating reunion, for he would not or could not have sex right away. "I grow tired, almost ill under repressed circumstances, and come home in the evening," Charmian recorded in her diary.[19] They went about their own social activities; when O'Brien had a dinner date with Theodore Dreiser, Charmian went off with her own friends. Finally, O'Brien virtually moved into her cottage, where he could write away from the telephone and "lion hunters." Fame having come late in life, he could little tolerate the claque of news reporters and fans who showed up at his door to disturb his work in Sausalito.

The couple now discussed their relationship more openly, agreeing that it should keep its charming sense of freedom—yet not too much freedom. One night Charmian framed photographs of Jack and hung them on her walls, while O'Brien read aloud from Jack's favorite author, Rudyard Kipling. O'Brien always respected Charmian's devotion to Jack; indeed, his knowledge of her ultimate loyalty may have provided the security he needed to stay with her. He must have sensed that in the end no man would replace Jack, and rather than be threatened, he saw this as a guarantee that he need not fear troublesome bonds.

Charmian and O'Brien separated to spend the year-end holidays with their relatives. At a New Year's dance at the Palace Hotel in San Francisco, Charmian, now fifty, took first prize for her costume, winning a purse. As the years progressed, Charmian's eye for unique and lavishly constructed clothes continued unabated. She approached clothes as works of art; she sought the finest materials on her various travels, and designed new outfits for Eliza to sew. If her wardrobe appeared opulent, it was successful in its disguise. Clever bargain hunting for fabrics and a demand for quality were the key, not flagrant expenditure of money. These beautiful outfits, which drew so much attention in public, nevertheless encouraged some to think of her as a wealthy widow. Charmian seemed unaware of the full impact these attention-getting outfits may have had on others: the misconceptions concerning her finances, the envy of other women, the appearance of frivolity. Among her friends, however, this dramatic flair was part of what made Charmian so interesting, and those who met her discovered that her conversation was sophisticated and enjoyable.

Certainly the effects of her artistic apparel were far from her mind the morning after the dance. "I enter this New Year [1921] helping Frederick O'Brien on his new book, *Mystic Atolls of the South Seas.* I am 'broke' but hoping for the best. My House is nearly done. Funny how this ancient Waterman pen of Howard Fisher's [a friend from the 1890s] is still the best and most reliable I ever had. What a lucky girl I am! The years pass—still I have love. And I have fame too, which may grow." As for Jack, "Sometimes I think about him for long. But it grows impersonal." She was hopeful that *The Book of Jack London,* as well as the revised edition of *Our Hawaii* George Brett had arranged, would finally increase her income. She was still a celebrity in her own right. The *Oakland Tribune* featured Charmian on the cover of its annual yearbook, proving with its pictures of her on horseback at fifty that she did indeed represent the "Spirit of California," a woman of "life and vigor and health and beauty."[20] The culture had finally caught up with her innate flapper personality.

Committed to remaining single, she reconsidered her ties to O'Brien. Although it is true that she did not seek permanence in the relationship, neither did she expect the disillusionment that followed. Putting her feelings in the third person some years later, she wrote: "[He was] so fastidious of his own feelings that he avoided hurt to others less his sense of wrong-doing disturb his own slumbers. He would not divorce his wife even though she wanted it, because he feared it would hurt her. One day, coming back from a ride, he stands waiting for her [Charmian] really enjoying her dismount. And she sees in his face the something meager, the lack of true companionship. But her loyalty and caring did not allow her to end things then. She waited, as women often do, for him to show signs of disaffection. Then she closed down, charmingly, relentlessly, until he, though relieved, was a bit breathless."[21]

Thus the relationship slowly shifted from ardor to companionship. When O'Brien left on another long trip in February, Charmian noted how blessed it was to be alone. Following his return, she wrote him explaining her relationship with Jack and her need for freedom. During her marriage, she had not felt restraint because she believed herself fitted "to be a real man's woman. But somehow I got to liberating myself." But like other men who think themselves liberal, she observed, Jack would "assert mastery, ownership in the most trivial matters."[22] During those moments she realized what freedom meant, that despite her natural inclination to regard a man as master, she was not bored with widowhood. Soon after receiving this letter, O'Brien went off to Hawaii once more to complete his manuscript.

In response to a 1922 query from the *Literary Digest* concerning career women, she asserted: "I am not for raising a family above all things. The woman with the brain and desire for professional life, business, politics, should not try to raise a family. Personally, I think every woman who has mind enough to know beyond doubt what she is best fitted for should fight to accomplish her end." This was a very contemporary attitude, but she added a remark more reflective of her lost life. "I nourish the 'good-old-fashioned' idea that the first desire and responsibility of the normal woman in a normal world is and should be to create a home for her man and their chicks."[23]

During the summer of 1921 Century distributed the two volumes of *The Book of Jack London,* including many photographs never published before. The reviews were mixed—deservedly so. As Lewis Mumford best summarized in his review in the *New Republic,* "It is one of the best, and one of the very worst examples of the [biographical] art that has come out of America during the last decade." What made the book excellent in other viewers' eyes was its utter frankness such that a "loveable, enthusiastic, very human Jack London" was revealed. The modern reader can see what Charmian was trying to do, how courageous and innovative her intentions were. But her style, with its florid, romantic drawing room touches, clashed disproportionately with her intentions. It was like staging a modern dance with costumes and music from *Les Sylphides.* Sometimes such incongruous mixtures conceive extraordinary artistic births; more often, as in this case, they spawn ludicrous miscarriages. Mumford alone recognized the reason: "These two volumes, however, might have been shorted by half [had she written] simple English. Had she been able to write clear, coherent prose, this titanic weakling [Jack] might have lived in the memory of men as a sort of American Cassanova."[24]

Yet, like many other reviewers, Mumford was not immune to confusing the merits of the book with those of its subject. Many of the laudatory reviews— and there were many—commented on Jack's character, not on Charmian's presentation. The reviewers liked him; ergo, the book must be a good one. Some of the deprecatory reviews went similarly awry. The *New York Times* critic, Archibald Henderson, took a pedantic tone: "There is something depressing in this recrudescence of the long-winded biography, and there is something of fatuity and futility in such works—the bulk wholly disproportionate to the merit or importance of the subject." Still, he astutely noted that Charmian lacked all sense of proportion; having been inundated with material, she simply entered all with equal weight. Much of the review was nonetheless a scurrilous attack on Jack, whom Henderson criticized as sophomoric and "a striking illustration of what a man of mediocre brain stuff, who detested writing, could accomplish by illimitable energy, undiminished perseverance, and a colossal ego."[25] Henderson's attitudes reflected those of most elite literary critics. Jack's memory was on the way to a quick burial in the annals of American literary criticism, an erasure so complete that even today most experts in the American novel and short story have read few of London's fifty-four published volumes.

Whereas Charmian's travel literature continues to satisfy, *The Book of Jack London* holds appeal primarily for scholars. The material that all the contemporary reviewers most admired, the romantic accounts of the couple's personal life together, exude a saccharine, unreal quality. For example, romantic expression then typically incorporated baby talk. Modern views of intimacy have changed so that our cynicism could lead us to conclude wrongly that Charmian misread or misrepresented their relationship. Her deference to Jack also grates against modern feminist views; it conjures the modern example of the ever-adoring upward gaze of Nancy Reagan toward her husband. The sentences lack the lilt and charm of *The Log of the Snark,* and the chapters vary widely in their structure, from entire letters to reconstructed conversations. And so with time the book has come to seem even less appealing. As with Caitlin Dylan's writings, too, it has been relegated to the musty corners of the library because somehow it does not fit our view of the artist that he shared an intimacy with a woman equal to his audacious drive and intelligence.

Because the book fails on literary grounds, it has been dismissed as an unreliable source of information. It is easy to single out the whitewashed passages: the elision of William Chaney and Jack's illegitimacy, the revised chronology of the affair leading to the second marriage, among others. Yet other sections are surprisingly frank. Charmian did not omit Jennie Prentiss's role in his life, a radical inclusion considering that even Jack had kept that racially sensitive information from public knowledge. She acknowledged his love for Anna Strunsky, and extensively quoted his letters to her. She tracked his mercurial moods, his dark periods and the destruction they wrought, without apology. She traced in detail his development as a writer, using his key correspondence with Cloudesley Johns to document her analysis. She did not avoid candid discussion of difficult periods in the marriage, for which she relied heavily on her diaries.

A strong editor could have guided the shaping of the material into a more taut and convincing one-volume account. The biography sold so poorly in the States that in 1930, when Century went out of business, Charmian was forced to buy the plates and remaining copies, to sell from her home by mail or to visitors to make up part of the loss.

The revised *Our Hawaii* appeared in the fall of 1921 as well, to similarly mixed reviews. "In spite of being badly written, the book derives some interest from its exuberant impressions and also from the biographical facts about the author's husband," concluded one critic. Perhaps the best description of Charmian's prose at its worst was the observation that she "must dress up her ideas in fancy costumes before parading them before the reader."[26] Frederick O'Brien prepared a full-page review for the *New York Herald,* which was curious for its almost total devotion to O'Brien's own experiences in the islands. By avoiding a direct review, O'Brien could save face, but his true estimation of the book was hinted at when he concluded, "The scores of pages of evidence of her love and admiration long since gone . . . [indicate] that the years since his death have been given to the preparation of his eulogy."[27] The most positive review was by Alexander Hume Ford in a Hawaiian newspaper—but Charmian had ghostwritten it for him. Despite that fraud, Hawaiian readers appreciated her observations even though they were not fully complimentary of the culture. Despite the American press, both this book and the biography of Jack would do well overseas, both in England and in translation.

In her diaries and letters Charmian showed little concern over negative reviews, perhaps because she had read through so many with Jack of his work. Rather, she was already planning her next two writing ventures: an autobiographical novel, *Charmette,* which never progressed beyond extensive note taking, and the completion of the novel Jack was writing the night he died, *Eyes of Asia* or *Cherry.*

O'Brien returned from his travels that fall, and behaved thoughtlessly at times because he was drinking heavily. When his wife, Gertrude, came to Sausalito, he had his secretary ask Charmian to go and visit her. Though furious over his impertinence, Charmian did visit Gertrude O'Brien, who thanked her for guiding his latest books to completion. The two developed a casual friendship.

The Shepard family became ever more important. Jack London Shepard was born to Irving and Mildred on August 5, 1921, "so wonderful ... the perfect body," Charmian noted. When Eliza went into the hospital for major surgery that summer, Charmian stayed by her, and noted with relief her quick recuperation. Although it was still a struggle to maintain the ranch, the harvest was rich with pears, peaches, prunes, apples, almonds, and honey.

The dramatic 1919 break between Charmian and Joan was in a curious way reassuring to two such dramatically inclined individuals. They were alike in other ways as well: hardworking, self-directed, highly curious, sensitively attuned to nature, fascinated by style, and comfortable with their erotic appeal. Had the episode on the ranch not occurred, they might readily have developed a more intimate connection based on shared worldviews. Instead, each had other interests to deflect her mind from the breech or any attempt to close it. Charmian had the ranch, the movie negotiations, her writing, and her lovers, while Joan had school and suitors.

Despite her academic excellence and determination to have a career, Joan was equally bent on a happy marriage. Having lost her father just as she thought she was regaining his affection, Joan would go through life unable to remain attached for long to a man. The first would be Park Abbott, an aspiring magazine writer with an interest in the cooperative movement, a softer kind of socialism. Following a brief courtship, Joan accepted his proposal, a decision that had tragic consequences for her old beau Charles Miller. The war had been especially cruel to Miller, whose parents were German immigrants. Fighting in the trenches against young men of his own heritage left him even more emotionally damaged than other infantry men. When he returned to California hoping to marry Joan, he was stunned to learn that she had committed herself to Abbott. His behavior became erratic, largely on account of drinking, and one night he was arrested for almost killing a man in a brawl. He was judged insane and committed to a mental institution, where he was to languish, probably undeservedly, for over two decades.

In June 1921 Joan married Park Abbott in a formal ceremony at Trinity Episcopal Church in Oakland, with Becky serving as maid of honor and the family doctor, William S. Porter, giving Joan away. Given Park's unpredictable and meager income, the couple moved in with Bess and Becky at 606 Scenic Avenue. Joan's longtime college friend Musa Evans also married that summer, though to a young man from a well-to-do-family. Musa would be a key support to Joan through the difficult years ahead.

Joan intended to go to graduate school, but she postponed that plan when she discovered that she was pregnant. Like her mother, Joan found herself to have a fierce maternal bent, and made her new son, Bart, her lodestar. He was, all agreed, a physically stunning baby, with curly blond hair, an endearing smile, and lively eyes, the kind of child featured in magazine advertisements. Little of his grandfather was evident in his face, but he would develop the same intense self-will. Joan doted on him, and Bess was charmed to have a grandchild in the house.

Musa also became pregnant, and Bess assisted at her home delivery of a daughter, Lee. While watching their youngsters play together, Joan and Musa would joke half-seriously that the two youngsters should marry and form yet another bond between the two families.

Always sensing that she was less important, Becky must have felt further crowded out by Bart's arrival. Yet her photograph album depicts scene after scene of joyful outings, Becky with one young man or another, or in the midst of girlfriends. She enjoyed the new freedom women her age were experiencing, the chance to crowd into an automobile for a day's outing, unaccompanied by adults. She especially liked dancing, and was less of a snob than Joan, who was shocked when Becky rode a streetcar in her evening gown during a date with a boy who could not afford a cab.

Some of Becky's friends had also been Joan's. She established a long correspondence with one young man who went east to Columbia University to earn his doctorate. Over several years the relationship deepened beyond friendship, particularly after they spent time together during a trip Becky and her mother made to Chicago in 1921. Following her graduation from Berkeley in 1922, Bess, Joan, Bart, and Becky traveled east to visit Maddern relatives there. During that stay, the newly minted professor courted Becky while she baby-sat for Bart at the hotel. He "told me he had loved me for ten years, since I was just starting high school," she later recalled. He proposed and promised to write her in California to let her know which of two teaching jobs he had accepted. Then he would come out west and marry her. The marriage never occurred. According to Becky, years later she overheard Joan telling a friend about "how she and mother laughed when they read his letter . . . asking permission to marry me; how she had mother write to tell him I was much too young."[28] Worse, Joan claimed it was she he had really loved, not Becky, and had proposed only because Joan had married Park. It appears that the man sent a number of letters to Becky, which Bess intercepted and destroyed. Finally, he stopped writing. Reflecting over this episode decades later, Becky proclaimed that his silence did not bother her at the time; she forgot him, and other interests distracted her.

It is a story of cruelty, and it has some credibility. It could well be that Bess put off the suitor, at least temporarily, because Becky was in fact not emotionally ready for the responsibilities of marriage. This was not the first or the last time she would protect Becky from potential troubles. Having gone through a traumatic marriage, too, perhaps she saw something in him that worried her. The unconvincing part of Becky's story is her claim to have been carefree for months afterward—at a time when she was hearing nothing from the man who had proposed to her. Surely this seeming rejection must have had a more profound effect on her, though her shrugging it off is consistent with her lifelong refusal to admit any possible ill-treatment by her father. To the outside world Becky insisted, on the one hand, that she was always being victimized in some way, yet on the other, claimed that the injuries did not matter.

Following this disappointment, Becky began to gain significant weight. Always tending towards plumpness, though in an attractive way, she now filled out her chemise-style dresses where they should have been loose. She returned to the university for a fifth year to earn her teaching credentials. When she completed that program in 1923, she decided not to teach after all, but instead attended a business college and went to work as a stenographer. Although she enjoyed the work, she resented that her contributions were, to her mind, supporting everyone else—when in fact all four adults in the household were working.[29] She also admitted not enjoying responsibility, she "didn't want to be anybody important."[30] Becky clearly felt second best in the household, yet was not willing to sacrifice the benefits of living in a large, attractive home with her family for company for living on her own under spartan conditions. As we will see, the truth was more complicated.

Despite the demands of motherhood, Joan was set on a career as a writer. To develop her portfolio, she worked part-time as a reporter for a weekly Piedmont paper, and was starting to compose short stories. While Becky drifted along, Joan continued to be driven and set high goals for herself. Her father might be long dead, but she was determined to prove herself to him.

# 14

# Fate in Their Own Hands

WOMAN'S SUFFRAGE HAD A SPECIAL meaning for women of Bess, Eliza, and Charmian's generation, who had supported the drawn-out battles with politicians, and observed in dismay the power of the opposition, as when members of the National Women's Party were force-fed in jail. For them the vote was the significant outcome, not the peripheral social freedoms that accompanied it. For her first vote, in 1922, Charmian marked an all Socialist ticket, as she would continue to do for the rest of her life (with the exception of supporting Roosevelt in 1936).

New admirers appeared. "Am full of music and also memories of last evening. Oh, men, my! It was high time for him to be sent away. One can't love 'em *all*, alas.[1] One evening she reread and burned the letters from seven previous lovers. Among the flirtations, another serious lover appeared. During much of the year Charmian's social life took her to the Swedish consulate in San Francisco. There she met someone identified in her diary only as "Prince," whose frequent attentions left her in an ebullient mood. Still, she reiterated to herself her conviction never to marry again, and spent her weekdays gathering notes for a proposed novel, negotiating with European publishers and translators of Jack's works, and working with animals on the ranch.

Also in 1922 her streak of misfortunes with the film industry ended. In April, Charmian went to Universal City to sign a contract for *Tales of the Fish Patrol*. This would result in eight two-reelers starring clean-cut Jack Mulhall. She also arranged another Universal Studio contract for *The Abysmal Brute*, which was produced as an eight-reeler starring British actor Reginald Denny. Later that year Hal Roach Studios contracted for *The Call of the Wild*, and Twentieth Century purchased rights to *White Fang*, perhaps to capitalize on the success of the dog story *Rin-Tin-Tin*. By now Charmian was an experienced negotiator, and was no longer tempted by multi-film deals promising large sums of money. Thus she accepted less money than in the past, along with a percentage commission for the sale. Because these contracts involved either established or up-and-coming film directors and performers, the movies were made quickly and with more skill than the Balboa productions, and would revive interest in Jack's works. In 1924, industry leader Thomas Ince negotiated for a sct of stories, but after he died mysteriously on William Randolph Hearst's yacht, the deal collapsed.

Now that the film arrangements were bringing in income to cover the ranch expenses and the house construction, in 1922 Charmian turned to Europe. This would be her first opportunity to meet the agents with whom she had corresponded for so many years. Her gracious social skills would serve her purpose well over the years, and result in a celebrity of her own, in particular in Denmark and France, although, with the steady erosion of the European economies, the continued popularity of Jack's and Charmian's books would not result in significant royalty income. Charmian depended as much as possible in her travels on the generosity of others; she stayed with friends, accepted arrangements made by agents, and bought tickets for the cheapest possible. She normally traveled as the sole passenger on freighters, typically for free. Her one extravagance on this and later journeys would remain purchases for her wardrobe. In letters she bragged to Eliza about the bargains she found.

Several days before her departure for Europe, Frederick O'Brien had lunch with her, and others held farewell parties for her in San Francisco. On December 8, 1922, she proved herself an "old salt" after boarding a Swedish merchant ship. To accommodate her health habits, she stored boxes of nuts, raisins, and figs in her cabin, and hiked several miles a day around and around the deck. As the only woman aboard, and one much at peace on the sea, she was a welcome addition to the officers' table, and on New Year's Eve danced a fox-trot with the wireless man so jauntily that they nearly went overboard in the revelry.

Her arrival in London almost seven weeks later was greeted with a whirl of invitations to shows, sightseeing, business calls at Mills and Boon, and interviews. She was guest of honor at the PEN dinner, where the group's president, G. K. Chesterton, introduced her to British literati. Accepting an assignment from *Women's Pictorial* for some articles on marriage and divorce, she noted that men "do not like to be told that it has been a man's world," in which helpmate, whose "body was at his disposition more than hers . . . had little recourse not to make life as unbearable as possible for the author of her woe." Thus she welcomed the liberalized divorce laws which provided women freedom from oppressive relationships. Divorce would not be necessary, she felt, if couples recognized "that each of them has lived a separate life previously, with its own sanctuaries, its peaceful privacies, its hours of priceless solitude necessary to growth." As for herself, "it pleases me that I enjoy liberty, independence, socially, and economically."[2]

The unofficial story of Charmian's European trips is found in her thick stacks of correspondence with European publishers. She made clear that she was to be consulted on all decisions to ensure that the translators were the best available, that the book illustrations were artistic and appropriate, that the books were produced cheaply enough for the average person to buy them, and that the advertising was tasteful. Whenever she learned of piracy, inept translations, or slipshod production, she excoriated the nearest agent. In Europe she sought out press interviews, doling out many quotable remarks. She knew how to play up to the local public, how to draw sympathy for Jack by emphasizing her role as devoted widow. The reporters had only favorable things to say about her, and the photographers posed her in the coy "glamour girl" shots so popular in that age. Charmian might bristle at being referred to as "Mrs. Jack London," but she enjoyed the showing-off if it meant more sales. On the street she felt as recognizable as Charlie Chaplin, so many people came up to her.

During this hectic trip Charmian also prepared an extensive diary, one that would eventually stretch over three hundred single-spaced typed pages, to be used as the *Snark* log had, with carbons mailed to friends in lieu of letters, the notes to be saved for a book manuscript. But it must have puzzled her correspondents, overwhelming as it was with names, places, meals, new clothes, but only rarely the surprising insight or clever description common in her previous work. Ironically, then, this most richly documented part of her life reduces to very little of substance, except perhaps to hint at an underlying loneliness, for in spite of all the socializing, she had to sit alone each day and type out her experiences. Yet it also hints at her continued self-discipline, and her ability to find pleasure in the smallest moments of the day.

Returning to New York in December 1923, Charmian dove into another round of social engagements. She met her most recent lover, now married and living in a cramped apartment in the New York suburbs, a sight that saddened her. She dined with the poet Edgar Lee Masters, a correspondent of several years, as well as Mary Claire O'Brien, the Pagan Poet, and her many performing artist friends. Sympathetic to those suffering in the Russian famine, she lent her voice to the American Committee for Relief of Russian Children. She also attended a benefit for Cecilia Loftus, a celebrated actress arrested for possession of "dope."

The highlight of this long trip had been Paris, where Charmian stayed with Anna Strunsky surrounded by her four children, in a large house with four stories, and four servants to manage it all. The rooms were like jewel boxes with their rococo hand-modeled plaster images of cupids and colorful flowers abounding. Anna's lifestyle had changed considerably since the time when, as a wandering radical, she had been detained in Russia as a potential subversive. Nonetheless, Anna and English retained their socialist theory, if not practice, and introduced Charmian to members of the local party paper, *L'Humanité*, which they helped edit.

Despite the lavish surroundings, the Wallings were no longer wealthy. For years they had spent beyond their means, as much to underwrite their political causes as their family's comfort. It did not help that Anna had invited her sister Rose and her family into the household and asked no contribution to the expense. Although living together, Anna and English were virtually estranged. He was annoyed by Charmian's repeated visits that year, complaining to Anna, "But 4 weeks! How preposterous! Neither you nor the children by any chance have one normal day while she is there. . . . I never want to see her again as long as I live."[3]

Oblivious to Anna's problems, Charmian kept a note in her purse: "In case of emergency: Notify Mrs. Walling." On her way home she thanked Anna for "those wonderful weeks in Paris" and her "marvelous hospitality."[4] If Anna was peeved by the visit, it was not evident in her "Charmian dearest" response the following month, nor in later letters. Only once had Anna shown strong anger toward Charmian: when, in 1920, Charmian would not support Walter Mc-Guinn's offer to make a film of *The Kempton-Wace Letters*.

If not for her children, Anna would have found little joy in life. In 1924, upon returning to New York, English ran for election as Democratic candidate for Congress but lost. Following World War I, the federal government stirred an anti-Soviet hysteria, leading to a "Red scare" during which Emma Goldman was deported. English found comfort in this new attack on a Russia he believed had failed in its revolutionary purpose. Now a stern anti-Bolshevist, he charged that even the stodgy *Book Review Digest* was subversive.

By 1925, having returned to the States, Anna realized that she must do something about their finances. English continued to travel whenever he wanted, visiting his mother in Florida every year and spending money on research for books whose earnings would never cover his costs. A letter from Charmian suggested a new option.[5] Worried over the ever-present danger of fire or theft on the ranch, she had sold Jack's handwritten manuscripts, along with part of his correspondence, to the Huntington Library. She knew that she could have made more eventually on the private market, but preferred that the collection be kept intact in a major library. Though Charmian did not disclose the price to Anna, she was able to pay off her biggest mortgage.

In despair over her own bills, Anna contacted the Huntington, informing them that she had a hundred letters from Jack London, and reminded them that she was the only person to have served as his collaborator. They were interested, but offered only three to five hundred dollars as their possible worth. Anna refused to part with these treasures for so little. She admitted to her mother-in-law, who had provided English's trust fund, that she had made a mistake from the start in not insisting that English find a financially rewarding career, for though he was a genius, he was not a breadwinner. When her sister's husband took a job in Washington, D.C., she invited Rose and her children to move in for three hundred dollars a month, partly for the income.

The money troubles were a symptom of the failure of their marriage. Although the Wallings attempted reconciliations during the late 1920s, they were not long-lasting, and only kept Anna on an emotional roller-coaster. In 1925 she blamed herself for remaining silent in the early years when English "could not think how he was hurting me, how he was inflicting words and tones upon me that I could never forget." Nonetheless, she loved him "boundlessly, endlessly," felt "infatuated, impassioned." Consequently, she fought with him, said "terrible, unpardonable things," even challenged him to find someone else.[6] In fact, he did.

Her sister Rose also faced marital problems. One day on a scrap of paper Anna wrote, "'When does a woman stop suffering over her husband's infidelity?' asks Rose. I know I shall never be unfaithful to you, my Own, but how can I expect that I shall always be irresistible to you. I must expect that your fancy will wander."[7]

Arriving home in the spring of 1924, Charmian sorted through the four hundred letters awaiting her response. Then she made a most courageous move: having resisted "temptation in London, Paris, Stockholm, Copenhagen, and New York," she bobbed her hair. The *Oakland Tribune* featured her new coiffure in an article, "Widow of Jack London Defies Cupid." She saw no reason for women ever to grow old, work being the key to the fountain of youth. "Women have their fate in their own hands," she told the reporter.[8] She crowed that *The Iron Heel* was selling well in France despite its being treated in the United States by "a capitalistic press" imposing a "conspiracy of silence." Hence shades of the old socialist remained, even after a year amid European wealth.

In October, Charmian would read on the front page of the *San Francisco Call* that her estranged stepdaughter Joan agreed about women's fate and the need for divorce as an option. In an interview after she filed for divorce against Park Abbott, Joan explained that she was not against marriage as an institution, but that it took more than the ritual words of a priest or judge "to institute a state of matrimony." Unfortunately, in her view, few people were capable of genuine love, and "to stay married without love is the cruelest torture in the world." Consequently, it is wrong to have laws that force a man and woman to live together when they no longer desire to do so."[9]

The precipitating episode was so painful to Joan that none of her descendants ever knew the truth until private notes dating from the period revealed the story: "The baby is dead, its spirit resting but a moment here on its swift journey for eternity. Untold pain and depths of heart-break crowd the little house with unbearable heaviness. The bright pink silk lining the little bed that will never be used." Joan had wanted many children. Now the daughter she longed for had not survived. For months Joan grieved, drew inward, and grew angry that Park was able to rebound more readily than she. "And again, you laugh." She composed poems to memorialize the loss of her daughter and of her marriage: "We pass heavy-hearted and slow along the barren way / Pain lives, dark and unsmiling, where once Love had her abode."[10] The loss was of more than this child. Surgery following the loss may have affected her fertility, for she would never again become pregnant.

The law permitted little of such truths in its briefs. Thus Joan's formal charges against Park included that he was slovenly and sullen, and would not let her name their son Jack. She asked for no alimony, requesting only twenty-five dollars a month maintenance for Bart. Although she was granted custody, Park was allowed half a year's visitation rights so that Bart would not be caught in the middle, as Joan and Becky had been. In theory, each parent would accommodate the other's needs, and when Bart was old enough, allow him to decide whom he wanted to live with. As a result he would spend months at a time with one or the other parent, and never felt pressure from either in making those choices.

Late in life Bart praised his parents for their decision. "My parents tried hard to see that I didn't get the kind of deal Joan and her sister got, where they were turned into missiles by their feuding parents. They never did the rigid kind of exchange that is so common today: weekdays with one and weekends with the other. These kind of agreements don't allow the child a choice." He also appreciated Joan's style of mothering, that she "never talked down to me [but] encouraged me to trust my own judgments."[11] In this regard too she chose to behave very differently from both her parents, who were so full of strictures and rules about ways of doing things.

What Bart did not realize was the undertone of hostility behind the negotiations. Park had been physically abusive; Bess was shocked one day to find black-and-blue marks on Joan, the result of his assaulting her during a vacation in Carmel. Surviving are Park's notes from the 1920s in which he obsessively documented Bart's time with him and Joan, observations about Joan's behavior that could be used against her, and accounts of Bart's health, including daily temperatures. Even after Park remarried, he seemed determined to punish Joan and accused her of not being true to their agreement. She kept the agreement, yet she also controlled the visitation periods, as suited her needs, so one can understand some of his anger. At the same time she relieved Park of the responsibility for child support when he was unable to pay, even when she was in financial straits. Within a few years Park became less disputatious, and the adjustments more smooth, matching Bart's recollection. Likely remarriage softened Park.

❧

Throughout the summer of 1924 Charmian labored on her latest writing project. *Cosmopolitan* had offered to publish the fragment of the novel Jack was writing the night he died, along with a second article by her describing how the story would have ended. The full-length manuscript of *Cherry* completed by Charmian is a most curious document.[12]

Jack's draft introduces Cherry, the sole survivor of a Japanese shipwreck on Hawaii many years before. Honu, the wealthy Polynesian patriarch who raises her, provides her with a Vassar education and European travels. Cherry's long disputations demonstrate the extent of her learning, most notably when she uses scientific ideas of the day to argue against intermarriage. "We have found it very expedient to keep our Herefords and Jerseys separate," she advises a guest. "Were you in charge with your layman's notions, our Jerseys would decline in butterfat, our Herefords would decline in beef, and all our rancher neighbors would be sneering at our scrubs." Yet, characteristic of Jack's ambivalent racism, she also decries the colonization of the non-white races, viewing them as separate cultures deserving of respect.

Interspersed with similarly interminable monologues are scenes of young, wealthy, handsome Caucasian men swooning over the Oriental beauty. She resists them, assuring Honu that she will never marry a man "who cannot rule me." Jack's handwritten manuscript stops at the point where Cherry observes Nomura, Yard Boy Number Four, a young Japanese man, "short, thick-set, almost massive, the muscles of the powerful shoulders plainly delineated under the single thickness of his garment." Nomura stares back at her, his nostrils flared.

Where Charmian picks up the story, the first impression is one of confusion. Some of her sentences take tortuous turns. "Seldom arising late, she was forehanded in nailing many a detail amiss, untying odd knots and generally overhauling the morale of the force under her hand. After which, alone or with some congenial enthusiast, or trainer schooling a youngster from the broodstable, she would return from a ride before the tenants of the interminable guest-wing and vine-clad auxiliary cottages were rubbing their eyes, as on the morning of her dash with Argyle." The words roll on, sometimes senselessly, and far out of proportion to the plot. Though skillful descriptions abound as well, lacy passages obtrude. The action, what little there is, staggers forward hesitantly, and more often just staggers.

Although Cherry is a typical Jack London heroine, a New Woman built on an exaggeration of Charmian's characteristics, she reduces to an at times ridiculous caricature. Cherry fancies costuming. She is a teetotaler. She invites a group of men to a swimming race and beats all but the Australian. She loves dogs and talks sentimentally about the ones that have died. She spends her time in self-education, studying languages or practicing her Chopin études. She goes into ecstasies while riding her horse. Being so accomplished and without fault, Cherry lacks believability.

The storyline meanders lazily for hundreds of pages. Suitors, indistinguishable from one another except by name, flow in and out of Cherry's life, bearing adulation and marriage proposals. She vacillates, rejects, then vacillates again. Her trances provide opportunities to explore her racial consciousness through their visions of Japan centuries ago. They provoke her to wear kimonos and learn the sake ceremony. Nomura hovers in the background, teasing her with his flute melodies, "their mad music timed to weird drums and trumpets heard in imagination, martial and male it was, in authoritative rhythm, as if leading a host to some sure goal."

At a grand Christmas ball, Cherry's behavior signals inevitable change. She wears a gown so clinging that except for the "blue gloss of a dragon-fly" she seems nude. (Charmian similarly attended a ball wearing a lacy Spanish scarf over her naked upper body.) Some guests, not recognizing her, wonder if she is part of the entertainment. "She was in miniature and perfection of maddening womanhood." Others describe her as "binary," a "twin-star," among other schizoid images. At the New Year's ball, she appears first costumed as a ten-foot coconut tree, then tiring of that, returns as a mermaid, only to finish the evening in her dragonfly gown. If Charmian intended self-mockery in these scenes, it is not evident in her writing.

The doubling, however, is characteristic of a pattern women adopt under patriarchal control. It is related to the defense mechanism of dissociation, splitting one part of the self from the other, usually to cordon off memories or feelings related to oppression. Women who have been beaten, abused, or raped will speak of separating themselves from the body being attacked. Doubling, however, is broader, because it requires duplicity, and may often be conscious. Seen in this light, Cherry's schizoid self-presentation is a commentary on the feminine role as Charmian experienced and understood it. She had been Jack's double, the part of his personality he repressed, but in the process had to suppress some of her own desires and feelings.

Charmian had in fact been facing this conflict in the final years of Jack's life, and with his death, she thrived in her unexpected independence. Bound more by convention, Cherry asserts her independence through her choice of mate. While in another Jungian-inspired trance, she realizes that Nomura is the concrete manifestation of her fantasy, that she must embrace her Orientalness.

Once her current Anglo suitor finds out, he mounts his horse, rides to the top of a volcano, and where "none to hear the animal's curdling cry, horse and rider launched upon thin air and toppled into the unknown depths." No one ever learns what happened to him.

Meanwhile, Nomura and Cherry fill a sampan with their goods, have a secret wedding, and sail off into the sunset. "To the shoulder of her choice of mate, blood of her blood, unafraid she pressed her forehead. . . . Almost diffident, like children, of their adventure, singing like children hand in hand, still their song was the song of the ages as they sailed into the night." The reference to immaturity resonates with the vision of marriage Jack urged upon Charmian—that she remain his "Kid," his "twin brother," that the two never lose the freedom of youth. Characteristic of Jack's romantic mating plots, an implicit "happily ever after" ends the story.

Charmian labored over *Cherry* almost continually for the next four years. *Cosmopolitan* magazine published a severe abridgment of what she sent them, leaving her humiliated and afraid that she would appear "silly" to readers unaware of the full tale. Though she wrote 80 percent of the manuscript, much of its contents seems, as she claimed to others, to follow Jack's plan. She had his notes for the book; she had discussed it with him extensively during the final days of his life. She firmly believed it to be an important vehicle for presenting Jack's attitudes on important social issues. The preoccupation with an idealized female character who captivates many men was increasingly common in London's later fiction, as were trances with their archetypal imagery. As in his weaker love stories, the plot of *Cherry* is almost nonexistent, and contains many ludicrous scenes, such as the suicide leap into the volcano. One cannot help but think of *Hearts of Three*, written for the movies, and wonder if some of the melodrama of *Cherry* was conceived with the screen in mind.

Since so much of the story indeed displays its roots in Jack's imagination, one must be careful in interpreting the story as an expression of Charmian's psyche. More relevant than the plot, perhaps, are her descriptions of Cherry's thought processes. Her descriptions of splitting into distinct personalities are uncannily realistic, as are the accounts of trance states, which Charmian had experienced since childhood. Another quality of Cherry's that may have been present in Charmian is a certain insensitivity to events occurring around her, an attitude born from two paradoxical sources: one being the ability to experience moments so deeply that larger connections are missed, the other being the inclination to see the world only through one's own unquestioned reality. Cherry is self-actualized and independent, but these traits lead her toward narcissism and away from empathy and the benefits of communion with others. Consequently, she is incapable of seeing her many male admirers as distinct individuals, but instead submits to the preordained mate, as Charmian had done in real life.

However tedious this draft, *Cherry* might have been revised into an entertaining book, given a skillful fictional technique, but Charmian, whose forte
was journalism, could not meet the challenge. By the end of the 1920s, she faced
the dreaded realization that she would not ever be able to put the book into a
reasonable condition. Upon publication of the *Cosmopolitan* version, Putnam's
asked to see the full manuscript, but eventually rejected it. Jack's last novel remains unpublished in completed form.

During this time Charmian also began her autobiographical novel *Charmette,*
though it would not advance beyond notes and sketches.[13] With some hesitation she revived her communication with Netta to learn about the Wiley and
Kittredge family histories. In recent years Netta and Edward Payne had preoccupied themselves with spiritualism, particularly summoning Jack's spirit, and
had regularly sent Charmian ouija board messages from him, which she ignored. Netta's egocentricity remained intact in old age. Once "Jack" told her,
"You [Netta] are my best friend that waits for heaven.———says you are the
best woman he ever saw."[14] To her great consternation, Netta was not able to
catch just who this other man was!

For years various mediums and spiritualists had contacted Charmian with
claims of receiving letters and even stories written by Jack. Charmian answered
all with a firm, clear statement that she did not share their beliefs and therefore
could not help in disseminating their documents. "This life is sufficient unto itself. When I die, if I am to see again those who have gone before—well and
good. If there is nothing but darkness, I won't know it, you see. So it is well either way, is it not?"[15] This resignation before the unknowable, this grasping of
life as it appeared from moment to moment, was unwavering throughout
Charmian's life, and provided the same source of inner security that any formal
religious doctrine might offer others.

Despite her rebuke, Charmian was often kind to these strangers, adding such
comments as "trusting your rheumatism is improved, for I know it is a terrible
misfortune." She was less gentle with Upton Sinclair, who wrote her excitedly
about a séance where Jack appeared with his "Squaw woman." Chiding him for
believing what Jack had rejected, she took the séance apart moment by moment
to show that none of it was mystical. She spoke of her childhood experiences of
spiritualism, when she learned the tricks of the trade. "I find the commonsense,
if pursued, is a rare possession and amounts to almost genius at times," she
pointedly added. "I'd rather inspire a good healthy smile or laugh in this world
than anything I can think of."[16]

Netta and Edward knew well Charmian's disdain of spiritualism, but undaunted, as true believers they made use of their "knowledge." In 1922 they con-

tacted the press, and soon stories appeared coast to coast concerning their communications with Jack. When Charmian learned that a book was under way, she warned Edward against adding a "ghostly" twist. There was nothing in the spiritual messages that could not be understood as the working of the unconscious mind, she admonished him.

Edward died in 1924, but Netta found a publisher in England for what would become *The Soul of Jack London.* She had been assisted by that most famous of contemporary spiritualists, Sir Arthur Conan Doyle, who provided a statement of his admiration for their work to be included in the book. Years earlier Doyle had been so convinced of "Jack's return to earth" that he had conveyed the news to Charmian, who received him courteously yet gently dismissed his claim.[17]

As a preface to the channeled material, the first section of *The Soul of Jack London* remains today an insightful essay on Jack's way of thinking, the battle in his mind between "the melancholy of materialism" and his "instinctive tendency toward idealism." The second section describes the Paynes' psychic communications with the writer. "Jack" had told them he accepted "a new understanding of the universe" and wanted to negate any follies he might have provoked by admitting to immortality and refuting materialism. Furthermore, "Jack" was very ready to discuss his personal failings with regard to the Paynes. "Jack London's habits that defiled the temple of his soul were light sins as compared to a certain occasion when he betrayed the love of his friends and neighbors by diverting their water supply into an artificial lake on his own ranch. This unhappy situation undoubtedly hastened his death and is an explanation of his many messages to us." Netta claimed to have spoken with him about his battle with John Barleycorn, for his phenomenal success could not cure his inner turmoil. She asked "whether you will finally and firmly lay hold on the verities." "Jack's" response was, "I am evil. The real essential in me was evil. To be great I must be good—the old platitude. I wronged you—I wronged many others." Thus could Netta and Edward prove that they had been right all along. And despite Charmian's objections, Conan Doyle used *The Soul of Jack London* to argue in an essay in the December 1927 issue of *Bookman* that the writing was indeed that of Jack from beyond the grave.

In 1925 Netta stirred up a new conflict, this time over finances. Since Jack's death, Charmian had been paying Netta fifty dollars a month toward her support. Eliza, as her financial agent in all matters, wrote and sent the checks. Netta wrote a vituperative letter complaining that, being "peculiarly sensitive to psychic impressions," she could not bear to see Eliza's handwriting on the envelopes.[18] Hence she demanded that the money be sent directly by Charmian, and on a quarterly system, or even better, placed in a trust that she could draw from directly without touching the capital. Charmian agreed to the latter option, and even allowed Netta to sell Charmian's Berkeley rental property on condition that the profits be added to the trust. Five years later Netta confessed that she had spent all that money.

Her aunt's bossy nature led Charmian on October 15, 1925, to write a new will, leaving almost everything to Eliza, "who by her unsleeping devotion earned and held my unswerving trust, respect, and love."[19] She bequeathed only five dollars each to her three closest relatives, including Netta. As Charmian explained in a letter to Eliza, only she understood the exigencies of the ranch and could run it according to Jack's wishes. Consequently, others' bequests were set at a minimum so that Eliza would not be inconvenienced in carrying out Jack's agricultural legacy.

Jack's daughters were not mentioned at all in Charmian's 1925 will, which is interesting because just months before she and Joan not only had reconciled but also were building a fast friendship. In late March of that year something impelled Joan to sit down and, without her mother's or sister's knowledge, pen a letter to Charmian. "I am a woman now, age 24," she wrote, and now realized it is "such a sorry state of affairs that we who loved him, should find it hard to know and love each other."[20] Touched by Joan's candor, Charmian answered warmly, apologizing for having written her off after the incident on the ranch. She hoped for "a frankness we can both be proud of as two intelligent women."[21] Joan suggested that they arrange a meeting through a mutual friend, "like a lover's rendezvous."[22] They traded letters briskly, with Charmian advising the younger woman how to become a paid lecturer, and even arranged an engagement for her. In June they discussed meeting under false pretenses, but neither really wanted the subterfuge. Nonetheless, Joan finally lied to her mother and met Charmian in San Francisco, where the two attended a movie version of *Adventure* together. "Charmian, I liked you—tremendously," Joan admitted afterward.[23] Charmian's letters to Hunter Kimbrough, an acquaintance of Joan's, expressed similar pleasure in this and other visits. She especially enjoyed Bart, a bright, sunny-dispositioned child, and asked Joan what books to send to him.[24]

The correspondence continued apace. Between the lines one can appreciate just why Joan sought Charmian out, and why the once-rejected stepmother reciprocated. Though she never told Charmian, Joan was still grieving over the loss of her baby girl. She did reveal other things about her home situation—the stifling atmosphere of living with her mother and disapproving sister. She desperately needed fresh counsel, and having learned so much about Charmian from mutual friends, she intuited correctly that her reaching out would not be rebuffed. The moment was right for Charmian as well, for with so many financial and other troubles in her life, she was proud to be asked to share her wisdom. Also, she saw in Joan traits that she much valued: a strong work ethic, independence, adaptability, and directness. The two readily slipped into a comfortable exchange, as though Charmian were a longtime favorite aunt.

Joan's letters combined optimism about her attempts to build a career as a writer and lecturer. The latter she pursued more out of financial need, for she did not always enjoy the people in the clubs that invited her to speak. George Sterling, now her mentor, recommended her to the Extension Division of the University of California at Berkeley, which booked her for lecture dates. Her programs consisted of discussing aspects of her father's life and reading aloud from abridged versions of his stories. She usually earned twenty-five dollars an appearance, which was not much pay, given her travel expenses and the many hours of preparation. When invitations took her into the California Central Valley, she lodged with her friend Musa to save money.

Joan's attempts to place her writing were frustrating. She sold a short story, "Youth Surrenders," to *Young's,* a journal which she described to Charmian correctly as pulp, and of little value. Her one hope developed when she signed a contract with National News to prepare sixty feature columns on the theme of "Woman to Woman," as well as a serial, which she would call *Sylvia Coventry.* These projects would keep her writing at a frantic pace through most of the latter half of 1925. What she could not foresee was that the columns would not be picked up, which meant several months' work with no financial payoff. The serial would not get wide circulation.

Joan confided these developments, disappointments, and expectations to Charmian in detail. Although she referred to her state of considerable indebtedness (often over $1,000 in bills due), she does not seem to have done so to manipulate Charmian, who shared her own tales of monetary woe. Nonetheless, Charmian did send Joan and Bart, known as Sonny, many gifts, and several times signed over royalty checks to the young woman. Charmian also used her social connections to create lecture assignments for Joan.

Throughout this remarkable exchange of letters, one request of Joan's stands out. She was thinking about writing a "slender little book . . . about Daddy as I remember him." He was "a wonderful father, as you know, despite everything."[25] She would avoid sentimentality, but rather present the relationship with sincerity and simplicity. Charmian urged Joan to wait, to "make a name for yourself on your own, without using him as a crutch, so to speak." She believed that it would make "a more beautiful dignified gesture in your life not to climb on this piece of work, but to lead up to it."[26] She worried that both daughters had suffered by being thrust into the limelight in ways they shouldn't have, and she believed in Joan's ability to find her own greatness. Joan responded to this advice with relief, admitting that it was others who were pressuring her in the matter, against her own better judgment. "Someday maybe, it will see light."[27]

In 1926 Joan introduced Charmian to the new man in her life, Charles Mala-muth, a gentle, portly young man who shared her admiration for socialism. A Russian émigré, he supported himself by translating Russian novels and was on the verge of attending graduate school in Slavic studies at Berkeley. Whereas Park Abbott had been sensitive and a dreamer, Charles was methodical and practical, and thus promised to provide stability to Joan's unsettled life. She had to help support the family, but she wanted more children, and avidly practiced the domestic arts: cooking, gardening, sewing. Although Joan had grown up a large-boned, imposing woman of strong opinion and hot temper, with inti-mates she was tirelessly nurturing and generous. Having seen the consequences of her parents' unhappy marriage, and gone through one herself, she put as much of her energy and resources into her private relationships as into her work and, later, her political activities.

Expecting a steady income from her syndicated writing, Joan and Charles bought a brown shingle house in the Berkeley hills, a large home with a view of the bay and San Francisco beyond. He taught at a private boys' school while at-tending Berkeley, and worked doing research for faculty members as well. Af-ter committing themselves to the house, Joan discovered that her contracts were not going to pay even the small amount she expected, so she signed with a New York lecture bureau, Leigh Emmerson. This meant that she would be traveling around the country for three or four months at a time. These were not good circumstances for a new marriage to thrive.

Bess watched over Bart while Joan went off on her lecture tours. The venues included universities, men's organizations, women's clubs, religious groups, and private schools, primarily in the Midwest and Northeast. Of the seven top-ics she offered one season, only one addressed her father. In one she discussed the story writer O'Henry, in another new trends in literature, and a third had her recounting stories by a variety of American writers. Another set of lectures explored the changing status of women, including their new role in politics, modern experiments in marriage, the crumbling of the double standard, and the challenges of new economic opportunities. Joan applied her dramatic training to good use, and received praise for her beautifully modulated voice and her ability to hold audiences spellbound.

Joan's attempt at fiction writing was much less successful. *Sylvia Coventry* was finally published serially in the *Oakland Tribune* from December 6, 1926, to February 24, 1927. The work combines elements of two of her father's novels, *Adventure* and *The Star Rover*. The heroine finishes college in the States to re-turn to her former home in Hawaii to live with her aunt Ruth and cousin Jack. A childhood friend, Jerry Cameron, has become a wealthy sugar plantation owner. One of London's love triad themes is established when Sylvia rebuffs Jack's proposal and goes to work as a welfare worker on Cameron's plantation.

The love story becomes immersed in a tale of danger and rescue as the heroine is bewitched by an ominous intruder and experiences various incarnations. Writing under great pressure, with little time to edit or reflect on the architecture of the work, Joan let the episodes wander and shift fecklessly. The characters lack development, and the incarnation scenes seem capricious additions to extend the story. Given her difficulties in selling her short stories, and her struggles composing the serial, Joan finally faced up to the fact that fiction was not her calling.

It would be the late 1920s before Becky would learn of Joan's friendship with Charmian. By then she too was unhappily married and raising two children, Jean and Jack (later called Guy). She had spent her early twenties making unwise decisions, at times, it seemed, out of sheer stubbornness just to counter her mother's counsel. Her temperament did not serve her well, for she tended toward indolence, inertness even, and showed little curiosity in life beyond reading (and, later, baseball). Well informed and of sprightly humor, she was a charming conversationalist whose photographs display the classic Jazz Age young woman. Less apparent was the burden of resentment, her sense that she was owed a better living.

Eager to leave her mother's home, though unwilling to support herself, Becky had accepted the proposal of Percy Fleming, a salesman twelve years her senior. Sixty years later she recounted her delight when Percy promised they would have a home of their own, and her still-hot anger that after the wedding he took her back to her mother's house, where they would live for the next twelve years. Once again she saw her mother as colluding against her. "I only liked my husband and it didn't last long," she recalled. "I lost all respect for him when I discovered he was a liar, a hypocrite, supremely selfish and only wanted a cook and a dish washer—not a wife." The result was "one empty, non-happy life . . . and I am ashamed that I let the time slip by and never did anything about it."[28]

The truth was much more complicated. Percy had proposed to Becky despite her having had a child out of wedlock by another man. Throughout her life, Becky succeeded in blanking out the story, which can now be told.

On May 7, 1926, a daughter was born to one "Florence Clark" at the Alameda Sanitorium. The attending physician, William Porter, listed the mother as white, twenty-three, a stenographer with no other children, and living at 606 Scenic Avenue in Piedmont. The father was identified as Charles Wellman, twenty-six, a clerk with no residence identified beyond "California." The baby, listed as Florence Clark Wellman, went home to be known as Jean. A story was fed to the newspapers that Joan was taking care of the infant daughter of cousins who had died unexpectedly in an auto accident.

Months earlier, Joan and Bess had discovered that Becky was pregnant. They created the cover story to protect Becky's reputation, and enjoined the cooperation of their longtime family doctor. Becky remained in denial about her condition, and after the delivery refused to bond with her baby, who was cared for by Bess. Thus, when Percy took Becky to live at her mother's home, it was in the hope that she would finally accept her daughter. Becky refused to do so. During her early childhood Jean assumed that she was adopted, though as she grew older, she suspected that she was blood kin—to Joan.

Some who were acquainted with Becky and Percy over the years describe Becky as an angry woman who treated her husband badly in public, while he was a milquetoast in her presence. Yet others said that he was the difficult one. Whatever the truth, their marriage was not contented. Often lost in the imaginary world of fiction, Becky remained at heart a loner, a woman who would depend on her mother to raise her child, all the while begrudging her presence. Becky never realized another great quality she shared with her father, that of being a rebel. Sadly, she was never able to find a cause beyond mundane ones through which to express her rebellion, her wish for a better world.

As she advanced through her fifties, Charmian seems to have lost some of her self-confidence and sense of herself as an active agent in the world. Rather, she responded to others as they wished, tossed herself into a social life of dubious satisfactions, and totally deprecated her writing abilities. Certainly some of these feelings of impotence and passivity flowed from external events: her aging, her inability to find financial relief, Netta's harassment, new physical ailments, the unending series of deaths of friends and acquaintances. Though she had chosen not to marry again, she realized the trade-offs she had made, and knew that she must learn how to cope with loneliness. A natural flirt, she was conflicted over her pleasure in teasing men and felt foolish about doing so at her age. Fortunately, the men were often flattered by her overtures, so she was harder on herself than others were.

She and Eliza continued their quest to retain the ranch property. With much regret, they subdivided a few parcels of the lowest acreage. They explored other uses of the land, both as a country club and as the site of an outdoor theater. In 1926 Irving Shepard could not afford to hire a single man to help with the harvest. Charmian tried to sell the extensive South Seas curio collection, only to be told that museums were not interested. At one point Eliza even considered accepting the proposal of a much older man with investments in the emerging California oil industry because of the financial security he would bring them. This was, however, a brief impulse she quickly dispelled. Neither woman would use marriage as a solution.

During the 1920s their prejudices led Charmian and Eliza to make some movie deals that proved very troublesome for a number of years. Charmian welcomed the proposals of Ralph Ince and David Thomas specifically because they were not Jewish; hence she believed that they would not take advantage of her, as some other Hollywood producers had. In fact, Thomas and his wife, Rose, had created an elaborate scheme to tie up a large portion of Jack's writings and defraud the women. In one scheme they gained the rights to a collection of short stories, planning to resell the rights to each individual story and make a windfall. In another they signed to produce *Eyes of Asia* in anticipation that Charmian would not finish the book on deadline and they could sue her for nonperformance. Through creative bookkeeping on Thomas's part, *Smoke Bellow* earned the women only $166, not the $10,000 they had been promised. The Thomas shenanigans became additionally troublesome when, during the late 1920s, all movie contracts became vulnerable as talkies came on the scene. Companies wanting to make a talkie had to buy the rights from whoever owned the silent rights, and in this case the Thomases were sitting pretty. By 1930 Charmian and Eliza had unsnarled most of this mess, but at considerable expense for lawyers and loss of expected income.

Also, Eliza had several operations requiring long recuperations, and diabetes with its debilitating effects would plague her last two decades. Typical of her uncomplaining attitude, she was a mainstay of Glen Ellen life, known for her kindness and contributions to community efforts. Gleaning—that is, taking the leftovers of a harvested crop—was one way ranchers could offer help to others. For example, Eliza promised Teodora Meglen, a local laundress with a dozen children, her second crop of grapes, and kept her word even when the market improved unexpectedly. As a result, the Meglens made enough to rent a building and stock a grocery store. Children in town called Eliza "Grandma Shepard," further evidence of her good reputation.

Eliza was a member of the Women's Improvement Club, among other local groups, and was instrumental in getting the Jack London Memorial Library built in 1923. That two-story structure also served as a meeting hall and community center during a time when the town still had dirt roads. With the waning of the Grand Army of the Republic, Eliza shifted her commitment to its successor, the American Legion, and during the 1920s served as national president of its auxiliary. True to her patriotic fervor, she was also active in the Daughters of the American Revolution. Nineteen twenty-six brought special honors in Washington, D.C., where she lived for a year while directing the American Legion Auxiliary. Among the highlights of her stay was a dinner invitation from President Coolidge, and her participation in the Women's Labor Congress. In 1928 Eliza once again filled an important role at a major peace conference. Consequently, she had the equivalent of a career of her own on top of managing the business interests of the ranch and literary estate.

For vacations, Eliza also went to Europe during this decade. Given the run-away inflation overseas, royalties were best kept within the country where they were earned rather than converted to U.S. dollars. Eliza particularly enjoyed Italy, perhaps because its climate was like that on the ranch. Though revealing much less than Charmian about her private life in letters, she obviously had love interests as well, for Charmian wrote a teasing approval of Eliza's shipboard affair during one Atlantic crossing. In Washington, Eliza had a romance with Cordell Hull, then a Democratic member of Congress who would go on to be-come Franklin Roosevelt's secretary of state. Hull was married to Rose Whitney, but according to family history, he proposed to Eliza, who refused him.

Since the women were separated more often than not, Irving and Mildred Shepard were now the one constant presence on the ranch. Charmian worried that the perpetual financial shortfalls would wear him down. She thought him an "exceptional fellow," wanted him to be happy, and appreciated his "fondness for the quiet & busy life in the country."[29] She also considered Mildred an ex-cellent "second," devoted to the ranch.

Whenever one or the other woman was away, lengthy letters continued their discussions and decisions about the farm, publishing rights, and movie rights. Eliza's style was formal and businesslike, with very little mention of her son Irv-ing, his family, local events, or mutual friends. Charmian's letters offered more narrative, incorporating tales of clothes shopping, gossip, and feelings evoked by her experiences. It was clear, though, that in all matters they were a tight partnership.

Of course, Charmian's lovers alone made her life more dramatic and emo-tionally rich than Eliza's. Frederick O'Brien told her at lunch one day that Rose Wilder Lane was suing him, claiming that she deserved co-author credit and half the profits from *White Shadows in the South Seas*. The suit could hardly have come at a more inopportune time, for his literary reputation had recently been fatally wounded by the appearance of a devastatingly clever parody of his works, *Cruise of the Kawa*, which stole his previously admiring audience away. *Kawa* readily convinced the cynical flappers and fun-seekers of the 1920s that O'Brien's South Seas romanticism was ludicrous. An undisciplined writer, O'Brien never wrote another long work, and virtually disappeared from the lit-erary scene in which he had so recently starred. Charmian helplessly observed his deterioration with considerable sadness.

When Houdini came to San Francisco in 1924, by mail he again insisted that Charmian revive their affair. On reflection she decided not to meet him. "Feel queer about Magic—but sense of integrity."[30] Still she thought of him, and appreciated his habitual communications. News of his premature death from peritonitis on October 31, 1926, flattened her. "I feel strangely stirred with regret. I scan his lovely profile with my magnifying glass," she noted in her diary.

When she learned that a youthful lover, Herbert Dugan, was dying of cancer, she sought the last chance to speak with him that she had lost with Houdini. Dugan survived for several years. The two enjoyed a special friendship during that period, she spending long hours at his bedside in conversation or reading to him. Still, she wondered what he thought of her—"old and sad, perchance."

One of the favorite men in Charmian's life during the 1920s was James Duval Phelan, son of an Irish immigrant who made a fortune in banking and real estate, served as reform mayor of San Francisco, and enjoyed three terms as U.S. senator. A noted patron of the arts, he enjoyed entertaining at his Villa Montalvo estate near the Santa Clara Valley. Phelan never married, the reason attributed by local gossip to the humiliating rejection of a proposal made in his youth. He had been a guest at the ranch over the years and was particularly fond of George Sterling.

After Jack's death Charmian became more a member of Phelan's inner circle, perhaps because they shared many other artist friends in common. She wrote him chatty letters, sent him Jack London bookplates and autographs; he replied with gifts of poetry and flowers, and encouraged her to continue her writing. They met up in Paris in late 1926, and may have traveled together, since a letter she sent him upon returning home referred to the "rout" of their "Roman days." When he was ailing and missed a California Writers' Club *bal masqué,* she teased, "I am sorry I did not have the chance to put my hands over your eyes and murmur, 'Oh, Jimmie! Have you forgotten—don't you know my voice!'"[31] He died soon afterward in May 1930.

As former suitors sickened or died, new ones continued to be entranced by her. A wealthy South African plantation owner proposed, and she was sorely tempted to be free of all her financial worries, but she refused thinking,. "Imagine me 10 years hence with a husband of 70!"

She grew anxious and insomniac as deaths of friends continued. A favorite aunt and uncle were killed in an auto accident; the only child of close friends, a youth beloved by Charmian, run over by an automobile. All those passing over were chosen, save one who tapped death directly and asked to be taken. In 1926, on the evening of a banquet he had arranged in honor of the visiting H. L. Mencken, George Sterling took a fatal dose of poison in his room at the Bohemian Club.

Mencken had recently published two of George's articles in the *Mercury,* his first significant publication in years. When Mencken said he was coming out to San Francisco for a visit, George planned celebrations, including the Bohemian

Club banquet, a spaghetti feed at a Montgomery block restaurant, and a "Buddhist meal" enhanced by exotic dancers in flimsy costumes. Sterling expected Mencken on a Sunday, but when a telegram arrived apologizing for a delay in his arrival, George fell off the wagon and began to work his way through the bootlegged supplies he had stashed for the parties. Mencken arrived late Monday night. On Tuesday he learned that George was so drunk he could not be roused. Joan London met Mencken that evening during a gathering at Idwal Jones's house, and wrote Charmian how "furious" the celebrity was over George's behavior, that everyone "feared what George might do when he discovered what he had done."[32] When George sobered up enough to realize that he had missed the banquet, he swallowed the cyanide he always carried with him, and was found dead the next morning.

Sterling's death brought a curiously rewarding opportunity for Charmian, an invitation to write a commemorative article for the *Overland Monthly*. The result, an essay of charming candor, is one of her best published writings. She described George frankly, yet presented his failings in terms that evoked understanding of the troubled man. "When he drank, he drank, anything and everything, without regard to combination. When he went on the waterwagon, he did it thoroughly, perhaps a year or more at a time, and was very proud of himself and the ease of his experiment. When he 'fell off,' he fell off with forethought and cheerful deliberation. . . . The world at large is prone lightly to consider an idiosyncrasy any departure from established custom. But George's case was the other way around. From committing deliriously outrageous pranks to the delighted horror of his circle, he balked consistently at being seen carrying any kind of parcel, no matter how neat and decorous."[33]

The essay was witty, particularly in its description of George's hashish parties, at which he'd make a paste and spread it onto sandwiches, providing massive doses of the drug to guests. In her discussion of his marriage, she candidly divulged George's infidelities without blaming him for Carrie's death. Were any proof needed that Charmian could have developed her writing talents, this essay provided it. Yet it was the last work of any substance she would ever publish; after 1926 only the most inconsequential articles appeared under her name, usually in obscure sources.

In scattered notes in her diary Charmian reviled herself as a "sybarite and a fool" for her behavior and noted her ongoing obsession with aging, describing herself as "sapped old woman." Finally, several movie deals brought in sufficient money for her to sit down and actually plan for her future. After paying off the outstanding ranch expenses, she decided to buy a car (for others to drive for her), and perhaps most important for her pride, to have a face-lift, which she arranged in Los Angeles, spending a winter alone there in a small proprietary hospital while the surgical changes, very primitive and painful then, took their course. Refusing to admit her vanity to friends such as Phelan, she said that she had been felled by a nasty flu.

On a second European trip, her spirits were revived. Three incidents stood out in her memory of this voyage. The first was a visit with Sybil and Babe Walters, who invited Charmian to join their crew for the Course Croisière, the annual race of the Yacht Club of France. It had been fourteen years since she had enjoyed such a sailing vessel, and taking second place added to her sense of achievement. Then, in Paris, her agent Louis Postif booked many publicity assignments for her, among the most satisfying a meeting with Alain Gerbault. Gerbault was an immensely popular celebrity, having been a tennis star and World War I ace who then set out for a six-year voyage around the world. A handsome and charming man, he was even the subject of popular songs. Naturally Charmian was very nervous about meeting him, not realizing that he would find much in common with a woman who'd had so many adventures of her own. They were guests of honor at several events, from which occasions they developed such mutual respect that Gerbault asked her to write the preface to his book *Atolls in the Sun*.

But her "Red Letter Day" occurred elsewhere on the trip. She had been corresponding with Jung (the letters, alas, now missing), who was, however, not in Zurich when she was free to visit him there. Instead she managed an appointment later in Vienna with Freud, "a small-featured slender man of 74, who to my horror was suffering cancer of the jaw and somewhat crippled thereafter from an operation. I learned a few things—Jung a mystic, etcetera. We got together sweetly and he prolonged the half hour somewhat."[34] If only we knew more of that meeting between the gregarious little American woman, dressed in a brilliant red suit with lavish trim, sitting there by the fire with the ailing genius who had discovered new psychological worlds for exploration.

What she did not remark upon in her diary was the level of acclaim and celebrity she had achieved. In Berlin, where her *Log of the Snark* had recently been serialized, 26,000 people attended an event in her honor at the Sportspalast. In Zurich, Vienna, Paris, and London as well she was feted and honored, often with leading writers serving as hosts. During this time of great public recognition, she was more likely to remark on performing artists and the plays or operas she attended. And as she would to the end of her life, she mused about what her dead mother, husband, and daughter might be like now. Joy would be almost a woman, she reflected, and wondered if she would enjoy sailing.

Charmian ended the 1920s with a flourish. Former lover Herbert Dugan's hopeful letters followed her from country to country, and she was bemused that he remembered long-ago Valentine rhymes he had sent her as a young man. On the long home crossing, she felt "really elated and disturbed inwardly by my un-expected and astonishing 'affair.' It gives unwanted zest."[35]

During this decade, too, writers first began to question the causes of Jack's death. In 1924 Upton Sinclair's *Mammonart* recounted Jack's "alcoholism," at-tributing his death to it. A closer reading of Sinclair shows that he, a humorless teetotaler, had been mocked by Jack. Sinclair repeated Jack's tales of "incredible debauches; tales of opium and hashish, and I know not what other ingredients; tales of whiskey bouts lasting for weeks." Though Sinclair even admitted that Jack "made fun of him," he failed to recognize that part of the fun was in seeing how he would react to such obviously overblown tales. Furthermore, Sinclair misled readers about their friendship, for he had met Jack on only two occa-sions, both times when he was on binges. Charmian attempted to correct Sin-clair's impressions, unsuccessfully, for he repeated the account in *The Cup of Fury*.

Then in 1929 an essay in *Bookman* resurrected the Crowd's rumor that Jack's death was a suicide. San Francisco reporters tracked down the doctors who had attended his death. Two were away in Europe, but one, Alan Thomson, "in-dignantly denied the suicide theory," explaining that "Jack London died of in-ternal poisoning brought about through kidney trouble."[36] With this report Charmian felt secure that the matter was at last resolved, though here she was wrong, as later events would prove.

Suffering the loss of friends and relatives, Charmian was led to make two ma-jor decisions out of a sense of her own mortality. First, she wrote a simple will leaving virtually everything to Eliza, in appreciation for her work and support. Second, she requested that after her death a museum be built in a fireproof structure (years later specified as her now completed home, Happy Walls) to contain all her memorabilia and photographic albums. A "responsible, *needy* person" should be housed there and put in charge so that the museum would never be unprotected. Her intent was "to keep all possible Jack Londoniana to-gether on the property bearing his name—'Jack London Ranch.'" If anyone doubted her certainty that it was the land on Sonoma Mountain that meant the most to Jack, this request sealed her determination and would point the way for its future use.[37]

# 15

# *The World Has Fallen*

In May 1930 Charles Malamuth filed for divorce, his charge being "that the defendant [Joan London] is guilty of extreme cruelty toward the plaintiff; that she causes him grievous mental suffering and humiliation; that she neglects her husband and her home in that she goes off for long periods of time on her own business, leaving him entirely alone . . . that she does not make room for him and does not prepare meals at home." He claimed that he never knew if or when she was returning from her speaking tours, and that humiliating gossip and speculation ensued. In addition, "she did not want marriage to limit her life as an individual, but she did not want me to get a divorce."[1]

She was irascible, agreed Paul Marenke, a philosophy professor from Berkeley who was often a guest at the house. He accused her of calling Malamuth names and behaving so badly as to break up bridge parties before the games were over. It was clear, he said, that she thought him and other of Malamuth's friends dull. There is probably some truth in these accounts. Joan was hot-headed and mercurial, and resembled her father with his feverishly active mind and his wanderlust. She preferred to think of marriage as an arrangement between loosely connected mates who respected each other's freedom. Indeed, one cannot but help notice the similarity to the match of Jack and Bess. Neither London *père* nor *fille* was content with a settled, conventional spouse.

Whether Malamuth was actually affronted by Joan's long trips out of town is less clear, for her lecture tours were required to support the family. His paltry earnings at Berkeley and from freelance translating work were insufficient for the couple's spendthrift ways. Worse, neither seemed to understand that they could not maintain the lifestyle of their childhoods. Bess London had labored to supplement her child support so that her girls could have all that was expected of an affluent middle-class family; Malamuth's parents had done very well financially and raised him in even greater comfort.

Joan's view of the divorce is unclear. She did not protest formally or countersue. In any case, Malamuth was the one about to take a long voyage, to Moscow, where he had just accepted a position as correspondent with the Associated Press. He explained his sudden departure from academia, to which he was so well suited, as the result of other professors in the Slavic Languages department being intolerant of his radical political beliefs.

How could a shy, scholarly young man on the West Coast be chosen for a key correspondent post, one that experienced journalists had vied for? The answer may lie in the way in which the Communist Party had insinuated itself into American journalism during the 1920s. Tass, the Russian news agency, had offices in United Press's New York building and hired Americans of solid party background to report Western news to Moscow. When the UP needed a new Moscow correspondent in 1927, the director walked over to the Tass office and hired Eugene Lyons, a reporter raised on the doctrines of both the Young People's Socialist League and the Wobblies. The Moscow correspondent for the *New York Times,* Walter Duranty, reported regularly to the OGPU, the predecessor of the KGB, and was swayed by Stalin to publish propaganda in that venerable newspaper until the horrors of the 1930s famine curtailed his collaboration. In any event, Malamuth's ties to the party likely played a role in his selection.

In Moscow, correspondents socialized with the Russian elite and the diplomatic corps, attending parties and celebrations at the various embassies. Thus Red-leaning journalists spent many evenings in full evening dress crowding around buffet tables stocked with caviar, imported fruits and vegetables, dozens of platters of meats and fine cheeses, and rich Slavic pastries. The most opulent parties were those sponsored by the Soviet government, which refused to allow anyone without a dinner jacket into the gilded chambers once belonging to the czar.

These scenes were an ironic contrast to the reality of life for most Russians. Starting with the food shortages of 1929, beggars began to appear on the streets, while "former people shops" sold the antiques, silver, furs, rare art, Oriental rugs, and jewelry of ex-aristocrats who had to sell their legacies to buy flour and milk. "Former people" were the *lishentsi,* those disenfranchised for incurring the displeasure of the regime. Excluded from most employment and denied rations, many died of malnutrition, disease, and suicide. Even affluent proletarians adopted asceticism, fearful lest any show of material success brand them *lishentsi,* or worse, causing their disappearance to an unknown end in prison. Meanwhile, runaway inflation increased foreigners' power to pay top prices, avoid rationing, and bypass the long lines at shops. A meal at the Grand Hotel in Moscow might cost the equivalent of a factory worker's weekly income, but foreign journalists could easily afford this luxury.

One American family that built a personal fortune based on ties to the regime was that of Armand Hammer, who gained trade favors and ran the only pencil concession in the nation. In 1930, after Stalin liquidated the Hammers' factories, the family returned to the United States, yet retained ownership of their Moscow home. If it was used to house foreign correspondents Dr. Hammer reasoned, the regime would be less likely to take over the building for its own uses. Consequently, Malamuth was one of a series of journalists to enjoy this sumptuous mansion with its gleaming marble stairways, rococo statuary and paintings, mounted animal trophies, cherub-friezed ballroom, cloakrooms large enough to serve as dens, and a vast kitchen equipped to prepare meals for hundreds.

Malamuth socialized with seasoned reporters who had observed the regime since the days of the Revolution. He joined them for an official swing throughout much of the country—a tour of factories and construction sites, state farms, peasant villages, dams and railroad lines, and other proofs of the nation's success. Their guides were gracious and distributed neat piles of figures to back up their claims of communist achievement. The public relations tour worked very well until, as Eugene Lyons put it, "forty-eight corpses joined our tour." These were professors, agronomists, and administrators of the food trust who were executed as a "counter-revolutionary society" during their visit.

Following that tragic experience the correspondents gave up their comfortable notions that future Russian gain required profound sacrifices. Lyons recalled that Malamuth became "like a man who has hoarded a fortune in banknotes, defended it with his life, and suddenly learns that the banknotes are mostly counterfeit." Lyons was fond of the young colleague whose gaudy socks compensated for his academic demeanor, and he was especially grateful to have him as translator one afternoon when Stalin agreed to a rare interview that made front-page headlines in the United States. Lyons was disconcerted to find the dictator a charming, friendly man lacking any affectation or falseness, but Malamuth, better informed about Russian society, discounted Stalin's engaging personality as characteristic of the gregarious Georgians.[2]

It may have been Malamuth's change in hard-line attitude that tempted him and Joan to reconcile, for in May 1931 she joined him in Moscow at the Hammer mansion. By then national demoralization was endemic, thanks to a decree that allowed those who informed on others to receive a quarter of all money and property seized by the government (though the government often found ways later on to acquire even that fraction). Small change literally disappeared as a result of the hoarding of silver and copper coins. Stories of forced labor and enslavement spread. To "liquidate unemployment," all able-bodied adults, including women with children, were given jobs. Joan arrived during a Moscow spring when the dung-colored mud matched the pallor of the people, who stank in their filthy, ragged clothes. Multiple locks bound every factory, shop, and residence door, while shabby watchmen stood by meager pile of bricks or boards to prevent looting. Jews, intellectuals, and professionals kept "little suitcases" packed—supplies for a quick escape from secret agents. In the stables and servants quarters of the Hammer mansion resided dozens of Russian squatters, whose children stood on tiptoe to gaze at the well-fed Americans in the main building.

As Eugene Lyons observed, "Joan had inherited much of her father's passion for social justice, which is the worst equipment for an appreciation of the U.S.S.R. Her abstract admirations had disintegrated almost instantly into seething angers and ironies between the time I had seen her in New York [that winter] and this reunion in Moscow."[3] Lyons admitted that her rapid disillusionment annoyed him, for it had taken her only a few days to recognize realities that he had taken three years to accept.

Joan also benefited from her father's special status in Russia. When the revolutionary leaders proclaimed that one of their first tasks was to build literacy, they singled out certain writers for mass publication. Very likely it was Lenin, a great admirer of Jack London, who had ordered the translation and distribution of his work, which transformed this turn-of-the-century Californian into an icon of Russian literature.

During the visit Joan drafted "From a Moscow Notebook," an account intended for publication though never completed.[4] Its theme was literary life in a country under severe political censorship, and it reflects the sudden shift in viewpoint Lyons had observed. The first segment follows the path taken two decades earlier by Anna Strunsky, to Yasnaya Polyana for a visit with the surviving members of the Tolstoy family still living there. Aware that even those with land were suffering, Joan delivered two suitcases full of necessities—a goose, flour, sugar, tea, vegetables, cheese, candies, and cigarettes. Madame Tolstoy and her daughter Sophie showed Joan around the house, which seemed strangely bare and unlived-in. Other of Tolstoy's adult children arrived, and the conversation drifted from English to Russian to French and German. Joan left feeling that she had been not in a home but at a museum filled with relics. She ended this section of her account, "As for the greater, more fundamental problems which so deeply concerned [Tolstoy], surely great progress has been made toward their solution."

A month later her account of visits with living Russian writers concluded much less optimistically. She regularly visited the Writers' Club located in the house once belonging to the wealthy revolutionary Alexander Herzen. She sought out the "proletarian writers," expecting to find courageous rebels and critics. Instead, she concluded, most were cowards. Onetime sailor Alexey Novikov-Priboy was proud of being known as the "Russian Jack London," although Joan found him a lackey of Stalinism. Another invited her to his "large and luxurious apartment" and showed off his den with its elaborately inlaid desk. The irony could not escape her of how well he lived compared to a highly trained geneticist who would not cast his findings in politically appropriate terms. Such writers she found to be "tightrope dancers," ready to compromise in exchange for material comforts from the regime. At least several "understood that a writer who is permitted to speak even in riddles is better than one who must remain silent because of the paper shortage [a common excuse for censorship], or must say 'yes' when he means 'no.'"

Thus, in just a few short weeks Joan tossed aside any lingering romanticism concerning socialism in Russia. Its literature was "blighted and dying," its most rebellious authors, such as Yevgeny Zamyatin, totally isolated and ignored. The hoped-for workers' state was "being suppressed by a political regime which is static and sterile." Rebel writers could not overthrow a bureaucracy, she sadly admitted, and wondered if anyone could.

Accompanying her on some of these visits was a young American poet and playwright, Edward Estlin Cummings. A recent arrival to Moscow, and too poor to afford the Intertourist Hotel Metropole, Cummings was taken in by the Malamuths, who invited him to make a bed in the den, where he slept naked. Joan entranced the poet, who found her gracious style, frank opinions, and well-informed conversation a relief from the drab, dirty, and dispiriting society. She also appealed to him physically, "the best looking female I never expected to see in that little bit of heaven on Hearth, Marxland."[5] He was relieved to find that she shared his disgust over the conditions afflicting the common people and the toadying behavior of so many artists and intellectuals.

Two years later Cummings used his Russian diary to create a mythic narrative around the experience. *EIMI* is a complex and powerful literary work, filled with linguistic idiosyncrasies that demand much of the reader. Recognizing its need for a key, in 1958 Cummings appended a preface in which he provided a chronology and identified various figures. Borrowing from *La Divina Commedia*, he honors Joan by calling her Beatrice, his inspirational guide. She is "Lack Dungeon's daughter (from the standpoint of the marxists; who've canonized her moderately popular father as a Great, i.e., Proletarian Writer)." She is also called "Turkess or Harem with respect to chief character number three—who's the TURK, sometimes called Assyrian or that bourgeois face or Charlie [Malamuth]."[6] Even with these clarifications it is difficult to reconstruct who is who, and who is speaking, for Cummings switches names for the same individual within a single scene.

*EIMI* depicts the Malamuths as a couple at ease with each other, quick to banter and tease playfully. Joan helps "Charlie" with his work by typing his dispatches. Cummings is charmed as they take him from one Russian scene to another, including drunken vodka parties, a jail, a circus (with an "antisocialist elephant"), several plays, and the Bolshoi Ballet. Throughout, "Charlie" provides expert background and analysis, thus reinforcing Cummings's disenchantment with anything collectivist. One evening Joan discusses her father, tells how she plans to write a book about him. Cummings is "led to believe that nothing in this celebrity's life became him like a meticulous exposé of sadistic vices enjoyed by animal trainers; also that his later years were swathed in obstreperously negative luxuries of most sheer frustration."[7]

Cummings's account also details the luxury enjoyed in the Hammer compound. Joan has a maid and a cook, who prepares a breakfast of three eggs, black bread with fresh cheese, creamy butter, and American coffee. Before going out, Cummings is forced by a maid to take a steamy bath, an extravagance beyond the reach of most Muscovites. During one evening of gallivanting he remarks that Joan is the only woman in any of the various settings who is wearing an evening dress. Malamuth's favored role as the only American correspondent fluent in Russian ensures first-class treatment, such as when he is ushered to the front of the line at Lenin's Tomb.

Despite the elite treatment, Cummings, and soon afterward the Malamuths, quit the country in disgust. Cummings would become extremist in his individualist antigovernment stance, while Joan and Malamuth aligned with Trotsky, the heretic expelled for his challenge to Stalin. For them socialism remained the best political-economic system, and they considered themselves, as Charles explained to a reporter, "a friend and at the same time a severe critic of the present Russian regime."[8]

Upon their return, the Malamuths moved in with Bess. Although the house was large, Becky's family now included young Jean and Jack, better known as Guy. Bart rejoined his mother as well. Understandably, the atmosphere in the large house was not always congenial. Becky's phlegmatic personality clashed with Joan's excess energy, and both resented Bess's assertion of maternal authority.

As for so many families during the Great Depression, it was pinched pockets that made this troublesome menage necessary. Percy Fleming worked at a small manufacturing company, while Malamuth cobbled together a meager income from lectures on Russian literature through the Berkeley Extension, and translations of Russian novels and plays, including one planned for film production by Cecil B. DeMille. Joan decided for the sake of the marriage to forgo further lecturing and concentrate on fiction writing.

In an interview about life in Russia, Joan focused on the situation of women there, who "were transformed almost overnight from mediaeval subjection to the most advanced status offered by any nation in the world today." Their civil equality, though, came at the cost of a "drab and colorless" private life. There was little time or energy left for romance—and romance "is just as real and important as independence."[9] Achieving a balance between romance and independence was a problem that would dog Joan throughout her life. Raised to be a wife, yet strong-willed and coming of age during the liberating 1920s, she could not resist the call of passion, but resented its luring her into an enclosure.

It may have been passion that resulted in the couple's final separation in September 1932 and subsequent divorce in 1934. Although it was Malamuth who finally pressed charges, he was still in love with Joan, and may have filed for divorce only at the urging of his family in Los Angeles, where he had gone to live. As in 1930, the press once again treated the personal tragedy as a source of fun, noting that Charles's complaints included Joan's listening to jazz on the radio when he needed rest and playing depressing Bach fugues on the piano when he was in a gay mood. The tabloid screeds held her up to moral ridicule, finding her behavior proof of the dangers of leftist politics. Given the trail of silly, scurrilous, and sensational stories about Joan during these years, it becomes more understandable that Becky would hide from public view.

The early 1930s were similarly troublesome for Charmian. In 1930, her House of Happy Walls still unfinished, she ordered repairs on the rundown cottage and bought a new range and vacuum cleaner—seemingly trivial domestic changes that in fact relieve long-standing daily irritations for those who are housebound. Small comforts mattered when so much around her was changing. James Phelan was dead, Frederick O'Brien was not in good health, and Eliza had suffered a major heart attack. When she learned that Cloudesley Johns had been evicted from his home, Charmian dug into some secret funds to buy his letters from Jack and asked Anna to assist him too. In October she slipped on a stair and broke her foot, ending the year on crutches. The anniversary of Jack's death reminded her of her visit with Freud and all her other brave acquaintances in that troubled part of the world. Events did not portend well for central Europe in the 1930s.

In late December an aristocratic twenty-two-year-old man, tall with lovely brown eyes and full lips (like Jack's) entered her home. Harvey Taylor, the relative of an acquaintance, came for assistance on a book he hoped to write—a comprehensive bibliography on Jack London and related material. "We 'click' much without much delay," Charmian noted. She discussed with him the possibility of marketing Jack's story "The Tar Pot" in a revised form, and of seeking out other publishing opportunities in New York City, where Taylor was about to move. Playfully she recorded her young admirer's endearments in her diary. He told her that he would return in the summer, having made her rich, and one day would travel to Paris with her. Charmian did not know whether to "laugh, cry, or feel an ass over the encounters with Harvey."[10]

She chose to laugh. Perhaps because she knew that he would be leaving shortly, Charmian saw him again, this time in public, deciding not to care what people thought. She worried still what would happen if she fell, and thus held back from any intimacy deeper than little hugs and brief kisses. "Move about in a thrall. Life is so full of surprises. And oneself is the most surprise of them all. I feel large-eyed, calm, under wonder, expectant."[11] At their last dinner together, Harvey said he felt mad and crazy, feelings she admitted to sharing. At the boat when he departed, the news photographers framed the two of them together, surely not suspecting that he was more than the protégé she claimed.

Taylor's first letters to her from New York were curt, though they included teasingly affectionate lines as well. He wished she were with him; he would do anything for her good. He told of Somerset Maugham's quip that the widow of a famous literary figure should never remarry, adding that Maugham said nothing about having "————" with the young literary manager away from home. On Valentine's Day he sent a wire to the effect that he was on "wires" of love. Charmian was smitten and at the same time frightfully embarrassed by her attraction to a man forty years her junior.

As Taylor established himself in New York, however, she received early signs that he was not listening to her regarding his business role. Against her wishes, he had stationery printed identifying him as "Literary Manager of the Jack London Estate." He ignored some of Charmian's queries, too, while making requests of her she thought questionable. A woman of fastidious politeness, she smarted when he did not thank her for various materials. Though on some days she thought him an "unlicked brat," her infatuation prevailed.

Friends were impressed by her vitality, and remarked often how well she looked. Rereading her youthful diary of 1895 set her dreaming. "I feel all disjointed—go all around with hands groping for the girl that was I. And I am that girl. Emmet [an early love]: 'I am too young to love you as I do.' And now, nearly forty years later, from Harvey, 23,3,000 miles away: "I love you.' Hell—what a widow!"[12] Taylor's brief reappearance in May led her to abandon all restraint with regard to him. Possibly he served as an outlet for frustrations over her writing failures. Provoked by several requests for biographies of Jack, and spurred on by a *Bookman* editor's claim that no Jack London biography had ever been written, she determined to reduce her two volumes to one. Though she edited the manuscript all spring, her attitude was hardly conducive to success. "I am a mess. Hate myself, but that's no help with weak pride."[13]

Throughout the summer Charmian sent Taylor what amounted to lengthy daily diaries that covered every experience occupying her hours: books read and plays attended, horseback rides, dinners with male admirers, nude sunbathing, lectures of encouragement, reminiscences of their dancing together. Intermixed with all this personal revelation were very explicit instructions to

Taylor as to what he could and could not do for the estate. Although her letters were in no way a reaching out for further intimacy, their sheer mass must have overwhelmed the inexperienced youth.

In late June, Taylor informed her that he had received $650 for "Poppy Cargo"—the revision of London's "Tar Pot"—but the payment just covered his expenses for the work he had done to sell it. He emphasized that he would more than make up for the money with movie commissions. Of course, Eliza and Charmian were the only ones who handled movie deals, and they questioned his presumption. Then Taylor arranged to publish an article on Jack's use of story outlines he had bought from Sinclair Lewis when that gawky youth was in need of money. Visiting the now famous author, he gained approval to prepare a definitive Lewis bibliography. Meanwhile, for his London bibliography, he took out an ad for orders in the *Saturday Review of Literature,* though he had no publisher (and the manuscript was never completed). Taylor must have been riding high now, so young, yet so trusted by one eminent literary figure and the famous widow of another.

As disturbing stories came back from friends in New York, Charmian chastised Taylor. She reminded him that he lacked authority to edit a collection of Jack's unpublished stories. No replies to her many letters followed. Then Charmian and Eliza learned that Harvey had torn the front page out of the rare original 1901 copy of *Dilettante* on which appeared a sonnet by Jack, and had sent the poem off for possible publication. Charmian was astonished at his thoughtless destruction of her property. She then wrote Fulton Oursler, supervising editor of the magazines Taylor had been dealing with, to inquire just what his payments had been. Oursler replied that he had paid $750 for "Poppy Cargo" and $1,184 for the Lewis materials. About the same time, Taylor finally wrote to say that he had been ill as a result of dental surgery for an impacted wisdom tooth, and had Sinclair Lewis not found him miserable in his apartment and paid off his bills, he would be in total misery. To add to his sorrows, he had suffered a ruptured hernia while taking some books from a shelf.

Ignoring his excuses, Charmian unleashed her fury. "Why have you done it? I can understand crookedness, and crookedness for its own sake. But I fail to comprehend why an intelligent young man, with his future to mold, deliberately risks that future by not being square. You sold the manuscript to *Liberty* for a red-letter price. I saw the article quite by accident. My misappropriated funds were in your bank account, instead of mine." She ordered him to return all her property, desist from using the stationery, and terminate all negotiations he might have entered into. "For the sake of your family I should prefer to settle quietly and directly with you."[14]

In spite of such forthright demands, Taylor did not understand the seriousness of the situation. He promised to return her property and repay the Lewis money over time, and acknowledged that he owed everything to her and had now lost her trust. But most of his response was a sustained whine about his bills and health problems and joblessness, along with stabs at Jack's writing as "third-rate" and unmarketable.

When, after a year had passed and Charmian still had yet to receive most of her precious manuscripts and photographs, she wrote to Taylor's mother. The woman apologized, distressed that her son had lost yet another job. Hearing of this correspondence, Taylor responded melodramatically. He begged Charmian not to bother the mother who had raised him and two other children following his father's suicide. He himself was seriously ill, about to have major surgery, and took solace that his life insurance would pay for his indebtedness to Charmian in case he died on the operating table.

Taylor survived; Charmian received her papers, if not the money. Taylor's bibliography of Sinclair Lewis eventually appeared in Carl Van Doren's book on the author. Lewis's major biographer, Mark Schorer, observed that Taylor's work contained many inaccuracies, as well as exaggerations of Lewis's publishing figures.

Charmian, meanwhile, was left with the follies of age, which are judged more harshly, and were so judged by Eliza. "What little pleasure I had in his company has faded, of course," Charmian wrote her "Sis." "But it hurts damnably to have you people here, whom I have chosen above my own people to live with and try to be happy with, begrudge me what little fun I can get. . . . Instead of censure and discordance, I need understanding."[15] Eliza never saw this letter, for it was Charmian's style to write down her angry feelings but not deliver them.

In December 1931 Frederick O'Brien was hospitalized with congestive heart failure, so ill he could have no visitors. Several days later, Charmian wrote optimistically that the shadow of death seemed lifted. He returned home when nothing more could be done for him, and there he died in early January. Having made an exception to her usual practice regarding funerals, Charmian joined members of his family at the memorial service. Sometimes later she remarked to a mutual friend that O'Brien never did any sustained work after their relationship ended. "He was a charming person—personage, if you please, and, sadly, his own worst enemy."[16]

Following O'Brien's death an acquaintance leaked information to reporters about his various lovers, causing the journalists to hound his widow, Gertrude, even breaking her gate and forcing entry into her house. They wrote hints about his "other wife," but without identifying Charmian. Gertrude consulted the exmistress and was grateful for Charmian's help in handling the press. Possibly these meetings explain subsequent news reports that Charmian and Gertrude intended to collaborate on the completion of O'Brien's last work, *On Paper Wings*, a project that never came to fruition. O'Brien haunted Charmian's dreams for months afterward. "He and I in more than one situation, trying to escape the pits. We do escape each time. But he's a dead weight. Half awake I realize my old lover *is* a dead man."[17]

Now sixty-two, Charmian found her life resonated with changes beyond her control. In the depths of the Great Depression, her small income shrank further, forcing her to forgo concerts and trips to the city; consequently she became isolated from her friends. She grew grateful for small savings, as when the Beaux Arts Association eliminated its five-dollar annual dues. Once she nearly had her electricity cut off. (And these were days when one could still enjoy, as she did one evening for a special celebration, a dinner of filet mignon, seafood cocktail, and vegetables for seventy-five cents.) She refused to join the Roosevelt team, however, and voted for Socialist Norman Thomas in 1932.

On the occasions when she did go to San Francisco, the once familiar sights of the city took on alien forms: "It occurs to me that I practically never see or meet any soul I know on the streets of San Francisco. Either I don't know anybody or the population is so big that one has no chance to fall in with acquaintances. Anyway, it's an unfriendly situation. Never see a hat raised. As a matter of fact, one doesn't see people meeting."[18] Of course the city had grown. What Charmian overlooked was how many of her old acquaintances were dead or ailing. The sight of the Golden Gate Bridge taking shape over the headlands disturbed her, for it cut off her favorite sailing views. The new Opera House, too, seemed a fiasco. For the first time in several decades her request for opening night tickets was returned, "not enough seats" being the reason. Recalling the grandeur of the premiere performances in the Civic Auditorium, attended by ten thousand people, she complained to Blanche Partington of the much smaller new house. When her favorite restaurant announced that it was going out of business, she could not afford a final commemorative dinner there.

Her social life revolved around a few remaining longtime friends, mostly through correspondence. To Blanche she confessed, "It seems as if I were being touched, folded in, every moment I am in your house. I can't describe it: just, perhaps, the deep feeling of faithful yours through thick and thin, and so much peaceful pleasure together, mixed with fun."[19] When strangers such as a San Quentin prisoner sought her advice on their writing, she initiated a long epistolary relationship. Anna Strunsky, Cloudesley Johns, and John Myers O'Hara still survived, though each suffered tragedies during this period.

In the late 1920s English had taken up with another woman, and lived with her for a time. Eventually he and Anna were divorced. He lived alone in a residential hotel in New York, while she settled in a Greenwich Village studio apartment. Anna's children were now in college or raising their own families, and she would have been much lonelier if not for her sister Rose's frequent companionship, and that of suitor Leonard Abbott. Rereading the account of Jack's death in *The Book of Jack London*, Anna mused that her life was over. "What is this obsession with English, who does not want me . . . ? I should take Leonard's love."[20]

Even up until the divorce, Anna's feelings for English vacillated. Despite his infidelity, she hoped he would return to her, and blamed herself as much as him for the marital failure. Finally, in 1933 she confessed it was wrong ever to have fallen in love with him. "I was never safe in his hands. He worked against me in the dark with my children, his mother, so passionately dear to me, my friends, and family." She accepted a truce and attempted a congenial friendship. One evening they sat in her flat writing letters to their children. Upon leaving he remarked, as if to excuse his behavior, "Well, you're all right." She felt "spurned as a woman," and developed a "real coldness" toward him.[21]

Yet in June 1936, when English left for Europe to do a lecture tour on behalf of refugee unionists, she wrote in her diary, "O, if I were sailing with you." After collapsing with pneumonia in September, he refused to let anyone notify Anna. He died in his hotel, a Dutch union organizer by his side. Anna went to Europe to attend the service in Amsterdam, and accompanied the body home, where a memorial was held in New York. Still ambivalent about English, Anna arranged a collection of essays in his memory. Her own depicted a flawless man, and elided any hint of rancor in his relationship with her or others. Significantly, neither her sister Rose nor Upton Sinclair would contribute. In his refusal, Sinclair suggested that Anna had repressed her true feelings toward English over the years "for the sake of her marriage."[22]

Cloudesley Johns and his wife were so sick and poverty-stricken that they eventually lived apart, though not from choice. John Myers O'Hara had lost everything in the Wall Street crash, and now supported himself by the sales from his treasured book collection. He bewailed his fate in his inimitable manner: "Charmian, it looks as though the 'ancien regime' is gone, the 'jeuness dorée' are no more. It is 'the dusk of the Gods.' I feel like Julian, the Emperor, must have felt when he heard the tragic words of doom. 'The world has fallen, beautiful is no more.'"[23]

Charmian's health worsened as well. She endured lapses of memory, dizzy spells, and other signs of hypertension, along with chronic hyperacidity. In 1934 she had an operation on tonsils and a thumb, and during the recuperation fell out of bed. Eliza's diabetes also worsened. "I have a disconcerting glimpse of what Sis and millions of other women have gone through with age looming whitely in the being walked over by the unheeding young. When I get really well and normal again, I must look to myself to survive," Charmian pledged in her diary.[24] She wrote Blanche of meeting an old white-haired deaf couple; she was shocked when the woman greeted her as a classmate from Mills. "They looked rich and how did they get so old? Heavens knows what they thought of me in my rig. I suppose I am what Jack called me—the kid that never grew up! But I think I look awful these days!"[25] Disappointments and sorrows accumulated. Film producers planning an expedition to South America invited her to go along for publicity and fund-raising purposes, but at the last minute the trip was canceled for lack of backing. Charmian concluded that it failed because she was no longer enough of a celebrity to attract investors. In fact, throughout the 1930s Charmian was often guest of honor at artistic events, and was treated warmly by spectators as the venerable literary widow. With age she seemed less able to acknowledge public recognition even though it continued.

Her diaries now listed the distressing international news—forewarnings of war ("Pogrom imminent in Germany—worst message in history") or catastrophes ("LA quake—500 killed"). The source of this interest in world events was the radio, which kept her company, at the expense of feeding her anxieties with its abbreviated, provocative announcements. On New Year's Day 1934 she reflected "I wish Mate could see me living my life—a funny sort of program. I miss access to many things—especially menfolk. But manage to put in many carefree if busy days, though strange worries lie beneath." She struggled on with her writing projects—revisions on the biography, a manuscript based on the *Dirigo* trip around Cape Horn, and brief articles for local newspapers—none to her satisfaction. Charles Malamuth offered to help her regarding the possibility of obtaining royalties from Russia, though this proved a hopeless cause.

The most wrenching adjustment followed the family's decision to turn the property into a dude ranch. When Irving Shepard first raised the issue, Charmian walked outside and thought she heard Jack in the hammock say, "It be work that shall break my heart."[26] Nonetheless, she cooperated in the plans, particularly in the purchase and care of horses. One day while riding she had one of her "beatitudes," or trance states, from which she awoke feeling young and interested, and rushed off to tell Irving that she would even serve as a guide for guests. Fortunately, the actual move out of her house proved untroubled, for she appreciated the contrast between the cottage, still in need of repair, and her beautiful new home.

The one favorable improvement was the estate's situation regarding movie rights. Charmian and Eliza finally unsnarled all the complications involving the Thomas fraud, as well as cleared up the ambiguities resulting from the introduction of talkies. Most significant was their sale of *The Call of the Wild* to Daryl Zanuck, whose career in the 1920s had been advanced by the success of his *Rin-Tin-Tin* movies. Now in command of a new major studio, Twentieth Century Fox, Zanuck realized that the story would be better if the emphasis were not on the dog but on John Thornton, as played by Clark Gable, who had been enticed over from MGM, with Loretta Young as his romantic interest. The movie's commercial success seemed guaranteed, and so it proved to be. Yet Eliza had sold the rights at a relatively low price, perhaps because the outcome was not certain for the fledgling company. The following year Twentieth Century produced *White Fang* with lesser-known character players, and lightened the story with comedy.

Charmian was little able to enjoy these developments. On August 5, 1934, Mildred Shepard heard Charmian singing as she rode over the field on horseback. Suddenly the song switched to a piercing scream. The horse had tripped over some wire mesh, throwing Charmian and rolling over her, leaving her, in her doctor's words, with "no left side." She wrote afterward:

> I took account of myself as a dying woman. For as Pattie rolled over me—assumably her hindquarters—and I realized from the great inevitable warm weight what was being done to my 108 pound skeleton by her half-long ton, or what I felt of it, that it was the end of Charmian. . . . I *directed* myself somehow as I know how, and learned without realizing it when my baby died and when Jack died, in every particular straightened myself, tried out my lungs to summon help and shrieked and shrieked for Irving acres away and *in the barn* and got him, and Bunnell [a ranch hand] simultaneously—and told them exactly how it happened, how I must be handled, and to get cot and shutter. Went into Mildred's house feet first.

She was not expected to live more than a few minutes. She experienced "Oriental dreams" of murder and thought it was "the end, Charmian," yet felt no fear. Taking stock, she concluded that this was perhaps the best time for her to go, for she had not made a success of her life since being widowed. Then she recalled how she had been singing just before the accident.[27]

Against expectations, she survived with few serious consequences. Throughout the years Charmian had kept up a regimen of daily calisthenics, and this may have accounted for her rapid healing. "The whole thing has been the most gorgeous experience," she assured Blanche.[28] In her diary she reflected on "how incredibly I was remembered and loved and helped, born on a lifting wave—wave upon wave. How happy I have been. I almost bless the mesh wire through which I visioned all around me the first week, for leading into such an epic experience—the greatest of my life."[29] When the insurance company told her to stop riding or else it would cancel her policy, she balked. It would be ten more years before Charmian would give up her horses.

Once more facing divorce, in 1933 Joan went to New York to deliver a manuscript to publishers there. It may have been *320 Panoramic,* a novel since lost that Bart recalled her writing when they were living in Berkeley. Her letters explain that she was writing yet another book, and was moving to Los Angeles. There Joan and Lillian Taussig, a female roommate took a house in Hollywood, where the two set up a personal assistance service—typing and running errands for the Hollywood set, who, despite the poor economy, still had money to spend. Perhaps hoping to break into screenwriting, Joan helped another writer complete a screenplay and completed several unsuccessful proposals of her own. Perhaps as a result of Charmian's influence, she was hired to write some publicity stories for Twentieth Century Fox's production of *The Call of the Wild.*

In the spring of 1934, Becky and Percy drove Bart and Bess down to drop the boy off for his spring semester of school. Now an adolescent, Bart sensed that his mother and Lillian were in a lesbian relationship. He had been raised by two unconventional parents, and this awareness did not bother him. He was proud to be seen on the street with his mother, always so well turned out and with striking looks that attracted others' admiration.

Joan and Bart once visited the set of *The Call of the Wild.* The stars posed for pictures with them, and Bart sensed the larger significance of his grandfather's legacy. The boy was not impressed with this aspect of Hollywood, nor would he ever be inclined to discuss his famous ancestor. What interested him more were the industry friends Joan made, such as Sacha Viertel, a screenwriter with a son, Hans, Bart's age. An immigrant, Sacha was a member of the Hollywood subculture committed to antifascist and leftist political beliefs. This group consisted predominantly of Hungarian refugees, whose unique background would infuse Hollywood creatively as they became prominent directors, designers, and actors. Though Bart had lived happily with his father, Park, on a remote ranch in Cobb, he equally enjoyed the stimulation of this cosmopolitan group, who conversed in several languages simultaneously. He seemed to thrive under the sometimes chaotic circumstances of his living arrangements, perhaps because through it all Joan was so devoted to him, whether in person or through almost daily letters when they were apart.

After little more than a year's stay in southern California, in late 1935 Joan moved back to the Bay Area without her companion. Charles Malamuth made overtures toward a reconciliation, but she was uninterested. No doubt to his later dismay, he would direct her to a meeting where she found her third husband.

Barney Mayes was a hypermasculine egotist who saw himself as the defender of radical purity on the San Francisco waterfront. He had been born in Russia and immigrated with his family to live in Kansas City, Missouri, when he was five. "Life was dirty and so was sex," he recalled of the slum where he grew up.[30] Leaving high school, he was introduced to radicalism by Wobblies lecturing about the Russian Revolution. "Marxism offered the working stiff self-respect and a historic role to play." Throughout the 1920s he worked for the Communist Party's Youth Worker League throughout the Midwest and New England. His unrelenting devotion and courage in the face of brutal police, company goons, American Legionnaire bullies, and the Ku Klux Klan propelled him quickly through the ranks, where he rose to become secretary of the League. The experience also convinced him that the communist vision, one more broad-based than the white male exclusivity of many unions, would better serve more workers.

During his years as an activist, Mayes's relationships with women were tainted by the party culture. Love and romance were considered bourgeois weaknesses, and social events often culminated with semipublic sexual encounters. Although he eventually had a steady woman companion, Ruth Reynolds, the wife of another comrade, party demands limited their ability to forge an intimacy. Continual impoverishment led to demeaning scrounging and sponging just to survive.

The couple grew disillusioned over what they saw as the lying, game-playing, and hypocrisy in the organization, as well as the infighting that followed Stalin's denunciation of Trotsky. Aligning with the latter's views, Barney and Ruth quit the League and formed a branch of the rival Communist League of America. There they discovered that most workers were no more interested in a Trotskyite radicalism than in a Stalinist one. Worse, the CLA lacked the largesse of the Soviet regime to support its activities. One evening Mayes and some black friends were arrested during a robbery of Detroit numbers runners. Following a stint in Jackson State Penitentiary, he moved with Ruth to southern California, before financial pressures forced what became a permanent separation.

Mayes's mission in life became to undermine the Communist Party infiltration of the unions. At that time, the party followed the dual union tactic, that is, set up competing unions to traditional affiliates of the AFL. The CLA saw this as a ploy to use workers for party purposes, and argued instead that the workers' rights could best be advanced by gaining control within the traditional unions. By 1934 Mayes was on the San Francisco waterfront, where longshoremen under the leadership of radical Harry Bridges succeeded in provoking a long and often violence-ridden general strike. Mayes decided that the maritime unions were ripe for the Trotskyite perspective—a perspective threatening to Bridges's Stalinist leanings.

Mayes was living in Berkeley when he met Charles Malamuth, who wanted to build a Trotskyite group in the Bay Area. Separated from Joan, Malamuth spoke often of her and his longing for her. He impressed Barney as "a genuinely warm and kind man" who had lost all his friends when he returned from Russia an anti-Stalinist. With Stalinists entrenched in the Slavic Department at

Berkeley, employment there was impossible, and he barely survived on bits of freelance translation work. Since Malamuth lived in a residential hotel, Barney agreed to provide his apartment for educational gatherings of Trotskyites. Meanwhile, to support his waterfront activism he worked for a professor at Berkeley, where New Deal funds maintained a variety of research projects.

It was 1935 when Barney met Joan, who appeared at one of his discussion groups. He was not very impressed at first. She interrupted him often, to the displeasure of other students. Besides, Barney later recalled, "As far as I was concerned, all intellectual dames, especially those around the radical movement I had seen, acted a little screwy, but it was something you put up with—at least that's the way I felt about it." Joan remained after the lecture and introduced herself, saying that she had heard about him from Malamuth. He was surprised by her interest in politics, because Malamuth had described her as essentially apolitical. She explained that "her Russian experience was causing a change in her." Joan also made it clear that she was interested in more than intellectual conversation. She asked to stay the night, and soon they were living together. "She was not the kind of person to beat around the bush when she was interested in something which made it easy for me to go along." Since Joan was a few years older than Barney, as he described it, "with her more varied experience sex became a vital part of our relationship."

Barney Mayes was unlike any man Joan had encountered before. One cannot help but think of the contrast London drew in various stories and novels between effete men of the mind and those of brawn, spirit, and intense physicality (the most notable example being Wolf Larsen in *The Sea-Wolf*.) With his thick dark hair and mustache, his swagger and vigor, Mayes exuded the rough sexuality portrayed by the movie gangsters so popular then. But like Wolf Larsen, he had educated himself in the erudite texts of those issues that fascinated him, thus revealing an intellect to match his imposing aura of barely controlled aggression.

Joan saw beyond Mayes's bravado and encouraged him to apply his facile mind in new ways. Consequently, when he was offered the editorship of *Voice of the Federation*, the weekly newspaper of the Maritime Federation of the Pacific, he accepted. He signed Joan on as his assistant, and throughout 1935 the two collaborated on writing, editing, pasting up, and distributing the publication. Being inexperienced in publishing, they borrowed books from the local library to teach themselves the many skills required. Under their masthead the paper grew in both size and prominence, gaining recognition nationally among the labor movement. Part of this improvement resulted from Joan's soliciting special articles from noted writers such as James T. Farrell, economists from major universities, and other labor experts. As a result of their political views, On April 20, 1936, the American Federation of Government Employees, Lodge

291, voted to expel them along with fifteen other members. Three days later they were expelled from the Union of Professional Workers as "disruptive Trotskyites."

Editing the *Voice* put Joan and Barney in danger. Their appointment had been made by the head of the Sailors' Union of the Pacific, Harry Lundeberg, on the recommendation of Norma Perry, a labor-minded radical who had been Harry Bridges's secretary. Perry had grown increasingly disenchanted with her boss's activities during the great strike of 1934. When her outspokenness led to her being assaulted by Bridges and expelled from the Communist Party, Perry then turned to the Trostkyites as the only hope of undermining Bridges on behalf of what she believed to be a better situation for the waterfront workers. Thus Barney and Joan were never surprised by the threats to their lives, as when some gun-toting Bridges goons charged into the office. Barney made sure he always kept a loaded rifle on hand, and he and Joan used subterfuges to make sure the copy got to the printer without being intercepted and destroyed. They also had their own protectors, including one called "Little Wop." For a woman of Joan's sedate upbringing, the danger and intensity of the waterfront rivalries was exhilarating.

During 1936 a series of brutal murders victimized the Sailors' Union of the Pacific. In one case a badly beaten nude body was found on the bay mud flats; in another, the death was caused by cutting the victim's leg arteries so he bled to death. A number of these crimes went unsolved, and Trotskyites such as Mayes greatly doubted the judgment of suicide or the verdict of self-defense that freed one of the accused. These events coincided with a waterfront strike combined with an employer lockout that persisted throughout 1936–37. Determined to control the sailors, Bridges came out against militant action, a position backed by the police chief's promise to tolerate "no gun men" against the employers. In December 1936, Mayes wrote a false headline reporting that Bridges and the Sailors' Union were nearing an agreement with the shipowners, thus provoking a major uproar on the waterfront that galvanized his opponent.

Bridges was a formidable foe. Backing his brilliant political maneuvering were two powerful allies: the local press, particularly the *San Francisco Chronicle,* which published anti-Lundeberg articles, and the liberal intelligentsia and artists, whose influence reinforced the widespread adulation of the charismatic union leader. Bridges used this event several months later when the strike ended to get the communists to put on the equivalent of a "Moscow trial" against Mayes. There he was accused of being anti–working class, a crony of the fascist German agents and Japanese military working against the Soviet Union. Mayes refused to "confess" but soon decided that it was time to leave the newspaper.

Joan and Barney next found employment with WPA-funded writers' projects on the Berkeley campus. Joan spent two years doing library research on the French Renaissance for a professor. They continued to speak out on labor issues, this time in unions in which they held membership. They moved to the first opulent house Mayes had ever lived in, a large brown shingle with a view from the Berkeley hills and a fireplace that really worked. As might be evident from Mayes's own form of expression, the two were never very compatible. Joan put as much energy into domestic activity (the house being the symbol for her of the basic unit of society) as into work and political activism. She was well educated, widely read, curious, and complex. Mayes was a true believer who interpreted life within a very narrow ideological framework. Furthermore, Mayes was a streetwise tough guy with none of Joan's exposure to opera, museums, and polite literary conversation.

Bart moved in with the pair to continue junior high school in Berkeley. He found Barney an inspiring man "who influenced me about as much as anyone except my mother and dad."[31] Barney and Joan encouraged Bart to join radical groups, such as the Young People's Socialist League and the American Students' Union on the Berkeley campus. When he was fourteen, he was arrested for illegally picketing Woolworth's in downtown Berkeley to support unionization of its warehouse workers. When the police realized that he was a minor, not a Berkeley student, they transferred him to juvenile facilities in Oakland. There a local reporter identified him as the Bolshevik grandson of the Bolshevik writer Jack London.

Bart had the striking boyish good looks and charm of his noted grandfather, and was readily accepted by the University radicals, except in one regard: sex. The women either shunned him or said they were not interested in "robbing the cradle." Between Barney's direction of his political reading and the thrill of getting arrested on various protests, Bart had little in common with high school peers.

Despite his brashness and commitment to the workers' cause, Mayes had moments of empathy for the various women he lived with. Of Joan he observed:

> A rejected daughter of a famous father, who grew up in genteel poverty was too much of a drawback for anyone to have to start out life with. Because she refused to live with him, after he left her mother and married Charmian, he compared her to a horse on his ranch who if in his opinion was no good, he would shoot dead. This highest paid author of his time and who signed his letters, "Yours for the revolution," allowed Joan, her younger sister and mother a miserable pittance to live on so that the mother became a tutor in math in order to keep the three of them going. . . . She was never able to survive the psychological crippling effect his

brutal abandonment of her had for the rest of her life. As we continued to live together this was a topic of conversation she would refer to many times and especially when we had been drinking. Later when I joined her to write her father's biography, this and many other facts came to my attention of what a rotten asshole for a human being Jack London was.

Nonetheless, Mayes was a heavy drinker, and it may have been during this period that Joan, too, became an alcoholic. Her family also noticed that Barney was physically abusive and wondered why she stayed with him. Bart understood that Barney was under a lot of pressure from Bridges's henchmen, and that this caused some of his spells of rage. He drew the line, however, when he and a friend came across Barney threatening Joan with a gun. They wrestled it away and calmed the situation, but Barney decided to leave. Against Joan's wishes, perhaps to escape this infelicitous household, Bart quit high school and joined the merchant marine.

Mayes had a way of absorbing Joan's work as his own. Clearly, he could never have managed editing the Federation paper without her writing, editing, and typing skills. Furthermore, he claimed to have originated the idea for and co-authored the biography of her father written during 1937–38, *Jack London and His Times*. But Joan was considering this project as early as 1925, and no evidence in her massive notes on the project shows the hand of a second researcher or writer.

What is more likely is that Mayes influenced Joan's thesis that her father was a socialist corrupted by money and capitalist temptations. Given her early childhood resentments, however, she shaped the text to ignore London's continued commitment to radical causes. For example, she knew that her father had officially resigned from the Socialist Party soon before his death in 1916. When she wrote to his old friend Ernest Untermann concerning this resignation, he provided a sophisticated account of London's reasoning. He explained that her father had quit the party organization, not the socialist cause, because he believed that the party leaders had lost sight of the workers and become self-absorbed bureaucrats who neglected their radical purpose. Joan ignored this information. She also completely omitted London's well-publicized 1913 interview concerning the Wheatland farmworker massacre. Rather, she used twenty-two chapters to cover her father's life up to 1907, and only three to cover his final nine years, the years when she knew him best. And, depending more on histories of socialism than her father's experiences, she suggested wrongly the significance of Daniel de Leon and Benjamin Kidd as major influences on his thinking.

Joan's reshaping of the facts is also seen in her letters to her hero, Trotsky himself, now living in Mexico. In July 1937 she wrote that she was writing a book on her father and asked if he could comment on Jack London's popularity in Russia. "Although my father has been much overrated as a revolutionary whose position seemed to be little further in advance of the typical Bernsteinian American Socialist Party of his time, he nevertheless seemed to have erratically approached a revolutionary position at intervals." In a later letter she emphasized that because her father had been "diverted by an insatiable desire for money," she intended to debunk him "both as a writer and as a socialist."[32]

Joan sent Trotsky a copy of her father's dystopian novel *The Iron Heel*. The story is presented as the rediscovered diary of a twentieth-century workers' revolutionary, Avis Everhard, concerning her underground ventures with her husband, Ernest, accompanied by a preface and footnotes appended by a scholar from the twenty third century. In an apocalyptic scene toward the end, the capitalist oligarchy sends troops to brutalize protesters on the streets of Chicago. Trotsky was deeply impressed by the work, which "surprised me with the audacity and independence of its historical foresight." He remarked that in 1907, when the book appeared, not even Lenin or Rosa Luxemberg had imagined so completely the "ominous perspective of the alliance between finance capital and labor aristocracy." Trotsky commended London's prescience in predicting the rise of fascism, which more than compensated for the "single 'errors' of the novel."[33]

Although Joan published Trotsky's lengthy encomium to her father, which offers a subtle response to her harsher evaluation, she essentially ignored its argument. Her conviction that her father had lost his socialist bent was logical in view of the role of money as the divisive element in her childhood experiences. To suspect her father of selling out to capitalism, as it were, makes sense from her limited perspective.

One can also see in Joan's correspondence with Trotsky a wish to please the father figure. In one letter she described how the National Committee of the Communist Party had suspended the state charter, and that a "Clarity Group" was "acting as vicious executors of the right-wing Stalinist stooges." She expressed her hope that the rank-and-file trade unionists seemed to be swinging to the left, and noted that the handful of Trotskyites she worked with were having "immeasurably greater" opportunities than several years earlier. This is also one of the few extant documents from the period containing a direct expression of Joan's beliefs.

Though Joan had finally committed herself to writing her father's story, she had neglected to inform Charmian. In fact, she had been out of touch with Charmian for a half-dozen years. Her timing proved most unfavorable.

# 16

## I Want Good Work Done on Jack London

FOLLOWING HER NEAR-FATAL ACCIDENT, Charmian adapted to life in Happy Walls. Slowly she withdrew into her new house, where she spent hours reviewing the past, rereading Jack's books, finding much that was new in them. The four Shepard children were now old enough to hike across the fields to visit or to do chores for her, and she enjoyed their company. "The grand thing about Mildred's children is that they never resent any orders and interferences—they seem to try to understand and show no anger or criticism of me, so far as I can judge."[1] Charmian was not the sweet, indulgent aunt; she insisted on respect for her habits and preferences. But at various ages each one seemed to become attached to her for a while, for she had much to teach them with her knowledge of horses, swimming, music, literature, and the world.

Some events touched Charmian more than they would less solitary people—the deaths of beloved horses, such as Pattie, who broke a leg while in foal, and of pet dogs. Over the years she had supported anyone who wanted her endorsement for a humane society project, and she wrote little essays protesting cruelty to animals. She also lent her celebrity to the protest against capital punishment. Like many in the 1930s, she tended toward pacifism, and was increasingly vexed as world crises accelerated in frequency and seriousness. When one dog disappeared, and she guessed it had probably been shot, she reflected on the cowardice of men who had invented firearms to fight unfairly. She preferred prizefighting, because it was honest, and sometimes the best man won.

For years Charmian fought on behalf of London's reputation, doggedly pursuing all published inaccuracies about him, protecting his private papers from the view of those she considered to be irresponsible grave robbers. In 1930 a journalist wrote that he was preparing three essays on Jack for the *Sunday School Times*. Charmian advised him to read her biography, and not to err by treating *Martin Eden* and *John Barleycorn* as autobiographical. So one can imagine how she bristled to find that the resulting pieces portrayed Jack as an atheist and a drunkard, the model of depravity. Seeking advice from an editor friend, H. S. Latham, she declared, "I want an atmosphere to get around of discouragement to all and sundry people writing trash about Jack London. There is a lot of it planned. I want to curb it. I want good work done on Jack London, good critical work that invites good discussion."[2]

A letter to the director of the Huntington Library was even more passionate. She decried the fact that "authors small or great" were so ready to write "biographies of dead men whose widows and families are still alive." For example, a famous writer warned her "that he had been approached by a publisher in New York City, who wanted him to undertake a biography of Jack London—and a scandalous one at that, or one written in a scandalous tone. The author wrote to them that if he did such a book, it would have to be based upon my *Book of Jack London* anyway, and what was the advantage of such a book?" She despaired that the heirs and relatives of such as London had any rights at all, for so many abused them.[3]

As Jack's literary heirs, Charmian and Eliza held only one right—control over publication of the author's private papers and any published works under copyright. That allowed them authority to stop distribution of Julie Bamford's memoir, which copied Jack's letters to her late husband without permission.[4] Furthermore, once someone is dead, laws of libel and slander no longer apply.

Charmian was long aware that her own biography of Jack was inadequate, and she was never able to abridge it to one volume. Someone else must provide the complete and accurate version while she and Eliza remained alive to pass on their knowledge. Finding such a person would not be easy. So far she had allowed no one to see Jack's private papers, but by the summer of 1936, she was convinced that she had found the person capable of doing the "good critical work." In early August, Charmian noted in her diary, "Everything lovely. All dressed and in house but Irv Stone's [sic] don't come. They did not verify my invitation. Too bad."[5]

Fresh off the success of *Lust for Life*, Irving Stone had written Charmian of his interest in doing a biography of Jack. His sudden renown at thirty-two had been most unexpected. When graduate study in economics at the University of Southern California convinced him that the academic life was not what he wanted, he began to write. Like Jack, for several years he tried various genres— novels, short stories, plays—and most were rejected. Realizing that he loved to do research, Stone concluded that biography most suited his talents, hence his embarking on van Gogh. *Lust for Life* was rejected by numerous publishers until his fiancée, Jean, took over the editing, and produced a much tighter volume, which was accepted immediately. One can see in retrospect why, newly married to Jean and financially secure, he should have identified with aspects of London's personality.

Stone could have chosen no better time to appear. Charmian's close encounter with death and Eliza's rapidly failing health had left the women even more anxious than ever to see a well-crafted, definitive biography of London in print before they died. Furthermore, when Stone contacted Charmian in 1936, she had been suffering fainting spells related to the onset of arteriosclerosis. Clearly he had learned of her vanity, for an early letter praised her biography, her figure, and her riding skills.

Stone finally arrived at the ranch on August 17, 1936. One can only guess at what transpired, given Charmian's diary entry the next day: "Can't help thinking of Stone—curious situation—though not exactly a novelty for me. My *Lust for Life* is a treasure of a book." The curious situation becomes clear in later entries and letters. By September 1 she was infatuated, "but nothing like last lovers." On September 15 she noted a "Red Letter Day" because Eliza had met her "the *whole* way about urgency of Stone doing biog. of Jack. And me."

Charmian's infatuation led her to send Stone a most revealing letter. She wrote to let him know how touched she was by his "saying that the day you spent here is one of the 'rare days' of your life," adding that she felt the same. "And right you are, most right, that the rapport we experienced is 'the rarest of all occurrences.'" She had felt in recent months that "some one would 'happen' to me to make me soar on my wings a little. . . . Hence, my naturalness with you." Consequently, "you blew in, 'Vincent,' at precisely the right time." Revealingly she added, "I have to be a child, but, oh I am wise! And a lovely thought comes to me. . . , When I am wise, I am right. 'Out of the mouth of babes,' and so forth, is not idle norm."[6] That is, she knew herself to be dominated by impulse, but believed it right to acquiesce to those feelings. An astute reader, Stone grasped her reference to being "a child," and built his characterization of Charmian around that theme.

Within several days of sending this letter, Charmian was feeling less trusting, since Stone informed her that he wanted to include a discussion of her early relationship with Jack. Her mind was "seething . . . blowing hot and cold," but she finally acquiesced, sensing this was her "last chance" to make the biography happen.[7] Furthermore, Eliza, usually very conservative in these matters, was now receiving letters and calls from Stone that secured her confidence as well.

Charmian had one other motive: to suppress Joan London's project. Since her trip to Russia, Joan had had little contact with Charmian. She had also become an alcoholic, and during her drinking bouts obsessed aloud about her father and his cruelty to her. Accordingly, she became resentful of Charmian, who had done nothing to spur this animosity. Hearing of Joan's new attitude, Charmian was dismayed to learn that she was planning to write a biography of the father she had rarely seen. Eliza "was wonderful and would do what I did not say—even rushing off publicity to stave off any shysters working with Joan."[8]

Over the next weeks Charmian met Stone in the city, sometimes she with a date, sometimes he with his wife, at times the two alone. At nightclubs Stone danced with Charmian. She remained uncertain about him. But after one night when he arrived alone, she recorded in her diary that he'd said, "It seems so long since I've seen you! It wasn't the same, the four of us in Berkeley," after which he knelt down and added, "I'll sit appropriately at your feet."[9] When asked about this fawning years later, Jean Stone explained that her husband had a story to get, and that flattering Charmian was necessary and effective.[10] It is, ironically, the view that Charmian would have taken in similar circumstances, that is, a writer needs to do whatever is necessary to get the material.

Following this courting, Stone drafted a permission letter, which further confused Charmian. She wrote him, "I do hope it [the permission letter] will relieve the tension you have been under. But then, so have I have been under tension with regard to this matter. I have not got happy about it yet—it's sort of a shock—even though I am going into it with my eyes open. The sort of enthusiasm I had concerning it at first has worn off, but I shall recapture it, or something better. You see, I am being frank with you."[11] He requested a change in wording to allow him to "use and publish about myself, in relation to Jack London, that which in our combined judgment seems necessary and suitable." Charmian conceded, eliminating "combined judgment" and replacing it with "anything which in your judgment seems necessary and suitable." To herself, she expressed the hope that he was "placated with her Great Gift."[12]

Following this episode, their notes and letters reverted to a chatty exchange of news. He wrote about visiting Jack's daughters: Becky was civil, but Joan, at work on her own book, understandably was not welcoming. (Joan wrote Upton Sinclair expressing her doubt that Stone, so unfamiliar with the radical movement, and also working with Charmian, could produce a constructive and valid account.) Otherwise the matter receded from her mind. The Stones moved back down to Los Angeles, for he had other projects as well as the London biography.

Charmian received her driver's license, and as her first solo trip drove to Los Angeles at the end of the year. On January 2 she met Stone for dinner. Finding him very "nervous and jerky," she concluded that he suffered "from overwork." While she was there, a plane carrying Martin and Osa Johnson, whom she was to meet, crashed into a mountain on its approach to Burbank. Because of the lengthy delays in carrying the injured five miles downhill to the closest hospital, a tuberculosis sanitarium, Martin could not be saved; Osa survived, though badly injured. The Johnson tragedy led Charmian to fill her diary with "sickening news"—other plane crashes, Jean Harlow's sudden death, floods in the Midwest, the *Hindenburg* catastrophe, word of persecution of Jews in Europe.

A new writing assignment brought welcome distraction. Mark Hennessey, who was preparing a book on the Sewall steel ships, asked Charmian to abridge her log of the journey of the *Dirigo,* Sewall's first big ship of its type, since he meant to cover the last voyage of its captain, Omar Chapman. Out of practice, she pieced together some text, enough for Hennessey's purposes.[13] But she felt only greater inadequacy that she could not turn the material into a real book. This would be her last published snippet of biographical information on her husband.

In June 1937, Irving Stone and wife Jean, now pregnant, moved at his request to the ranch so that he could work with the mass of materials Charmian still retained. Her diary entries point to many misunderstandings and conflicts:

> June 18: We've decided he's very young. I say he's naive, very . . . amateurish . . . awful in saddle and a poor companion.
>
> June 22: Stone works in basement a long time. I have my house locked all over.
>
> June 26: Eliza tells me of Stone's babbling all over Santa Rosa.
>
> June 27: Jean Stone took some people into my old room at my cottage— My Holy Place.
>
> June 30: Not very happy. This Stone matter is assuming proportions I do not like. He's a snake not "in the grass" but "under the pillow." Bullet-headed. . . . Find Eliza letters that Stone has been howling for.
>
> July 1: I was almost ill last night from Stoneing with Detective Stone, and his strange threat, as if I care!!! . . . Eliza sweet and worried about how I looked when Stone got through with me. She comforted me and said that if we didn't like him, we could send him down the hill.
>
> July 4: Stone's friends come from L.A. and he overdoes everything for the benefit of friends—kissing, etc., on arrival.
>
> July 10: Stone is trying very hard to be nice—asks if my name is Clara. Aunt Netta is telling everything she knows. And my hands are tied.
>
> July 13: Stone comes to grill me. I choose Book Room and he types. I face bookstacks. He says Aunt N. holds I lived with Jack before marriage. What an aunt. Bunnell [a ranch hand], he says, claims evidence!! What happy souls. We work amicably enough and I stay for dinner at headquarters [the Shepard house]. . . . Bring layette to Stones. . . . Stone loosens up and says, "Oh, I know that Jack loved you." I almost got sentiment[al] about things.

Despite her qualms, Charmian handed over Jack's love letters, insisting that Stone read them in her presence.

What she did not know was that Eliza had let him see other forbidden material, Charmian's diaries from before her marriage to Jack, which had been sequestered in a safe hidden behind a secret door in her bookcase. Stone noted this in the 1977 acknowledgments to a reprint of his book, and added that the diaries had since disappeared. They were part of what Charmian destroyed in April 1938, according to her statement that "any papers, letters, or books per-taining to the Jack London estate, and to my property . . . have been so destroyed with my full understanding and special permission."[14] Exactly what she burned was never itemized; thus a mystery remains regarding the completeness of the Jack London archives.

After Stone mentioned "filth about Netta"—her aunt's simultaneous intimacy with Roscoe Eames and Edward Payne—Charmian decided to be "mutinous" and cooperate instead with Joan.[15] Other factors turned her against Stone. There were the generational differences, with age looking condescendingly upon youth, which tended to patronize in return. Personal preferences were also a source of some of the growing antipathy, such as her contempt for Stone's being a "poor rider." Charmian found him crude and unmannerly, as did some ranch guests. Possibly these judgments can be attributed to Charmian's residual anti-Semitism. Jean and Irving Stone were northeastern Jews, used to a more assertive and direct style of interaction than the California-bred Charmian. She also noted their similarity to several Los Angeles movie men who had cheated and deceived her. Although she was not conscious of the Stones' Jewish identity during this time, it would enter her mind later. Consequently, with their bold personal style, unwittingly provoked negative reactions from Charmian.

Further indications alerted her that Stone was not preparing the book she had hoped for. In a letter to Blanche Partington, Charmian reported learning that Stone "picked over all the garbage heaps in Alameda County, Los Angeles County and San Francisco . . . all that 'research' with a rather prurient mind—before coming to Eliza and me. If he had gone about it decently in reverse, it would not have been a succession of blows in the face." She described his methods as "extremely amateurish. And yet, he contrives masterpieces." Furthermore, she believed that much of the work was actually done by his wife, who arranged his materials and repeatedly rewrote his drafts. Nonetheless, she advised Blanche to "give the man an interview and be done with it," and "embroider your friendship with Jack all you like."[16]

In the summer of 1937 Charmian went to the Bay Area to stay with relatives. During this time Stone left the ranch—or was asked by Eliza to leave. Charmian no longer had direct contact with him. Gradually, others shared similar reports about his interviews. Charmian's cousin Beth Baxter described how Stone had appeared unannounced and "upset mother and me terribly. It looks like we are going to have one of those modern sensational biographies about Uncle Jack." They were shocked when he called "Uncle Jack a suicide, without claiming knowledge of many affairs with women, which we said, we knew nothing about, how can he know so much." When he made a remark about Charmian's having been "just a stenographer, glad to get a home even if it meant breaking up someone else's happy home," they countered that Charmian had been very popular in Berkeley, and had had plenty of admirers and proposals. "He said he was writing the kind of a book Jack would approve of. I said that if he hurt anyone in it or caused any unhappiness that Uncle Jack would certainly not approve of it at all—that Uncle Jack never hurt anyone if he could possibly help it—he did look kind of funny when I said that."[17]

Baxter intimated that Stone had been swayed by Bessie's view of things, and indeed he appears to have been. Like any biographer, on some issues he found it difficult to separate his personal values from his judgment of his subject. Or perhaps he was thinking of his readers, who in 1930's America had rejected the looser morals of the 1920s. In portraying Charmian as the wicked husband-stealer, he could produce more reader sympathy for Jack. By doing so, however, he confronted Charmian with perhaps the most unseemly episode in her life: her false friendship with Bess during the adultery, behavior neither she nor Jack ever acknowledged, let alone regretted.

Stone's surviving research notes substantiate some of these claims.[18] He had a gift for eliciting telling details from his respondents. Notes from interviews with the same individual contain odd contradictions, suggesting that he may have phrased his questions to support preconceived ideas. For example, early in her interview, Glen Ellen resident Mrs. Robert Hill described Charmian as intelligent, well-read, and accepted in the community, whereas at the end she portrayed her as high-handed and preoccupied with childish and trivial things.[19] Of course, Stone was venturing into new territory to fulfill the vision he had of a dramatic, engaging biography. London was one of a long list of individuals whose lives he wished to illuminate for a large reading public as a conduit for bringing history to those who were uninterested in scholarly tomes. Still new to the game of historical research, he had to create his own rules as he went along, and cannot be faulted for the attempt. He was persistent and thorough, if perhaps too eager to force others to bend to his views.

Though well meaning, Stone's letters to others included the same cloying adulation that he had expressed in his first notes to Charmian. Cloudesley John wrote back voicing strong objections to Stone's inaccuracies; Anna rejected his flattery. But others did not. Jimmie Hopper, one of the few surviving members of the Crowd, told Stone that a physician at Jack's death bed had found a piece of paper on which Jack had calculated the number of morphine tablets necessary for a fatal dose, though Hopper, who lived in Carmel, was apparently only elaborating George Sterling's gossip. Another woman wrote that she knew of another probable divorce and a third wedding for Jack.

Two persons in particular deprecated Charmian. Her aunt and childhood guardian Netta Eames, who had always belittled her niece, remained true to type. Most tellingly, she wrote Stone, "I always use the same appellation, 'Childie.' . . . This is my pitying way of picturing her, as the 'Childie' I raised from infancy left to me when her blessed mother died." She swore that she had known nothing about the love affair between Jack and Charmian, a forthright lie she withdrew later when Stone confronted her. Inflating her own importance, she claimed that Jack and Bess had come to her "two days after the marriage" for help on sexual problems.[20]

Another uncomplimentary informant was Eliza, who made passing references to Charmian in the haystacks with Allen Dunn, said that dinner table discussions had been over Charmian's head, and, most astonishing of all, disclosed her fear that Jack would leave her alone on the ranch with Charmian. This last comment is incomprehensible and completely out of character. If Eliza indeed was so fearful, then why did she join in partnership with Charmian so willingly from the beginning? A talented, competent woman, she could easily have left after Jack's death and supported herself as well, if not better, than through taking on the ranch with its persistent indebtedness. If Eliza did in fact say such things, what can explain it?[21]

Eliza was quite favorably taken with Stone. He wrote addressing her as "Mama Shepard" and intimated that he considered her, not Charmian, to be the most expert and reliable witness. Trusting Stone, she admitted to some of her negative feelings. It was Charmian who had always handled the press, who had learned to be distrustful of any journalist, however, appealing. Eliza little suspected that a clever journalist will ingratiate himself to obtain such information. Finally, Eliza's illness had left her frail and in need of reassurance. Her loyalty to Stone, though, soon ended as well.

After Charmian made up her differences with Joan, she invited her to the house and agreed to let her examine papers both at the ranch and at the Huntington Library. This reconciliation was critical to Joan, because she had no legal right to see or quote from her father's papers. The offer could not have been easy for Charmian, for in 1930 she had repeatedly commented in her diary on her dismay over the lectures Joan was giving in New York. Eventually even Eliza was privy to Charmian's arrangement, and cooperated in preventing Stone from knowing of it. Joan in turn reassured them that her mother was similarly frustrated over Stone's interviewing techniques. Worse for Bess was the discovery after he left that several photographs were missing from the albums she had shown him, taken apparently when she briefly left the room.[22] Consequently, during the fall and winter of 1937, Joan spent several periods of up to a week on the ranch, where Charmian let her see the same personal files she had shown to Stone. By October she was happy to have Joan around, and appreciated her affectionate company.

When Charmian had sold material to the Huntington Library, she believed it included only business and other impersonal papers, but she learned now from informants that Stone must have found additional private letters as well. Consequently, she asked Joan to make note of anything significant while she was going through the archives there. Joan told of finding Stone's notes penciled onto folders, and her surprise at "what he considers important." She reassured Charmian that the letters there were of either a business or "semipersonal" nature, except for a few concerning the purchase of Sinclair Lewis plots. Then Joan wrote of finding the "Amy" telegram, the mysterious message suggesting that Jack was having an affair in New York.[23] Charmian responded that she knew Stone had already seen that document. Having been forewarned, she had introduced the item "quite naturally and laughingly," and was amused she could do so when "he had no idea I knew he had seen it."[24] By now a cat-and-mouse game was in full force, with Charmian and both biographers manipulating and at various points deceiving one another.

In April 1938 Charmian provided Joan permission to quote from Jack's writings, advised her on dealing with publishers, and sent her money to see her through the writing expenses. In May, Charmian left for Europe on business, but not before seeking a way to cut Stone out of potential film income. In September her agent struck an agreement with MGM to make a film based on *The Book of Jack London*. Furthermore, she arranged that Bess, Becky, and Joan would receive $5,000 each from the contract.

Although Charmian had prepared herself for the worst, Eliza, who had retained some sympathy for Stone, was shocked by the first installment in the *Saturday Evening Post* of *Sailor on Horseback*. Although Rose Wilder Lane had uncovered the facts of Jack's illegitimacy years before, she had not made much of the man thought to be his real father, William Chaney. In contrast, Stone elaborated an extensively detailed portrait of the astrologer, for he believed Jack to be a reproduction of his father. In doing so, he challenged what Eliza may have inculcated in her son Irving, who believed that he was a blood relation of Jack London. Unlike Lane, Stone drew John London as a sympathetic, gentle, simple man whose faults rested in his being too subservient to Flora's manic whims. Like her, however, he presented sections of London's fiction as biographical fact, a fallacy easy to commit, given the parallels. Stone was nevertheless a more skillful writer than his predecessor, more adept at rhythmic narrative and lively description.

Sensitive to the distortions of her early family life, particularly the images of poverty and family disorganization, Eliza was so indignant over Stone's disloyalty that she asked Charmian to send him a letter terminating their agreement. Charmian accordingly asserted that she had granted him full access to write "a free and untrammeled judgment of [Jack] and of myself in relation to him" in expectation that he would "use that privilege fairly, cleanly, and with the sensitive understanding of an intelligent and cultured man." Instead, he had "abused that privilege; and . . . converted what you assured me would be a distinguished appreciation of Jack London and his place in Life into a scandal-mongering serial aimed to secure sensationalism without justice."[25] Even this did not stop his efforts to negotiate with the estate, for in early 1938 he wrote Eliza about a possible movie based on his book, to be called *A Giant in the West.* When Eliza replied that his earlier permission included no movie rights, he urged her to remind Charmian that she would be portrayed by a popular screen star like Myrna Loy.

As the installments of *Sailor on Horseback* appeared in the *Post,* Charmian felt successive waves of disgust and shame at seeing the most intimate details of her and Jack's life painted garishly for ready gossip. A woman of an earlier time, she failed to anticipate the growing frankness in journalism. Although their affair had taken place during the heyday of yellow journalism, when local lovers' comings and goings pushed national news off the front page, Charmian and Jack had always carefully managed their activities or cajoled friendly reporters to prevent disclosure.

Probably the most disturbing material for her was that concerning Jack's death. Dr. Allan Thomson, who in 1928 swore to the world that Jack had died of uremic poisoning, now allegedly asserted that the gossip about Jack's committing suicide was true. Thompson publicly denied that he had said so, yet a surviving letter from him to Stone hints of a gossipy vendetta against the two women. Furthermore, his wording intimates that it was Stone who had discovered the "evidence" of suicide.[26] (William Porter, another of Jack's doctors, had already warned the women that Stone was trying "very hard to say the death was due to other things than uremia," as well as making other sensational claims.)[27] As with so many situations in the book, Stone cleverly reported some of the facts, and by omitting others, perhaps even fabricating some, constructed a most convincing argument for the gullible reader, though one that has not held up under the scrutiny of subsequent scholarship.

When reviews of the book appeared, Charmian had further proof that the biography she had expected to introduce Jack once more to the public was in fact a "perpetration." *Sailor on Horseback* was featured on the front page of the Sunday *New York Times* book review section on September 18 in an essay by Hassoldt Davis which emphasized London's "unfortunate alliances with women," his "failure at nearly everything," and his "continuous and secret drinking." Stone's praise for such works as *The Iron Heel* and *Martin Eden* was concluded to be "nonsense." While hailing Stone's vivid account, Davis questioned the appropriation of London's own writings without citation, and his "overenthusiasm" for the subject. Similarly, the *New Republic* found Stone "overworshipful and unduly romantic about a mere adventure writer . . . a febrile he-man faker," whose "decline as a writer" went unmentioned.[28] One senses from the reviews that Stone's intentions had been sincere, that he wished to extol London, yet failed in allowing his emphasis on the tawdry to overwhelm his laudatory message. Consequently, Stone was so effective at exposing London's weaknesses that he convinced his reviewers that the man was lacking in virtue.

Many wrote Charmian letters critical of Stone's work. One correspondent sent her a copy of an article from *Ken* magazine, which published segments of Jack's *John Barleycorn* alongside Stone's writings to prove that he had appropriated "the dead master's words, without quoting, save indirectly and lamely in one instance." Questioning whether much of the book could be credited to Stone, the reporter concluded, "Transposing the first person to the third does not constitute literary interpretation. It merely adds the face of the clown to the mask of the ghoul."[29]

Other friends provided emotional support. Cloudesley Johns fumed that Stone had used some of his letters with neither quotation marks nor credit, and cheerfully reported on the poor sales of the book.[30] Charmian devoured all such news with no small glee, especially a report that in a year-end poll of fifty literary experts, only three mentioned Stone's book among the most important publications of the year; and that the price of the volume was slowly but surely decreasing in the booksellers' efforts to clear their shelves.

Despite news of negative reviews and meager sales, *Sailor on Horseback* poisoned Charmian's thoughts, seeping in to spoil her daily pleasures. Being a trusting person, one inclined to think well of Stone, she could not understand why he should have written as he did. Consequently she accounted for his actions by suggesting that he was slightly off-balance, confused. When even that did not hold up as a reasonable explanation, she took up another. As Jack had fallen back on anti-Semitic sentiments to express his grudge toward Judge Samuels in 1910, so did Charmian once she discovered that Stone had likely been, in her odd spelling, a "Stine." She dug for evidence, hounding several academics for confirmation that his college association, Sigma Nu, was "a Jewish fraternity." Thus, the same woman who could agonize over the fate of European Jews felt exploited by "that shyster," and failed to recognize her own anti-Semitism.

Eventually Charmian ceased distorting Stone's name in her diary and letters. Though she considered a lawsuit, she eventually rejected the notion, concluding that it would only bring publicity to the book; she would rather it died on the shelves. Before it did, however, the second printing was released with a new subtitle, *A Biographical Novel*, the publisher's response to reviews critical of its fictionalizing.

Given the delay in gaining access to her father's papers, Joan London's *Jack London and His Times* did not appear until 1939, by which time Stone's book had cornered the market. As she later explained, she never felt part of her father, and thus wrote the book in the third person. This oddity, noted by almost all the reviewers, could not disguise that it was a *cri de coeur,* a symptom of her as yet unresolved suffering over her father's seeming unfairness and abuse.

Though persuaded by George Sterling that her father killed himself, Joan nonetheless hedged in her account. She suggested that London was suicidal, the result of his subordinating his socialism to false capitalist values. As evidence, she noted that both Dr. Porter and Dr. Thompson agreed that he had taken a large amount of morphine, and that the latter believed it was an intentional overdose. Since her book lacked references, a reader would not know that her source was *Sailor on Horseback,* and that Dr. Porter had strongly countered that claim in a letter to her.

Despite certain deficiencies, *Jack London and His Times* remains useful today. Although Joan covered much of what had appeared in earlier biographies, she produced the most lucid and coherent account. Significantly, she had known some figures, such as Flora London, Jennie Prentiss, and the Madderns, more intimately than Charmian, and in adulthood had been befriended by many of Jack's associates. In addition, she was a careful, accomplished social historian, who contextualized London's life in a manner no one else has since achieved.

*Jack London and His Times* received consistently positive reviews, and was judged superior to *Sailor on Horseback.* One critic praised Joan's "special emphasis on West Coast events and personalities; and her industry and shrewd insight." The *New Yorker* noted that the work avoided soft-pedaling, and was "absorbingly handled." Consistently held up for commendation was the writing and organization. Unlike in reviews of *The Book of Jack London* or *Sailor on Horseback,* the subject was little confused with the value of the work; *The New Republic* even concluded that Joan "underestimated his achievements." Perhaps the most perceptive review was by a Berkeley student, future movie reviewer Pauline Kael, who acknowledged the "first-rate biography" and Joan's "fairness, objectivity, and good taste," though "less justifiable is condemnation of a man whose actions seem incomprehensible to her."[31]

Charmian went to Europe, where she remained on business for almost a year during 1938–39. The first months she passed in Germany. One might have expected rich descriptions of that country, steeped now in imperialistic expansion and blatant hostility toward its Jewish citizens. But she wrote scarcely a word of political comment in her diary, focusing instead on the people she met and various social events. Nonetheless, she was aware of changes, noticed the silence at night on streets that had previously been full of joyous crowds, wondered why so many of her press interviews were repeatedly postponed, forgotten, or canceled at the last minute. Possibly she was self-censoring out of fear the diary might be confiscated.

Illness also prevented her full comprehension of the shocking events around her. As she wrote a friend, "When I left home, Eliza looked like death. I didn't look very much alive myself, and felt worse. Had two severe lapses with my eyes, and being somewhat of a nerve wreck, couldn't let well enough alone on the five weeks voyaging though the Canal to Hamburg, Germany." She read so much on the ship that her eyes gave out. "For nearly five months I did not use them, even on newspapers, and so did not know much about what was going on, until I got enmeshed in the well-remembered Crisis Week in Paris."[32]

The mood in Paris was considerably different. She joined in the general revelry of the last celebration before certain devastation to come, scurrying to concerts and parties with her many friends in that city. Since her earlier visits had ensured the competent translation and production of Jack's books, she could bask in the pleasure of seeing how popular and widely read Jack was outside the United States.

Denmark was another story. As in the other northern countries, it was Charmian herself who had won over the reading public, and she was embarrassed to hear that her books were currently outselling Jack's. The popularity was unwelcome. "Last night I was so tired sitting through four hours of foreign speeches, dead tortured with tobacco, that I welcomed departure and peace. But that is *my job,* for Mate, for publishers, for host and hostess."[33]

With England, the final leg of the tour, came some promise of rest at a friend's house in Sussex. In London, this woman born on the California frontier gave her first television interview, which led to many other invitations for social and publicity purposes. Now sixty-seven, she was still the indefatigable dancer, and however tired, attended balls to dance with the young men. (Several years later, she would note, none remained alive.)

While she was overseas, Charmian learned of the terrible fate that had befallen her old nemesis, Bess London, who suffered a stroke so severe that the paralysis left her permanently bedridden and unable to speak. Charmian was saddened to hear the news, and did not take any pleasure in it. The tragedy had painful consequences for Becky as well. She had just persuaded her husband to move the family out of the Scenic Avenue house into their own home in Alameda. Now Bess would move in with them, leaving Becky once again without the independence she desired. Since she was also working full-time at the stationery store Percy had bought, she understandably resented that Joan would have less daily involvement in their mother's care.

More pressing to Charmian was Eliza's health. One evening, while in the twilight between wakefulness and sleep, Charmian had a vision. "Suddenly, like a bright ray of sunshine, you, my sister Eliza, stepped right through a doorway, stood in the frame, smiling, bright, alert, just like yourself when you are well and welcoming me. It was so splendidly vivid, so vital, so reassuring, that I was fairly shocked with the pleasure of it."[34] Though Charmian had no faith in spiritualism, she had always retained an open mind about extrasensory perception, perhaps because Eliza was known for her uncanny predictions and experiences. Charmian recorded the exact date and time of the "visitation," translated it into ranch time, and asked whether anything special had happened to Eliza then. To their mutual astonishment, Eliza explained that she had come out of a coma that day, and in the process had had a similar vision of Charmian bathed in light. As she walked toward Charmian in her reverie, she gained consciousness.

With Eliza improved, Charmian sent her "Sis" long, chatty letters about her new friends, her attendance at banquets in her honor, the wonderful bargains she found on clothes, and the latest gossip about Irving Stone. A major theme was the care of the horses on the ranch. For example, "Please tell Mr. Couch to train Blaise to stand 'tied to the ground'—reins hanging down in front. It would give me a lot of pleasure to have him reliable that way—I used to tie Star Bird, so, when I wanted to lie down on a mountain meadow among the yellow lupins, etc."[35] Such explicit instructions continued for many more lines. Given her love for her horses, upon returning home in mid-1939 Charmian was shocked to realize how stringy and weak her muscles had become, how difficult it was to ride.

Production for the film biography was now under way. Charmian hoped for better casting than had occurred with "low brow Gable" in *The Call of the Wild*. She preferred that Myrna Loy would be cast in her role. Although Spencer Tracy was assigned to play Jack, war put him in uniform. The movie was eventually released as a second-billed feature starring Michael O'Shea and then-starlet Susan Hayward, and the story was reduced to a piece of anti-Japanese propaganda. Louise Beaver played "Mammy Jennie," though the script never explained why a black woman should be so caring toward a white boy. The most realistic feature of the film was the costuming, which was based on photographs in Charmian's possession.

In the fall of 1939, Gabriel Heater, the popular radio commentator and interviewer, invited Charmian to appear on "We, the People." She did not want to go, for Eliza was ailing. Since all the expenses were covered, permitting her to fly to New York and stay at first-class hotels, she relented to Eliza's urgings, and agreed as well to visit friends at various points across the country during her return.

Several days after the radio broadcast, on September 29 Charmian received a cable informing her that Eliza had died that morning on the ranch. The local paper featured her passing on its front page, and commented at length on both her activities as a "devoted, patriotic woman" and her love for the outdoors. Repeated mention was made of her character, of her being a "distinguished, kindly woman" who "never tired in what she had undertaken to perform."[36] Her relation to Jack was described as "half sister," and simply "sister" in a briefer obituary two days later. The services were under the auspices of the Women's Auxiliary post that she had founded, and one of the six pallbearers, in defiance of tradition, was a woman.

"Can it be? What an anniversary in my life. I rove over future—immediate and further. . . . How our apprehensions overtake us. I'm glad I fortify myself in advance. I'll never again fear for Eliza. But miss her counsel—God!"[37] True to Charmian's belief that funerals were not for the living, she kept to her original itinerary, taking several weeks to return home to face the enormous vacancy left by Eliza's passing.

# 17

# He Loved Me More

WITH THE PUBLICATION OF *Jack London and His Times,* Joan remained hopeful that she could become a self-supporting writer. She and Barney Mayes collaborated on two books based on their familiarity with waterfront union events. *Corpse with Knee Action,* a mystery, was published in 1940 under the pseudonym B. J. Maylon. The "knee action" refers to the slicing of the victim's leg arteries, a means by which several seamen were murdered in the 1930s. The detection is done by an ex-boxer turned reporter, Bill King, who has written exposés of anti-union figures in San Francisco. King and Stella Holmes, a woman he encounters on the San Francisco waterfront, discover the first corpse on a boat. Two waterfront union leaders are arrested for the crime, and when King finds another body, he develops doubts that the first murder was union-related.

From this point the chase is on. King discovers that Stella's name is phony, and is puzzled to find her sitting in a Chinese restaurant with the head of a dope ring. After two goons, Shrimp and Kitz, assault Stella, King intervenes and takes her to Ching, a close friend, who helps the two out. Other bodies appear, along with car chases, threatening letters, and double-crosses. There is a corrupt medical doctor in the guise of an advocate for eliminating corruption in government and business, a private investigator disguised as a threatening stranger, and a cast of colorful minor characters serving as red herrings. In the end, disguises are unveiled and the real murderer is exposed in a clever tie-up.

The plot is too complex, fraught with characters who show up at the magic moment, and lacking in sufficient development of motivation. Nevertheless, the tough, racy dialogue richly evokes the underside of life on the Embarcadero and in Chinatown. The high level of violence, chases, and gunplay reflects the action of 1930s B movies. Though hardly a significant piece of detective fiction, it is a fascinating, rollicking story. The reviewers agreed. They quibbled over the melodrama, the uneven narrative, and the improbable circumstances of the plot. Yet they acknowledged that the book had "rough and ready excitement" and a "rather well worked-up surprise ending."[1] With more shaping, it might have been an accomplished thriller.

Their next book, *Embarcadero,* was never published.[2] This roman à clef, for which Mayes was the main author, is a more powerful work, and one of scholarly interest for its insight into the Trotskyite side of the 1936–37 turmoil on the waterfront. The antagonist is Bennett, the dockworkers' leader aligned with the "Comics" or "Communal" Party, a thinly veiled version of Harry Bridges. As the story opens, members of the sailors' union are discussing a job action which Bennett "and his Commies" want to stop. "They got all the gravy in the big strike [of 1934], and . . . the shipowners didn't even give us our own hiring hall!" The leading protaganists are more blended. Kurt Geel, head of the Sailors' Union, seems more like Barney Mayes than Harry Lundeberg; Madge, an ex-communist activist, resembles Norma Perry, with her astute sense of strategy. George Sligh, an East Coast union worker, seems a romanticized version of Mayes, particularly when he meets Vera O'Brien, who, with her "wide shoulders, diminished somewhat by the broadness of her hips and . . . muscular but well-shaped calves," is a sweeter version of Joan. Undisguised are Little Wop and his Animals, the counter to Bennett's goons, who protected Barney in real life from Bridges's men.

The story follows union gatherings and behind-the-scenes strategy meetings in response to the threats from Bennett, the ship owners, and the police. Even patriotic groups intervene, hoping to get the sailors to help "clean the unions of reds." Workers are beaten and murdered (via sliced leg arteries), only to send Little Wop and his gang off in happy retaliation. Whiskey and sex ("Vera, the balloon goes up tonight!") offer the characters relief and remind the reader how all-encompassing the cause was to the participants. Throughout, the smartest character is Madge, who perceptively analyzes situations and individuals, and provides the real direction to the men. Although Trotsky's name is never invoked, various dialogues reveal why the sailors are both ardent anticapitalists and anticommunists.

While some elements of the story are pure entertainment, the vividness of the scenes and the directness of the language place the reader well within the perspective of the Sailors' Union. Adaptations of actual headlines from the period introduce each chapter, and particular events, such as the washing up of a chained shipmate's body, are incorporated accurately as well. One senses the conviction, passion, and often terror that permeated the conflict. The story ends, as in life, with mixed results. The Sailors' Union wins its strike and joins the American Labor Congress, but the Longshoremen's Union has also gained further support among the uptown businesspeople and police. George Sligh is shot dead, a symbol of the pyrrhic victory.

After these manuscripts were completed, Joan and Barney continued to write. He embarked on another mystery plot, while she began working on *Pie in the Sky*, a history of depression social movements such as Sinclair's EPIC campaign, the Townsend Plan, and Ham'n'Eggs. Harcourt Brace was interested, but the war clouds scared them away from offering an advance. Joan hoped to sell some chapters to magazines to provide income until the book was completed, though she never did. She also received tempting messages from her Hollywood agent, Spencer Valentine (the same used by Charmian, who perhaps introduced them), regarding a movie based on her biography of Jack. Again, nothing resulted, and the couple continued to wonder how they would pay their next set of bills.

Interestingly, it was the first decently paying job for each that would set the stage for their breakup. Recognizing their zeal for the labor cause and their respective talents, in 1940 the California Labor Federation hired Barney to be an organizer and Joan to set up the library and research service for the organization. This meant that Barney would be traveling throughout the state on an expense account, and Joan would commute daily to San Francisco on the ferry and put in regular hours.

Joan proved an exceptional choice; she would stay with the organization for over twenty years. Her strong work ethic and love of research compensated for her lack of training in reference library work. She was given full responsibility to organize the unit, which meant deciding on every detail, from the placement of a desk to organizing the bibliographic filing system and purchasing reference materials.[3] Once she had that system in place, she devoted most of her time to researching material for court cases, writing and editing the CLF weekly newsletter, and ghostwriting many of the union leaders' speeches. In the newsletter, Joan displayed a talent for taking technical economic reports and presenting them for non-experts.

Although Joan was the only woman holding a professional position in the organization, she did not encounter particular difficulties in being accepted by her peers and bosses. In her demeanor she was typical of Hollywood depictions of career women, such as those Rosalind Russell often portrayed. She dressed stylishly, was impeccably groomed and well mannered, but no prude; she held her own at the bar after work, quipped readily during male banter, and especially enjoyed prizefights. Forty years later men who'd worked with Joan spoke of her wistfully as beautiful and principled.

Typical of the day, she was paid much less than the men. In 1943, the earliest year for which data are available, she earned $3,620, while Barney Mayes, who lacked a college education, was paid $5,450 plus expenses. Similar income discrepancies between her and other men with the same responsibilities continued until her retirement. Even so, she was the highest-paid woman worker on staff.

She and Barney now lived alone. With Joan's full approval, Bart had quit high school after the eleventh grade and left home. He hitched to the Viertel home in Hollywood, hoping to get his friend Hans to join him. Upon arriving, he found the living room filled with guests who were engrossed by a man speaking in French about the Spanish civil war. The speaker proved to be the noted novelist André Malraux. Hans Viertel eventually moved to the Bay Area to share an apartment with Bart, who joined the merchant marine and continued his radical activities in the Bay Area. As in the past, Joan wrote him frequent long, letters expressing her worries about him, giving advice, sending money or gifts, and keeping him up to date on the latest disputes among the Bay Area radicals. And she was very happy when he announced that he had visited her best friend Musa's daughter, Lee Pence.

"Betrothed" in utero by their playful mothers, Bart and Lee had played together often during their childhood. Eventually, though, the two lived too far apart for frequent visits.[4] Lee saw Bart briefly once when he was living in Hollywood and was taken aback by the "wild hulk with lots of uncombed black hair." Raised to be a proper lady, Lee told her mother that Bart was "very uncouth," and she did not want to see him again. Later Lee went off to Berkeley, where she lived in the Presbyterian student center. One evening she heard two motorcycles, and looked out to see her brother and "somebody you'll want to see," who turned out to be Bart, well beyond his wild hulk stage. She accepted a date and learned, among other things, to drink beer. At Christmas he showed up at her mother's home in Pasadena with an engagement ring, and took her to a New Year's party at the Viertels' filled with Hollywood directors and stars. Lee was a breathtaking natural beauty, a perfect counterpart to Bart's muscular handsomeness.

Soon after, Lee fled north to move in with Bart and Hans Viertel in their cottage in Berkeley. Joan accepted this illicit living arrangement, and invited the couple to eat many dinners at her house to save money. Bart gave Lee a reading list of political books, most of which she borrowed from Joan. Lee had no training in domestic skills, and found Joan always willing to share a recipe or explain how to shop for food and clean house. When Musa began to fuss over the situation, Joan suggested that the couple get married, which they did before a justice of the peace.

Soon after the United States entered the war, Lee gave birth to two daughters in rapid succession. Bart became a San Francisco longshoreman. Joan often dropped in to visit after work at the labor federation. They found her a wonderful grandmother, generous with money, eager to pay for music and drawing lessons and more. One day Joan invited them to a reception for a concert pianist well regarded by the bohemian and social set. Since they lacked good clothes, they sold their Model A roadster, and Bart bought the only suit he ever owned. Both Charmian and her house guest Anna Strunsky were at the party, and they invited the engaging young couple to visit. Bart and Lee's family eventually became the center of Joan's life, so much so that Lee thought the mother-son relationship too intense.

Joan regularly informed Bart of family doings—the condition of "Nana," his grandmother Bess, and news of Becky. Cousin Jack Fleming upset his mother when he followed Bart's lead and quit school to become a seaman. In May 1940, Joan reported, he "signed on a ship going to the Mediterranean, so poor B[ecky] is having cat fits . . . I don't blame her for worrying."[5] Joan also updated Bart on the ongoing political conflict among the radicals over U.S. participation in the war. The Communist Party was very much in support of the Soviet Union's joining with the Allies, and the Socialist Party tended to go along as well. The Workers' Party took as its wartime banner "For the Third Camp: Neither Washington Nor Moscow," in support of countries opposing both Germany and Russia. Its members participated in the armed services and war industries, but openly criticized the loss of labor rights gained just a few years previously. Joan, Barney, and Bart found themselves among the radical minority by siding with the Workers' Party.

Barney's new position with its frequent travel strained the relationship. He lost interest in Joan sexually, embarked on affairs, and began to drink more. He resented her for providing the first "bourgeois" life he had ever known—a well-ordered home with good food and furnishings—for it clashed with his radical purity, his belief that an activist had to suffer along with the working class. His ideology did not, however, prevent him from accepting good pay. He was successful at his job, and gained, if anything, too much self-confidence.

During a labor convention in Los Angeles, Barney looked up a screenwriter friend of Joan's and had "frantic sex" with her. He asked her to meet him in San Francisco, but two days before her arrival she took an overdose of sleeping pills. To assuage his guilt, he left Joan, taking only his clothes, leaving her with all the equity in the house as well as the mortgages. Soon after that Bart took a job far south in San Pedro. Thus, now in her early forties, Joan was living alone for the first time in her life.

During the early 1940s Charmian seldom left Happy Walls. Finances may have restricted her here, for she learned that before her death, Eliza had negotiated the equivalent of seven years' advances against future royalties from Macmillan. Charmian felt bitter that she had been told nothing of this move, that money she was counting on would not be available. Furthermore, she realized that she was unlikely to earn anything on the basis of her own writing.

Among her few excursions were a visit in September 1940 to see King Hendricks, an English professor from Utah State University, and then to stay with

Anna in New York. "And Anna fills in tragic gap in 1901 [the year of Anna's relationship with Jack]. Terrific! Unhappy, naughty J. L. It *was* too bad." In disclosing no more than this in her diary, Charmian leaves us tantalized, wondering how "naughty" Jack had been—unless he had kept even Charmian unaware of his original intention to leave Bess and marry Anna.

Retaining traces of her Victorian upbringing, Anna still refused to succumb to Leonard Abbott's desire for an intimate relationship. Or perhaps her resistance was due to Abbott's having to compete with Jack's memory. With English dead and appropriately memorialized, she returned to her biography of her first love. She explained to Charmian that she felt she owed it to Jack to write something in his honor. Few of the draft pages that survive add much to our knowledge about his life, apart from her own dealings with him, for it is clear that she relied heavily on Charmian's biography. Her account of their relationship, however, is poignant for its still apparent longing for her lost love. More significant for those familiar with only Jack's side of the story as reflected in his letters to her is the admission that she was equally impassioned and wanted to marry him. This preoccupation with Jack London forty years after their involvement matched with Charmian's similar reliving of her marriage to all who wished to listen.

Anna stayed at the ranch in 1943 when she visited the Bay Area for the first time in thirty-nine years. She arrived just after the launching of a Liberty Ship named in Jack's honor, and stayed both in San Francisco and on the ranch for several month, attending a New Year's party with Charmian. There are stories, perhaps apocryphal, that when the two women met after his death, the conversation included the exchange: "He loved me more. . . . No he loved me more!" Anna's continued preoccupation with Jack is evident in the inscription to her *Violette of Père Lachaise,* presented "with all my love" to Charmian. Below her signature she added, "His youth did not perish in the funeral pyre, when, as ashes, he was returned to the elements—for this is the test of greatness that it lives beyond itself."[6]

What Charmian never learned from Anna was that Irving Stone had corresponded with her. During the 1940s he embarked on a biography of Eugene Debs, *Adversary in the House,* and cozied up to Anna as he had with Charmian years earlier. Anna sent him accounts of her experiences with Debs, and lent him books and copies of letters as well. Once the book appeared in 1947, Stone apologized to her for not having included information about English, but the demands of the novel form for a wide reading public required that he omit "good and valuable men."[7]

Because she lacked regular household help, and indeed did not want any, Charmian seldom had overnight guests. But she did enjoy entertaining anyone who came through the area with a hope of talking about Jack. One young woman left a recollection of such a visit. In the living room, "tapa draperies were drawn, even during the daytime, and the lighting was content to remain inside the huge, black, wooden cannibal bowls that served as chandeliers. The upholstered cushions about the sunken fireplace and raised window seats were black leather." The wooden floors were covered by a scattering of Oriental rugs and tanned skins of game animals. When the guest noted "several bouquets of long dead flowers festooned with cobwebs," Charmian explained "that she liked them better when they had passed, the colors were so subtle."[8]

Similarly, book collector George Tweney recalled how, when he visited her during the war, Charmian virtually floated into the room, dressed in a long, voluminous robe, her sparkling eyes suggesting her openness. "It was obvious to me she had been very much in love with Jack, and that she accepted her years with Jack as having been almost idyllic in nature. To what extent her memories and her feelings had conditioned down through the years, I cannot say. She was eager to show me many of Jack's books, and she brought out many pictures to lay before me, detailing first one, then another in response to my interests."[9]

New Year's Day 1940 rolled in "with good health—determined health. It's the one and only thing I have to depend on for courage." In fact, she did not have good health. The diaries suggest to even the most casual reader that all was not well. Notes and lists enclosed in boxes cross-hatch the pages, the words stroking in different directions, pages crammed with a tiny, almost indecipherable backhanded scrawl. Eventually one discerns patterns, notices that the boxes slanted vertically along the seam contain world news, while large, central, horizontal squares enclose notes of daily activities. But the overall effect is one of a desperate attempt to organize confusion. Activities are listed literally: the songs on the radio, the temperature, news headlines, practice schedules for the piano, horseback rides, minor accidents and illnesses. And of course there is the continuing list of deaths, including those of celebrities: the pianist Paderewski, comic W. C. Fields, New York mayor Fiorello La Guardia, and novelist H. G. Wells, among others. In 1943 Armine von Tempski, thirty years younger than Charmian, died unexpectedly of heart failure. One morning she opened the paper delighted to see the name of her flyer friend Alain Gerbault, only to find it was an obituary. (Gerbault had left for the South Seas in the early 1930s and was reported missing soon afterward. In fact, he had written Charmian regularly from Pago Pago, where he was "discovered" again, living in near-starvation in 1944, and soon succumbed.) Then there were the many associates from happier days—photographer Arnold Genthe, San Francisco conductor Alfred Hertz, local music critic Mason Redfern, Finn Frolich—whose passing removed favorite companions in the city. Another lifelong friend, albeit primarily by correspondence, was the actress Pauline French, who now sent indecipherable letters from a mental hospital.

Irving Shepard came by one day to say that Irving Stone was once again stirring up potential problems, likely related to the filming of Charmian's biography of Jack. She and Shepard flew to Los Angeles to settle the matter, and visited the movie set. Charmian was pleased with Susan Hayward's portrayal, and taken aback when Milo O'Shea hugged her the very same way Jack had. But Stone's influence continued, for Charmian discovered the *Encyclopedia Americana* had changed its entry to state that Jack had committed suicide.

For the most part she enjoyed what remained in her life. She continued to ride, attend literary functions and concerts, and practice piano. She finally voted for a candidate outside the Socialist ticket, picking Roosevelt in 1944.

In 1941, arterial disease was inducing ever more serious symptoms. On February 7, she recorded: "After a bad night, had a heavy morning sleep. Awful incident of helpless left hand. Quietly I meet paralyzed future and make plans. Circulation comes back to ineffectual fingers of left hand and left side of mouth after hard exercises." While the doctor told her that her problems was neuritis, that her heart was splendid, she still puzzled over the continued weakness of the left side of her body. She countered the symptoms with a new exercise regimen for herself, studied her work and eating habits, and proclaimed a new attitude of "I must be well" each day. "Having nobody TO LEAVE, no child," she returned all letters she had received from Anna, explaining that she was doing the same with all her old correspondents.[10]

One of the few people she saw, though not often, was her aunt and former guardian. In 1934 she had agreed to help Netta find a publisher for her novel *Deseret,* which was based on the Wiley family's experiences in Salt Lake City.[11] When Netta remarried in 1937, Charmian agreed after many years' separation, to meet the older woman. Only Netta could have responded that she dreaded to see Charmian, who would be so old now. She did withstand the shock, though within a year Netta was widowed again when her beloved third husband died from exposure after breaking through an icy pond during a hike on Mount Shasta. Later Netta wrote to say that she had received a "vision" advising her to absolve Charmian of any more responsibilities for her upkeep, which she did. Though spirited and healthy, Netta was effectively prevented by advancing blindness from further machinations. Charmian made her peace with the old woman, but when Netta died in 1944, Charmian was unable to finish the obituary she had planned. Bitter memories of Netta's collaboration with Irving Stone stayed her hand. Nor did she attend the funeral.

Her final years were marked by a reaching into the past, a completing of old tasks. She tried writing again, with hopes of producing at least two of the several books represented by piles of notes about her desk. One was to be her account of the *Dirigo* voyage. To refresh her memory, she sent long lists of questions to Nakata, now a dentist in Hawaii. Could he sketch their rooms on the deck? What were the mates' names? Who fed the chickens? Did the men chew tobacco? Nakata filled in her failing memory with fine details, but his assistance was fruitless, for she would never finish the book.

Even more curious was the decision to begin a new biography of Jack, starting from scratch. The remnants of that work reveal a tragic tale of the changes in her mental functioning. The notes resemble her diary: pages filled with boxes, the typescript laid out in various directions on the page. And onto a page would be pinned tiny pieces of paper, on which were pinned other, even tinier pieces of paper. One might expect the pinned notes to be all on the same topic, but they were not. The collection formed a hopeless jumble of material, proof that her organizational skills, never strong to begin with, had virtually deteriorated. It was difficult enough for her to scribble labels on an anecdote—"Childhood," "Mate and Me"—let alone link related items. Nevertheless, she sat at her desk day after day, struggling to reconstruct the puzzle, but it was like asking herself to translate a passage from French, a language once known but now long forgotten.

Final proof of her loss of editorial skills is found in her last published work, a short essay prepared for *Redwood Empire Woman,* a monthly magazine produced by the Sonoma County Branch of the League of American Pen Women. Charmian had been an organizing member of the group, frequently hosted its meetings, and provided much encouragement to local women writers. As this one paragraph from the five making up the work testifies, the essay was a sad burlesque of her earlier writing, fraught with trite expressions and quaint figures of speech:

> Alone, now I look back upon further travels among proud empires seemingly, alas, being crumpled; places of rare beauty, rare romance. And ever, homing, I compare them with this magnificent Redwood Empire of our own—of which my exquisite acres are a portion. When in foreign parts, I lay their loveliness against My Mountain scenery and realize there is nothing to surpass it—never does it suffer by comparison with Valley of the Moon and whole majestic Redwood Empire of an unparalleled and beloved Californian region. Blest are we who claim it all as our own heart's privileged! It is a veritable Mecca for thousands of undisappointed wayfarers, who often use the word "privilege" when they set foot in it, and yearn for it ever afterward!

However difficult the struggle to prepare a few crude paragraphs for publication, the diaries she maintained with ease. "This is my 26 cents Woolworth diary. Diaries are fun." And so they seemed, for she could enter successes along with disappointments. At seventy she went out to cut a foot-thick redwood tree by herself, earning a satisfaction that kept her glowing for days. At seventy-one she attended a costume ball at the Fairmont Hotel, taking her turns around the floor as often as possible. At seventy-two she continued to ride her horses, falling off with regularity, though not enough to stop her. (And she worried about gaining weight: "106 pounds stripped—more than I can remember in years. Clothes are tight.") On her seventy-third birthday, "feeling almost as much. It's comically absurd, me, with this body and spirit." She spent New Year's 1944 on the couch, writing to a friend in England, surprised when "I Want to Be Happy" ran through her mind just as the Crosby Bobcats took up the tune on the radio.

Despite her failing health, during the early 1940s Charmian consulted on several films, in each case inviting the stars and crew to the ranch to acquaint themselves with the original atmosphere, to show them photographs or writings that might help them in their production. Columbia made *The Adventure of Martin Eden,* starring Glenn Ford and Evelyn Keyes (changing the plot to follow instead another book of Jack's, *The Mutiny of the Elsinore).* Monogram distributed *Alaska,* based on the short story "The Flush of Gold." And Warner Brothers produced *The Sea Wolf,* unquestionably the masterpiece of the London genre films, directed by Michael Curtiz and starring Edward G. Robinson as the most vivid and convincing Wolf Larsen of the many to be represented on the screen before or since. Charmian met a wide range of Hollywood celebrities during these years but was never starstruck. What mattered to her was that the directors and actors do well by Jack; they were to be lackeys in his service. As for other noted people who visited the ranch—national and international figures in various fields—she did not often deem their appearance worth a mention in her diary.

More than anything else, she concerned herself with the world turmoil. Page after page of events swirl by in her diary: "I hate to think of the Nazis so close to Russian oil in Caucasus. Ghastly prospect in France. Laval will work with Hitler . . . Winter strikes Japs in Aleutians . . . Women as a group are capable of serving on federal juries. And nation-wide movement—some states are still in medievalism . . . Deportation from France of 70,000 Jews by French (?) Government."

In 1944 Joan sought out Charmian once more, writing, "It's a mad world, and growing madder, and good things are becoming more and more precious."[12] She visited the ranch, and encouraged Bart and Lee to accept Charmian's invitation to stay for several days.[13] Lee found Charmian "a rather frail little woman" who explained that they would have to fend for themselves during their stay. Lee went into the kitchen, which was well equipped and well stocked, and made dinner. She described Charmian as "gay, funny, and a good conversationalist," who still focused her life on Jack, preserving his desk, books, and papers as though he were still around to work. Jack's clothes hung in the closet alongside the array of artful handmade gowns and dresses Charmian had been saving since adolescence.

One afternoon while Charmian napped, Lee and Bart poked around the house. They discovered two guests rooms still in the final stages of construction on the first floor. A secret stairwell took them up to a tiny kitchen and pantry next to Charmian's enormous bedroom, which covered most of that floor. A luxurious bed and a Greek-style chair sat at one end, with her grand piano at the other. Though used to luxury, Lee had never seen so dramatic or romantic a room. Charmian wrote Anna how delighted she was to have the couple's company, "so wrapped up in each other."[14]

Charmian welcomed the reunion with Joan, and offered her some grass mats from the South Seas to help furnish her latest home in Berkeley. Plans to visit Joan were curtailed after Charmian had a bad fall in the bath. Joan offered sympathy and concern that Charmian's letter following the accident did not sound like her old self: "Too tired, too lonely. And maybe a good talk and a lot of laughter would be a tonic," Joan suggested.[15]

Joan too was lonely, but in the midst of a crowd, for she had turned her place into a salon for Berkeley leftists. On evenings and weekends after work at the labor federation she welcomed people for educational meetings, informal intellectual discussions, and general festivity. The late 1930s had brought a major breach among socialists, who clashed over whether to support the Soviets, who, however degenerate, deserved backing against capitalist nations, and those who saw nothing in Russia worth defending, particularly since news of the purge trials. The latter group, a small minority, were cursed as "Hitlero-Trotskyites," primarily intellectuals who defied the party's calumny. Joan attracted many of these, such as Sidney Hook, Mary McCarthy, Irving Howe, Dwight MacDonald, and others who would become major social critics. Frequent guest Stan Weir recalled Joan as very nurturing, always introducing people to one another and making a haven for leftist castaways.

Among those who joined in the meetings was, surprisingly, Becky, who "comes faithfully to all educationals and public meetings," Joan informed Bart.[16] One participant recalled how, not being well read in political theory, Becky was exploited by some of the others. Her daring to attend Joan's meetings hints at a much deeper unhappiness in Becky, for she had always defined herself in contrast to her older sister and been defiantly unconcerned with political and social issues. Unlike Bart, Becky's children, now almost adults, were not particularly close to their mother. Yet even with the war encouraging women's independence, Becky remained tied to the man she now despised.

Joan lived in a brown shingle house with a cottage in back. She was "picking

comrades out of my hair," joking that she would have to move into the basement since her home had become the party headquarters.[17] In fact, with the inflation that followed the end of the war, she realized she could no longer afford
the upkeep of her home, which often housed self-invited guests from the
movement. Familiar with the latest economic data as part of her job, she reminded Bart that the cost of living since 1941 had gone up 83 percent in San
Francisco, and these statistics were notoriously low. Her monthly commutation
book now cost $8.50, up from $2. When Bart's union went on strike, she apologized for being unable to help him out. She finally decided to move into the
cottage, where she would have more privacy and time to write, and rent out the
main house.

Although she evicted several people, one remained, a young man attending
Berkeley on the GI Bill. She let him live with her rent-free and cooked his meals.
Soon she found herself once again in a relationship haunted by domestic violence. Although Park and Barney had beaten her, in neither case were the as-
saults a typical occurrence. Her new boyfriend, however, was so brutal that
friends worried for her safety.

Following an operation in 1945, Charmian amused everyone with her determination to keep the rails on the bed down. But it was a most serious matter to her
to be treated like an adult. As usual, she turned her pain into an adventure, another kind of experience, by tracing its effects on her mind in her journal. For
almost a year she stayed bedridden, living with Irving and Mildred Shepard so
they could care for her during her recuperation. Her shaky diary scrawl betrayed that her tiring body was dying. She mistakenly wrote "Death of My Man"
on November sixteenth, not the twenty-second. Strange misspellings material-
ized: "My mate would have clased [clasped] me in one arm and with the other
hold the letter of Gody's [Godey's] Lalies [Ladies] magagin [magazine] editor
and promised to publish her stuff. The dear think [thing] must have been
among the treasures left by my dainty Lady Aunt Ninetta Eames and other
names—that one of the tiny three sisters of whom I was the daughter [indeci-
pherable word] of Dayelle Wiley, wife of my gallant father "Kit" [Kitt] from his
surname Kittredge."[18] Nevertheless, once recovered she continued to attend
PEN meetings in the city, her only trips away from home now.

Gradually the diaries and letters chart the loss of long-cherished activities.
When the War Writers' Board asked her to prepare something for them, she
declined. "I must conserve my energies, which are low, and under the threat
(which I pray is not too serious) of renewed attacks of the rather terrifying sudden paralysis of nerve force. I feel that I *must* not undergo this again." Still she
offered to write something, so long as it did not involve her experiences with

Jack, a topic that "took so much" out of her. Next to go was the riding. "Horses in my mind all the sleepless night. Am I, Charmian, *through*?" Her hands became shakier. "Practice piano in evening. Begins to show. Wonder where the pianist is."[19]

The diaries increasingly recalled episodes from the past, of the time when, as a nine-year-old at her aunt Carrie's ranch, she first rode the old workhorse, of Edward Payne and his discourses on life, of her favorite horse, Hilo, and the feel of his energy between her legs. And, more than anything, of Jack. "I think of Jack London so often. If he were, 'What did I tell you, Mate Woman?' he'd say if he were here. 'Come here, I want to kiss you again.'"[20]

And then the diaries stopped—though not Charmian.

In 1947 life ended for Bess Maddern London, a saving grace after years of being able to do little beyond make the slightest facial gestures from bed. Even through that terrible ordeal she conveyed warmth and composure to visitors, who wondered how she could cope with the loss of so many functions. Her brief obituary recognized her primarily as Jack's widow.

The funeral became the focus for a conflict between Becky and her daughter Jean. Now a young woman, Jean so resembled her mother at that age that pictures of the two in their early twenties could be confused.[21] By then Jean knew the truth of her parentage, but had learned of it from Percy, who was frustrated by Becky's treatment of her teenage daughter. When the funeral arrangements were complete, Becky told Jean not to attend, apparently out of fear that others would see the obvious resemblance between the two and realize their relationship.

Becky's shame was felt as well by Jean, for it would be the 1970s before a child born out of wedlock did not also bear social opprobrium along with the mother. For most of Jean's lifetime, she would know secretly that she was a "bastard," and even kept the truth from her own sons. Forced into complicity, she kept from them as well their blood legacy from Jack London. (The sons guessed the truth eventually, partly as a result of their acquaintance with Bart's children, who knew the facts and hinted at them.) The societal censure was so severe during those decades, though, that Becky and Jean could not have a satisfying mother-daughter relationship.

In 1947 Joan was in an auto accident that severely crushed her facial bones. Despite plastic surgery, her appearance was changed significantly. Very likely she had been drinking when she crashed the car, and afterward she never drove again—but she didn't need to, for by now she had a permanent chauffeur.

She had finally evicted her abusive student lover. Never comfortable living alone, Joan married once again in 1948, this time to Charlie Miller, her boyfriend from her teenage years. Miller had spent most of his adult life in an Ohio asylum following his emotional breakdown in World War I. Upon his release, he made his way back to the Bay Area, somehow located Joan, and persuaded her to marry him. Miller, who had become a stonemason white at the institution, was a passive, agreeable man, happy to wait on Joan. They moved over the mountain from Berkeley to Pleasant Hill, where they bought a ranch house with a large yard, where Joan would spend hours on weekends gardening.

Meanwhile, Bart's marriage had collapsed. Lee took her two daughters back to her parents' home, where she was relieved to tuck them in under percale sheets and otherwise enjoy the comforts she had known as a child. Although the breakup was rancorous, each partner soon remarried: Bart to Helen Dalzell, a divorcée with three children, and Lee to her divorce lawyer. Throughout, Joan remained supportive of everyone, maintaining a steady correspondence with her former daughter-in-law while welcoming her new one. She enjoyed domestic activities in her free time, sewing clothes for her family, cooking for guests, and caring for her constant crowd of dogs and cats. One cat was unable to walk, but she refused to put it down. Joan was always able to nurture more readily than accept nurture.

With the rise of the cold war, Joan's Trotskyite activities made her suspect. Union leaders came under particular scrutiny by Red-baiters, and Joan did not want to compromise her colleagues at the labor federation. Her tactic, in the words of one associate, was "silencio," a careful monitoring of her speech and activities.

In fact, the FBI had been watching her for several years, noting such "subversive" acts as being on the mailing list of the Industrial Workers of the World, writing the governor a letter in support of a Workers' Defense League case, contributing to civil rights groups, and performing in a play called *The Judge Saw Red*. In 1947 the monitoring increased. Joan's file would extend to over three hundred pages, most covering her activities as financial director of the Bay Area branches of the Workers' Party and International Socialist League between 1947 and 1951.[22] Interestingly, one person who provided some information on Joan was Charles Malamuth, now firmly in the anti-Soviet camp.

An FBI mole had infiltrated the party, whose regular meetings seldom attracted more than a dozen individuals. That meant the informant was someone highly trusted and well known to Joan and her comrades, who sometimes included Bart. That agent's reports were highly detailed minutes, describing individuals' expressed beliefs along with organizational finances and plans, such as a rummage sale to raise money. As an anti-Stalinist group, it had no support from the Soviets and was at best a collection of optimistic, idealistic revolutionaries with no resources to effect change. Joan, like the others, hoped that Stalin would fall and Russia experience a true socialist revolution, which then would set the stage for increased activity in the United States. Where the group was more effective was in local issues, supporting strikers, joining in national union lobbying (such as attempting to defeat Walter Reuther as president of the CIO), and backing local black leaders in civil rights matters. But much of their effort was distracted by theoretical concerns and paranoid fears that Stalinists would infiltrate them and the groups they backed.

In 1952 Joan expressed "silencio" in action as well as at work. She decided that her involvement was too threatening to the California Labor Federation and her colleagues there, that she did not want to be the cause of attracting Red scare proponents any further. Consequently, she went on inactive status from the party, though did not change her opinions or commitments to socialist revolution where the workers controlled production and profit.

Her withdrawal may also have been out of concern for Bart and his family. He and Helen had three more daughters, one named Chaney in honor of her paternal great-grandfather. Like his grandfather, Bart developed alcoholism, and after a diagnosis of narcolepsy went on permanent disability. After that, he and Helen expanded their bohemian lifestyle, which would include communal farming, as well as long stays in Mexico and Hawaii, where expenses were low. During periods in California, they too were under FBI surveillance. Helen became accustomed to the sudden appearance of agents at her door, demanding information on her mother-in-law, well after Joan's withdrawal from the Trotskyite groups. Throughout, Bart retained his very close relationship with his mother, who continued to encourage and nurture him from long distance.

Thanks to Park Abbott, the family acquired a retreat that would become a place for reunion and restoration. At the end of the war, two large ranches in Yosemite Park were in the hands of the county, which decided to auction off parcels of the land to relieve it of responsibility. Park was now a contractor and major leader in the Berkeley cooperative movement, which was seeking ways to put ownership of businesses and living spaces in the control of volunteer groups. He saw the auction as an opportunity for his politically committed friends, many of whom brought in only modest incomes, to develop their own recreational retreat. The bidding, which started at five dollars a lot, was apparently not well publicized. Consequently, Park's network of friends, which included Joan and Charles Miller, bought most of the lots at rock-bottom prices.

Foresta, as the community became known, offered all the benefits of Yosemite with the addition of privacy. It perched high above the valley floor, with Half Dome rising in the distance, and was close to the main road leading down. The land was heavily forested, with a stream running through the center of the settlement, which formed cascades and pools as it tumbled down the mountainside. Miller used his stonemason skills to build a massive hearth, the centerpiece of the cabin he and Bart built. Park built his family a home on a knoll across the creek.

By this time Joan's feelings toward Charmian and the Shepards had hardened. She had described Charmian in *Jack London and His Times* as "largely misunderstood," someone who deserved neither the credit nor the blame for much that had happened to Jack London. She was "a woman of average intelligence and more than ordinary courage" who had the ability "to adapt herself goodnaturedly to unpleasant circumstances." Joan acknowledged Charmian's talents, her conversational acumen, her popularity. Always the historian, Joan noted how, being a breaker of traditions, Charmian would draw detractors, yet overall she had managed "to achieve extraordinary freedom without being socially ostracized." Most significant, she had done a better job of being Jack London's wife than anyone would have expected. By the 1950s, though, Joan was describing Charmian as vain, childish, inane.

Part of Joan's turnabout may have been the result of reflecting on her own failures in life. As she explained to Bart, she developed a sense of rage one day upon recalling "the countless, intelligent efforts I had made to accomplish things—which got nowhere—while constantly mediocre talents were receiving recognition and remuneration." She named popular books she had thrown into the fire. Adding to her anger, she heard that *The Star Rover* was being made into a motion picture "and thought of all that money going up to Glen Ellen."[23]

On January 12, 1953, Joan and Becky appeared together in public for the first of what would be many events honoring their father. The California Historical Society unveiled a plaque at the branch of the American Trust Company on Third and Brannan Streets in San Francisco to commemorate their father's birthplace. The original house had been destroyed in the 1906 earthquake and fire. That they were present, and not Charmian, marked the passing of an era.

Shortly before his death Jack had told a reporter, "I would rather that my spark should burn out in a brilliant blaze than that it should be stifled by dry rot. I would rather be a superb meteor, every atom of me in a magnificent glow, than a sleepy and permanent plant."[24] And so he was, though unlike a meteor, he seemed intent on leaving behind considerable evidence of his passage: through his fiction, his ranch and his agricultural innovations, his socialist writings, and the word-of-mouth tales of his adventures. It was Charmian who would be satisfied to live for the moment, to leave in the end only ashes.

She had once told a friend she wished never to die "by inches." Her wish was not granted. By 1950 senility left her unable to care for herself. She could still tell stories of her life with Jack, and even in advanced age retained her appealing charm. The Shepards devotedly saw to her care. While they respected her independence, her determination to live alone in her house, they ensured that family members and friends stopped in regularly to see that she was well, or to drive her to the beauty shop. She loved to be taken with several other older women to Vella's ice cream parlor or the Sebastiani movie house in Sonoma. Anna Strunsky still wrote, but all the others from Charmian's life with Jack had passed away or were too feeble to communicate.

One day in 1953 Irving Shepard entered Happy Walls and found Charmian on the kitchen floor, her hips broken from a fall. The Shepards moved her back into the cottage where she had lived with Jack, for it was just across the field in sight of their own home. The nurses who came in did not always have an easy time with her, for the spirit that had caused Charmian at seventy-five to throw down the rails of her bed remained at eighty-two, and she would not be babied or cajoled.

Physically she remained in excellent health, even better than in her seventies, the chronic ailments and frequent colds having given up their siege. Mentally, while she could manage the logic of a specific situation, her poor memory confused her sense of time. At lunch one day she looked up at Mildred Shepard and very politely inquired, "And who are you?" Knowing that Charmian's lapse was momentary, Mildred simply answered, "Why I'm Irving's wife—you know me."[25] The one person Charmian always recognized was Irving, so she quickly made the comparison and beamed back at Mildred.

Hearing of Charmian's decline, Joan, Bart, and his family went to visit Charmian, aware that it would be for the last time. When they arrived at her door, Irving Shepard refused them entry, so they were not able to make a farewell. By now neither he nor Joan regarded the other fondly. She may have appeared to him too ready to exploit Charmian, while in Joan's mind he was an interloper enjoying the legacy she and Becky deserved. His rejection on this occasion was not necessarily personal, however, because he kept others from disturbing Charmian as well.

One day in January 1955 Charmian's nurse called Irving to the house. Charmian was being unusually obstreperous and uncontrollable over her evening meal. Irving had always been able to calm her down during these excitable periods, so he went, mollified her, and returned to his late dinner, only to be called again. Patiently he returned to calm her, then again a third time. Entering his home after this last visit, he told Mildred that Charmian had just died, presumably of heart failure. Later they realized that her state of anxiety had likely resulted from her fighting for oxygen those final hours.

They sent her body to Santa Rosa for cremation. Charmian had not wanted any fuss, so Mildred made certain that their minister conducted the simple, brief ceremony she would have found in good taste. Then the family took her ashes and placed them, as Charmian had requested, into an unmarked grave on the ranch, under the large volcanic rock that covered Jack's urn.

The brief obituary in the January 15 *New York Times* mentioned the things that had mattered most to her so far as her public reputation was concerned: her tie to her mother as a writer, her adventures with Jack, her work on his behalf after his death, and her House of Happy Walls. A more personal memorial in the local Sonoma paper added the loss over which devoted friends would grieve, "the charm of Charmian, her engaging smile, her splendid intellect, the eternal light she gave to Jack London."[26]

Several years before her death, Charmian signed an agreement to sell the bulk of the remaining Jack London materials on the ranch to the Huntington Library. The eight thousand items included personal letters, small manuscripts, notes, and other material. The library was also given full rights to grant access to any and all Jack and Charmian London manuscripts and correspondence, with the understanding that property rights and copyrights would remain in the family. Thus any publication of copyrighted materials had to be cleared with Irving Shepard. In 1959 Shepard sold to the Huntington Library Jack London's personal library of over five thousand books and pamphlets, along with the Cloudesley Johns correspondence so critical to appreciating London's formative period as a writer. Because the most prominent London scholar at the time was King Hendricks, Shepard donated a large quantity of London-related material to his university, Utah State. Much of this consisted of carbon copies of correspondence already in the Huntington, along with much original material relating to Charmian and Eliza, including Charmian's private library.

During the 1950s Anna also accepted the role of distributing valuable historical materials in her hands to safer keeping. In 1953 she sold 155 of Jack's letters to the Huntington for $1,500. She distributed English's papers to several locations, including the State Historical Society of Wisconsin and Yale University. Other of her own private papers would end up at the Bancroft Library at Berkeley, the Huntington, and Yale. (That distribution would make research on the Wallings comparatively difficult since the sources were so widely separated.) She sent off the notes on her Russian trip to a Moscow scholar, Vil Bykov. As young scholars became interested in the period of her youth, she welcomed interviews, so long as they were not personal. She had been fortunate to have known noted people of her day and was gracious in sharing her recollections.

Anna's final public appearance as a close friend of Jack London's was in 1960, when she visited Glen Ellen for the last time. In 1959 Irving and Mildred Shepard gift-deeded land, incorporating the House of Happy Walls, the Wolf House ruins, and Jack and Charmian's burial spot to the state of California. This was done partly to fulfill a codicil Charmian had added to her 1938 will: "In case of my death, it is my wish that my home, 'House of Happy Walls' is not to be lived in by anyone except a caretaker. This building & its arrangements are peculiarly an expression of myself and its ultimate purpose is that of museum to Jack London & myself. It can be used for the purpose of revenue." The next year the Sonoma Valley Chamber of Congress agreed that it should work toward the establishment of a state park on the ranch. At first, state officials were cool to Shepard's offer, but the legislature welcomed his gift and authorized the park.

Shepard provided "one of the biggest bargains in the history of park property acquisition," announced the *Santa Rosa Press Democrat,* yet the state listed the value of the fifteen acres as $150.[27] Shepard also offered gratis to Sonoma County five and a half acres over a mile-long right-of-way through his ranch so that the public could reach the parkland. In addition, he contributed personal furniture, artifacts, and clothes from Jack and Charmian's cottage to place in Happy Walls. When the state asked for more than fifteen acres so as to have a more convenient footprint, Shepard added some of the ranchlands as well. Finally, he negotiated a role as unpaid consultant on the exhibits so that Jack London would be portrayed accurately and respectfully.

On September 24, 1960, a rare reunion of Shepard and London kin met during the dedication ceremonies. So many people arrived that the mile-and-a-half road up from Glen Ellen was filled with parked cars. Irving and Mildred Shepard beamed as the plaque on the front of the partially completed museum was unveiled. Though the temperature reached one hundred degrees, visitors stayed to hear Anna Strunsky speak at length of her relationship with Jack. Despite Anna's being in her ninth decade, her voice remained strong and her delivery dramatic. Joan was introduced to the crowd's applause as well.

Joan's family was there with her. While socializing afterward, Mildred Shepard pulled one of Bart's daughters aside, put an arm around her, opened the other out wide over the landscape, and said, "All this is your heritage. Why don't your people every bring you up here?"[28] It was a kind gesture, well meant and accepted as such. Nonetheless, it would be many years before Bart's children would begin to understand this inheritance. In meeting Anna, who impressed them with her graciousness and intelligence, they began to understand more about their great-grandfather, apart from their grandmother's conflicted experience.

Just as Charmian had outlived virtually all her friends and relatives, so did Anna. Her dear companion Leonard Abbott died in 1953. By 1957 she had survived all of her brothers. In 1963 came what was likely the worst loss, that of her sister Rose, who had been her lifelong support and confidante. On February 26, 1964, Anna's daughter, also named Anna, went to her mother's apartment and found her dead on the floor. She was surrounded by her notes about Jack London.

# 18

# Jack London Had Two Daughters

FOR JOAN, RETIREMENT IN 1962 meant neither rest nor recreation but a manic flurry of writing projects shaped around three very different topics. The first was a collaboration with a fellow labor advocate, Henry Anderson. At that time, agribusiness influence in government cast anyone working on behalf of the farmworkers as "radical." A sociologist who added public health to his professional training, Anderson had suffered from the long reach of corporate power as an instructor at the University of California at Berkeley. In the late 1950s he received a grant from the U.S. Public Health Service to study folk medicine among the Mexican farmworkers, and in the process realized how badly this labor force was being treated. Although he was not an activist then, outside pressures led university administrators to order him to abandon the project, after which they destroyed his eight hundred–page report.

Having become persona non grata at Berkeley, Anderson assumed a more political stance and accepted a position as director of research with the Agricultural Workers' Organizing Committee for the AFL/CIO. He came to know Joan from his visits to the library at the California Labor Federation. After leaving the research job in 1962, he helped form Citizens for Farm Labor as a means of expanding the base of support for the pickers.

Anderson was immediately impressed with Joan. Although she was not very vocal during discussions, perhaps because she was so much older than most other members, he found her one of the best participants. She never missed a meeting, served on the executive committee, and helped research and compose testimony. Because of her experience, Anderson invited her to collaborate on a history of the farmworkers' organizing attempts. Their proposal brought a contract from Thomas Crowell Publishers, and they set to work on *So Shall Ye Reap*.

Joan used the minor fame attached to her father to speak out on behalf of labor in general and farmworkers in particular. In one talk she reviewed her father's stance against "injustice, oppression, grinding poverty in a rich land."[1] In another she recounted his rebuke of the ranch owners and deputies responsible for murder in the infamous Wheatland Hops riots of 1913, and argued that his socialist writings retained immediacy fifty years later.[2] She reviewed the history of exploitation of farm labor, with its abuse of the most helpless or disenfranchised in society—Chinese, Japanese, Mexicans, children, women, prisoners, reform school inmates, Filipinos, Dust Bowl Okies, braceros. In addition to being excluded from social security and the Fair Labor Standards Act, farmworkers had little disability protection, and many regulations were not enforced in the fields. Sanitation facilities were absent, and housing, when available, consisted of shacks. Child workers were kept out of school. Joan described recent examples of sheriffs roaming fields with shotguns, billy clubs, and sidearms in an attempt to provoke violence and further stir anti-union sympathies. Always careful to back herself up with statistics, Joan noted that a head of lettuce in the 1960s cost one cent to pick while selling for twenty-three cents, and cited a nine-year-old laborer whose foot had been crushed by a cattle feeder.

Although Joan's passion came out in her speeches, she ran into disagreements with Hank Anderson regarding the tone of their book. She agreed with their editor that in order to appeal to their major market, the East Coast liberals, they should not be too sentimental or portray an "angel theory of farm workers," nor should they present an anti-grower, anti-government diatribe. Here her father's influence is evident, for London's most powerful social writings, such as in *The People of the Abyss,* rely on facts to make their argument. Anderson was confused, for he thought they had agreed to avoid that approach, influenced by John Steinbeck's documentary chapters in *The Grapes of Wrath.* Eventually he came around to her view.

More affecting the delays and disagreements was their method of working. Since both were used to being independent researchers, Joan and Hank divided the labor so that she would concentrate on the social history of the movement, while he would craft biographical sections on key leaders at each stage. Thus they had few meetings, but depended instead on exchange of materials and comments by mail. Upon reading the first draft, their editor expressed disappointment over the split in tone and style, whereby the historical material was more impassioned, staking out clear positions against child labor and the bracero program, while the biographies were more interesting but also more diffuse in focus. Joan cut Hank's biographies in half, while Hank reduced much of her social history, despite assurances that they had the utmost trust in each other. They further frustrated their publishers by not meeting their deadlines, partly because of all the changes that were occurring contemporaneously in the farm labor movement.

Despite their disagreements, they were clear about their primary purpose: to produce a history of the farmworker movement based on meticulous research yet written in a style that was straightforward and avoided professional jargon. In accord with Joan's belief that they must not extol a true believer view, they criticized some in the union movement along with the growers who prevented unionization from taking hold in the fields. Furthermore, they demonstrated that César Chavez was successful in leading the farmworkers not only on the basis of his charisma but also as a result of his having emerged from the ranks. They focused as well on those from an earlier era who deserved recognition for laying the foundation. These included Father Thomas McCullouch, grower Fred Van Dyke, and economist and organizer Ernesto Galarza. Chavez, they argued, had capitalized on workers' knowledge of these earlier activists and the battles they had led. Interweaving these personal stories with the larger history provided an inviting tale for non-specialists.

Besides working on *So Shall Ye Reap*, Joan began two more personal manuscripts. The first was a book about her grandfather William Henry Chaney. Envisioning a biography of him as a pioneer astrologer, she contacted Gavin Arthur, a nationally known astrologer in San Francisco, to collaborate on or at least write an introduction to her work. Joan complained to her friend Dale Walker of the various biographers' misrepresentation of Chaney as an "itinerant astrologer."[3] The portrait was one of fecklessness and irresponsibility, when in fact Chaney had lived during a time of great mobility. Placed in context, Joan asserted, Chaney was "like many Americans of his time, who sought more favorable environments for their hopes and ambitions . . . when the frontier was moving swiftly to the west and southwest, industry was growing by leaps and bounds, the status of Jefferson's 'common man' was diminishing, the schism between haves and have-nots was widening, and the rapid development of railroad lines made long journeys possible and not prohibitively expensive."[4] Furthermore, from interviewing specialists she realized that Chaney's astrology originated in his study of astronomy. He became known among devotees as the father of modern American astrology for his writing and publishing of ephemera and guides.

Joan's notes for this project demonstrate the depth and thoroughness of her historical research. She read key histories, such as Charles Beard's *American Party Battle*, Harold Laski's *American Democracy*, and James Connolly's *American Fishermen*, along with scholarly articles on the history of Maine, maritime technology, and nineteenth-century religion. She developed a file of "mistaken ideas about Chaney" in published sources. She created a multicolored chart of national elections between 1848 and 1860 to clarify for herself the political parties and key events during this rapidly deteriorating time for the nation. She developed a chronology of political protest parties between 1872 and 1901. Most difficult was tracking down copies of Chaney's publications, which, apart from his *Common Sense* articles, were not in libraries. Throughout she used precise questions to guide her reading. "Why did he decide to study law? What drew him successively to the Whig, Democratic, and Native American (Know-Nothing) parties. It's exasperating but fun, nonetheless."[5]

She prepared an article for *American Book Collector*, "W. H. Chaney: A Reappraisal," that hints at how she intended to restore the reputation of the man, considered "a charlatan and something of a crackpot," but for whom her father should have felt no shame. To achieve this, though, she stretched her interpretation to present Chaney's life as the story of a troubled youth turned genius. She excused his rejection of his probable son as the result of his confusing "sterility" with "impotence," and thus believing that he was incapable of fathering a child. Though acknowledging the man's prickly personality, she pressed her evidence toward the conclusion that Chaney's peripatetic life moved "in that mainstream of nineteenth-century American idealism best recognized today by the names of his three contemporaries: Emerson, Thoreau, and Whitman." Here, in reappraising the man, she went too far, but her intention was to defend her father's reputation. No longer would he be known as the bastard child of a ne'er-do-well crank.

Joan's third project was an account of her early life in relation to her famous father, a book she had planned to write since early adulthood. The impetus to complete this work came from a collection of new associates. During the 1960s she had been "rediscovered" as a result of revived scholarly interest in London. Consequently, many lay and academic researchers contacted her for information and reminiscences, and in the process engaged her in a reevaluation of her father. Though most of these people esteemed her and became friends, several took advantage.

Two Bay Area residents became frequent visitors as well as research assistants. Tony Bubka was a labor historian interested in London's socialism and his support of the working class. His friend Jim Sisson was a retired English professor who spent his days retrieving London's more obscure writings, such as his poetry, plays, and earliest compositions, toward developing a comprehensive bibliography. Sisson's retirement had been forced upon him when a rare and horribly disfiguring genetic skin disorder left him without a nose and left ear, and sent him to the hospital regularly for skin graft operations. A genteel southerner, Sisson handled his frightful disability—which led some to run away from him—with grace. To associates, he was known as cultured and articulate, with a wry sense of humor and unending kindness. Self-imprisoned in libraries, he became among a handful of London scholars, known for his meticulous attention to both detail and reasoned interpretation. Sisson and Bubka shared their latest research with Joan, as well as providing a sounding board for her ideas.

Especially pleasing to her was Bubka's discovery of new evidence of London's social commitments later in life. For example, he located a letter of Jack's printed in the *Miner's Magazine* of 1913 that stated, "If opposing the burning of Negroes at the stake is harmful to Socialism, then Socialism . . . ought to be destroyed." He also did extensive research on London's "Definition of a Scab," which was being used in the publications of the farmworkers' movement. Similarly, he located Jack's response to the Wheatland Hops riots of 1913, where he argued that the violence had been perpetrated not by the workers but by the employers and the state. Interestingly, Joan would claim she had read this piece when it first appeared, as though this article had been the source of her politicization. This provided a moving rhetorical effect, but it was similar to what her father had done in his writing: doctoring a real situation with fictional elements.

Approaching her with a very different scholarly topic was Eugene Lasartemay, co-founder and longtime president of the East Bay Negro Historical Society. Having lived and studied East Bay African American history for decades, Lasartemay was familiar with oral accounts of Jennie Prentiss's life and her influence on Jack London. He had traced the family history of Jennie and Alonzo through official records and interviewed those whose families were close to her. In the process, he became convinced that her place in London's history deserved more prominence, and sought assistance from Joan for his project. A supporter of civil rights causes since the 1930s, Joan needed no convincing to share her memories of Jennie with him. She also agreed that the Jack London State Historic Park should include a portrait or photo of Jennie in its museum display, an addition that took some years of lobbying on Lasartemay's part to accomplish.

Others developed epistolary relationships. Al Shivers was a young literary scholar who had written a dissertation on London, and in the process became dubious of Irving Stone's claim that Jack killed himself with an overdose of morphine. Joan wrote to him that her father was on a suicidal path "whether his death was from uremic poisoning or an accidental or intentional overdose of morphine."[6] Despite Dr. Porter's insistence that the death was natural, she believed that the doctors had lied on the death certificate to prevent loss of Jack's life insurance.

Despite her resistance, Shivers became convinced on scientific grounds that Jack's death was not a suicide. His questions forced her to face her biases, including the fact that she had never read the death certificate. Furthermore, she found evidence among her own notes, such as prescriptions of her father's, that supported Shivers's claim. Through his experience as a pharmacist, and assisted by Joan's information, Shivers published a convincing argument. After Joan read his essay, she came to accept his conclusions, writing him, "That is [sic] makes me personally glad that he did not take his own life goes without saying."[7]

One person she wrote concerning her change of heart regarding her father's death was Hensley Woodbridge, a Spanish professor at Southern Illinois University who became fascinated with London and was in the process of cataloguing everything that Jack wrote or had been written about him. Woodbridge and Shivers both kept Joan apprised of various machinations in the "London industry"—the growing number of critics and biographers making major career investments in studying the man. To further that scholarship, Woodbridge singlehandedly undertook what would become the most important outlet for the revival, the *Jack London Newsletter,* which published influential scholarly articles.

A common topic among all these men was the role of Irving Shepard in discouraging or preventing scholarship. Anyone requesting permission to quote from London's unpublished writings was asked to share the proceeds of any work. Joan learned of this from her childhood friend Franklin Walker, now a noted scholar of California history, who had attempted a literary biography, with Shepard's approval, during the 1950s. After considerable research, when Walker sought permission from Shepard, he was required to sign an agreement handing over half the royalties. Woodbridge wondered how someone who had not done half the work, with all the investment of money that required, could demand half the profits. Walker never completed his work, but instead published *Jack London in the Klondike.* Woodbridge heard through the grapevine that Walker had finally obtained permission to publish his study provided he mention nothing about London's paternity. Indeed, the book begins by quoting London's fallacious claim that his "father was Pennsylvania-born, a soldier, scout," in other words, John London. And his foreword notes that no manuscript material used in the book could be quoted elsewhere without permission of Irving Shepard, a curious warning given that "fair use" policy under copyright law allows scholars use of brief quotes once the manuscript material appears in print.

Unlike Walker, writer Richard O'Connor could not even obtain permission to view the archives at the Huntington Library. Woodbridge knew O'Connor, and had interceded on his behalf with Irving Shepard, who apparently was planning to republish Charmian's biography and did not want any competition. A freelance biographer with a bent for social history, O'Connor consequently found himself forced to resort to the unreliable work of Irving Stone and Rose Wilder Lane, along with often inaccurate news and magazine articles from London's time. Given O'Connor's understanding of the Progressive Era, his *Jack London* was a more subtle and perceptive look at London than the work of earlier writers, yet he was hampered by the sensational and often invalid material in his sources. In response to his book, Jim Sisson compiled a lengthy list of errata, which, however, was never published.

Joan chastised O'Connor for writing the kind of biography that emphasizes "the unlovely aspects of the subject's life" to the point where they overshadow the accomplishments. She challenged him to produce evidence regarding her father's drinking and sexual exploits. Too much, she said, seemed based on "malicious gossip," or *John Barleycorn*, which could not be taken as fact (a point in which she erred). She admitted liking much about his book, but thought that O'Connor should have explained how her father "wrote daily winning a desperate struggle against the hidden causes."[8]

Other gossip published as fact only incensed Joan further, and led her to discuss Irving Shepard as a man driven by greed. She mocked how he had "wrung every cent possible out of my dad's literary estate, and dared to sign his name to *Jack London's Tales of Adventure*, which I cannot imagine him having written [edited]." She saved newspaper clippings, including one a friend sent by San Francisco columnist Herb Caen, which read, "Add cracks in the Iron Curtain: Irving Shepard, Jack London's nephew and heir, just rec'd his first royalty check from Hungary, where London's books have long been big sellers." That Shepard identified himself as a blood relative of London was not new to Joan, but she bristled to learn that the first major collection of London stories, a volume edited by Earle Labor of Centenary College in Louisiana, quoted Shepard to that effect. What sealed her own vows of vengeance, though, was the appearance in 1966 of *Jack London: A Bibliography*, which spoke of "not only the many editions and translations [of London], but also the motion pictures, which must have poured—and are still pouring . . . though in smaller amounts—millions into Glen Ellen for Charmian and Irving Shepard."[9]

Especially upsetting to Joan and her associates was the publication of *The Letters of Jack London*, listing as co-editors Irving Shepard and King Hendricks of Utah State University. Joan thought the one-sided presentation greatly distorted the truth, especially about her relationship with her father. Woodbridge found the editorial work, particularly the annotations, inadequate, and observed that letters to Bess London in particular neglected to provide the full context to allow readers to see beyond Jack's view of events. He complained to Joan of the many positive reviews appearing in the papers, which he attributed to the fact that the book was being assigned to reviewers ignorant about London. Thus she was pleased to learn that the *Times Literary Supplement* had commented unfavorably regarding London's letters to Bess and his daughters.

Joan's animosity toward the "other family" had become so vitriolic that even her closest friends were unaware of Charmian's earlier patronage. Joan's standard account by then, which all believed, was that Charmian had refused her permission to see her father's papers. (After Joan died, her descendants were surprised to discover the extensive correspondence that had long lain unnoticed at the Utah State University library.) Her comments about Charmian throughout the 1960s, both private and public, grew meaner; she called her childlike, a moron, a wicked witch, silly and vain. In time Joan determined to change the focus of her childhood story. Along with protesting "visiting rights only" for divorced fathers, she would add "*implicit* criticism of Charmian and Shepard . . . no accusations; just enough of the facts" to lead readers to the conclusions she wanted.[10]

When tragedy struck the Shepard family, however, Joan was too well brought up to let her personal feelings prevent an expression of sympathy. In 1965 Irving and son Jack were riding a tractor on the ranch when it overturned, killing the younger man. Mildred Shepard thanked Joan for her condolences, and told her they had been preparing Charmian's old cottage for Jack and his family when the accident occurred. Mildred also expressed dismay that a month earlier the old Frohling-Kohler winery structure, with the second story Jack had added for guests, had burned down.

In her resentment of the Shepards, whom she supposed to be wealthy beneficiaries of an estate to which she and her sister were entitled, Joan overlooked the economics of maintaining the ranch. The Shepards continued to operate the dude ranch well beyond the years of the depression simply because they needed the income to supplement their farming. London's book royalties in the States had dried up; in addition, many of the translations around the world had been published in violation of international copyright law, or in the case of the Soviet Union, in countries not signatory to that agreement. Movie sales certainly did not bring in "millions" of dollars, and in a number of cases resulted in costly litigation. The book royalties Shepard shared with various writers brought in paltry earnings.

Joan also could not know how much Irving Shepard disliked being responsible for the literary estate. He was at heart a man of the land, a private person like his mother, Eliza, and he found the pressures of being connected with Jack London onerous. Nor could Joan appreciate his devotion to the memory of both Charmian and his mother, his accepting the burden of honoring the legacy Jack had passed to them. He was much more aware than Joan of all the people over the years who had exploited the women or tried to abuse their goodwill. And among those he considered exploiters was Joan herself, who to his mind had appeared in Charmian's life only when she wanted something from the older woman. That perception was inaccurate, but it played a major role in preventing any rapprochement between the two families.

Apart from the matter of finances, Joan felt insulted that Shepard had never informed her directly of the many publications. She was also vexed that she could not quote her father's letters to her in her own book without Shepard's permission. This seemed the final insult resulting from her father's 1911 will.

Another scholar with whom Joan corresponded was Vil Bykov. They had met in the 1950s when he had come to California to gather research for a book. She became wary of him when he visited Irving Shepard before seeing her, and then, at his first interview, instead of asking questions talked about his meeting with Anna Strunsky. She was also suspicious of him, wondering why a Soviet literature professor was allowed to travel in the company of scientists during the height of the cold war. Charles Malamuth, now remarried and living in Los Angeles, suggested that Bykov was the "guardian," an English-speaking academic trusted to watch and report on his comrades to officials. Nevertheless, Joan encouraged Bykov, in hopes that her knowledge and point of view would shape his research.

When Bykov's book was published, Malamuth translated it for Joan, and summarized it as a "poor literary product." She was taken aback by the "whitewash job" of Jack's political beliefs and was aghast at Bykov's excusing Jack's racism. She developed a three-page list of factual corrections, which included errors in dates, story titles, and references. As for substantive errors, she denounced his repeating her father's tale of childhood poverty. "[Flora] and Mammy Jennie always indignantly denied that they were as miserably poor as Jack made them out in his books. Oh well, I don't think I shall ever win this argument; my dad was much more persusasive."[11]

Malamuth encouraged Joan's proposed book on her childhood, adding that it should be her primary activity, for she was a good writer who would be absolutely honest and "spare nobody." Although he liked the idea of the history of the farmworkers' movement, he reminded her to provide a "balanced perspective," one that included such topics as increased mechanization, changes in food marketing methods, and such. In recent years Charles had shifted more to the right, perhaps like many former communist sympathizers, in response to the full exposure of Stalin's brutality. His knowledge of the Soviet Union back to the early days made him a valuable senior research associate on communist strategy and propaganda at the University of Southern California. To Joan, though, he revealed nostalgia for his earlier years of activism. "Remember the time Jim Rorty and I were arrested in the Imperial Valley," he recalled wistfully.[12] Following Malamuth's sudden death in 1965, one of his sisters told Joan that he had never loved anyone else. Joan knew that his family had not welcomed his second wife, Renee, and was disappointed that their bitter animosity toward his widow continued.

One person who had moved fully to the right politically was Barney Mayes. Mayes had married a well-to-do woman, and became known in the 1950s for his flashy appearance at the Bay Meadows racetrack. In 1966 he called Joan out of the blue at two in the morning, "pleasantly drunk," though coherent.[13] "I'm a ca-*pit*-alist now!" he announced "with gentle self-scorn." In "slightly drunken sentiment" he told Joan what a nice person she was, and was pleased to hear how Bart was doing.[13] Despite all her problems with Barney over the years, Joan was gratified to know he was thriving.

Events at two schools were pleasing to Joan each in its own way, in the 1960s. One occurred at Sonoma State College, which had developed from being an extension of San Francisco State University. Its first official campus after it became independent was a group of apartment buildings in Rohnert Park, about forty-five miles north of the Golden Gate. Many of its founding faculty were Berkeley graduates or residents, and of liberal persuasion, so it was not surprising that a dormitory was named Jack London Hall. Joan attended the opening ceremonies, and quickly became popular with the faculty. One group became known for raucous partying that lasted throughout the weekend at a country home. Joan was remembered for her ability to sing protest songs all night long without once repeating a tune, as well as holding her liquor with the best.

In addition, overdue recognition came in 1966 when the library and English Department at the University of Washington put on a display of London first editions and sponsored a meeting commemorating the fiftieth anniversary of the writer's death. Most of the books were from the collection of George Tweney, who urged that Joan be invited as guest of honor. The trip was a wonderful balm. It began with her first airplane ride. Joan took pleasure in being housed at the unpretentious Tweney home. There she met Dale Walker, a young writer who had collaborated with Richard O'Connor on a biography of John Reed, admirer of the Russian Revolution. Joan and Walker shared many interests, and would correspond frequently afterward. At the commemorative event Joan gave a prepared speech before the audience of 150, addressing her father's formative years as a writer, and read aloud from his letters to Cloudesley Johns.

As a result of that visit, the University of Washington Press decided to republish *Jack London and His Times* as part of its Americana Library, a series intended to reprint "books of recognized and unusual importance that have been out of print and hard to find." Joan prepared a new introduction noting that the social problems that had most concerned her father still remained. After acknowledging the eclipse of interest in his works among critics, she reminded her readers how popular London remained around the world, for he had become among the most widely translated of American authors. She acknowledged, too, the weaknesses in his ideas, notably his Anglo-Saxon glorification, yet reminded readers that his popularity rested in his "unshakable belief in man's ability to rise to incredible heights of courage" and "his compassion for the poor and hatred of everything that deforms human spirit." His confusions and contradictions, she suggested, were "poignant proof of his active engagement in the battle between 'good' and 'evil.'"

It is clear that in her seventh decade Joan had laid to rest the ghost of her father and come to take pride in his achievements. Asked to compose the biographical sketch for *The Reader's Encyclopedia of American Literature*, she emphasized London's political writings over his fiction. Works she chose to highlight were *Martin Eden* ("in which a struggling writer achieves success, but having rejected socialist aims . . . finds life meaningless"), *The Road, The Iron Heel, The People of the Abyss,* and *The War of the Classes.* Having had much experience now with the complexities of social activism, and the enormous force of those who would squelch it, she appreciated her father's unrelenting stance on social justice for the working class, though it threatened his other endeavors. She admired his prophetic voice, his visionary warnings about capitalism and the dangers of technology.

Her perspective on her mother and Charmian also shifted. She now perceived how her mother's narrow, stubborn stance limiting the conditions for Jack's visits with the girls was to be faulted as much as his hostility and refusal to compromise. Each had provoked the other, and at any point Bess just as much as Jack could have changed the outcome. As for Charmian, despite finding her character unattractive, Joan continued to see her as the right mate for her father. She even believed that had Bess allowed the girls to go to the ranch, Charmian would have treated them well. In a letter to Adela Rogers St. John, who had visited the ranch as a child, Joan concluded, "It is impossible to blame anyone for the tragedy of our relationship; not my mother, who was a truly fine person, not my father, not Charmian, not myself."[14]

Unfortunately, Joan's progress on the book was continually interrupted by the demands of *So Shall Ye Reap,* the Chaney biography, and political activities, which always drew her away from the desk. In 1967 she earned what she could only have considered an honor—repeated mention in the California legislature's *Fourteenth Report of the Senate Factfinding Subcommittee on Unamerican Activities.* She was recognized chiefly for her work with Citizens for Farm Labor, a group "ranging from those sincerely concerned with the plight of the workers, [to] those whose participation in the Free Speech Movement and the activities of the Marxist new left organizations is well known." Clearly placed among the latter group, Joan was singled out for teaching college students "techniques of picketing and boycott activities," and involving them in the Delano grape strike. (Joan had many notable peers in that report, which listed leading scholars from universities and Democratic politicians prominent in both state and federal government, such as Willie Brown and John Burton.)

She may even have been responsible for the farm labor unionists' invoking Jack's definition of a scab. César Chavez noted that her father would be marching side by side with the strikers were he still alive. London's commentary, he said, provided "terrific ammunition" during the California Subcommittee on

Agricultural Workers hearings. He invited Joan to read Jack's story "The Mexican" aloud to the strikers, and thanked her for being a "loyal friend."[15]

Joan also attended the many antiwar rallies in the East Bay during this time, and was active in Women For Peace. She always appeared in fashionable dress, and was rather peeved that demonstrators did not pay more attention to their appearance. To her, being politically committed did not mean giving up comportment and style. She thought all the fuss over the proper activist "uniform" took energy away from the real purpose of protest.

Joan kept Bart and Helen, now living in Mexico, informed of local events. She sent clippings about the various marches and boycotts, and continued to recommend the latest politically oriented books. When the Free Speech Movement broke out in Berkeley, she went to the rallies, and found hope in the fact that there were people such as Mario Savio who were ready to carry the work forward after her generation was gone. She tried hard not to be pessimistic, but the actions of newly elected Governor Ronald Reagan left her unsettled. She worried about what he and his right-wing appointees would do to social welfare and education. Several of Bart's daughters were activists as well, and Joan heartily approved when they joined an antiwar protest at the San Francisco Opera's season premiere.

Joan was so energetic in public and so devoted to her causes that few people knew she was playing a masquerade. Both she and husband, Charlie Miller, were seriously ill. In late 1966 Charlie had had a bad fall and suffered bleeding ulcers. His recuperation demanded much of Joan's time, for he needed her help to move around the house, and he was put on a highly restrictive diet and an intrusive schedule of drug therapy. When Park Abbott was diagnosed with prostate cancer, Joan visited him often during his repeated hospitalizations. Around the same time she began to suffer from symptoms of what proved to be cancer of the pharynx, likely from years of chain smoking. Yet for as long as possible she kept the news from virtually everyone, even her son. To keep Hank Anderson from worrying, she made excuses to avoid meetings, working primarily by mail. It would be many months before he learned the truth about her condition.

Over the next several years she, Charlie, and Park endured surgery, chemotherapy, and other debilitating treatments. Besides leaving an already hotheaded Joan even more prone to irritability, they also limited her work, and thus income to meet her bills. As she explained caustically to a friend, retirement from the labor federation had left her with only the inadequate pension granted women retirees, far inferior to that of the men. A film project on Chaney collapsed, as did several television writing opportunities. One editor who read the manuscript of her childhood memoir praised it as "beautifully written, informative, and quite interesting" but too localized (meaning Californian in focus), and thus better suited for a university press.[16]

Despite these disappointments, Joan saw increasing signs of revived interest in her father. In 1968 the Port of Oakland decided to redevelop a waterfront neighborhood, Jack London Square, and hired an advertising man, Russ Kingman, to develop publicity linking the site more directly to its historic roots as the environs of London's youth. Kingman had served in the navy, worked as a terrazzo craftsman, and been a Baptist minister before turning to advertising. Although he had little familiarity with London, he soon became a fanatical admirer who would spend the rest of his life glorifying the writer.

The gregarious, energetic Kingman called Joan, who praised him to others and in her usual manner set out to help him in any way possible. She sent him names, addresses, and detailed information on a variety of people who could assist him in his work, including Hensley Woodbridge, George Tweney, key figures in Oakland literary circles, and collectors. She told him about the *Jack London Newsletter,* saying, "Be sure to use my name when you contact these people. It will be your *bona fides.*"[17]

Kingman found in her lists one name that suggested a terrific publicity stunt. Dick North was a magazine editor in Alaska who claimed to have found a cabin where London had scrawled his name in 1898. Both North and Franklin Walker had been cautious in identifying the cabin as London's, but when Joan saw a photograph of the signature, she agreed that it was similar to her father's handwriting. In 1969 Kingman arranged a trip to the site, accompanied by actor Eddie Albert and a member of the Oakland police department, Ralph Godfrey, who was to assist in the verification. Russ visited Joan before leaving to have her sign a half-dozen copies of her biography for him to distribute as gifts to officials. Kingman would return in triumph, asserting that the cabin was genuine. (It would eventually be split in half, one part remaining in the Yukon, the other sent to Jack London Square in Oakland, where in full reconstruction it stands today.) What was never publicized, though, was Godfrey's official report, which Joan received. After running scientific tests on the material as well as comparing the signature to fifteen others London wrote at the same period, Godfrey concluded that the signature was not authentic.

Perhaps this report explains why the Oakland Museum, which was the first to be offered the structure, turned it down. This rejection upset Becky as stupid, and shortsighted, and for once motivated her to act on her father's behalf. The president of the museum board was a former boyfriend from her early twenties. She wrote him to plead for a reversal, but he never responded. This silence must have caused special pain, for Becky had kept clippings about the man over the years, a most telling act on the part of a woman who destroyed virtually every memento.

As far as can be determined, Joan apparently never shared Godfrey's report with her other contacts. By now she had become, like Kingman, an ardent apologist for her father, and was thus unlikely to expose the findings. What sealed Joan's devotion was a memo Tony Bubka discovered while researching at the Huntington Library. On a scrap of paper, undated, Jack had scrawled:

> Absolute detailed study of Joan and me—from her standpoint
> where she loses me crystallizes with the little person in a pigeon-hole
> Whole talk, he hard.
> Her terrible, radiant father's rare visits.
> She is not big enough, & at twenty realizes too late her mistakes.

At first this puzzling message flooded Joan with "old, aching memories,"[18] though upon reflection she concluded that her father loved her very dearly, and that his terrible letters to her had been an expression of momentary rage. Otherwise, why would he record this idea, which was so typical of the way he began to plan a story or novel? To reach this conclusion, though, she had to ignore the overarching point of the note: that *she* had been the one to make mistakes.

By 1969 Joan was dying, although she disguised her pain from all but her closest friends and family. Her strong nurturing instinct compelled her to focus her attention on nursing Charlie and comforting Park. Since neither she nor Charlie now drove, she became more isolated in Pleasant Hill, which had poor public transportation to Berkeley and Oakland. She could no longer travel to the beloved cabin in Foresta. Nonetheless, her letters remained focused on current events, her son's large family, and the pleasures of gardening. Jim Sisson's sharing of his experiences with chemotherapy and radiation provided unique supportive counsel. When he gave her bulbs for her spectacular garden, she split the collection and gave half to Becky.

Unlike her sister, Becky aged with heartiness and no serious ailments. Yet her animosities toward her husband, Percy, were little disguised. When his eyesight prevented him from driving at night, she complained of being trapped at home with him. Her grudges toward Joan remained, though were expressed behind her back. Having missed an opportunity to attend a party at Joan's house, she confessed to Sisson that she could not help being catty, and asked if Joan had let anyone else talk. While to Joan's face she supported the childhood memoir, she shared her disapproval with others. In any event, she was certain no one would publish it. The sisters had only one noteworthy disagreement, when Becky decided to sell her half of the books signed by their father to the University of the Pacific. Joan had never wanted to see the set broken up, but was unable to persuade Becky to hold onto the books until both could agree on a disposition.

Nevertheless, during Joan's final months, Becky updated others on her sister's suffering and expressed sympathy that her dying was so difficult.

During the late spring of 1970 Charlie Miller's health failed steadily, without any apparent reason. Following a brief hospitalization, he died on August 14 of what proved to be pancreatic cancer. Joan wrote to tell his friends how grateful she was that he had little pain until the end, at which point "the hypos were right there." Her own carcinoma, she assured them, had vanished, but arthritis was causing her much discomfort.[19]

In fact, the cancer had spread to her esophagus. Having tried various alternative therapies, with what she believed was some success, she decided to go to a clinic in Tijuana, Mexico, for the popular "cure" then, Krebiozin. The treatment had no effect, and by early January 1971 the tumors were pressing so hard on her windpipe that she could barely swallow, and was on oxygen. Bart became so distraught that Joan wound up consoling him rather than seeking his comfort. Accepting her fate, she asked to be taken back to Oakland to die in a hospital there.

During her final days Joan prepared detailed notes for Bart. He was to stop delivery of the newspaper, have the gas, electricity, and phone at her home turned off, and file change of address cards. He was to ask the funeral director for information. She indicated who was to be called and who written to following her death. To the end, Joan was concerned for her son, who was drinking heavily throughout this episode.

Joan then detailed how her material goods should be distributed. Becky was to get her chaise longue and a small chest of drawers that had belonged to their grandmother Maddern. The Yosemite cabin would go to Bart. Grandchildren were granted possessions suitable to their interests. Aware that Bart was not completely reliable, she named two of his children co-executors. She indicated what was to be sold—unsigned London first editions, manuscripts, a painting by Maynard Dixon—and specified that the profits be shared *not* equally but "on basis of need, health, education, etc." of the heirs.

Joan survived beyond expectations. She wanted to live long enough to see the reviews of *So Shall Ye Reap*, which had just been published. Bart's wife, Helen Abbott, contacted William Hogan at the *San Francisco Chronicle* and advised him of Joan's condition. Consequently, he arranged that a review of the book be moved forward on the schedule, and it was read to her just before she died on January 17.

Although Joan had not wanted any funeral service, a simple memorial was held at St. John's Presbyterian Church in Berkeley. Among those providing eulogies were Robin Lampson, who recounted meeting her when he was sixteen, labor leader Jack Henning, who paid tribute to her firebrand commitment to the cause, and Jim Sisson, who praised her research and writing. Afterward,

Joan's ashes were placed alongside Charlie Miller's under a rock altar beside the Foresta cabin. On February 8, 1971, the California State Senate unanimously passed a resolution expressing its sympathy to Joan's family and eulogized her "as a warrior for labor with a passion for economic justice from early adulthood to the very end of her life."

During her final years, with much regret Joan had started to sell off some of her personal materials related to her father. Various negotiations were under way at her death, which meant that Bart had to take them over. Losing his mother had sent him into a major alcoholic binge, clouding his thinking; in addition, he had little experience or interest in financial matters. As a result, he was ripe for exploitation.

Even before Joan's body was cremated, several people called Helen and Bart to say that Joan had promised them one or another set of materials. A noted book collector offered a larcenous $125 for sixty-six books in her library, which included many London first editions. One London buff insisted that Joan had promised him the mission chair that once belonged to her father. Another wanted to look through her den for objects of interest. Fortunately, Dale Walker heard of these maneuverings. He advised Helen of the real value of various goods, and kept her and Bart from being taken advantage of. Most disturbing, though, was the occasion when they found Joan's den ransacked, with papers spilled all over, though nothing of value had been removed from the house. This intrusion made sense only if it had been committed by either the FBI or someone from the London network.

Bart did complete the formal sale in progress of some manuscript materials. One set of letters ended up at the Huntington Library. Another set of documents, which included most of Jack's letters to Joan, Joan's correspondence with such significant figures as Trotsky, and the photograph album her father had kept of her early years, was sold to a private collector.

Joan had specified that Tony Bubka, Jim Sisson, and George Tweney were to edit her volume for publication. It was an unlikely arrangement, and Tweney wrote Becky that he doubted the work would be completed. She was grateful to hear that, and reminded Sisson that she would prefer that the manuscript disappear. Nevertheless, Bart had made a promise at Joan's deathbed to see the work published. He approached the University of Washington Press, which welcomed the project but suggested that a scholar familiar with London prepare an introduction to the material. Richard Etulain, a noted western historian who had edited an issue of *Western American Literature* devoted to London, accepted the assignment. Although the manuscript ended essentially in early 1915, with only some brief commentary on its concluding chapter, what existed was finished writing, in need of little additional editing or doctoring. What Bart did not realize was how Becky would respond, or the difficulties Etulain would encounter.

With Joan's death, Becky's status within the Jack London community was suddenly elevated. Previously Joan, being the elder daughter and the only one publicly discussing their father, had received all the attention, and in some cases the aggravation. Friends and associates of Becky all agree that to this point she hardly ever spoke about her father, and distanced herself from Joan's apparent grandstanding. Now people were calling Becky up and knocking on her door to talk about her father or ask her to appear at an event as his blood proxy.

Becky was hesitant at first. When Russ Kingman proposed what would become an annual Jack London Birthday Banquet, she was not very excited about being guest of honor, and confessed to her son that she did not want to be the only "lady" present. In 1972 she hesitantly agreed to be guest of honor at the University of the Pacific for the formal installation of its Jack London Collection. The retirement of her husband in 1971, however, provided further motivation for Becky to leave the house whenever possible. All he wanted to do was sit around, she complained to Bart, so she began taking long trips and welcomed excuses to go out. Thus by 1973 she was much more visible as a celebrity by virtue of her paternity, thanks to the offices of Kingman, who began to invite her to other publicity-related events. In the process, she revealed to him and his wife, Winnie, her long-suppressed unhappiness over her childhood.

Hearing that Bart wanted to go forward with his mother's book, Becky finally became direct about her feelings. She told him that he did not have permission to use her name, that she wished to be excised completely from the book as though she had never existed. Her preference was that the manuscript be burned. "You have no means of knowing what Joan thought in 1916," she added. "No amount of research can discover that."[20]

Even before Joan died, Kingman had begun deprecating her character, despite having had scant direct contact with her. The reason perhaps was her rebuffing his public relations orientation, for she agreed with George Tweney and others that events such as the log cabin stunt were "crass commercialization." Joan may also have detected in Kingman a wish to present London in a mythic way, whereas she demanded (as her father would have) candor and frank discussion of failings. After all, who had better exposed his great characters flaws than Jack himself in works such as *John Barleycorn* and *The Little Lady of the Big House*? Kingman's whitewash was well intended, but not for her the alternative to Irving Stone's emphasis on the pathological. Becky, by contrast, preferred the idealization of her father, and viewed Kingman as the perfect spokesperson to replace Joan. (Jim Sisson was understandably very upset when Becky told a reporter that Russ was the "premier London scholar.")

During the early 1970s the Kingmans moved to Glen Ellen, where Winnie capably managed a used bookstore while Russ devoted himself full-time to anything related to Jack London. Gregarious and inquisitive, he began writing and calling anyone who could provide information on some detail of London's life, and entered the results by fountain pen on notecards. Eventually he would incorporate his activity under the Jack London Research Center, where he made his growing collection of dissertations, books, photographs, and files freely available to others. He also embarked on a richly illustrated biography, one that he said was to be "neither definitive nor scholarly," nor provide references, but instead offer a revised account of London's life that debunked the errors of earlier works.[21]

Kingman was, much like his hero, a man of extreme virtues and weaknesses. He was generous with his time and resources, for example, corresponding by hand with each individual student in a junior high school class studying the author. He provided free lodging to impecunious scholars visiting the area. As Jim Sisson had been previously, he was in a sense co-author or co-editor of several books that did not give his name on the title page, for he answered pages of questions from scholars who relied on his microscopic eye to supply the details for an annotation or passage. Nevertheless, he came to see his interpretations as the correct ones. For example, he denied that London had a problem with alcohol, and spoke scurrilously of other biographers to strangers who visited his store. Unlike Sisson, he bragged about the lists of errata he had compiled of others' research, though these "errors" included opinion as well as fact.[22] In time he pronounced himself the "world's expert" on Jack London, when he was arguably only the "world's greatest fan."

Russ was also tremendously loyal to his friends, and defended them as fiercely as he did his view of Jack London. His protection of Becky solidified as the result of a crime in 1983. Her husband had died the year before, and she was at home alone when two robbers broke in. Although she was not harmed, she was understandably fearful afterward. Estranged from Guy and Jean, she welcomed an invitation to move to Glen Ellen with the Kingmans. Russ added a small apartment to the bookstore, with the long-term view of its housing the research center after Becky's death.

This move was possibly a lifesaver. Becky had privacy, comfort, and companionship when she wanted it. There were hundreds of books in the store for reading, and steady entertainment from San Francisco Giants baseball and 49ers football broadcasts. She often welcomed strangers who wanted to speak with her and hear her stories about her father. Journalists began to publish her memories of her childhood with her perfect father. "He made a huge difference in my life, I can tell you that. I never again met anybody who was that much fun!" she told one.[23] As for the custody battle, she explained that their mother "was afraid we would be wild Indians if we came up here, because Daddy would teach us how to ride and we'd tear all over the ranch and do a lot of walking and all of that, and she was trying to bring us up as ladies."[24] She repeated many of these stories at various public events as well, usually arranged by Kingman.

That remark about being raised as ladies hints at how much Becky and Joan misunderstood each other. Joan had resented Bess's emphasis on propriety, although she had divulged that displeasure only to her friends. Similarly, had Joan been less immersed in her many activities, she might have taken time to notice the latent rebel in Becky. Although they had remained cordial throughout their life, they had never discovered deep truths about each other. Instead, an unwritten taboo formed around the source of their disagreement—their father—and prevented the full intimacy that might otherwise have developed.

Knowing of Becky's unhappiness over Joan's version of the "window incident" in Joan's manuscript, Kingman objected to the editor at the University of Washington Press. He represented himself as Becky's literary representative, and demanded to see a copy of the manuscript, which was provided.[25] He accused Joan of being a "very bitter and unhappy woman," called her story "an untruthful version," and threatened a lawsuit.[26] There was no legal basis for blocking the book, since it did not quote Becky, nor did it represent her in an unfavorable light. Nonetheless, the editor sought ways to prevent further conflicts and appease Becky.

When the editor suggested that the window incident be excised, Bart refused. He had promised his mother that he would allow no alterations, and added that scholarly dissent should be handled in the usual way, through further publication by those who disagreed. He described a recent meeting with Becky, who was very upset that Andrew Sinclair's biography *Jack* claimed that their father "terrorized" the girls. He was surprised by her anger and suspected that she was being influenced by Kingman. She had seen the manuscript and made no corrections, he protested, but he did not realize that Becky had doubted the book would ever appear.

The editor made another recommendation, to change the title to *Jack London, My Father,* as a way of indicating that the version was not the recollection of both daughters. In rejecting this change, Bart missed an opportunity to end the dispute. Nevertheless, the editor assured Becky that he would give her a final look at the book and its introduction. Etulain also offered to add a long footnote to the window incident in which her version would be explained. Becky warmed up to Helen and Bart again, and sent them newsy letters about herself, her children, her good treatment by the Kingmans, and her health.

During the 1980s Becky gradually lost her sight, and severely missed reading. She tried Library for the Blind tapes, for she wanted unedited books, but thought that the delivery of the reading was not good enough. Ironically, Becky had been a volunteer Braille transcriber for many years in order to provide her father's books to the blind, yet she was unable to read Braille well. By 1988 her letters displayed many fewer words on a page, scrawled large enough so she could see them as she wrote. Her hearing was failing as well. Nonetheless, she kept in good spirits and turned up the radio louder. Never timid about calling herself "just another old lady," Becky handled the changes of aging with grace.

Preparing her will in 1986, Becky appointed Russ and Winnie Kingman as executors. She was very specific about who was to receive which items, including individual books, pieces of jewelry, china, paintings, and furniture. Most was divided among Guy, his wife, Winona, and Jean. Because Guy was in debt to her for $13,000, she bequeathed that amount to Jean. Among small monetary bequests was one for $100 to the Jack London Foundation. Bart was to receive a small chest of drawers, a gift from her father. The Kingmans were to receive only "any and all books not chosen by my children."

Russ was to serve as literary executor, "to withhold permission and not grant that my name be used unless it be beneficial to my estate," a request unsupportable by law, and "to monitor and check all copyrights of books and other writings, published and unpublished, of my father, Jack London." This was in reference to an earlier clause assigning Jean "all royalties, income or profits from any and all endeavors of my father" to which she had "any right, title, interest, or claim by right of descent, including but not limiting to any and all lawsuits." These references to her father's royalties may seem odd in light of their having reverted to Charmian and the Shepards. But in this way Becky left a glimmer of hope that someday her descendants would have at least some of what was rightfully hers.

Other obstacles appeared to hamper publication of Joan's book. Although the collector who bought Joan's letters had agreed to make the materials available to scholars, Etulain was unable to see them. A productive scholar with other projects under way, he fell behind schedule. In frustration he finally pulled out, and the University of Washington canceled the project.

At that point Bart met Malcolm Margolin, whose Heyday Press specialized in California history. He agreed to produce the work in paperback, but ran into another objection when Milo Shepard, who became literary executor of the London estate following his father's death in 1975, refused to permit quotes from the "wounded colt" letter. What he wanted instead proved easy for Margolin to provide—the full text of the letter as an appendix, which ironically only served to support Joan's perspective.

Bart prepared a brief introduction that cogently put *Jack London and His Daughters* in context. It was, he said, Joan's attempt to understand her father's abandonment and the conflicting loyalties forced on her by her parents. Even more, he emphasized, her intent was to offer a reminder of the consequences of using children as pawns. "She loved her mother so very much. She adored, was dazzled by, her father." Noting that the manuscript remained unfinished, he reflected that "even if the book had been completed, however, the unanswered questions might still never have been resolved."

In fact, the last 40 percent of Joan's time with her father takes up only 8 percent of the book. More significant, the missing information concerns the rapprochement that occurred during 1915–16, as well as Joan's realization in adulthood that her mother, however well meaning, was equally responsible for the custody conflict. "What has taken longer . . . than anything else, and [is] more painful to look at and accept, was to admit that Mother's adamant refusal to let us visit him at the ranch . . . was wrong," Joan wrote. There was no doubt that Bess "was punishing Daddy for having left her."[27] Although the book states that Jack "took his own life," she no longer believed so at the time of her death. Despite these omissions, the account stands on its own with regard to her original purpose, for it is a poignant, eloquent narrative of growing up in a divided family. Had her father been just an average person, its value would stand still as a testament to a pattern of childhood that became increasingly familiar as the century progressed. It is Joan's masterpiece.

Despite appearing in 1990 under the imprint of a regional press, *Jack London and His Daughters* received prominent reviews, and it was selected as a feature of the Quality Paperback Club. Bay Area papers called its insights "a valued contribution to our knowledge of London" and declared it contributed "a key piece to the colorful mosaic of California life and literature." Reviewers from other regions recognized the broader theme, that of the child as a victim of divorce. In that regard, noted one, it was "a brilliantly written, philosophical, melancholy work."[28]

In the Bay Area *Jack London and His Daughters* also attracted several feature stories that took note of Becky's disapproval. Most likely Kingman, the former public relations man, stimulated some of this coverage. He often stated his dislike for the book, as when he remarked with some satisfaction to Henry Anderson that he had sold only three copies, and did not expect to sell any more.[29] He did not question Joan's writing ability, just her failure to put the blame where he thought it belonged: upon her mother.

Bart Abbott, by then suffering from cancer, made appearances on radio and at bookstores to publicize the book locally. Had the title remained *Visiting Rights Only*, as Joan originally planned, it might have sold better. Lacking good nationwide distribution and marketing, it eventually ended up in remainder bins. Thus Becky had little reason to be concerned about its consequences for her and her father's reputation.

By 1991 Becky was frail, on some days too weak to take an automobile ride or even to turn on the radio. That November she had a bad fall and was sent to a convalescent home named in honor of her father. She was unable to build up the strength to walk again. Wheelchair-bound, she still kept her childhood teddy bear as comfort. Jean, who lived in Sacramento, decided to transfer Becky to a convalescent home nearby. On March 26, 1992, she died there. Her ashes were scattered at sea.

Becky's death touched the large network of London fans and scholars who had met her at various conferences and events. Russ Kingman called her "Little Mary Sunshine," which suited her well those final years. She had come on the scene just when a renaissance of interest in London was occurring, and she was the only person left to convey Jack London's story through firsthand knowledge. Her profile, a replica of her father's, was also a reminder that London was once flesh and blood, not just an abstraction. One could see, too, how she, like her sister, had been dazzled by her father, and understand one's own fascination with that complex, larger-than-life individual.

# Epilogue

ALTHOUGH BECKY LONDON NEVER received her emotional or financial
due from her father, she was able in her final years to enjoy the fruits of renewed
evaluation of his life and works. Prior to the 1970s, Jack London was seldom addressed by literary scholars. Ignored after his death, he was discounted by leading critics in the 1950s; graduate students in American literature need not have
studied him to qualify as experts in the field.[1] His best stories were missing from
college anthologies, and apart from *The Call of the Wild* and *White Fang*, which
were read by some schoolchildren, American students were unlikely to be exposed to him. Some readers later found him through *Sailor on Horseback*,
which never went out of print and caught enough of Jack's spirit to turn them
into fans. They found, however, that they had to resort to well-worn copies at
local libraries or from used bookstores if they wished to explore beyond his
best-known novels.

By the 1960s the literary climate was showing signs of reassessment. Essays
began to appear in key scholarly journals, and new editions of London's novels
came out in paperback, accompanied by insightful introductions. In 1965 King
Hendricks and Irving Shepard's edition of *Letters from Jack London* for the first
time revealed information previously available only to those few with access to
the Huntington Library. Franklin Walker's *Jack London and the Klondike* in 1966
offered an essential corrective on London's earlier years. Hensley Woodbridge,
John London (a book dealer), and George Tweney published *Jack London: A
Bibliography* in 1966, and Woodbridge started the *Jack London Newsletter* in
1967. Far from a brief bulletin, the *JLN* spurred study of London, particularly
among younger literary scholars, and many of its papers were groundbreaking.
It also broadened the field by including excellent work by undergraduate and
graduate students, along with papers by foreign scholars, including Francis La-
cassin in France, Vil Bykov in Russia, Victor Tambling in Great Britain, Mario
Maffi in Italy, Li Shuyan in China, and Eijii Tsujii in Japan, which has the greatest concentration of London scholars outside the United States. Joan London,
whose biography of her father was reprinted in 1968, enjoyed hearing of these

projects, and corresponded with a young Louisiana professor, Earle Labor, who would become a major force in the revival.

After Joan's death, Becky was drawn further by the parallel emergence of activities among readers and collectors. The attractively produced first editions suddenly interested collectors, who avidly searched out and drove up the price of even the more commonly available volumes. Russ and Winnie Kingman initiated the annual Jack London Birthday Banquets, which attracted fans and scholars from around the world. Becky attended these even before moving in with the Kingmans, and though modest about her place of honor at the head table, clearly appreciated the attention. An accountant, David Schlottman, started *What's New about Jack London*, a newsy offering catholic in its coverage (references to London in news articles, crossword puzzles, movies, and such). At banquets Schlottman distributed *The Wolf*, usually consisting of essays or reprints of articles on London, which Becky proudly autographed. Another devotee, Mike Bates, for several years published *Jack London Echoes*, for which Becky wrote a column, "In My Mailbox," addressing questions about her father.

Becky's affectionate 1974 reminiscence of her father in the *Pacific Historian* led to her further public recognition.[2] During 1976, the centennial of London's birth, requests for her presence at various events increased. That year *Modern Fiction Studies* and *Western American Literature* each devoted an issue to essays on London, and scholars sought to break into the tightly controlled programs at professional meetings. Russ Kingman, having moved to a larger space in Glen Ellen, created the Jack London Foundation, began a monthly newsletter, and sponsored other activities to promulgate word of London's life and works, notably in schools.

Both scholarship and fan activities expanded during the 1980s. Becky made brief speeches at fundraisers for the State Historic Park and for the Jack London Foundation, as well as at writers' groups. With Russ Kingman's assistance, several movie possibilities were explored, using her as a consultant. Most significant for her would be an event on January 11, 1986, when the U.S. Postal Service issued a Jack London stamp as part of its Great Americans series. Almost to the end, despite failing health, she continued to appear at the annual birthday banquets.

The sweet, even shy Becky who appeared in public was not always the same woman behind the scenes. As I have shown, she was determined to suppress or at least modify Joan's manuscript on their childhood. In addition, by coming to public notice just when interest in London was growing, she was able to have a singular influence on the scholarship. Why Becky idealized her father and demonized her mother and older sister remains open to conjecture. Certainly that stance deflected any further exploration into her past, with what was for her still the disgraceful, mortifying episode of her daughter's illegitimacy. Whatever her motive, her opinion became established truth, for it is very difficult to question the assertions of a gentle, kindly old woman.

Becky reinforced her father's view of Bess Maddern as small-minded and mean-spirited, and by implication undeserving of such an important man. Thus Russ Kingman's 1979 biography, apart from brief asides ("a fine woman"), portrayed Bess fully in Jack's terms as humorless, not enjoying company, prudish, and demanding: "She was selfish, cruel, jealous, and cared little for anybody else."[3] After quoting at length Becky's view of the window incident, Kingman added, "It was only logical that the two daughters would be nearly as incompatible as their mother and father, since Joan was a carbon copy of her mother, and talking with Becky is like having a chat with her father."[4] Normally a scrupulous researcher, Kingman never held Becky's statements up to his usual insistent scrutiny. My own work, *American Dreamers,* published in 1988, was similarly slanted by familiarity with and affection for Becky, as well as Kingman's repeated derogation of Joan. Though I feel that I was more subtle than Kingman in my portrayal of Bess, I repeated Jack's charge that she was "microscopic" and "shallow," sexually cold, unfeminine, and wary of guests. My evidence is perhaps even more convincing because it includes quotes from Joseph Noel and Joan London. But in retrospect it is clear that I was selecting evidence to fit a preconceived notion. Ironically, though I absorbed Kingman's dislike of Joan London, I found her biography lucid and cogent. One could find homologies as well in the way Russ and I handled Flora London and Anna Strunsky.

One biographer, the British writer Andrew Sinclair, suggested a new outlook on Bess, Flora, and Anna, but neither Kingman nor I was receptive to his interpretation. Sinclair presented the women through Jack's eyes, yet avoided accepting that version as complete. Rather, he portrayed the women as victimized by a tormented, domineering American male, a man who shunned his mother, bullied his wife, and put money ahead of love when it came to Anna. Nevertheless, since Jack's relationships with women are a minor theme in the larger arc of his story, Sinclair's different views are easy to miss. Apart from rightly rejecting his pathological portrayal of London, Kingman and I had personal reasons for ignoring Sinclair. We were each deep in our research, which would take many more years, when we discovered that Sinclair had been sanctioned by the estate to do a biography. With a long list of books behind him, we suspected that he would make a speedy trip through the archives and prepare a facile presentation. I knew of Sinclair's accomplished history *The Better Half: The Emancipation of the American Woman,* yet was too blinded by envy to pick up his feminist thread when preparing my first book.

With regard to Jennie Prentiss, however, my *American Dreamers* stands apart from the rest by refusing to refer to her as "Mammy Jennie." (Sinclair's index even reads, "Prentiss, Virginia *See* Mammy Jennie.") For years I had heard her called such by scholars and fans, so casually as to deny her any rightful role apart from that of serving Jack London. The only well-known photographs show her standing beside a baby carriage with young Joan, that is, in servitude, and even then her features are hard to discern. To hear or read such a name used as if it were objective, not racist, grated. Still, I did not know much about Jennie Prentiss's life apart from Jack until Eugene Lasartemay and Mary Rudge wrote *For Love of Jack London* in 1991. Unfortunately, they wove fiction into the history, and made some factual errors in discussing Jack's life that were appropriately enumerated in a negative review by Kingman.[5] Those deficiencies aside, however, enough remained, some of which I could corroborate through other sources, to lightly sketch her presence. Her feelings and motives remain muted by history, but today one can glimpse more of her authenticity, and realize that there was much more to her life than being wet nurse to a white baby who grew into one of the most famous men of his day.

Becky's eventual hostility toward Joan also influenced scholarship. In taking sides with Becky, Russ Kingman belittled Joan, whose radicalism and multiple marriages offended his personal beliefs. One graduate student who planned to do a dissertation on Joan stopped to talk to Kingman before going on for a meeting with Bart Abbott. Kingman so convinced her that Joan was an unworthy person that she canceled the later appointment and changed her dissertation topic.[6] The Jack London State Historic Park continues to ignore Bess and Joan, while placing on prominent display a photograph and long statement about her father by Becky. Visiting there, one would not know that the elder daughter wrote two books about London and lectured on him around the country.

The most prominent scholar to address Bess, Joan, and Becky in recent years so completely accepted Becky's versions as valid that she overlooked evidence contrary to her arguments. For example, in her 1992 review of *Jack London and His Daughters*, Jacqueline Travernier-Courbin correctly noted Becky's displeasure with the book, as well as Jack and Bess's thoughtless decision to marry though not in love. But her overall attack is on Bess as "resentful, manipulative, vengeful, and dangerous to [the children's] psychological well-being," a woman motivated by "jealousy, spite, and vengefulness."[7] She points, among other incidents, to Becky's story of how her mother and Joan prevented her marriage to the man she loved. The argument makes sense if one attributes total validity to Becky's version. But as Travernier-Courbin notes at the start of her essay, one cannot depend on a single voice to relate any story. In granting full credence to

Becky (and Jack), she must deny any credence to Joan, who is depicted as over-identified with her mother.

As should be evident by now, the family dynamics were much more complex. That Joan and her mother had a special bond cannot be denied, for as the elder daughter she bore special responsibilities, many imposed by her father as much as her mother. As though to emphasize her defense of both the father and younger daughter, Travernier-Courbin repeats the theme in her review of *The Letters of Jack London,* and even accuses Joan of being "incredibly rude" and "totally lacking in courtesy" toward Charmian after Jack's death, which the correspondence clearly disputes. And it is ironic that the woman with so little voice in the matter, Bess, is so facilely characterized, masked as it were by the claims of others. Hating to write letters, she left her daughters to represent her view, and like many siblings, they disagreed.

Interestingly, Becky did not influence the intellectual handling of Charmian. Although I did not publish my book until 1988, my talking with and corresponding with others about my revisionist views of Jack's second wife helped change previously held views. At one birthday banquet I gave a dramatic reading of Charmian's writings from her life with Jack, including descriptions of some loving moments and his death. Suddenly I realized that Becky was sitting right beside me, and I felt embarrassed by my insensitivity. But when I sat down she thanked me warmly for the presentation. Her writings show no malice toward Charmian. Some years later she stated, "Charmian and Daddy were very happy all the years they were married and I think that's the main thing in life, to make other people happy. Then you're happy yourself."[8] Her perception was consistent with her idealization of her father, who, from her child's point of view, wanted her on the ranch, while her mother refused. And unlike Joan, left out of all the estate negotiations, Becky would see only the end result, the financial support and gifts from Charmian. There is a sweet poignancy to Becky's few stories of her father, which she held as close as she did the teddy bear he had given her.

Yet my valorization of Charmian in *American Dreamers* little extended Charmian's voice in scholarship, beyond causing her to be acknowledged more often as a constant and useful presence in London's life. Her most significant writings, *The Log of the Snark* and *Our Hawaii* (both editions), remain little cited where one might expect a reference, as with regard to London's Pacific Rim literature.[9] Nor has any literary scholar addressed the place of these books in the travel genre on their own merits, apart from the relation to London. Though Charmian's books appear regularly in bibliographies, they remain for the most part unexamined. In fact, they are all very hard to locate, being out of print or locked up in special collections, despite Charmian's request that her "own books of travel, *all* of them . . . and also my *Book of Jack London,* be at all times kept on sale" in the Happy Walls museum.[10]

Another source of misrepresentation was ironically the publication of the authoritative three-volume set of *The Letters of Jack London* by Stanford University Press. Although the editors were often careful to provide background in their annotations, they could not include the detail that would situate each item vis-à-vis the recipient or individual being discussed. These letters are a boon to those who cannot visit the archives, but it must be remembered that the standards of document analysis require much more than taking them at face value. Unfortunately, too often the other side of a correspondence is missing or difficult to access. To the extent that this was the case here, then my conclusions must be tempered. It could be, for example, that Becky did write her father more often than the existing evidence suggests.

Taking into account all the possible sources of error in attempting biography, it is a wonder any of us do. Given those caveats, what can one conclude?

My intentions in this study were several. One was simply to narrate the lives of the mothers, wives, daughters, stepsisters, and love interests of Jack London using the latest information available. Second, I hoped that tracing these women's lives from their perspective would provide a corrective to previous scholarship that depended either on London's own perceptions or on cultural stereotypes and themes about womanhood. Third, the issue of gender was to guide my analysis of the various women's relationships with London and among themselves. Key here was the notion of patriarchy and changing conceptions of femininity and masculinity during the Progressive Era. Finally, the interpretation would incorporate California as a defining region, paying attention to such matters as its economic opportunities, laws, artistic life, and special connection to the landscape during the time under consideration.

With regard to patriarchy, I wished to note that the expression of male dominance results in typical actions, such as silencing women, denying their point of view and needs, suppressing or censoring their sensuality and sexuality, and enclosing or restricting their activities. As a reciprocal response, some women incorporate into their self-image and presentation commensurate behaviors: passivity and unassertiveness, deference to others' needs, alienation from or denial of their bodily and sense experiences, and narrow notions of acceptable behavior. Such were in fact characteristic of the discourse pressed on nineteenth-century women, leading to what historians have dubbed the Cult of True Womanhood. As has been shown, both the California experience and the rise of the New Woman nationally during the Gilded Age and Progressive Era offered a strong rationale for avoiding these restrictive adaptations. Thus women such as Flora, Netta, and Charmian all challenged convention, though not without censure. Jennie Prentiss and Eliza Shepard were more conventional, though not out of response to masculine demands, and each was hardly housebound. Bess London had strong inclinations toward the new model, but, deserted with two small daughters, demanded her legal rights for economic support, and in the process entangled herself in a mean-spirited dance with her ex-husband. Both she and Anna Strunsky referred to the rhetoric of love as a rationale for their self-abnegation and deference.

Most striking to note is how even today deeply structured notions of femininity influence the perception of these women, and it matters not whether the scholar is male or female. The subtext has little changed. As the historian Caroll Smith-Rosenberg has revealed, the androgynous New Woman of a century ago was ultimately bound by the precept of maternity. Thus Anna, Bess, and Charmian each challenged Victorian femininity in some regard, and each was allowed a certain freedom *for a time,* but ultimately they all expected motherhood to be their defining status. And given the Darwinian influence, with reproduction tied to the survival of the species, motherhood bore an additional weighty cultural purpose beyond establishing femininity. For Anna and Charmian this is most evident in their responses to corporeal failure, to the loss of their babies and the wretched self-doubts that followed. For Bess we see it in her fiercely placing her children before anyone else, even her husband, quite in line with the expectations of the day.

The issue of maternal loss runs through the recent commentary on Jack London's writings. As Jeanne Reesman reminds us in her study of his short fiction, "the search for the mother persists in a way that the anxieties about the father do not."[11] In his final Hawaiian stories, the search becomes more transcendent, as in "The Water Baby," with its "thought of my return to my mother and of my rebirth from my mother into the sun."[12] This search directed London's life as well, and it should not be surprising that we return to the mammy figure and its particulars. Mammy is strong, loyal, faithful, and asexual, thus never a threat to the existing order. Despite encompassing these qualities, the dour, life-soured Flora had no chance compared to Jennie Prentiss, who eventually lost Jack's support when she too aligned with his first wife. Of the three maternal figures from his childhood, only Eliza prevailed. Yet by the time she came to the ranch, she'd brought along her own son and was much more London's business partner than the coddling stepsister of his childhood.

From his wives and lovers London expected the same qualities, though with asexuality replaced by fidelity. Their New Women skills and interests, whether clerical, artistic, or athletic, were admirable both in themselves and for their potential service to his needs. "Mammyness" is not a reciprocal relation; the man need not return these virtues. Still, one should be careful not to reduce these relations to convenient analytical categories, nor is my argument here the old one of sexual oppression and female victimization. Whatever the explicit balance of power on London's side, it was not total; otherwise there would not have been so many dramatic events that caused him (and the women) consternation. Anna refused his proposal, Bess denied him his daughters, and Charmian challenged his concept of the manly right to philander.

In terms of the common expressions of patriarchy, Jack was inconsistent. His attempts to silence Flora and Bess failed. Rather than stifle Anna's and Charmian's creative impulses, he encouraged them. He wanted Bess to be more expressive sexually, and adored Charmian for that quality. In Bess and Joan in particular, he found himself up against formidable opponents who would not quietly accede to his demands, and who used subtle manipulation to revive communication after a breach. When angry at Flora and Jennie, he still dared not withdraw financial support for fear of the damage to his reputation, which he had so carefully constructed, of the successful self-made man. With Becky he had little connection until the final two years, when he started to notice her as more than the figure in Joan's shadow.

If anyone was fully enthralled by patriarchy, it was London himself, yet the culture offered only confusion. No New Man courted the New Woman. There were Teddy Roosevelt's Bully Men, who proved their might against strange nature and strange lands. (Add from this study the stories of Martin Johnson and Frederick O'Brien.) In reality, the primary outlet for virile self-assertion was the bureaucratic battlefield of market capitalism. "Work, work whether you want to or not," wrote David Graham Phillips, another novelist raised on Horatio Alger stories.[13] There was even a model of muscular Christianity, of Jesus the burly carpenter plying his trade, a portrait very different from the effeminate image hanging in the parlor. Success was proof of one's exercise of the manly virtues.

Men were also being held to account for much that was wrong with society. In the magazines for which London wrote, editors, ministers, and social commentators attacked male rule and questioned whether men had the makings to create a worthwhile society. They had built a great economy, no doubt, but at a cost to their souls. In devoting themselves to materialistic success, in venerating individualism, men had created an unjust society breeding poverty, slums, child labor, disease, and other social ills. Furthermore, the hardworking patriarch was never at home, hence not much of a father. And as if it were not enough that he was too busy, he was also not busy enough, for he was wasting his time on liquor and carnality.

London's own writings followed the trajectory of this growing argument. His quick acceptance of the New Woman as his standard white heroine, as in the strong women of his Yukon stories, reflected his recognition that change was at hand. Frona Welse challenges her patriarchal father in *Daughter of the Snows,* while Dede Mason reforms Burning Daylight from his corrupt businessman's ways. *The Little Lady of the Big House* represents his most explicit deconstruction of masculinity in its mockery of the virility-obsessed yet sterile Dick Forrest. Ultimately, the New Woman has power over men's darker impulses, and must be encouraged in her assertiveness and revered for taking on this awesome duty.

In life, however, London was understandably less able to carve clear and consistent choices. Though his fiction follows the popular discourse of criticism aimed at men, he was more conventional in his own expectations. He would ask to be judged for meeting his duty in supporting so many households, and he deserves praise for it. However much in debt, he made sure that the monthly checks went out to Bess, to Flora, to Jennie, to Netta, eventually to Eliza, and their dependents. He gave to supplicants of all sorts, fed and housed guests for weeks at a time, supported dozens of ranch workers and their families during his final years. In so overstressed and overworked a life, his querulousness toward some recipients merits a dollop of mercy. There were at his core good intentions—the desire for a more just world, where children would not lose an arm in factory machinery or die from drinking sewage poisoned water, where the few would not live lavishly on the fruits of others' labor, where the soil would not be depleted by wasteful farming practices. Combine that generosity and idealism with the often-reported features of his personality—his enthusiasm, his boyishness, his energy, his endless curiosity—and one sees a most beguiling person.

One must acknowledge these traditional qualities to understand the actions of the women in his life. Why would Flora stick by her son even after he was shocked to learn of his illegitimacy? Why would Jennie Prentiss give him $300, an enormous sum in 1891, to buy a boat? Why else would Anna die surrounded by notes about her experiences with him, or Bess never lose her love? Why would Charmian and Eliza spend their lives carrying on his literary and agricultural legacy when they could have sold the land and made other choices promising fewer troubles? Why would Joan find it so difficult to let go, or Becky cling to her remembrances? The gains from their relation to London were often outweighed by the costs, emotional and otherwise. To reduce the equation to gender—that they were somehow being compliant, or subservient, or deferential to the patriarchal power structure—does not hold. As London accepted after meeting Charmian, love is real, however much it is overlooked in the postmodern critical autopsy. It was not submission that led Charmian during Jack's final terrible months of suffering to "so beautifully [turn] the darts of his barbed comments to her and others and at the dinner table [as] she played Rachmaninoff to soothe him."[14]

Love made life difficult for Bess once Jack discovered his passion first for

Anna, next for Charmian. (It was perhaps less difficult for the woman in Hawaii, who reputedly rejected him by leaving a note in an ashtray.). It naturally engulfed his daughters. It was law, not cultural beliefs concerning gender, however, that through its support of patriarchy really complicated matters. Some legal scholars believe that there was a serious error in the settlement of the estate, that the daughters deserved rights to half of their father's royalties for life.[15] The shift in control from Charmian to the Shepard line was most unusual in the extent to which it cut out Jack's blood descendants. What became apparent to me during my research was how that breach had led to so many misunderstandings on either side of the line. Though Joan and Charmian attempted a healing, they were unable to achieve it, at no blame to either.

Less important than the money, ultimately, was the emotional toll on Joan and Becky following their father's death. Charmian and Eliza bore the burden of continuing his legacy but also reaped the rewards and public recognition. As widow and surviving stepsister, they found that the relationship expanded opportunities for self-expression and adventure, however difficult at times. Over-identified not with her mother, as Russ Kingman believed, but with her father, Joan tied herself to him with unhappy consequences. She was "Jack London's daughter" to the press, usually in some pejorative sense. As Joan's lifelong friend Robin Lampson observed after her death, "What a brilliant career she might have had, not necessarily in writing, but somewhere in the field of stage, music, singing . . . if only she had been able to enjoy *her legitimate share* of her father's enormous earnings and of . . . his royalties after his death."[16] She might even have achieved renown as a historian, where her writing talents most lay. Instead, she was never able to maintain an intimate functional relationship with a man, and that, combined with her drinking, added to the story of promise unfulfilled.

Becky fled public notice, even before bearing Jean, and unlike Joan was quick to adopt her husband's name. She too had an unsatisfactory marriage, but, being more traditional, doubtless felt bound by the need for her husband's financial support. She lived a modest life as a businesswoman, working at the stationery store and serving as caretaker to her ailing mother. Despite her later criticism, Becky never alienated herself from Joan, but true to her sense of propriety maintained friendly relations. Were it not for the Kingmans, Becky would have received none of the fruits of her father's legacy at all. Unlike Joan, she never expressed rancor toward the Shepards nor wished for recompense. Nonetheless, in her will she left her father's royalties to her descendants, just in case.

Apart from their not seeking reconciliation with the daughters, the Shepards acceded to Charmian's wishes by preserving the bulk of the land, and eventually turning it over to the state. If they erred, it was perhaps in so tightly restricting access to the materials at the Huntington Library. Irving Shepard did so with good intentions, having seen how Charmian and Eliza were repeatedly exploited. But the result was to foster accounts that perpetuated the errors of Rose Wilder Lane, Irving Stone, and Joan London. Even today, encyclopedia editors refer to those works when challenged. After Irving Shepard's death, his son Milo responded to the renascence of interest in London by granting permission more often and more broadly.

The estate has little value now in terms of royalties, for London's works went out of copyright, and today anyone may print and profit from them. Most of his works are now available in E-texts on the Web. The Park Service owns and controls the thousands of negatives of the rich and significant array of photographs taken by Charmian and Jack. London's image has been appropriated by advertisers without benefit to the estate. With so many of the key private papers in print, or used as the basis for recent biographies, movie and television producers have access to the material without the contracts required in the past. Consequently, though there was intermittent income in the past for Charmian and the Shepards, this is no longer the case. And as they would have been the first to point out, the income went right back into preserving the land.

For the descendants of Joan and Becky, wounds remain unhealed. After Bart Abbott's death, Helen began to go through his correspondence and only then realized the extent to which others had acted to create a slanted view of Flora, Bess, and Joan. Bart's daughters from both marriages followed Helen's lead and began to research and discuss their family history. The documents could not answer their many questions, because the truth is rarely pure. When anger led to blame, they discovered those blamed need not have acted out of pure malice. Then Jean died, and her sons learned the truth of their bloodline and realized that they too were part of the story. They joined in the dialogue with Bart's daughters and Helen. In time, these family members became vocal at scholarly meetings, challenging what they saw as a skewed interpretation of London and the women in his life. At least one form of reparations was due, they implied, and the record should be corrected. This book is the first response to that call.

London's impulsive last will seems cruel, and it is not clear that he would have changed it much had he had the chance, nor been disappointed with the results. As his late letters indicate, he wanted his daughters to be like his Man Comrade vision: strong and fearless, loyal and true, yet without losing their femininity and ultimate maternity. He expected them to make their way in the world, as he had, and he trusted Charmian to see to that end. There would have been no supporting them in adulthood. He would clearly have approved of Joan's activism, even her messy private life, but been puzzled by Becky.

He would perhaps have been disappointed, too, that Anna failed to meet his expectations of literary or political acclaim. He might have been sorry that his mother and foster mother had such difficult last years, for he was not heartless. That Charmian saw to his worldwide publication and reputation through her management of his literature, that she and Eliza exploited Hollywood to save the ranch, would have garnered his applause. He might even have come to admit that he was not, after all, a self-made man.

# Acknowledgments

WITHOUT THE TRUST AND SUPPORT of members of two families—the Abbotts and the Shepards—this book could not have been written. Particularly noteworthy is the fact that, despite the breech between the two family lines, none of them conveyed any wish other than that I develop my book and interpretation without prejudice. That says much about the honor and kindness of all involved, and their wish that the story be complete.

From the start of my interest in Charmian London, Irving and Mildred Shepard opened their home and hospitality to me and enabled me to view materials not yet sent to the Huntington Library. During a time when part of the London papers were kept separate and generally unavailable, the Shepards permitted me complete access. Following his father's death, Milo Shepard continued that support and encouragement, and guided me in appreciating the agricultural life, its attractions and demands. His graciousness, generosity, and patience over the years formed a steady grounding point through times of despair that the work would ever be completed.

Helen Abbott did more than share her boxes of letters and photographs from Joan and Becky. She reminisced in full, lush paragraphs, and always sent me off with fresh-baked bread. She prodded and argued, kept pushing documents in front of me. She directed me to people to interview, and offered a more subtle understanding of the different choices Joan and Becky made in life. Her daughter Tarnel Abbott unwittingly became a research assistant, for as her curiosity was piqued, she located new sources and shared them with me. Up to the end, Tarnel kept coming up with new thoughts and material to enlighten me on key episodes.

Librarians are the stalwart beavers for projects such as this. Many provided efficient assistance and guidance at the Huntington Library, Merrill Library at Utah State University, Oakland Public Library, Bancroft Library in Berkeley, Special Collections at the University of California at Los Angeles, State Labor Archives at San Francisco State University, and Ruben Salazar Library at Sonoma State University. Serving from afar were those at the State Historical Society of Wisconsin, Indiana University, and Yale University. Special thanks to

Sue Hodson of the Huntington for her assistance, and Greg Castillo at the California Labor Federation library, who opened his files so I could see the full array of Joan's work there. Although we often disagreed, Russ Kingman was unstinting in his help at the Jack London Research Center in Glen Ellen. After his death, Winnie Kingman showed the same bigheartedness, which meant that I was able to benefit from various of Russ's correspondence and research files.

Several people graciously volunteered copies from their private collections of Charmian London documents, including Mel Smith, Judy van der Veer, and Margaret Guilford-Kendall.

Besides members of the Shepard and Abbott families, others, some under anonymity, offered extensive memories of Joan and Becky in particular. Henry Anderson knew Joan best during the 1960s, when they were in activist groups together. Jack Henning remembered her from his long tenure at the California Labor Federation. Winnie Kingman was Becky's protector and close friend during her final years. Stan Weir was in the midst of the radical Berkeley activities of the 1940s, and knew both Joan and Becky from that time. Archie Green also filled me in on labor issues, especially the complicated dealings on the San Francisco waterfront, and directed me to Barney Mayes's unpublished autobiography. George Tweney provided a lively account of visits with Charmian.

Garlands to those who read an early version of the draft to identify areas for improvement and clarification: Candy Donnelly, James Donnelly, Catherine Pyke, and Marlise Tellander. James Williams's incisive criticism of a later draft provided the right combination of niggling and intellectual challenge to spur a total revision.

Over the years, several people active in the London scholars' community have been constant in their encouragement. My E-mail colleague Susan Irwin Gatti gave almost daily cheer. Hensley Woodbridge, Tony Williams, Earle Labor, Jeanne Reesman, Andrew Furer, and Kazuhiro Kobayashi all contributed to the dialogue in valued ways.

James Boylan sent invaluable research material from his work on Anna Strunsky and William English Walling, and kindly answered a variety of picky questions. Fellow biographer Kenneth Silverman kept me buoyed with his notes of encouragement and confidence in my ability to handle this complex topic.

Among colleagues at Sonoma State University, Daniel Markwyn ably directed my further understanding of California history, while Robert Coleman-Senghor shared ideas regarding London and biography in general. During my graduate history seminars, I regularly shared my ongoing research, and I appreciate the interest and comments of students in those classes.

In a day when publishing is no longer a "gentleman's profession," it has been a delight to find otherwise in editor Bruce Wilcox, whose cordiality and wisdom added so much enjoyment to the process. We shared a good laugh the day we realized that he had been an editor at the University of Washington Press when the troubled communications involving Russ Kingman and Becky London were complicating the possibility of publishing *Jack London and His Daughters*. It seemed propitious that he should now be editor of this project, and in a sense make up for the earlier loss to Joan. In overseeing the manuscript production, Carol Betsch maintained the friendly atmosphere, quickly responded to my concerns, and handled my episodic hysteria with aplomb. Copyeditor Amanda Heller proved the best I have ever had assigned in my thirty years of writing. She was fearless and always correct in her amendments, questions, and elisions. Much of any grace and clarity in this work rests with these three.

Once more, bouquets to my husband, Michael, and daughter Kendra, who suffered through my doubts, anxieties, and frustrations over these many, many years. But no thanks to the evil three, the late Pavarotti, Mickey, and Kita, whose nagging, mewing, and dirty pawprints on research notes was not appreciated!

# Notes

Much of my research at the Huntington Library was done under an earlier cataloguing system, when correspondence was filed alphabetically in boxes. It was later rearranged with each document assigned an identification number. For that reason, not all of my references to that collection include the current call number. Furthermore, some of the most important documents were still at the home of the Shepard family, and are most likely now at the Huntington.

In some instances I have not attached notes where the source is easily discernible. In particular, where dates are attached to quoted remarks of Charmian London's, the source is her diary, now at the Huntington Library. Accordingly, where dates are attached to quoted remarks from the correspondence of Jack London, the source is *The Letters of Jack London,* 3 volumes, edited by Earle Labor, Robert C. Leitz, and I. Milo Shepard, with the permission of the publishers, Stanford University Press. Copyright 1998 by the Board of Trustees of the Leland Stanford Junior University. Finally, quotations within discussions of literary works are taken from those works unless otherwise noted.

Abbreviations used in the notes:

AS      Anna Strunsky
ASWY    Anna Strunsky Walling Papers, Manuscripts and Archives, Yale University Library, New Haven
*BJL*    *Book of Jack London,* 2 volumes, by Charmian London
BL      Bancroft Library, University of California at Berkeley
CKL     Charmian Kittredge London
HA      Helen Abbott
HEH     Henry E. Huntington Library, San Marino, California
JL      Jack London
JLFRC   Jack London Foundation Research Center, Glen Ellen, California
*JLHD*   *Jack London and His Daughters* by Joan London
*JLHT*   *Jack London and His Times* by Joan London
*LJL*    *The Letters of Jack London,* 3 volumes, edited by Labor et al.
ML      Merrill Library, Utah State University, Logan, Utah
SH      Home of Irving Shepard, Glen Ellen, California

## Preface

1. Dana Garcia suggested this project and helped on early research.
2. I analyze a number of consistent errors in seven biographies appearing up to 1974 in "The Social Construction of Biography," *Modern Fiction Studies* 22 (Spring 1976): 51–71. See, for example, Irving Stone, *Sailor on Horseback,* chap. 7; Richard O'Connor, *Jack London,* 374–75; Kevin Starr, *Americans and the California Dream,* 154–60. Virtually omitting Charmian altogether were Philip Foner, *Jack London—American Rebel,* and Joan London, *Jack Lon-*

*don and His Times.* The best introduction to Earle Labor's contribution up to that time is *Jack London.*

3. James Boylan, *Revolutionary Lives.*
4. Clarice Stasz, *The Vanderbilt Women; The Rockefeller Women.*


## 1   Mrs. Prentiss, Mrs. Chaney

1. Jennie Prentiss told stories about her past to Becky and Joan London when they were children. These accounts are reported passim in *JLHD* and in unpublished accounts recorded during interviews with Becky at the JLFRC. The only complete study is by historian Eugene P. Lasartemay and poet Mary Rudge, *For Love of Jack London,* an error-ridden work that must be approached cautiously yet cannot be discounted. See my review in *Jack London Journal* (1995) for a full evaluation. Lasartemay and Rudge give Tennessee as Jennie's birthplace, but I have relied on Joan London, who was told by Jennie that her name originated with the state of Virginia.

2. Lasartemay and Rudge identified the plantation, and I found a possible listing for Jennie in the 1860 census, where she is identified as a "Negro," another indication of the looser culture of slavery in Tennessee.

3. See, for example, Elizabeth Fox-Genovese, *Within the Plantation Household: Black and White Women in the Old South* (Chapel Hill: University of North Carolina Press, 1988); Anne Firor Scott, *The Southern Lady: From Pedestal to Politics, 1830–1980* (Chicago: University of Chicago Press, 1970); Deborah Gray White, *Ar'n't I a Woman: Female Slaves in the Plantation South* (New York: Norton, 1985). As with most monographs on slavery, these books emphasize data from the Deep South and eastern seaboard states.

4. Chase Curran Mooney, *Slavery in Tennessee,* traces the laws and practices of that state and interprets them in light of personal records and account books from various slaveholds. He distinguishes three cultural regions of slavery, the Parker plantation being from what he calls Middle Tennessee. Except for chapter 4, "Slave Life," which seems an apology for the institution, this is a good overview of the regional differences within the state.

5. The classic study here is Eugene Genovese, *Roll, Jordan, Roll: The World the Slaves Made.*

6. Dorothy Hershberger of Canton, Ohio, provided copies of unpublished papers ("Flora Wellman: Her Early Life" and "Jack London: Feminine Influences") that provide information on Wellman genealogy and the family's role in local history. See also *JLHT*, 2–6. Joan London reflects more on how Flora's youth shaped her personality in *JLHD*, 120–23.

7. Lasartemay and Rudge trace the Prentisses to Tiffin in Seneca County, probably because that is the town where Alonzo enrolled in the army. The International Genealogical Index, however, lists the marriage of Ruth McConnell to Alonzo Prentiss on April 7, 1842, in Putnam County, south of Toledo. Census records of 1840, 1850, and 1860 show Alonzo and Ruth's parents, the McConnells, living there as well. Prentiss's military pension records identify three children: Thomas William, born 1843; Lyman Edwin, 1849; and Ruth Edna, 1856.

8. Alonzo Prentiss's mulatto status is claimed by Lasartemay and Rudge, *For Love,* 6. His pension records state "no records found" of any medical treatment while in the army.

9. Joan London made extensive research notes on Chaney in anticipation of completing a full-length biography. See MI 681, HEH. She assisted her friend Fulmer Mood in preparing "An Astrologer from Down East," *New England Quarterly* 5 (1932): 769–99. My check of their primary sources corroborated their research and conclusions.

10. W. H. Chaney, *Primer of Astrology and American Urania,* 139. Chaney weaves detailed biog-

raphical material throughout his astrological discourse, presenting himself as a case example. Wry self-effacement runs through, as when he refers to himself as of "unsymmetrical and lumpy appearance" (123) and an "idiot in financing" (161).

11. On Chaney and astrological humanitariansm: ibid., 1–3, 11–14, 111–12.
12. Chaney's third marriage: ibid., 169ff.
13. ibid., 157.
14. Chaney on Flora Wellman: *Primer,* 118.
15. William Chaney to JL, June 4, and 14, 1897, as reprinted in Russ Kingman, *A Pictorial Life of Jack London,* 18–21. The originals are in the Irving Stone collection, UCLA.
16. The full collection of *Common Sense* is available at HEH.
17. Joan London Miller, notes for a biography on William Chaney, MI 681.
18. Chaney on Abigail Duniway: *Primer,* 140–41.
19. Ibid., 34, 119, 139.
20. Affadavit of Flora London, June 9, 1898, Civil War pension file of John London.
21. See note 15.
22. Inscription in *The Cruise of the Dazzler,* September 24, 1916, Oakland Public Library. "Well, it took a long time to pay back what I borrowed from you with which to buy the 'Razzle Dazzle.' . . . And here is loving you, and always lovingly, Your white pickaninny, Jack London." Years earlier Jennie angrily reminded Jack not to call her Mammy, but he refused to accede to her request.


## 2   Johnny, Jack

1. As quoted in *BJL* 1:24–25, Mills and Boon ed. The American edition omits three paragraphs of Jennie Prentiss's account to Charmian London.
2. The early family history of John London was researched by Jim Ricfenstahl and is available at the JLFRC. His careful investigation revealed a number of factual errors in Charmian London's *BJL* regarding Jack's stepfather.
3. Records of the Veterans' Administration, Civil War pension file of John London, document these ailments.
4. Deposition of Daphne V. Prentiss, October 16, 1900, Civil War pension file of John London.
5. Dolores Nason McBroome, *Parallel Communities,* describes the special relationship of blacks to other ethnic groups in the Oakland area.
6. See photograph of the Prentiss house at 2060 Pacific Avenue, Alameda, in Lasartemay and Rudge, *For Love,* 109. The London home there no longer exists.
7. *BJL* 1:35–36.
8. See Christopher Gair, *Complicity and Resistance in Jack London's Novels.*
9. For an introduction to the popular culture of women's domesticity during this period, see Barbara Ehrenreich and Deirdre English, *For Her Own* Good, (Garden City, N.Y.: Anchor, 1978); Peter Gabriel Filene, *Him/Her/Self* (New York: Harcourt Brace, 1975); Glenna Mathews, *"Just a Housewife"* (New York: Oxford University Press, 1987); and Harvey Green, *The Light of the Home.*
10. This and other recollections are part of *Jack Liverpool,* an unfinished autobiographical novel. Box 24, folder 4, ML.
11. Frank Irving Atherton, *Jack London in Boyhood Adventures,* 28–30.
12. A major earthquake on October 17, 1989, destroyed a freeway through the neighborhood of Jack London's youth. Before rebuilding began, it was necessary to comply with Section 106 of the National Historic Preservation Act, which resulted in archaeological investigation in

depth of twenty-two city blocks by the Anthropological Studies Center of Sonoma State University. The findings unearthed artifacts that led to a new understanding of the social and cultural history of this heterogeneous working-class community of the late 1800s. The major findings are reported in Suzanne Stewart and Mary Praetzellis, eds., *Sights and Sounds: Essays in Celebration of West Oakland.* Prior to reading this work, I envisioned London growing up in a racially segregated neighborhood.

13. For the Woman's Relief Corps and patriotism, see Cecilia Elizabeth O'Leary, *To Die For,* and John Higham, *Strangers in the Land.*

14. Jack and Charmian London Collection, box 24, folders 3 and 4, ML.

15. See, for example, John F. McClymer, "Late Nineteenth-Century American Working-Class Standards," *Journal of Interdisciplinary History* (Autumn 1986): 379–98. This study demonstrates that "working class" then was not synonymous with "poor," and identifies consumer goods markers for distinguishing levels of income.

16. "Pioneer Head of Lincoln School Taught J. London," *Oakland Tribune,* February 9, 1927, 32.

17. JL to Ina Coolbrith, December 15, 1906, JLFRC.

18. Atherton, *Boyhood Adventures,* 27.

19. Ibid., 41.

20. See oral interviews with Jane Disard Wright and Theo Bruce, great-granddaughter of Isaac Caudwell, in Lasartemay and Rudge, *For Love,* 131–33.

21. London recounts his socialization to alcohol in his masterly account *John Barleycorn: Alcoholic Memoirs.* There he analyzes with incisiveness the relationship between masculinity and drinking—his expression as an amateur sociologist at its best.

22. See excerpt from report, "California Jute Mills, Oakland," in Reda Davis, *California Women,* 12–13.

23. *BJL* 1:141.

24. Lasartemay and Rudge, *For Love,* 132.

25. As quoted in Franklin Walker, ms. notes for biography of Jack London, 22–23, HEH.

26. Georgia Loring Bamford attended the high school at the same time as Jack. Her memoir, *The Mystery of Jack London,* reflects the attitudes of a conventional middle-class schoolmate toward this grown man with so much more worldly experience.


## 3    Those California Women

1. Given the state's size and significance in U.S. history, it is surprising how little scholarship has addressed California women overall. For an introduction, see Joan M. Jensen and Gloria Ricci Lothrop, *California Women.* Much of the available scholarship either is biographical, highlighting the development and contributions of particular women, or else singles out a narrow group by role and time period. The various sources with which I am familiar lend support to the broader themes suggested by Jensen and Lothrop, at least for the period 1865–1920.

2. As quoted in Jensen and Lothrop, *California Women,* 21.

3. The full texts of Chaney's letters are in Russ Kingman, *A Pictorial Life of Jack London,* 17–21.

4. The full set of JL inscriptions to his mother are in Carolyn Johnston, *Jack London,* chap. 1, n. 5. In personal communication Johnston reports she saw these books at SH.

5. The most sophisticated analysis of London's self-marketing is Jonathan Auerbach, *Male Call,* chap. 1; see also *Martin Eden,* chaps. 23 and 24, for a fictionalized presentation reflecting London's own method.

6. JL to Edward [Ted] Applegarth, November 14, 1898, *LJL* 1:19–20.

7. JL to Mabel Applegarth, November 30, 1898, *LJL* 1:23–26.

8. "Jack London," *Overland Monthly* (May 1900): 417–25.

9. I viewed all the primary materials (letters, poems, stories, diaries) relating to Dayelle ("Daisy") Wiley at SH.

10. Much of the information on Charmian's childhood comes from unpublished notes for a never-completed autobiographical novel, *Charmette,* SH. See also Netta Payne to CKL, November 30 and December 7, 1937, box 15, folder 13, ML.

11. The many letters from Netta Eames to CKL throughout her life corroborate this characterization of her as manipulative, derogatory, and insensitive toward her ward.

12. Raine Edward Bennett, "The Intimate Jack London," *San Francisco* (March 1976).

13. JL to Cloudesley Johns, March 10, 1900, *LJL* 1:167–69.

14. "An Oakland Boy's Success as a Story Writer," *Oakland Tribune,* November 22, 1899.

15. *The Editor* (November 1900), JL Scrapbook microfilm, HEH.

16. *Boston Beacon,* December 22, 1900, JL Scrapbook microfilm, HEH.

17. George Hamlin Fitch, *Impressions* (September 1900), JL Scrapbook microfilm, HEH.

18. *The Critic* (August 1900), JL Scrapbook microfilm, HEH.

19. For more detail, see Mark Pittenger, *American Socialists and Evolutionary Thought, 1870–1920.*

20. Letters from JL to Cloudesley Johns dated June 7, 12, 23, and July 5, 1899, *LJL,* 1:79–94, provide the most detailed explication of London's views on Anglo-Saxonism at the time. The quoted passage is from a letter dated December 12, 1899, *LJL* 1:133.

4  *"Gitana Strunsky"*

1. This and subsequent quotes concerning the event: AS, memoir notes published in CKL, *BJL* 1:319–21.

2. JL to AS, December 19, 1899, *LJL* 1:133–35.

3. JL to AS, December 21, 1899, *LJL* 1:135–36.

4. On Anna's family background and youth: James Boylan, *Revolutionary Lives,* chap. 1.

5. "The Golden Wedding," unpublished manuscript, Strunsky Walling Collection, BL, box 1.

6. AS, as quoted in Boylan, *Revolutionary Lives,* 9.

7. AS, "Jack London," notes for biography, ASWY, folders 392–93, contain Anna's recollections of the relationship. These pages are repetitive, out of order, and incomplete.

8. Boylan, *Revolutionary Lives,* 16.

9. JL to AS, January 15, 1900, *LJL* 1:143–44.

10. JL to AS, February 13, 1900, *LJL* 1:156–57.

11. JL to AS, April 6, 1900, *LJL* 1:179.

12. JL to Ninetta Eames, April 3, 1900, *LJL* 1:178.

13. JL to Cloudesley Johns, October 3, 1899, *LJL* 1:115–16.

14. Joan London, *JLHD.* After the divorce Joan repeatedly heard her father speak to her mother about the "good times" the couple had always had.

15. JL to AS, April 6, 1900, *LJL* 1:179.

16. AS, "Jack London."

17. JL to AS, May 2, 1900, *LJL* 1:183.

18. JL to AS, July 31, 1900, *LJL* 1:198.

19. AS, "Jack London."

20. Jack London and Anna Strunsky, *The Kempton-Wace Letters,* 210.

21. AS, "Jack London."

22. JL to Cloudesley Johns, January 23, 1899, *LJL* 1:88–91.
23. JL to AS, January 6, 1901, *LJL* 1:235.
24. Melissa Maddern told Joan London the story, as reported in *JLHD*, 3–4.
25. *JLHD*, 8.
26. A wealth of biographical material on George Sterling is available in the Cecil Clemens papers, BL. These consist of letters, notes, and interviews with people Clemens approached about preparing a never-completed biography of the poet. Quote is from Adolphe de Castro to Cecil Clemens, October 5, 1942, BL.
27. First published in *The Delineator* (January 1904), and included in *Revolution and Other Essays* (1910).
28. Bess London to Lurline [Montgomery], March 27, 1902, JL 9401, HEH.
29. Fragmentary notes, ASWY, folder 300.
30. JL to AS, "Saturday Evening" [?1901], *LJL* 1:261–64.
31. I made this connection upon receiving Charmian's copy of Browning's poems as a gift from Milo Shepard. Ticks in the index note "My Star," which is the first poem in the volume. London also wrote a poem to Charmian calling her "Star of my life, my hope, my light." JL to CKL, ca. January 1903, Pacific Book Auction Catalogue, 1993.
32. Flora Wellman London to AS, ca. April 1904, Walling Collection, Box 3A, HEH.
33. AS, "Jack London."
34. JL to AS, June 10, 1902, *LJL* 1:297–98.
35. Flora Wellman London to AS, August 20, 1902, Walling Collection, box 3A, HEH.
36. JL to AS, August 25, 1902, *LJL* 1:306–8.
37. JL to AS, August 28, 1902, *LJL* 1:308–9.
38. AS, "Jack London."
39. Elsie Whitaker Martinez, oral interview conducted by Franklin D. Walker and Willa Klug Baum, BL. Several years later, teenage Elsie married Xavier Martinez.

5   *Damned Hard on the Woman*

1. These photographs are at the offices of the State of California Parks and Recreation Department in Sonoma.
2. "Jack London Had *Two* Daughters," *Jack London Foundation Newsletter* (October 1990): 1–4.
3. JL to Cloudesley Johns, August 26, 1903, *LJL* 1:381.
4. JL to AS, December 20, 1902, *LJL* 1:328–30.
5. JL to George Brett, January 20, 1903, *LJL* 1:337–38.
6. David Mike Hamilton, *"The Tools of My Trade,"* 153.
7. JL to AS, February 3, 1903, *LJL* 1:342.
8. Jo Anne Sharpe, "William H. Chaney Appearances in *The Adept*," *Jack London Foundation Newsletter* (January 1975): 12–14.
9. CKL, "Jack London Afloat," *Sunset* (1903): 190–91.
10. JL to Frank Putnam, March 9, 1903, *LJL* 1:347–48.
11. All information concerning London's earnings are based on calculations from entries in Russ Kingman, *Jack London.* The totals reported here and elsewhere should be considered conservative, because internal evidence suggests that the figures reported are not complete.
12. JL to Carrie Sterling, September 15, 1905, *LJL* 1:520–26. Quotes in this section are from this version of his account of the events leading to his affair with CKL.
13. Joseph Noel, *Footloose in Arcadia*, 113–14.

14. CKL destroyed these diaries in 1938.
15. JL to CKL, June 18, 1903, *LJL* 1:365–67.
16. JL to CKL, July 1903, *LJL* 1:370–71.
17. JL to Cloudesley Johns, August 26, 1903, *LJL* 1:381.
18. JL to CKL, September 28, 1903, *LJL* 1:391.
19. CKL to JL, scrap of letter, n.d. [ca. 1903], HEH.
20. *JLHD*, 17–19.
21. *JLHD*, 19–21.
22. Jack maintained a clipping service and kept all his reviews and other newspaper mentions over the years in enormous scrapbooks, HEH.
23. AS to George Brett as quoted in Boylan, *Revolutionary Lives*, 33.
24. AS, notebook, August 14, 1903, Strunsky Walling Collection, BL.
25. JL to CKL, September 24 and 28, 1903, *LJL* 1:389–91.
26. AS, notebook, December 17, 1902, Strunsky Walling Collection, BL.
27. AS, notebook, February 21, 1904, Strunsky Walling Collection, BL.
28. [JL to CKL], January 4, 1904, *Pacific Book Auction Galleries*, February 1993 catalogue. The catalogue includes a copy of the first page of the letter, which has no salutation and is described as unsigned. The handwriting is JL's and a note "Return" on the top is in CKL's hand.
29. JL to Eliza Shepard, as copied in body of letter to Corinne [Maddern], April 4, 1904, typewritten copy, HA. In typescript and format the letter is identical to that prepared for the manuscript of *Letters from Jack London*, edited by King Hendricks and Irving Shepard. The letter was not printed in that volume, nor did Hendricks and Shepard print the extensive correspondence of JL to CKL during his trip to Korea.
30. JL to Corinne [Maddern], April 4, 1904, HA.
31. Will Maddern to JL, n.d., photocopy of original, HA.
32. JL to CKL, March 11, 1904, *LJL* 1:419.
33. JL to CKL, July 6, 1904, *LJL* 1:431.
34. "Absurd and Vulgar, Says Miss Strunsky," *San Francisco Chronicle*, June 30, 1904.
35. JL to AS, July 23, 1904, *LJL* 1:436.
36. Three of Jack's wills are at HEH: July 19, 1905; December 4, 1905; and May 24, 1911. All have dated codicils as well.
37. JL to Blanche Partington, September 21, 1904, *LJL* 1:444–45.
38. JL to CKL, September 29, 1904, *LJL* 1:446.
39. AS to Katia Maryson, September 2, 1904, as quoted in Boylan, *Revolutionary Lives*, 42.
40. Eliza Shepard to AS, December 4, 1904, HEH.
41. *JLHD*, 26.

6   *Deceivers and Deceived*

1. The full poem is in Boylan, *Revolutionary Lives*, 43.
2. The most complete biographical information on Walling: ibid., esp. chaps. 8–12.
3. William English Walling letters to AS during this time are in folder 210, ASWY.
4. Rose Strunsky to AS, November 1905, folder 86, ASWY.
5. The speech was expanded into "Revolution," an essay in *The War of the Classes*.
6. JL to Cloudesley Johns, June 7, 1905, *LJL* 1:490–91.
7. *JLHD*, 46.
8. CKL diary, May 10, 1905, JL 248, HEH.

9. JL to Caroline Sterling, September 15, 1905, *LJL* 1:520–26.
10. Joseph Noel, *Footloose in Arcadia*, 154.
11. Various promotional booklets on Jack London for Macmillan repeat these themes. These are reprinted in *Jack London Journal* 5 (1998): 136–67. As editor James Williams points out, even those booklets written in the third person display the hand of London in sections.
12. *San Francisco Chronicle*, June 30, 1904.
13. JL used these descriptions regarding CKL and Bess in several letters over the years, and according to Noel, used the same terms in talking to his male friends.
14. On masculinity during the Victorian and Progressive eras: E. Anthony Rotundo, *American Manhood*; Mark C. Carnes and Clyde Griffin, eds., *Meanings for Manhood*; Peter Filene, *Him/Her Self* (New York: Harcourt Brace Jovanovich, 1975); Mark Carnes, *Secret and Ritual Manhood in Victorian America*.
15. On new models of fathering: Robert L. Griswold, *Fatherhood in America* (1993), chaps. 1–4.
16. All quotations are from London's July and December 1905 wills in HEH.
17. For the *Snark* plans, see *Nautical Quarterly* (Winter 1981): 69.
18. AS to CKL, October 6, 1905, HEH.
19. *San Francisco Chronicle*, November 18, 1905.
20. King's letters, poignant in light of his ignorance of Anna's real intentions, are in folder 73, ASWY.
21. Cameron King to AS, April 4, 1906, folder 73, ASWY.
22. As quoted in Boylan, *Revolutionary Lives*, 104.
23. Ibid., 97.
24. AS, "Revolutionary Lives," 10–11, Strunsky Walling Collection, BL.
25. Jack London, "The House Beautiful," in *Revolution and Other Essays*.
26. George Sterling to Ambrose Bierce, as quoted in Franklin Walker, *The Seacoast of Bohemia*, 15.
27. Mary Austin, *Earth Horizon*, 303.
28. CKL to Blanche Partington, March 8, 1907, Partington Family Collection, BL.
29. *JLHD*, 67.


7   *Like Children at a Circus Parade*

1. CKL, *The Log of the Snark*, 20.
2. Ibid., 16.
3. See JL to George Brett, *LJL* 2:685–87.
4. *JLHD*, 72.
5. *JLHD*, 72–73.
6. Armine von Tempski, *Born in Paradise*, 198–99.
7. *Log*, 39.
8. *Log*, 34.
9. *Log*, 78.
10. As quoted in Vil Bykov, "Anna Strunsky's Parcel," unpublished ms. Bykov's article quotes extensively from a manuscript about her Russian journey that Anna sent him during the last year of her life. I am grateful to James Boylan for providing a translated copy.
11. *JLHD*, 105.
12. JL to Eliza Shepard, March 19, 1908, *JLJ* 2:745–46.
13. Quotations from Bess London to JL, March 24, 1907, ML. This letter is obviously misdated. First, Bess and Milner were not yet engaged in early 1907. Second, a letter Jack wrote on Oc-

tober 27, 1908, refers to his having "just received" her letter of March 24, and responds to points in that letter.

14. Quotations from JL to Bess London, October 27, 1908, *LJL* 2:762–68.
15. JL to Ninetta Eames, February 5, 1909, *LJL* 2:789–91.
16. JL to Becky London, October 28, 1908, *LJL* 2:768.
17. *JLHD*, 102.
18. JL to Eliza Shepard, February 4, 1909, *LJL* 2:792.
19. These letters could have been left on the *Snark* when it was abandoned, thus not necessarily signaling any intended rejection on Jack's part.
20. *Oakland Tribune*, April 22, 1909.
21. JL to George Sterling, October 31, 1908, *LJL* 2:770.
22. *Log,* 436.
23. *Log,* 482.
24. *Revolutionary Lives,* 143.
25. William English Walling, "The Race War in the North," *Independent*, September 3, 1908, 519–34.
26. Mary Ovington, *The Walls Came Tumbling Down,* 132.


8   *Mother-Girl, Mother-Not*

1. CKL diary, September 2, 1909, HEH.
2. CKL to JL, August 4, 1909, SH.
3. CKL diary, December 19, 1909, HEH.
4. Carrie Sterling to Blanche Partington, as quoted in Franklin Walker, *Seacoast of Bohemia,* 66.
5. As quoted ibid., 86.
6. CKL diary, March 23, 1910, HEH.
7. Mary Austin, *Earth Horizon,* 304.
8. CKL diary, April 30, 1910, HEH.
9. Emma Goldman, *Living My Life,* 468–69.
10. Candace Falk, *Love, Anarchy, and Emma Goldman,* 133.
11. As quoted in Peter Dreyer, *A Gardener Touched with Genius,* 154.
12. See my "Jack London and Eucalyptus: Not a Folly," *Jack London Newsletter* (1987) for an explanation of how his decision to plant was based on current agricultural expertise.
13. Netta Eames to JL, June 12, 1909, HEH.
14. CKL diary, June 19, 1910, HEH.
15. CKL diary, June 20, 1910, HEH.
16. Lailee van Dillen, "Becky London: The Quiet Survivor Talks about Her Father," 34–39.
17. *JLHD,* 110.
18. *JLHD,* 154–55.
19. CKL diary, July 11, 1910, HEH.
20. Adela Rogers St. John, *Final Verdict,* 352–64.
21. Bess London to JL, November 4, 1910, HA.
22. Joan London to JL, December 26, 1910, HA.
23. CKL diary, December 18, 1910, HEH.
24. Bess London to JL, January 4, 1911, ML. This is a retyped copy, which appears to have been done on Charmian's typewriter.
25. JL to Bessie London, January 8, 1911, 969–71.

26. *JLHD*, 164–65.
27. Becky London, "The Window Incident," January 1, 1979, JLFRC.
28. Joan London to JL, March 4, 1910, as quoted in *JLHD*, 165. I was unable to locate the original of this letter.
29. Joan London to JL, March 5, 1911, HA.
30. *JLHD*, 166.
31. JL to Bess London, January 8, 1911, *LJL* 2:969.
32. Joan London to JL, October 22, 1911, HA.
33. Joseph Noel, *Footloose in Arcadia*, 221.
34. Ibid., 223.
35. *New York Evening World*, January 6, 1912.
36. CKL diary, January 29, 1912, HEH.
37. AS to JL, January 29, 1912, JL 120129, HEH.
38. Max Eastman as quoted in Steven Watson, *Strange Bedfellows*, 161.
39. AS to JL, January 18, 1913, JL19864, HEH; April 1, 1913, JL19866, HEH.
40. CKL diary, February 8, 1912, HEH.
41. CKL to Anna Strunsky, February 8, 1912, ASWY.
42. As quoted in Boylan, *Revolutionary Lives*, 190.
43. AS to Rosalind Walling, May 6, 1911, ASWY.

9   *Bitter Harvests*

1. CKL, "Cape Horn Journal," SH.
2. CKL diary, March 8, 1912, HEH.
3. "Cape Horn Journal," March 17, 1912.
4. Ibid., April 16, 1912.
5. CKL diary, May 23–29, 1912, HEH.
6. CKL to Anna Strunsky, June 12, 1912, HEH.
7. "Cape Horn Journal," April 29, 1912.
8. Joan London to JL, June 21, 1912, HA.
9. CKL diary, August 27, 1912, HEH.
10. On Martin Johnson's career: Pascal Imperato and Eleanor M. Imperato, *They Married Adventure*, esp. chaps. 3–4; Martin Johnson to JL, December 8, 1910, HEH.
11. CKL diary, December 4, 1912, HEH.
12. CKL diary, December 27, 1912, HEH.
13. CKL to Benjamin de Casseres, November 3, 1912, private collection of Mel Smith.
14. L. Rudio Marshall, "Mrs. Jack London's New Viewpoint," *Overland Monthly* (May 1917): 401.
15. JL to CKL, November 6, 1912, *LJL* 2:1096–97.
16. JL to Minnie Maddern Fiske, July 30, 1910, *JLJ* 2:918–20. This letter also discusses the eucalyptus plantation.
17. JL to William W. Ellsworth, March 1, 1913, *LJL* 2:1131–32.
18. Dick Forrest expresses these ideas in London's *Little Lady of the Big House*.
19. CKL diary, March 11, 1913, HEH.
20. CKL diary, April 10, 1913, HEH.
21. Allan Dunn to JL and CKL, June 20, 1914, ML.
22. Joan London to JL, April 1, 1913, HA.
23. Joan London to JL, April 8, 1913, HA.

24. Joan London to JL, April 20, 1913, HA.
25. Joan London to JL, May 7, 1913, HA.
26. JL to Joan London, May 9, 1913, *LJL* 2:1159–60.
27. Joan London to JL, May 25, 1913, HA.
28. JL to Joan London, May 28, 1913, HA.
29. JL to Joan London, May 31, 1913, *LJL* 2:1181.
30. JL to Jack London, June 19, 1913, HA.
31. Joan London to JL, July 3, 1913, HA.


## 10    A Ruined Colt

1. JL to Joan London, August 24, 1913, *LJL* 3:1218–19.
2. Joan London to JL, August 27, 1913, HA. Page 2 is missing.
3. JL to Joan London, August 29, 1913. *LJL* 3:1220.
4. JL to Joan London, August 31, 1913, *LJL* 3:1221.
5. Joan London to JL, September 2, 1913, HA.
6. Joan London to JL, September 13, 1913, HA.
7. JL to Joan London, October 11, 1913, *LJL* 3:1257–60.
8. Joan London to JL, October 28, 1913, HA.
9. Based on correspondence with a rheumatologist, Russ Kingman supported the lupus theory, while Andrew Sinclair in *Jack* favored the Salvarsan explanation.
10. Fire forensics specialist Robert Anderson of San Jose State University took a team to Wolf House. A nontechnical version of their conclusions is at www.parks.sonoma.net/firecause.html.
11. CKL to AS, November 14, 1913, HEH.
12. CKL diary, August 31, 1913, HEH.
13. For a well-balanced discussion of these negotiations, see Tony Williams, *Jack London: The Movies*, chaps. 2, 3. I read all the relevant court documents and correspondence, HEH.
14. Notarized statement, January 6, 1914, JL25207, HEH.
15. CKL, notes for *The Book of Jack London*, HEH.
16. JL to CKL, January 1914, as quoted in Pacific Book Auction catalogue, 1993.
17. JL to CKL, January 29, 1914, *LJL* 3:1294–95.
18. CKL to AS, October 14, 1913, HEH.
19. CKL to AS, ca. 1914, HEH.
20. AS to William English Walling, January 30, 1913, as quoted in Boylan, *Revolutionary Lives*, 201–2.
21. William English Walling to AS, February 1914, as quoted ibid., 202.
22. *JLHD*, 75.
23. JL to Joan London, March 5, 1914, *LJL* 3:1303.
24. Joan London to JL, March 9, 1914, HA.
25. Lailee van Dillen, "Becky London," 37.
26. *JLHD*, 174.
27. "Becky London," 36.
28. CKL to Paul Eldridge, June 11, 1914, private collection of Mel Smith.
29. JL to "Comrades of the Mexican Revolution," February 11, 1911, *Los Angeles Citizen*.
30. JL to Ralph Kasper, July 25, 1914, *LJL* 3:1339.
31. JL will, holograph copy, Sonoma County Museum. The codicil is dated April 17, yet on April 15 CKL notes in her diary that *Collier's* editor Edgar Sisson had wired them about Mexico

and they left immediately. They took the train from Oakland on April 16. Perhaps, being en route, Jack thought it best to give Glen Ellen as the location, or he may simply have got the date wrong, though that would have been much out of character.

32. JL to Joan London, July 5, 1914, *LJL* 3:1340.
33. Joan London to JL, February 1, 1915, HA.
34. JL to Joan London, February 4, 1915, *LJL* 3:1419–20.
35. MI Box 37, file 13, HEH.
36. AS to JL, October 13, 1913,
37. This and other reminiscences are in the Cyril Clemmons collection, BL.
38. In the course of my research, I learned that the psychologist Barrie Stevens completed a manuscript of over a hundred pages based on interviews with Dr. Nakata. Despite help from her surviving relatives, this material, which they believe had been lent or given to a Canadian scholar, was never located.
39. Luther Burbank, "The Training of the Human Plant" (1906), reprinted in Peter Dreyer, *A Gardener Touched with Genius*, 238.
40. JL, "My Hawaiian Aloha," 23–33, in CKL, *Our Hawaii*, rev. ed., addresses this theme in detail.
41. This information was revealed by the granddaughter of the woman, who wished her and her family to remain anonymous. The informant knew nothing about Jack London; thus I was able to question her in ways that ensured she could not have known that she was providing corroborating information.
42. JL to Eliza Shepard, June 28, 1911, as quoted in Pacific Book Auction catalogue, 1993.

## 11  Your Silence Is Now Golden

1. CKL diary, November 26, 1915, HEH.
2. JL to Joan London, August 25, 1915, *LJL* 3:1490–92; Joan London to JL, September 6, 1915, HA.
3. JL to Joan London, September 16, 1915, *LJL* 3:1500–1501.
4. JL to Joan London, August 25, 1915, *LJL* 3:1490–92.
5. Baby Bee [Becky] to JL, October 19, 1915, HA.
6. *Jack London Foundation Newsletter* (October 1990).
7. JL to Joan London, November 12, 1915, *LJL* 3:1518–19.
8. On London and war: *BJL*, vol. 2 (British ed.), 347–50.
9. CKL to AS, May 18, 1915, HEH.
10. Penduffryn notes, SH.
11. An extensive array of these reviews are found in the Jack London scrapbooks, HEH.
12. *Conservator* (March 1916).
13. *North American Review* 202 (November 1915): 778.
14. As quoted in Boylan, *Revolutionary Lives*, 218.
15. *New York Times*, November 17, 1915.
16. Emma Goldman, "The Black Scourge of War," *Mother Earth* 12 (June 1917): 102.
17. AS to English Walling, January 27, 1917. See Boylan, *Revolutionary Lives*, 227.
18. JL to Joan and Becky London, August 22, 1916, *LJL* 3:1566–67.
19. *JLHD*, 177.
20. JL to Bessie London, October 12, 1916, *JLJ* 3:1586–88.
21. Sophie Loeb to "Wolf," September 30, 1916, HEH.
22. *BJL*, vol. 2 (English ed.), 383.

23. Ibid., 386.
24. "Jack London Had *Two* Daughters," *Jack London Foundation Newsletter* 2 (October 1990): 3.
25. "George Sterling in High Tribute to Jack London," *San Francisco Examiner,* November 27, 1916.

## 12 Widows

1. CKL diary, January 1, 1917, HEH.
2. CKL to Frederick Bamford, 12–14–16, Franklin Walker Collection, HEH.
3. The correspondence between CKL and Willard Growall concerning the long-protracted estate settlement is in ML, box 10, folder 3 and box 12, folder 8.
4. CKL to George Sterling, James Hopper, Frank Strawn-Hamilton, and Upton Sinclair, December 13, 1916, carbon copy, SH.
5. CKL to Frederick Bamford, December 20, 1916, HEH.
6. L. Rudio Marshall, "Mrs. Jack London's New Viewpoint," *Overland Monthly* 48 (May 1917): 400–401.
7. CKL to Willard Growall, February 21, 1918, ML.
8. Willard Growall to Eliza Shepard, March 7, 1918, JL6943, HEH.
9. CKL to Eliza Shepard, April 10, 1918, ML.
10. Robin Lampson to Russ Kingman, March 2, 1971, JLFRC.
11. Willard Growall to Eliza Shepard, October 12, 1918, JL6959, HEH.
12. CKL diary, June 20, 1917, HEH.
13. New York *Evening World,* December 22, 1916.
14. Marshall, "New Viewpoint," 404.
15. Joan London to CKL, July 2, 1917, HA.
16. Joan London to Al Shivers, October 2, 1969, HA.
17. Joan London, "London Bridge," 5, HEH.
18. Robin Lampson, eulogy for Joan London memorial service, January 21, 1971, HA.
19. Lailee van Dillen, "Becky London," 34–39.
20. These photo albums were given to Helen Abbott by Becky London. I made copies for research purposes.
21. Joan London to Al Shivers, January 15, 1964, MI 913, HEH.
22. CKL to W. H. Metson, November 11, 1918, HEH.
23. CKL to Anna Strunsky, February 18, 1922, HEH; *San Francisco Chronicle,* January 5, 1922.
24. CKL to Rose Wilder Lane, September 19, 1917, HEH. The October issue appeared on the newsstands in September.
25. Rose Wilder Lane to CKL, September 22, 1918, box 10, folder 13, ML.
26. Charles Fields to CKL, January 2, 1918, HEH.
27. Charles Fields to CKL, March 19, 1918, HEH.
28. CKL to Charles Fields, December 13, 1917, HEH.
29. CKL to Louise Clark, February 16, 1919, HEH.
30. CKL diary, December 18, 1917, HEH.
31. CKL diary, December 2, 1917, HEH.
32. O'Hara's other books include *Poems of Sappho, Songs of the Open, Eben Muse, Manhattan,* and *Threnodies.*
33. John Myers O'Hara, n.d., HEH.
34. CKL diary, February 24, 1918, HEH.

35. CKL to Eliza Shepard, January 24, 1918, box 10, folder 13, ML.
36. The affair with Houdini is reconstructed from the CKL diary entries, HEH.
37. See, for example, CKL diary entries, February 26, March 3, 13, and 17, 1918, HEH. For more perspective on this relationship, see *Houdini* by Kenneth Silverman, who learned of the relationship from me.

### 13   Every Woman Should Fight to Accomplish Her End

1. Ed Towse, review of *Our Hawaii*, (Honolulu) *Sunday Advertiser*, May 12, 1918.
2. AS to CKL, October 18, 1918, Walling Collection, box 5, HEH.
3. Correspondence between CKL and Hobart Bosworth on this and other film matters is in HEH. Bosworth had apparently discussed this sequel with Jack when he was alive.
4. Williams, *Jack London: The Movies*, 89.
5. AS to CKL, April 14, 1920, Walling Collection, box 5, HEH; AS to CKL, April 11, 1920, ASWY.
6. CKL diary, November 26, 1918, HEH.
7. CKL to AS, October 26, 1919, HEH.
8. CKL to Aunt Netta [Payne], March 6, 1919, box 15 folder 12, ML. Marked "I did not send this letter."
9. CKL to Joan London, May 1, 1917, HA.
10. CKL to AS, October 26, 1919, HEH.
11. CKL to Joan London, May 5, 1919, HEH. Marked "Not to be sent" and "Never was sent, '37."
12. Joan London to CKL, May 1, [1919?], HA.
13. CKL to Martin Johnson, March 27, 1918, HEH.
14. *Bookman* 52 (December 1920): 299.
15. *Bookman* 59 (March 1924): 55.
16. CKL diary, June 23, 1920, HEH.
17. This and other of CKL's private library books are in ML.
18. As quoted in CKL diary, June 17, 1920, HEH.
19. CKL diary, October 12, 1920, HEH.
20. "The Spirit of California," (Oakland) *Tribune Yearbook, 1924*, 28–29.
21. CKL notes for *Charmette*, SH.
22. CKL to Frederick O'Brien, April 21, 1921, HEH.
23. CKL to *Literary Digest*, October 23, 1922, HEH.
24. *New Republic*, March 29, 1922; C. B. Hawes, *Atlantic* (January 1922): 400.
25. *New York Times*, July 15, 1922.
26. Unidentified copy typed by CKL, SH.
27. *New York Herald*, February 19, 1922.
28. "Jack London Had *Two* Daughters!" *Jack London Foundation Newsletter* 2 (October 1990): 5.
29. Becky London interviews, JLFRC.
30. Lailee van Dillen, "Becky London," 37.

### 14   Fate in Their Own Hands

1. CKL diary, November 11, 1923, HEH.
2. CKL, "Marriage and the New Divorce Laws," *Women's Pictorial*, August 18, 1923; "How We Made Our Marriage a Success," *Woman's Pictorial*, August 23, 1923.
3. William English Walling to AS, Walling Collection, box 6, HEH.

4. CKL to AS, February 9, 1923, ASWY.
5. CKL to AS, April 27, 1925, ASWY.
6. AS diary, November 9, 1925, ASWY.
7. Undated note, Strunsky Walling Collection, BL.
8. *Oakland Tribune,* September 7, 1924.
9. *San Francisco Call,* October 31, 1934.
10. Joan's poetry with notes on the loss of the child, dated November 1923, are in MI 745, HEH.
11. Sam Hardin, "Interview: Bart Abbott," typescript, HA.
12. The full manuscript of *Cherry* is in HEH. Jack London's draft appeared in *Cosmopolitan* (September 1924), while the October issue provided a précis of Charmian's book-length version.
13. Notes for *Charmette,* SH.
14. Netta Payne to CKL, February 22, 1917, HEH.
15. CKL to C. Luker, February 22, 1917, HEH.
16. CKL to Upton Sinclair, July 21, 1930, HEH.
17. Doyle's correspondence with CKL is at both ML and HEH.
18. Netta Payne to CKL, May 25, 1924, ML.
19. CKL will, October 15, 1925, ML.
20. Joan London to CKL, March 24, 1925, HA.
21. CKL to Joan London, March 26, 1925, HA.
22. Joan to CKL, March 30, 1925, HA. Charmian destroyed her 1925 diary; thus the information for this year is more sketchy.
23. Joan to CKL, May 7, 1925.
24. Mel Smith kindly gave me copies of Charmian's and Joan's letters to Hunter Kimbrough, 1927–29, which are now at HEH. Charmian may have had an affair with Kimbrough, brother-in-law to Upton Sinclair.
25. Joan London to CKL, May 18, 1925, HA.
26. CKL to Joan London, May 25, 1925, HA.
27. Joan to CKL, May 30, 1925, HA.
28. Becky London, "Becky's Life," JLFRC.
29. CKL to Eliza Shepard, July 23, 1926, ML.
30. CKL diary, November 1, 1924, HEH.
31. The correspondence from CKL to James Phelan is at BL.
32. Joan London to CKL, November 24, 1926, HA.
33. "George Sterling: As I Knew Him," *Overland Monthly* (March 1927): 1–7.
34. CKL diary, January 21, 1930.
35. CKL diary, February 30, 1930.
36. C. Hartley Grattan, "Jack London, *Bookman* 68 (February 1928): 667–80.
37. CKL, museum bequest, January 13, 1927, JL21001, HEH.

15   *The World Has Fallen*

1. "Jack London's Daughter Too Much Like Her Father," *American Weekly,* June 1, 1930, photocopy, JLFRC.
2. Eugene Lyons, *Assignment in Utopia,* chap. 8.
3. Ibid., 418.
4. For quotations, see "From a Moscow Notebook," MI 693, HEH.
5. E. E. Cummings, *EIMI,* 92.

6. Ibid., ii.
7. Ibid., 142.
8. "Soviet Lacks Glamour, Says Joan London," *Oakland Tribune,* undated photocopy, JLFRC.
9. Ibid.
10. The discussion of Charmian and Harvey Taylor is based on their correspondence, SH Quote is from CKL diary, December 24, 1930, HEH.
11. CKL diary, January 8, 1931, HEH.
12. CKL diary, March 31, 1931, HEH.
13. CKL diary, July 7, 1931, HEH.
14. CKL to Harvey Taylor, November 24, 1931, HEH.
15. CKL letter to Eliza Shepard, ca. 1931, HEH.
16. CKL to Michael Monaghan, May 6, 1933, HEH.
17. CKL diary, June 7, 1932, HEH.
18. CKL diary, June 2, 1933, HEH.
19. CKL to Blanche Partington, October 27, 1932, Partington Family Collection, BL.
20. Undated diaries, ca. early 1930s, folder 356, ASWY.
21. As quoted in Boylan, *Revolutionary Lives,* 266.
22. Upton Sinclair to AS, March 28, 1938, Strunsky Walling Collection, BL.
23. John Myers O'Hara to CKL, 3-3-35, HEH.
24. CKL diary, June 11, 1934, HEH.
25. CKL to Blanche Partington, July 23, 1934, BL.
26. CKL diary, March 21, 1934, HEH.
27. CKL diary, December 31, 1924, HEH.
28. CKL to Blanche Partington, August 30, 1934, BL.
29. CKL diary, August 5, 1934, HEH.
30. This and subsequent quotes are from Barney Mayes's unpublished autobiography, Labor Archives, San Francisco State University.
31. Unpublished Bart Abbott interview with Sam Hardin, HA.
32. See Joan's letters to Lev Trotsky, July–August 1937, MI 924–6, HEH.
33. *JLHT,* 313–15.

### 16   *I Want Good Work Done on Jack London*

1. CKL diary, August 18, 1935, HEH.
2. CKL to H. S. Latham, April 25, 1931, HEH.
3. CKL to Leslie Bliss, April 29, 1931, HEH.
4. The correspondence to and from Julie Bamford is in ML, box 10, folder 1; box 11, folder 2.
5. CKL diary, August 2, 1936, HEH.
6. CKL to Irving Stone, September 1, 1936, SH.
7. CKL diary, September 10 and 11, 1936, HEH.
8. CKL diary, September 15, 1936.
9. CKL diary, October 7, 1936, HEH.
10. Personal communication, Jean Stone, April 8, 1993. In a well-balanced evaluation of Charmian at that time, Jean Stone observed her to have "no world but herself," yet she was a "magnificent female animal" with strong sexual appeal even in her mid-sixties. What the Stones could not have realized was how physical changes were affecting Charmian's personality, and that she was in the early stages of senility.
11. CKL to Irving Stone, October 9, 1936, HEH.

12. CKL diary, October 13, 1936, HEH.
13. "Diary of *Dirigo*," in Mark W. Hennessy, ed., *Sewall Ships of Steel.*
14. Witnessed and notarized statement of CKL, April 13, 1938, JL25151, HEH.
15. CKL diary, July 21, 1937, HEH.
16. CKL to Blanche Partington, July 24, 1937, Partington Collection, BL.
17. Beth Baxter to CKL, "Thursday the 26th" [1937?], HEH.
18. These materials were at UCLA when I saw them in the 1970s, but I was refused access later when I hoped to review and reevaluate the materials. This obstacle has necessarily left my account more one-sided than I would prefer.
19. Carolyn Johnston provided me with access to her copies of several of Stone's interviews from the UCLA archive.
20. Netta Eames Payne to Irving Stone, July 2, 1937, UCLA.
21. I was privy only to letters Stone wrote Eliza Shepard, HEH, not to his research notes about conversations with her or any she may have written him.
22. While looking over an album with Helen Abbott, Charmian pointed to places where photographs had been removed and said that Joan had told her those were the ones Stone had taken. Virtually all of Joan London's letters to CKL are at ML, box 14, though I used copies owned by Helen Abbott.
23. Joan London to CKL, January 1, 1938, HA.
24. CKL to Joan London, January 3, 1937, HA. The context clearly places the letter in 1938.
25. CKL to Irving Stone, August 2, 1938, SH.
26. Dr. Allan Thompson to Irving Stone, October 29, 1937, UCLA.
27. Dr. William S. Porter to CKL, August 10, 1937, SH.
28. John Chamberlin, *New Republic*, September 21, 1938.
29. *Ken*, August 25, 1938.
30. Cloudesley Johns, August 19, 1938, SH.
31. *New York Mirror*, September 26, 1939; Roberts Taply, *The Nation*, November 25, 1939; *New Yorker*, November 4, 1939; *The California Grizzly* (April 1940); clipping in Miller collection, MI 1114, HEH.
32. CKL to Judy van der Veer, February 15, 1939, private collection of Judy van der Veer.
33. CKL to Eliza Shepard, July 31, 1938, ML.
34. CKL to Eliza Shepard, January 30, 1939, ML.
35. CKL to Eliza, December 14, 1938, ML.
36. Herbert Slater, "Mrs. Eliza London Shepard Succumbs at Valley Ranch," *Santa Rosa Press Democrat*, September 30, 1939.
37. CKL diary, September 30, 1939, HEH.

## 17   He Loved Me More

1. See reviews in *Saturday Review of Literature*, July 6, 1940; *New York Times*, July 7, 1940; *Time*, August 5, 1940.
2. HA provided a carbon copy of *Embarcadero*, which serves the basis for this précis and selected quotes.
3. Joan London, "Guide to the [California State Labor Federation] Library," ms. index, California State Labor Federation, San Francisco.
4. This account is based on Lee Miller, "My Life with Jack London's Grandson," unpublished ms.
5. Joan London to Bart Abbott, May 14, 1940, HA.

6. This presentation copy is in the circulating collection of San Francisco State University Library, an unexpected boon that arrived through interlibrary loan.
7. Irving Stone to Anna Strunsky, May 29, 1947, Walling Collection, HEH.
8. Marjorie Gardner Hodapp, "Charmian London," unpublished ms., 1963, Sonoma County Library, Santa Rosa.
9. George Tweney, telephone interview, July 27, 1995.
10. CKL to AS, July 1, 1940, ASWY.
11. Although later correspondence shows that the novel was to be published by a man named Hamlin, the manuscript and book have vanished. Considerable searching by librarian Diane Price proved fruitless.
12. Joan London to CKL, June 17, 1944, HA.
13. Miller, "My Life."
14. CKL to AS, July 19, 1944, ASWY.
15. Joan London to CKL, October 9, 1944, HA.
16. Joan London to Bart Abbott, July 10, 1946, HA.
17. Joan London to Bart Abbott, October 1, 1946, HA.
18. CKL diary, November 16, 1945, HEH.
19. CKL diary, December 27, 1945, HEH.
20. CKL diary, January 11, 1946, HEH.
21. I was going through photographs at HA's home and remarked over one portrait how gorgeous Becky was as a young woman. HA responded that the portrait was of Jean.
22. Federal Bureau of Investigation, San Francisco File 100–10017.
23. Joan London to Bart Abbott, September 17, 1953, HA.
24. Ernest Hopkins, "Jack London Is Dead," *San Francisco Bulletin,* December 2, 1916.
25. Personal communication, Mildred Shepard.
26. CKL obituary, *New York Times,* January 15, 1955.
27. H. Hunter Culwell, "Jack London Real Estate in Public Domain," *Jack London Newsletter* 1 (July–December 1968): 68–75. A state parks employee, Culwell served as the first historic guide for seven years, and had access to state documents and interviews in preparing this history of the origin of the park.
28. Personal communication, HA.


## 18   *Jack London Had* Two *Daughters*

1. Notes on Jack London speech, MI 761, HEH.
2. Speech on Jack London and unionism, MI 760, HEH.
3. For a memoir of Walker's friendship with Joan, supplemented by extensive quotes from her letters, see Dale L. Walker, "Letters from Joan London," *Pacific Historian* 22 (1978): 12–25.
4. Joan London, "W. H. Chaney: A Reappraisal," *American Book Collector* 17 (1966): 13.
5. Notes for the Chaney biography, MI 682–3, HEH.
6. Joan London to Al Shivers, August 14, 1962, MI 912, HEH.
7. Alfred S. Shivers, "Jack London: Not a Suicide," *Dalhousie Review* 49 (1969): 43–57. Joan London to Al Shivers, August 13, 1939, HEH. Joan also expresses her support of Shivers's theory in a letter to Hensley Woodbridge, June 30, 1968, MI 953, HEH.
8. Joan London to Richard O'Connor, January 22, 1965, MI 896, HEH.
9. Joan London to Al Shivers, March 10, 1964, JL15461, HEH.
10. Joan London to Bart Abbot, November 9, 1966, HA.
11. Joan London to Charles Malamuth, June 4, 1964, MI 890, HEH.

12. Charles Malamuth to Joan London, April 20, 1964, MI 662, HEH.
13. Joan London to Bart Abbott, October 24, 1966, HEH.
14. Joan London to Adela Rogers St. John, April 25, 1963, MI 907, HEH.
15. César Chavez to Joan London, October 6, 1967, MI 223, HEH.
16. Martin Mann to Joan London, July 1, 1964, MI 299.
17. Joan London to Russ Kingman, April 7, 1968, HA.
18. Joan London to Bart Abbott, April 6, 1969, HA.
19. Joan London to Bart Abbott, August 14, 1969, HA.
20. Becky London to Bart Abbott, September 22, 1973, MI 399.
21. Kingman, A Pictorial Life of Jack London, 11. "[T]his biography lays no claim to being either definitive or scholarly."
22. After the publication of my American Dreamers, Kingman sent me a twenty-seven-page handwritten list of errata, the bulk of which concerned difference in interpretation.
23. Becky London to Elgy Gillespie, The Scotsman, April 27, 1990.
24. Becky London to Dick Alexander, San Francisco Examiner, November 18, 1990.
25. I used this copy, then in the JLFRC, when preparing *American Dreamers*. Without knowing that Joan had left a son who held her literary rights, I quoted directly from it. In 1996 Helen Abbott, who was going through her husband's papers, discovered this violation of copyright by myself and Andrew Sinclair. Her call to reproach me led instead to the invitation to use Joan's papers in her possession.
26. Russ Kingman to the University of Washington Press, February 11, 1981, JLFRC. An interview with him in The Scotsman, April 27, 1990, repeats phrases used in the letter, and is the source quoted here.
27. "Afterword," unpublished notes for JLHD, HA.
28. Oakland Tribune, July 1, 1990; San Francisco Examiner, June 10, 1990; Denver Post, July 22, 1990.
29. Henry Anderson to Bart Abbott, June 29, 1990, HA.

*Epilogue*

1. Only six doctoral dissertations addressing London were completed during the 1950s. For a full listing, see Earle Labor, *Jack London*, 163, n. 3.
2. Becky London Fleming, "Memories of My Father," *Pacific Historian* 18 (Fall 1974): 5–10.
3. Russ Kingman, *A Pictorial Life of Jack London*, 229.
4. Ibid., 228.
5. *Jack London Foundation Newsletter* 3 (July 1991): 4–6.
6. Susan Gatti, personal communication.
7. Quotations from Jacqueline Travernier-Courbin, "A Daughter's Last Message," *Thalia* 12 (1992): 90–99; "Jack London: 'A Pretty Good Correspondent,'" *Thalia* 12 (1992): 100–109. Had the author consulted the correspondence at ML, which includes that between Joan, Becky, and Charmian, as well as letters involving settlement of the estate between Charmian and the executors at HEH and ML, she would have drawn some different conclusions, as I do here.
8. Becky London interviews, JLFRC.
9. A refreshing exception is James Slagel, "Political Leprosy: Jack London and the *Kama'aina* and Koolau the Hawaiian," in Leonard Cassuto and Jeanne Campbell Reesman, eds., *Rereading Jack London*, 172–91. Slagel refers to Charmian's accounts as evidence in understanding London's identification with Hawaiian culture.

10. CKL, museum bequest, January 13, 1927, JL21001, HEH.

11. Jeanne Campbell Reesman, *Jack London,* 69.

12. Earle Labor expounds on this theme in *Jack London,* 127–29.

13. As quoted in James R. McGovern, "David Graham Phillips and the Virility Impulse of the Progressives," *New England Quarterly* 39 (September 1966): 341.

14. Finn Haakon Frolich, "Sea Dog and Sea Wolf at Play in the Valley of the Moon," *The Californians* 8 (January–February 1991): 23.

15. Several lawyers investigated the settlement and came to the conclusion that it ignored law granting the daughters a right to royalties, but that there was no longer value in the estate to challenge it. Files of correspondence provided by HA.

16. Robin Lampson to Russ Kingman, March 2, 1971, JLFRC.

# Selected Bibliography

## The Principals

FLEMING, BECKY LONDON

"Memories of My Father." *Pacific Historian* 18 (Fall 1974): 5–10.
"Jack London Had *Two* Daughters." *Jack London Foundation Newsletter* 2 (October 1990): 1–4.
"Becky London: The Quiet Survivor Talks about Her Father." Interview with Lailee van Dillen. *The Californians* 9 (January–February 1992): 34–39.


LONDON, CHARMIAN KITTREDGE

"A Rival of Blind Tom in California." *Overland Monthly* 35 (1900): 240–43.
"Jack London Afloat." *Sunset* (1903): 190–91.
"Cross-Saddle Riding for Women." *Out West* 21 (1904): 27–37.
*The Log of the Snark.* New York: Macmillan, 1915. (British editions split into three titles: *Voyaging in the Wild Seas, Jack London in Southern Seas,* and *A Woman among the Headhunters.* London: Mills and Boon, n.d.)
*Our Hawaii.* New York: Macmillan, 1917. (British edition is *Jack London and Hawaii.* London: Mills and Boon, 1918.)
*The Book of Jack London.* 2 vols. New York: Century, 1921. (British edition, which contains material expurgated from the American, is *Jack London.* 2 vols. London: Mills and Boon, 1921.)
*Our Hawaii (Islands and Islanders).* New York: Macmillan, 1922. (Also referred to inaccurately as *Our Hawaii.* Revised edition. British edition is *The New Hawaii.* London: Mills and Boon, 1923.)
"How Jack London Would Have Ended *Eyes of Asia.*" *Cosmopolitan* (November 1924): 78ff.
"George Sterling—As I Knew Him." *Overland Monthly and Out West Magazine* 85 (March 1927): 1–7.
"My Husband—An Old Contributor." *Overland Monthly* 90 (1932): 106–7.
"Diary of *Dirigo.*" In Mark W. Hennessy, ed. *The Sewall Ships of Steel.* Augusta, Maine: Kennebac Journal Press, 1937.


LONDON, JOAN

*Sylvia Coventry.* Serialization in *Oakland Tribune*, December 6, 1926–February 24, 1927.
"Youth Surrenders." *Young's Magazine* (November 1925): 290–96.

"No Latin, No Greek." *College Humor* (September 1927): 53, 84.
*Jack London and His Times: An Unconventional Biography.* New York: Book League of America, 1939.
*The Corpse with Knee Action.* [B. J. Maylon, pseud. Barney Mayes and Joan London.] New York: Phoenix, 1939.
"The London Divorce." *American Book Collector* (November 1917): 31–32.
"W. H. Chaney: A Reappraisal." *American Book Collector* (November 1966): 11–13.
*So Shall Ye Reap.* [With Henry Anderson.] New York: Thomas Y. Crowell, 1970.
*Jack London and His Daughters.* Berkeley: Heyday Books, 1990.


WALLING, ANNA STRUNSKY

*The Kempton-Wace Letters* [with Jack London]. New York: Macmillan, 1903.
"Women and the Russian Revolutionary Movement." *California Women's Magazine* (August 1905): 1–2.
"David Graham Phillips: The Last Years of His Life." *Saturday Evening Post,* October 21, 1911.
*Violette of Père Lachaise.* New York: Frederick A. Stokes, 1915.
"Rosenfeld's Poems." *New Review* (March 1915): 178–79.
"Memories of Jack London." *The Masses* (July 1917): 13–17.
"Foreign Born." *Conservator* (July 1917): 68.
"What Auto Suggestion Will Do for You." *Psychology* (August 1924): 32–34.
"Class Freedom in Russia." *Labor Age* (January 1929): 29.
"La Vie Exemplaire de Jack London." *Les Lettres Français* (March 1948): 1, 8.


*Firsthand Accounts*

Atherton, Frank Irving. "Jack London in Boyhood Adventures." *Jack London Journal* 4 (1997): 14–172.
Austin, Mary. *Earth Horizon.* New York: Houghton Mifflin, 1932.
Bamford, Georgia Loring. *The Mystery of Jack London: Some of His Friends, A Few of His Letters, A Reminiscence.* Oakland: Georgia Loring Bamford, 1931.
Chaney, W. H. *Chaney's Primer of Astrology and American Urania.* St. Louis: Magic Circle Publishing Company, 1890.
Cummings, E. E. *EIMI.* New York: Grove Press, 1933.
Eames, Ninetta. "Jack London." *Overland Monthly* 35 (May 1900): 417–24.
Glotzbach, Bob, ed. *Childhood Memories of Glen Ellen.* Glen Ellen, Calif.: Regeneration Resources, 1992.
Goldman, Emma. *Living My Life.* New York: Dover, 1970.
Frolich, Finn Haakon. "Sea Dog and Sea Wolf at Play in the Valley of the Moon." *The Californians* 8 (January–February 1991): 14–23.
Hendricks, King, and Irving Shepard, eds. *Letters from Jack London.* New York: Odyssey, 1965.
Henry, James, ed. *Give a Man a Boat He Can Sail: Letters of George Sterling.* Detroit: Harlo, 1980.
Johnson, Martin. *Through the South Seas with Jack London.* New York: Dodd, Mead, 1913.
Johnson, Osa. *I Married Adventure: The Lives and Adventures of Martin and Osa Johnson.* New York: J. B. Lippincott, 1940.
Labor, Earle, Robert C. Leitz III, and I. Milo Shepard. *The Letters of Jack London.* 3 vols. Stanford: Stanford University Press, 1988.

London, Jack. *Martin Eden.* New York: Macmillan, 1909.

——. *Burning Daylight.* New York: Macmillan, 1910.

——. *Revolution and Other Essays.* Macmillan, 1910.

——. *John Barleycorn: Alcoholic Memoirs.* New York: Century, 1913.

——. *The Valley of the Moon.* New York: Macmillan, 1913.

——. *The Little Lady of the Big House* .New York: Macmillan, 1916.

——. *On the Makaloa Mat.* New York: Macmillan, 1922.

Lyons, Eugene. *Assignment in Utopia.* New York: Harcourt, Brace, 1937.

Martinez, Elsie Whitaker. *San Francisco Bay Area Writers and Artists.* Oral history interview with Franklin D. Walker and Willa Klug Baum. Regional Oral History Office, Bancroft Library, University of California, Berkeley, 1969.

Noel, Joseph. *Footloose in Arcadia: A Personal Record of Jack London, George Sterling, Ambrose Bierce.* New York: Carrick & Evans, 1940.

Noto, Sal, ed. *With a Heart Full of Love: Jack London's Inscriptions to the Women in His Life.* Berkeley, Calif.: Twowindows Press, 1986.

Ovington, Mary White. *The Walls Came Tumbling Down.* New York: Harcourt, Brace, 1947.

Payne, Edward Biron. *The Soul of Jack London.* London: Rider, 1926.

Pearce, T. M., ed. *Literary America, 1903–1934: The Mary Austin Letters.* Westport, Conn.: Greenwood Press, 1979.

St. John, Adela Rogers. *Final Verdict.* Garden City, N.Y.: Doubleday, 1962.

Sinclair, Mary Craig. *Southern Belle.* Phoenix, Ariz.: Sinclair Press. 1962.

Sinclair, Upton. *Mammonart.* N.p.: Upton Sinclair, 1925.

——. *Cup of Fury.* Great Neck, N.Y.: Channel Press, 1956.

Sisson, James E. "A Memorial to Joan London." *Jack London Newlsetter* 4 (January–April 1971): 1–8.

von Tempski, Armine. *Born in Paradise.* New York: Literary Guild of America, 1940.

Walker, Dale. "Letters from Joan London." *Pacific Historian* 22 (1978): 12–26.


*Secondary Sources*

Anderson, William T., ed. *A Little House Sampler: Laura Ingalls Wilder and Rose Wilder Lane.* New York: Harper and Row, 1988.

Auerbach, Jonathan. *Male Call: Becoming Jack London.* Durham, N.C.: Duke University Press, 1996.

Bagwell, Beth. *Oakland: The Story of a City.* Novato, Calif.: Presidio Press, 1982.

Bassow, William. *The Moscow Correspondents: Reporting on Russia from the Revolution to Glasnost.* New York: William Morrow, 1988.

Bowers, William R. *The Country Life Movement in America: 1900–1920.* Port Washington, N.Y.: Kennikat Press, 1974.

Boylan, James. *Revolutionary Lives: Anna Strunsky and William English Walling.* Amherst, Mass.: University of Massachusetts Press, 1998.

Breton, Pierre. *Klondike Fever.* New York: Carroll and Graf, 1985.

Carnes, Mark C. *Secret Ritual and Manhood in Victorian America.* New Haven: Yale University Press, 1989.

Carnes, Mark C., and Clyde Griffen, eds. *Meanings for Manhood: Constructions of Masculinity in Victorian America.* Chicago: University of Chicago Press, 1990.

Cassuto, Leonard, and Jeanne Campbell Reesman, eds. *Rereading Jack London.* Stanford: Stanford University Press, 1996.

Cornford, Dan, ed. *Working People of California.* Berkeley: University of California Press, 1995.

Davis, Reda. *California Women: A Guide to Their Politics, 1885–1911.* San Francisco, 1911.

Dreyer, Peter. *A Gardener Touched with Genius: The Life of Luther Burbank.* New and revised edition. Santa Rosa, Calif.: Luther Burbank Home & Gardens, 1993.

Dubbert, Joe L. *A Man's Place: Masculinity in Transition.* Englewood Cliffs, N.J.: Prentice-Hall, 1979.

Falk, Candace. *Love, Anarchy, and Emma Goldman.* New York: Holt, Rinehart, and Winston, 1984.

Foner, Philip. *Jack London: American Rebel.* New York: Citadel Press, 1947.

Gair, Christopher. *Complicity and Resistance in Jack London's Novels: From Naturalism to Nature.* Lewiston, N.Y.: Edwin Mellen Press, 1997.

Genovese, Eugene D. *Roll, Jordan, Roll: The World the Slaves Made.* New York: Pantheon, 1974.

Green, Harvey. *The Light of the Home: An Intimate View of the Lives of Women in Victorian America.* New York: Pantheon, 1983.

Hamilton, David Mike. *"The Tools of My Trade": Annotated Books in Jack London's Library.* Seattle: University of Washington Press, 1986.

Haughey, Homer L., and Connie Kale Johnson. *Jack London Ranch Album.* Stockton, Calif.: Heritage Publishing/Valley of the Moon Natural History Association, 1985.

———. *Jack London Homes Album.* Stockton, Calif.: Heritage Publishing, 1987.

Hedrick, Joan. *Solitary Comrade: Jack London and His Work.* Chapel Hill: University of North Carolina Press, 1982.

Heller, Adele, and Lois Rudnick, eds. *1915, The Cultural Moment: The New Politics, the New Woman, the New Psychology, and the New Theatre in America.* New Brunswick, N.J.: Rutgers University Press, 1991.

Higham, John. *Strangers in the Land: Patterns of American Nativism, 1860–1925.* New York: Atheneum, 1985.

Hoch, Paul. *White Hero, Black Beast: Racism, Sexism, and the Mask of Masculinity.* London: Pluto Press, 1979.

Imperato, Pascal James, and Eleanor M. Imperato. *They Married Adventure: The Wandering Lives of Martin and Osa Johnson.* New Brunswick, N.J.: Rutgers University Press, 1992.

Jensen, Joan M., and Gloria Ricci Lothrop. *California Women: A History.* San Francisco: Boyd and Fraser, 1987.

Johnston, Carolyn. *Jack London—An American Radical?* Westport, Conn.: Greenwood Press, 1984.

Kaucher, Dorothy. *James Duval Phelan: A Portrait, 1861–1930.* Saratoga, Calif.: Montalvo Association, 1961.

Kennedy, Richard S. *Dreams in the Mirror: A Biography of E. E. Cummings.* New York: Liveright, 1980.

Kingman, Russ. *A Pictorial Life of Jack London.* New York: Crown, 1979.

———. *Jack London: A Definitive Chronology.* Middletown, Calif.: David Rejl, 1992.

Labor, Earle. *Jack London.* New York: Twayne, 1974.

Lane, Rose Wilder. *He Was a Man.* New York: Harper, 1925.

Larrowe, Charles P. *Harry Bridges: The Rise and Fall of Radical Labor in the United States.* New York: Lawrence Hill, 1972.

Lasartemay, Eugene, and Mary Rudge. *For Love of Jack London: His Life with Jennie Prentiss—A True Love Story.* New York: Vantage, 1991.

Lewis, Oscar. *Bay Window Bohemia.* New York: Doubleday, 1956.

May, Elaine Tyler. *Great Expectations: Marriage and Divorce in Post-Victorian America.* Chicago: University of Chicago Press, 1980.

McBroome, Delores Nason. *Parallel Communities: African Americans in California's East Bay: 1850–1963.* New York: Garland, 1993.

Mintz, Steven. *A Prison of Expectations: The Family in Victorian Culture.* New York: New York University Press, 1993.

Mood, Fulmer. "An Astrologer from Down East." *New England Quarterly* 5 (1932): 769–99.

Mooney, Chase Curran. *Slavery in Tennessee.* Westport, Conn.: Negro Universities Press, 1971.

Muscatine, Doris. *Old San Francisco: From Early Days to the Earthquake.* New York: G. P. Putnam's Sons, 1975.

Norton, Mary Beth. *Founding Mothers and Fathers: Gendered Power and the Forming of American Society.* New York: Random House, 1996.

O'Brien, Frederick. *White Shadows in the South Seas.* Garden City, N.Y.: Garden City Publishing, 1919.

O'Connor, Richard. *Jack London: A Biography.* Boston: Little, Brown, 1964.

O'Leary, Cecilia Elizabeth. *To Die For: The Paradox of American Patriotism.* Princeton: Princeton University Press, 1999.

Perry, John. *Jack London: An American Myth.* Chicago: Nelson-Hall, 1981.

Pittenger, Mark. *American Socialists and Evolutionary Thought, 1870–1920.* Madison: University of Wisconsin Press, 1993.

Praetzellis, Adrian, and Mary Praetzellis. "'Utility and Beauty Should Be One': The Landscape of Jack London's Ranch of Good Intentions." *Historical Archaeology* 23 (1989): 33–44.

Reesman, Jeanne Campbell. *Jack London: A Study of the Short Fiction.* New York: Twayne, 1999.

Rice, Richard B., William A. Bullough, and Richard J. Orsi. *The Elusive Eden: A New History of California.* 2nd ed. New York: McGraw-Hill, 1996.

Riley, Glenda. *Inventing the American Woman: A Perspective on Women's History.* Arlington Heights, Ill.: Harlan Davidson, 1987.

Rosenbaum, Fred. *Free to Choose: The Making of a Jewish Community in the American West.* Berkeley: Judah L. Magnes Memorial Museum, 1976.

Rotundo, E. Anthony. *American Manhood: Transformations in Masculinity from the Revolution to the Modern Era.* New York: Basic Books, 1993.

Schlereth, Thomas. *Victorian American: Transformations in Everyday Life (1876–1915).* New York: Harper Collins, 1991.

Schwartz, Stephen. *From West to East: California and the Making of the American Mind.* New York: Free Press, 1998.

Sherman, Joan. *Jack London: A Reference Guide.* Boston: G. K. Hall, 1977.

Shi, David E. *In Search of the Simple Life.* Salt Lake City: Peregrine Smith, 1986.

Silverman, Kenneth. *Houdini: The Career of Erich Weiss.* New York: Harper Collins, 1996.

Simon, Rita James, ed. *As We Saw the Thirties.* Urbana: University of Illinois Press, 1967.

Sinclair, Andrew. *Jack: A Biography of Jack London.* New York: Harpers, 1977.

Starr, Kevin. *Californians and the American Dream, 1850–1915.* New York: Oxford University Press, 1973.

———. *Inventing the Dream: California through the Progressive Era.* New York: Oxford University Press, 1985.

Stasz, Clarice. "Charmian London as a Writer." *Jack London Newsletter* 11 (1978): 12–26.

———. "The Social Construction of Biography: The Case of Jack London." *Modern Fiction Studies* 22 (1976): 51–71.

——. Review of Lasartemay and Rudge, *For Love of Jack London*. *Jack London Journal* 2 (1995): 195–98.

——. "Jack London's Delayed Discovery of Fatherhood." *Jack London Journal* 3 (1996): 146–61.

Stewart, Suzanne, and Mary Praetzellis, eds. *Sights and Sounds: Essays in Celebration of West Oakland*. Rohnert Park, Calif.: Anthropological Studies Center, Sonoma State University, 1997.

Stone, Irving. *Sailor on Horseback*. Boston: Houghton Mifflin, 1938.

Takaki, Ronald. *Strangers from a Different Shore: A History of Asian Americans*. New York: Penguin, 1989.

Traprock, Walter E. [pseud.]. *The Cruise of the Kawa: Wanderings in the South Seas*. New York: Putnam, 1921.

Viertel, Salka. *The Kindness of Strangers*. New York: Holt, Rinehart, and Winston, 1969.

Walker, Franklin. *Jack London in the Klondike*. San Marino, Calif.: Huntington Library, 1966.

——. *The Seacoast of Bohemia*. New and enlarged edition. Santa Barbara, Calif.: Peregrine Smith, 1973.

Watson, Steven. *Strange Bedfellows: The First American Avant-Garde*. New York: Abbeville Press, 1991.

Wexler, Alice. *Emma Goldman in America*. Boston: Beacon Press, 1984.

Williams, Tony. *Jack London: The Movies*. Los Angeles: David Rejl, 1992.

Woodbridge, Hensley C., John London, and George H. Tweney. *Jack London: A Bibliography*. Georgetown, Calif.: Talisman Press, 1966.

# Index

London, Jack: biographical slants toward, x–xi; paternity of, 11–12; infancy, 13–15; childhood, 16–19; and African American community, 20, 28; adolescence, 29–30; first publication, 31; hoboing, 32–33; socialism, 34–35; mercurial temperament, 36–37; and Applegarths, 41–46; in Yukon, 46–47; early writing, 47–50; Anglo-Saxonism, 53–55; meets Anna, 56–59; marries Bess, 60–61; and stereotyping of Jews, 63; views on women and marriage, 64–65; as new father, 66–67; and George Sterling, 68–69; proposes to Anna, 73; in England, 74–75; reconciles with Bess, 77; attracts other women, 78–79; starts affair with Charmian, 80–82; success of *Call*, 85; at Russo-Japanese War, 90–91; with Blanche, 94; visits with daughters, 95–96; socialist activities, 101–3; break with mother and Jennie, 104; daily life with Charmian, 105–6; marriage and socialism, 107–9; 1905 will, 109–10; in Carmel, 116–17; *Snark* trip, 120–23; drinking problems, 124; fights Bess and Milner, 130–32; social Darwinism, 133; tropical illness, 134; 1909 will, 135; and friends, 140–43; and agriculture, 143–45; at birth of Joy, 146–47; "cruel pattern" regarding visitation, 149–53; 1911 will, 154; success and finances, 155; manic in New York, 156–57; meets the Wallings, 158; promises temperance, 162–63; ranch endeavors, 169–71; and film producers, 172–75; revives relationship with daughters, 175–77; reaction to house fire, 178–79; "awful letters" to Joan, 180; copyright problems, 180–83; love for Charmian, 183–85; "ruined colt" letter, 186–87; financial difficulties, 187–88; in Vera Cruz, 188–89; warm letters to Joan, 190–92; affair in Hawaii, 194–95; reunites with daughters, 197–99; kidney problems, 199–200; new psychology, 201; renewed fight over finances, 205–7; and Sophie Loeb, 208; death, 209–10; reviled by book reviewers, 241; characterized by Mayes, 286; in Joan's biography, 287–88; portrayed by Stone, 297–99; suicide disputed, 327
—Writings and *film adaptations*
"The Abysmal Brute," *246*
*Acorn-Planter,* 193

*Adventure,* 33–34, 123
*Before Adam,* 115
"The Bones of Kakekili," 201
*Burning Daylight,* 108, 141, 143–44, 147, 228, 353
*The Call of the Wild,* 46, 79, 85, 88, 101, 224, 302, 345
*Children of the Frost,* 77
*The Cruise of the Dazzler,* 63
*The Cruise of the Snark,* 124
*A Daughter of the Snows,* 63, 352
"From Dawson to the Sea," 48
*The Game,* 94
*The God of His Fathers,* 46
"The Golden Poppy," 70
*Hearts of Three,* 196, 208, 254
"The House Beautiful," 115, 177
*The Iron Heel,* 108, 115, 125, 184, 250, 288, 303
*Jerry of the Islands,* 193–94
*John Barleycorn,* 151, 162, 168, *173, 188,* 223, 289, 329, 339
"The Kanaka Surf," 108
*The Kempton-Wace Letters,* 64–65, 72–74, 76–78, 83, 86, 128, 184, 230
*The Little Lady of the Big House,* 108, 169–73, 190, 230, 353, 339
*Lost Face,* 121
*Love of Life and Other Stories,* 110, 129
*Martin Eden,* 43, 124, 223, 289, *313*
*Michael Brother of Jerry,* 193
*Moon-Face and Other Stories,* 110
*The Mutiny of the Elsinore,* 181, 228, *313*
"My Castle in Spain," 115
*On the Makaloa Mat,* 201, 230
*People of the Abyss,* 74, 88, 324, 333
"Planchette," 110
*The Red One,* 201, 230
*Revolution and Other Essays,* 99, 108, 115
*The Road,* 33, 115, 129, 135, 333
*The Sea-Wolf,* 77, 86–87, 94, *173, 181–82,* 228–29, *313*
*Smoke Bellew,* 167, 262
*The Son of the Wolf,* 52–53
*The Star Rover,* 190, 228
*Tales of the Fish Patrol,* 246
"The Tar Pot" ("Poppy Cargo"), 274–76
*Theft, 146*
"To the Man on the Trail," 48–49

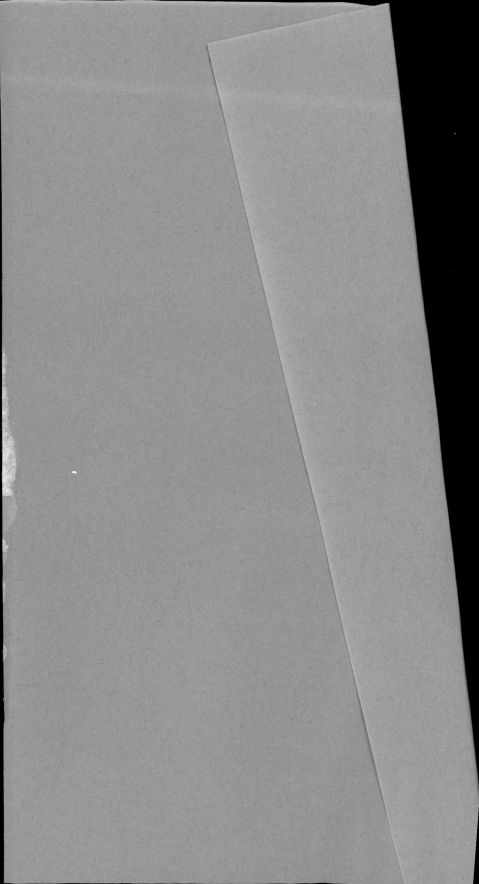